A SOCIAL AND RELIGIOUS
HISTORY OF THE JEWS

Late Middle Ages and Era of European Expansion
1200—1650

VOLUME XVIII

THE OTTOMAN EMPIRE, PERSIA, ETHIOPIA, INDIA,
AND CHINA

A SOCIAL
AND RELIGIOUS
HISTORY OF
THE JEWS

By SALO WITTMAYER BARON

Second Edition, Revised and Enlarged

Late Middle Ages and Era of European Expansion
1200–1650

VOLUME XVIII

THE OTTOMAN EMPIRE, PERSIA, ETHIOPIA, INDIA,
AND CHINA

Columbia University Press
New York   1983

The Jewish Publication Society of America
Philadelphia   5743

COLUMBIA UNIVERSITY PRESS

NEW YORK, GUILDFORD, SURREY

COPYRIGHT © 1983 COLUMBIA UNIVERSITY PRESS

ALL RIGHTS RESERVED

ISBN: 0-231-08855-8

LIBRARY OF CONGRESS CATALOG CARD NUMBER: 52-404

PRINTED IN THE UNITED STATES OF AMERICA

Clothbound editions of Columbia University Press Books are Smyth-Sewn and printed on permanent and durable acid-free paper.

CONTENTS

CONTENTS

A SOCIAL AND RELIGIOUS HISTORY

OF THE JEWS

PUBLISHED VOLUMES

THE OTTOMAN EMPIRE, PERSIA, ETHIOPIA, INDIA, AND CHINA

LXXV

OTTOMAN EMPIRE

PRACTICALLY ALL the countries, both Christian and Muslim, discussed in the last volume were gradually reunited under the powerful Ottoman sultanate. To contemporaries it appeared like a God-given or God-inflicted "miracle" that, in the course of three centuries (1280–1580), a regime which had started through the conferral of a small fief in northwestern Asia Minor on Ertojul, the chieftain of a small Turkish clan allegedly numbering no more than 400 families, became one of the leading world powers. The name of Ertojul's son Uthman or Osman (1286–1324), served to identify forever after the specific Turkish group from among the various Turkmen emirates (so-called *bergliks*) which had been established during the constant flow of immigration of Central Asian nomads since the eleventh century. As Ottomans or Osmanlis these Turkish tribesmen, long since converted to Islam, happened to be located in the northwest corner of the Anatolian Peninsula in close proximity to Constantinople on the European side of the Dardanelles (ancient Hellespont). This geographic location made them the natural vanguard of the Islamic expansion against the declining Byzantine Empire at its most vulnerable point. Because they were permeated with the spirit of an Islamic Holy War against infidels they became the *ghazi* warriors whose main objective was to expand the reign of their faith over all neighboring areas. At the same time they were also driven by the desire to acquire new land. In both capacities they attracted a considerable inflow of warlike and land-hungry Turkomans not only from the neighboring marches but also from the vast areas of Iran and Central Asia which had come under the domination of the oppressive Mongolian regimes.

From these small beginnings the Ottoman dynasty, which included a number of highly gifted and long-reigning monarchs, expanded in the following three hundred years into an enormous empire. Under Suleiman the Magnificent (1520–66) and his successors, it extended from the Iranian border in the east to that of Morocco and the Adriatic Sea in the west and from northern Hungary and the Marmora Sea in the north to the Sahara, the Sudan, and Yemen in the south.[1]

A phenomenal rise of this kind understandably aroused the curiosity of both contemporaries and modern historians concerning its reasons and effects. They noted, in particular, that the Ottoman expansion proved more durable than the Mongolian conquests by Jenghiz Khan or Timur (Tamerlane) which, though extending over a much greater area, fell apart within a very short time while leaving a permanent imprint on the conquered populations. We recall the impact of the "Turkish menace" on the European nations during the fifteenth and sixteenth centuries. To be sure, when at the end of the sixteenth century the situation became stabilized and was followed by the constant weakening of Ottoman power, this horror of Turkish expansion gradually gave way to a renewed deprecation of the Turkish civilization and to a partial repetition of the Byzantine thirteenth-century underestimate of Turkish might and cultural attainment.[2]

The causes of the initially rapid Ottoman expansion in Anatolia undoubtedly lay in the relatively small density of its native population and the collapse of its rather superficial Hellenistic culture. Even in antiquity it was clear that Hellenism had deeply permeated only the population of the larger cities, whereas the countryside continued worshiping its local deities or followed the lead of such expansive Eastern religions as that of the Mithras cult. It was not without reason that the Romans viewed the eastern peasant masses as heathens, the term *paganus* identifying both peasants and polytheists. Some modern Turkish nationalists have insisted that the majority of the farming population had always consisted of descendants of the ancient Hittites. While forced to admit that the Hittites themselves did not represent a homogeneous ethnic group and that we still have residua of six different Hittite dialects, half of which belong respectively to the Indo-European and the Semitic groups of languages, these scholars explained the quick Turkicization of Anatolia by the historic continuity of the peasant population from the pre-Hellenistic period. During the flowering of the Panturkish movement in the interwar period some spokesmen insisted that the immigration of Central Asian and western Turkic tribes into Asia Minor merely paved the way for the liberation of their related ethnic masses, long oppressed by the small number of Graeco-Roman conquerors. Even if one dismisses these fantastic historical reconstructions, one cannot doubt that the successive waves of eastern nomads reaching Asia Minor between the eleventh and fourteenth centuries uninterruptedly reinforced the manpower of the Turkish warriors and builders of a new economic structure, both urban and rural. It has been estimated that at the beginning of the Osmanli expansion there were more than one million Turkoman nomads in Anatolia and that their numbers rapidly grew when the Turkish conquests opened up for them ever new territories for permanent settlement.[3]

Similarly controversial were the evaluations of the effects of the rapid Ottoman expansion on the conquered populations and the Mediterranean civilization at large. With the growth of Turkish national fervor, a considerable number of Turkish scholars, including such competent historians as Mehmet Fuat Köprülü and Ömer Lutfi Barkan, emphasized above all the beneficial effects of Turkish pacification of vast areas in Europe, Western Asia, and North Africa which had theretofore suffered from interminable wars and sanguinary domestic conflicts. They also pointed out that the Turkish abolition of formal serfdom liberated untold masses of unfree peasants. One is reminded in this connection of the aforementioned apologists for the *Pax Mongolica* of the thirteenth century, anticipating in some respects the *Pax Britannica,* of the nineteenth century. Both schools of thought overlooked, of course, the wholesale slaughter of the civilian population by both the Mongols and the Turks during their original conquests. Certainly, the *Pax Britannica* was built over the last three centuries with proportionately far fewer original victims.[4]

In contrast, Balkan nationalists, especially Bulgarians and Serbs, were prone to denigrate the beneficial effects of the Turkish regime even after the initial "barbaric" periods of occupation. Typical of that school of thought is Dimitri Angelov's exclamation, referring to the catastrophe which befell the Greeks in Asia Minor around 1300:

the [Turkish] conquest had as its result the mass destruction of material goods, the ruin of entire cities, the massacre, deportation, and enslavement of thousands of inhabitants, in one word, the general and enduring decline of all productive forces of the country.

The Turks, Angelov added, had neither the superior culture nor the superior organizational talents, as claimed by their recent historians.[5]

Transcending these nationalistically inspired controversies, Western scholars tried to come to grips with the enigma of the Ottoman expansion by insisting on the weaknesses of the surrendering states, the persistent economic decline of the native populations, the sharp divisions between the Eastern Churches and Western Catholicism which made many Eastern Orthodox hate the Latins more than the Muslims, and other debilitating factors—all of which made these areas ripe for occupation by a determined foreign power. Such determination was nurtured among the Turkish conquerors by the *ghazi* spirit of the Holy War against infidels, the traditional avidity of steppe peoples for new land, and the historically more accidental fact of a long enduring dynasty with a succession of gifted, sometimes inspired, rulers. With a modicum of education, the sultans were able to build a powerful military and bureaucratic structure, and clearly to perceive, and at crucial moments to exploit, the weaknesses of their immediate enemies and the far-reaching fratricidal animosities among the Western peoples. The program of Ottoman succession to the Byzantine Empire was clearly enunciated as early as 1394, when Bayezid I secured the title "sultan of Rum" from the shadow caliph of Cairo.[6]

The emergence of the Ottoman Empire could not have come at a more propitious moment for the European Jews, whose position in the fourteenth and fifteenth centuries had reached a new low point. Their expulsion from England (1290), France (1306, 1394, and in the late fifteenth century), the Iberian monarchies and their dependencies (1492, 1496–97); their massacres in, and banishment from, various parts of the Holy

Roman Empire and Hungary in the Black Death era and the subsequent decades; and finally, from many Italian principalities and city states including even the partial banishments from the theretofore relatively tolerant States of the Church (1569, 1593)—all forced those Jews who remained true to their faith, including numerous secret Jews disguised as New Christians, to seek new shelters. While the relatively small number of Ashkenazic Jews could flock into the newly rising Commonwealth of Poland and Lithuania, the Mediterranean Jews, both Sephardic and Italo-Greek, far more numerous, wealthy, and self-assertive, could find only limited openings in the North African Islamic possessions. But their masses, set in motion especially by the severe Iberian persecutions, needed much larger and more promising outlets. Such new socioeconomic opportunities opened up to them in the rapidly expanding Ottoman Empire, some of the far-sighted rulers of which realized the great benefits their country could derive from these culturally and economically advanced Iberian and Italian arrivals. They were also convinced that as sufferers from Christian intolerance these new immigrants would become more loyal servants of the Ottoman Porte than the more numerous Christian subjects of the conquered Balkans and vicinity. Needless to say, even more welcome were the renegades from both Christianity and Judaism, many of whom, with astonishing speed, became devoted Muslims and deeply loyal patriots of the Ottoman regime.

On their part, the Jews greatly benefited from their freedom of travel, the new ramified opportunities in industry, commerce, medical practice, and government service, as well as from their extensive internal communal self-government, which enabled them to undergo also a new cultural and religious renaissance. The Turkish communities thus rivaled those of Poland and Lithuania in the leadership of world Jewry. Although their own golden age of the sixteenth century coincided with the Spanish *siglo d'oro* and they never forgot their original Spanish culture and language (down to the twentieth century their masses continued to speak Ladino, a basically Castilian dialect despite its numerous borrowings from the

Hebrew and from their Slavic and Turkish neighbors), they adjusted themselves with amazing speed to their new multinational Ottoman environment.

SLOW BEGINNINGS

At first Osman and his son Orkhan (1324–60) gradually enlarged their territory by fighting both the Byzantines and the other Turkman rulers of the Peninsula. Orkhan, in fact, by marrying Theodora, daughter of Emperor John Cantacuzenus, for a while played the role of the emperor's ally. This gave him the opportunity to intervene in the internal Byzantine affairs and thus to enlarge his own sphere of influence. Among the major conquests of father and son were the occupation of the three Anatolian cities of Nicomedia (renamed, in Turkish, Izmid or Izmit), Nicaea (renamed Iznik), and Brusa (in Turkish, Bursa). Turkicization of these and other major cities was pursued with great zeal by the conquerors, bearing testimony to a rising Turkish national feeling. It contrasted with the later practices during the occupation of Syro-Egyptian areas, where the Arabic names of the conquered localities underwent little change. This combination of the nascent Turkish national sentiment with the traditional Islamic drive for expansion contrasted with the divisiveness, religious as well as ethnic, characteristic of the Byzantine Empire. Medieval Turkish historians were not slow in extolling the ethnoreligious spirit which animated the early Osmanli conquerors. For example, Oruj praised the Ottomans as

Ghāzīs and champions striving in the way of truth and the path of Allāh, gathering the fruits of *ghazā* and expending them in the way of Allāh, choosing truth, striving for religion, lacking pride in the world, following the way of the *Sharī'a,* taking revenge on polytheists, friends of strangers, blazing forth the way of Islam from the East to the West.

Although the predominantly Sunni Osmanlis had to accommodate a number of Shi'ites, especially devout dervishes, they were united in fighting the Holy War against Christians. This sentiment became quite strong among the Muslims in that period of Counter Crusades which had led to the final destruction of the Latin Kingdom of Jerusalem in the preceding years. In contrast, the Christians saw in their recurrent defeats, especially the destruction of the expeditionary army sent by Emperor Michael III in 1302, a sign of the divine wrath over their sinful government.[7]

More importantly, exceeding even their Mongolian prototypes, the Osmanlis, upon the conquest of a city like Brusa (Bursa), are said to have eliminated all males and enslaved all women and children, dispersing them over many localities. They rapidly replaced that population by settling there many Turkoman nomads and by allowing other nationalities, including Jews, to resettle in the city. In 1333, but seven years after their conquest, Ibn Baṭṭuṭa called Brusa "a great important city with fine bazaars and wide streets." Soon after Orkhan erected there a mosque which became a renowned landmark of early Turkish architecture. The conquest of Nicaea (Iznik) further underscored the Turkish advance, since only a few decades earlier the city had served as the capital of the Laskarid Empire. From there that dynasty succeeded, by appealing to Greek nationalism, in overrunning the Latin possessions in the Balkans and in restoring in 1261 the Byzantine Empire to its pre-1204 position. Most significantly, Orkhan ventured for the first time to cross the Dardanelles to Europe and, aided through the preceding destruction of its powerful fortifications by a violent earthquake in 1354, he succeeded in occupying Gallipoli, a great commercial and military center of Byzantine power (1357). From there the road was open to the conquest of Thrace, leading in the 1360s, shortly after Orkhan's death, to the conquest of Adrianople. This city, renamed Edirne, was speedily converted into the capital of the Ottoman state. It is in connection with these conquests that Archbishop Philotheus, himself a captive taken by the Turks in Gallipoli, mentions a curious group of "Chiones," who adopted Judaism. This may possibly have been but an intermediate step, as has been suggested, for their ultimate conversion to Islam, although one does not see why they needed that roundabout way. Certainly, conversion to Islam could be accomplished in an even less formal ceremony than that to the Jewish faith.[8]

With this initial occupation of a sizable European area, the expansion of Ottoman power took on a new complexion. It also marked a turning point in the destinies of Mediterranean Jewry. We hear very little about Jewish residents in the Anatolian cities before and during the early period of Ottoman domination. The paucity of the Jewish population in the area contrasted sharply with the conditions at the beginning of the first millennium C.E. At that time, we recall, the Jewish population of the Peninsula may have numbered as many as one million persons. Some of its famous cities embraced important Jewish communities dating back to the Greek period before their occupation by Achaemenid Persia. However, from the outset the Jews of the area seem to have been subject to both considerable hostility on the part of their neighbors and strong assimilatory pressures. The Jewish interlocutor of Aristotle who, according to Clearchus of Soli, "not only spoke Greek but had the soul of a Greek," may well have been typical of a large group of Jews in the area. In the days of Herod, Nicolaus of Damascus had to be sent from Jerusalem to help plead the cause of the Jews before the Roman authorities when the local Greek citizens tried to curtail their rights. Later on their progressive Hellenization made them open to strong Christian conversionist efforts. It was no mere accident that the founder of "Gentile Christianity," the apostle Paul, had been a native of Tarsus and had concentrated many of his missionary activities on the Hellenistic inhabitants of Asia Minor and the Balkans. Among his successors was Marcion, a sharp enemy not only of the Jews but of Judaism as such, which he tried to denigrate as the worship of an inferior God. While the regnant ecclesiastical circles repudiated Marcion, much of that hostility seems to have continued underground. At the same time the Hellenization of the cities but not of the countryside continued apace. It undoubtedly induced a great many Jews to join the New Church and ultimately to disappear from the Jewish scene. It is also likely that whatever remnants of Jewry of both the Rabbanite and Karaite variety that continued to live in Anatolia suffered even more severely from the four successive decrees of forced conversion issued by Heraclius,

Leo the Philosopher, Basil I, and Romanus I Lekapenos in the seventh, eighth, ninth, and tenth centuries, respectively.[9]

It is small wonder, then, that upon their conquest the early Osmanlis found relatively few Jews in the occupied cities. It appears that Brusa, the Ottoman capital in 1326–61, had an important Jewish settlement before Orkhan's conquest, and that, like the rest of the population, it had suffered greatly from the plague and the internal disorders. However, in contrast to the majority of Christians, many Jews, who had fled the city before the occupation, were allowed to return and to reestablish their community in accordance with the traditional Islamic law, the *shari'a*. They doubtless were subject to a poll tax and other special imposts but otherwise they enjoyed full religious freedom and much communal autonomy. Their residence on a Jewish street in the center of the city, which also included a synagogue built soon after their return, was recorded by early Turkish historians. Before long the city became a great center of commerce and industry, in which Jews and a number of other ethnic groups, including Europeans, developed far-flung commercial relations. The newly erected Muslim hospitals, allegedly serving a population of 200,000 (doubtless a gross exaggeration), "admitted poor people, be they Christians, heathens [Muslims] or Jews," according to Johann Schiltberger, a German who had been taken captive at Nicopolis in 1396 and subsequently spent several years in Brusa. There also existed a few other smaller Jewish communities in the Anatolian possessions.[10]

More important, however, were the European communities conquered by the Turks in the course of the fourteenth century. Gallipoli, which was the first to fall into Turkish hands, in 1354 (although temporarily recaptured in 1366 by the crusading Count Amadeus of Savoy but speedily returned to Turkish sovereignty) had accommodated a Jewish settlement perhaps in unbroken continuity from ancient times. If in the 1160s Benjamin of Tudela had found there a sizable settlement of 200 Jewish families, the decline of the Byzantine Empire in the subsequent two centuries and the recurrent plagues must have reduced that number. But there is no question that the Ottoman conquerors extended their toleration to a Jewish group which was to increase rapidly by immigration from other endangered localities. The number of Jews under Ottoman rule gradually increased with the Ottoman expansion into the Balkans under Orkhan's son and successor, Murad I. Occasional names of Jewish scholars from both sides of the Straits also attest the continued cultivation of Jewish learning among these scattered Jewries. Some savants, however, may have fled in periods of greatest disturbance and we find quite a few Jewish scholars bearing the name Anatoli in other Mediterranean communities.[11]

FROM MURAD I TO MURAD II

Under a similar title Franz Babinger described the second major phase in the Ottoman expansion in the nine decades of 1362 to 1451. During the reign of Murad I (1362–89)—which tragically ended with the sultan's assassination by a Serbian, Miloš Obilić (Kabilovich) and both men's subsequent glorification in patriotic poems by their respective conationals—practically all of Bulgaria and most of Serbia had been conquered. Murad's son, Bayezid I, nicknamed Yildrim (the Thunderbolt, 1389–1402), at first continued these conquests in both the West and East. But he was suddenly stopped by Timur (Tamerlane) who, at the momentous battle of Ankara in 1402, destroyed the Turkish army and took Bayezid prisoner. The result was the inglorious death, in a Mongolian prison, of the first Ottoman "sultan" to bear this title with the formal consent of the shadowy caliph residing in Cairo and with the noteworthy approval of the Mameluke rulers, who had theretofore tried to reserve it for their own regime. Because of this unexpected turn of events, the sons of Bayezid divided the Empire among themselves, opening up new opportunities for the resuscitation of Byzantine power and the rise of various national irredentas.

Even when in 1413, after reigning in Anatolia for ten years, Meḥmed I succeeded in reuniting the empire, the power of the monarchy was seriously undermined by the social revolution initiated by Sheikh Bedr ed-Din and his pupil Bürklüce

Mustafa. Among others, these innovators found a follower in a converted Jew Torlaq Kemal (his original name probably was Samuel, the usual equivalent of Kemal), who is said to have assembled a partisan force of some 7,000 men. Their spiritual leader, Bedr ed-Din, emphasized above all the equivalence of all religions, although when pressed into an anti-governmental position he allegedly declared: "Henceforth the dominion is mine and the throne has been granted to me. I am to be called the king, the Mahdi. I shall unfurl my flag and rise up" in arms. Apparently with less messianic Pretensions, Bürklüce Mustafa went further and demanded the community of all property among men. According to the well-informed Byzantine historian Michael Ducas, he preached to the Turks the ideal of "voluntary poverty, taught that with the exception of women, everything should be common property, food, clothing, cattle, and agricultural tools." Whether he realized it or not, he thus followed in the footsteps of his fifth-century Persian predecessor Mazdak, but he and his peasant listeners were deeply imbued with the sexual ethics of Islam and refrained from postulating any promiscuous relationships with women. While this revolution ended in 1416 with Kemal's death in battle, the crucifixion of Mustafa, and the hanging of Bedr ed-Din, the heritage of their effective propaganda left some noteworthy traces in Turkish society down to the nineteenth century. Murad II (1421–51, with important interruptions when he abdicated in favor of his fourteen-year-old son Meḥmed and then returned to power) resumed the Ottoman expansion with great force and, in 1444, decisively defeated the Crusaders led by King Wladislaus of Hungary at the battle of Varna. He penetrated the Peloponnesus and parts of Albania, and reoccupied Serbia, although he could not conquer the strongly fortified city of Belgrade. In short, by the end of his regime practically the entire Balkan Peninsula and most of Anatolia came under Ottoman rule.[12]

The Turkish conquests opened the gates of the Balkan Peninsula to the ever-swelling waves of Jewish immigration. Despite the reverses it had suffered during the first two decades after Bayezid's defeat at Ankara, the Empire now included older and new Jewish communities. Adrianople, which had a long, if insufficiently recorded, history of Jewish settlement since ancient times, included at the time of the Ottoman conquest an old "Greek" community of Jews which continued well into the twentieth century. True, because of the absence of reliable documentary evidence, the events leading to the occupation of the city by the Turks and their effects upon the Jews have not been fully clarified. The medieval Ottoman historians give the impression that the entire population was removed by the conquerors, with many inhabitants being slain and others, particularly women and children, carried into captivity. On the other hand, some local rumormongers subsequently spread the tale that, even before the Turkish occupation, Jews had sided with the besieging Turks, for which services they were rewarded with an especially favorable privilege after the city's annexation. Neither assertion is supported by solid evidence. But if most Jews, too, were forced to depart, they seem to have speedily reestablished their quarter alongside that of the newly immigrating Turks. Steadily reinforced by new Jewish arrivals from other cities, including Constantinople, and from other lands, they were soon joined by other ethnic settlers. In any case, before very long, Edirne, serving under its new Turkish name as the Ottoman capital—an event which Murad I broadcast to all Muslim rulers in the adjacent lands—began to prosper; it grew in population, and became a fairly typical Turkish city.[13]

After the crucial victories at Maritza in 1371, at Kosovopolje in 1389 (notwithstanding Murad's death there at the hand of the assassin), Nicopolis in 1396, and Varna in 1444, all of Bulgaria, most of Serbia, the bulk of the formerly Byzantine possessions in the south, and even sections of Albania, Walachia, and Hungary came under Turkish domination. At that time Bulgaria alone included at least four Jewish communities: in its capital, Tirnovo, Sofia (ancient Sardica, later the capital of the third kingdom of Bulgaria), Vidin, and Pleven. Nicopolis, too, had a Jewish community before the 1396 battle between the great Western and the Turkish armies at its gates; it embraced a growing Jewish population after its rebuilding under Turkish rule. Most important of all for Jewish history was the Turkish conquest of Thessalonike (better known as Salonica) which had played a considerable role in the history of the Jewish people in ancient and medieval times and was destined to become one of the leading Jewish communities in the modern world. In the fourteenth and early fifteenth centuries, it was a long-suffering city with constantly changing masters; it achieved enduring peace only after the final Ottoman occupation. In fact, the Turks had conquered it first in 1383, and again in 1391 and 1413, but lost it each time to the Greeks after a few years. By 1423 the Byzantines ceded it to Venice which, with its powerful navy and vast financial resources, was in a better position to hold on to it. However, after a protracted war with the Republic of the Lagoons, Murad II occupied Salonica for good in 1430. We are told that its 1423 population of some 40,000 had dwindled to but 7,000 at the time of the Turkish occupation because so many inhabitants had deserted it at the time of the Turco–Venetian hostilities. But it was not very long before the city regained its important position as a major Aegean harbor and attracted a rapidly increasing Jewish community. It was soon to become one of the few metropolises with a permanent Jewish majority, a situation which was not fundamentally altered until the Nazi Holocaust. In Anatolia, too, the few existing Jewish communities were now included in the Empire, especially Ankara, which in the twentieth century was to become the capital of Turkey. Smyrna (in Turkish and Hebrew, Izmir), though important in ancient times, seems to have harbored very few Jews before the Turkish conquest. Subsequently, however, it became a major emporium of international trade, in which Jews played a significant role, as well as a center of Jewish intellectual life and Hebrew printing.[14]

Turkish methods of warfare seem to have been less damaging to Jews than to their non-Jewish neighbors. Generally warfare was very cruel on both sides. Even Murad I, who was often praised as a mild-mannered, humane person, emphasized to his commander during his first attack on Salonica that "countries of infidels must constantly be devastated." As part of that scheme, the Ottoman strategists often used irregular auxiliaries (so-called *aqinji*) as a first line of attack. By letting loose such gangs of men bent upon slaughter, plunder, and arson, they so thoroughly scorched the countryside that the cities, even if strongly fortified, were deprived of their usual means of supply. Together with the terror which struck the population at large, these preliminary guerrilla-like hit and run assaults served to soften the enemy so that the regular Turkish armies encountered less vigorous resistance. However, looking forward to the postwar administration, Murad I also informed his commander: "Your governors which you will appoint for the interior of the country shall be righteous persons so that the condition of the subject population be good. . . . As to the Muslims who will be under your regime, you ought to supervise their marital relations. But you should also keep the other *rayas* [subjects] in good condition, do them no violence, and do not molest them." In other words, absolute ruthlessness during the campaign was to be followed by a just regime in order to heal the wounds and to foster the well-being of the entire population. Murad II is highly praised even by such Byzantine writers as Laonis Chalcandyles and Ducas as a man who kept his promises unwaveringly and, despite his numerous conquests, was a lover of peace. "He never sought any people's total destruction," states Ducas, "when the vanquished sent envoys to him asking for peace, he received them in a friendly fashion, granted their request, terminated the war and became a friend of peace."[15]

As far as the Jews were concerned, they suffered relatively less from the *aqinji* raids, since few of them lived in villages. After the four Byzantine expulsions and the constant warfare and turmoil raging for generations through the entire peninsula, even their urban population must have dwindled far below that found by Benjamin of Tudela. Few cities seem to have had enough Jews to form a community or to own a synagogue. Hence they were less likely to be victimized by the ruthless type of warfare, while they were able to benefit even more than their neighbors from the ensuing peace, an economic revival and the governmentally sponsored immigration of settlers from the outside. At the same time there is no evidence that Murad I was in any way influenced in favor of Jews by his wife, Mara, originally Tamar, daughter of the Bulgarian Queen Theodora, who according to tradition was a converted Jewess. Mara was not only a renowned beauty but also a very generous person and, as such, a heroine of many folk poems recited for generations. Certainly, whatever political influence she may have had on her husband did not save her brother, the last medieval Bulgarian tsar, Shishman III, who though for a long-time Murad's ally was ruthlessly slain when he became the sultan's enemy. Nor is there any evidence that Mara's son, Bayezid I, showed any particular preference for Jews.[16]

One of the greatest advantages of the expanding Ottoman regime for Jews and other minorities was the basic uniformity of the fundamental laws governing the entire empire. It replaced, to a large and ever-growing extent, the enormous variety of laws and usages under which they had theretofore lived not only in the formerly independent countries and the Venetian or Genoese colonies, but also in the numerous feudal subdivisions of the old Byzantine Empire. Although the Ottoman rulers maintained much latitude in preserving local customs and in transferring relatively small tracts of land to the custody of chosen landlords in the forms of semifeudal *timar*s, the basic principle of government that all conquered lands belonged to the sultan remained in force. The underlying traditional Islamic law, the *shari'a,* and its constant adjustment to changing needs by a ramified specific legislation, the so-called *qanun*s issuing from the sultan's absolute authority, increasingly permeated the entire fabric of the Empire. At the same time, the new order allowed for considerable self-government of the various groups in the population along ethnoreligious and cultural, rather than territorial lines. (This evolving *millet* system will be more fully analyzed in Chapter LXXVIII.) With such a combination of political and economic unity and reliogiocultural diversity, buttressed by their great military power, the Ottoman empire builders established an imperial structure which, for centuries to come, was to play a vital role in the destinies of the Mediterranean world, including its Jewish segment.[17]

There was, however, a fundamental difference between the Ottoman colonization of Anatolia and that of the European possessions. In their efforts to repopulate cities and villages devastated by wars, their own included, the Turkish rulers, as we shall see, not only welcomed new settlers but also often forcibly transplanted inhabitants from one area to another. In Anatolia these efforts were concentrated primarily on settling Turks, rather than Greeks and other ethnic groups, and thus on converting the area into a predominantly Turkish-speaking Muslim area. This task was facilitated by the presence on the Peninsula of a great many Turkoman tribesmen, who had first settled there in the eleventh century and continued to immigrate from Central Asia long after the rise of the Ottoman power. Asia Minor thus became the mainstay of the Turkish nationality until the present day. In Europe, on the other hand, Murad I acted along similar lines only at the beginning of his reign, when he tried speedily to convert Adrianople-Edirne into an imperial capital. Soon thereafter he, and still more his successors, realized that the millions of Greeks, Slavs, Albanians, Armenians, and Walachians could not readily be displaced and that from them, whether or not converted to Islam, would have to come most of the manpower needed for the resettlement in the depopulated territories.

Illustrating this new orientation, was the conquerors' expropriation of but few Christian religious institutions. Only in Adrianople did the Christian churches and other monuments disappear and, according to Nicholas Iorga (writing at the beginning of this century), "not a trace has been preserved of the numerous Christian churches of the past." Elsewhere, however, not only houses of worship for the masses of Christian inhabitants, but also monasteries were allowed to continue their habitual operations. This is true of such famous centers of learning as the monastery on Mount Athos and also of some smaller institutions. For example, an official register of the district of Brancovica (Vilq) for 1455 recorded the presence there of three monasteries, each of which accommodated only one to four monks. Yet even this tiny number of personnel sufficed to keep up their cloisters' limited functions. Jews apparently had even less difficulty in keeping their synagogues since, after his conquest of Anatolian Brusa, Orkhan had allowed them to continue worshiping in their old building.[18]

In their march toward world conquest, however, at first the

sultans occasionally found it more expedient to control vassal principalities in Anatolia and the Balkans rather than to occupy them outright. Such dependencies were obliged to pay regular tributes and, when called upon, also to furnish armed contingents for Ottoman campaigns. In the case of a leading merchant republic like Dubrovnik, the initial tribute was set at 1,500 ducats annually. It was gradually raised until it reached 12,500 ducats in 1481. More remarkably, in the days of Murad I and Bayezid I, the Byzantine Empire itself was forced to pay the Ottomans an annual tribute of 30,000 gold pieces or 15,000 Venetian gold ducats (1379–1403). After Bayezid's defeat at Ankara and the ensuing domestic turbulence in Turkey, to be sure, these payments were suspended. As we recall, Venice even entertained the ambitious plan of conquering Gallipoli, and thus setting in motion the ultimate removal of the Turks from the European continent. However, under Murad II the Ottoman Empire so quickly regained its strength that, in 1422, the sultan could attempt to conquer Constantinople. His attack failed, but Byzantium now had to pay annually 300,000 slightly depreciated aspers then valued at 9,090 Venetian gold ducats.[19]

Personally, Murad II was not vindictive. While insisting on severely punishing Christian rulers who had broken their promises to keep peace, we are told by Ducas, "his anger was never of long duration." Whenever the vanquished party sent envoys to ask for peace they were received in a friendly fashion, their proposal was accepted, and the war discontinued. Yet among his numerous innovations, one proved to be of great historical importance for all Ottoman subjects: the formation of a new military elite corps of Janissaries. He did it by the so-called *devshirme* (gathering), consisting of a systematic selection of young boys, chiefly from among the prisoners of war. These youngsters were removed to Anatolia and placed in villages for a long enough time to learn Turkish and to be thoroughly indoctrinated with Islamic teachings and practices. Particular stress was laid on the doctrine of the world's division into the "World of Islam" and the "World of the Sword" sooner or later to be conquered by a holy war. Then came a period of training in military skills similar to that given to the

Mamelukes in Egypt. Together with the palace guard, likewise taken from young captives especially trained for that duty, this elite corps was to play a great role in all subsequent wars as well as in domestic affairs. From the outset the Jewish child captives, even if not quickly ransomed by their coreligionists, must have been exempted from both these branches of service, since Islamic law had long since forbidden their forced conversion. Even later, when some Jews participated in the military ventures of the Ottoman Empire, we do not hear of Jewish Janissaries. In time, to be sure, this corps lost some of its idealism and, bent upon profit, resented possible Jewish competitors for royal favor. Its members often squeezed out substantial payments from individual Jews or their communities. But at the beginning the few Jewish communities under Murad II's regime must have been grateful to a government which enabled them to live a fairly secure life with relatively little discrimination and ample opportunities for making a decent living.[20]

On the whole, the new regime treated its Jewish subjects in accordance with the traditional provisions of Islamic law. Nor were the lower officials and judges necessarily antagonistic to the "infidels." From the time of Murad II (1437) comes to us a curious report about a Sofia Christian soldier who, after arriving in Adrianople, publicly blasphemed against the Messenger—a capital crime. He was immediately surrounded by an angry mob and dragged to court. Rejecting all the openings for an effective defense offered him by the Muslim *qadhi,* the soldier stubbornly insisted upon the truth of his assertion, and even slapped the judge's face. Understandably, he thus brought upon himself a martyr's death. This story may be but an apocryphal part of the vast Christian martyrological literature illustrating a Christian's religious steadfastness in the face of death. But it does show that, at least occasionally, Muslim judges-theologians were known to overlook serious pecadillos of an "unbelieving" subject. Jews were also given full opportunities to cultivate their own religion, in both the Rabbanite and Karaite forms, and to run their communal affairs along established ways. There also was an incipient revival of Jewish learning, cultivated by both native and immigrant scholars. In

Vidin, at the time of the Ottoman conquest, we hear of a Rabbi Moses ha-Yevani (the Greek) and his teacher R. Shalom of Neustadt, evidently an immigrant from an Ashkenazic community, perhaps from Hungary after the decree of expulsion of Jews issued by King Louis the Great in 1360. Perhaps already in the days of Murad II another immigrant rabbi, Isaac Ṣarfati, was so impressed by the favorable conditions of life of Ottoman Jewry that he issued a much-quoted circular, addressed to the Jews of Swabia, the Rhineland, Styria, Moravia, and Hungary. Contrasting the prospective readers' insecurity of life under Christian masters with the conditions prevailing in the Ottoman Empire, he wrote:

Brothers and teachers, friends and acquaintances! I, Isaac Ṣarfati, though I spring from French stock, yet I was born in Germany, and sat there at the feet of my esteemed teachers. I proclaim to you that Turkey is a land wherein nothing is lacking, and where, if you will, all shall yet be well with you. The way to the Holy Land lies open to you through Turkey. Is it not better for you to live under Moslems than under Christians? Here every man may dwell at peace under his own vine and fig-tree. . . . And now, seeing all these things, O Israel, wherefore sleepest thou? Arise! and leave your accursed land for ever![21]

MEḤMED THE CONQUEROR (1451–1481)

Murad II's work was continued without interruption by his young son, Meḥmed II, subsequently named Fatih, the Conqueror, by an admiring world (1451–81). With his reign prematurely ended in a somewhat mysterious way (perhaps by the then widely used method of secret poisoning) when he reached the age of fifty-two, the third phase of the Ottoman expansion reached a new height. Meḥmed, equally distinguished as a military commander and as a statesman, succeeded in both, greatly extending his country's boundaries and in consolidating the earlier conquests. One of his initial acts of government consisted in the epochal conquest of Constantinople in 1453. This great imperial center of Eastern Christianity (renamed Istanbul in Turkish) soon became the new Ottoman capital and, having quickly undergone a thoroughgoing

Turkicization, has ever since remained the economic and cultural center of the Turkish world.

Far-sighted Meḥmed began with the reconstruction of the depopulated and ruined city almost immediately after its occupation. He not only opened its gates to new settlers and invited most of the older residents to return from their places of refuge, but he also instituted forcible transfers of inhabitants from other localities. According to a Turkish historian of the time, he first dispatched messengers to all his lands saying: "Whoever wishes, let him come, and let him become owner of houses, vineyards, and gardens in Istanbul." In a similar report the Greek Kristovoulos of Imbros adds that the order was aimed at having "as many inhabitants as possible transferred to the city, not only Christians, but also his own people and many of the Hebrews." Finding that this invitation did not attract enough settlers, the sultan gave orders

to dispatch families, both rich and poor, from every province. The Sultan's servants were sent with orders to the qāḍīs and the military commandants of every province and, in accordance with these orders, conscribed and brought very many families. These newcomers were also given houses, and this time the city began to flourish.[22]

As a result Constantinople, the population of which had declined to some 30,000 persons in the first part of the century, witnessed an increase to 97,956 by 1478. Characteristically, the census figures for that year show that, within the first quarter century after the conquest, the formerly overwhelming Christian majority had dwindled to but a little over 30 percent, while the Muslims constituted the majority of nearly 60 percent, and the Jewish community numbered some 10 percent of the population.[23]

Jews undoubtedly belonged to the most eager settlers following that invitation. To begin with, the existing Jewish community of the Byzantine period seems not to have been totally uprooted during the siege. Franz Babinger, otherwise a most careful scholar, was wrongly assuming that the Jews of the Balat quarter were the only ones not to suffer much during the first three days after the conquest when the Turkish soldiers were given free rein to slaughter the local inhabitants and to expropriate all the goods they could lay their hands on.

We recall the eyewitness testimony of the Venetian surgeon Nicolò Barbaro that in their final assault on May 29, some besiegers disembarked "by the Giudecca, so as to have better opportunity of getting booty." Nor did any Jewish source imply that the capital's Jewish population had escaped its devastation by the victory-intoxicated Turkish soldiery—an event which, if it had happened, might have been celebrated later by the Istanbul Jews in a Purim-like festival, as happened in many other localities on similar occasions.[24]

It appears, however, that the siege was not total and that during the nearly eight weeks of its duration (April 6–May 29), some ships bringing supplies could still reach the city. Similarly, quite a few individuals could escape the early horrors of the occupation by residing in such foreign colonies as that of the Genoese in Pera. At any rate, while descriptions of the conquest and accompanying "atrocities" circulated widely in horror-stricken Europe, we find few echoes thereof in the contemporary Jewish literature. Certainly, within a very short time the organized Jewish community resumed its ordinary course on a higher plane and in a more favorable climate.[25]

After the conquest of Constantinople, Mehmed embarked upon his renowned career as conqueror in West, North, South, and East. From his early youth he was dreaming of becoming a second Alexander the Great. Whether or not he knew foreign languages, especially Greek and Latin, he was able to acquaint himself with the biography enshrined in many legends of the equally youthful hero of the ancient world. He had available a reworking into Turkish of the *Iskander-Name* (Alexander Story) by Ahmadi (died in 1413). In general he was a studious young man. Before starting his campaign against the ancient Roman-Byzantine capital he spent many sleepless nights in studying the maps of the city with its fortifications and access roads so as to plan a quick occupation before the expected rescue forces of the Venetian navy and the armies of the European allies could reach the area. As a result, he was very impatient when the siege extended over some eight weeks. Secundino, a Greek who participated in the negotiations for surrender, was not alone in warning the West of Mehmed's insatiable ambition to conquer neighboring countries, including Italy. In response, Pope Nicholas V deluded himself into believing that he could organize a successful crusade against the invader despite the sharp internal conflicts among the European nations. Even less realistic was Pius II's effort to persuade the sultan to become a Christian. In his letter to Meḥmed the pope argued that "a bit of water" would suffice to make him a convert to Christianity and thus legitimize his assuming the title of emperor of the Christians and Orientals. The pope added:

All Christians will adore you and make you their arbiter in their conflicts. All the oppressed peoples will take refuge with you as their common protector. . . . You will thus be enabled to suppress the tyrants, to protect the good, and to fight the evildoers.[26]

Understandably, the Venetians with their long experience in the Balkans and the Aegean islands knew better. They hoped that the pope could unify Western Christendom for common action, but in the meantime they became embroiled in a protracted war with Meḥmed (1463–78), which ended in the loss of most of their footholds on the Balkan coastline, except Modon and Coron. Equally futile proved to be the resistance of Scanderbeg (Iskander Bey, originally George Castriota, *ca.* 1404–1468), one of the most renowned folk heroes in Albania, extolled in ballads for centuries thereafter. After many partial victories against larger Turkish forces he was finally defeated and executed. In short, within the thirty years of his reign Meḥmed not only consolidated his father's conquests, but also extended them westward to the Adriatic Sea, Bosnia, and Herzegovina, and reaffirmed his overlordship over Walachia and Moldavia. Most spectacularly, a Turkish naval expedition led in 1480 to the Ottoman occupation of Otranto, an important bridgehead on the Appenine Peninsula. This conquest opened vistas of Turkish annexation of southern Italy and ultimately of Rome and the powerful northern republics. At the same time, beginning with Lemnos in 1455 one Aegean island after another surrendered to the Turks; among them Negroponte (ancient Euboea) which harbored an important Jewish community. A sufficient number of local Jews speedily emigrated to the Turkish capital to form there, as we recall, a separate "Negropontine" congregation. Only Rhodes fended off a Turkish attack in 1480—Jews suffered severely on that occasion—but fell to the Ottomans 42 years later (January 1, 1523). For the first time Meḥmed also succeeded in the conversion of the Black Sea into a Turkish possession. He put an end to the empire of Trebizond, as well as to the Genoese colonies including Kaffa. In 1474 he even converted the Crimean Tatars into vassals of his empire, ready from time to time to send auxiliary forces to support Ottoman expeditions. Finally, the sultan eliminated the major strongholds of the pre-Ottoman Seljuks in Anatolia by occupying Karaman in 1474. He thus became an immediate neighbor of the Mameluke Empire and in contact with Persian-dominated Iraq, both of which also were soon to fall into Ottoman hands. In most of these areas Meḥmed encountered Jewish communities which, like the predominantly Christian populations and the increasing number of Shi'ite Muslims, shared, before long, the positive, and the negative, aspects of Ottoman rule.[27]

At the same time Meḥmed devoted himself to the reorganization of the Empire by enacting a number of ordinances, codifying the existing laws, centralizing the administration, and establishing an absolute rule. To be sure, his regime was in many ways oppressive and extortionist. According to a contemporary estimate by Theodorus Spanduginus (Spandoni), no less than 873,000 persons had become victims of Meḥmed's warfare. His fiscal policies were also quite ruthless. Five times during his reign he depreciated the currency by forcing the population to exchange six silver coins for five. It was an indirect war tax of one-sixth of the value of the currency. Nor did he seem to oppose outright falsification of coins, especially of the then regnant gold coin, the Venetian ducat. In general, he husbanded his revenues well. Aided, as we shall see, by the Jewish doctor Ya'qub of Gaëta, who was equally gifted as a physician and financier, Meḥmed usually managed to spend less than he received from revenues flowing into the Treasury through his ramified system of taxation. He thus was able to accumulate funds in the Treasury, despite the extremely costly wars which he waged against enemies on various fronts. By establishing a fairly uniform system of taxation, however, Meḥmed's policy proved to be much more beneficial to the subject population than the diverse and often arbitrary extractions of revenue by the previous feudal lords and petty rulers. Once again Jews, along with the other religious groups, were subject to special taxes, but these were, on the whole, rather moderate and, because they were often administered by their own leaders, were tempered with a good measure of social justice.[28]

Meḥmed's numerous enactments, not all of which have as yet been published, sought to redress especially the balance among the rural inhabitants and to promote commerce and craftsmanship in a most effective way. To facilitate adherence to these diverse acts of legislation he issued a code of laws (*qanunname*), summarizing some older, and more recent, enactments including his own. Curiously, he evinced so great a respect for established mores that he also codified, at least in part, the customary laws observed in diverse sections of his empire. Because of the two sides of his complex personality, which combined a quest for justice with occasional sanguinary and tyrannical acts, he merited both the condemnation of his European enemies, who equated him with the Antichrist and devil personified, and the high praise showered on him as a glorious and just ruler not only by the Turks but also, for example, in an exaggeratingly laudatory biography of the sultan by the Greek Kristovoulos of Imbros.[29]

The "Conqueror's" sense of justice manifested itself particularly in his treatment of religious dissenters. While he disliked the dervishes and their turbulence, he considered it a matter of good policy not to antagonize them unduly. Although a devoted Sunni, he harbored considerable sympathies for the Shi'ite point of view and did not discriminate against Shi'ite officials. More importantly, from the outset he tried to deal fairly with the Empire's large Christian population. After the conquest of Constantinople he faced the immediate problem of how to treat Constantinople's Oecumenical patriarchate. This central ecclesiastical authority for millions of Greek Orthodox worshipers in his own land and beyond, by its very constitution and age-old tradition, had been intimately tied to Byzantium's Caesaropapist imperial office. At the same time Meḥmed, who had at his service a widespread intelligence network in many lands, was undoubtedly well informed about the considerable misgivings felt by many Greek-Orthodox clerics and laymen regarding their episcopate's ethical standards. Moreover, many staunch believers were appalled by the prospects of an intervention of the West-European powers and their insistence upon the union of the Churches. Remembering the harsh reign of the Crusaders in 1204–1261, many undoubtedly felt like the Grand Duke (*megas dux*) Lucas Notaras, who contended that he would rather see "the turban of the Turkish sultan than a Latin mitre on the streets of his city."[30]

A leading exponent of the Turkophile orientation was the monk Gennadios (Georgios Scolarios) who suffered persecution from his superiors on this score. It was only natural for the sultan to inform the Greek-Orthodox leaders that they must elect a new patriarch and to suggest that Gennadios receive the appointment. The monk, captured by the Turks during the siege and sold into slavery in Adrianople, was now installed as the new patriarch (January 6, 1454). Thus foundations were laid for the famous *millet* system which granted the non-Muslim religious groups in the country full ethnoreligious and cultural autonomy. The decree of appointment (*bérat*), to paraphrase Georgios Phrantzes' summary, granted to Gennadios (1) inviolability of his person; (2) permanent tax exemption; (3) the renewal of the same privileges for all his successors; (4) similar rights to be extended to the rest of the clergy. Clearly, freedom of religion and worship was also included. The early operations of that system appeared so satisfactory to the Church that in his 1480 letter to Doge Giovanni Mocenigo of Venice, the then Patriarch Maximos glowingly described the existing conditions. He pleaded that similar treatment be extended by the Venetian authorities to the Orthodox on the island of Crete, and added:

The great and excellent autocrator who confesses a different creed has nevertheless granted the Christians and all dissenters full liberty of religion and conscience. Last year he received petitions from people residing in Great Walachia [Thessaly] who wished to do violence to the Armenians so as to force them to adopt the true religion and become Orthodox, but he [the sultan] through letters addressed to them ordered that God's law remain free of force.

In this way developed a long-range symbiosis between the Orthodox masses and the Ottoman regime, which continued despite the divisions within the Orthodox Church itself and the subsequent relative independence secured within it by the Bulgarian and Serbian "autocephalous" Churches.[31]

Almost immediately thereafter, similar treatment was extended to the Jewish faith. It appears that Meḥmed's predecessors reigning over tiny Jewish communities had few incentives to try to impose any kind of central organization upon them. After 1453, however, the Jewish community of Constantinople was rather sizable and the sultan was eager to attract more and more Jewish settlers. He realized that the Jewish community would itself benefit from a more authoritative leadership with easier access to the throne and the ability to represent the Jewries of the whole empire before the Ottoman authorities. As a result, the sultan might thereby also exercise more direct control over this increasingly important segment of his subject population. Looking for a leader to whom he could entrust a position somewhat similar to that of the Orthodox patriarch, his choice fell on Moses b. Elijah Capsali. According to the report included in his grandnephew Elijah b. Elqanah Capsali's historical narrative, the sultan first tried to ascertain the rabbi's probity and attitude toward Islam, and in disguise attended a court session in which Moses had to pass sentences in civil litigations. To his satisfaction he found that Capsali had decided a case against a rich and powerful member of the community in favor of a poor man whose claim was legally valid. Subsequently Meḥmed summoned R. Moses to his court and during the conversation inquired about the general rabbinic attitude toward Ishmael, the reputed progenitor of all Muslims. In reply, Capsali could quote from the Talmud a number of complimentary references to this elder son of Abraham, the recognized ancestor of both religious groups. While we have neither the exact date nor the text of his original decree of appointment, Capsali's induction may have resembled in a lower key that of Gennadios. Later Jewish tradition claimed that the rabbi's position was placed ahead of that of the patriarch which, though unsupported by any Turkish documentary evidence, may have taken place when, in later generations, the Jews had become a large, affluent, and highly influential part of the ethnoreligious structure of the empire.

Certainly, the regime could rely on Jewish loyalty much more unequivocally and permanently than on that of the more numerous and concentrated Christian groups subject to blandishments from their powerful coreligionists outside the country.[32]

One of the major problems still awaiting elucidation is the extent to which the chief rabbi's authority extended over Istanbul's Jewish sectarians, especially Karaites and Samaritans. We know that in Egypt the Mamelukes treated all these groups as part of the Jewish community, headed by a single *nagid*. True, even in Cairo Karaites and Samaritans often appeared before the authorities, independently represented by their own chiefs. In fifteenth-century Istanbul the Turks found very few Samaritans but an increasingly flourishing Karaite community. In fact, headed by such outstanding scholars as Elijah b. Moses Bashyachi and Kaleb b. Elijah Afendopolo, the Karaites were then undergoing a great religiocultural renaissance and produced some of their most authoritative works of law and theology. Yet, we do not seem to have any evidence that the Ottoman authorities were fully aware of the depth of these divisions within the Jewish community. We shall see, in another context, that both Rabbanites and Karaites were affected by internal dissensions, resulting primarily from the differences in mores and rituals brought with them by the new immigrants from their respective countries. While the more numerous Rabbanites could, before long, form as many as forty-four congregations in the capital alone, the relatively few Karaites were linguistically, culturally, and ritualistically separated into two main groups: the old Mid-Eastern settlers who spoke the local languages and were open to important religious reforms, and the new arrivals from the Crimea who were staunchly conservative and for a long time continued using their special Judeo-Tatar dialect. Yet, it appears that for a long time even the official tax registrars lumped together all these varieties of Jews; they were apparently satisfied to leave the central and local fiscal administration mainly in the hands of Rabbanite leaders.[33]

We must bear in mind, however, that despite, or perhaps because of, his forceful personality and his attempts to impose his will on other Jewish communities of the Empire, Capsali's orders were often disregarded by the provincial rabbis or congregations. From an interesting letter, probably written by R. Eliezer ha-Shimeoni (who first served as rabbi of the Ashkenazic congregation and was later elected as the spiritual leader of the Catalan synagogue in Salonica, where he died in 1530), we learn of at least one case of such "disobedience." In this epistle, addressed to Capsali shortly before his demise in 1496 or 1497, the writer complained that, some three years before, the chief rabbi, because of some false allegations, had commanded him to desist from administering divorces in his congregation and from single-handedly issuing sentences in civil litigations. From these obscure allusions, it appears, Capsali had found fault with either a phrase in the particular writ of divorce or some other procedural detail, which may have conformed with an Ashkenazic tradition but was unfamiliar to the chief rabbi, who was of Candiot origin. In any case, the Salonican rabbi who, deeply offended, had at first wished to give up the rabbinate altogether, yielded to the entreaties of the leaders of his congregation and, "with the consent of all the [local] sages," continued to administer justice and to adjudicate authoritatively matters pertaining to marriages, divorces, and ḥaliṣot.[34]

The developments of the Christian Churches and the Jewish communities under the sultans after the fall of Constantinople reveal marked differences, as well as similarities, however. To the Balkan Christians their subjection to a non-Christian regime was a relatively novel experience and all along the Orthodox Church regarded itself, to use Steven Runciman's felicitous phrase, as a "great Church in captivity." The synagogue's captivity, on the other hand, had been an established millennial experience long before the rise of the Ottoman Empire; it now merely flourished under a relatively stable and less oppressive regime. Curiously, even in daily life there existed many crypto-Christians who, having been converted to Islam, did not dare publicly to revert to their former faith, because such conversion was officially classified as a capital crime. In contrast, many Jewish immigrants now settling in the Muslim Middle East left the Iberian Peninsula, where they had lived as crypto-Jews under the perennial danger of prosecution by the Inquisition, while upon arrival in the Ottoman Empire they could freely profess their Jewish faith. Similarly, there was a great temptation for the Muslim conquerors, including Meḥmed II, to convert the large and beautiful Christian churches into mosques, whereas the existing synagogues were, for the most part, small and unpretentious, often outwardly undistinguished from private houses. There certainly was little incentive for expropriating such buildings for Muslim worship. On the contrary, when Meḥmed instituted the policy of forcibly repopulating Istanbul with Jewish settlers from other communities he must have realized that the new arrivals would require additional places of worship. Indeed, as a result of the simultaneously growing Jewish immigration from other lands, new synagogues were springing up all over the Empire, further stimulated by the differing rituals in the divine services conducted by the diverse groups of Jewish immigrants. For this reason the old Muslim law, echoing the ancient and medieval Christian enactments which had prohibited the erection of new synagogues without special governmental permits, at first went into total discard and had to be reintroduced by Muslim legislators in the later period of stabilization.[35]

On the other hand, both denominations enjoyed the right to tax their own members. In fact, Meḥmed the Conqueror and several successors sometimes granted to Jewish (or Christian) leaders the task of collecting not only their own denominational, but also state taxes. Jewish communities could distribute the load among their families according to their own judgment regarding the best interests of their members. Characteristically, the enforcement of denominational taxes was placed on a par with that of the state revenues. At a person's death, both kinds of tax arrears had priority over all other obligations of the estate, including a wife's dowry, which normally was separated from the assets before any other debts were paid. Nor was it the law that each denomination be distinguished externally by different colors of headgear, shoes, and the like, as overtly discriminatory in the Ottoman environment as in the West. Meḥmed himself issued strict regulations concerning the specific colors of the attire to be worn by his highest officials. The viziers had to wear green clothes, while the chamberlains were to appear in scarlet red, the muftis in white, and the ulemas (scholars) in purple garments. Generally, the officials of the Porte were distinguished by their yellow shoes; those of the palace wore bright red. The "badge," therefore, had lost much of its derogatory implications and was mainly a part of a multicolored system of costumes displayed by a civilization which laid great stress on external appearances, especially on formal occasions.[36]

Concerned primarily with empire building and the reorganization of his administration, Meḥmed realized that he could not get along with Muslim officials alone. While reserving the highest offices to men professing Islam (among them quite a few former slaves raised in the Islamic faith after their captivity), he could safely entrust many lower positions to Christians and Jews. From the beginning of his reign Meḥmed found an outstanding counselor in a new arrival from Italy, Ya'qub (Jacopo) of Gaëta. Although probably quite young, Ya'qub was a well-trained physician when he was first employed by Murad II. He is said to have later identified an ailment of the suprarenal capsules (subsequently named Addison's disease after Dr. Thomas Addison of Guy's Hospital in London, author of a pertinent analysis published in 1855). Very early after reaching Adrianople Ya'qub caught the eye of young Meḥmed who persuaded his father to send the doctor to his residence in Magnesia (Manisa), Anatolia. Ya'qub speedily became a confidant and mentor of the young prince and followed him in 1451 to Adrianople and, later, to Istanbul, serving both as a physician and as one of the chief advisers in political and financial affairs. This versatile doctor quickly advanced to a position of *defterdar,* the equivalent of a modern finance minister, who, though ranking below the grand vizier, was reporting directly to the sultan. Using his familiarity with the Western systems he was also able to advise the sultan on international and fiscal affairs as well as on problems of bureaucratic reorganization. Ya'qub later was said to have served as vizier and borne the title of pasha. It is frequently assumed that, before his appointment to these high offices, Ya'qub had at least to pay lip service to Islam, but there is no official record of his conversion. The strongest argument advanced in favor of conversion is derived from a document attesting that four of Ya'qub's sons, bearing Muslim names, received in 1489–90 gifts from a Muslim pious foundation (*waqf*). This conclusion is by no means cogent, however, since in another document relating to an Istanbul *waqf*, written in Meḥmed's lifetime (1481, reproduced in an extant copy of 1495), three Jewish physicians named Musa (Moses), Elias, and Avraham, appear as owners of property belonging to a Muslim hospital. They probably served in some capacity on its medical staff; the hospital's statute expressly stated that it should have in its employ "two physicians of whatever nationality, provided that they are able to apply [proper] remedies and are celebrated for their skill in operations." There also are other recorded cases of members of the same families indiscriminately bearing Muslim, along with Christian or other non-Muslim names. In any case, a century later (in 1571), some of Ya'qub's descendants still were professing Jews; they appealed to a rabbi in their litigation relating to their hereditary tax immunity with the Jewish community of which they were members. It also appears that, while serving as one of the sultan's most influential associates, Ya'qub had more than one occasion to help his Jewish coreligionists.[37]

Remarkably, in 1452, quite early in Meḥmed's reign and his court physician's career, the sultan conferred upon his Jewish favorite a noteworthy privilege. When Ya'qub temporarily lost the original copy, Meḥmed did him the extraordinary favor of issuing a second decree repeating the first privilege in full. However, shortly thereafter the first copy came to light and the family cherished both copies for generations. In fact, our knowledge of this text is derived mainly from its Hebrew translation, inserted more than a century later (in 1571) into a responsum by the distinguished Salonican rabbi, Samuel b. Moses de Medina (1505/6–1589), on the occasion of a controversy which had arisen between Ya'qub's descendants and the leaders of the Istanbul Jewish community. To prove their point Ya'qub's progeny submitted a version of their privilege to the rabbi. After praising Ya'qub as "the glory of scholars and the ornament of physicians, the Galen and Hippocrates of his generation," the sultan enumerated in this document a number of major taxes, as examples of the numerous imposts from all of which Ya'qub and his offspring were to be permanently exempted. Meḥmed added:

I hereby decree and establish and exempt the said physician and all the issue of his loins, [making them] exempt [from all future taxes] for ever. . . . No rod shall oppress them, they shall dwell alone in sure dwellings, calm and peaceful and delighting themselves in the abundance of peace, with joyfulness and with gladness of heart. And if any man dare to ask of any of these men any of the things that are written here, or [even] speak about them with his lips, then there shall fall on him the curse of God (may He be blessed), of His holy angels and of man, and the curse shall be upon him until he becomes an example to all his beholders.

In his sentence settling the controversy, the rabbi unhesitatingly confirmed the validity of the decree and decided that the community had no right to impose any tax upon the privileged family.[38]

In keeping with the mores of the time, the Venetian rulers tried to bribe this influential Istanbul diplomat. Even publicly, envoys arriving from other countries were expected to bring precious gifts not only to the sultan but also to his chief counselors. According to experienced Ragusan observers, the Turkish negotiators "are generally very strict, but they soon relent . . . [and] do everything for money; he who pays more proves successful." This issue led to a long-lasting debate when documents found in the diplomatic archives of Venice revealed that the Venetian Senate had tried to persuade Ya'qub to poison Meḥmed and thus to remove that most feared adversary from the scene. The physician was promised, upon the sultan's death, Venetian citizenship with high honors and the payment of the enormous sum of 200,000 ducats in new currency. Ya'qub seems to have played the game along with the Venetian authorities, possibly with Meḥmed's knowledge, as he did in 1465, when he informed the Venetian *bailo* in Istanbul that the sultan had already been converted to Christianity. Perhaps by entering this "conspiracy" he had hoped to divert the attention of the Venetians from achieving their goal through other intermediaries. They did, indeed, try to achieve the same result in fourteen such attempts over 23 years—in 1475–77 by enlisting the cooperation of another Jewish court physician, Vlaco—equally in vain. Aware of these designs and constantly in dread of assassination, the sultan isolated himself from his entourage. Indeed, each foreign envoy entering his chambers was supposed to be escorted by two Turkish attendants firmly holding his arms. Ultimately, all these precautions proved futile and the distinguished sultan died mysteriously at the age of fifty-two, apparently from a poisoning instigated by his own son, Bayezid. Ya'qub, however, evidently remained the sultan's loyal adviser to the end of his life.[39]

BAYEZID II (1481–1512)

Bayezid II generally continued his father's policies, though with a greatly diminished élan. Whereas in official documentation Meḥmed had called himself "Meḥmed, son of Murad, ever victorious Khan" and only occasionally applied the grandiloquent title of "Sultan, also by the Grace of God, King and Emperor of both Continents of Asia and Europe," Bayezid sometimes added the boastful phrase "and of the Rest of the World." In another document he described himself more briefly: "Sultan Baiazith, by the Grace of God, the Supreme Emperor of Asia and Greece." Yet, from the outset he had considerable difficulty even in seizing the reins of government in his own country. At first his younger brother, Jem, aided by the grand vizier, made a strong bid for succession. It was only with the help of other dignitaries and particularly the Janissaries that Bayezid vanquished Jem's troops and forced him into permanent exile. During the interval the Janissaries staged a regular riot against Christians and Jews in Istanbul. They even made a special search for the chief rabbi, apparently because they resented Capsali's earlier reprimand of some Jewish youth for having taken part in their licentious bouts. Only by chance did the rabbi escape detection and probable assassination. To appease his elite corps the sultan had to grant it total amnesty for the bloodshed and a considerable raise in wages. Even after his defeat, moreover, Jem's presence in Rhodes or France for the following fourteen years hindered

Bayezid in undertaking any major military action, since he was afraid of an armed intervention of the Christian powers in favor of his rebellious brother. But even after Jem's death in 1495 Bayezid's military activities were mainly holding actions aiming at preserving the Ottoman conquests.[40]

Though of a largely pacific disposition and known as a lover of books and music, Bayezid was constantly embroiled in campaigns along various fronts. Unwittingly he thus added some possessions to his empire. A particular instance was his war with Venice, which had been irked by his building up the Turkish navy (according to an exaggerating Italian report, it was supposed to have been manned by crews, one-third of whom consisted of Jewish sailors). He ended it by adding many Venetian strongholds, including Coron and Modon, to his Balkan territories. In the North he defeated King John Albert (Jan Olbracht) of Poland in 1497 and thus reaffirmed Turkey's control over the Black Sea and, at least for a time, its overlordship over Moldavia. In Asia, too, he fended off threatening attacks from Isma'il, the new Ṣafavid ruler of Persia. When, for the first time, the Ottomans were seriously involved with the still powerful Mameluke Empire because of Bayezid's attack on Cilicia, a Mameluke dependency, neither party wanted a protracted confrontation and peace was reestablished on the basis of the status quo.[41]

Bayezid's reign coincided with one of the greatest Jewish migratory movements of the early modern period. The expulsion of the Jews from Spain and Sicily in 1492 and from Navarre in 1498, combined with the forced conversion of the Jews in Portugal in 1496–97, the opening of its frontiers for Jewish emigration in 1507, as well as the banishment of Jews from the Provence and other French areas in the 1490s, and from the Kingdom of Naples in 1510–11 all set in motion waves of Jewish migration to the eastern Mediterranean with growing momentum. To be sure, we recall the enormous difficulties encountered by Jewish exiles in crossing the sea even to neighboring Italy or North Africa. It is also very likely, although we do not have convincing documentary evidence to this effect, that the Spanish authorities looked with a jaundiced eye on attempts by Jews to settle in the Ottoman Empire, an archenemy of Spain. When, in 1492, Granada surrendered to the Catholic monarchs, the treaty specifically allowed the free departure of the Granada Muslims to North Africa but expressly prohibited their emigration to Turkey. In this respect the widespread sentiment expressed in the well-known ironical saying attributed to Bayezid—"You call Ferdinand [of Spain] a wise king; him, who by expelling the Jews has impoverished his country and enriched mine!"—did not escape the attention of the Catholic monarchs. From the outset they must have perceived the incongruity of providing an enemy with enterprising new settlers equipped with considerable skills and capital. Certainly, if the Palermo elders protested against the Spanish decree of expulsion of the Sicilian Jews because their city would thereby be deprived of skilled workers for the production of weapons and agricultural implements, that loss to Sicily undoubtedly accrued to the benefit of the Ottoman economy and armed forces. In any event, an ever-increasing number of Jews succeeded in reaching Istanbul, Salonica, and other major Turkish cities. Salonica, in particular, because of its favorable location as an Aegean harbor and its underpopulation, attracted a great many Jewish immigrants. To quote Samuel Usque's pertinent observation written in 1545:

There is a city [Salonica] in the Turkish kingdom which formerly belonged to the Greeks, and in our days is a true mother in Judaism.
. . . The majority of my children who have been persecuted and exiled from Europe and many other parts of the world have taken refuge in the city and she embraces them and receives them with as much love and good will as if she were Jerusalem that old and ever-pious mother of ours.

Before the end of the century the local rabbi, Samuel de Medina, discussing a legal problem in which that fact mattered, emphasized that Salonica already had a Jewish majority of the population.[42]

Jewish immigration was not limited to major cities, however. In a recent study of the provincial community of Trikala, Thessaly, Nicoará Beldiceanu has shown that, while the official registers of 1455 fail to mention the existence of a Jewish community in a population at that time numbering almost 2,500 persons, in 1506 the city embraced 260 Muslim hearths,

29 widows, 1 bachelor; 318 Christian hearths, 38 widows and 24 bachelors; as well as 19 Jewish hearths. The total population had thus increased to about 3,100 persons, among whom the Jewish community numbering some 100 souls constituted an important segment. A passage relating to Jews in the document reads: "They ought not to be prevented from departing in order to engage in commerce or to exercise their crafts. But if they leave they must designate a guarantor [*kefil*] for the payment of the capitation tax." In general, Bayezid II prohibited Jewish emigration from his country because of the ensuing loss to both the Ottoman Treasury and economy.[43]

The Iberian immigrants, in particular, immediately formed congregations of their own according to their respective towns or districts of origin on the Iberian Peninsula. In Salonica, for example, they began with a congregation called *Gerush Sefarad* (The Expulsion from Spain) to commemorate that momentous event in their history. It was followed by the congregations of Castilian, Majorcan, Catalan, as well as of Portuguese, Lisbon, and later Evora groups, each quite autonomous and cultivating its own ritual. Before long there existed two Sicilian congregations which in the latter part of the sixteenth century quarreled with each other so that the case had to be brought to the attention of R. Samuel de Medina.[44]

Proud of their great cultural heritage, all these Jewries cultivated their original Spanish language, predominantly of the Castilian variety which they spoke with great fluency. In fact, half a century after the expulsion a Spanish visitor, Gonsalo de Illescas, reported that the Jews of Salonica, Constantinople, Alexandria, Cairo, Venice, and other mercantile cities regularly used Spanish in their conversation. "I have known in Venice many Jewish children from Salonica who spoke the Castilian language as well as, or better than, myself." Of course, in time, that language received many admixtures. Even in their relations with Jews of other origins, the Romaniots (often called the Gregos), Askenazim, Italians, and others who spoke languages of their own, they had to use other media. Since in their daily business and social connections the majority of Jews constantly had to deal with these polyglot groups, many of them developed the facility of conversing in many languages.

This circumstance made them particularly useful for the service as dragomans (a semi-official designation of interpreters) who, going far beyond their linguistic mediation, often served as trusted agents for foreign diplomats and merchants in negotiations with local authorities and businessmen. Understandably, in the course of time their original purely Castilian speech incorporated a considerable number of loan words, phrases, and occasional sentence structures not only from the Hebrew but also from the Turkish, Slavic, Greek, and later on Arabic environments. Instead of becoming a mere jargon, however, the resulting Ladino dialect became a language in its own right with its own literature and cultural validity. Because they were as usual quite conservative in their domestic and synagogue relationships, the Sephardim preserved enough of the original Castilian vocabulary, pronunciation, and other linguistic ingredients to arouse the curiosity of modern students of the medieval Castilian language which, in its native Spanish habitat, had been submerged by the centuries of linguistic evolution.[45]

At first the local Jews, many of them fairly recent arrivals themselves, were quite hospitable toward the newcomers. Unlike some of their North-African coreligionists, they viewed particularly the immigrants from the Iberian Peninsula as martyrs for the faith, treated them with compassion, and often took them into their homes until they could find other accommodations. They also seem to have instituted charitable collections for the "redemption of captives," a category of sufferers, with whom they identified the exiles from Spain and Portugal and who had long enjoyed a high priority in the traditional scheme of Jewish philanthropy.

Rather than considering the new arrivals as likely competitors for jobs, commercial opportunities, housing, or food supplies, most of the local Jewish residents seem to have felt, as was later expressed by R. Moses b. Joseph di Trani, that they "ought not to interfere with any man arriving from the end of the earth if he wishes to engage in business and make profits, for the local people will profit from it together with him." With the passage of time, however, the differences in appearance, habits, and outlook of the various groups necessarily led

to intercommunal friction. The Germans, for example, depre-
cated both the Romaniots and the Sephardim as lacking in
rabbinic learning, whereas the Mediterraneans looked down
upon the Ashkenazic arrivals as uncultured and, in worldly
matters, uncivilized people. More importantly, each group also
brought with it different rituals and interpretations of certain
details in talmudic law and regarded its own way of life and
traditions as superior to those of the others. At times even the
regional differences in the home countries of both the Ashkenazim and Sefardim—promoted by the long-lasting political
and feudal divisions and perpetuated in the various custumals
which had proliferated especially in Central Europe in the
fourteenth and fifteenth centuries—created much friction between the congregations of the same fundamental rite. These
divisions assumed such dimensions that a leading Polish halakhist, R. Solomon Luria (1510–73), commenting on the accepted Sephardic-Askenazic breach, observed that there was a
real threat that the Jews would have not two Torot but 613
Torot.[46]

Moses Capsali, rather than mediating between these diverse
heritages, often tried to impose upon all groups a certain uniformity of observance in consonance with his own original
background developed by generations of Cretan Jewry. This
attitude is well reflected in several responsa from his pen which
have reached us. He probably encountered few objections when
he insisted that cantors must not receive their posts through
the interference of secular authorities, and when he attempted
to prevent individuals from outbidding one another in the acquisition of houses, a measure necessitated by the arrival of
masses of immigrants which undoubtedly created a great
housing shortage in many war-ravaged cities. Both these rabbinical decisions were fully in line with the long-established
Jewish communal procedures. However, in the most delicate
aspects of family purity the minute differences in the laws of
divorce could easily lead to differences of opinion whether a
particular woman was not legitimately divorced and, hence,
whether her children by another husband were to be condemned as "bastards" in the technical sense. Here, R. Moses
tried to follow only the lines accepted by the Balkan-Aegean

Jews, naturally arousing much opposition from the other groups. Similarly, he invoked the old law that marriage ceremonies should be conducted in the presence of ten adult male Jews. The purpose of that regulation was to give each wedding wider publicity so that neither party could conceal its earlier marital ties in other lands. However, precisely in this matter the Ashkenazim brought with them a tradition of disregarding that provision because many tiny German communities could not assemble a quorum of ten adult men for every wedding.[47]

Capsali's rigidity is further illustrated by his ordinance forbidding the incoming Sephardic Jews to wear their accustomed scarves (*sudarim*) on their clothing on Sabbath. Although the new arrivals explained to the rabbi that this was part of their attire, hallowed by an old custom in their native land and hence was not a detached object which by Sabbath law Jews were prohibited from carrying from a private into a public area, Capsali remained adamant in his outlawry. This stubbornness naturally created much resentment. On one occasion his roughshod tactics actually brought the chief rabbi into a highly embarrassing situation. A messenger arrived from Palestine bearing the curious name Moses 'Esrim ve-Arba' (Moses [the Man of] Twenty Four, a name which enemies interpreted to mean that he was only learned in the twenty-four books of Scripture, whereas it was really derived from a German place name, Vierundzwanzig Höfe in Württemberg). The question arose whether he should be allowed to preach in the synagogue of R. Elijah Mizraḥi who was later to officiate as chief rabbi. For some reason the local congregation did not wish to listen to him, but Capsali forced it to allow him to preach. Such an intervention by the chief rabbi in the inner affairs of a congregation caused widespread dissatisfaction and at least four other communal leaders loudly objected to the rabbi's high-handedness. Ultimately, the controversy assumed an almost international dimension, when the messenger continued his journey to Italy and there obtained from R. Joseph Colon, one of the outstanding rabbinic authorities of the generation, a sharply worded letter of condemnation of Capsali. To be sure, Colon later regretted having acted without first conducting a full-fledged investigation of the merits of the case and eventually sent his son to Istanbul to offer Capsali personal apologies. But all these incidents only demonstrated that Meḥmed the Conqueror's original expectation that by establishing a chief rabbinate in Istanbul he would be better able to control the Jewish communities of the entire Empire was unrealistic. In the long run Ottoman Jewry learned to live with an increasing variety of groups and approaches and, perhaps because of that plurality, was able to develop an even more flourishing and pulsating cultural life.[48]

From the outset this ability to continue living their accustomed way of life at home and in the synagogue and speaking their own languages, while adjusting to the political and economic exigencies of their new environment, helped many new settlers to devote their creative energies to the pursuit of learning. Embracing in their midst a large number of scholars, theologians, and writers, these new arrivals contributed mightily to the rise of the general cultural level in the population. Symbolic of their contributions to the Ottoman civilization was their pioneering in the art and business of printing. Just as in Portugal, where printed Hebrew books appeared before the publication of the first Portuguese volumes, so did the Constantinople and Salonican Hebrew presses precede in time any similar establishments in Turkish, Greek, or Slavic letters. There even appeared a Hebrew incunabulum, in the shape of an edition of the well-known code of laws by R. Jacob b. Asher, *Arba' Ṭurim* (The Four Pillars) which was published in 1494 in Constantinople by the brothers David and Samuel Ibn Naḥmias. Within a few decades the Turkish Hebrew prints began competing with those of Venice and Amsterdam on the world market. We shall see that, from the point of view of content, too, these publications made significant contributions to Jewish and, to a lesser extent, to general studies. In this fashion, the Balkan Jewries were fully prepared to work side by side with the old and established Jewish communities of the Syro-Egyptian and North-African varieties with whom they were soon to share their common Ottoman regime.[49]

NEW HAVEN OF REFUGE

Ottoman expansion could not have come at a more propitious moment for medieval Jewry. The last three centuries of the Middle Ages marked a period of growing intolerance toward Jews and Judaism among the Christian nations. The ensuing wave of expulsions and forced conversions in Western and Central Europe sent many exiles in quest of new homes. While the simultaneous emergence of the Polish-Lithuanian Commonwealth into the ranks of the major European powers enabled it to absorb thousands of refugees from neighboring lands, the expansion of Turkish power into the Balkans and the Aegean islands opened up new settlement opportunities for the much larger masses of Mediterranean Jews uprooted from the Iberian Peninsula, southern France, and southern Italy. Many pious Jews may well have seen in these new developments an encouraging omen that, to quote an old rabbinic saying, God often "provides a remedy before the affliction." For generations thereafter the Ottoman Empire became the main haven of refuge for the persecuted Western Jews.

Such friendly treatment of Jewish refugees was facilitated by two internal developments in the Turkish-dominated lands. Although for the most part pious Muslims, the early rulers of the Anatolian Turkish possessions issued special enactments which in some respects deviated from the all-embracing law of Islam. True, they professed rigid adherence to the *shari'a*, and often adjusted the requirements of their own administration to the teachings propounded by qadhis learned in the various branches of Islamic law. But time and again, they, and still more their fifteenth-century successors, especially Meḥmed the Conqueror, had to issue ordinances (*qanuns*) at some variance from the official Islamic law. Such a conflict had indeed become manifest in the early introduction of the *devshirme*, which clearly violated the Old Islamic principle of tolerating surrendering *dhimmis*. Yet, the leading rulers of the growing Empire realized that the demands of realpolitik had at times to override the considerations of strict orthodoxy. It was doubly imperative to make whatever readjustments of the law were required for the evolution of the *millet* system which, for centuries thereafter, was to govern the relationships between the Muslim majority and the respective non-Muslim minorities.[50]

Developments of this type were facilitated by the growth of the Ottoman Empire into a multinational state. It was simply impossible for the conquering Turks to assimilate all the Christian nations which came under their sway in rapid succession. Developments in multinational empires had played a decisive role in the history of medieval Jewry everywhere and now made itself felt with redoubled strength in the Ottoman area. Only multinational Poland, though an overwhelmingly Christian nation, could become the most religiously tolerant country in Christian Europe at least until the new counter-reformatory and nationalistic regimes of the seventeenth and eighteenth centuries endeavored to convert the entire Commonwealth into a predominantly Catholic and Polish national state. Even then it could not completely depart from the modicum of a toleration of Jews and other religious minorities in contrast with the exclusivity of the Western nation-states before the Peace Treaty of Westphalia. The Ottoman Empire which, to the very end, was dominated by a Turkish minority ruling over a variety of ethnoreligious groups, had a double motivation to be tolerant toward Jews whose loyalty appeared much more dependable than that of some other ethnic groups with brethren living as free nations across the borders. This situation prevailed until after the First World War when the Republic of Turkey, through the loss of its non-Turkish-speaking provinces, became a national state and pursued strongly nationalistic policies.

TURKEY'S GOLDEN AGE

URING THE sixteenth century the Ottoman Empire's multinational character received a new coloring by its expansion to the Indian Ocean and the Sahara. It now embraced a multitude of new peoples divided by language, faith, and deep-rooted regional and local traditions. Even the Arabic-speaking majority in the new provinces conversed in a variety of dialects, so that Iraqi and Algerian farmers could hardly communicate with one another. The growth of the Shi'ite minority injected a strong element of diversity into the dominant Muslim religion. So did the adherence of the various provinces to one or another of the four major schools of Muslim jurisprudence. Although the ulama (Turkish, ulema, the scholars and judges constituting the body of mullahs) of these schools had long learned to live with one another in relatively peaceful relations, their followers often ardently cherished their different customs and interpretations, as well as applications, of the universal *shari'a*.

The Christian minorities, too, were deeply divided by sectarian differences. In contrast to the Balkans, where the Christian populations predominantly accepted the teachings and practices of the Greek Orthodox Church and submitted to the governance of its unified ecclesiatical establishment, the various Eastern Churches evinced numerous dogmatic and ritualistic disparities which added much color to, but also created frequent internal dissensions within, their religious life. Apart from such large concentrations of diverse sects as those of the Egyptian Copts, the Lebanese Maronites, and the Armenians, the sectarian divisions among the Christian communities throughout the Asian and African provinces were too deeply rooted to be overcome by the administrative uniformity of the new regime. Nor were, as we shall see, even the far smaller Jewish communities entirely homogeneous. Yet, it was this very multinational and multisectarian agglomeration of peoples which proved at first to be a source of strength to the upsurging Empire, although it also ultimately became—especially in the era of the overpowering force of modern nationalism—a major factor in its disintegration.

FROM SELIM TO SELIM (1512–74)

The sixty-two years of the reigns of Selim I, nicknamed *Yavuz* (the Grim, 1512–20), Suleiman the Magnificent (1520–66), and Selim II (1566–74) marked the apogee of Turkish power and may justly be called the Golden Age of the Ottoman Empire. When its imperial expansion was brought to a halt in the last quarter of the sixteenth century, the Turkish ruling classes lost much of the dynamism created by their sense of universal mission to establish a world empire through an unceasing "holy war." Moreover, Suleiman who, known in the West as the Magnificent, was more precisely described in Turkish historiography as Suleiman the Lawgiver (*Qanuni*), left behind memorable achievements in Ottoman legislation and administrative organization. These were matched by the glory of Turkish architecture, poetry, and jurisprudence, as exemplified by the works of the great architect Sinan (aptly called by Franz Babinger "the Michelangelo of Turkey"), the poet Baki, and the Grand Mufti Abu Su'ud.[1]

From the Jewish point of view even more important were the particular areas of Ottoman expansion during the sixteenth century. In 1516–17 Selim I conquered Syria and Egypt, taking over the entire Mameluke Empire. In 1534–35 Suleiman annexed Iraq. All these territories, representing the old heartlands of both Islam and Eastern Judaism, now became part of the Ottoman Empire until World War I. While during the last three centuries of the Middle Ages both civilizations had lost much of their creative élan, their adherents nevertheless remembered the centuries of the Islamic Renaissance and the millennia of biblical, talmudic, and geonic Jewish culture. Outwardly, too, as the ruler of Mecca and Medina, each Turkish sultan became the *khādim al-haramain* (protector of the holy places), which greatly enhanced his prestige throughout the Muslim world. By conferring upon each sultan the duty to protect all Muslim pilgrims streaming from the various lands in fulfillment of their religious obligation to visit Mecca at least once in their lifetime, this title also gave him the opportunity for political interference outside his own borders. Moreover, in putting an end to the shadow caliphate, which had been transferred from Baghdad to Cairo and was fully controlled by the Mameluke rulers, these conquests paved the way for the assumption of the title caliph by the Ottoman rulers who, proud of their Turkish ancestry, obviously could not claim direct descent from Mohammed, as did certain dynasties in Persia, Yemen, and Morocco. The Jewish communities of Cairo, Damascus, and Baghdad, and particularly those of the Holy Land, now began again playing a role in world Jewish affairs, a role which had been denied them during the preceding three centuries. In the West, too, the decisive campaigns against the Austrian Habsburgs, culminating in the siege of Vienna in 1529, extended the Ottoman power over the central part of Hungary, including Buda, and established its overlordship of Transylvania.[2]

Even after the battle of Lepanto of 1571, in which the Ottoman navy suffered a major defeat and which was celebrated in European countries as an epochal victory, Grand-Vizier Muḥammad Sokolli could boast that, if the sultan were to issue an order to rebuild the fleet in great splendor so as "to cast anchors from silver, to make riggings from silk, and to cut the sails from satin" this feat could be speedily accomplished. In fact, within a year the reconstructed Turkish navy was again fit for new battles and, as a result, Selim II was able to add Cyprus permanently to his empire. He also succeeded, by ejecting the Spaniards from Tunis in 1574, in converting the entire North African area of Libya-Tripolitania, Tunisia, and Algeria into Turkish provinces and in achieving a lasting political and cultural influence on Morocco. Only Crete in the Aegean still remained as an outpost of the great Venetian colonial empire until it, too, had to be surrendered to the Ottomans in 1687. But these achievements were counterbalanced by the "liberation" of Buda and most of Hungary by Austrian troops in 1686.[3]

All these momentous events took place in the full light of

history. Since the underlying developments were of importance to both the peoples under Ottoman rule and their European neighbors, an enormous amount of documentary material and other sources of information have become available for extensive international research. The Ottoman archives, both central and regional, have become an inexhaustible resource for Turkish and foreign scholars. Clearly, a great deal is yet to be done to make the materials thus assembled fully open to independent investigation, and decades of intensive research will be required to publish the more important documents and to analyze them in connection with other sources. But what has already been accomplished over the last century and a half since the pioneering work of Joseph von Hammer-Purgstall begins favorably to compare with the historiographic achievements of the Western European nations. These countries themselves, moreover, because of their extensive economic and diplomatic relations with the Porte, also include great documentary treasures in Turkish and other languages in their archives and in manuscript collections assembled in their libraries. In connection with these documents some scholars have made careful studies of the Turkish chancery procedures, paleography, and diplomatics.[4]

Because all developments in the Ottoman Empire had long fascinated Western European observers, we also possess much pertinent information in the diplomatic reports submitted to their governments by foreign ambassadors and consuls. For more than a century many astute observations included especially in the dispatches of the Venetian representatives in Constantinople-Istanbul have been used to great advantage by historians. A legion of Christian and Jewish travelers and pilgrims also recorded their experiences in European Turkey, western Asia, and North Africa. This travel literature has likewise been extensively utilized by Western historians. Since Jews played a considerable role in the Ottoman economy and politics, many of these foreign observers, whether friendly or hostile to the Jewish people, included in their descriptions interesting facts, sidelights, and anecdotes relating to Turkish Jews. Moreover, a vast array of data has been made available through the Jews' own increasingly proliferating local literature. The hundreds of volumes of Hebrew *Responsa* alone contain, in both inquiries and replies, relevant information not only on legal and religious aspects of Jewish life but also on the daily life, economic activities, and cultural concerns of the masses of the Jewish population and their leaders. Thus far, less attention has been paid to the large Hebrew homiletical and ethical literature and belles lettres, which include independently rich information on other aspects of Jewish life, while the Ladino popular letters, particularly poetry, have been the subject of investigation primarily by philologists and literary historians.[5]

GROWTH OF JEWISH COMMUNITIES

The impact of the Ottoman expansion under Selim I, Suleiman, and Selim II upon the Jewish communities made itself immediately felt. Unlike the previous conquests which, with few exceptions, embraced only small and struggling Jewish communities, the new annexations included such old centers of Jewish life and learning as Baghdad, Damascus, Aleppo, Jerusalem, Alexandria, and Cairo. Even Buda (Turkish, Budun; German, Ofen) had a rather well-established Jewish community which had weathered many storms during the preceding centuries. Most of these communities had good reasons to greet the new regime with much favorable anticipation.

Conditions varied from province to province. In Babylonia-Iraq, for example, the recovery from the Mongol "deluge" of 1258 had been very slow and incomplete. We know very little about the Jews in that formerly populous and affluent capital of the Great Caliphate under the later rulers, the Julairids (1340–1410), the Black Sheep Turkomans (1410–69), and the White Sheep Turkomans (1469–1508). The subsequent reign of Persia's Safavid dynasty did not bring about any major change in the policy of a somewhat ambiguous toleration. As we shall see, the predominance of the Shi'ite state religion did not create an atmosphere favorable to a Jewish communal and cultural renaissance. On two occasions in the seventeenth century, the Persians came close to a total suppression of Judaism. Understandably, Iraqi Jewry welcomed the Turkish troops upon their arrival in 1534. Except for a brief interval in 1623–

38, when the city and province again came under Persian rule, they remained an integral part of the Ottoman Empire until World War I. Regrettably, the four centuries here under review (1250–1650) belong to the darkest periods of Jewish history in Iraq, belying the old adage that a people is happiest when it has no history. In the case of Jews the obscurity largely resulted from the sharp decline in both their number and the level of their learning, with the ensuing drying up of Jewish literary contributions and a paucity of extant historical records. Even in 1570–90, after half a century of Ottoman rule, the Jewish population of the entire province of Baghdad counted only 603 families in a general population of 68,636 households. Robert Mantran's observation that, as a result of the Ottoman expansion, "compared with the immediately preceding periods, she [Baghdad] achieved a return to celebrity, enrichment by many buildings, and a share in the Ottoman world power" did not quite apply to its Jewish inhabitants.[6]

One of the immediate effects of the new conquests on the Ottoman Empire at large was that, for the first time in its history, it now embraced a decisive Muslim majority of the population. By professing Sunnite Islam, moreover, this majority to a very large extent also removed the previously recurrent menace of Shi'ite subversion. For the Jews this change had both favorable and unfavorable results. By significantly contributing to the internal peace within the Muslim majority and with the growing acquiesence of the Christian minority, most Jewish communities could now look forward to a long period of relative domestic peace. This feeling was reinforced by the absence of foreign invaders from most Ottoman territories. Only along the imperial periphery in Hungary and the western Balkans, as well as the territory facing Persia, did some foreign troops threaten from time to time. But the large expanses of the Empire now suffered only from the perennial plague of piracy on the Mediterannean Sea. If the ensuing heightened consciousness of Muslim superiority at times nurtured manifestations of religious intolerance, it also removed some of the inhibitions characteristic of minority regimes based on force alone. It may also have reinforced the realization by the government circles that total Islamization of the religious minorities would dry up a very important source of imperial revenue and in other ways undermine the economic and cultural well-being of the country.[7]

In all these respects Selim I's conquests of parts of Armenia and the entire Mameluke Empire, followed by Suleiman's successful campaign into Persia and the occupation of Iraq, reduced the danger of Persian interference for many years. Not only was Persia militarily greatly weakened, but it realized that it had escaped total annihilation by the Turkish troops only because of its great distance from the focal areas of Ottoman power and its own extreme "scorched earth" policy. Moreover, as the new protectors of Mecca and Medina, the Ottoman sultans became the preeminent monarchs in the world of Islam. Selim I had already been hailed by contemporaries with the exclamation: "Now all of the territories of Egypt, Malatiya, Aleppo, Syria, the city of Cairo, Upper Egypt, Ethiopia, Yemen, and lands up to the borders of Tunisia, the Hijaz, the cities of Mecca, Medina, and Jerusalem, may God increase the honoring of them completely and fully, have been added to the Ottoman Empire." This new position in the Muslim world was underscored when Suleiman added to his numerous titles that of caliph. A rationalization of his right to do so without being able to claim, as did the earlier bearers of this honor, direct descent from Mohammed, was offered early in his regime by the grand vizier and scholar Lutfi Pasha.[8]

As a result of this rapid expansion of Ottoman sovereignty and the ensuing broadening of economic opportunities for all residents through the length and breadth of the Empire without travel restrictions (except for Mecca and Medina, which barred access to "infidels"), Jews speedily increased in population and in the number of communities they formed. The conscious governmental policy to resettle inhabitants into areas which required new manpower actually enhanced Jewish dispersal. Following the example set by Mehmed II in reshaping the population of conquered Istanbul, Suleiman the Magnificent is said to have repopulated the newly conquered Hungarian capital of Buda (1543). From several complementary, if partially confusing, reports by Aladár Ballagi and other chroniclers, it appears that the Buda Jewish quarter at first fiercely resisted the Turkish onslaught behind its wall. During the siege Jews, we are told by various writers, lost 3,500 fighters. Occupying the quarter by storm with the aid of their superior artillery, the Turks allegedly

gave the Jews the choice of either departing with them or remaining in Buda. . . . After three days of deliberations, they [the Jews] decided unanimously to stay on in Buda. This reply angered the Turk and he ordered that the Jews be divided into three groups: Adult men from thirty or forty on formed one group; a second embraced young men twenty [and over]; and a third included all women and children. Each group had to choose [separately] where they wanted to live. When the Turk heard that they all decided to remain in Buda, he ordered the slaying of all older Jews, while the young men of twenty, as well as the women and children were carried away with him.

We do not learn from this and other accounts whether, like other captives, the Buda Jewish prisoners were sold into slavery or, what is more likely, were handed over to the existing Jewish communities for resettlement and rehabilitation. But even if in some cases imperial Jewry had to ransom these "slaves," they doubtless quickly joined their coreligionists as members of their respective communities in the Balkans and other Ottoman possessions. True, many Jews, along with other inhabitants, seem to have left Buda before its occupation. In fact, the Hungarian Queen Maria (widow of Louis II who had died on the battlefield of Mohács) issued a decree in part reading: "Those Jews who, because of their fear of the Turks, had fled from the city together with their possessions are not to be allowed to return; their houses become the property of the state." She added that Jews who had remained behind should be exiled, but they were to be permitted to dispose of their homes.[9]

Nevertheless, before the final occupation, many Jews remained in the city and, according to the contemporary historian Joseph b. Joshua ha-Kohen, "the heads of their community came out of the city, prostrated themselves before the sultan and surrendered the city to him." It is frequently assumed, that, because most Christians had fled from Buda before the siege, the Jews were the only organized group left behind to negotiate such a surrender. In recognition of the

Jews' collaboration, Suleiman granted a perpetual tax exemption to their leader, Joseph son of Solomon—his descendants were later known in Turkey as the families of Salto and Israel. The privilege specified that they should be exempt from a number of specific taxes, including the poll tax, not be forced to billet soldiers, and be permitted to acquire ten male and five female non-Muslim slaves from among the new captives. This privilege was renewed by several successive sultans. Even in 1865, after the reforms enacted in Abdul Mejid's era (1839–61) going under the name of *Tanzimat,* which tried to reduce the existing special privileges, the sixty-five families of Salto and Israel then living in Istanbul and its vicinity secured from the sultan another confirmation of their tax-exempt status. We hear less of forcible transfers of Jews elsewhere, although, after the conquest of Cyprus in 1570, Selim II ordered a large-scale removal of 2,000 Jewish families from Safed to the newly conquered island. This order, as we shall see, was apparently not carried out because of local resistance, Jewish and non-Jewish.[10]

Far more important was the voluntary immigration of Jews. Regrettably, we do not have even approximate data as to how many Spanish and Portuguese refugees found their way into the Ottoman Empire in the decades following their exodus from Spain and Portugal. Certainly, the figure of 10,000 Spanish Jewish refugees supposed to have settled in Italy and Turkey, mentioned by their well-informed leader, Don Isaac Abravanel—who himself took refuge in Italy—refers only to the first wave of migrants. The pertinent passage is included in his messianic tract *Ma'ayene ha-Yeshu'ah* (Springs of Salvation) which was completed in December 1496 and reflected the contemporary reality, also attested by other sources, that the vast majority of Spanish exiles first found their way into neighboring Portugal. Small groups also settled in Navarre, Provence, and North Africa. As a result of the subsequent persecutions, however, the stream of emigration to the Ottoman Empire took on mass proportions. As usual, the more numerous, populous, and well organized the existing Jewish communities in the eastern Mediterranean became and the more opportunities for making a living they offered to recent arrivals, the more they attracted wanderers looking for a new life in the hospitable Turkish environment. The mere fact, moreover, that some members of a family had already settled in Constantinople, Salonica, or other Turkish cities greatly facilitated the initial adjustment of such newcomers. That is why the Jewish communities in the Balkans grew by leaps and bounds during the sixteenth century. Constantinople's Jewish settlement, for example, which by 1478 had already grown to some 10,000 souls, continued to increase so as to reach more than 18,000 persons before the death of Chief Rabbi Elijah Mizraḥi in 1524. It continued growing until by the middle of the century it exceeded 30,000 persons and thus became by far the greatest Jewish community in the early modern world.[11]

Salonica too, which as we recall had to be forcibly repopulated after its conquest by the Turks in 1430, a century later had become "a city whose majority is Jewish," according to R. Samuel de Medina, one of its outstanding leaders in the second half of the sixteenth century. The change in Jerusalem was equally startling. In the last decades of the Mameluke regime the city had witnessed a decline from the 250 Jewish families encountered there by Meshullam da Volterra in 1481 to but 70 families reported by Obadiah di Bertinoro seven years later. Their living conditions were even more abysmal. According to Bertinoro,

Jerusalem is for the most part a desert and, needless to say, is not surrounded by a wall. The people living there, as I was told, consist of 4,000 families and from the Jews there have remained today only 70 impoverished families who lack all sustenance. There is practically no individual who is making a living and, if he is lucky to do so for one year, he is called a rich man in this place. There are also many widows, old and lonely, from the Ashkenazic, Sephardic, and other linguistic groups; in short, there are "seven women for one man." . . . [For this reason the elders] welcome all new settlers, honor and respect them, and constantly expostulate for the misdeeds they had previously committed.

Conditions greatly improved after Bertinoro took over the leadership and introduced numerous reforms, but its full flowering came only in the years following Selim the Grim's entry in 1516. Similar increases took place in many other communities in Palestine and elsewhere. Greatly depopulated Iraq—where Baghdad had counted only some 1,250 Jews at the time of the Turkish conquest and the second largest city, Başra, probably had even fewer Jewish inhabitants—embraced but a total of over 15,000 Jews when it was visited by Jean Baptiste Tavernier in 1632. These examples can easily be multiplied. However, of even greater importance was the larger geographic spread of the new arrivals and their formation of new communities in many smaller localities.[12]

INTERNAL STRAINS

Such mass immigration had obvious advantages as well as drawbacks. Clearly the influx of highly educated, skilled, and trained businessmen, artisans, and physicians, as well as prominent rabbinic scholars, enabled the Jewish communities to rise to new levels of prosperity, political influence, and cultural attainment. At the same time the great variety of traditions, mores, and languages the immigrants brought with them from various lands, where even persons stemming from the same areas often betrayed considerable differences in habits and outlook, injected an element of instability and conflict into Jewish communal life. Within the three major divisions between the original settlers, the "Romaniots," the Ashkenazim, and Sephardim ("Italians" were often counted among the Romaniots, but more frequently joined the Sephardim), there were many subdivisions, resulting in the growth of individual congregations which were at times antagonistic to one another. Almost every larger city with a substantial Jewish population as a rule embraced congregations of different origin, each claiming complete independence. If, in order to prevent extreme fragmentation of Jewish communal life, the talmudic rabbis, taking a cue from the unrelated biblical prohibition of *lo titgoddedu* (you shall not cut yourselves; Deut. 14:1), had already forbidden the Jews to form independent subcommunities (*agudot agudot*), the sixteenth-century Ottoman scholars had to reconcile themselves to these assertions of independence. A typical comment by R. Joseph Ibn Leb explained:

Even in Salonica, where every man speaks the language of his people and where, on arriving from their exile, each linguistic group has established a congregation of its own, no member transfers from one congregation to another. Each congregation supports the poor of its own linguistic group and each is entered independently in the governmental registry. Thus every congregation appears to be like a city in its own right.

This practice remained in force, although Ibn Leb had to add the reservation that in exceptional cases, the majority of the congregation could force each group to adhere to a city-wide ordinance adopted by it. In fact, even in ancient times the sages had to take notice of differences and thus recognize the right of each locality to issue ordinances of its own without violating the prohibition against communal separatism. But in Turkey such fragmentation went so far that frequently a faction dissatisfied with a congregation's management or because it was led by ambitious and power-hungry individuals, staged an exodus from that congregation and formed a new association of its own. Thus there arose in Salonica two "Catalan," two "Lisbon," two "Sicilian," and no less than three "Calabrian" congregations (under different names). Such groups were always characterized by separate houses of worship, but many also had schools and cemeteries of their own. In smaller cities, on the other hand, costs would have become prohibitive to run all institutions independently and most of them had to husband their resources for a common Talmud Torah school, a common cemetery, and even a common slaughterhouse.[13]

Some members, however, tried to use the opportunity of leaving a congregation merely to evade its taxes. The recurrent plagues in the cities sometimes furnished a welcome excuse. Because a pestilence usually put to flight a number of inhabitants, who spent months, even years, in another locality before returning to their old residences, absentees often claimed to have left their original community for good and hence were not obliged to contribute to the taxes imposed upon its members. Communal leaders usually dismissed such claims without much ado. More difficult was the problem of the relatively few privileged families to whom, on account of their purportedly distinguished services to the country, the government had granted a perpetual tax exemption. In such cases any collection of their usual share in taxation by congregational bodies, even when it could be enforced by purely spiritual sanctions, would antagonize the governmental authorities. Furthermore, the incipient operation of the system of "capitulations," for which the foundations were laid in the Franco-Ottoman treaty of 1569 (which harkened back to the older privileges granted by the Byzantine, Mameluke, and Ottoman authorities to the Venetian and Genoese merchant colonies), opened up new possibilities for tax evasion by some of the wealthiest members, who succeeded in obtaining the "protection" of one of the treaty powers. In many cases the communal leaders could only try to persuade the privileged "outsiders" to make voluntary contributions to the communal chest, contributions which occasionally even exceeded the amounts which might have been collected from their formal taxes.[14]

Remarkably, however, we hear little about rivalries between congregations for the admission of new members through grants of the exclusivist so-called *ḥezqat ha-yishub* or *ḥerem ha-yishub* (right of settlement) which played such a great role in the medieval and early modern Ashkenazic communities. The majority of the new arrivals in the Ottoman Empire had come from the relatively freer societies on the Iberian Peninsula where admission of members depended more on the kings and local lords than on the Jewish communities. The situation in fourteenth-century Aragon is well illustrated by the privilege issued in favor of the Jews of Alcolea by Infante Alphonso on August 1, 1320, which extended to them royal protection against local interference. Article 15 of that decree reads in part:

Every Jew is free to come to Alcolea with the intent to settle and live there unharmed and secure. He is also to be allowed to move from that locality to whatever other area he may wish to go, be it Ours or [belonging to a] foreign ruler. He shall further have the right to transfer there all his possessions and his family without obtaining any special permit from Us or from any of Our officials.

The only reservation consisted of a promise that the authorities would see to it that, before leaving Alcolea, such a Jewish resident would pay all outstanding debts to his creditors. The subsequent reversals of these friendly policies came to the fore also in this respect during the anti-Jewish propaganda after 1391 and is reflected in the sharply intolerant Castilian legislation, especially in Juan II's comprehensive decree of January 2, 1412. Among its numerous provisions Article 16 declared that "no Jew or Moor, man or woman, shall leave Valladolid or any other place in order to live in another locality, under the penalty of the loss of all possessions and his or her life [cuerpo] being at My mercy." In neither period, however, did the Jewish community seem to enjoy the authority to regulate such Jewish migratory movements to the extent it did in Poland and Lithuania during the early modern period. In the Ottoman Empire even the government interfered relatively little with the movements of people, except for such emergency measures as were taken from time to time to repopulate a newly conquered area deserted by many of its inhabitants. Under ordinary circumstances, the relatively open society of sixteenth-century Turkey allowed the Jews broad freedom of movement and ample opportunities for trade and craftsmanship in many localities. As R. Samuel de Medina phrased it, "This realm is wide open without a wall . . . and everyone anxious to do so may come in and attend to his business. . . . Hence no Jewish court of one city may prevent a Jew of another city whether of this or another country from entering and freely trading in it." Such a general mobility also obviated any formal admission to residence by cities or their ethnoreligious subgroups. This basic difference between the conditions in the original Ashkenazic and in the Sephardic communities also makes understandable Rashi's strict interpretation of the talmudic application of the Deuteronomic prohibition (14:1) to communal separatist movements. Rashi, who lived in the tiny eleventh-century community of Troyes, condemned the formation of a new association by discontented members as "giving the impression of two groups professing two different faiths [torot]." No such explanation would have been applicable to the Ottoman environment. Yet in their general conservatism the rabbis could refer to the talmudic outlawry of communal separatism as an existing law and hence prohibit even (unjustified) individual transfers from one congregation to another. But they saw no reason for holding down the enrollment of new arrivals in any existing congregation in order to lessen competition in business or trade.[15]

Not surprisingly, immigrants arriving from the northern countries, deeply inured to the restrictive systems prevailing in the ancient Babylonian and medieval Franco-German communities, felt that local merchants had to be protected against competition by outsiders. It was the West Balkan community of Ioannina which inquired from R. Samuel de Medina as to whether "visiting merchants could legally be kept out of the city"—that is, whether its leaders had the right to influence the local Turkish authorities to prohibit nonresident traders from selling their goods in the city. The Salonican rabbi, himself of Sephardic ancestry and facing an entirely different cosmopolitan community, took pains to explain to his inquirers:

Let me first reiterate that the law pertaining to this case is not as simple as it appears to the local rabbi. The reason (for the difficulty) is that the opinions expressed in the Talmud and by the halakhists of former generations regarding such cases do not apply to our own time, for in their times Jews lived in countries governed by different rulers, whereas we Jews live under one sovereign who imposes no restrictions on travel or on commercial activities on any of his subjects.

While his historical reference to ancient Babylonia was not quite accurate, R. Samuel was definitely right in contrasting the situation in feudally fragmented northern Europe with the generally centralized administration of the Ottoman Empire. Therefore his decision that it was "illegal to deny the nonresident merchants the right to sell their products" in Ioannina corresponded to the realities of the Empire and encountered no objections on the part of the other rabbinic leaders.[16]

In relation with the outside world, however, the communities often needed city-wide leaders functioning as committees of *memunim* as in Salonica or under a single *sheikh al-Yahud* as in Damascus. In Istanbul the chief rabbi was at first supposed not only to lead the entire Jewry of the city but also to exercise jurisdiction over the other Turkish Jewish communities. This system largely broke down, however, as we have seen, after Mizrahi's death and would not fully resume again until the nineteenth century. Sporadically one or another Jewish community would decide to form a union of local congregations. Such a compact is reported, for example, in the city of Patras which, falling back on old Byzantine traditions, adopted an ordinance:

> We the holy community of ancient [!] Patras through the under-signed agree to maintain all the ordinances existing from previous generations and not to separate each congregation [from the others; there were four such congregations named Mustarab or Greek, Si-cilian, Spanish, and Apulian], not to speak of individuals, but to be bound . . . by oath so that, though each may pray in a different synagogue, with respect to the welfare of the entire holy community we are like one. Any man or woman who will deviate [from this rule] shall be separated and banished from our community.

However, the very fact that such agreements were sporadic and, if adopted, required constant renewals (indeed often went into total oblivion) kept up a certain feeling of instability in most communities.[17]

Intracommunal relations were further complicated by the arrival of former Marranos. The Spanish *conversos* appeared doubly suspect to non-Iberian Jews because their history reached back to 1391 when a great many of their Castilian and Aragonese ancestors had adopted Christianity under duress as the only alternative to death at the hand of pogromists. Some of them had found their way back to Judaism in the following decades, but a large segment had outwardly lived as New Christians, while continuing to profess Judaism in the secrecy of their homes. When a century later many of these Marranos arrived in the Ottoman Empire their Jewish origin became quite questionable, since their parents or grandparents may have been born to non-Jewish mothers. According to Jewish law, any child of an unconverted Christian woman was con-sidered a born Christian who could be admitted to the Jewish fold only after a formal act of conversion. It was doubly diffi-cult to say, therefore, which particular Marrano immigrant was of identifiable Jewish descent. Some Turkish rabbis, especially if they themselves were of non-Iberian descent, assumed an intransigent position. For example, R. Benjamin b. Mattathiah of Arta, echoing sentiments expressed by R. Isaac b. Sheshet Perfet after 1391, wrote:

> Those who submit to the advocates of conversion and do not leave their country to save their souls [are not to be considered Jews]. Al-

though at the beginning they were converted by force, thereafter they have freed themselves from the yoke of the Kingdom of God and broken the fundamentals of the Torah; they have thus voluntarily followed the laws of the Gentiles and sinned against all the commandments of the Torah. Moreover, [some of them] have actually persecuted the unfortunate Jews living among them, denounced them [to the Inquisition], in order to eliminate the name of Israel from their midst; they also informed the authorities about those *conversos* whose hearts still turned toward Heaven and had found ways to serve the Lord in secrecy. Such men are full-fledged evildoers; they are disqualified from testimony [in Jewish courts] and inferior to regular Gentiles. They are to be humbled and not elevated; although at the beginning they had been forced converts, today they have no part in the God of Israel.

A diametrically opposing view was taken by the Salonican rabbi Joseph b. Solomon Ṭaiṭaṣaq and his pupil Samuel b. Moses de Medina. Referring in particular to the Jews arriving from Portugal, De Medina insisted that "all Portuguese Marranos while marrying, both man and woman, intend to emigrate and to settle in a locality where they would be able to serve the Lord, God of our fathers and to observe His law." He also quoted Ṭaiṭaṣaq as well as an earlier decision by R. Ṣemaḥ Gaon who taught that "a forced convert arriving with the intention of repenting, so long as we believe that his father was a Jew, we also assume that his mother was Jewish, not Gentile."[18]

Remarkably, there seems to have been little discussion in the Ottoman Jewish circles about the requirement for Marranos arriving in the Empire to have been circumcised. Of course, before leaving the Iberian Peninsula, performing circumcision even on himself placed a man in constant jeopardy of being investigated by the Inquisition. True, the distinguished mystic and messianic dreamer, Solomon Molkho (Diogo Pires) asserted: "one night I performed the convenant of circumcision while no one was with me and the Holy One Blessed Be He for His name's sake helped and healed me. Although the pain was great and I fainted from my suffering, while the blood was flowing like a bubbling spring, the Merciful Healer cured me in less time than I dared hope." But this probably was an exceptional self-sacrificing act performed by a relatively small minority of *conversos*. The majority must have delayed such action until after their escape to a safer environment. In Italy we hear of cases of uncircumcised New Christians, who nevertheless attended services in the synagogue, performed all other duties of professing Jews, and were considered as such by themselves and their neighbors. Even the liberal Leghorn community, however, refused one such individual participation in the honors connected with the divine services and did not allow him to don phylacteries. Evidently in the Ottoman Empire circumcision was taken for granted, although we have no documentary evidence concerning its frequency, the time lag between the arrival of a Marrano immigrant and his family joining the community as a full-fledged member, and similar other details. Despite these complications, during the sixteenth century entire groups of Marranos arriving together were able to found independent congregations in Istanbul, Arta, Vallona, and Smyrna; they even established two "Lisbon" congregations in Salonica.[19]

This problem had direct legal implications with respect to Marrano marriages. The question often arose whether a married woman arriving from the Iberian Peninsula had to prove that she had been properly divorced or, if her husband had died without leaving a child, she needed a release from his brother, a levir. An ordinance, adopted by the leaders of the Salonican congregations about 1493 under the impact of the expulsion from Spain, took the extremely liberal position that if a woman had been married to a Jew while they were under the conversionist ordinance, even if they were betrothed in the presence of Jews living there who had the waters of baptism on their heads, one does not have to pay any attention to such betrothals and she is free to marry any Jew prepared to take her in either the conversionist locality or anywhere else after their escape from the conversionist regime. Thus we have the rule in this city of Salonica that any woman arriving from Portugal or Castile is not suspect about any marriage vows she might have taken after conversion and we allow her to marry anybody. . . . Since there are no qualified witnesses at the wedding, the marriage is null and void. If she happens to be subject to the requirement of levirate marriage, no such duty exists at all and she needs neither a writ of divorce nor a *ḥaliṣah* ceremony in order freely to marry.

An additional argument in the same vein was presented by Joseph Ibn Leb, who pointed out that, after the expulsions, no marriage on the Iberian Peninsula could have been attested to by professing Jews and hence had no legal validity at all. In these controversies one frequently detects differences in individual temperaments among those motivated by pity for the victims of the Inquisition and others who wished to adhere more strictly to the letter of Jewish law. To be sure, even some of the advocates of a narrow interpretation were prepared to make some exceptions. A magnetic personality like Solomon Molkho—who had grown up in Portugal as a Christian and had served there as a royal courtier—had become such a dedicated preacher of Jewish redemption, a penetrating cabbalist, and one defying all dangers of prosecution by Italian inquisitors, that he fascinated even such a stalwart Jewish leader as the great codifier Joseph Karo. But most other refugees could readily become objects of dissension in their new Turkish Jewish environment.[20]

Differences in marriage customs also affected other Jewish groups coming from different lands, even if they had no religiously controversial past. To begin with, the minute legal requirements, developed over centuries in different countries by rabbinic interpretations and decisions, were often strictly adhered to by the new arrivals in the Ottoman Empire as well. For example, from time immemorial Jews were extremely careful in following standard formulae in their writs of divorce; textual deviations, however minor, were often considered a sufficient reason to invalidate the document and thereby annul the divorce. Less drastic, but of some importance, were also the consequences of oversight regarding certain regional variants. Solomon A. Rosanes pointed out no fewer than sixteen such formal differences in the formulas used among the Jewish communities of the Ottoman Empire. For example, in Adrianople, Brusa, Salonica, Smyrna, and Sidon each writ of divorce was dated with both the day of the week and the month. In Istanbul, Gallipoli, and Alexandria, on the other hand, the writs were dated only by the day of the month. Even more remarkably, a minor difference in spelling of the same Hebrew or Aramaic word sufficed to raise questions about the writ. As seemingly minor a divergence as whether a man's patronymic was indicated by the Hebrew word *ben*, as was customary in most communities, or by the Aramaic word *bar*, used in Salonica, also was far from negligible in reality. More substantive differences arose, especially in the case of the *'agunot*, with respect to the validity of some testimony about their husbands' purported deaths. Some of the more lenient rabbis were inclined to accept less fully authenticated rumors so as to make it possible for the suffering widows to remarry, while others were so horrified by the specter of a technically married woman entering a forbidden union with another man that they insisted upon ironclad evidence. Regional differences also arose in regard to the requirement of the presence of ten adult male Jews at every wedding. As late as 1567, the Salonican rabbis felt it incumbent upon themselves to repeat that requirement in a sharp ordinance signed by R. Samuel de Medina and several associates. Considered sufficiently important for R. Moses Almosnino to copy it verbatim for future reference, the pertinent proclamation offered an interesting motivation that sheds light on the existing conditions in the community. It read:

Our eyes have seen that many servants have nowadays broken through the fence of righteous and modest daughters of Israel living in the recesses of their houses. They [the servants] have spread rumors they they had betrothed [the young women]. They have also persuaded bad and sinful witnesses of their ilk to testify about their evil deeds. As a result, some daughters of Israel have become like *hefqer* [exposed to public contumely]. For this reason we have found it necessary to renew an ordinance enacted by our sainted forefathers to excommunicate every man who is called an Israelite who will betroth a woman, adult or minor, either by himself, through his or her representative, or through her father . . . unless these betrothals take place in the presence of ten adult free Jews.

This procedure—on which both the Romaniot and Sephardic Jews were so insistent that the "Castilian" community in Fez had placed it ahead of all other regulations in its famous collection of ordinances—had long since been disregarded by the Ashkenazim and could lead to much local friction.[21]

A similar division arose with respect to gifts (*siblonot*) given to fiancées by the men to whom they were bespoken. Already the talmudic sages were divided regarding the nature of such gifts. Some of them (like R. Huna and Rabah) suspected that such gifts might have been used by would-be bridegrooms to make the required marriage vows by handing their potential brides, in the presence of witnesses, objects worth more than a *perutah* (the smallest coin). In such cases, as Rashi explained it, the woman concerned would not have been able to marry anyone else without obtaining from that donor a writ of divorce. The Sephardim generally adopted the more stringent interpretation, whereas the Ashkenazic communities, even in their homelands, treated such gifts as simple expressions of friendship and, at most, as signs of courtship. In the Balkans, even the Sephardim were in considerable disagreement on this score. While in Istanbul and Sofia the gifts were considered a serious problem, in Salonica they were taken much more lightly. An interesting case, shedding light on existing marriage customs, is recorded in the *Responsa* of R. Elijah Mizrahi in a judgment probably rendered while he was serving as chief rabbi in Istanbul. A young man residing in the capital arranged with his potential bride living in Salonica to postpone their betrothal until the two arbiters selected by them set the wedding date and decided the amount of dowry to be given by the bride's father as well as the size of the "supplementary" provision (above the legally required minimum) for the bride to be inserted into the marriage contract. In the meantime, however, the would-be bridegroom sent some gifts to the lady in Salonica, "where they do not suspect such gifts." Subsequently, the Salonican father brought his daughter to Istanbul, where they were visited by the mother of the prospective bridegroom, who presented the young lady with a gold-studded comb. All this happened before the arbiters announced their conclusion that the couple was not mutually suitable and the projected betrothal was called off. Yet some precisionists raised the question whether the intervening gifts did not represent a hidden betrothal. While R. Abraham Ibn Ya'ish strongly argued against such an assumption, Mizrahi raised several objections to a simple declaration that the lady was free to marry anyone else.[22]

Of considerable importance also was the conflict which arose between the so-called Pulian (Apulian) and almost all the other Salonican congregations concerning the ordinance, adopted in 1534 by the majority of congregants in Arta, which forbade a fiancé to visit his betrothed, as well as men and women to dance together in public. Although this regulation was approved by the other Salonican groups, the Apulians, who had come from Renaissance Italy with its greater *joie de vivre* and less puritanical customs, sharply objected. Invoking their communal autonomy, they ultimately prevailed so that their members were exempted. Similarly, when the Hungarians had brought with them the more stringent custom of abstaining from work during the entire mourning period for the destruction of the Temple of Jerusalem on the first nine days of the month of Ab, the other congregations did not follow suit. But they did not question the right of the Hungarian elders to punish their own congregants who violated that custom. Most importantly, the problem of polygamy, though of relatively minor practical concern, became a major theoretical issue. While the Romaniots followed the example of the Ashkenazim and observed the ban against plural marriages, originally proclaimed by R. Gershom, the Light of the Exile in the tenth century, the Sephardim, who had never formally accepted that proclamation, were not automatically subject to such restrictions. Even when the Salonican congregations issued a general local ordinance outlawing multiple marriages, sporadic cases of second marriages by members of the Sephardic congregations appear in the records; although generally condemned by the non-Sephardim, they were not formally annulled by any courts. In one case, however, when a husband, without divorcing his wife and apparently unable to secure permission from his rabbis to marry another woman, performed such a betrothal in the presence of a Muslim *qadhi*, the reaction of the community at large was instantaneous. Yet it took about a year of communal pressure before the man was persuaded to divorce his second wife. It may be assumed that most of these deviations were rather exceptional, since, as in the North African communities formed by Spanish refugees in Algeria, the custom had long been established in Ottoman lands for many Jewish marriage contracts to add a clause forbidding the husband to marry a second wife without either divorcing the first and paying her marriage settlement in full, or at least receiving her formal consent. We must not forget, however, that forcing a husband to give a writ of divorce to his wife, even if agreed upon by the couple before their marriage, was not devoid of complications. Controversial views held by various rabbis on any such enforced writ are reflected even in the major Karo-Isserles code of laws.[23]

Regrettably, most of our information about the family life of Ottoman Jews is derived from rabbinic responsa; these replies, as a rule, deal with complicated legal problems arising from exceptional occurrences beyond the ken of local rabbis to resolve. It may be taken for granted that, in addition to the law-enforcement powers of the communal leaders, there was the strong pressure of public opinion which made the majority follow long-adopted patterns of life without major deviations. Nevertheless, the mutual forbearance toward diverse practices and mores, even if it occasionally lead to heated debates, added to the vitality and creative élan of these relatively young communities. In the course of time, however, the differences between the individual congregations diminished. It was merely the force of tradition which kept the two Catalan congregations in Salonica alive well into the twentieth century. But the growing equalization, imposed by a common language like Ladino in the Balkans and Judeo-Arabic in the Syro-Egyptian and other North-African communities, served as a major leveler, not necessarily to the advantage of intellectual creativity.

ECONOMIC ADJUSTMENTS

Communal divisions, including their effects on the members' marital life, had ramifications in the economic sphere as well. For example, the problem of the 'agunot frequently arose from husbands having been murdered away from home, a circumstance which particularly affected peddlers. We learn, for example, that in Damascus numerous Jews, artisans and merchants, made a living from supplying surrounding villages with goods and services. The artisans usually spent a few days or a week in a village performing all the repair jobs needed by the peasants and then moved on to the next locality. Many tried to spend the Sabbaths at home but those who had to travel greater distances often returned to their families only for holidays, including Passover, Hanukkah, and Purim. While staying in a particular village or Bedouin camp, they were on the whole hospitably received. According to a contemporary pilgrim, Israel of Perugia, "the gold- and silversmith, weaver, cobbler, and shoe repairman are quite successful, for on their journeys through villages and small towns the Arabs are very hospitable toward them, give them bread, honey, and fruit free of charge, and do not bargain down their wages." However, on open roads all travelers were exposed to attacks by highwaymen and many vanished without leaving a trace. The resulting legal uncertainties to the families at home were often differently handled by different rabbis.[24]

Ritualistic traditions in their great diversity frequently also affected the income of different groups of Jews. For instance, the adhesions in ritually slaughtered animals' lungs, detected during the required close post-mortem examination, totally disqualified their meat for consumption among the Ashkenazim and Romaniots, but they had long been treated more leniently by the Sephardic rabbis. No lesser an authority than Joseph Karo gave this disparity an economic interpretation. He wrote:

The reason why the sages of Castile have been less exacting in regard to adhesions was that the Gentiles in those countries for the most part staunchly refused to consume meat of animals slaughtered by Jews. As a result, if [Jewish butchers] had followed the hard line, they would not have been able to sell such disqualified carcasses to non-Jews, and the resulting losses of money to the Jewish community would have been very substantial.

This decision was in line with the great concern already evinced by the talmudic sages for large losses of sustenance to Jews. Similarly, the old restrictions concerning the sales of houses to Gentiles may have lost their importance in communities where Jews lived in their own quarters. According to R. Samuel de Medina, it was assumed that "no Turk would wish to live among them [the Jews]." But outbidding a neighbor's concession or rental housing was strictly forbidden. In Salonica an all-communal ordinance went so far as to forbid all Jews from trying to take over premises vacated by a coreligionist, unless they had remained unoccupied for fully three years, thus preventing unfair competition. We are told, however, that some Salonican sages themselves expressed reservations on this score "because such practices are likely to cause ill-will among the inhabitants of the land and the Turkish owners of real estate are much perturbed about them."[25]

The existing shortages and ensuing price inflation in the middle of the sixteenth century are well illustrated by the experiences of the De Medina family. R. Samuel had to wait a year before he could secure living quarters. Since each acquired right (*hazzaqah*) had considerable monetary value, as it did in Rome and many other major Jewish communities, Samuel's older brother and chief financial supporter, on one occasion, sold his *hazzaqah* to a dwelling for 4,000 akçes (aspers); he allegedly could have obtained for it 100,000 akçes ten years later. Only the fact that the Jewish quarter in Salonica was not legally restricted to a given area prevented the institution of "acquired rights" from becoming a serious drawback to the life of the inhabitants, as it became in the papal capital in the seventeenth and eighteenth centuries. Yet even in Salonica the controversies arising from the existing *hazzaqot* were a perennial source of intracommunal friction. The inflationary pressures, generated all over Europe through the influx of New World silver, soon spread to the Ottoman Empire. They were aggravated there by the frequent official currency depreciations. The ensuing price rises on one occasion caused R. Samuel de Medina to complain that the neighborhood farmers who supplied wool to the flourishing Salonican Jewish clothing industry were "devouring [the fruits of] our sustenance and toil," a situation made worse by Jews outbidding one another in their purchases. The ensuing rise of real estate values in Salonica undoubtedly exceeded that of most other Turkish cities because of its speedy absorption of successive waves of new settlers and the additional shortages caused by frequent conflagrations. On the other hand, many rabbinic leaders also evinced egalitarian concerns. In some cases they actually insisted that the donors of implements of worship for the synagogue must not reserve their use for themselves but must share them with the rest of the congregation.[26]

In matters of taxation, too, the rabbis not only insisted on upholding the existing differentials in the poll tax rates between the rich, the middle class, and the low-income groups, thus maintaining a modicum of progressive taxation, but they also made further adjustments according to their sense of justice. For example, to safeguard taxpayers against unscrupulous elders some sages taught that no community had the right to impose loans on members. In one interesting case, it was a governmental authority which forcibly collected a loan from the community at large, though the amounts contributed by individual members varied according to their financial capacities. When the loan was not repaid for many years, the lenders abandoned all hope of ever receiving any return on their investment. But to their surprise the government suddenly repaid the loan and the original contributors expected to get back their shares. The opposition argued, however, that since, according to talmudic law, abandonment of hope for the return of one's property was a sufficient cause for loss of ownership, this bonanza should be distributed to all families in equal amounts, a view which finally prevailed. Intercommunal cooperation was also often needed for the collection of taxes from new arrivals. Usually freed from local imposts for a period of time, some tax evaders tried to prolong that immunity by claiming that they had continued to pay taxes in their former communities. At the same time they assured their previous compatriots that they were being taxed in their new residences and hence had become subject to double taxation. It appears that in most cases the leaders succeeded in making short shrift with such would-be tax dodgers by exchanging information with other communities. Quite early the seven oldest Iberian congregations in Salonica, known as the *Gerush-Sefarad* (Spanish Exile), Castilianos, Catalanes, Aragon, Ishmael (Andalusians), Portugal, and Lisbon, reached an agreement about which congregation was to play host to incoming immigrants from their home countries. When in doubt membership was to be decided by casting lots. In the meantime, all revenues collected from as yet unassigned newcomers (some of whom undoubtedly arrived with capital and quickly went into business) was to be divided equally between the seven congregations.[27]

Fiscal and other communal attitudes toward new settlers assumed increasing urgency among the sixteenth-century Turkish Jews not only because of the masses of immigrants steadily arriving in the various parts of the Empire, but also because of the growing mobility of the Ottoman population. As usual, with respect to Jews, we are best informed about rabbis leaving one community to take a post in another. To mention but one example, the distinguished codifier Joseph Karo (1488–1575), who as a child had to leave his native Toledo in 1492 and Lisbon in 1498, in his adult life served as a spiritual leader of congregations in Nicopolis, Adrianople, Salonica, Istanbul, and finally Safed. To be sure, rabbis, even if personally quite wealthy, were exempted from all governmental and communal taxes. However, numerous laymen who for commercial, family, or other reasons likewise changed their residences very frequently might have become the victims of double taxation. Incidentally, the rabbis' Muslim counterparts, the ulema (jurists-theologians), were likewise extremely mobile, not only because, like many of their medieval predecessors, they were in search of new local traditions, but also out of a general scientific curiosity and in pursuit of new career opportunities.[28]

Remarkably, we have but few data about the reaction of the general public to the Jewish mass immigration. Occasionally, to be sure, we hear rumblings of discontent concerning the alleged importation of certain diseases by the newcomers. However, unlike North Africa, Turkey had been the scene of syphilitic infections even before the mass arrival of the Western Jews, and rumors attributing the spread of leprosy and other skin maladies to these new settlers are mentioned in only a few instances. Nor do we hear many complaints about the rise in the cost of living because of the rapidly increasing number of consumers, such as were voiced in North Africa a century earlier. Probably Turkey, being a very productive land, on whose grain exports Venice and other countries greatly depended, would have made such accusations rather meaningless. In fact, most visitors to Syria and Egypt were astounded to find the cost of living exceedingly low. Most people must have realized that the constant governmentally sponsored depreciation of currency was the main inflationary factor. Yet, there were other subjects of contention. On one occasion we even hear of an uprising against the Jews in Bulgarian Nicopolis because of their alleged usury. In Salonica and Istanbul, too, we are told, the local Greek population complained about Jewish moneylending in a petition addressed directly to Sultan Suleiman. However, unlike the situation in Europe, where Jews often dominated the money trade, the Balkans and the Afro-Asian provinces of the Empire embraced many Armenian, Greek, and even Muslim money changers and lenders, some of whom actually extended credit to Jews.[29]

More threatening, therefore, could have been the revival of the old myth of Jewish ritual murders. Curiously, the two Blood Accusations recorded in the early sixteenth century occurred not in the great centers of Jewish life on the Balkan Peninsula or in the Syro-Egyptian cities, but rather in two Anatolian localities whose Jewish population was very small and whose presence, as far as we can tell from other sources, had generally evoked few hostile reactions. The case in Amasia is particularly instructive. An anti-Jewish group of local Armenians, perhaps motivated by simple envy, greed, or revenge for some alleged injurious Jewish action, conspired to have one adult Christian, who had occasionally performed household chores for Jewish families, temporarily disappear from the city. They immediately spread the rumor that Jews had killed him in order to make use of his blood for their unleavened bread on Passover. A number of Jewish suspects were arrested and one Joseph Abiyyab, a physician, was burned at the stake. However, a local Jew detected the alleged victim in another city and persuaded him to return to Amasia and appear before the local qadhi. As a result, the court physician, Moses Hamon, induced Suleiman to issue a firman in 1553–54, renewing a decree by Meḥmed II which had ordered all Blood Accusations against Jews to be referred to the Diwan in the capital, rather than to be adjudicated by the local authorities. This order was reconfirmed by Selim II and Meḥmed III.

While the episode in Amasia thus had caused no long-term harm to the Jewish community, it was an ominous sign of the instability of Jewish life even in the Turkish environment. A number of other ritual murder accusations in Anatolian Toqat and other Ottoman localities followed down to the nineteenth century; they reached a climax in the notorious Damascus Affair of 1840. It is noteworthy that, although most of the accusations arose from suspicious or willful distortions by Greeks rather than Muslims, the Greek Church did little to stem their reappearance. Not until 1873 did the Ecumenical Patriarchate of Istanbul take a stand against these libels. Even then it couched its repudiation in vague general phrases—opponents might have called them weasel words—rather than in outright condemnation, such as had been voiced over the centuries by Roman popes, beginning with Innocent IV in 1146.[30]

Under the existing power constellation, moreover, any enduring or whimsical dislike of Jews by a highly placed personality could appear as a real threat to all imperial Jewry. This was particularly the case at the beginning of Suleiman's reign, when Ibrahim Pasha, the sultan's grand vizier and intimate friend, evinced deep-seated anti-Jewish feelings doubtless stemming from his original Greek ancestry. Fortunately for the Jews, he committed a serious blunder and played into the hands of his enemies. They included Suleiman's favorite wife, Khurrem, called in the West Roxalana, and the influential court Jews of the time, who caused a sudden reversal in the sultan's sentiments and the grand vizier's execution in 1536. According to a tale, which had circulated in the Jewish community, the grand vizier had tried to overcome by a trick the sultan's staunch resistance to the idea of expelling the Jews from his country. He arranged for a secret underground tunnel to be dug from his quarters to the imperial bedchamber. On three successive nights he impersonated Mohammed and in the Messenger's alleged voice exhorted Suleiman to put an end to the Jewish people, Islam's inveterate enemy. It was only after Moses Hamon learned of this plot that the cabal was detected and the culprit executed. In fact, however, Ibrahim, for many years (1523–36) the guiding spirit of the Ottoman administration and its meritorious reformer particularly of the newly in-

corporated province of Egypt, fell from grace primarily because of his overbearing posture and his alleged schemes to
replace Suleiman on the throne.[31]

DOCTORS, MERCHANTS, DIPLOMATS

Moses Hamon's intervention in securing a protective decree
for Jews accused of ritual murder was a typical example of
how the Jewish community at large could benefit from the
contacts between highly placed Jews and the ruling circles in
Istanbul. As we recall, the great influence achieved by Ya'qub
of Gaëta, whether or not he ultimately converted to Islam, had
a beneficent impact on the still small and struggling Jewish
communities under Meḥmed II. Now the vastly increased
and ramified Jewish settlements in the Empire, much more
affluent and politically important, had more frequent opportunities to invoke the aid of dignitaries who professed their
religion. The most direct access to the throne was given to
court physicians like Ya'qub, who took care of the health of
the sultan and his family, including hundreds of inmates of
the imperial harem and their attendants. Usually there were a
number of doctors in the sultan's service, preferably chosen
from among the Muslim members of the profession, but open
also to "infidels," particularly Jews. Some Jewish physicians arriving from the Iberian Peninsula and Italy had, even before
their settlement in the Ottoman Empire, enjoyed a great reputation for their medical skill and found ready acceptance
among the ruling classes of the Empire.

The growth in number of Jewish court physicians is well
reflected in several official documents. One register, dated
1536–37, records four or five Jewish practitioners along with
thirteen to fifteen Muslim colleagues. Twelve years later (1548–
49) a similar register mentions thirteen to fourteen Jewish
doctors and seventeen Muslim physicians. Understandably, the
official post of chief physician was given to a Muslim, regardless of his personal qualifications in comparison with those of
the other candidates, whose respective positions were reflected
in their salaries. Moses Hamon, who in the mid-1530s was the
highest paid Jewish doctor, received 45 aspers (akçes) daily,

which was less than one-half the salary of the chief Muslim medical officer. Twelve years later Hamon's salary had increased to 75 aspers and was almost equal to that of the Muslim *hakim-bashi*. In 1536–37 Moses, although listed in the fourth place, received the highest salary while the Jewish recipients, including Moses' son Joseph and other relatives, were paid much less down to 8 aspers a day. Possibly these younger members acted in the capacity of assistants until they grew into maturity and secured higher posts on their own. It stands to reason that those who resided at court were provided with free lodging, food, and many services, so that they could live a comfortable life with their families. Moses Hamon and family, however, occupied a large mansion in the Jewish quarter, probably because they wished to live among Jews and close to their synagogue. Very likely, some of these court physicians were also allowed to have a private practice outside the imperial palace.[32]

Court services of the Hamon family began with Moses' father, Joseph the Elder, who seems to have arrived from Granada, where his father Isaac had functioned as a court physician of one of the last Muslim rulers. After settling in Constantinople, he functioned in a similar capacity for Bayezid II and Selim I. A rumor, perhaps originating in the aforementioned stories about Ya'qub, attributed to Joseph a leading role in the poisoning of Bayezid II, staged by his son Selim. Supposedly, as a sequel, Selim, instead of being grateful to his co-conspirator, ordered him to be executed. In reality, however, Joseph served Selim for six more years. He accompanied the sultan on his campaign against the Mameluke Empire, during which he seemingly died a natural death in Damascus in 1518. This is, indeed, the impression one gains from the obituary address delivered by R. Joseph b. Meir Garson and especially from the fact that Joseph's son Moses succeeded him without a break.[33]

Moses Hamon (*ca.* 1490–1554), became the most prominent member of his family as both a practicing physician and a writer of medical works. One of his treatises on the diseases of the mouth was the earliest essay on dentistry ever written in Turkey; it was composed not very long after the publication of a similar work in the West. He was also a distinguished collector of books and manuscripts—he was said to have spent 8,000 ducats on the copying of manuscripts alone—and accumulated an outstanding library. Among his most precious possessions was a noteworthy manuscript of the first-century Greek treatise on drugs by Pedanius Dioscorides, which had already been of great interest to Ḥisdai ibn Shapruṭ, a participant in its new Arabic translation in tenth-century Cordova. In recent generations this manuscript has been one of the show pieces of the National Library in Vienna. At the same time Moses was very active in Jewish communal affairs in Istanbul and beyond. He tried to mediate in a notorious Salonican controversy between a tyrannical lay leader, Baruch, and the head of a distinguished rabbinic academy, R. Joseph Ibn Leb, by summoning Baruch to the capital. His efforts, however, proved in vain and, on his return to Salonica, Baruch went so far as publicly to slap the face of R. Joseph. Hamon was more successful, as we shall see, in persuading Suleiman to intervene in behalf of Doña Gracia Mendes when, during her temporary stay in Venice, her entire property was threatened with confiscation because of her secret profession of Judaism. His medical ministrations, on the other hand, received the praise of such foreign visitors as Nicolas Nicolay, who had accompanied the French ambassador Aramon to Istanbul in 1551–52, although a less friendly German observer, Hans Dernschwam, on his journey through the Middle East in 1553–55, generally blamed the Turkish Jewish doctors for their imperfect knowledge of Greek and Latin and their unfamiliarity with Western medicine. Moses Hamon's downfall, soon followed by his death in 1554, may have been connected with the internal palace intrigues which in 1553 had led to the temporary removal of the pro-Jewish Rustem Pasha, the sultan's son-in-law and grand vizier since 1544. All this, however, did not prevent Joseph the Younger, Moses' son, from continuing to serve at the courts of Suleiman and Selim II. One of the greatest services Joseph performed for the Jewish community was his securing in 1568 the sultan's renewal of the wide-ranging privilege of the Salonican community. Like his father he also acted as a patron of Hebrew poets. His son, Isaac, continued the family's medical career at court. Isaac's incorruptibility was recorded in connection with a Spanish envoy's futile effort to bribe him to intervene with the sultan in favor of a truce between Spain and the Ottoman Empire. Isaac emphatically declined, a procedure which was not common among the diplomats of that broadly mercenary age.[34]

Moses Hamon's intervention for Gracia Mendes (before her marriage in Portugal called Beatrice Benveniste, sometimes also Beatrice de Luna), bore richer fruit than he could expect. Within a few years (in 1552) she arrived in Constantinople after a triumphant entry via Dubrovnik and Salonica. True, during her latest Italian residence in Ferrara she enjoyed relative peace under the liberal government of Ercole II d'Este, although she seems rather openly to have professed Judaism there, which she had been unable to do during her remarkable career in Flanders, England, France, and Venice, mentioned in our earlier volumes. In Ferrara she also could unfold her true Jewish spirit through her numerous benefactions not only to Jewish individuals but also to Jewish cultural efforts at large. It was partly under her inspiration that, in 1553, the poet Samuel Usque published his classical Portuguese volume *Consolaçam as Tribulaçoens da Israel* (Consolation for the Tribulations of Israel). In dedicating the volume "to the very illustrious lady Doña Gracia Nasi" the author emphasized, that he did it "not out of blind devotion, though I am your protégé," but rather because "you are the heart in the body of our people: in the remedies you have offered you have always shown that you feel our people's sufferings more poignantly than anyone else." In the page describing her activities Usque compared Gracia with the ancient Jewish heroines, Miriam, Deborah, Esther, and Judith, and summarized her contribution up to the point of her departure for Turkey in a way which adumbrated the far greater impact her work was to make under her complete freedom of action in the Ottoman capital. He wrote:

Her inspiration greatly encouraged your [Jewry's] needy children in Portugal, who were too poor and weak to leave the fire, and to undertake a lengthy journey. She generously provided money and other needs and comforts to the refugees who arrived destitute, sea-sick

and stuporous in Flanders and elsewhere. She helped them overcome the rigors of the craggy Alps in Germany and other lands, and
she hastened to alleviate the miseries caused by the hardships and
hazards of their long journey. She offered you her compassion and
divine largesse in the sudden dire distresses you faced when you
were exiled from Ferrara. She provisioned the rich at a time when
they could not use their wealth. She helped the masses of destitute
people. She denied no favor even to her enemies. . . . Thus with
her golden hand and angelic purpose, she lifted the majority of our
people in Europe from the abyss of this hardship and countless others where poverty and sin had hurled them. She continued to guide
them until they were in safe lands, and until she had returned them
to the obedience and precepts of their ancient God.[35]

Gracia's stay in Italy belongs to the stormiest periods of her
life. Apart from the difficulties of maintaining a Christian front
while professing Judaism in secret, she was embroiled in
weighty family dissensions. She brought with her not only her
daughter Reyna and her nephews João (Joseph) and Bernardo (Samuel) Miguez (or Miques), but also her younger sister Brianda and the latter's daughter called Beatrice *la chica*
(the Younger). Brianda did not share Gracia's devotion to Judaism, enjoyed her life in Italy, and really did not wish to move
to Turkey. Neither was she an observant Christian. Before long
she began demanding from Gracia her and her daughter's
share in the large inheritance left behind by her husband,
Diogo Mendes, who in his will had specifically entrusted his
entire estate to Gracia's exclusive management. We need not
pursue here the details of the litigation between the two sisters
in which the Venetian government and ultimately also the Papacy, the king of France, and the sultan became involved. The
most dramatic part occurred when Joseph abducted little Beatrice, apparently with her consent, took her to the States of
the Church and allegedly married her in Ravenna. According
to the report of the Austrian ambassador to Venice, Dominik
de Gaztelu, otherwise unconfirmed, the marriage was consum-
mated, although, as we shall see, this escapade did not prevent
Joseph from marrying Reyna, the bride's cousin, nor Joseph's
brother Bernardo who had joined them in the flight from
Venice, from marrying young Beatrice in Turkey a few years
later. Very likely this whole flight was merely a subterfuge

to withdraw the prospective heiress from the clutches of the *Signoria*. Not surprisingly, this affair caused an international sensation. The Venetian authorities reacted violently. On July 21, 1549 the Council of Ten in a speedily convoked special session unanimously adopted the following resolution:

João Miquez shall be banished in perpetuity from Venice, from all the lands and cities of the Republic, and from its ships whether armed or unarmed; whenever in the future he should be caught and delivered to us, he shall be hanged between the two columns of Saint Mark until he dies. Those who will capture him even in a foreign country and deliver him alive into our hands shall be given 2,000 ducats out of his [João's] property which will be confiscated, or in the case of default out of the moneys of the Signoria. Those who will kill him even in a foreign country and will be able to prove that assassination will be given 1,500 ducats as stated above. In both cases they will also be paid a lifetime pension of 200 ducats from the Treasury of the Council of Ten.

Clearly, behind this extremely severe resolution and the high price placed on Joseph's (and his associates') capture, lurked not merely the Council's desire to punish an abductor of a young lady for the purpose of marriage, but rather the attempt to justify its intended seizure of the Mendes possessions. This proclamation remained without results, however, and merely added impetus to Gracia's decision to leave for Turkey, a design which, with the intervention of the powerful and greatly feared sultan, she finally carried out by reaching Istanbul in the summer of 1552. Before long she was joined not only by Joseph and Samuel but, after their reconciliation, by her sister and niece.[36]

Although not of a retiring disposition, Gracia herself did not engage in any major political activities despite her excellent connections with the Porte and some members of the diplomatic corps in Istanbul. On the one occasion when she ventured into the field of international politics the undertaking ended in failure. We recall how, guided by emotions rather than a sense for realpolitik, she sharply reacted to the tragic deaths of the twenty-four Marranos on the inquisitorial pyre (plus one by prior suicide) in papal Ancona. With the aid of her son-in-law, Joseph Nasi, she succeeded in persuading the sultan to intervene in behalf of the Turkish Jews who then happened to be in Ancona on business—they included some former Marranos serving as business agents of her own firm—and thus to spare them untold hardships, if not death. But she was unable to save those "relapsed converts" who were not the sultan's subjects, and hence could freely be condemned by the Inquisition. Gracia's subsequent reaction was punitive rather than purposeful. We recall that she endeavored, with the assistance of several prominent rabbis, to induce all Jewish traders in the Ottoman Empire to switch their exchanges of goods with central Italy—theretofore channeled through the port of Ancona—to Pesaro in the neighboring duchy of Urbino. This boycott not only proved to be economically unsound, because Pesaro could not compare with Ancona as a center for the distribution of goods, but it also created many internal Jewish problems, particularly the dangers threatening the surviving Jewish community in that papal city, perhaps even in all the States of the Church. The ensuing discord among the Turkish rabbis about the validity of the temporary ban, and their inability to agree on its continuation, brought the entire enterprise to naught. The dissension was aggravated by the resentment of many non-Sephardic Turkish Jews against their former Marrano coreligionists. Some of these doubtless felt like the chief opponent of the Ancona boycott, R. Joshua Soncino of the famous family of printers by that name, a native Italian, who was serving as a rabbi in Istanbul. He insisted that "these Jews who formerly lived according to Gentile mores in Portugal but decided to dwell under the wings of our Godhead and practice the laws of Moses and Judaism, did not have to establish a residence in another Christian country even if they received many promises [of immunity]. . . . If I could find someone [in authority] who would join me, I would excommunicate anyone who had been forced to convert in Portugal and later selected a residence under another Christian regime." It was from this rigid point of view that he could allow himself to state that the youthful prank committed by the prince of Urbino against the synagogue and scrolls of law in Pesaro, had brought greater contumely on the Jewish people than the papal execution of the twenty-four Marranos in Ancona. At the same time R. Joshua maintained his equanimity and, as we shall presently see, in other cases affecting the Mendes family he impartially sided with Gracia.[37]

Doña Gracia spent most of her energies on her far-flung commercial undertakings and philanthropic endeavors. She must have been a very effective businesswoman who, aided by her nephew, equally brilliant as a merchant, banker, and diplomat, successfully tried to salvage as much as possible of the fortune she had left behind in Flanders, France, and Italy and profitably to invest her capital in new undertakings of an international scope. More successfully than many other Marrano capitalists, she prepared the ground for the transfer of some of her resources to Turkey before arriving in Istanbul. In this respect, too, the fact that Joseph had remained behind in the West for more than a year after her departure enabled him to add to these resources in various ways. Of course, he could not liquidate all the firm's investments. For example, one of its largest outstanding assets, the 150,000 écus which Joseph claimed to have advanced over the years to the king of France became, as we shall see, the object of a prolonged controversy between France and the Ottoman Empire. Nevertheless, through its numerous agents the House of Mendes was able to continue doing business in Ferrara, Venice, Lyons, and other commercial centers of Christian Europe.

In the early years of her life in Turkey, to be sure, Gracia lived under the cloud of Brianda's aforementioned claim to her and her daughter's inheritance rights. She had good reasons to distrust her hedonistic sister's ability to manage her property. The matter was finally settled in 1554–55 when R. Joshua Soncino and other Jewish authorities decided that, since Brianda's and Beatrice la chica's inheritance claims were based on the estate left behind by Francisco, who had died as a Christian in Portugal, the Portuguese law favoring Gracia governed its allocation. It was also owing principally to Gracia's efforts and considerable financial sacrifices that a large part of the family fortune was saved from the rapacity of Emperor Charles V and other Christian rulers. Other pitfalls in Gracia's business career arose from her unavoidable use of foreign agents who did not always prove trustworthy. In a much-discussed case, Gracia, upon departing from Ferrara in 1552, left behind 18,000 ducats with two Marrano agents, Agostino Enriquez and Duarte Gómez. The two men were supposed to add 3,000 ducats each and to manage the total amount of 24,000 under the arrangement that half the profits would go to Gracia and the other half be divided between them. In other words, after deducting their business expenses, they were each to share in 25 percent of the profits, contrasted with their investment of but 12½ percent of the capital. It appears that Enriquez submitted regular annual accounts without having to pay out her share of the profits to Gracia. However, when after seven years (in 1559) the lady requested him to send the accumulated funds to her in Turkey, the agent demurred. For a long time thereafter he failed to answer her letters and when, through Turkish intervention, the D'Este authorities began demanding action, Enriquez put up counter-claims for expenses going beyond the originally agreed upon amounts. Finally, fearing a lawsuit before Ferrara courts where he knew that he would lose, he suddenly declared himself to be a professing Jew, named Abraham Benveniste, and demanded that the matter be decided by a rabbinic court. R. Joshua Soncino and other authorities, consulted in this matter, decided in favor of Gracia (apparently in 1562). However, all these difficulties were overcome with the aid of Don Joseph Nasi and his political allies and the Mendes fortune apparently continued to grow from year to year.[38]

At the same time, Gracia spent a substantial part of her large income on subsidizing Jewish communities and individuals throughout the Empire and beyond. This generosity was in compliance with the old Jewish tradition, upheld with particular vigor in medieval Spanish Hebrew letters, that it was part of the divine guidance of history to bestow wealth and political connections upon certain chosen individuals so that they would be able to help their people. In Istanbul Gracia established a new synagogue with an adjacent academy, the guidance of which she entrusted to the famous scholar R. Joseph Ibn Leb. Curiously, this new synagogue called Della Señora, or in Hebrew *Shel Ha-Geveret ha-Ma'aṭirah* (the Magnificent or, more literally, the Crowning Lady), caused a disturbance in the capital's Jewish communal life. Because much of the budget of the two institutions was covered by the generous patroness, quite a few members of other congregations—either to ingratiate themselves with the influential lady or to reduce their contributions to congregational expenses—transferred out of their former houses of worship to the new synagogue. Thereupon some leaders of the older groups vigorously protested and submitted the matter to rabbinic jurisdiction; the controversy finally reached the generally recognized authority of R. Samuel de Medina in Salonica. Arguing that since, unlike Salonica, the capital did not have an intercommunal agreement against raiding members of each other's congregations, the rabbi decided that Istanbul's Jewish residents had a perfect right to choose their membership in any newly founded congregation. We do not know whether the Señora in some way compensated the older congregations for their losses, but peace was quickly reestablished. Remarkably, we do not hear of Gracia's direct contacts with the imperial *seraglio* which, because of the increasing influence exercised by the sultan's wives and concubines on the affairs of state, became more and more significant politically and economically. She seems to have left all such relationships either to the court physicians or to such women-agents as Esther Kyra, who for decades supplied the harem ladies with desired goods and information (see below). Most remarkably, however, the passing of Doña Gracia was nowhere recorded with any degree of precision. Notwithstanding the great admiration in which she was held by Turkish Jewry we do not even possess the text of a single obituary or funerary oration. To be sure, the great Salonican preacher, Moses Almosnino, briefly referred to such eulogies he had delivered in her honor in both Salonica and Adrianople. But he mentions these addresses in passing in his collection of sermons, *Sefer Me'ammeṣ koaḥ* (Increasing Strength, with reference to Proverbs 24:5), published in Venice, 1588. A leading Hebrew poet of the metropolitan circle, Saadiah Longo, composed a dirge in Gracia's memory. But neither writer bothered to mention the exact date of her demise or her burial place. However, it seems that she died in late 1568 or early 1569 in Istanbul.[39]

DON JOSEPH NASI

Much more spectacular was the career of Gracia's nephew, João Migues (often called Miques or Micas; *ca.* 1514–79). Born in Lisbon to an influential father Agostinho (Samuel) Migues who in 1518–25 taught medicine at the University of Lisbon, he and his brother Bernardo seem to have joined their aunt Gracia during her emigration from Portugal to Flanders in 1536. Both adolescents grew up among the upper bourgeoisie and aristocracy in Antwerp. In 1540 and 1542, respectively, Bernardo and João entered the university of Louvain where João, in particular, closely associated with a fellow student, the future Holy Roman Emperor Maximilian II. It was this youthful association which doubtless influenced Maximilian in 1567, on the occasion of his sending Bishop Anton Veranchich (Verantius) of Gran (Esztergom) on a peace mission to Istanbul, to send with him a present for the new duke of Naxos. The bishop praised Joseph for the assistance given to him, despite the mention in his reports of July 23, and December 2, 1567 that the duke of Naxos was an apostate from Christianity, allegedly lured away because he would thus be able to marry wealthy Gracia's daughter. Veranchich also alluded to a rumor current in the diplomatic circles in Istanbul that the sultan intended to send Don Joseph as his ambassador to Vienna. Upon his return from that mission, after the conclusion of the Austro-Ottoman truce of February 17, 1568, the bishop admitted on May 28 that, without an apparently interest free loan from the duke, the Austrian mission would have found itself in a very embarrassing position. It is small wonder then that in addressing, during that year, a letter to the influential Jewish courtier in the Turkish capital the emperor himself began his epistle with the line: "Maximilianus Spectabilis et magnifice sincere nobis dilecte salutam." Returning to young João's career we do not know when and why he left the university and joined the Spanish army in Flanders. As a dashing, handsome young cavalry captain he seems to have cut quite a figure in the entourage of Emperor Charles V. These contacts later served him in very good stead when he joined the wealthy business firm of his uncle Diogo Mendes. We recall that, despite many vicissitudes, Diogo played a great role in the leading mercantile circles of Antwerp which at that time was a prime emporium for world trade. After his death the firm's survival hung in balance because of Charles V's perennial shortage of funds and the growing anti-Marrano sentiments in the Spanish-Flemish bureaucracy which later led to the attempted expulsion of the New Christians from Antwerp (1549–50). Anticipating this contingency João persuaded his aunt to transfer most of her funds to safer places abroad. In 1544 Doña Gracia herself succeeded in leaving Antwerp for Aix-la-Chapelle "for health reasons" after promising Queen Maria, Charles V's sister, to return to the Low Countries. When she failed to do so the queen tried to confiscate as much of the Mendes property as possible. It took João two years to negotiate with the emperor and his sister for the release of all Mendes possessions against a cash settlement of 100,000 florins in addition to a shipment of precious stones, worth some 30,000 écus, previously seized by the Flemish officials. Finally, in 1546, having settled his accounts with the ever-impecunious emperor, João rejoined the family during the years of its stay in Venice and Ferrara.[40]

Ultimately, however, at the end of 1553, João joined his aunt in Istanbul. Equipped with a formal safe-conduct and traveling on an armed ship sent for him especially by his aunt, he safely crossed the Adriatic to Dubrovnik and proceeded in the company of Janissary bodyguards to the capital. About his early sojourn in Constantinople, we have a rather curious report from Andrés Laguna, a Spaniard posing as a doctor, who in his autobiographical *Journey Through Turkey* reminisced:

The first days that Juan Micas was living in Constantinople as a Christian, I went to him every day and begged him not to do such a thing as to become converted to Judaism for the sake of four *reals* of money, for one day the Devil would take them from him. I found him so firm [in his Christian faith] that naturally I went away consoled; for he assured me that he would not go to visit his aunt again, and that he wished to return to the West at once. You can judge my surprise when I learned that he had already become one of the Devil's own. When I asked him why he had done this, he said that it was so that he should not remain subject to the Spanish Inquisition.[41]

We do not know what induced Miguez at this point to pretend to wish to remain a Christian, because he must have known that his aunt expected him and his brother publicly to profess Judaism. In fact, both men underwent circumcision and assumed the Hebrew names of Joseph and Samuel Nasi. In June 1554, within seven months after his arrival, Joseph married Reyna in an impressive ceremony, which was followed by several months of festivities in honor of the newlyweds. No one seems to have raised the question of a possible conflict with his purported previous "marriage" to Beatrice the Younger in a public ceremony, allegedly attended by a multitude of people, at the Cathedral in Ravenna. Nor did anyone mention that, shortly before his departure to Turkey, Joseph was supposedly still trying to persuade the Papacy to confirm the validity of the Ravenna wedding ceremony which could have been useful to him in reclaiming both his "wife's" money (in the meantime taken away from him) and the Mendes fortune from the Venetians. It certainly was not too difficult for Joseph, shortly before his settlement in Turkey, to explain to the French diplomat, Louis de Lansac (de Saint Gelais) that all he wanted was an intervention of the sultan with the Venetians to return to him both his wife and his possessions, which allegedly included 100,000 écus in cash. One must not forget, however, that from the Jewish point of view there was no legal obstacle to his marrying Reyna. To begin with, as we recall, the Turkish Sephardim, like their ancestors in Spain and Portugal, had never formally accepted the ban against plural marriages issued in the tenth century by R. Gershom the Light of the Exile and hence everyone was theoretically entitled to marry a second wife, particularly under unusual circumstances. But in the case of Reyna even that rule did not have to be invoked, for, as we recall, all Marrano marriages in Christian countries, performed under the ever-present threat of the Inquisition, were considered null and void by the Turkish rabbinate, unless they were accompanied by other weddings in accordance with "the laws of Moses and Israel," and in the presence of ten adult male Jewish witnesses. Everybody who may have heard of the Ravenna Christian ceremony—if it ever took place—knew that it was merely a stratagem employed by the Mendes family in its legal battle with Venice. Hence even Beatrice the Younger's subsequent nuptials with Bernardo in Istanbul in 1555 were completely legal in the eyes of the most exacting Turkish rabbis who generally viewed with horror any new union by a woman, however remotely suspect of still being married to another man.[42]

Thenceforth Don Joseph could freely dedicate himself to the upbuilding of the family business. Regrettably, we have few details about the firm's far-flung enterprises in several countries. In fact, many aspects of the Jewish and general economic history of the Ottoman Empire in the sixteenth century are still in the early stages of investigation. There is no question, however, that, under favorable circumstances, as Halil Inalcik explained, capital formation was relatively easy. So was the ready availability of credit at a moderate rate of interest even from the Muslim lenders despite the consistent opposition thereto by the authoritative Muslim jurists. We know, for example, that Don Joseph's Greek rival, Michael Cantacuzenus, apparently a scion of the famous Byzantine imperial family, made an enormous fortune by farming salines, collecting tax revenues from Moldavia and Walachia, and through other enterprises. He committed the mistake, however, of not hiding his wealth behind the façade of modest living as did most of his wealthy Greek compatriots, but rather built for himself a magnificent palace almost rivaling in splendor that of the royal residence. Because of his ruthlessness he was nicknamed *Shaitanoglu* (the Devil's son) by the Turks. Arrested in 1576, Michael was freed on the intervention of Grand Vizier Mehmed Sokolli (Sokollu or Sokulluh). But when he quickly resumed his former ways of living Murad III ordered his rearrest in 1578. Without formal trial he was hanged and his whole fortune confiscated. Such arbitrary methods, often employed by the Turkish bureaucracy, illustrated the risks run by all successful businessmen. Perhaps because, shortly after her arrival in the capital, Doña Gracia lent the sultan 10,000 ducats, and because thenceforth she and Joseph closely collaborated with Grand Vizier Rustem to the end of his life in 1561, Don Joseph succeeded in actually rising on the ladder of success from year to year. That he continued doing so even in the face of the new Grand Vizier Sokolli's animosity, was a testimony both to his dexterity and to Sokolli's realization that Joseph was rendering important services to the Turkish regime. Even in the last five years of his life, when his influence was waning, the Jewish diplomat still was an esteemed citizen, showered with favors by both the Ottoman court and some foreign powers, and he peacefully died in his own bed in 1579.[43]

We are relatively best informed about Don Joseph's business undertakings connected with government concessions, records of which are generally better preserved. In some areas he had a near monopoly of the wine trade. Although the consumption of alcohol was prohibited to Muslims, the high-quality wines of the Greek islands, including those produced from Joseph's own vineyards in Naxos and vicinity, were extensively consumed in the Empire and much sought after in foreign countries. Perhaps the very type of "coloring" added to Turkish wines of the time, which did not appeal to such visitors as Hans Dernschwam, may have exerted a special attraction for those who over many years had cultivated their taste. We recall, in particular, his large export trade of wine to Poland, known to us from Polish sources. Introduced in 1562 to King Sigismund Augustus by a flattering letter from Suleiman—Joseph was called in it "a gentleman worthy of all honor, faithful and favored by Us, Our servant and *mutafariq* [nobleman-courtier]"—he further gained these royal favors through a loan of some 150,000 ducats to the Polish Crown and certain courtesies to Polish envoys. In return Don Joseph received highly laudatory letters from the Polish king and also, in the face of much local opposition, both Christian and Jewish, he obtained in 1567 an important commercial privilege from the king. But even here the specific details of the trade conducted by his agents to the end of his life and beyond are yet to be fully elucidated. Similarly, Gianomore (probably identical with Salomon Giemnero, mentioned below), one of Joseph's Jewish agents, secured a concession from the Polish government to be the sole exporter of wax (another very important item in international trade) to Turkey. Poland's infringement on that contract through admission of other exporters elicited a protest from Selim II who emphasized that

since We always extend Our benevolence to persons who have distinguished themselves by their loyalty and deeds to Our imperial throne,

We hope that because of the contacts and ties you have with Istanbul, the city of righteousness, you will act in consonance with the privilege in their possession and fully restore their [exclusive] lease. We also wish that their privilege regarding customs duties and other matters should suffer no delay, but be speedily implemented [March 17, 1568].

With the cessation of Turkish pressures after the deaths of Selim and Joseph and under the impact of generally changing economic and political conditions, the trade between Poland and the Ottoman Empire greatly declined, resulting also in the financial ruin of the Mendes firm's Jewish agents in Lwów.[44]

Apart from such international exchanges Don Joseph also collected considerable revenues from farming certain customs and tolls, and later on as duke of Naxos and the Cyclades archipelago also from taxes gathered from the local populations. Of course, much of that revenue had to go to the Turkish Treasury. Tax farming had already been for some time a favorite occupation of wealthy Turkish Jews. The acute French observer, Pierre Bellon de Mans, who had visited Turkey about 1547 (before Don Joseph's arrival), commented that

they [the Jews] have taken over the traffic and commerce of Turkey to such an extent that the Turk's wealth and revenue is in their hands. They set the highest price on the collection of tributes from the provinces and the harbor dues [harborage] from ships, and other things like these. . . . I have often had to make use of Jews and to keep company with them. Hence I have easily learned that theirs is the subtlest and most malicious of nations.

On the other hand, Joseph's business and personal expenses were likewise enormous. He not only lived very lavishly but, according to existing custom, he constantly had to deliver costly presents to the sultan and high officials, as well as to foreign ambassadors and visiting dignitaries. Like his aunt, moreover, he also was a philanthropist helping coreligionists in need and contributing a good deal to the Jewish communal budgets in Istanbul and elsewhere.[45]

Don Joseph's far-flung business relations drew him into the field of international political affairs as well. Even more than other countries, the Ottoman Empire depended, for its knowledge of conditions in other lands, on intelligence reports either by professional spies or by interested business associates. While a number of foreign states were represented by their ambassadors at the Porte, the sultans, taking pride in the fact that other sovereigns had to negotiate with them at their imperial residence, only occasionally sent envoys, usually lower ranking officials, on specific missions abroad. Hence, from the time of Murad II, it became customary to collect information through business agents located in other capitals, some genuinely representing firms at home, others using that camouflage in order to obtain or verify pertinent information. Joseph was in an especially favorable position to collect dependable data and valuable insights into developments in other countries. According to the French Ambassador Jean de la Vigny, Nasi "has the best means of hearing about anything happening in the West, better and earlier than anyone in the world; he immediately communicates these data to the sultan." Another observer mentioned that Don Joseph's name "was known all over the world." Some objectors, particularly Spaniards, liked to classify that activity as espionage. Even a near-contemporary French historian called Don Joseph "the greatest spy in the world." The fact was that, as subject and councilor of the sultan, he felt obliged to perform his patriotic duty and let the Turkish government know certain facts which he had learned before anyone else. This was no cloak and dagger affair, but rather simple information obtained in the course of his business activity, or from correspondence with his agents or customers. A close parallel may be drawn from the Rothschilds in the early nineteenth century who were frequently consulted by their respective governments about recent developments in other lands.[46]

Outsiders often misjudged such activity. We recall the canard heard in Amsterdam about the international exchanges of information which allegedly took place regularly between representative Jews from Salonica and Venice and the leaders of the Amsterdam community meeting in Amsterdam every Sunday. They were supposedly thus quickly able to provide, well ahead of their competitors, reliable information about mercantile and political trends evolving in both the Levant and Atlantic areas. This rumor was a pure invention; but the fact remained that Jews residing not only in these three cities but also in other mercantile centers often communicated with one another and, at times, even entered into family unions. We recall that the Jews of Buda were accused by some enemies of telling their coreligionists arriving from the Balkans about what was happening in Hungary so that these visitors upon their return to Istanbul were able to submit that information to the Turkish authorities. Certainly, the entire Ottoman intelligence service did not compare with the effective espionage network developed by Philip II of Spain. We must also remember that Joseph never was a Spanish subject; even in Flanders he lived as a "Portuguese" resident alien. He may actually have viewed with apprehension certain manifestations of the Spanish ambition to take over Portugal, an ambition which was to be fulfilled in 1580, one year after his death. In contrast, Philip II's intelligence network included some non-Spaniards, such as the head of the Maltese Order, and, at times, even the Greek Orthodox patriarch of Constantinople who thus committed treasonable acts against his own country. However, probably even more valuable than the submission to the sultan of more or less reliable facts was Don Joseph's ability to evaluate them. With his keen perception of the existing realities and his precise knowledge of many leading individuals among the ruling circles in the Western lands, he was able, probably better than anyone else, to review the welter of often contradictory data supplied by agents abroad and to help the Ottoman Diwan to assess their true significance. He thus enabled it to make rapid and far-reaching decisions. We may well understand, therefore, the saying attributed to Suleiman that for him Joseph "was the true mirror in which he saw all the developments in Christendom and from which he obtained information about all countries."[47]

Don Joseph's influence at court was sometimes used even by such outsiders as a newly elected Greek Orthodox patriarch of Constantinople. Since every election of an ecclesiastical chief required governmental confirmation, we are told, the patriarch paid Don Joseph a visit, accompanied by a customary present (in this case 1,000 ducats), and asked him to intervene in his behalf. After a while a beautifully illuminated firman, issued by the Turkish chancery, confirmed the election. We possess Moses Almosnino's eyewitness report to the scene when the patriarch, on receiving the document from Don Joseph, wished to kiss the diplomat's hand, which Joseph understandably refused. Regrettably, we are not told which patriarch thus approached Don Joseph. Most likely it was Metrophanes III after his first election by the Holy Synod in 1565, rather than the more eminent Jeremias II Tranos who succeeded him for the first time in 1572. Such a rather humiliating visit of a leader of the Greek Orthodox Church to a Jewish courtier can be understood only against the background of that Church's general disorganization and its frequent mistreatment by the Muslim authorities of the time.[48]

Despite the prevailing vagaries in international relations of the period Don Joseph's activities reflected his general anti-Spanish animus. Otherwise not a vindictive person, he could assert, four years after he had escaped the clutches of the Venetian Council of Ten, which had placed a high price on his head, that he held no grudge against the *Serenissima*. In fact, in 1567 that very Council unanimously voted to revoke its earlier resolution. However, his enmity to Spain went deeper. Personally, he and his immediate relatives seem to have suffered little from the Spanish Inquisition. They had left Portugal before its own counterpart of the Spanish Holy Office was fully functioning—the delay was partly the result of their own efforts in Rome—while Diogo Mendes' occasional difficulties in Antwerp were the effect of governmental, rather than inquisitorial, persecution. Yet almost to the last years of his life Joseph made deliberate efforts to undermine the overwhelming power of Spain, the greatest and most dangerous enemy of the Ottoman Empire. Undoubtedly, he felt that such a policy was dictated by the genuine interest of both his newly adopted fatherland and world Jewry. He was willing, therefore, not only to side, more or less permanently, with France, the perennial ally of Turkey against the Habsburg powers, but also to try to be helpful to all other movements fitting the overall Ottoman imperial designs.

It was for this reason, for instance, that Nasi was in touch with the Protestant Consistory of Amsterdam in its political activities, which before long led to the Dutch War of Independence. He is said to have encouraged these restless Spanish subjects to rebel against their oppressors by asserting that "Philip, the King of Spain, would become so involved in fighting the Ottoman army that he would be unable to give much thought to Belgian affairs" (November 4, 1566). While the existence of such a letter, reported by Fabiano Strada, is otherwise unconfirmed, there is good evidence to show that the envoy, sent to Istanbul in 1569 by William of Orange, the leader of that anti-Spanish revolt, resided in Don Joseph's home and was apparently introduced by him to the sultan. Seven years later William was also to try, as we recall, not only to secure financial support from German Jewish bankers, but apparently also to persuade, through them, the prominent Jewish diplomats in Istanbul to help increase the tensions between Spain and the Porte and thus cause the diversion of some Spanish forces to the Mediterranean area. If nothing tangible came out of these negotiations, it was certainly of some aid to the Dutch "rebels" to know that their uprising had genuine sympathizers in the powerful Ottoman Empire. In another area, too, as early as 1569, Joseph suggested to the French allies of Turkey that King Henry II's brother marry the sister of the childless Sigismund II Augustus of Poland and thus become a strong candidate for succession to this last scion of the Jagiellon dynasty. As is well known, something of that kind happened four years later when Henry de Valois was elected king of Poland, though on Henry II's unexpected death a few months later, he fled to Paris to assume the more coveted crown of France. Joseph's 1569 proposal also included a marriage between Henry II's sister and King John II Zapolya of Transylvania, a move which, through such family ties, might have strengthened the coalition of the three anti-Habsburg powers. On occasion Nasi also tried to support smaller popular movements as when, in June 1563, he extended a welcome to Sampiero da Bastilica, the renowned freedom fighter against the oppressive Genoese regime in Corsica. When Sampiero's illness—which the Genoese envoy ineffectually tried to convert into a fatal malady by conspiring with the "rebel's" doctor—contributed to the ultimate failure of his mission to enlist Ottoman help for the uprising, Joseph lent him money for departure.[49]

It is small wonder that these far-reaching interventions by the Jewish duke greatly annoyed the king of Spain and his councilors. In reaction, on October 26, 1569, Philip II wrote a noteworthy letter to Marquis Fernando Francisco de Avalos de Pescara, his viceroy in Sicily. It related to a mission of Juan (Giovanni) Barelli, commander of the Order of St. John, in connection with some ambitious anti-Turkish plans initiated by the Order's Maltese grand master, Parisot de la Valetta. With the aid of some Turkish traitors, this chief of Christian corsairs, a counterpart of the North African Muslim buccaneers, endeavored to arrange to blow up the Ottoman arsenal—which reminds us of the actual explosion in the Venetian arsenal shortly thereafter which was to be attributed to Don Joseph's agents (see below)—to stage an uprising in the Morea, and in various other ways to undermine the Ottoman military power. After briefly discussing these plans Philip II added:

You should also know that Juan Micas, duke of Naxos, is the person most responsible for inspiring the machinations being conducted [in Turkey] to the detriment of all Christendom and of Our kingdoms. He has great insights [*intelligencias*] into what goes on at this Court and in other parts of My kingdoms. It would, therefore, be of great service [to Us] to have him in Our hands, and for the agent [Barelli] to bring him [Joseph] along dead or alive. Though I do not wish to get involved in this undertaking, Barelli will do it provided he is given a safe-conduct which would enable him securely to enter Our kingdoms and estates [together with Joseph]. . . . In case he should be unable to get him alive, but would have to kill him [*menester quitarle la vida*], after accomplishing this task, he would also receive some compensation.

In other words, the king ordered the marquis to cooperate with Barelli and to see to it that, after kidnapping the duke, Barelli would have no difficulty in crossing, together with his prisoner, the frontier to Spanish-dominated Sicily. Evidently, Philip preferred to have Joseph alive, doubtless because he would thus be able (if need be, with the aid of torture) to extract from the prisoner some valuable information about conditions and leading personalities in Turkey and other lands.[50]

In this connection, the Simancas archive possesses a number of documents relating to the activities of one Agostín Manuel, a renegade Jew from Istanbul. After his arrival in Sicily he claimed that, through his brother serving in Don Joseph's entourage, he had information that the Jewish diplomat was ready to change masters, to come to Spain, revert to Christianity, and to serve Philip II against Turkey. It appears that it was Manuel who brought with him a memorandum, allegedly addressed by Don Joseph to Philip II in cipher, asking that, for the purpose of settlement in Spain, he be given a safe-conduct granting the Mendes family total immunity from prosecution by the Spanish Inquisition and secular courts. This document, undated and unsigned, was perhaps a simple forgery, or else, if it was indeed written at the end of 1571, it may have represented a temporary aberration of a man who, under the impact of the Turkish defeat at Lepanto, feared being executed or at least being deprived of his great fortune because of his earlier "hawkish" stand in the war—a fate often befalling even grand viziers for a crucial advice gone wrong. Certainly, Selim's behavior was anything but reassuring. On October 7, 1571, the very day of the crucial battle, the sultan had left his capital for Adrianople with perfect equanimity. Sixteen days later, on learning of the great debacle of his fleet, he hastened back to the capital and, almost immediately, dismissed Pertev Pasha, one of the two admirals who had commanded the Ottoman navy. Furthermore, all the pasha's possessions were confiscated. Nor was Joseph oblivious of what happened after the failure of the ambitious and imaginative campaign against Muscovy in 1569–70. Inspired by Sokolli, the Turkish attack which, if successful, was to culminate in the construction of an Ottoman-controlled Don-Volga canal, speedily ended in the retreat of the Ottoman forces. Thereupon the sultan informed his grand vizier that "the costs and the losses will be totalled and you will have to make them good!"[51]

It is thus barely possible that, in a momentary panic, Joseph tried to open for himself an avenue of escape. Hence, even if it was authentic, the memorandum in question represented no more than an impulsive reaction, speedily regretted by its author. All along Philip II, nicknamed the "Prudent," treated the entire affair with much greater caution than did some recent investigators. The king had been warned, on October 10, 1570, by his envoy to the Holy Roman Empire, Count de Monteagudo (on the basis of information received from the emperor), to be on his guard in dealing with Don Joseph. Nevertheless, the Spanish authorities pursued some approaches aimed at securing an armistice with the Ottoman Empire until 1574, when whatever hopes they may have entertained to enlist Joseph's cooperation ended in his outright refusal. While this entire affair is still full of obscurities, the elucidation of which may come only from the discovery of new archival documents in both Spain and Turkey, the data now available give the impression that even in these negotiations Joseph subtly pursued his general anti-Spanish policy. If Philip II, ever since 1567, had tried without overtly acting in this direction to get under the umbrella of the negotiations for an armistice then being conducted by Maximilian II with the Porte, and thus to achieve a respite from the ever-threatening resumption of large-scale Ottoman hostilities, Joseph may have been endeavoring, through dissimulation and the pretense of being a friend of Spain, to drive a wedge between the two branches of the Habsburg dynasty. In fact, the truce, concluded between the Holy Roman Empire and the Porte on February 17, 1568, did not include Spain and, most importantly, two years later the Austrian Habsburgs refused to join Spain, the Papacy, and Venice in the anti-Turkish alliance during the Cypriot war.[52]

All these activities were overshadowed by the grand gesture made by Selim II when, in one of his first acts of government, he appointed Joseph duke of Naxos. He could not easily make him a vizier, because such high posts were restricted to Muslims, including converts to Islam. With this limitation the sultans usually took the best men they could find without regard to their ethnic origins. It has been shown that of the 48 grand viziers who held the real power behind the throne in the years 1453 to 1623, only 5 were of Turkish descent, no less than 36 were recruited from among Christian renegades, including 11 Albanese or Yugoslavs, 6 Greeks, and so forth. Some of these potentates belonged to the most illustrious leaders of the Ottoman Empire. If Ya'qub of Gaëta reached, as it is claimed, the position of imperial treasurer, this appointment would increase the probability that by that time he was professing Islam at least outwardly. A story had it that Suleiman had offered a high government post to Joseph Hamon the Elder, on the condition that he adopt the Muslim faith. The doctor supposedly replied that, if he or his family had been prepared to relinquish their Judaism, they could have lived peacefully and prosperously in their native Spain. Don Joseph's elevation to the duchy of Naxos was, therefore, a breach of tradition because it involved his serving in a capacity similar to that of a *sanjak* or governor not only of the island of Naxos, "the pearl of the archipelago," but also of a number of neighboring Cyclade islands. His legally undefined status was that, without belonging to the regular Turkish bureaucracy, he was not quite the semi-independent vassal on a par with the voivode of Walachia or Moldavia or the rulers of Dubrovnik.[53]

We do not possess the original decree of appointment, but it seems to have been fairly well summarized in Moses Almosnino's *Extremos y Grandezas de Constantinopla* (pp. 77 f.):

Thereafter when he [Selim] assumed the reign and left Constantinople in order to stay in the military camp . . . he [Joseph] joined him and, upon arriving in Philoppopolis [Selim] did him the favor of conferring upon him the rule of Naxos . . . Paris and Ante-Paris, Milo, Santorin, and other islands connected with these which are inhabited, in addition to others which are deserted, so that he may do, or leave undone, things in this his domain according to his wish.

This did not mean, of course, any transfer of sovereignty which remained with the sultan. In fact, for generations past the dukes of Naxos of the Crispo dynasty, who had since 1372 claimed to rule over "the oldest duchy in Christendom," had been under Venetian overlordship. In 1540, however, the Turks took over the duchy. For a while Suleiman left the last duke, John IV Crispo, in control, except that he had to pay an annual tribute of 4,000 ducats (out of a total revenue of 8,000–9,000 ducats) to the Ottoman Treasury. But in 1566 John was deposed and for a time languished in an Istanbul prison. To make the task of the new duke easier, on November 24, 1567 Selim ordered the qadhi of Galata to see to it that all former Greek inhabitants of the islands who resided in Galata (and perhaps also in some other cities of the Empire) be forced to return to their former residences. At the same time he forbade Muslims from settling in any of these localities under the excuse that there were no mosques on these islands. Five days later the sultan instructed the qadhi of Chios personally to proceed to Naxos and supervise the collection of the capitation tax from all non-Muslims. So pleased was the new "Duke of Naxos, Count of Andros and Paros, Lord of Milo and the Islands" (as he sometimes called himself in official correspondence) with his new dignity, that he hastened to Naxos and even missed the great celebrations occasioned by the enthronement of his friend Selim in the capital.[54]

To the end of his life, Don Joseph was ably assisted in Naxos by his lieutenant Francisco Coronello, a New Christian descended from the last chief rabbi of Castile Abraham Señor. Joseph saw his major task as stimulating the economy of the islands under his regime. With special reference to his own near-monopoly over the Turkish wine trade, he cultivated high-quality vineyards in Naxos and opened up new markets for that renowned beverage; he also replaced the existing social disarray by a reign of law and order. Nevertheless, the Greek Orthodox population of the island resented the rule of a professing Jew. It must have been particularly aggrieved by certain untoward incidents. For example, during Coronello's brief captivity on November 8, 1571, Don Joseph's auditor and councilor, Doctor Samuel Cohen, had to exercise in behalf of the "regnant" duke the right to nominate the priest Marco Belogna as "chaplain and guardian" of a local monastery named D'Annonciata. Cohen also ordered the new guardian to "supervise the monastery and rule it in a manner customary in the past, so that all praise him." This document, preserved by the family Coronello, was countersigned by another of Don Joseph's officials, his secretary Joseph Cohen. However, the aggravation for the Greek majority of the population must have been somewhat mitigated by the recollection that such nominations had long been presented by ducal officials who for the most part had been equally disliked Roman Catholics. In any case, the old regime was hated as both Catholic and oppressive, whereas Don Joseph, although paying the Ottoman Treasury an annual tribute of 6,000 ducats, or 50 percent more than his predecessors, seems to have been quite helpful to many of his "subjects." For example, in 1568 he persuaded the sultan to order the Turkish navy to inflict a decisive defeat on a corsair who, for years past, had interfered with shipping to the Cyclade islands and often raided one or another settlement. Yet, after Joseph's demise in 1579 Murad III appointed no immediate successor to bear his title. The Coronellos, however, remained on the island and belonged to its Christian aristocracy well into the twentieth century.[55]

Joseph's elevation to a distinguished dukedom created a sensation in the West. Even more dramatic was the conflict generated between the two allies, France and Turkey, because of his and Gracia's insistence on the repayment of a large debt of 150,000 écus owed them by the Crown of France. The House of Mendes claimed to have invested 100,000 of that amount when Henry II issued the great public loan going under the curious name of "Grand Party," preliminary to his "excursion" into Germany which resulted in the incorporation of Metz, Verdun, and Toul into the French realm. After his arrival in Istanbul Joseph continued to perform valuable services for France and particularly for the French ambassadors. As early as October 26, 1553, Louis de Lansac reported home that he had borrowed money from Joseph without interest. Lansac also mentioned "Michas' " readiness to be of service to the king of France, asking in return for the aforementioned French recommendation to the sultan to help him "rescue his wife and possessions held by the Venetians." On November 29, 1556 Henry II issued such *lettres patents* in favor of "Joseph Nacy, called Don Juan Miques, Our argentier [bursar] for the Levant, he being of the Hebrew nation." A year later the king wrote "to Our dear and well beloved Joseph Nacy, hitherto called Don Juan Miques, Our argentier for the Levant who for some time past had liberally loaned Us from his funds." All along Joseph befriended the respective French ambassadors, one of whom was the first dignitary to rush with his personal congratulations on Joseph's marriage to Reyna. Whenever the question of the repayment of the accumulated loans came up, however, the French regime made easy promises, which it had no intention of keeping. By 1560 disillusioned Joseph declined the formal appointment as French argentier under the excuse that such an official function might conflict with his services to the sultan. Once Ambassador Guillaume de Grantier Seigneur de Grandchamp actually signed a Document acknowledging the large debt and promising its repayment in the somewhat reduced amount of 125,000 écus in two installments six months apart. (After payment the ambassador was to receive a commission of 10,000 écus in jewelry.) Unfortunately for Joseph, Grandchamp was the least worthy of the sixteenth-century French ambassadors to the Porte, and his promise apparently had not been authorized from Paris.[56]

After years of fruitless waiting Don Joseph finally persuaded the Turkish government to proceed with a drastic action. We recall the old medieval tradition that local creditors were entitled to seize the goods of burghers stemming from the place of residence of a defaulting foreign debtor in order to satisfy their own legitimate claims. To be sure, no such procedure seems to have been applied to the property of private traders for the satisfaction of creditors of their reigning monarch. Nevertheless, the sultan issued in November 1568 an order that all ships then stationed in the French pavilion of the harbor of Alexandria be seized and one-third of their goods sold up to the amount of the 150,000 écus claimed by the Mendes family. As a result three French and two Messina ships were sequestered. It is small wonder that this action created a furor all over Europe, particularly since some of the ships seized were not even owned by Frenchmen but were merely temporarily accommodated in the French part of the harbor. In fact, the ships themselves were not held for any length of time, but the goods located on French bottoms were quickly disposed of. As it turned out, the disposal of the goods through a forced sale yielded Nasi less than 70,000 écus, possibly because the revenue had to be shared with some Turkish officials in Istanbul and Alexandria. Although we have just seen that Henry II knew all along that Don Joseph was "of the Hebrew nation," the French regime now used the excuse that the money borrowed from the Mendes family did not represent a legitimate royal obligation because, living in France as clandestine Jews, their entire property was, according to French law, subject to confiscation. As a result, the French claimed not only reparations for the damages caused to the owners of the merchandise seized in Alexandria, a claim pursued as late as April 16, 1579, a few months before Joseph's demise, but at first also demanded Nasi's execution; of course, without success. Nevertheless, this affair, much discussed all over Europe, contributed somewhat to the temporary weakening of the alliance between the two powers, a development which would have come about in any case because of the growing French preoccupation with its raging civil war of religion. The high-handed Alexandrian procedure, largely ending in failure, probably also played into the hands of the Turkish enemies of Don Joseph, including the powerful Grand Vizier Meḥmed Sokolli.[57]

From this experience Joseph might have learned, as did many other creditors of states in that and other periods, that tangling with a powerful regime, even with the support of one's home government, for the most part ended in frustration. The Ottoman national interest still dictated close collaboration with France in combating Philip II's expansionist policies. Within less than a year after the Alexandrian episode (October 1569), the two countries concluded a treaty, published in French under the heading, "Articles Conceded by the Sultan to the King [of France] and His Subjects . . . for the Security and Traffic . . . of the Levant." It was this treaty (and not, as has often been assumed, the unfinished exchanges of 1535) that laid a firm foundation for the comprehensive system of "capitulations." Based on the numerous privileges previously granted to Venetian and Genoese merchants and the actual practices which had evolved in the treatment of other foreign traders, that system was destined to play a significant role in the subsequent history of the Jewish and other minorities in the Ottoman Empire. Notwithstanding his temporary reverses, Joseph's prestige in Selim's court apparently was still high enough for him to influence the preparation of that treaty.[58]

More significantly, Joseph seems even to have cherished dreams of further advancement. At least rumor had it that, after his elevation to the lordship of "the oldest duchy in Christendom," he yearned for the even higher title of king of Cyprus. For many years past, many Turkish statesmen had cast covetous glances on this neighboring island, the closest Venetian colony to the shores of the Empire. According to a dispatch of 1562 from the Venetian representative Donini, Selim, then heir apparent to the throne, "had several times expressed the wish to add the island of Cyprus to the Empire, in order to leave behind a memorial for himself." As usual searching for an historical excuse, the advocates of the conquest argued that, since the island had for a time been under the suzerainty of the Mameluke kings of Egypt, the Ottomans, as successors of the Mameluke regime, were entitled to reestablish another Muslim overlordship there. At first, an attempt was made to persuade Venice to surrender the island voluntarily in return for some concessions elsewhere. Being unable to persuade the *Signoria* even to raise its annual tribute to the Ottoman Treasury from 3,000 to 4,000 ducats, Selim and Sokolli—prompted, it was said, by Don Joseph—decided on a military attack, which in 1570–71 led to the quick conquest of Nicosia, a somewhat longer siege of Famagusta (to August 6, 1571), and soon thereafter to the complete occupation of the island. It was widely suspected that the duke of Naxos now hoped to become the titular king of Cyprus under Ottoman suzerainty.[59]

Perhaps there was some connection between these alleged high-strung expectations of the leading Turkish Jew and the attempts of the Ottoman administration to colonize the newly acquired island with Jewish settlers. However, as we shall see, several steps taken by the Ottoman government in 1573 and 1576–77 were not carried out because of the staunch defense on the part of the Safed Jews, supported by the local authorities and, probably also, by some influential coreligionists in Istanbul. The opponents pointed out, in particular, the great damage such deportations would cause to the Turkish provincial administration in Damascus and the imperial Treasury. Similarly ineffectual seems to have been a later attempt to force a group of 100 Jews, who traveled with their families from Salonica to Safed, to be diverted to Famagusta "because they are needed there from all points of view." Thus all such designs for the colonization of Cyprus with Jewish settlers were abandoned, while Muslims, recruited from among Turks and other ethnic groups, constantly increased in number. Even later, when the established Jewish community gradually increased in numbers and socioeconomic stature, it never played a major role in the island's modern history. At the same time the "Turkish" minority grew into a significant segment of the population, creating the well-known international complications of recent years. In any case, there is no solid documentary substantiation for the rapidly spreading Western assertion of Nasi's royal aspirations. Even the ambitious duke probably was given no encouragement by his friend Selim, while the objective difficulties for such a move were enormous. But in Western eyes Joseph was generally considered the chief "culprit" responsible for the Turkish conquest.[60]

Neither Joseph nor the sultan's other counselors seem to have anticipated the sharp reaction by the Pope, Spain, and Venice, which gradually led these three powers to form a league to stem the advances of the Turkish steamroller. Supported by some smaller principalities, its combined navies ultimately overwhelmed the Turkish fleet in the famous three-hour battle of Lepanto (October 7, 1571). The story of that battle and its aftermath, more important to Venice and the West than to the Ottoman Empire, has been mentioned above, with the necessarily brief selection from the amply available documentation; it need not be repeated here. Suffice it to say that, while Selim and Sokolli kept their sang-froid—we recall the grand vizier's proud boast about the Ottoman Empire's ability speedily to rebuild a far more costly navy than the one lost at Lepanto—the duke of Naxos may have become panicky for a moment. But, as we recall, there is no trustworthy record of any such temporary "aberration" by the duke of Naxos in either the Turkish or the Jewish sources and he seems to have undisturbedly continued his career in Istanbul. To be sure, his influence in Selim's final years was gradually waning; after the sultan's death in December 1574 it diminished further. The new sultan, Murad III, a despotic personality thinking in terms of a new generation, seemed to dislike equally both Don Joseph and Sokolli. But he cautiously left the irreplaceable grand vizier in office until Sokolli's assassination in 1579. He also continued friendly relations with the "great Jew." Moreover, for reasons which remain unclear, the House of Mendes apparently suffered sharp business reverses, perhaps because its chief had been ailing for years before his death on August 19, 1579. According to the French ambassador, Jacques de Germigny, Joseph's estate, which was immediately sequestered by the Treasury, yielded barely enough revenue to restore to the duchess of Naxos her original dowry of 90,000 ducats. We do not know, however, how much the Treasury collected from the duke's other assets and how much the three Turkish officials in charge of the estate's administration embezzled for their private benefit—actions for which they were later convicted and severely punished. Doña Reyna, who may have been able to salvage some other possessions, continued living for eight more years in her splendid palace of Belvedere or at her second residence in a neighboring village. She also maintained some of the cultural interests of her mother and her husband, and supported two Hebrew printing presses. But otherwise she lived in quiet retirement.[61]

On the whole, in all his high diplomatic activities Joseph was principally guided by the Ottoman imperial interest, the satisfaction of his own ambitions, and the pursuit of private business advantages. With the exception of the boycott of Ancona and the Tiberian project (about which more anon), both initiated by Gracia, he did not think primarily in Jewish terms. Evidently, he did not consider the possibility that his latest international enterprise, the war with Venice over Cyprus, might seriously endanger the survival of the Jewish community in the City of the Lagoons. We recall that, in its reaction to the war which began with the great explosion at the Venetian arsenal, sometimes blamed on Don Joseph's agents, the Council of Ten decreed the expulsion of the Jews from the Republic. Only in consonance with established traditions, the Venetian authorities postponed the execution of this decree for two years, when their compact with the Jewish community was to expire. It was fortunate for Venetian Jewry that interveningly the situation changed and war was drawing to its close, with a peace treaty concluded with the aid of another Jew, the physician Solomon Ashkenazi. Similarly, in his earlier efforts to promote the marriage of Henry de Valois to a sister of the last Jagiellon king of Poland so that the French prince could claim succession after the latter's prospective death, the duke did not weigh the likely impact of Henry's election on the status of Polish Jewry which, in this its formative period, greatly depended on royal support. Certainly, a French prince, coming from the overheated atmosphere of sectarian conflicts in Paris, which before long resulted in the Saint Bartholomew massacre of August 24, 1572, was the least likely to become a patron of Jewish economic and cultural endeavors. Nonetheless in Western public opinion, as reflected in the contemporary diplomatic correspondence and literature, Joseph was sometimes called "the great Jew," as well as the "great spy," and the enemy of Christendom. Even in England, which was a direct beneficiary of his anti-Spanish policies, he served as a model for Christopher Marlowe's influential caricature of a Jewish banker, Barrabas in *The Jew of Malta,* and to some extent also for the figure of Shylock in William Shakespeare's *Merchant of Venice.*[62]

Domestically, on the other hand, Nasi continued with many benefactions to his fellow Jews, including subventions to authors desirous of seeing their works in print; interventions in behalf of communities seeking favors at court, such as Moses Almosnino's aforementioned 1569 mission to secure a confirmation of Suleiman's *Magna Carta* of 1537 for the community of Salonica; or help in settling intracommunal controversies. Occasionally he seems to have participated in some scholarly and religious debates, although he used more common sense arguments than, as was mostly the case in such discussions, quotations from established authorities. Rejecting, for example, widely held "superstitions," he contended that "one must not rely on evidence from feeble-minded persons, or from exaggeration-prone men and women." Out of such debates he was induced to publish in 1577 a small Hebrew polemical tract, *Ben Porat Yosef* (Joseph Is a Fruitful Vine), written in cooperation with Rabbi Isaac Onqeneira. He received for it more than his due in encomia from some of the most authoritative rabbis of his generation in their introductory approbations of this booklet. At times he also extended a helping hand to proselytes. For instance, in 1575 a French nobleman, Roveries, owner of three chateaux in the vicinity of Lyons, decided to adopt Judaism and to proceed to religiously tolerant Turkey. Subsequently victimized by a dishonest New Christian depositary with whom he had left 30,000 ducats, he lived in destitution in Istanbul until he received support from Don Joseph. According to the near-contemporary Jewish apologist, Immanuel Aboab (ca. 1555–1628), some doubters of Roveries' motivations received from the proselyte the poignant reply, "I did not come to seek the Hebrews, but the God of the Hebrews and their Law; of them you can assuredly say no ill." Moreover, through the very fact that a Jew could exercise so much power at court, his political clout accrued to some benefit for the rapidly growing Turkish Jewish communities. It is noteworthy that, except for the Ancona and Tiberian enterprises, as well as the litigation with Brianda, in all of which the initiative came from Doña Gracia, the great diplomatic achievements of the first Jewish duke in centuries found only a relatively faint echo in the contemporary Hebrew letters, save for some commemorative poems and obituaries written by such personal friends as Saadiah Longo and Moses Almosnino.[63]

Remarkably, Don Joseph seems to have had practically no enemies among the Turkish Jews. Despite their great divisions and frequent internal conflicts, they all seemed to agree that the Mendes family had done well by the community. Whatever opposition Gracia's or Joseph's actions may have elicited, as was the case with regard to the boycott of Ancona, it was voiced in objective terms without rancor. To be sure, during the controversy over the French debts, the French envoy, Guillaume de Grandchamps, secured the testimony of a Jewish agent Daud (David), that Joseph had "maintained secret correspondence against the Porte with the pope, Spain, the duke [grand duke] of Florence, the Republic of Genoa, and other enemies of the sultan." When this accusation was disproved, Daud was banished to the island of Rhodes and excommunicated by the rabbinates of Istanbul and other cities. This ban was revoked only after Joseph's death in consideration of Daud's good behavior in Rhodes. Initiated by the island's rabbis, who pleaded for mercy toward a repentant sinner, this revocation was accepted by the mainland rabbis, including even so staunch a friend of the Mendes family as R. Joseph Ibn Leb.[64]

More serious was the enmity toward the duke evinced by another Jewish diplomat who frequently found himself in the camp opposing Don Joseph: Solomon Ashkenazi (*ca.* 1520–1602). We have had occasion to discuss the Udine doctor's public activities in connection with the Turco-Venetian War of 1570–73 and his subsequent efforts in behalf of Henry de Valois' election to the throne of Poland. It is truly remarkable how quickly this physician, who had settled in Istanbul in 1564 after serving for sixteen years at the court of Sigismund II Augustus in Cracow, gained access to the highest governmental circles. As a native of Udine in the *terra firma* of the Venetian Republic, and with relatives and friends still living in the area, he apparently found easy entry to the officials of the Venetian colony, and quite early became a close friend of Marcantonio Barbaro, the Venetian *bailo* in the Turkish capital. He probably also served as his physician. Barbaro, on his part, apparently introduced him to Sokolli to whom he seems likewise to have extended some medical ministrations. When in 1570 war broke out over Cyprus, Barbaro, though representing an enemy power, was not forced to leave Turkey but was allowed to stay on indefinitely under a sort of comfortable house arrest. This semi-isolation did not prevent him from communicating with the grand vizier—probably, on occasion, through Ashkenazi's mediation. When the time came for peace negotiations, Ashkenazi was, therefore, in a position to pull his weight. Familiar as he was with the domestic situation in Venice, he may well have received information that some of the republic's leading merchants and statesmen were getting tired of a war which not only cost the *Serenissima* the huge amount of 12,000,000 ducats, but also seriously interrupted its profitable trade with the Levant. On pure business calculations it was far less expensive to give up Cyprus and to conclude a peace treaty which provided for Venetian payments of an indemnity of 300,000 ducats over a period of three years.[65]

In this connection the Jewish question likewise emerged. Since early in 1573 the terminal date for the punitive expulsion of the Jews from Venice was speedily approaching, it was easy for the protagonists of peace, such as Barbaro, to advocate a revocation of that hostile decree. According to the contemporary Jewish historian Joseph ha-Kohen, it was a Venetian diplomat (he mentions Giacopo Soranzo, possibly inspired by Barbaro) who asked the doge to convoke the Council of Ten. He supposedly addressed the Council as follows:

What folly have you committed by [decreeing to] expel the Jews? You should have known that this would have a bad ending. Who was it that increased the Turk's power, where did he find the craftsmen to produce for him the battering rams, the guns and artillery, the swords and shields, in order to destroy the Christian forces, except the Jews who have been expelled by the kings of Spain? And now you, too, have decided to banish the Jews residing among you so that they would have to leave the country and add strength to our enemies! You should also know that the Jews have considerable influence among the Turkish dignitaries holding high positions in the empire. I swear, that in this decision you did no good [to our country]. You must also ascertain to whom you will turn for help if the Turkish armies should come upon you. To the pope or the king of Spain? You well know that they are broken reeds and you already have experienced how unreliable their assistance is.

One need not take that address at its face value; it probably was one of the usual artifices of contemporary historians who, in imitation of Livy, inserted into their historical narratives imaginary speeches in order to express what they believed to have been the main motivations of leading historical figures at a particular moment. Considerations of the kind attributed to Soranzo dominated indeed the thinking of the Venetian Senate which, within four months after the successful conclusion of the peace negotiations, abrogated the decree of banishment by a vote of 104 to 69 (July 7, 1573). This action culminated a year later in Ashkenazi's triumphant entry into Venice and his appearance (on September 3, 1574) at a session of the Council of Ten as the official representative of the Ottoman Empire to negotiate a Turco-Venetian détente. We also recall that, with the prestige thus won, Solomon could also lay claim to having promoted the election of Henry de Valois to the throne of Poland much more effectively than the French ambassador to the Porte, François de Noailles, bishop of Dax, who tried to take full credit for himself. This move by Ashkenazi—parallel to that of Don Joseph—is doubly noteworthy because, having but recently come from Poland, where he had lived for years close to the center of power, he should have more readily realized the perilous nature of that election to the status of Polish Jewry. Both statesmen were absolved of their responsibility only by Henry's sudden abandonment of the Polish crown in favor of the French. Less successful was Ashkenazi's support of Duke Alphonso II of Ferrara's candidacy for succession to Henry in the new election of a Polish king.[66]

For a long time thereafter Solomon, who survived both Don Joseph and Sokolli by twenty-three years, continued to play a political role in international affairs. But these activities took place under greatly changed circumstances during the reign of Murad III, and they will be discussed below, together with some other stars in Jewish diplomacy, especially David Passy and Alvaro Mendes (Solomon ibn Ya'ish).

PROTOZIONIST EXPERIMENT

One of the most memorable activities of the Nasi family related to the project of opening a Palestinian haven of refuge for the Jews of the Christian world. It developed from Doña Gracia's original effort to find a permanent resting place for her late husband in the Valley of Jehoshaphat. She had his remains exhumed and transported from Portugal to the Holy Land. This was in keeping with the old Jewish tradition, noted also by Christian visitors to the country, to consider burial of a body in the holy soil an assurance that it would be among the first to be resurrected. According to George Sandys, a distinguished "poet-adventurer," who visited the Holy Land in 1610–11, shiploads filled with Jewish bones were arriving in Jaffa for transshipment and burial in Jerusalem. "They say that through that action they assure additional pleasure for their souls and that they would be the first to stand before the tribunal on the general Day of Judgment." Moreover, this was a period of widespread messianic expectations, especially

among the Jews of Italy, which must have deeply affected Doña
Gracia during her years of sojourn in Venice and Ferrara.[67]

Gracia may actually have expected to follow her husband
and to provide for her own burial somewhere on the consecrated soil of Palestine. It appears that these thoughts propelled her to choose Tiberias as a locale where she might spend
her last years and find her final resting place. Tiberias recommended itself for various reasons. To begin with, its natural beauty was extraordinary. The much-traveled John Sanderson, who in 1601 visited the Lake of Tiberias region, claimed
that he had never seen so impressive a landscape. Its medici-
nally renowned warm springs at that time attracted annually
between 1,000 and 3,000 visitors seeking relief from their ailments. Most importantly, the city had been a renowned center
of Jewish learning during the centuries following the Fall of
Jerusalem. It was there, as we recall, that the work on the
Mishnah and most of the Palestinian Talmud was brought to
fruition and that it had also been the great center of the Ma-
sorah and its final textual revision of the Holy Scriptures. Many
pious Jews remembered also R. Johanan's ancient saying, repeated by Maimonides in his authoritative code, that the end
of days will be ushered in from Tiberias. Nonetheless, by the
sixteenth century, Tiberias had become so desolate, and its
ruins were inhabited by so many snakes, that it had many
empty spaces which cried out for additional settlers. It was
easy, therefore, for Gracia to approach the sultan (apparently
in 1560) and ask for permission to colonize the city with Jews,
promising to pay taxes far in excess of what the Turkish
Treasury was collecting up to that point. After a short investigation Suleiman decided to accept that proposal and to set
aside a designated area around Tiberias which had numerous
trees and land "appropriate for the cultivation of silk and the
plantation of sugar cane." The sultan formally transferred that
area to a newly established foundation (*waqf*) sponsoring a soup
kitchen in Damascus (June 15, 1560). In this way two days
later this property could be allotted to the Nasi family through
a long-term lease under the protection of the Muslim authorities, religious and secular.[68]

Out of this simple beginning developed an enterprise which

made a considerable impression on contemporaries and has since been the subject of extensive debates among Jewish historians. The main source, written by the contemporary Jewish chronicler Joseph ha-Kohen not many years before his death in 1578, revealed how important this development appeared to the careful and selective historian in his treatment of contemporary events. Departing from the major theme of his work *The Valley* or *Vale of Tears*, which concentrated on the description of persecutions and other misfortunes afflicting Jews through the ages, he devoted several paragraphs to the great success of Don Joseph Nasi's scheme without mentioning in this connection the role played by Doña Gracia. After stating that Joseph had left Portugal and finally reached Turkey, the chronicler continued:

He found favor in the eyes of Sultan Suleiman who loved him greatly. The monarch gave him the ruins of Tiberias and seven adjacent villages making him chief and lord over them. Don Joseph sent there R. Joseph b. Ardiṭ [Ibn Arduṭ], his employee, and ordered him to build the wall around the city. Ibn Ardiṭ found favor in the eyes of the monarch's son [Selim] who granted him a salary of sixty piasters a day. He [the sultan] also sent along eight men from his entourage and handed him [Ibn Arduṭ] a privilege signed and provided with a royal seal. He also recommended him to the pasha of Damascus and the district governor of Safed, ordering them "to do everything that this man would ask them for." Another order was issued in behalf of the sultan commanding all builders and porters in the area to proceed to Tiberias and to work on construction there, under the sanction of severe punishment [for disobedience]. They [the laborers] found there plenty of stones [for building], for Tiberias had been a large city before its destruction; it had included thirteen synagogues in the days of R. Ammi and R. Assi [fourth-century talmudic sages]. The monarch also ordered the inhabitants of the seven localities to prepare mortar for the buildings. There was plenty of sand around, since the Lake of Tiberias [Kinneret or the Sea of Galilee] was in the vicinity.

That Ibn Arduṭ was thus given an official post and provided with a salary which compared favorably with those paid most of Suleiman's court physicians indicates the seriousness with which the government viewed the project of Tiberias' rehabilitation.[69]

Some such concession was granted to Don Joseph, probably

in 1563, although we do not possess any text of the sultan's pertinent orders. Regrettably, the respective collections in the Istanbul archives have a serious lacuna for the crucial years 1560–64. However, Joseph's success is partially confirmed by a dispatch from the French ambassador, De Pétrémol, dated September 13, 1563. After reporting about rumors circulating in the Turkish capital concerning Joseph's colonization scheme, the ambassador added with great excitement: "In this way, it is believed, he plans to turn himself into a king of the Jews. That is why he so urgently demands the money from France." This brief remark by De Pétrémol has given rise to endless discussions. Some scholars believed that the future duke of Naxos really contemplated establishing a Jewish principality under the suzerainty of the sultan but autonomously governed by himself. Today there is a growing consensus among scholars that no such ambitions could have been seriously entertained under the then prevailing conditions in the Ottoman Empire. The sultans may have allowed semi-sovereign rulers on the periphery of the Empire, like the kings of Yemen or Transylvania or the still more independent kings of Morocco who continued bearing their old titles. It was noteworthy enough that in 1566 Selim II granted Joseph the right to take over the title of duke of Naxos, which merely meant an exchange of one vassal duke by another. But to create vassal kingdoms in the middle of the Empire went against the grain of basic Ottoman policy. Even after the conquest of Cyprus or of the various North African realms the sultans speedily converted them into regular provinces under the administration of ordinary governors (begs). It was hardly imaginable that a new kingdom would be carved out of a tiny territory within a province which extended into Syria and had been governed by a pasha in Damascus for half a century.[70]

At the same time, the Turkish administration certainly desired to attract new settlers to many relatively deserted places. In this way their soil could be redeemed for cultivation, industry and commerce could expand and, in part, be newly introduced. The greatly increased sedentary population would also offer a welcome permanent defense against the roving bands of nomads. Most significantly, any new settlement of this kind would also generate much additional revenue for the Treasury and ultimately be a source of strength, rather than a liability, for the Turkish authorities. It was undoubtedly in this sense that the offer of a Jewish magnate like Joseph to pay for the privilege of colonizing Jews in Tiberias appeared attractive to Suleiman and his son. The offer was to pay 1,000 ducats annually, which at the existing rates equaled six times the value of the 13,000 aspers theretofore collected by the fiscal agents (according to the 1560 document). The immediate downpayment of a larger sum was also alluring. Hence the establishment of a new Jewish colony serving, under a partially autonomous regime like that of Naxos, as a haven of refuge for Jewish exiles from Christian Europe was a distinct possibility, especially under the reign of Joseph's close friend, Selim II.[71]

Clearly, the mere removal of legal difficulties did not guarantee the upbuilding of the new Jewish settlement. From the outset the undertaking faced some opposition from the local Christians and Muslims. Generally, intergroup relations in the Holy Land at that time were very tense. We learn from Fray Pantaleõa de Aveiro who, some time before 1565, arrived in the country in the company of sixty monks led by Bonifacio di Ragusa, that even the Turks and the Moors (Arabs) residing in Jerusalem "hated each other mercilessly and their relations with one another were based entirely on cheating." This observation was confirmed by Guillaume Postel, who for years had studied the mid-Eastern populations from close range, and who contended that, despite the general unity of the world of Islam, the non-Turkic Muslims hated the Turks more than the "infidels." He insisted that, while the Tartars, Persians, Arabs, and other Muslims "would demand nothing from a Christian or a Jew, or at the most despoil him of his goods, they would put a Turk to death in the most cruel way they could invent." Curiously, De Aveiro, perhaps himself a Portuguese New Christian, evinced considerable interest in the Jews of the area. While himself harboring a strong anti-Jewish bias, he claimed that in Jerusalem the Jews were the most hated group of the population. It is not surprising, therefore, that immediately after the enactment of the first order of 1560 the relatively few Christians inhabiting Tiberias evinced fears that the new Jewish arrivals might appropriate their ancient Church of St. Helena and convert it into a synagogue. Bonifacio di Ragusa, serving as custodian of the Franciscan Order in the Holy Land, complained about it to Rustem Pasha. The grand vizier promised an investigation which must have revealed that these fears were entirely based on the Christian clerics' misunderstanding of the nature of the Jewish "house of worship," which could be located even in a small section of any private dwelling. Many pious Jews of the time would, very likely, have hesitated to pray in a locale which had once been consecrated for the worship of another faith. As late as 1630, indeed, the visiting friar Eugène Roger mentioned the Tiberian synagogue as being located in a warehouse.[72]

More threatening was the reaction of the Arab population. One of its fanatical old sheiks may have overheard Jews speaking about the aforementioned rabbinic tradition that the final salvation would start from Tiberias. Out of a misunderstanding or malice, he spread the rumor that he had found in an old book the prediction that, if Jews rebuild Tiberias, this event would mark the beginning of Islam's downfall. Thereupon the workers building the wall laid down their tools and left the city. However, when the pasha of Damascus learned of this flagrant disregard of direct royal orders, he sent a detachment of soldiers, seized two ringleaders and punished them severely, and the erection of the wall proceeded without further molestation. Its completion in the month of Kislev 5325 (November 5–December 4, 1564), close to Hanukkah and hence vividly reminding the participants of the Maccabean renovation of the ancient Temple, filled the new settlers with great hopes for the future. On the whole, to be sure, this was not a very large undertaking. The wall's circumference most likely amounted to but three-quarters of a mile. Yet within these narrow confines a number of buildings were constructed on Gracia's order; she may have planned to inhabit one during her declining years. She probably did not come to Tiberias, however, since her arrival in the Holy Land would certainly have been recorded by some contemporaries.[73]

A small Jewish settlement rapidly followed these early moves. Don Joseph, who seems to have become the moving spirit after

1563, proceeded with the practical problem of colonization by persuading some older Jewish fishermen living along the shores of the Sea of Galilee to develop their trade in the new community. In the neighboring villages assigned to him by the sultan he planted many mulberry trees and apparently found Jewish newcomers skilled in the production of silk and silk garments. He imported Spanish wool, and probably also Merino sheep of high quality, so that a new textile industry could lay the foundations for a self-supporting Jewish community. Furthermore he protected the inhabitants of these villages against fiscal and other demands from local feudal lords and government officials, who sometimes also tried to interfere with their pursuits. To increase the Jewish population rapidly he also made it known among the European communities, especially in Italy, about that new outlet for their emigration. Italian Jewry, particularly in the Papal States, was then going through the anguish of great persecutions initiated by Paul IV in 1555. This reversal in the old papal policy of moderate toleration was soon to culminate in Pius V's decree of expulsion of all Jews residing in the States of the Church except for the residents of Rome, Ancona, and southern France. Many Jews of central Italy were now ready to abandon their ancestral homes and proceed to the Ottoman Empire. We have interesting documentation in a letter addressed by the small community of Cori in the Campagna, the entire membership of which made preparations to transplant itself to the new Palestinian settlement. The writers spoke enthusiastically of "the Crown and glory and grace and honor of the prince, the lord and noble . . . Don Joseph to whom the Lord God caused to be given the land of Tiberias, wherein God chose him to be the sign and symbol for our redemption." They had learned that this benefactor had sent ships to Venice and Ancona to transport those who were ready to come to the Holy Land. They added: "We have indeed learned that many have already set out and crossed the seas, with the assistance of the communities and the aforementioned Prince. It has been told us, moreover, that he seeks especially Jewish craftsmen, so that they may settle and establish the land on a proper basis." In view of their great poverty, however, the Cori Jews needed assistance to reach the harbor in which ships waited to transport them to Palestine free of charge. In 1569, after the promulgation of Pius V's decree of expulsion, a large group of 700 refugees assembled in Pesaro and Senigaglia awaiting transshipment to the Holy Land. Their circular among the Italian communities asking for assistance seems to have borne some fruit.[74]

Regardless of these promising steps, about which we possess few other contemporary records, the progress of colonization was very slow. It is possible that the energy initially displayed by Don Joseph about 1563 greatly diminished, not only because of the difficulties of building a new colony from scratch, but also because beginning three years later, as we know, his new assignment as duke of Naxos and the Cyclade islands required much of his care. At the same time he realized that he could not stay away from Istanbul for any length of time because the unending palace intrigues might have undermined his status even with such a long-time friend as Selim II. His far-flung business activities and his constant efforts to collect the debts due him from the kings of France must also have diverted his attention from the details of his and his mother-in-law's colonization scheme. Gracia's death may have further reduced his emotional involvement in a project whose realization under the then prevailing conditions would have overtaxed the resources and mental energies of a man far less preoccupied than Joseph with matters of great international importance like the Cypriot war of 1570–73.

Events in neighboring Safed must also have been quite discouraging. That important center of a Turkish district, as we recall, embraced a flourishing Jewish community whose outstanding halakhic and kabbalistic sages left a permanent imprint on the culture of world Jewry. However, the attitude of the local officials changed for the worse in the last quarter of the sixteenth century. We recall that, as early as 1573 under the friendly regime of Selim II, an effort was made to help repopulate the recently conquered island of Cyprus with Jews from Safed. At first this transfer was meant to be a punitive action against some Safed Jewish "thieves," according to a denunciation by a Jewish informer who was speedily excommunicated by the rabbis. In 1576–77 the plan was converted into direct orders to transplant first 1,000, later reduced to 500, wealthy and productive Jewish merchants (and probably highly skilled artisans) to Cyprus. The order of October 10, 1576 stated explicitly: "I command that as soon as [this order] arrives without delay . . . you register one thousand rich and prosperous Jews, and send them, with their property and effects and with their families, under an appropriate escort to the said city [Nicosia]." As a result, numerous Jews, poor as well as wealthy, fled from Safed, some becoming a burden on other Jewish communities. Because of the ensuing uncertainty Jewish trade was nearly suspended and the Treasury's revenues of 1,500 florins from Jewish poll taxes, and 10,000 florins from their payments of customs duties and other imposts, were in danger of drying up. Jewish representatives argued, therefore, that

if it is decided to deport them [the Jews] to Cyprus, the Public Revenue will lose the above-mentioned amount of money and the town of Safad will be on the verge of ruin. The Treasury of Damascus will suffer a great loss [since the collection of] their poll-tax, [impositions on] their houses liable to pay extraordinary levies ('avāriż-ḥāne), custom-duties, stamp-duty on broadcloth (çoka damġasi), customs on felt (keçe), and the tax-farm of the dye-houses (boya-ḥāne) will [all] be discontinued. Their houses will also remain deserted; no buyer will be found [for them]. Their landed property will go for nothing. [In short,] considerable loss and damage will result.

This argument, supported by the local administration, elicited a governmental firman of May 23, 1578 (confirmed by another of January 5, 1579) to suspend the deportation totally. These imperial orders did not prevent the beglerbeg of Cyprus in the spring of 1579 from suggesting to the Porte that a group of 100 Jews, whose ship, on its way to Palestine, stopped at Famagusta, be forcibly detained and settled in that city—a recommendation speedily approved by the sultan (June 1579). Although this order, too, seems not to have been carried out, the local Turkish officials may have felt encouraged to use all sorts of subterfuges to squeeze out funds from individual Jews and the community at large. Together with other adverse factors, such as plagues, famines, the general economic decline, and the continued hostility of the Muslim population, which

viewed with disfavor the growth of Safed Jewry, and the proliferation of its synagogues and academies, the oppressive regime cast a pall on the Jewish immigration to the Holy Land,
including that to Tiberias.[75]

Nevertheless, the enterprise thus set in motion was not
abandoned completely. Subsequent visitors found there a
Jewish community, small but bravely facing the difficulties of
pioneering in a novel semitropical environment. Nor was the
official scheme of upbuilding the Jewish colony formally revoked by the government. Although Ottoman law generally
provided that any privilege granted by a sultan automatically
expired upon his death, this did not apply to the Tiberias
firman because, we are told, that document, originally issued
by Suleiman the Magnificent, was co-signed by Selim, his heir
apparent, and the latter's son Murad. It appears that, precisely
in order to prevent such an expiration, Don Joseph secured
these additional signatures to indicate that the government
planned to maintain the new community in its privileged position for an indefinite period. In fact, after a relatively short
interval a new sponsor appeared on the scene. We shall see
that in 1585 another Jewish diplomat, Alvaro Mendes (apparently not related to the Nasi family), after a stormy career in
India and Western Europe, settled in Istanbul as a professing
Jew, named Solomon ibn Ya'ish. Speedily advancing at court,
he likewise became a duke, this time of Mytilene (ancient Les-
bos), and played a significant role in international diplomacy.
He, too, took an interest in the Tiberian colony and even dispatched his son Jacob there, probably to supervise its further
development. To the father's chagrin, however, Jacob became
a learned student of rabbinics and mysticism and lost all interest in worldly affairs. When Solomon died in 1603 the colony
lost again its influential protector. But it seems to have carried
on for a time, although on his visit (about 1630) Eugène Roger
found within its wall only 10 to 12 Jewish (alongside 25 Muslim) families whose spiritual guidance was provided by a rabbi
who came from Safed once a week to instruct them and to
conduct their divine services. Yet its very persistence prepared
the community for playing a certain role in the subsequent
evolution of Palestinian Jewry.[76]

REUNIFICATION OF MOST MEDITERRANEAN JEWRIES

An outstanding characteristic of the Golden Age of the Ottoman Empire was the establishment of the reign of law and order over the vast expanses of the Balkans, Western Asia, and North Africa. With the aid of a well-designed central administration and of a combination therewith of much provincial and ethnoreligious autonomy, the regime was enabled to resolve, at least temporarily, many of the tremendous difficulties inherent in the great diversity of interests and traditions among the Empire's population. Almost everyone outside the military caste was indubitably grateful for the *pax ottomanica* reigning through the length and breadth of the imperial lands outside the frontiers facing such enemies as the Habsburgs in the West and Persia in the East. Under Suleiman and Selim I and II, moreover, the Turkish soldiers— whether recruited from the Janissaries and the "men of the household" (*ghilman*) or sent into battle by the feudal lords who were the mainstay of the Turkish military system—had their hands full with the prolonged hostilities at the various boundaries of the country. They and their auxiliary troops still had plenty of opportunity to enrich themselves from the booty of the newly occupied areas even if a campaign ended in retreat. Above all, the opportunities for industry and commerce opened up by the new conquests and consistently encouraged by the government, and the protection granted Turkish traders through the awesome power of the sultans, domestically and internationally made possible the flowering of a new economy. This process became doubly necessary because of the steady growth in the population and the general rise in the standard of living.

Jews benefitted not only from the new affluence and orderliness, but also from the greater opportunities for cultural advancement. After their centuries-long fragmentation since the fall of the Great Caliphate, the Jewish communities in the Mediterranean world—who had theretofore always constituted the majority of the Jewish people—now saw themselves largely united under the umbrella of one, rather friendly regime. Except for Italy (whose Jewish settlements had, after the expulsions from Sicily and Naples and the new antagonism generated by the incipient Counter Reformation, been concentrated in a small area in the north) and for semi-independent Morocco, practically all Mediterranean Jews now lived in the Ottoman Empire. The Venetian Jewry, moreover, the largest and most influential segment of the Jewish inhabitants in the northern parts of the Apennine Peninsula, continued to maintain close commercial and cultural relations with its Turkish coreligionists through both the Venetian surviving colonies such as Crete and the Republic's East Adriatic dependencies. In fact, the "Levantine" Jews of Venice were actually endowed with special privileges in many Turkish emporia. Only the growth of Polish and Lithuanian Jewry into the largest Jewish community in the seventeenth-century world offered a parallel to the rise and splendor of Ottoman Jewry. But the Sephardic and Romaniot communities now lived almost exclusively under Ottoman rule and its system of legislation characterized by great stability and basic protection of human rights. The Jews reciprocated with a growing sense of Turkish patriotism. R. Samuel de Medina expressed the prevailing sentiment when he condemned the occasional Jewish lawbreakers by stating that "he who does not respect the honor of our great and pious king, may his majesty be enhanced, would be better off, if he had never been born. For we are obliged . . . to pay obeisance to his word and fulfill his commands and ordinances just as we are obliged to keep the commandments and ordinances of the King of the Universe." [77]

With the great freedom of movement guaranteed by legal and administrative enactments, communication between the various Jewish communities became very intensive; it was further facilitated by the influx of Spanish-Portuguese refugees into all these areas, which helped overcome some of the older differences in local origin and tradition. To be sure, Mehmed II's original intention to establish, through the chief rabbinate of his new capital, a central spiritual leadership for all Ottoman Jewry, similar to that of the Istanbul patriarchate of the Greek Orthodox Church, was speedily undermined by the Empire's rapid territorial expansion and the influx of masses of Jewish immigrants with their internal divisiveness and quest for communal self-determination. The rise of such new great centers of Jewish learning as those of Salonica and, for a time, of Safed, likewise reduced the power and prestige of the Istanbul chief rabbinate. Yet, the intrinsic unity of the Jewish people toward the outside world and its basic adherence to its age-old heritage of unity within the diversity in its traditions and mores helped it to create a new amalgam of a basically homogeneous ethnoreligious entity. Making use of the vast opportunities offered it by Turkey's Golden Age the re-grouped Mediterranean Jewry, too, now enjoyed a new efflo-rescence. It too may have legitimately classified the sixteenth century as another Golden Age of its own.

Alas, these conditions did not continue indefinitely. The very rapidity of the Empire's growth and the ensuing enforcement by the authorities of a somewhat superficial, rather than an integral, unity in part masked its inherent weaknesses which, under changed national and international circumstances, came strongly to the fore. It is not amazing, therefore, that this Golden Age almost suddenly ceased and gave way to an era of turbulence and incipient disintegration. The Jewish com-munities, too, could not remain unscathed.

LXXVII

INCIPIENT STAGNATION

THE PERIOD from the death of Selim II in 1574 to the assassination of Ibrahim in 1648 marked a creeping stagnation in the societal and political life of the Ottoman Empire. This was not a steady development. Owing partly to individual monarchs and partly to the changes in the Mediterranean world at large, there were numerous ups and downs. Thus under the reign of Murad III (1574–95) the decline was masked by certain advances which, in the long run, proved counterproductive. The decline was accelerated under Murad's short-lived successors Meḥmed III (1595–1603), who, upon coming to power, ordered the execution of his nineteen brothers in accordance with the traditional law of fratricide; Aḥmed I (1603–1617) who died at the age of twenty-eight; Osman II (1618–22), not to mention the two brief reigns of three and fifteen months of an outright imbecile, Mustafa I (1617–18, 1622–23), who was removed in each case because of his mental incapacity to rule.

These manifestations of decay were somewhat reversed under Murad IV (1623–40), but at great cost to the internal strength of the Empire. The underlying negative factors continued to operate more intensively under the weaker regime of Ibrahim (1640–48), although they were temporarily reversed in the following four decades (1648–87) in a new upsurge under the effective reign of Meḥmed IV, which was symbolized by the occupation of Crete and the second great siege of Vienna.[1]

DEEPENING CRISIS

It is noteworthy that the early symptoms of imperial decay did not escape the attention of at least some keen Turkish contemporaries. As early as 1596–97, a short time after Murad III's demise, a Bosnian scholar, Ḥasan al-Kafi Aḥizari, issued a missive (*risala*) on "Philosophic Principles Concerning the World Order" in which he pointed out numerous shortcomings in Ottoman public life. He was followed three decades later by Kuchu Bey, adviser to Murad IV, in a similar tract reflecting the deepening malaise during the intervening period. Curiously, Jewish leaders, though cognizant of the Empire's growing administrative weaknesses and their deleterious effects on the Jewish communities, limited themselves, as we shall see, to a variety of complaints about specific events or practices which adversely affected the Jews along with the rest of the population. Some foreigners, too, particularly Frenchmen who maintained close relations with the Ottoman Empire, sensed the damaging changes in the entire Ottoman society of the period, although some others continued to romanticize about anything taking place in Turkey. Modern scholars have generally agreed with Ahizari's and Kuchu Bey's observations and expanded on them with fuller documentation.[2]

Externally, the decline manifested itself mainly in the loss of the imperial drive which, during the preceding two centuries, had raised the power of the Osman dynasty from one ruling over a small principality in Anatolia to that of a commanding world power. The military steamroller, which before the reign of Murad III was still expanding the frontiers of the Empire in many directions, came virtually to a halt. The frontiers, achieved under Selim I, Suleiman the Magnificent, and Selim II, were now more or less stabilized, the few minor advances being counterbalanced by retreats. To be sure, the European colonial powers, Venice and Genoa, Spain and Portugal, remained definitely shut out from the eastern Mediterranean and North Africa after the conquest of Cyprus in 1571 and that of Tunis in 1574–79, as well as by the Moroccan victory at Alcazarquivir (Al-Qsar al-Kabir) in 1578. Not until two centuries later were the Western powers able to resume their penetration of the Maghrib. In the course of the seventeenth century, however, the Ottoman suzerainty of Tunis and Algeria was gradually weakened by the emergence of their semi-independent begs; it speedily disappeared in Morocco, which continued to conduct its own foreign policy. Crete, the only residual Western colony in the eastern Mediterranean still left under Venetian domination, was occupied by the Turks in 1669–1715. At the same time, however, the northern Ottoman frontier in Europe was gradually receding. Although the Turks succeeded in holding on to their share of Hungary, their continued control was achieved at great cost in manpower and money (it has been estimated that the thirteen-year war with the Austro-German Habsburgs, which ended in 1606 with the peace treaty of Zsitvatörök, cost the Ottomans 15,500,000 ducats) and resulted in the first formal recognition of mutual equality between the sultans and the emperors. This egalitarian relationship was demonstrated by the cessation of Austria's annual tributes to the Porte and the establishment of a regular Austrian embassy in Istanbul. The Habsburgs now could increasingly share with France "Protection" over the sultan's Catholic subjects, enabling them at times to interfere in the inner affairs of the Ottoman Empire. They were also able to hold off any Turkish intervention in the Thirty Years War which, at certain critical moments, might have spelled disaster for the Austrian-led Catholic alliance. In the meantime the part of Hungary which remained under Turkish domination was rapidly declining, so that, for instance, Buda's trade became less intensive than that of Belgrade. With some exaggeration a contemporary complained: "This is the country which was once a genuine paradise. But nowadays its misery is so great that he who is not accustomed to it, would wish to weep blood!"[3]

Another significant result of the Ottoman loss of forward momentum was that Turkish overlordship over Transylvania, Moldavia, and Walachia became very shaky. Imperial influence at times declined to the point where the Walachian voivode Michael the Brave was able to defeat Turkish armies. Poland-Lithuania, which had been benevolently neutral through most of the sixteenth century, now turned into a permanent enemy, glorying in its role of a "rampart of Christendom" against further Muslim advances. Most threatening, as it turned out, was the growth of Muscovite power. By freeing itself from the supremacy of the Golden Horde and steadily advancing toward the Black Sea through the destruction of Tatar power, Muscovy gradually became the archenemy of the

Ottoman Empire and increasingly claimed to be the legitimate inheritor of old Byzantium. No more favorable were the developments in Asia. While Murad III, in a difficult twelve-year war (1578–90), was able to expand the frontiers of the Ottoman Empire through the annexation of several formerly Iranian provinces, these gains were nullified under his successors by the several military campaigns of the distinguished Persian shah, 'Abbas I (1588–1629), who was extolled by the Italian envoy, as a "most just, courteous and brave man, beloved by his people, and gladly followed and obeyed by all." To be sure, the occupation of Baghdad and Mosul by the Persians was reversed during the last year of Murad IV's reign (1639); they thenceforth remained an integral part of the Ottoman Empire till World War I. But these military encounters were mutually exhausting and caused a constant drain on Ottoman manpower and financial resources.[4]

Internally, the situation was not much better. Because the forward motion of the Turkish army and navy had practically come to a halt, the expected remuneration of the conquering hosts through booty in foreign lands greatly diminished. At the same time the Treasury became ever more impoverished. As a result of the disorganization of the entire administrative machinery, the annual revenue from the *kharaj* collected in the European possessions gradually declined from 20,000,000 to 5–6,000,000 ducats. Unable to meet their expenses, the sultans resorted to the old trick of reducing the silver content of their coins, so that the value of the ducat, which had still retained its nominal gold value (it weighed 3.49 grams), gradually rose from the equivalent of 40 aspers (akçes) to 60, 120, and ultimately 200 aspers. Naturally, such a depreciation of the currency, combined with actual coin clipping by both the government and individual dealers, generated a galloping price inflation. Not surprisingly, many Jews, some of whom were engaged in aspects of the money trade, were often blamed by their enemies for debasing the currency. Even a royal ordinance issued on May 27, 1572 under the friendly regime of Selim II and addressed to the qadhi of Istanbul complained of "the large quantity of false money circulating in the empire and particularly in the capital" and added: "Since the Jews and other individuals are in the habit of making this sort of money, which does not prevent its entering into My Treasury, I command that these coins be removed from circulation and that they should not serve as currency in commercial transactions." The qadhi was told to make the appropriate public announcement through town criers and to order the owners of such forged coins to throw them into the sea, while those who possessed underweight currency should deliver it to the Mint for melting and recycling. Of course, Jews may have had their share of coin clippers, but they were but a tiny minority among their fellow money changers. Many undoubtedly heeded the strong condemnation of currency manipulations by their revered rabbi, Samuel de Medina. Calling Jewish counterfeiters traitors to their ruler, the rabbi rhetorically declaimed, as we recall, that "he who has no respect for the honor of our monarch, the great and pious king, may his Majesty be extolled, would be better off if he had never come into the world."[5]

Remarkably, we hear of but few aspersions cast on the Jewish officials employed in the governmental mints. In fact, under Murad III, Nessimi (a physician or son of a physician), the Jewish superintendent of the Istanbul mint, was told to stop the *simdji bachi* himself from further interfering with the minting and from producing false coins with the aid of a "protected subject" Constantine, evidently a Christian (September 18, 1583). As another means of protecting the coinage he was later ordered to stop the practice of shipping small coins across to Anatolia altogether (August 11, 1584). As a result of the growing deterioration of the coinage and the ensuing decline of their "real" wages, the Janissaries and the court guard often mutinied, these effects thus illustrating the growing laxity in military discipline. Many lords of feudal *timar*s, too, were now able successfully to evade sending their men to war. Moreover, the Janissaries, now increasingly recruited from the local population rather than through the *devshirme* of youthful non-Muslims, who were raised as well-trained and deeply indoctrinated soldiers, gradually became rather inferior combatants.[6]

The negative impact of the constant currency devaluations and occasional revaluations upon the economic life of Turkish Jewry must have exceeded that on Turkish society at large.

The profits probably derived therefrom by the relatively small number of speculators and unethical moneymen were far outweighed by the confusion generated among the large majority of Jews by every sudden decline or rise in the value of coins in circulation. Pious individuals and their rabbinic leaders also were gravely concerned about the untoward ethical aspects of devaluation. They considered it tantamount to "robbery" on the lenders receiving a smaller return than the amounts originally lent, particularly if the loan had been extended, according to the law, without interest charges. Revaluation had the opposite effect of "robbing" the borrowers. A later Turkish rabbi contended that "it is generally known how much ink has already been spilled on matters relating to the value of the currency." Even ordinary merchants and craftsmen must have been seriously hampered by the difficulties of planning ahead under the ever fluctuating value of coins. Potentially even more ruinous were the effects of these sudden arbitrary and ill-conceived governmental moves on this lifeblood of all commercial and industrial exchanges—moves which were further aggravated by the lack of generally accepted Jewish and Muslim legal safeguards in this field.[7]

The havoc played by the currency fluctuations with ordinary commercial transactions is often reflected in the contemporary rabbinic responsa. For example, R. Moses b. Ḥayyim Alshekh (died some time after 1593) was once asked to resolve a controversy between two Jewish merchants in Damascus, mentioned only with the customary fictitious names of Reuben and Simon. Reuben had advanced a certain sum to Simon, who was traveling to Aleppo, asking him to acquire there some "Frankish" clothing for Reuben's account. Simon was to receive only the very low commission of 1 percent. At that time the "current" ducats were worth 38 "pieces" (silver coins) in Damascus, but only 37 "pieces" in Aleppo. Before the transaction was completed, however, the value of the ducat was officially raised to 40 pieces, which was tantamount to a more than 5 percent devaluation of the silver coins, then the main medium of exchange. The mutual accounting was further complicated by a temporary drop in prices after the proclamation, although these quickly returned to their original level (probably in gold coin equivalents) while the deal was still pending. In his reply the rabbi was in a quandary to decide first whether Reuben's original advance was to be considered a loan. In this case the antiusury laws would have had a considerable bearing on the ultimate resolution of the conflicting claims of the two merchants.[8]

Civil administration was further weakened by the corruption spreading among officials up to the highest circles of government. Even the relatively honest and truly distinguished Grand Vizier Sokolli, who had started as an impecunious captive, left behind an estate valued at 22,000,000 ducats after his assassination in 1579—more than was owned by the Treasury at that time. One of his early successors, Sinan, received in 1591 a substantial annual salary of 2,263,000 aspers, which was about fifteen times the salaries given to the next-highest officials, the viziers. But he evidently had other sources of revenue, overt or clandestine, and was able to accumulate a "fabulous" fortune. The only remedy for the government was, under one excuse or another, to condemn grand viziers and other dignitaries to death and to confiscate their estates. The ensuing disastrous fiscal debacle of this system was reversed only by Murad IV by Draconian means at the cost of many lives and the fear for survival of even his closest advisers. Cruel and tyrannical by nature, this sultan made it clear to his viziers that they were no more than his slaves. With the use of these terror tactics he succeeded in reassembling a treasury of 30,000,000 ducats. A Venetian envoy actually described Murad as "the richest of all the princes that ever emerged from the House of Osman." However, even his drastic measures could not stem such adverse fundamental trends as the rapid increase in the Ottoman population, which far outstripped the growth in the agricultural and industrial output of the country. The simultaneously increasing exploitation of the peasants by the landlords added to the internal tensions and impoverishment of the masses. Not bound to the soil along the Western patterns, many peasants fled to the cities, thus swelling the hosts of the unemployed and underemployed populace. Even without that landflight agricultural productivity, a mainstay of the Turkish domestic economy and the export trade, probably did not increase until the introduction of newer technological methods in the nineteenth century. Assuming a more or less stationary crop of 64–80 kilograms of wheat per hectare in the entire area under cultivation, the total yield must have barely sufficed to meet the needs of the domestic consumption. Combined with the difficulties of transportation, continued exportation of some grain abroad from certain areas, and occasional years of bad harvests from natural causes, this system created frequent regional imbalances and near-famine conditions in certain localities.[9]

Other basic sources of Ottoman weakness originated from the growing influence of the harems on the reigning monarchs. While some of the sultans' favorite consorts, or the valideh sultans (queen mothers) were more intelligent and adroit politicians than their husbands or sons, their activities largely consisted of a variety of successful or disastrous palace intrigues. Most of the other ladies were primarily interested in luxuries, often supplied only by imports from foreign countries; they had little understanding for political or economic realities. From the point of view of the religious minorities, including the Jews, the growing influence of Muslim theologians and jurists, the ulema, and that of the grand mufti, the chief Muslim ecclesiastical officer and permanent member of the imperial Diwan, further undermined their feeling of security. It also often interfered with the undisturbed pursuit of their business, which otherwise might have accrued to their own and the country's benefit. If, according to a Polish envoy in Istanbul, the muftis as a class were antagonistic to the Catholic Church, such animosity doubtless also colored their attitude toward other "infidels," including Jews. When Sultan Ahmed I, wishing to duplicate his mother's construction of a beautiful mosque in Istanbul, built another called the Ahmedia at the annual cost of 1,830,000 scudi, at a time when the imperial Treasury was nearly empty, such benefactions raised the specter of insolvency for the once prosperous and flourishing regime. In short, these deficiencies might speedily have ruined any great power. It really was a testimony of the intrinsic vitality of the Turkish masses and the vigor of the legal and administrative system established by the earlier sultans and fully reorganized under Suleiman the "Lawgiver" (the nickname given to the "magnificent" sultan by his Turkish contemporaries) that the Empire survived without suffering even greater damage. However, since these adverse factors were never completely remedied, they ultimately produced those deep symptoms of internal illness which were to justify Otto von Bismarck's designation of nineteenth-century Turkey as "the sick man of Europe."[10]

NEW COURT DOCTORS AND COUNSELORS

As usual, these changes, though drastic in a cumulative sense, proceeded rather slowly in the eyes of contemporaries. In the first third of the period 1574–1648, here under review, the number of Jewish court physicians and other advisers to the sultan and grand viziers actually increased. The most important physician-diplomat of the older school serving the Crown to the end of Murad III's life and beyond was Solomon Ashkenazi. After his success following the Cypriot war he had a prolonged dispute with the French over his claim to have helped Henry de Valois to become king of Poland. Henry himself, after ascending the throne of France, sided with his ambassador François de Noailles, bishop of Dax, and refused to pay any compensation for Solomon's services. Perhaps out of spite against France the Jewish diplomat promoted the aforementioned attempts to secure a Turco-Spanish armistice and, in 1586, as the sultan's official representative, he signed the pertinent agreement between the two powers. While personally practicing medicine, especially among the court dignitaries, Solomon, on the side, engaged in commercial activities through third persons. In time he was assisted by his three sons, who as part of the reward granted him by the Venetian Senate had received extensive schooling in the City of the Lagoons at the Republic's expense. He also had a brother, Isaac, residing in Vienna. On one occasion, as we shall see, Ashkenazi is said to have been instrumental in averting the consequences of Murad III's wrath aroused by the appearance of a Jewish woman in luxurious attire. He allegedly played a role in the rise of Ferhad Pasha to the grand vizierate, but he also got along well with Ferhad's successor, Sinan Pasha. According to the reports by the Austrian envoy Bartelomeo Pezzen, he was also active in 1591 in behalf of the candidacy of Emanuel Aron to the voivodship of Moldavia, perhaps because of Aron's alleged Jewish ancestry. Solomon died around 1602, leaving behind a family whose estate apparently remained untouched by the authorities.[11]

Among his sons Nathan played a certain diplomatic role when he was delegated by Aḥmed I to deliver some papers to the doge in Venice. Having been received there with diplomatic honors, he was acclaimed by the Levantine Jewish congregation in Venice at a special Sabbath service. On his part, he subsidized the publication of an important Hebrew work, the responsa of Rabbi Moses Alshekh, which appeared in Venice in 1606. In this endeavor Nathan was aided by his stepmother Bula Iqshati, whom Solomon had married after his first wife, with whom he had lived in Poland (she was casually mentioned in the responsa of rabbis Solomon Luria and Moses Isserles), had died in Istanbul not long after 1564. Bula probably received no formal medical training but, through assisting in her husband's ministrations, seems to have acquired sufficient expertise to help cure Sultan Mehmed III (or Aḥmed I) from *Veroli* (syphilis). She seems to have become very friendly with many ladies of the court, especially Mehmed's queen mother from the Venetian family of Baffo, who had some Jewish blood flowing in her veins. Through the sultana, who had been quite influential in her husband Murad III's time but now fully dominated her young and inexperienced son, Bula continued to exercise considerable influence on the affairs of the state.[12]

The most influential Jewish lady at court was Esther Kyra. The term *kyra,* or as it is sometimes mentioned in its diminutive form *kyriatsa,* the equivalent of the English title Dame, is a derivative from its corresponding Greek masculine form, *kyrios* (lord). The first Jewish *kyra,* recorded in various Turkish documents and historical records, often unreliable and conflicting, seems to have performed certain services for the ladies of the sultan's harem which were considered so beneficial to the state that Suleiman issued a decree permanently exempting her and her descendants from various imposts. A renewal of this decree dated in 1534 was handed to her grandson Kurd in 1548. According to the only extant copy from the days of Osman II (died 1622), this decree was reconfirmed by Selim II, Murad III, Meḥmed III, Aḥmed I, and Osman II. Yet for some reason this first Jewish *kyra,* about whose antecedents we know very little, adopted Islam in 1548 under the name of Faṭma. She died soon thereafter, leaving behind a husband, Mosheh, and two sons, Elia (Kurd's father) and Joseph. It has also been plausibly suggested that she had belonged to a Karaite family in Kaffa and had entered the service of Suleiman's queen mother while the young prince served as governor of Kaffa and later Magnesia. This *kyra* continued her ministrations at court after Suleiman's coronation in Istanbul in 1520, and long after his mother's demise in 1534.[13]

Far better known, especially through her activities also within the Rabbanite Jewish community, was another Jewish *kyra* named Esther who was married to a physician, Elijah Ḥandali, scion of a prominent Istanbul rabbinic family. Having served the ladies of the harem under Suleiman and Selim II, she maintained her varied activities during the reigns of Murad III and Meḥmed III. As early as 1566 Samuel Shulam, in the Foreword to his meritorious edition of Abraham Zacuto's important historical work, *Sefer Yuḥasin* (Book of Genealogies), thanked Esther for her financial aid which made that publication possible. After describing her deceased husband Elijah as a prominent Jewish citizen, Samuel extolled his sponsor as "a God-fearing, wise woman, a lady great in her deeds," whose charitableness extended far and wide. Esther's first patroness at court seems to have been Suleiman's favorite daughter Mihrumah, married to the influential Grand Vizier Rustem. Even after the death of her husband in 1561 and her father in 1574, Mihrumah continued to exert considerable influence on the affairs of the state. The enormous riches amassed by Rustem and herself over the years (in 1576 Stephan Gerlach estimated her income at 2,000 ducats daily or more than 700,000 ducats in a Muslim lunar year) must have secured her a high position at court, quite apart from her contacts with her brother Selim and her nephew Murad. Esther's influence seems to have increased further under Murad III, when foreign representatives, including the Venetian *baïlo*, Paolo Contarini (1580–83), sought her support at court. She now was the most important Jewish protégée of Murad's favorite wife, Baffo (Siyese), whose influence reached even greater heights when her son, Meḥmed III, became sultan in 1595. All along her friend Esther was instrumental in securing privileges for individual Jews and even in persuading the sultan to entrust certain high offices to one or another non-Jewish candidate. According to custom, such contenders rewarded their protectress with handsome gifts, often outbidding one another. Ultimately, however, her support of a particular newly appointed military commander brought about her downfall. Although in this case the Jewish community greatly appreciated her services, she was heartily disliked by the Janissaries, who sided with the opposing candidate. In addition the *kyra* was widely blamed for the sudden depreciation of the Turkish currency ordered by the sultan which, among its other effects, resulted in the reduction of the "real" wages of the Janissaries and the Sipahis of the imperial household (see below). These unruly elite corps immediately staged an uprising against the *kyra* on March 30, 1600, seized her, made her ride on horseback through the streets of Istanbul and, although to save her life she allegedly adopted Islam, killed her together with most members of her household. Esther's younger son survived by accepting conversion to Islam, in which faith he lived to the end of his life. Esther's entire estate, worth some 100,000 ducats, was confiscated—a procedure widely practiced after the death of most fallen dignitaries—and used for the additional wages paid the Istanbul garrison for a whole year, thus helping end the revolt.[14]

This tragic end of a gifted and much deserving woman was witnessed by John Sanderson. After many years of intermittent living in the Middle East and then serving as an English consul in Istanbul, Sanderson was an acute observer and generally accurate reporter. Because of its detailed, if gruesome, eyewitness description, his account is fully reproduced here:

I can not lett passe to relate that a Juishe woman of the greatest credett and welth in Constantinople was brought out of hir house and stabbed to death in the Viseroys yeard; thence, *by a window in*

*the Serraglio wall, where the Grand Signior, Sultan Mahomet, stood to see,
shee was* drawne with ropes to the publiquest place in the citie, and
ther, betwene a peramide pillor erected by Theodotiouse and the
brasen tripled serpent, laid for the doggs to eate, who did devoure
hir all save the bones, senowes *of her legges,* and soules of hir feete.
Hir head had bine caried uppon a pike throughe the citie, and alike
hir shamefull part; also many smaule peces of hir fleshe, which the
Turks, janesaries, and others caried aboute tied in a little packetred,
shewinge to the Jewes and others, and in dirision said: Behould the
whores fleshe. One slice of hir I did so see passe by our house in
Galata. Hir eldest sonn in like manner the next day [was] cruelly
stabbed and murthered in the said Viseroyes court, dragged thence,
and laid by his mother; but was so fatt and ranke that the doggs
would not cease uppon him, or else they were sasiate with the wom-
ans flesh the day before (*who was a short, fat trubkin* [little squat
woman]). So together with his mothers bones the next day was this
bodie burned *in that place.* Her second sonn became Turke to save
his life; so would his dead brother, yf he could have had the favoure.
The third sonn, a younge youth, thier wrath beinge apeased, they
permitted to live. This was an acte of the Spahies, in spight of the
Great Turkes mother; for by the hands of this Jewe woman she [the
Valide sultan] toke all hir bribes, and hir sonns weare Chefe Customers of Constantinople, who toke all the gainefull busines into thier
owne hands, doinge what they lusted. The mother and childerin
weare wourth millians, which all went into the Great Turkes cof-
ers.[15]

Apparently also short-lived was the most spectacular diplomatic career made by David Passi. Previously little known in
the historical literature, his career came to light through recent investigations of both long-recorded diplomatic reports
by European envoys and some archival researches in both
Turkish and Polish collections. These documentary data on
Passi, however, cover only the years 1585–94, leaving his earlier and later activities in the dark; they will hopefully be elucidated by some future discoveries. We do not even know
where he came from. While Cecil Roth interpreted the name
Passi, similar to the better known Alfasi, as indicative of his
being a native of Fez, Morocco, the contemporary English
statesman Lord William Cecil Burghley called him an Italian,
while Judah Serfatim, Solomon ibn Ya'ish's agent, regarded him
as a Portuguese, perhaps because he placed him in the category of the more familiar Marranos. At his first mention in

the English diplomatic correspondence from Istanbul on August 9, 1585, referring to "News from Italy," the English government was informed that "the Grand Signor had invested David Passo [!], a rich Hebrew and nephew of his physician, into the Duchy of Nixia [Naxos] in the Archipelago, in the jurisdiction of the Duke who is here [in Istanbul[?], which Jew has been in the city [of London] for a long time." However, this report seems to have been the result of some confusion of Passi with Alvaro Mendes, who had indeed lived in London (and Paris) for many years before settling in Istanbul (see below). On October 30, 1585, in a dispatch of the Venetian representative Lorenzo Bernardo, Passi appears as the author of a political memorandum read during the audience of the French ambassador with the "magnificent Pasha" (grand vizier). On November 25, 1585 Bernardo informed his government about two newly arrived Englishmen, one of whom was "in constant conferences with David Passi, the Jew, who is always ready to take a part in such matters." Rumor had it that these negotiations aimed at some simultaneous action of the English and Turkish navies to counteract Philip II's expected attack on England, "though everyone holds it certain that the Sultan will not be able to move on account of his own political position and the difficulties of the Persian war." A month later the two Englishmen left "in company with a Jew belonging . . . to the household of David Passi" on a mission which Bernardo could not explain.[16]

Subsequently Passi is recorded as a frequent, sometimes daily, attendant at meetings of the highest council with the sultan, grand vizier, *qapudan* (naval chief), and occasionally also with such other dignitaries as the commander of the Janissary corps. We have a graphic description of this mysterious diplomat in the following dispatch addressed on January 5, 1591 by another Venetian ambassador, Hieronimo Lippomano, to the Doge and Senate of Venice:

I have been forced to admit David Passi, the Jew, to my confidence, for I found that the Sultan himself had ordered the Grand Vizir to consult with Passi, to listen to him, to favour him. The Grand Vizir refused, whereupon the Sultan said that slaves like the Vizir he had in abundance, but never a one like David, probably alluding to all the information about Christendom with which Passi furnishes the Sultan. Passi is a man of natural ability, and sufficient knowledge. I carefully weigh and balance all he says, but I have frequently had occasion to find him correct; and so I think it well to attach him as much as may be, for he is able to do great harm and great good.

Some of the topics in these high-level discussions related to the build-up and location of the Turkish navy, as well as Ottoman relations with Spain, France, and other Christian powers. In 1588 Passi also appeared as a representative of Dom Antonio, the pretender to the throne of Portugal, who forced the unfriendly English representative, Edward Barton, to treat Passi hospitably as his plenipotentiary. Barton's reluctance may perhaps be explained by Passi's association with Dom Antonio, which must have placed him in a collision course with Don Alvaro Mendes, then a recent arrival in Constantinople. As we recall, for years past Mendes had been a most influential representative of the Portuguese pretender at the courts of France and England. By that time, however, the relations between Alvaro and Antonio had become quite strained. Passi may also have served as the superintendent of the mint, the post previously held by another Jew, Nessimi.[17]

Before long Passi played a crucial role in the crisis in Polish-Turkish relations which emerged early in the reign of King Sigismund III (1587–1632). Theretofore the two powers had maintained a mutually benevolent neutrality in the wars raging between the Ottoman Empire and the Habsburg powers, on the one hand, and the Polish–Muscovite conflicts on the other hand. Officially Poland and Turkey had even negotiated in 1552, 1562, and 1568 treaties of "perpetual peace" and, toward the end of his reign, Sigismund II Augustus (1548–72) had come close to concluding a formal alliance with the Porte aimed at the rising power of their common enemy, Ivan IV of Moscow. In these negotiations Joseph Nasi played an important role. In the following years, however, these peaceful relations deteriorated owing to Poland's growing aspirations for control over Moldavia, which had for a long time been an Ottoman dependency; the frequent raids of Polish-dominated Zaporogian Cossacks on the neighboring Turkish lands; and the reciprocal attacks of Tatars, then the sultan's vassals, on the southeastern Polish provinces. In 1589–90, Murad III denounced the "perpetual peace" and appeared to be making preparations for the invasion of Poland. At one point Turkish troops fighting in Moldavia actually crossed the Polish boundary, but speedily turned back. To face that danger, Sigismund and his chief adviser, Jan Zamoyski, who served both as chancellor and as hetman (generalissimo) of the Polish armed forces, took some necessary defensive measures. However, neither the Poles nor the Ottomans were ready for a large-scale confrontation, their finances being in serious disarray. Even Stephen Báthory's militarily successful campaigns on Poland's eastern front left the Polish army in a state of exhaustion, while the prolonged and difficult war with Persia, though ending with a favorable peace treaty in 1590, left behind a strong desire for peace in the ruling circles in Istanbul.[18]

At this point David Passi entered into the negotiations. Regrettably, the extant documentation does not furnish us with a clear picture of the sequence of events. Our major source consists of the correspondence between Sigismund III and his chancellor and particularly of two lengthy letters written by Zamoyski and the king. Phrased with caution and alluding to developments understandable to their recipients but not to outsiders, their meaning is often obscure. However, the chancellor, averring that the situation was quite confused and claiming that "we have neither a secure peace nor a definite war," suggested, as he had apparently done before, that a major delegation be dispatched to Istanbul "with full power," that is, primarily with discretion to spend a considerable amount of money on the customary gifts to the sultan and his advisers, in order to smooth the way toward reestablishing peaceful relations. Sigismund now realized the mistake he had made by not sending such a generous delegation before, but he tried to justify it by the lack of funds. In his letter to Zamoyski he bitterly complained of his fiscal crunch: "the arrears on the wages to the soldiers are drawn out and will continue to be extended so long as we shall not be sure of peace; other soldiers newly engaged will all demand pay, where do we get the money? Almost everywhere the capitation tax remains uncollected. . . ." Under these circumstances Sigismund and his chancellor were happy that the Turkish troops had withdrawn from Polish territory, especially if from reports he had received during the preceding year about the growing unrest among the Turkish sipahis Zamoyski believed that these internal difficulties had been responsible for the withdrawal.[19]

At this juncture Sigismund was ready to authorize a fairly large expenditure. One source speaks of Passi expecting to receive between 10,000 and 15,000 ducats and of his cooperating beglerbeg (governor-general) of Rumelia, which included most of Turkey's European possessions, being promised 5,000 to 10,000 ducats. It was perhaps in this connection that the second Polish envoy to Turkey, Jan Zamoyski (the chancellor's namesake), was allowed to bring along letters of credit (called *membranes*) for 15,000 ducats to be handed to Passi. However, this may have been intended only as repayment of a previous loan, which had enabled the ambassador to purchase presents for the Ottoman dignitaries, since some earlier gifts shipped from Poland had allegedly been lost in transit through the Black Sea. (This rumor may have been circulated by the Polish delegation itself merely to cover up the previous envoy's negligence in not bringing along the expected cadeaux—at that time considered a serious breach of diplomatic etiquette in all negotiations with the Porte.) It also was perhaps on Passi's initiative—through Barton or through his predecessor William Harborne, who had been the architect of the Turko-English cooperation but had left for London in the fall of 1588—that Queen Elizabeth wrote a letter to the sultan. The queen argued that a Polish–Turkish understanding was of vital interest to England since, in the case of a war between those two powers, she might be deprived of the usual supply of Polish grain on which her country greatly depended. Through all these intrigues, moves, and countermoves, the underlying desire of both countries to avoid hostilities reasserted itself without any loss of "face" for either government. It concluded in a renewal of the old Turco–Polish treaty, signed in Istanbul by envoy Zamoyski in 1591. As a result Passi not only received his appropriate "gift" as well as interest on the loan, but probably also obtained the right to remove from Poland some merchandise which the local government had sequestered. Possibly Passi had been a silent partner in the continued extensive trade between Turkey and Poland conducted under special privileges by Joseph Nasi and his successors for many years which, however, after the duke's death in 1579 had turned "sour" and ultimately resulted in the bankruptcy of Joseph's original employees. Be this as it may, at the beginning of 1591 Passi's prestige was quite high in Istanbul and abroad.[20]

However, these very Turco-Polish negotiations (during which both King Sigismund and his chancellor called him David Basha or Pasha, though they knew that he was a Jew) led to Passi's downfall. Grand Vizier Sinan, characterized by Ibrahim Pasha as "a faithless and devilish man," who increasingly resented his Jewish competitor's influence on the sultan, now finally found an opportunity to accuse David of a serious indiscretion. Enraged by Passi's rather careless warning to Zamoyski that the grand vizier's conciliatory letter to him had been issued without the sultan's authorization, he ordered Passi's arrest and sent him off in a galley for banishment in Rhodes. Probably Sinan's intention was to have him murdered on the way, but in some unknown fashion Passi escaped that fate and soon thereafter even returned to Istanbul. However, Sinan had long suspected Passi of spying in behalf of Spain (a suspicion which he theretofore could never prove), and had his Jewish rival arrested again in 1593 for trying to help a newly arrived Spanish representative, Guillaume de Savoie, to secure another armistice or even a peace treaty with the Porte. Passi had indeed committed the faux pas of allowing Guillaume, on arrival in Istanbul, to reside for a time at his home. When on Ibn Ya'ish's urgings, doubtless intended to help England, the sultan declined the Spanish offer, Guillaume recognized the futility of his mission and embarked on his return voyage. However, Sinan arranged for him to be arrested and, after extended torture, to obtain the desired "confessions." When soon thereafter Guillaume died in prison, the letters he carried with him, and seemingly another letter written by Passi which was intercepted, led to the Jewish diplomat's renewed imprisonment. After 1594 all traces of his activities vanish from the record. It is possible, however, that having gone through the vicissitudes of three arrests, each combined with a serious threat to his life, Passi, when faced by another personal crisis not recorded in the sources, decided to adopt Islam and thereby to secure forgiveness for his "crimes." If so, and if Abraham Galanté's suggestion that he changed his name to Ḥalil and subsequently appeared in the Turkish records as the high dignitary (*kaimakam*) Ḥalil Pasha and Murad III's brother-in-law is to be accepted, he was somehow involved in the tragic death of Esther Kyra in 1600. Because he had failed to save her life, we are told, the kaimakam was deposed. At any rate, even before his purported conversion, Passi seems to have been little concerned about Jewish affairs, although his aid to Dom Antonio may have stemmed from the fairly general Jewish and Marrano resentment of Philip II's takeover of Portugal in 1580.[21]

Galanté's suggestion, to be sure, of Passi's identity with Ḥalil Pasha (a well-known figure in the Ottoman government at the turn from the sixteenth to the seventeenth century) is supported only by an occasional reference in the sources to Ḥalil Passo instead of Pasha. If further research should prove it to be true, it would still fail to resolve the mystery of Passi's years before 1585 and after 1600. Perhaps in view of his meteoric rise and fall it may not be too venturesome to suggest that he was none other than the David (Daud) who, after serving for some time as Joseph Nasi's confidant, turned against him and, in testifying before the French ambassador Guillaume de Grandchamps (in 1566–67), denounced Don Joseph as a Spanish spy. Although this unwarranted accusation brought down upon David the wrath of both the Turkish authorities and the Istanbul rabbinate and resulted in his exile to Rhodes, after the duke's death in 1579 and that of R. Joseph Ibn Leb in 1580, under pressure from Don Joseph's antagonist, Solomon Ashkenazi, he was forgiven and allowed to return to the Turkish capital. He may even have rejoined what remained of the Nasi entourage, which would help explain how, as David Passi, he could suddenly play such a significant role at the Porte in 1585–94. It also was perhaps his earlier association with Nasi that had brought him into contact with Poland and enabled him, like his master, to engage in trade with that country. The Nasi connection may further explain why, after Don Joseph's death, he could harbor aspirations to succeed him as duke of Naxos and make more understandable his meteoric rise, his repeated sudden downfalls and recoveries, and even his ultimate conversion. However, this hypothesis, advanced here with great hesitation, must await further confirmation from as yet undiscovered archival sources.[22]

Among the outstanding Jewish diplomat-businessmen serving the Porte was Alvaro Mendes, who on previous occasions intervened in Passi's behalf and had three times helped to free him from prison. Yet he was also partly responsible for David's downfall. This prominent Jewish diplomat has been discussed here in various contexts including his promotion of Dom Antonio's struggle against Philip II. Suffice it to recall that his interest in the Portuguese "pretender" may have been stimulated by his kinship with Dom Antonio's mother, who had been of Jewish descent. However, in time, partly as a result of Dom Antonio's fickleness and the growingly entrenched power of the Spaniards, he seems to have given up the hope of liberating Portugal and decided to move to Istanbul at the age of sixty-five, after having had a rich and varied career in many lands. Born in Portugal in 1520, Alvaro acquired considerable expertise in the jewelry trade, which led him in his twenties to a protracted sojourn in the Indian province of Madras. After amassing a fortune there, he returned to Portugal where, as he was to reminisce in 1593, he performed many services for the Portuguese kings, "through which they gave me the greatest honours that ever they gave to any man that came from the India, in so much that the king gave me free the custome of all my precious stones, which he never gave to any Visrey [Viceroy]." He also was made knight of the high Portuguese Order of St. Iago de Compostella. Subsequently he settled in Paris where he became friendly with King Henry III and his leading councilors. From the French capital he made many journeys to London, where, through his brother-in-law Rodrigo Lopez, Elizabeth's court physician, he likewise found entry to the highest governmental circles.[23]

All along, however, Alvaro appears to have planned a haven of refuge in the Ottoman Empire in case the tentacles of the Spanish or Portuguese Inquisition should ever reach out toward him. As early as 1572 he succeeded in obtaining from Suleiman the Magnificent a strong recommendation to the Venetian authorities to facilitate the journey of his father and family to Turkey. This move, made in absolute secrecy, apparently escaped the attention of the inquisitorial and diplomatic agents, so that he could continue living in Paris and visiting Italy and England without bringing upon himself the ever threatening prosecution. For some reason, however, in 1585 he decided to move to Istanbul, profess Judaism in public after undergoing circumcision at the advanced age of sixty-five, and change his name to Solomon ibn Ya'ish. He had undoubtedly traveled on the special Turkish safe-conduct issued to VIPs and his arrival was probably greeted with pomp similar to that extended to Doña Gracia and Don Joseph, particularly since, in addition to his vast diplomatic "savvy" and connections, he brought with him a fortune estimated at between 850,000 and 1,000,000 ducats. Almost immediately after his arrival he was made duke of the island of Mitylene and heir to the privilege granted to Don Joseph to continue with the colonization of Tiberias. We do not know the precise reasons why he was not granted succession to Joseph's dukedom of Naxos. Possibly, the French efforts to secure the restoration of the old Crispo family to that long-held dignity and certain disturbances in the Cyclade Archipelago in 1583 prevented the sultan from appointing another duke soon thereafter. Perhaps it was Joseph's success in raising the revenue from those possessions to 13,000 ducats annually, out of which he paid only 6,000 to the Treasury, which whetted the appetites of the regime to collect the large balance as well. At any rate, neither the vizier Cigala, a Christian renegade, nor David Passi, both of whom had tried to secure that high dignity, were able to attain it.[24]

Because of his former London connections, Solomon immediately became a friend of the English merchant-diplomat William Harborne. When Harborne's successor Edward Barton tried to avoid contacts with the Jew, formerly so well seen in the highest circles in his country, he was rebuked by Lord Burghley. Ultimately, in connection with some complications which arose for him in 1592, Queen Elizabeth wrote a personal letter in Solomon's behalf to the sultan to defend him against his enemies' allegations. She wrote in part:

Since we have found him, being a man of consequence, most ready in the furthering of business and our affairs for many years, we desire to signify to Your Majesty what opinion we have of him. Now we can truly testify that not only we ourselves but also many other Christian Princes have wished him to tarry and dwell in our Kingdoms because of his virtue, honesty and industry where, without doubt, he could have lived quietly in all plenty and abundance, but when he chose rather to dwell at Constantinople in your dominions than anywhere else in the world, the artifices and lies [artes et fraudes] of the Ministers of the King of Spain prevented him from resting even there in safety.

Curiously, in his letter of thanks to the queen, written in Spanish, Solomon used the date 28 July 5352, of the Jewish era or 1592 C.E. He referred here to a long communication he had received from the English chancellor of the Exchequer on the queen's order to which he was replying at length concerning his own services to her. He concluded: "I promise to be at her service all my life with complete loyalty announcing her heroic deeds and praying that her Majesty long continue to reign and that all her enemies be destroyed." We recall that, according to the dispatch of Bernardino de Mendoza, the Spanish ambassador in Paris, to Philip II of May 23, 1587, Solomon claimed in a letter, which Mendoza had in his hand, that "your Majesty's [Philip's] truce with the Turk would have been concluded but for him. Your Majesty, he says, demanded the inclusion therein of the Pope, the duke of Florence, and other princes of Italy, and he used influence with Luch Ali [the grand vizier] to demand, on the part of the Turk, that the queen of England also should be included." In general, Ibn Ya'ish had long used all his influence at the Porte to prevent a Spanish–Turkish rapprochement.[25]

In retrospect we can doubly appreciate Ibn Ya'ish's insistence on the inclusion of England in the 1587 armistice agreement between the two powers, if one were to be concluded at all, since we know how helpful the mere possibility of a Turkish attack on Spain in the Mediterranean was to prove to England in her hour of peril in the following year when she faced the invasion of Spain's "Invincible Armada." Later on, according to a dispatch from the Venetian ambassador Giovanni Moro of October 9, 1588, Alvaro "was the first to report that the Spanish armada had been routed by the English," in contrast to the Ragusan representative who contended that the Spaniards had won. It appears that it took two months after the battle, fought between July 31 and August 8, for the news to be accepted as reliable by the grand vizier. Subsequently, however, Ibn Ya'ish, like Don Joseph before him, apparently moderated his anti-Spanish stance. In 1594 and 1597 he actually promoted the idea of a Turco–Spanish peace. Doubtless for this reason it was possible, despite the general prohibition for any professing Jew to enter Spain after 1492 under the penalty of death, for Ibn Ya'ish's representative, Joseph Serfatim, to be received hospitably by the Spanish king and other dignitaries in Madrid and quietly to proceed from there to London.[26]

Generally, we know very little about Alvaro's business activities and his involvement in Jewish affairs which were of less interest to the foreign diplomats in Istanbul. Even in London, where everybody knew that Rodrigo Lopez belonged to a New Christian family, we hear very little about his brother-in-law's Jewish ancestry. One also wonders whether, while in London, Alvaro had participated in some of the secret Jewish divine services held by the then nascent Marrano community. We only have the later testimony of his agent in London, Solomon Cormano, who came there as a professing Jew, that, while in the English capital, "he and all his trayne vsed publickely the Jewish rytes in prayinge, accompayned wth divers secrett Jewes resident in London." This "boast" was reported to Lord Burghley by the English envoy in Istanbul, Edward Barton, in a long letter of August 15, 1592. Among other complaints Barton claimed that he had received Burghley's letter of April 11 on August 3, but in the meantime that letter, as well as Queen Elizabeth's epistle to the sultan, had been shown by Alvaro's "servant" (doubtless referring to Cormano) "in every tauerne and bragging of them, interpretinge them, at his pleasure to the coṁon people." Even during Ibn Ya'ish's stay in Istanbul we cannot tell how orthodox his lifestyle was and, except for his moderate effort in Tiberias, what kind of services he performed directly for the Jewish community or its scholars. But he seems to have financed the establishment of a new Jewish academy bearing his name; it was led by the distinguished scholar R. Joseph b. Moses di Trani. These and probably other services rendered by him must have been significant enough for the clerk of the Privy Council to refer to Solomon in 1594 as "the greate Jew that is at Constantinople" and to mention "the Care he hath, being a Jewe, of his Brethren and Kynsfolk." Solomon was, indeed, revered by his co-religionists, and his death in 1603 was widely mourned, although we have no recorded texts of obituaries or poetic lamentations written on this occasion. Nor do we know much about any of his descendants except for his scholarly and mystically inclined son who had settled in Tiberias, repudiating the glamorous existence he might have led in the Turkish capital.[27]

Next to these leading individuals we learn, again for the most part from the foreign diplomatic correspondence, about other prominent Istanbul Jews who performed sporadic diplomatic functions. For example, Isaac b. Joseph Hamon, of the distinguished medical family established at the sultan's court by Moses Hamon, is recorded to have refused in 1578 a substantial monetary gift from the Spanish ambassador for help in securing an armistice with the Ottoman Empire. We recall that the duke of Naxos had at that time been prepared to support such a move and that the first truce was actually proclaimed two years later and repeated several times thereafter. Hamon, however, who like his ancestors loyally served the sultan as both court physician and councilor, rejected the offer, arguing that Spain wished only to gain time in order the more effectively to attack his country at some future date. On the other hand, he was a "devoted and faithful servant" to the king of France, according to a letter written by the French envoy Jacques de Germigny. In fact, Henry III agreed to give Rabbi Isaac 100 écus in recognition of his friendship. Another prominent Jewish physician, Jacob Ruben, served Sinan Pasha, while Israel Celibi participated in negotiations between the sultan and Austria, as well as Tuscany. In the days of Osman II

(1618–22) an unnamed Jewish lady tried to promote the candidacy of a wealthy Greek, Locadello, to the voivodship of Moldavia. Through her friendship with the sultan's sister she was able to introduce Locadello's partisans to the grand vizier and other dignitaries upon whom Locadello lavished much of his bounty. It probably was only the sultan's strangulation on May 20, 1622, twenty days after the above report by the Venetian envoy was written, that frustrated that undertaking. Nor must we overlook the growing role in international relations played by Jewish dragomans. Although never reaching the heights of the Greek Phanariots of the eighteenth and nineteenth centuries, these overtly humble "interpreters" often exerted considerable influence on the thinking of high Turkish and foreign officials. But, as we shall see in another context, their heyday was to come in the period *after* 1650.[28]

Not surprisingly, the earlier success of Jewish diplomats induced some naïve would-be followers, or even outright impostors, to try to take a part in vital diplomatic negotiations. In 1599, for example, in the midst of the long and arduous Austro-Turkish wars of 1595–1603, some Jews and Turks, fourteen men in all, led by a Spanish Jew, Don Gabriel Bonaventura, appeared before Emperor Rudolph II in Prague, offering him their mediation for securing peace. They pretended to have been authorized to do so by Sultan Meḥmed III. They evidently overestimated the emperor's gullibility. Bonaventura landed as a prisoner in the tower of Buda, while the others were condemned to hard labor. In many cases, however, our information about what one or another influential leader had actually done for the Ottoman Empire or its Jewish community is extremely limited. For example, in a meritorious study on R. Moshe Benvenest, Meir Benayahu has assembled valuable data on that learned doctor's background and family (which included a number of scholars), but was unable to identify exactly the nature of the services rendered by him to the sultan or to the Jewish people. Certainly, the two Hebrew poems published by Benayahu (one of which may not even refer to R. Moshe), mention—as is often the case—generalities rather than specific details. We are not even certain about the rabbi's part in Siavush Pasha's involvement in the Turco-Spanish negotiations which led to the grand vizier's permanent exile.[29]

SLOW DOWNGRADE

The conspicuous role played by a number of Jewish diplomats during the reign of Murad III should not blind us to the gradual deterioration of the Jewish status in the Empire. To be sure, Murad III was personally an unfriendly man who treated all his advisers quite roughly. His whimsical tyranny and utter cruelty in war and peace (he annihilated, for example, the 30,000 men of the Baghdad garrison and another 30,000 civilians, including women and children, after the city's surrender in 1638) doubtless struck terror among would-be rebels and helped restore some order in the growingly chaotic society at a high cost to its long-range stability and prosperity. Despite his occasional nightly excursions into the streets in disguise to learn the feelings of the population, Murad had little contact with the masses. The few impressions he secured from such haphazard meetings with individuals from the heterogeneous population of the capital were insufficient for him to feel the pulse of Istanbul's 700,000 inhabitants. Without the aid of better informed, though hardly unbiased, advisers he undoubtedly misinterpreted much of what he had heard and seen. He knew even less about the large majority of the imperial population living under diverse environments in the European, Asiatic, and North African provinces.[30]

Under one such impulse, we are told, Murad decided to take a drastic measure against Jews. On hearing that a wealthy Jewish lady had appeared on an Istanbul street clad in satin attire, with much jewelry, one piece of which was supposed to be worth 40,000 sultanas (Turkish gold coins), he allegedly wished to exterminate all Jews, men, women, and children, throughout the Empire. This is undoubtedly a vastly exaggerated report of the sultan's irate utterance. Such a universal genocidal decree, which would have been unprecedented in the annals of Islamic countries, probably stemmed from the Jewish rapporteur's overheated recollection of the story in the Book of Esther. Except for the Almohade Empire, no major Muslim country had ever enacted even a decree of forced conversion of all Jews or Christians. The deranged Egyptian Caliph Al-Ḥakim, as we recall, limited himself to the destruction of Jewish and Christian houses of worship. Whatever Murad's real intention may have been, after an intervention, at the request of Solomon Ashkenazi, by the talented queen mother Kiusem (the real power behind the throne) and the head of the Janissaries, the sultan merely ordained that thenceforth no Jew or Christian should publicly appear in luxurious attire, especially not in satin clothes. He also sharpened the existing regulations concerning the distinguishing headgear of all non-Muslims.[31]

In reaction to Murad's clothing regulations the Jewish communal leaders, particularly R. Joseph b. Moses di Trani (Mitrani in Hebrew), issued a sumptuary ordinance of their own. The governmentally instituted cone-shaped Jewish hat to replace the turban also evoked a responsum from R. Samuel de Medina to an inquiry concerning the permissibility of wearing such a hat on a Sabbath, because of the general rabbinic prohibition against erecting a tent on that day of rest. Needless to say, R. Samuel answered in the affirmative and upheld the imperial decree. He could the more calmly accept this imperial decision, as he must have realized that distinguishing attire and special colors were the rule, rather than an exception among the ethnoreligious groups in the Empire. Certainly, in his own residence, Salonica, with its Jewish majority, the varying clothing and headgear of Turks, Greeks, Serbs, Armenians, Franks, and others stood out as much as those of the Jews. Neither did Murad III's renewal in 1584 and 1593 of the prohibition against appointment of "infidels" to the position of provincial governors seriously disturb Ottoman Jewry. In the rare cases that he, or one of his successors, would wish to entrust a non-Muslim favorite with such a high office, he could violate that prohibition with perfect impunity.[32]

None of the restrictive measures taken by Murad III marked major innovations in the Turkish legislation concerning Jews. Basically, they merely restated the tenor of many decrees and juristic interpretations long hallowed by the *shari'ra*. Even when in his first year in office (1575) the sultan allowed the qadhi of Istanbul to issue a sharp regulation forbidding both sellers and purchasers from transferring Muslim slaves to Jewish owners under the severe penalty of hard labor on galleys, this ordinance was essentially to serve as an implementation of similar general prohibitions enacted by the earlier qadhis of the capital in 1559 and 1560. In fact, the decree of 1560 had specified that no excuses for transgressions of this kind be accepted and insisted that the qadhis be held personally responsible for its implementation. On the other hand, in firmans issued in 1583, 1584, and 1585 Murad insisted on protecting the rights of the Jewish community in Istanbul to use freely its cemeteries "situated on the Heskany on land belonging to *waqf*s of the late Sultan Bayezid." These ordinances were aimed at some Muslim builders who had begun erecting houses there on as yet unused plots, undoubtedly in response to the needs of the rapidly growing population. Some violators even tried to remove existing tombstones under the excuse that they were helping to conceal thieves. The sultan not only forbade further encroachments of this kind but he also ordered complete restoration of Jewish control over the entire area within its original boundaries. If, according to some reports, Murad's successor Mehmed III generally favored Christians over Jews, this policy was not maintained under the regime of Ahmed I. Nor did the new code of laws (*qanunname*) which was issued by Ahmed in emulation of the great codification by Suleiman the Lawgiver (it restated more recent enactments seeking to reduce the influence of the military on the conduct of civil affairs) directly impinge upon the traditional status of Ottoman Jewry.[33]

Nonetheless, the changes in the existing power structure brought about a deterioration in the Jewish status far greater than is reflected in the existing laws. To be sure, some of the ulema understood the causes for the general decline of Ottoman society and government which followed the sixteenth-century "golden age." As early as 1596–97, we recall, in his small tract on the art of government in Arabic and Turkish Hasan al-Kafi (al-Kiafi) Ahizari of Bosnia had emphasized, to quote V. J. Parry's summary,

that justice was becoming ill administered in the empire, that incapable men untested in long years of service rose to the highest offices of state and that the Ottoman armies had lost much of the obedience and discipline, the courage and skill, which distinguished them in former times; the sultans had fallen into a life of ease and self-indulgence; viziers intrigued one against the other; the influence of women had become marked in the conduct of affairs; there was no regular mustering of the armed forces and their equipment; the soldiers often committed grave excesses against the subject populations of the empire; and failure to adopt the latest techniques of warfare had led to defeat in battle with the enemies of Islam; negligence, corruption, favouritism and greed now bade fair to ruin the Ottoman system of government.

Some of these shortcomings were further elaborated by Murad IV's adviser Mustafa Kuchu Beg in his *risala* (missive) to the sultan. To be sure, the much-resented neglect by the monarchs of their traditional function of personally commanding the armies in the field (Meḥmed III and Aḥmed I took personal charge of the military operations only in critical moments in Hungary and against the Anatolian rebels) might have accrued to the benefit of the Jews and other minorities, since he thus was able more directly to intervene in their behalf against local potentates in other regions. However, this neglect merely symbolized the monarchs' growing aversion to dealing with the detailed operations of the governmental organs, which was also reflected by their frequent absenteeism from the sessions of the Diwan.[34]

While Aḥizari's warnings evoked little reaction in the influential government circles, those by Kuchu Beg apparently bore some fruit. Written in 1630, they doubtless made an impression on Murad IV, who had just grown into adulthood and began ruling the Empire with a firm hand. In general since Aḥmed I the power of the ulema was on the ascendancy. This factor had both beneficial and adverse effects on the Jewish status: beneficial, in as much as the experts in Islamic law were for the most part prone to emphasize some of the protective provisions of the *shari'a* concerning the "peoples of the Book." However, they were also likely to stress the more orthodox facets of their law and advocate measures leading to the conversion of Jews and Christians to their "true faith." Yet, there seems to be no evidence that any of the great Turkish theologians fully followed the more extremist teachings of the Mameluke thinker Ibn Taimiya.[35]

Lack of strong central controls in the legal field made itself doubly felt in the heterogeneous Ottoman Empire, largely held together by its loyalty to the monarchy. This loyalty, or at least fatalistic acceptance, was reinforced by constant indoctrination and by rigid enforcement of the imperial will (even if it often appeared arbitrary and unreasonable), with drastic penalties for disobedience. In some respects, this was characteristic of all absolutist and totalitarian regimes, but was doubly important for the Ottoman Empire, as was noted by an acute English observer, Sir Henry Blount, on his visit to Turkey in 1634. Among other matters, he noted with special emphasis:

> The maine points wherein Turkish *justice* differs from that of other *Nations* are three: it is more Severe, Speedy and Arbitrary. They hold the foundation of all *Empire* to consist in exact *obedience,* and that is exemplary severety which is undeniable in all the World, but more notable in these States, made up of severall Peoples different in *Bloud, Sect,* and *Interesse,* one from another, nor linkt in affection or any common engagement toward the publique good, other than what meere terror puts upon them. . . . Therefore the *Turkish justice* curbs and executes, without either remorse or respect which all accept.

As far as the Jews were concerned, it was precisely that great diversity of cultures under the same imperial scepter which generally favored greater religious toleration and alleviated for them the hardships of arbitrary rule.[36]

Weaknesses at the top were further aggravated by the frequent changes in succession to the throne. The short-lived reigns of the monarchs during the quarter century between the two Murads; their accession to the throne at too early an age (Aḥmed I was 13–14 or 16–17 [according to different records]; Osman II, 14; Murad IV, 12 years of age when they were invested with the supreme office); the two brief reigns (3 and 15 months, respectively) of the incompetent Mustafa; the assassination of Osman II in 1622 and of Mustafa in 1623 were all manifestations of a decline of the royal power, completely unprecedented in the previous three centuries of Osmanli history. Conditions in the Ottoman Empire paralleled in some respects the contemporary "time of troubles" in Muscovy (1603–1613). Nor was there any stability in the highest offices of the bureaucracy. Whereas their predecessors, especially Rustem and Sokolli, had helped administer the Empire over a period of 17 (1544–61, with a brief interruption) and 14 (1565–1579) years respectively, even Sinan Pasha, who held office for relatively many years, was deposed no less than four times. On the first occasion he was completely disgraced and sent into exile, to be recalled after a short absence. In his 1607 report home, the French envoy François de Salignac, observed, "There is lack here of everything, especially of people able to assume command; also of money." At the beginning of Murad IV's reign in 1622 the financial pinch was so severe that there was no money even for the customary gifts to officials. As Khadji-Khalifa explained it, "They had previously drawn funds out of the Treasury with full hands in order to appease the mutinous soldiers, so that nothing remained."[37]

These adverse factors naturally also influenced the Empire's standing in the world. The Ottoman imperial expansion in the Mediterranean world came to a halt. Beginning in the 1580s the deadlock achieved between the Spanish and the Ottoman Empires caused both to turn most of their attention to other regions. While Philip II's orientation increasingly shifted to the Atlantic Ocean, Turkey concentrated its efforts in the areas bordering on Persia and made some (ineffectual) attempts to dispute the Portuguese supremacy on the Indian Ocean. Because as protector of the Muslim pilgrimages to Mecca and Medina (*khadim al-haramain*) the sultan had to counteract both Persian and Muscovite interference with pilgrims from the more distant areas, the Empire became involved in a more or less constant warfare with Persia and was bogged down in the Caspian and Caucasian areas. The Muscovite expansion in these regions also threatened the age-old alternate commercial route from central Asia to Europe. No less damaging to Ottoman interests was the ideological contrast between Istanbul and Moscow. The great élan of the "Holy War," which had animated the Ottoman armies and their commanders in the previous generations and had carried them from victory to victory, had practically died down. The main enemies now were the Persians who, though hated as Shi'ite heretics, could not really be considered enemies of Islam, while in the West the long-lasting stalemate in both Hungary and the Mediterranean largely deprived the Ottoman leaders of any hope of an early breakthrough. At the same time the Muscovite march on Kazan and Astrakhan bore all the earmarks of a Christian "holy war." The Russian St. Hermogenes, who defined its objective as "that their [the unbelievers'] lips which spoke falsehoods be closed, the Jewish and Muslim obstinacy and false defamations be ended, and the pernicious heretical teaching be uprooted" fully mirrored the religious enthusiasm which characterized the incipient Russian drive toward world domination. Yet, as we recall, instead of pursuing the policy of a Turco-Polish alliance against the common enemy in Moscow, both countries got involved in conflicting aspirations for overlordship over Moldavia and in 1620 even opened direct hostilities against one another.[38]

The reorientation of Ottoman policy away from the Mediterranean also contributed to the weakening of the influence of Jewish advisers, since the great expertise possessed by Jewish counselors like Don Joseph Nasi, Solomon Ashkenazi, and Solomon Ibn Ya'ish, all stemming from Western countries, was not matched by their followers with respect to the eastern and northern areas. Not even the leaders of Egyptian Jewry, which for centuries past had maintained close contacts with India, could prove equally helpful to the regime in fighting the superior naval forces of the Portuguese or of their more powerful Dutch and English successors in the Indian Ocean.[39]

Nor was the domestic situation more reassuring. Beginning with the death of Murad III, local and regional uprisings of discontented subjects multiplied throughout the Empire. One of the longest-lasting and deeply rooted was the rebellion in Asia Minor, which enemies dubbed the *Khuruj-i Jalaliyam* (the Bandits' Revolt, 1595–1610). Joined by many former warriors, and actively supported by numerous *Sipahi*-landlords, some of whom had failed to obey the call to arms, this movement reflected socioeconomic as well as sectarian, particularly Shi'ite, grievances. In Lebanon, an uprising led by the Druze chief Fakhr ad-Din resulted in the establishment of a semiautonomous regime between 1590 and 1613 and again, after Fakhr's return from a European exile, for another seventeen years in 1618–35. Other local or regional revolts were led by ambitious district or provincial governors. While Fakhr found it convenient to preach religious freedom and, during his stay in Europe, enjoyed the protection of Cosimo II of Tuscany and Philip III of Spain, the Walachian voivode, Michael the Brave (assassinated in 1601) utilized the Austro-Turkish war temporarily to expand his domination over Moldavia and Transylvania. On one occasion, he assembled the Turks and the Jews of a region and indiscriminately slaughtered them. Similarly, when some governors of the eastern provinces tried to assert their independence, their short-lived regimes cost many lives among the rebels, the loyal Turkish forces, and the local population.[40]

Whatever may have been their motivations, all these uprisings contributed to a state of unrest which directly or indirectly adversely affected the Jews. Even when they were not specifically aiming at Jewish neighbors, their participants often looted houses and shops of the area under their control, while their leaders for the most part financed the revolts by imposing arbitrary tributes upon the local inhabitants. "Infidels" were usually the most helpless and rewarding objects of exploitation. At times Jews also suffered from uncontrollable disasters. According to a French report of April 1589, the memorable attack by the palace guard on the imperial residence in Istanbul resulted in a fire which at first affected only a few Jewish houses "in which, as usual, all the pashahs had found refuge." When this fire was speedily extinguished the pashas left. But almost immediately thereafter a much larger conflagration destroyed an area two leagues long, consuming 6,000 dwellings, including "all Jewish quarters" in that district. In many cases, however, attacks were more particularly directed against Jews. For example Safed, which because of its proximity to Tiberias and the attempt by Jewish leaders to colonize the area aroused a more than usual enmity among the local population, was nearly destroyed by Druze rebels in 1589. Among the Jewish refugees escaping to Damascus was the famous poet Israel b. Moses Najara. Earlier persecutions took place in 1587–88. To be sure, the vitality of the community was not completely sapped and it recovered sufficiently for a Franciscan visitor of 1599 to make some curious observations on the life in the city.

In his travelogue, mixing biblical legends with contemporary realities, Aquilante Rocchetta reported:

Safet, in which Queen Esther was born, is today inhabited by Hebrews, and is ruled by them, according to a concession granted by the Turk, as it is said, to a Hebrew lady [Gracia Mendes]. Here the Hebrews occupy their principal seats and attract a multitude of rabbis and priests because they hope that the Messiah will first appear in this place. Hence they pay much money to the Turk so that the city should not be inhabited by any but themselves.

The city and community were destroyed again by an assault of the Druze mountaineers in 1604, to recover but slowly in the following decade. This recovery was once more interrupted by a Druze attack in 1634–35, in connection with another uprising against the government, and again in 1656.[41]

An even more fundamental weakness affected the two mainstays of the Ottoman regime: the army and the bureaucracy. The Janissaries, that elite corps which marched in the vanguard of Ottoman expansion in the preceding generations, lost much of its fighting power. Although increasing in number from 7,866 in 1527–28 to 53,499 in 1669–70 (the corresponding growth of the Sipahi forces from 5,088 to 14,076 men was relatively slower), the Janissaries were now recruited for the most part from local Turks, rather than from prisoners of war selected through the *devshirme* system. No longer did they undergo that prolonged period of indoctrination and rigid discipline which characterized their predecessors. With the cessation, moreover, of the successful campaigns in Europe and the "scorched earth" policy on the Persian front, the prospects of large loot in newly occupied territories greatly diminished. Although the cost of maintaining the corps went up from some 15,500,000 aspers in 1527 to 134,000,000 in 1670 (the simultaneous increase of the Sipahi was from 31,000,000 to 69,500,000 aspers), the constant depreciation of currency caused a decline in their wages' purchasing power to such an extent that, for this reason alone, they were often forced to rebel against the regime. The frequent changes on the throne and the reign, for the most part, of weak rulers, likewise took its toll.[42]

Jews, even in Istanbul, were often chosen targets for pillage by Janissaries. With every change of the regime another opportunity arose for an assault on Jewish quarters and extortion of ransom from Jewish leaders. These animosities did not necessarily prevent the Janissaries from securing Jewish help in their own financial dealings. At least after the uprising of 1740, the British envoy Everard Fawkener reported to the Foreign Office about their employing an influential Jewish agent (without mentioning his name), and added: "It is not easy to imagine the credit this Jew . . . has in that body, and applications are made by the pretenders to them to him. . . . I have had applications from Officers of rank even as high as Colonel, for recommendations to him." The other major source of military power, the Sipahis, increased their pressure on the subject population in their *timar*s. They extorted more and more revenue from the peasants and also dealt roughly with Jews who had contact with them. Under these circumstances, it was remarkable that the Turkish army still maintained sufficient fighting qualities for able sultans like Murad III and Murad IV to maintain their sovereignty over all provinces previously conquered and even occasionally to add to their possessions.[43]

With the instability in the office of the central vizierate (there were no less than 26 changes in the 43 years between Sokolli's death in 1579 and Murad III's accession to the throne in 1623), the power of the provincial and local governors was greatly enhanced. However, there was an even larger personnel turnover in second- and third-tier posts, and dismissals or transfers of locally very powerful satraps were the rule rather than the exception. It is a matter of record that in less than half a century (from 1574 to 1622) the high office of governor-general or viceroy of Egypt was held by no fewer than 23 officials who thus averaged no more than two years in administering that great province. When in Algeria the beglerbeg had to start sharing his power with centrally appointed governors, these men were from the outset appointed for only three years. Not all of them lasted even that long. It has also been established that during the entire 145 years of Ottoman occupation of Buda (1541–1687) some 100 officials were recorded as having held that rank (some with interruptions). Similar brief tenures also existed in the offices of provincial governors in Damascus, Aleppo, and elsewhere. Consequently, most of these officials tried to accumulate as much wealth as they could during their short terms of office. The popular adage concerning the ancient Roman governor of Syria, Ventidius Cumanus, that he had "entered rich Syria poor and left poor Syria rich," was equally justified about numerous administrators of Ottoman provinces in the seventeenth century. One of the worst, as far as Jews were concerned, was the governor of Jerusalem Meḥmed ibn Farukh, who in 1625 succeeded in extorting money from the Jewish inhabitants and their communal leaders under all sorts of excuses and trumped-up charges. Time and again he imprisoned some of the outstanding rabbis, including the highly revered Ashkenazic sage, R. Isaiah Horowitz, and held them for ransom. As a result, the Jewish community not only exhausted its own resources, but had to borrow 60,000 aspers from Muslim neighbors, an amount which quickly increased by an annual interest of 10,000 aspers, or a rate of 16.66 percent. The Jews fared even worse during Ibn Farukh's temporary absence, when he led a caravan of Muslim pilgrims to Mecca. Leaving his brother-in-law, Osman Anas, in charge of his office, he gave him the opportunity to enrich himself at Jewish expense within a few months. It required persistent, and doubtless also costly efforts of the Jewish leadership in Damascus and Istanbul before Ibn Farukh was deposed on the sultan's order. Similar cases of exploitation repeated themselves on many occasions in that city and elsewhere.[44]

Few victims, however, were able to secure even that modicum of redress. True, Jews and other oppressed groups were able to send petitions directly to the Porte. Josef Matuz regards this safety-valve as a testimony for the Ottoman Empire's functioning as a *Rechts- und Wohlfahrtsstaat*. As a matter of record, some sultans indeed made special efforts to respond to grievances addressed to them by individuals in distress which came to their attention. But in practical life the relatively few cases when redress was secured were no more helpful in relieving the pressures on the masses of the mid-eastern fellahin and impecunious urbanites than did the similar petitions and poetic litanies submitted by contemporary Polish villeins mentioned in our earlier description of conditions in Eastern Europe in the seventeenth century. Possibly the Turkish Jews were in the more fortunate position of finding some coreligionists able and willing to appeal in their behalf to influential dignitaries at the Porte, although, for instance, Joseph di Trani's trip to Istanbul in 1599 on a mission for the endangered Jewish community of Safed resulted only in some financial aid to the impoverished Safed Jews from alms of their well-to-do brethren in the capital.[45]

The extortionist practices of the administrators knew few limits. Even the French embassy officials were often blackmailed into paying ransom by borrowing substantial amounts from Jews or Turks at high rates of interest. In 1665, a period of relatively greater stability in the Ottoman Empire, Louis XIV had to insert into his instructions to the newly appointed ambassador, Denis de la Haye Vanteley, that he should "influence the sultan to send out intelligent officials, in company of a Frenchman designated by the ambassador [to various localities], in order to liquidate the debts caused by those who had committed outrages against Frenchmen and annul all promises made by [these] Frenchmen to Jews and Turks with respect to interest and usury." Similar instructions were issued to departing ambassadors in 1670 and 1685. Characteristically, the same Frenchmen, who doubtless were grateful to the lenders for helping them out in emergencies, often evaded repaying the loans. In 1632 one such recalcitrant debtor in Aleppo, whose consul was told by the pasha to see to it that the loan be repaid, suggested to the consul that "the Jew be punished through a boycott [batellation] by the French nation and that, in order that his own countrymen could tell him that he [the lender] had acted wrongly, the boycott should include the whole Jewish nation."[46]

A remarkable illustration of a far-fetched command addressed to a Jewish communal leader on the basis of an historical recollection was the order given in 1586 by another governor of Jerusalem, Abu Sifon, to the famous kabbalist R. Ḥayyim Vital Calabrese. Hearing on a Friday, the Muslim weekly day of rest when the city's noises subsided, an underground flow of waters and learning that it probably came from the waters of Giḥon "the upper springs" of which, according to the biblical tradition (II Chron. 32:30), had been "stopped" by the ancient Israelitic King Hezekiah, the governor ordered R. Ḥayyim to see to it that these waters "shut off by your king" be instantaneously reopened. In fear for his life R. Ḥayyim escaped to Egypt. Much more frequent were simple legislative chicaneries, such as were used by Bibir Meḥmad Pasha, governor of Damascus in the 1620s. To extort funds from the Jewish community, he placed the city's gallows in front of the synagogue and hanged there a condemned criminal. He allowed the corpse to dangle for three days and three nights in the hot Syrian climate until the Jewish community secured its removal by a substantial douceur. He also allowed his son, whom he appointed chief of police, to make intensive searches in Jewish homes, allegedly to discover the sources of wine imbibed by Muslims in violation of their religious law. On such occasions, the inspectors were able not only to confiscate containers of wine but also to rob the owners of other possessions for their own and their chief's benefit. However, when these practices, which were paralleled by similar extortions from the Muslim majority, came to Murad IV's notice, he ordered the governor's execution; it took place on October 5, 1623.[47]

These negative factors in Turkish life were greatly aggravated by the ever-deepening economic crisis. The gradual shift of the center of world trade from the Mediterranean to the Atlantic and the fact that the Ottoman Empire's productivity was not keeping pace with the speedy growth of its population increasingly undermined its role in world affairs. At the same time, because of the internal turmoil, the recessional trends then prevailing in the entire Western world affected the Ottoman Empire even more severely than some of the West European countries. The growing price inflation alone upset many customary ways of living. According to the estimate presented by so competent a scholar as Ömer Lutfi Barkan, the price index, which had gradually risen from 50 to 182 between 1490 and 1575, jumped to a high of 631 by 1610, slowly to decline to 424 in 1630. These gyrations must have played into the hands of many speculators but were undoubtedly ruinous to the large mass of the population, including the majority of Jews. Interrelated with these price rises was the deterioration of currency, whether by government fiat or through private initiative. As early as 1584–86 the new aspers, weighing 0.384 grams each, were the equivalent in value of only 1/120th of the Venetian ducat. Before long the price of the ducat went up to 200 aspers. In part this was the effect of the flooding of European countries with silver brought by the Iberian "silver fleets" from the American colonies. In addition the depreciation of a currency in one country deeply affected that of other lands, as when a mass of inferior Polish coins penetrated the Turkish markets.[48]

We have no evidence about the role Jews played in these international transactions, although through their active participation in world trade they must have been among the first to react to these international trends. We recall that some Jews were accused of coin clipping by their neighbors in the mid-sixteenth century. Reference has also been made above to the differences of opinion among the rabbis, then and after, about the legal consequences for existing contracts of the frequent devaluations and revaluations of the coinage because of the rabbinic anti-usury laws. These differences were discussed by the sixteenth-century Istanbul savant Joshua Ḥandali in a little tract, reproduced in his responsa. Yet the temptation to replace the silver content of a coin by inferior alloy often was very alluring. In vain did some rabbis protest against that spreading evil. Asked about two Jewish culprits who had previously been excommunicated because of that transgression, R. Solomon b. Abraham ha-Kohen wrote:

It is true that I would have preferred not to be questioned about the law concerning a man performing this ugly work, which is a sin in the eyes of God and of God-fearing men. His transgression is, in my opinion, so severe that if his life depended on me I would tear him to pieces like a fish. But what can I do if the generation is not ready for it? . . . The legal rule is to treat such persons as outlaws, not to sit within four ells from, nor trade with, them . . . until they desist from doing the aforementioned work and take upon themselves all punishments provided by the communal leaders with the proper safeguards that they would not return to their evil ways.

Communal reactions of this kind might have discouraged some coin clippers. But, with the dissolution of the social bonds under the semianarchical conditions of the period at the turn from the sixteenth to the seventeenth century, communal safeguards were probably futile in the face of the great gains available to successful operators and the possibility of their evading, with the aid of the corrupt imperial bureaucracy, the penalties provided by state laws.[49]

IMPACT ON THE JEWISH COMMUNITIES

It is not surprising that Jews suffered with the rest of the population from the increasing decline in the Ottoman society's moral and material values. One of its most important manifestations was the great weakening of communal controls within the respective Jewish groups. Because of the easy accessibility to the Muslim authorities through bribes, overt or clandestine, almost any wrongdoer in the community could escape the consequences of his misdeeds by securing immunity from the local Muslim governor or judge. The Jewish leaders, to be sure, tried to uphold the principle of Jewish judicial self-government and, in most cases, controversies among Jews still were adjudicated at Jewish courts. But they could no longer prevent powerful individuals from repairing to general courts or administrative officials if they expected more favorable decisions there. The old adage that informers—that perennial evil in many Jewish communities—were to be uprooted by all means at the community's disposal, including the imposition of a death penalty where Jewish judges had the authority to issue death sentences, as they did in medieval Spain, seems to have lost much of its deterrent power. In actual practice we learn very little from the contemporary rabbinic sources about the condemnation of delators and the carrying out of any court sentences against them.

A major example of such loosening of communal controls was the presence of Jewish collaborators with extortionist officials. Even such a tyrannical chief as Ibn Farukh found local Jews ready to assist him in his cruel exactions from their coreligionists. For example, when the governor accused some new

Jewish settlers in Jerusalem of having established themselves during the preceding three years without the requisite government authorization, and threatened to impose severe penalties on the individuals concerned and the community at large, he found informers within the community to identify for him these alleged lawbreakers. Otherwise under the then prevailing chaotic conditions in the Holy City he would have been at a loss to know the names of the new arrivals and the dates of their settlement. Even under the more orderly conditions of the sixteenth century the mass immigration of Jews and other foreigners took place quite openly and without specific consultation with the Muslim authorities. Now Ibn Farukh had to be placated by substantial gifts. He also secured the same type of cooperation when, after exhausting this source of revenue, he extended his search to arrivals within the past ten years. Neither the aforementioned special tract describing the general sufferings of the Jews under his oppressive regime, nor the few rabbinic sources referring to these exactions, mention any names of informers or measures taken to punish them. Evidently the rabbis did not dare to antagonize the superiors of Ibn Farukh and his brother-in-law to whom they could have appealed but who might actually have been inclined to encourage such denunciations by Jews of Jewish violators of state laws.[50]

Sometimes the aid of corrupt officials was invoked by individuals for carrying out nefarious designs even in the most intimate area of family life, where the autonomy of the respective denominations was most carefully safeguarded. A noteworthy case of such violation in Jerusalem is recorded in a contemporary responsum by R. Jacob b. Abraham Castro: A wealthy Jew cast his eyes upon an attractive young girl aged nine whom he wanted to marry. He sent two messengers with the requisite funds to the girl's father, asking him to go through with his daughter's betrothal in absolute secrecy, for he did not wish to divorce his wife or to inform his children of his new matrimonial venture. The girl's father roundly refused. But when soon thereafter he left on a business trip to Egypt, the persistent admirer persuaded, with the aid of a local Muslim official, the girl's elder brother to give the needed consent. Upon his return, the irate father wanted to cancel the compact, but was told by the brother and mother that they would both be severely punished by the local authorities and was forced to yield. Apparently Rabbi Castro was in no position to help the unhappy father and child in their predicament. Evidently under the existing chaotic conditions, the rabbi could not even threaten the overbearing suitor that, if he repaired to a Muslim authority against the judgment of a Jewish court, he would be excommunicated. Such breaches of communal authority often had to go unpunished. Some lenders, for example, obtained from the borrowers a sworn promise that, if the installments provided for in the contract became overdue, the creditor would be entitled to sue the delinquent debtor before Muslim courts and to charge him the additional costs of the suit and collection. In one such case, R. Moses Alshekh, though invoking the authority of R. Asher b. Yeḥiel in favor of stringent reprisals against the guilty creditor, merely suggested some compromise between the parties, "because both of them behaved wrongly."[51]

On the other hand, in that general state of lawlessness some Jewish communal organs, too, overstepped their authority; for example, in their relations with the Karaites. During that period of turmoil the socioeconomic and cultural position of the Karaite community had generally declined even more sharply than that of the Rabbanites. After their great renaissance during the fifteenth and early sixteenth centuries the Karaites' spiritual stagnation progressed at a rapid pace. The contrast between the two communities was intensified by the cessation of any new Karaite immigration into the Ottoman Empire, such as had existed during the period of the Ottoman expansion into the Crimea and other parts of the Black Sea region. After the Muscovite conquest of Astrakhan in 1556 Turkish influences north of the Black Sea diminished and the general and Jewish manpower supply from that area was greatly reduced. At the same time the Rabbanite Jews were still arriving in considerable numbers from other lands. Quite apart from individuals, we learn of forty Marrano families, expelled from Venice in 1549, planning to settle as a group in the Balkans. The same held true for the exiles from the Papal States under

Pius V and Clement VIII. Deprived of such reinforcements and witnessing a general decline of their intellectual leadership, many Karaites voluntarily submitted themselves to rabbinic authority and even adopted certain regulations and interpretations from the Talmud which they had theretofore repudiated as a matter of principle.[52]

It seems, however, that their majority still continued to adhere to their own ancient lunar calendar and kept the holidays on the basis of the appearance of the new moon, rather than according to the Rabbanite astronomic computations. On one such occasion R. Joseph b. Moses di Trani took a most drastic action to prevent their celebration of the Day of Atonement on a date different from that observed by the Rabbanites. When two Karaite shopkeepers opened their stores on the Rabbanite Day of Atonement, he summoned them before his tribunal. Since they refused to close their stores and thus created a public "scandal," the rabbi sentenced them to death and so informed the Muslim authorities, which hanged both Karaite resisters. This extraordinary action may serve as an illustration of a Jewish community which, though no longer enjoying the right to inflict capital punishment, could attain similar results merely by informing some Muslim officials of an alleged breach of the law.[53]

Yet, one must not draw overly broad conclusions from an exceptional incident. Otherwise there were numerous misunderstandings and even certain overt differences of opinion among the Rabbanites themselves with respect to how they should deal with that persistent minority. Nevertheless, for the most part, the two communities managed to live side by side in relative peace. At times the Rabbanites and Karaites closed ranks against attempts by outsiders to interfere with their religious institutions. For example, after 1538 the leaders of both groups jointly insisted that the old cemetery in Cairo, which had originally belonged to the Karaites, should remain in Rabbanite possession. The majority group pledged itself to provide the necessary guards and "to make good any injury caused by a Rabbanite to a Karaite or vice versa."[54]

REGIONAL AND LOCAL VARIETIES

The Ottoman Empire's growing political and economic crisis under Murad III and his successors was partly the result of its precipitate growth and its inability to overcome the enormous regional and ethnoreligious differences of its population. There was a lack of homogeneity even in some basic economic factors. It has been shown that whereas a kilogram of wheat cost 11 aspers in Semendrovo, in neighboring Siren and Szegedin, the price was 14 aspers. The standard of life also differed very greatly. We recall Muḥammad Sarakhsin's eleventh-century observation about the great regional disparities in annual incomes of the people residing in the various cities of the Great Caliphate. With some modifications such differences also applied in the early modern Ottoman Empire because of its vast expanse and the difficulties and costliness of transportation. Understandably the cultural and political diversities were even more startling.[55]

The sharpest differences existed between the three major areas: (1) Rumelia covering most of the European possessions of Turkey, together with numerous islands in the Aegean, Ionian, and Mediterranean seas; (2) western Asia and Egypt including particularly Anatolia, Syria, Palestine, and Iraq; and (3) North Africa, especially west of Egypt, consisting of the previously independent states of Tripolitania-Libya, Tunisia, and Algeria, with their fluid frontiers extending to the Sahara. In addition each of these three groups of provinces had Ottoman dependencies, principally Moldavia and Walachia, and the Crimea in Europe; Yemen and other parts of southern Arabia in Asia; and, for a short while, Morocco in North Africa. Of these dependencies Morocco quickly regained its independence and, after a transitory occupation by Turkish forces in the sixteenth century, it was able to pursue its own foreign and military policies with little interference from Istanbul. In the cultural sphere on the other hand, the Ottoman developments played a considerable role not only in these dependencies but in the entire Muslim world and even, to some extent, in West-European affairs. Many of these differences affected, of course, Jewish life as well. The attentive readers of previous chapters must already have noticed the considerable variations in life and thought among the Jewries scattered in the vast empire. Obviously, we must limit ourselves to stressing but a few highlights in the general and Jewish areas.[56]

The European provinces showed the greatest variations from the other lands, as well as among themselves. This was the effect of the rapid conquests of the fifteenth and sixteenth centuries of populations which had had a long history of diverse ethnogenesis behind them. In many areas the majority of the population remained Christian, especially in the countryside, and the generally effective efforts of the Turkish regime to develop a centralized administration governing these heterogeneous masses fell short of changing their ways of life and beliefs. True, conversion to Islam proceeded apace without the use of force. Even without organized missions Islam was a very successful missionary religion and has remained so in many parts of the world until the present day. In Ottoman-ruled Europe such conversions were facilitated by the great initial losses suffered by the local populations during the Ottoman conquest—whether inflicted by Turkish regular armies or by their even more cruel auxiliary forces designed to strike terror among the prospective victims and thus weaken their resistance—and their replacement by both Turkish immigrants and captive converts to Islam brought back from other battlefields, especially to Istanbul, Adrianople, and other Balkan cities. There also was a considerable amount of conversion by Christians and Jews seeking higher careers in government or marrying outside their fold. *Dhimmi* criminals and others wishing to escape punishment for transgressions against state laws often found it expedient to adopt Islam and thus secure amnesty. To be sure, some enlightened rulers like Suleiman wished to discourage conversion for worldly reasons. According to Sir Henry Blount referring to thousands of would-be converts appearing before the sultan, "when they explained that they wished to do so in order to bee eased of their heavy taxations," Suleiman refused to have them converted and doubled their taxation. While conversions from Islam to any other faith were strictly prohibited and became quite rare, those from other faiths to the dominant religion were encouraged by the existing power structure. Hand in hand with the Islamization of individuals and groups went conversions of churches into mosques, which were not limited to the immediate aftermath of conquests. For instance, a famous Salonican structure, originally built as a mausoleum for the pagan Roman Emperor Galerius (305–311) and later serving for more than a millennium as a distinguished Christian house of worship, was now, at the instigation of Sinan Pasha, suddenly transformed into a Muslim sanctuary. In the following generations it was known as the Hortaci Mosque. This alteration took place in 1589–91, more than a century and a half *after* Salonica's definitive incorporation into the Ottoman Empire. Such proceedings are recorded in many smaller localities. Certainly, the mere loss of one's accustomed house of prayer, often combined with the inability to raise the funds for building another, even if such was permitted by the authorities, may have induced many a hesitating Christian to accept conversion. This factor operated less strongly among Jews. The conquerors themselves doubtless were not attracted to the mostly small and unimpressive buildings or chapels in which Jews had theretofore worshiped. Moreover, suspicions of the loyalty of some Christians to the new regime were much stronger than those aimed at Jews, who had hardly any reason to yearn for the restoration of the former Byzantine or another oppressive Christian regime.[57]

Yet, because the Greek Orthodox faith had become deeply rooted in the Balkan populations, especially among the peasant majorities, wholesale Islamization, which often also led to Turkicization, was largely limited to the major cities and was only partially successful in the smaller towns, villages, and hamlets. In any case, the aforementioned transformation of Buda, which, apart from its initial human losses at the Ottoman conquests, witnessed so constant a stream of emigration of its native Christian population to neighboring lands that the large majority of its Christian families totally disappeared from the city before its reconquest by the Habsburgs in 1687, was quite exceptional. Other major cities, including the two successive Turkish capitals, Adrianople and Istanbul, even after quickly securing Muslim majorities always retained sizable

Christian minorities, however deeply divided among themselves. They consisted of Greeks, Bulgarians, Serbs, Albanians, as well as Armenians and "Frank" Catholics and soon Protestants of various nationalities. In the countryside the divisions largely continued along territorial lines. Despite the incessant internal migrations, large stretches in the western Balkans, especially Morea, still had their Greek majorities, while Bulgaria, Serbia, and Hungary retained their respective Slav or Magyar numerical preponderance. This is particularly true of the countryside, while the cities witnessed the settlement of large numbers of persons belonging to the other ethnic groups in the Empire. Albania, perhaps the most zealously nationalistic and rebel-minded among these conquered European populations, though subject to many Greek, Turkish, and Slavonic influences, continued to develop its independent culture.[58]

The Jewish community in European Turkey likewise retained for a long while the diversity of the members' origins. Many communities continued to embrace congregations of descendants of the original inhabitants of Byzantium going under the name of Romaniot, of numerous arrivals from the Iberian Peninsula known as Sephardim, in addition to "Sicilian" or other Italian and Ashkenazic groups. Yet, the amalgamation of these various strains proceeded apace far more speedily than the corresponding integration in the non-Jewish majorities. After all, these congregations were Jewish, different only by somewhat diverse rituals and, at first also, in speech and inherited mores. But in time these relatively minor differences could not prevent the emergence of a preponderant Sephardic culture and the dominance of its Ladino language in the daily speech of the large majority of Balkan Jewry. To be sure, in the western Balkans many Jews retained their traditional Greek speech. Some Jews coming from Central Europe brought with them their Yiddish speech. There also remained certain ritualistic differences, some even within the same groups. For example, the West-Balkan community of Patras, divided into the four usual congregations, saw its Romaniot group persisting in reciting the paragraph in the highly significant silent prayer (*'Amidah*), *li-meshumaddim al tehi tiqvah* (Let there be no hope for apostates, while heretics and informers shall quickly be eliminated) instead of the more generally accepted formula *ve-la-malshinim* (Let there be no hope for informers). In that generally strictly monogamous community we learn of a childless wife who resisted being divorced by her husband after ten years of married life as recommended by many rabbis. She demanded that she be permitted to stay with her husband while allowing him to marry another consort. But these were minor deviations that could be tolerated by the leading rabbis of the generation, largely recruited from Sephardic circles. Only the situation of the Karaites and Samaritans was basically different. Though they were often treated by the government and society at large as members of the Jewish minority, they cherished their own traditions to such an extent that over the centuries they successfully staved off assimilation to the Rabbanite majority. They did it, to be sure, at the high price of a rapidly declining membership so that in the nineteenth century even the Karaite sectarians amounted to only a few thousand, and the Samaritans to but a few hundred persons within the Empire.[59]

Equally great was the diversity of conditions in the islands taken over by the Ottoman Empire from different previous sovereignties. Many of them, like Negroponte, were quickly incorporated in the centralized Ottoman administrative structure. We have seen that in the Jewish case such an absorption led to the emptying of the Jewish settlement on the island and the emigration of most Jews to Istanbul. On the other hand, the conditions prevailing in Naxos had many unique aspects created by the takeover of a semisovereign power by a Jewish duke under Ottoman suzerainty. Most noteworthy was the evolution of the Jewish communities in some of the largest islands, such as Rhodes and Cyprus, which were annexed by the Turks in 1522 and 1571, respectively. (The changes brought about by the gradual Turkish conquest of Crete in the late seventeenth and early eighteenth centuries are beyond the purview of the present treatment.) In 1522, when Suleiman evicted the Hospitalers from Rhodes, he tried to attract Jews to the island by granting them a number of extraordinary privileges. As summarized by Abraham Galanté, the royal firman included the following provisions:

1. The Jews should be exempt from taxation for a period of one hundred years;
2. they should enjoy the benefits [of exploitation] of the sulphur mines on the island;
3. they should have the right to accompany their funeral corteges to their last destinations and lament their deaths, even when passing Muslim quarters;
4. they should be able to secure kosher meat at the same price and under the same conditions as prevail regarding meat sold to Muslims;
5. each family should have the right to obtain from the government free housing [upon arrival].

We do not know to what extent these provisions were put into effect. But evidently the general treatment of the older and newer Jewish residents was sufficiently favorable for the Jewish community to develop peaceably and to continue more or less undisturbed until World War II.[60]

In contrast, when Selim II and Murad III tried to enforce Jewish colonization in Cyprus, particularly by transplanting Jews there from the large Jewish community of Safed, they encountered enough resistance, as we recall, even from the Turkish authorities in the Holy Land, to abandon these plans. Evidently, under the rapidly deteriorating economic and political conditions of the time, Jews evinced little desire to settle in the unfriendly atmosphere of an island which had a strong Christian heritage and utter lack of any Turkish patriotism. Hence the small Cypriot Jewish communities failed to grow in number and affluence in the subsequent generations. Culturally, too, they seem to have been quite backward. This was partly the fault of the Venetian administration which, ending at the height of the Catholic Counter Reformation, belied its own frequent assertions of independence from the Papacy and generally followed its intolerant directives especially in the colonies. In 1553, when Julius III, under the inspiration of his Grand-Inquisitor Gian Pietro Carafa (who soon thereafter became Pope Paul IV), ordered the burning of the Talmud, the Venetian authorities in Cyprus collected all available copies not only of the Talmud itself but also of some commentaries thereon and other works derived from it, and staged public bonfires in various localities. The result was that even under the Turkish domination the state of Jewish learning on the island was minimal. This came to the fore in a noteworthy incident in Limasol which created quite a stir in rabbinic circles in Istanbul and Safed. From a responsum by Joseph b. Moses di Trani, one of the leading rabbis of the generation, we learn that at one time a young Jew of Nicosia fell in love with a beautiful eleven-year-old girl in Limasol. By forging the consent of her brother (in the father's absence) residing in Nicosia, he succeeded in betrothing the child in Limasol. When this ruse was detected two Safed rabbis suggested that the simplest way out was for the girl, still a minor, to exercise her right of refusal of a marriage arranged by her relatives. Concerned about the ability of the child's advisers to use the proper form for such a refusal—any legal inaccuracy might have invalidated the document—they proposed that it be written in the language included in the Maimonidean Code or in that of Jacob b. Asher. In this connection they expressed the hope that a copy of either book would be found on the island— certainly a sign of intellectual poverty for any Jewish community of that period. Joseph di Trani, however, disagreed and insisted upon a formal divorce with a full-fledged writ to this effect.[61]

Of a different order were the conditions in the Asian provinces. Here, too, Jewish life under Turkish domination in Anatolia differed greatly from that in Syria and Egypt after Selim I's conquest in 1516–17 or in Iraq, which was dominated by Turkey after 1529 with a relatively short interruption in 1624– 38. Anatolia, the cradle of Osmanli power, was converted into the heartland of the Turkish nation through the slow infiltration of Turkomans over several centuries. Even under the Roman-Byzantine rule the Hellenization of the vast peninsula had been quite superficial. The Christian faith introduced by one of its natives, the apostle Paul, took root more in the cities, with their originally numerous Jewish inhabitants, than in the countryside, where the peasants, often called *pagani* by the ancient Romans, long adhered to a variety of polytheistic beliefs and rituals. Later on as a part of the Byzantine Empire under constant attack from the eastern tribes, Anatolia had proved less and less hospitable to the Jews. Particularly under the impact of the four decrees of forced conversion issued by the Byzantine emperors during the seventh to tenth centuries, they dwindled to tiny minorities before the rise of the Osman dynasty. Because Greek culture and Christian faith had long been greatly weakened, the new rulers, steadily reinforced by Turkoman immigrants, succeeded in converting the entire conglomerate of principalities gradually occupied by them into a predominantly Muslim and Turkic entity. The Greeks, Jews, and Armenians, still appearing in some numbers in various cities, constituted but an ever dwindling fraction of the population. The Anatolian *sanjaks* thus became the most Turkish of all the provinces of the Empire. This process of Turkicization did not prevent the rise of many dissenting groups, whether represented by socioreligious reformers like Sheikh Bedr ed-Din, with his militant Turkish and Jewish followers, by Shi'ite dervishes, or by the Čelali rebels of the sixteenth century. But their Turkish character and their Muslim faith as such was never in question. The Jews, who all through the Late Middle Ages must have considered Anatolia an uncomfortable place to live in because of the constant wars between Byzantium and the Great Caliphate and its successor states, continued to dwell in but a few Anatolian localities even after the consolidation of the Turkish regime. Only the former capital, Brusa (Bursa), which played a significant role in international affairs, appears to have had a Jewish community of some 2,300 persons in the late sixteenth century. But this number seems to have dwindled to 700 persons a hundred years later. We also have, as we recall, some evidence of Jewries in Amasia, Magnesia, and finally in the rapidly growing city of Izmir (Smyrna), but they left few records behind and the reconstruction of their history before 1650 has thus far not been very successful. In any case, they played but a minor role in Jewish life in the Empire.[62]

Quite different was the situation in Syria, Egypt, and the other possessions taken over from the Mameluke Empire in 1516–17, followed by the occupation of Iraq in 1529. Here Tukicization proceeded very slowly. While in Europe and even in Asia Minor Islamization usually led to the adoption of the Turkish nationality, in the newly acquired Asian possessions, which had been the birthplace of Islam and had a splendid heritage from the Islamic Renaissance, the idea of a local *jihad* was quite meaningless. The large Arabic-speaking populations, for the most part professing Sunni Islam like the Turks, could not be subjected to a process of mass conversion like that accomplished over centuries in Anatolia and less effectively in the European provinces. At the same time there was no sizable Turkoman immigration in the sixteenth and seventeenth centuries and the relatively few Turkish officials and soldiers, though exerting a powerful political and administrative influence, did not suffice to lend a truly Turkish character to these cities. This was doubly true in the countryside. There also were pockets of different ethnic and cultural groups, like the Druses and Maronites in Lebanon, including some villages which continued speaking in remnants of their old Syriac-Aramaic language (similar to the ancient Jewish settlement in Peki'in, see below). There also were remnants of ancient Assyrians and larger populations of Kurds who staunchly adhered to their ancestral traditions.[63]

The very size and populousness of the area, as well as the rapidity of its conquest within twelve years, 1517–29, made the process of assimilation much more arduous. After all the lands thus added exceeded in both area and population the entire Ottoman Empire at the beginning of Selim I's regime in 1512. Moreover, the chaotic conditions of the declining Mameluke Empire and the great power of the provincial emirs, who were semisovereign in their respective territories, could not be completely eliminated by the centralized power of the Porte. In fact, almost immediately after the incorporation of Syria and Palestine, two native governors appointed to administer these provinces tried to revive the old emir rebelliousness by dreaming of achieving complete independence from their new masters. Although these efforts proved futile and the powerful Grand Vizier Ibrahim quickly suppressed these revolts, a certain tradition of unruly independence continued to animate much of the provincial leadership in the following generations. The half century from Selim I's conquest to the death of Selim II did not suffice to introduce fuller integration into these vast areas before the onset of the economic and political downgrade at the end of the sixteenth century undermined the authority of the Porte everywhere, but particularly in the outlying areas.[64]

For the Jews, these epochal transformations which took place in their original heartlands of Babylonia, Palestine, and Egypt appeared as signs of the approaching Messiah. One of the early reactions was that of R. Abraham b. Eliezer ha-Levi (*ca.* 1460–1530), an Iberian exile who became a leading figure in Istanbul and Jerusalem. In the 1520s he preached that the Ottoman expansion was a sign of the downfall of Christianity and would usher in the final redemption which he predicted would come in the year 5291 (1530–31). There were others who felt that, on the contrary, the cooperation of the Christian world with the Jewish tribes who had allegedly retained some independence in the Middle East—there were exaggerated rumors about their presence and great power behind the legendary river Sambation—found its extreme expression in the spectacular propaganda journey of David Reubeni, assisted for a time by Solomon Molkho. As we recall, in 1525, Reubeni proposed to Pope Clement VII an alliance between the West and a Jewish tribe, 300,000 strong, living in the desert of Tabor, in order to destroy the Ottoman regime. The expected victory would be followed by a restoration of the Jews to an independent kingdom in the Holy Land. In his epistle to the Falashas of 1525 R. Abraham contended:

It appears that in the year 5284 [1524] the redemption had begun, even though it has not yet become manifest where it has taken place. My heart tells me that the children of the tribe of Reuben and some others from the remaining tribes have started out and moved from their place to other areas in that year and that through them a number of their brethren have already been redeemed.

Such predictions impressed even a realistic jurist (on the side also a successful businessman) like David Ibn abi Zimra.[65]

The emotional reaction among the masses was both deep and widespread. Many individuals actually began making preparations to join the hosts of exiles returning to their Palestinian homeland. As we shall see, it even helped generate a major movement among the leading Palestinian rabbis, headed by Jacob Berab and Joseph Karo of Safed, to initiate moves preparatory to the coming of the Messiah, such as the reestablishment of a Sanhedrin, the last major institution to survive in Palestine after the fall of Jerusalem in 70 C.E. To remove the main obstacle, namely the regulation that the membership in a Sanhedrin was restricted to men who had received the ancient form of ordination long since discontinued, Berab and a representative assembly of 25 rabbis in Safed decided, in consonance with a Maimonidean suggestion, to start a series of ordinations by appointing Berab as the first newly "ordained" rabbi who could subsequently ordain others. These in turn could confer an ordination upon some of their outstanding disciples until the number of seventy ordained scholars would be available to form the first Sanhedrin. These high hopes were quickly dashed by the continuing reign of Islam and the growing power of the Ottoman Empire and caliphate. Within the Palestinian rabbinate, it was particularly the realistic "spoiler," R. Levi b. Jacob Ibn Habib of Jerusalem, who spoke up against the exaggerated messianic expectations and also successfully repudiated the legitimacy of the new ordination.[66]

In the meantime, however, both these hopes and the realities of the international situation brought masses of Jews into the successor provinces of the Mameluke Empire, including the Holy Land. Nevertheless the way of life for both Egyptian and Palestinian Jewry continued to be influenced by the local traditions more strongly than in the other parts of the Empire. All of world Jewry now felt the impact of the teaching of the Palestinian leaders. At the same time new centers of Jewish life and learning were springing up in the former Mameluke provinces, some of which proved to be quite enduring. After the great upsurge of the sixteenth century, however, the Jews of Palestine, Syria, and Egypt felt the growing oppression by the local Turkish tyrants like Ibn Farukh to an even greater extent than did their European coreligionists in Rumelia. Very frequently redress against the excesses of the provincial pashas and their subordinates could be obtained from the Porte only by petitions submitted to it through some influential Istanbul Jewish spokesman. But it was in the nature of things that such interventions from Istanbul occurred only on rare occasions and temporarily benefited one or another town, whereas the local bureaucratic outrages continued unabated elsewhere and often became generally a permanent feature of life. Nonetheless, compared with the lack of security in most European countries in the last medieval generations, the mideastern Jewries found life more tolerable. Nor must we forget that the existing records were likely to reflect more frequently both the governmental excesses and occasional protective actions than the ordinary rhythm of daily living among the masses under the reign of the sultans even in its periods of relative decay.[67]

In some respects Egypt stood out among the East Mediterranean provinces of the Empire. It had a long heritage of state capitalism reaching back to the ancient period. In the Faṭimid period, for example, it was the exception among all Muslim lands, we recall, in extending its state controls to a requirement of individual passports for travel within the country. This tendency was further reinforced by the late Mameluke rulers who developed a highly centralized monopolistic economy entirely controlled by the government in Cairo. They adhered to this system to the very end, despite its obvious damage to the economy at large felt in all walks of life both by the Muslims and by the "protected peoples." In their effort not to interfere with the province's internal management, the Turks left much of the local controls as they were, except for transferring certain fundamental decisions to Istanbul. The Egyptian governors, or rather viceroys (beglerbegs), still enjoyed more autonomy than did most of their compeers in other parts of the Empire.[68]

An illustration of this semi-independent behavior is offered by the career of Ibn Velisseir, an influential Jewish businessman in Istanbul and later in Cairo. His was a typical story of what happened to many Jewish leaders, especially after the onset of the Empire's decline. Quite early in his career Ibn Velisseir became acquainted with a high Turkish official Ḥusain in Istanbul who was then speedily advancing within the ranks of the imperial bureaucracy. All along the Jewish businessman provided the dignitary with all kinds of merchandise, including clothing and military uniforms, on credit and offered advice whenever asked. From time to time the official paid varying amounts which temporarily reduced his indebtedness, but also continued incurring new debts until at the end of thirty years he owed his Jewish friend 25,000 piasters. At that moment the patron was promoted to serve as viceroy of Egypt. The new beglerbeg wished to take his trusted Jewish adviser to Cairo but the grand vizier personally insisted that he be accompanied by another Jewish counselor. On his arrival in Cairo, however, Husain Pasha disregarded the grand vizierial order and started using the services of his own favorite exclusively, thus incidentally also emphasizing the relative independence of his office. After prolonged bickering the two Jews compromised and Ibn Velisseir paid his rival 7,500 piasters in settlement for the latter's claim to a share in the joint profits. With the usual change of fortunes of high Turkish officials, however, the viceroy was recalled after but two years and together with his Jewish favorite returned to Istanbul. There Ibn Velisseir found himself confronted with his rival's new claim for a complete accounting of all the income he had received while in Cairo; and a demand for the payment of the balance of his share notwithstanding the previous compromise. Ibn Velisseir was saved only by the intervening retirement from office of the grand vizier. In general, Jews were very active in serving as advisers to various ranking Turkish officials in Egypt, including the aghas (commanders) of the Janissaries who were in charge of collecting much of the imperial revenue from the provinces. It is, indeed, mainly in this area that we have important information about Jewish economic activities in Egypt. Otherwise, too, it stands to reason that, while pursuing their traditional occupations in crafts and commerce, they suffered from Turkish official oppression in a much milder form than under the late Mameluke regime.[69]

We have even less reliable information about the Jews living in the third major area under Turkish domination, Tripolitania, Tunisia, and Algeria, during the first century of Turkish rule. Here the traditions of Berber independence made themselves so strongly felt that before long the beys appointed by the sultan became more and more mere figureheads. The actual control over the administration switched to the *deys* who were elected for short terms by their fellow members of a five-man supreme council. While invested with full administrative power the deys were subject to curious limitations which must have made many of them very unhappy individuals during their periods of tenure. They were obliged to live a solitary life in the castle from Saturday morning through Thursday noon every week, being allowed to join their families only on Friday, the Muslim day of rest. Although recipients of substantial salaries, amplified by "gifts" from the subject population, including Jews, they did not possess the free disposal of that income which was closely supervised by the council. The description of a *dey* by an eighteenth-century secretary of the Danish consulate applied in the seventeenth century as well. He was, as Schonberg wrote: "a rich man who had no power over his fortune; a father without children; a husband without a wife; a nobleman without freedom; a king of his slaves and a slave of his subjects." Yet among his Jewish advisers he or the council found aides who helped administer the country, collect its revenues, and perform some of its public functions. Regrettably, our specific information about the Jews of these North African countries between 1550 and 1650 is extremely limited.[70]

At the same time Ottoman controls of one kind or another extended over dependencies which were not subject to the detailed regulations and administrative operations of the imperial regime. A clear case of such vassal states was the Moldavo-Walachian area. The Danubian Principalities as they were later called enjoyed a large measure of independence which differed from period to period as a result of the ever changing conditions of power. During the period of decline of the imperial overlordship Michael the Brave could at times defeat Turkish armies and join the hostile power of the Habsburgs. At other times the two duchies were ruled by fairly loyal native or foreign voivodes who, appointed by the sultans, seriously viewed their obligation to furnish auxiliary troops to the Turkish campaigns. In other periods the relationship dwindled to mere tributes paid by the Rumanian rulers to their overlords in Istanbul. But such tributes were often paid also by such foreign rulers as the Byzantine emperors or the Austrian Habsburgs. The tribute as such was by no means a symbol of dependence, but often appeared to have served as mere ransom paid to a bellicose neighbor in order to stave off his predatory "excursions" into one's territory. The fate of the Jews in such Ottoman dependencies was clearly affected more by the will, or even whim, of the duke or one of his subordinates than by the occasional decisions of the padishah in Istanbul. The same held true for the Crimean and other Tatars who, from time to time, became vassals of the sultan, even furnishing him auxiliary contingents for his campaigns, but at other times totally disregarded his wishes with impunity. Another semidependent area was that of Yemen. During his conquest of the Mameluke Empire Selim I also occupied Yemen together with the rest of the Arabian peninsula and incorporated it into the Ottoman Empire. Frequently, however, as in the Middle Ages, some local dynasties held sway over sections of Yemen and vicinity whether or not they acknowledged some nominal Ottoman overlordship. Since in contrast to the two preceding dependencies, Yemen embraced a considerable number of Jews whose cultural creativity was quite high, their settlements were able to develop a lively communal and cultural life of their own, somewhat at variance from that of the other Ottoman Jewish communities.[71]

CONSOLIDATION VERSUS STAGNATION

Beginning with the last quarter of the sixteenth century Jews suffered from the negative economic and political developments along with their non-Jewish neighbors. In fact, their harassment by the authorities increased disproportionately while the narrowing of the economic opportunities affected them even more adversely because of their more sensitive occupations in commerce and industry. However, they had some compensation for these losses in the growing consolidation of their internal life.

During the rapid expansion of the "Golden Age" Jews built up a communal structure of vast proportions in a haphazard way. Each group of newcomers arriving on Ottoman shores was able to erect a synagogue and organize a congregation along its own traditional patterns, in fact with some innova-

tions of their own liking. Since the government interfered little with the internal processes of religious and educational life
within the respective communities, they could indulge in their
freedom of choice in a way which endangered the very existence of an overall community. To be sure, far-sighted leaders
from the outset noted the inherent dangers of such anarchical
growth. Quite early they persuaded the congregations to adopt
certain joint resolutions and ordinances, in Hebrew *taqqanot,*
which were designed, for example, to limit unfair competition
in trade or in housing, supervise basic moral behavior, establish the authority of rabbinical courts transcending the boundaries of individual congregations, and open educational opportunities on a community-wide basis, such as the Salonican
Talmud Torah. All along they had to recognize the diversity of
tradition even in marital life. They were fully cognizant of the
different legal interpretations and practices, which in the very
realm of halakhah had developed over the ages in diverse parts
of world Jewry. However, by insisting on a line of continuity
and reconciling minor differences which left the basic similarities inviolable by mutual understanding and concessions, they
succeeded in maintaining a modicum of unity within diversity
in the face of the obvious need for common action in a new
country with its perennial needs and perils of adjustment.

These processes of mutual accommodation became doubly
imperative under the pressure of a general decline. Intercommunal and intracommunal solidarity now became a matter of
highest urgency, especially since cases of defiance of the majority will by wealthy and powerful members multiplied. Aided
by a corrupt Turkish bureaucracy, influential businessmen and
tax farmers were often able to break ranks in pursuit of their
selfish desires. To make the communal will prevail required a
combination of sagacity, profound knowledge of Jewish law,
and an effective appeal to the masses. This was indeed the
fruit of what might be called a long period of consolidation of
the early achievements during the difficult days from Murad
III to Murad IV.

One such effect was the growing predominance of the Sephardic element in Ottoman Jewry. Arriving in the country
with greater traditions of learning, more expertise in trade and

finance, in craftsmanship and professional skills, as well as in rabbinic learning, the Iberian exiles and their offspring soon dominated the communal scene by virtue of their intellectual superiority. Without forcing the old Romaniot Jews or the arrivals from Central Europe to join their own congregations they automatically became the leaders of the community at large and before long absorbed much of the various other groupings into their own communal organizations. In the Balkans particularly, where the long-weakened survivors of Byzantine persecution and of internal discord became a dwindling minority within the Jewish communities at large, the predominance of the Castilian language and the Spanish-Portuguese ways of life became a simple reality. Before long there developed a new Ladino dialect which, by absorbing some elements from the local Greek, Slavonic, and Turkish tongues gradually evolved into a full-fledged new language. Less pronounced was that preeminence in the Asian and African provinces where Arabic, or some sort of Judeo-Arabic, continued to rival the Ladino speech in daily life, though no longer in the area of cultural achievements. In matters of general Jewish interest, moreover, Hebrew remained the main medium of communication between the various groups and constituted the ultimate basis of unity in religion and culture throughout the vast expanses of the Ottoman Empire.

SOCIOECONOMIC TRANSFORMATIONS

DESPITE THE chronological and territorial variations described in the last two chapters, the Ottoman Empire revealed a remarkable stability in its administrative structure and its impact upon the economic and social developments throughout the vast Empire. Such constancy was promoted, during the two centuries of rapid expansion of Ottoman power (1400–1600), by the victorious march of the Ottoman armies, as well as by the general acceptance of the prevailing doctrine that "all classes of society have to serve and promote the power of the ruler" (Halil Inalcik). The sultans reciprocated by enhancing their country's productive capacity through a regime of law and order, the building of roads, bridges, and maritime facilities, enhancing domestic and international trade, pursuing well-calculated fiscal policies, and maintaining powerful, mobile armed forces. To be sure, conditions varied not only between such major areas as the European, Asian, and the North African provinces, but sometimes even from one district to another. In a noteworthy study of four administrative divisions (*sanjaks*) in Ottoman-dominated Hungary, Josef Kabrda has shown that the two northern districts, predominantly inhabited by ethnic Hungarians, differed greatly from the two southern districts, one of which had a large Slav, and the other a similarly large Vlach minority. Because of the perseverance of customs and mores among the numerous religious and ethnic groups, generally tolerated by the Turkish administration, these areas displayed great demographic, economic, and cultural vigor, contrasting with their relative stagnation during the fourteenth century. Only frontier regions, exposed to frequent incursions of hostile armies or marauders, often lost residents who fled across the border, and were sometimes declining in both populousness and affluence.[1]

The great difficulties of communication existing in the large expanses of the Empire were aggravated by the differences in mores and languages in the heterogeneous population of the Balkan Peninsula: Anatolia with its Turkish majority, the Syro-Egyptian provinces with their predominantly Arab population, and the North African provinces which, though likewise predominantly Arabic-speaking, owed much of their culture to their Berber ancestry. Yet there gradually developed some basic similarities in their social and political structures. This underlying unity owed much to the effective centralization of the administrative apparatus in Istanbul, combined with considerable freedoms left to the provincial bureaucracies, the feudal lords on their smaller or larger fiefs in the countryside, and the various local ethnoreligious and professional groups. Keeping a balance between these often conflicting sources of power was not easy. Monarchs of great ability like Meḥmed the Conqueror and Suleiman the Magnificent, aided by brilliant advisers, succeeded in lending the country the appearance of a unified organism. Their governmental machinery was running quite smoothly for the benefit of both the ruling classes and the masses of the population. Under less able monarchs, however, with inferior counselors, that machinery often creaked and at times seemed to come to a halt. But until the late seventeenth century the Empire's intactness was usually restored quickly and the line of continuity remained unbroken.

As far as Jews were concerned such smooth operations, even if frequently marred by excessive extortions and arbitrary acts of individual bureaucrats, sharply contrasted with the disarray prevailing under the late Byzantine and Mameluke administrations. They were particularly important for the growing Jewish merchant class, as well as for its Armenian and Greek counterparts, which enjoyed a special patronage of the government. In their actions and legislative enactments the great rulers, especially Meḥmed the Conqueror and Suleiman the Magnificent, pursued policies reflecting the attitudes described in a mid-fifteenth-century counseling handbook advising the public to

look with favor on the merchants in the land; always care for them; let no one harass them; let no one order them about; for through their trading the land becomes prosperous; and by their wares cheapness abounds in the world; through them the excellent fame of the Padishah is carried to surrounding lands; and by them the wealth within the land is increased.

Notwithstanding the numerous infringements of such freedoms by self-seeking government officials and the continued opposition on principle to the ethics of commerce by many Muslim intellectuals, these generally sympathetic views held by the autocratic rulers assumed an ever greater significance for Turkish Jewry. They played an important role in converting the Empire into one of the largest, most affluent, and culturally creative historic centers of Jewish life. Hence, what happened in the Ottoman Empire between 1450 and 1650 was of vital importance for world Jewry at large. It marked, particularly, the high point in the evolution of the Sephardic communities throughout the Mediterranean world.[2]

DEMOGRAPHIC TRENDS

This highly significant evolution was illustrated by the rapid growth of the Jewish population. We shall presently see that the demographic data available for the Ottoman Empire in the early modern period are, in many respects, more satisfactory than those pertaining to most Western countries. True, the enthusiastic assertion of Louis Henry, one of the leading contemporary historical demographers, could not be justified even in sixteenth- and seventeenth-century Turkey. Henry, whose *Manuel de démographie historique* has become a handy tool for international research in this complicated field, could proclaim that "contrary to what a superficial view might suggest, historical demography is not simply a marginal part of demography. It is demography itself, just as demography, being a study of human populations in time, is history itself." If taken literally, this assertion would make shambles of the study of all history in the prestatistical period. However, in the case of the Ottoman Empire we are able to salvage at least some fairly reliable demographic data from the extant archival records. Remarkably, the Ottoman administration quite early perceived the importance of such data, if for no other reason than to make the collection of taxes, and to some extent also the call to arms, more effective. Understandably, the fiscal and military purposes made, for instance, the Anatolian peasants deeply suspicious of governmental censuses, a feeling persisting until the present day. Hence, all along many inhabitants appear to have evaded being counted. However, in periods of great governmental power, supported by the idealization of a reigning monarch through constant indoctrination, the authorities seemingly reduced such evasions to a reasonable minimum.[3]

More serious was the concentration of the census takers on prospective taxpayers. Thus they had to leave out whole classes of the population, such as children below the age of twelve, women who were not heads of households, the infirm and impecunious—one need only remember the hosts of beggars encountered by any tourist in a typical Middle Eastern city—as well as the legally tax-exempt groups of officials, military personnel, and the Muslim (sometimes also Christian and Jewish) clergy. Less important numerically was the omission of the permanently tax-exempt individuals and families, such as Ya'qub of Gaëta and his descendants mentioned above. However, by establishing a reasonable multiplier, one can deduce from these records not only approximate figures of the total population in a specific locality or district but also many other demographic data of major significance.[4]

A great virtue of these censuses was their detailed enumeration of households, whether headed by men or women, and of bachelors. They have the additional advantage over other contemporary records of this type in their repetition of the enumeration in the same localities from time to time so that one may trace prevailing trends, especially the growth or decline of particular communities. True, the suggestion made in 1541 by the retired Grand Vizier Luṭfi Pasha that such censuses be conducted every thirty years did not quite materialize. But some lists were compiled more frequently, especially during the regime of Suleiman the Magnificent. In the seventeenth century, however, the censuses became quite irregular. Of course, even the sporadic counts had their merits and compared favorably with what was available in many other lands. The religious minorities, including Jews, were usually designated as such and listed in the registers (*defters*) with the same thoroughness because of their payment of special taxes in addition to the regular imposts. The general reliability of these registers and their submission, as a rule (often together with brief summaries), to the central and provincial administrations were another basic asset of incalculable importance. So was the uniformity of the methods of enumeration employed by the census takers over the years in various parts of the Empire which facilitated comparisons, chronological as well as territorial. Finally, we owe it to the officials in charge of the Ottoman archives that a great many of these lists have been preserved to the present day and have gradually been opened to research during the last half century. Needless to say, not all the extant materials have as yet been examined. In fact, the very location of some of them has but gradually been ascertained in recent years. Nevertheless, the enormous number of *defters* known to be extant prompted, as early as 1940, Barkan's enthusiastic assertion that they offer "a living tableau of Turkey, abundantly documented, and presented in the eloquent language of millions of ciphers."[5]

At the same time we must also realize the serious deficiencies of the Ottoman system. In the first place the amounts of taxes listed were based on expectations rather than actual payments. Only in exceptional cases do we get from other sources some actual records of local revenues which may then be, with some difficulty, compared with the respective assessments. Secondly, the lists are incomplete not only because of the aforementioned deliberate omission of all non-taxpaying classes, but also because they fail to mention why certain individuals recorded in one list are not entered in the following enumeration a few years later, and vice versa. Nor do we know to what extent transients were listed in the locality which they happened to be visiting at the time of the enumeration or in their permanent residences, or perhaps in neither. In view of the great mobility of the Ottoman urban population, the question of transients is not to be underestimated. Most importantly, it is almost impossible fully to ascertain whether and when new arrivals and new births were included, while persons deceased were deleted from the records. In comparison with seventeenth-century France and England, students of Ottoman demography are hampered by the absence of parish records concerning births and deaths. Occasionally, to be sure, we learn about local customs, such as existed in Basra during the early sixteenth century, for the tax collector to go around town with a kettledrum to gather a fee for each birth or death of any member, rich or poor. However, even there this procedure was abolished in 1551. Similarly, the report by Aḥmad b. ʿAbd al-Wahdab al-Nuwayrì (d. 1332) that in some provinces of the Mameluke Empire the officials in charge of the capitation tax forced the *dhimmi* chiefs to list daily all male births (as prospective taxpayers thirteen years later) and deaths in their respective communities, may have reflected more wishful thinking than actual practice even in the days of the more orderly fiscal administration during the third reign of Sultan An-Naṣir b. Qalaʿun (1309–1340). No such procedure is recorded immediately before or after the Ottoman occupation of the Mameluke provinces in 1516–17. Nor did the financial reform of the collection of the capitation tax by the Ottoman authorities in 1594–95 yield any such detailed demographic records. It may also be noted that Jewish communities themselves in both East and West were very late in adopting any system of registering births, marriages, and deaths, and no material of this kind was available to either contemporaries or later historians. There are, of course, numerous other deficiencies owing to human error, incomplete preservation of the records prepared, some losses occasioned by fire, water damage, and the like.[6]

For these reasons, as well as for the fundamental question of interpreting the figures given, we must have recourse to other sources of information and additional methods of evaluation. In some cases the mere enumeration and identification of localities, especially villages, where larger or smaller groups including Jews were mentioned in the sources have opened up new vistas on the demographic possibilities of entire areas. Such an approach, utilized early in this century by Karl Lamprecht for parts of medieval Germany, proved quite helpful, for example, to Isaac Ben-Zvi in searching for traces of Jewish settlements in early modern Palestine.[7]

Of great help have also been the various legal sources. While the governmental enactments as such, some of which are actually included as preambles to the census rolls, are in the realm of normative postulates, rather than of daily realities, one may assume that at least in periods of strong governmental controls they were largely applied in practice. Other juridical sources, such as documents preserved in the archives of the qadhis, have likewise proved very useful. In handling testaments of deceased persons, especially, these Muslim judges often recorded the names of prospective heirs and the amounts to which they laid claim. The family relationships between such heirs were also given, thus often rounding out the picture furnished by the censuses. They have the additional advantage of mentioning small children below the taxpaying age. To some extent this is also true of the rabbinic responsa if either the inquiry or reply goes into sufficient detail. Similarly, wherever notaries were needed to record specific transactions, their records, if extant, often help to add a human dimension to the dry census ciphers.[8]

Still another source of important information is derived from data supplied by the numerous foreigners living in, or visiting, certain parts of the country. Envoys of foreign powers domiciled in Istanbul often made it their business to mention important demographic and economic facts in their reports home. Travelers visiting various cities, too, sometimes referred to total numbers of their inhabitants or to those of specific groups of the population. It may be assumed that much of that information was obtained from informed local citizens. In this connection we must not forget the relative accuracy of many medieval oral traditions, especially in the Middle East, when compared with often unreliable oral communications today. Finally, important demographic figures were often found in the contemporary historical literature—Turkish, Arabic, and Western.[9]

Another worthwhile line of investigation which has hitherto been rather neglected with respect to the Middle East is the relationship between a city's or quarter's area and the likely number of its inhabitants. Today—as in Graeco-Roman antiquity—most Middle Eastern cities are highly congested. In the turbulent medieval and early modern times, however, conditions greatly differed from locality to locality and, even more, from period to period. Yet, a vigorous attempt to come to grips with whatever data are available concerning these topo-demographical relationships may contribute fresh insights concerning the probable size of the respective populations.[10]

Notwithstanding the availability of such rich resources we must remember the warning sounded by T. H. Hollingsworth:

Historical demography is a difficult subject. The collection of data is laborious, requiring checking and a watch for hints of underenumeration. The analysis is often subtle, since errors in the data need to be assessed. The conclusions may seem too trivial to be worth so much effort. Yet the historical demographer's aim is to produce the best conclusions that can be drawn from the extant material. Scholarship that tries to do more must be in vain.

Hollingsworth refers, in particular, to Goren Ohlin's critique of certain approaches to historical demography.[11]

AUXILIARY CONSIDERATIONS

An evaluation of the specific demographic data thus assembled depends on the availability and examination of numerous extraneous sources which facilitate their more dependable interpretation. Broader social trends, both positive and negative, often help explain the rise or fall in the existing populations. To the positive factors we must count in the first place domestic peace. During their final consolidation in the sixteenth century the large expanses of the Ottoman Empire enjoyed long periods of peaceful conditions. Whatever wars were fought usually took place on the frontiers, particularly those facing the Habsburg empires and Persia. But the large majority of the Ottoman provinces faced no immediate external enemies. This situation changed in the "period of troubles" between the reigns of Murad III and Murad IV (1595–1623).

But domestic peace was soon thereafter reasonably well restored. Of equal importance was the country's orderly administration which, too, was more characteristic of the sixteenth than of the early seventeenth century. Further consideration must be given to whatever data are available about the fertility of the soil. On the whole, as we shall see, the Empire was rich in agricultural produce which, under normal conditions, sufficed to maintain the population and offered surpluses for export.[12]

Attention must also be paid to such social factors as the average age of marriage. The Middle East was generally characterized by early marriages and the ensuing greater rate of fertility of women. The frequency of polygamy among the predominantly Muslim population was undoubtedly responsible for the relatively large number of bachelors recorded in the *defter*s. It may thus have contributed to a smaller increase in population, as may also have the absence from their families of many males fighting on the frontiers or living in all-male fortified localities like Tarsus in Asia Minor. Certainly, the occasional figures recorded of children begotten by sultans and other dignitaries having large harems were exceptions which doubtless contributed but little to the increase of the total population. Moreover, some contraception was even then practiced in milder or more drastic forms (through coitus interruptus, herbal potions, abortions, and even infanticide). While our sources of information on these obscure aspects of family life are extremely limited, the few available hints must be seriously considered.[13]

Jewish population growth was far less seriously affected by either polygamy or military service (from which Jews were for the most part excluded). But probably even more than their neighbors they must have felt the impact of the religious factors impeding birth control. From ancient times they interpreted the two passages in Genesis (9:1, 7) referring to God's blessing of Noah and his sons, "Be fruitful and multiply and replenish the earth," as constituting the first commandment recorded in the Torah. The demand to have children was amplified by the rabbis in various statements referring to family life. In a discussion, for instance, as to whether a man, all of whose children had died in his lifetime, was still obliged to father new offspring R. Johanan, representing the majority opinion, insisted that such a man had not yet fulfilled his moral obligation. R. Johanan's opponent, R. Huna, who claimed that children, once born, helped their fathers to live up to that religious postulate, had to justify his opinion by an extralegal mystical argument. He quoted the statement of R. Assi (or Yosi) that "the son of David will not come until all souls [of the departed] will have come [to the heavenly Treasury of souls], for it is written: 'For the spirit that enwrappeth itself is from Me, and the souls which I have made [Isaiah 57:16].'" This argument, somewhat akin to the Augustinian doctrine of a total number of souls inhabiting heaven, did not find acceptance among the majority of Jews. In fact, the widely prevailing notion found its sharpest expression in the statement by the second-century sage, R. Eliezer, that "any Jew who does not procreate is like one who sheds human blood, for it is written [in the context of the original "commandments"]: 'Whoso sheddeth man's blood by man shall his blood be shed; for in the image of God made He man'" (Gen. 9:6). It was in this vein that many marriage laws were discussed in the Talmud and the later rabbinic literature. Connected with the birth rate was the average life expectancy, another important factor which, when ascertainable, throws much light on the growth or decline of any population. Certainly, if on the average any newborn child could be expected to live to the age of thirty-five the ensuing total population would have been much larger than one based on life expectancy of but thirty years. Of course, the data referring to these difficult problems are extremely meager. But for that very reason they ought to be exploited to the hilt.[14]

Among the powerful negative factors we have to consider first the man-made disturbances. Wars had deleterious effects on population growth not only because of the numerous casualties among the combatants, but also through their destructive effects on the civilian population in occupied areas. We recall the old Islamic distinction between cities which surrendered voluntarily, the inhabitants of which were allowed to continue living peaceably by paying special taxes, and those which had been taken by force, whose population might readily be exterminated or forcibly converted to Islam. Frequently, detachments of irregular raiders (*akinjis*) were sent in advance of the Turkish armies to kill, plunder, and remove captives in order to strike terror in the hearts of the people to be conquered and thus to undermine their resistance to the regular troops. In addition, during their early conquests in Anatolia and the Balkans the rulers opened the gates to a large influx of Turkish settlers, including some Turkoman nomads who were still arriving in Anatolia in large numbers, into areas occupied by force. Only thus can one explain why so many localities, urban and rural, were quickly converted into Muslim settlements. By the middle of the fifteenth century Skoplje (Üsküp) had 22 Muslim as against 8 Christian quarters. Some localities in Thrace had Muslim majorities of 80 to 90 percent, while in others the total population was greatly reduced. These drastic methods may have been gradually moderated during the Ottoman expansion. Yet the ensuing depopulation of many cities is well attested by the Ottoman *defter*s themselves.[15]

Suffice it to cite the example of Hungary, whose Turkish possessions were acquired in successive campaigns especially in 1526 and 1541. There entire districts rapidly declined in population. It has been shown that, as early as 1547, that is, within six years after the final conquest of Buda, only 238 Christian families from the original Christian population of some 5,000 persons, remained in the city, according to the official register. This number was further reduced to 223 families by 1580, to 14 in 1627, and to only 1 family at the time of the city's reoccupation by the Austrians in 1687. A similar process of depopulation took place in the district of Simontonya according to the *tahrir defter*s for 1546, 1551–52, 1565, 1580, and 1590. The decline of the Christian population alone, of course, did not necessarily reflect a similar diminution in the number of all inhabitants. Hungary may have been exceptional—not only because of the evidently rapid progress of Islamization in its cities, but also because all through the Turkish regime it was an exposed frontier province with great external and internal disturbances. Many Christian inhabitants, especially of the upper classes, were probably leaving their respective towns for both western Hungary which had come under Austrian domination, or Transylvania which, though under Ottoman suzerainty, remained a predominantly Christian area. Yet everywhere else, too, protracted military campaigns left behind them a trail of devastation and loss of life which could not be rectified for a number of years. Nicopolis, which in 1396 had been the locale of Bayezid I's decisive victory over the Hungarians led by the future Emperor Sigismund, played a considerable role under Ottoman rule during the sixteenth century. But in 1599–1600 it was so thoroughly devastated by Michael the Brave of Walachia that it was not yet rebuilt when it was visited in 1613 by the Hungarian traveler Tamas Borsos. As a result of such disturbances the Empire often had to strain its manpower and financial resources to hold on to some such forcibly occupied new provinces. As observed by Gyula Káldy-Nagy, "the cost of maintaining its line of defense [against the Austrian Habsburgs] required an annual investment of funds, in comparison with which the combined tributes paid by the emperors and the princes of Transylvania assumed a merely symbolic character." The resulting pressures further undermined the natural growth of the population. Similarly, on the eastern front, the retiring Persian armies pursued a "scorched earth" policy so as to make it impossible for the conquerors to live from the produce of the occupied land. There it took a long time after each campaign for the people of Iraq and neighboring lands to regain their demographic strength.[16]

Close to the warlike disturbances came those generated by the numerous revolts in various provinces. Even the heartland of the Ottoman Empire, Anatolia, suffered greatly during its so-called Çelali revolt, while Egypt was the scene of frequent uprisings of the masses. Even more numerous were the rebellions of the Janissaries and other discontented soldiers clamoring for higher wages; their assassinations at times reached out to the very throne. As a rule, however, they were not satisfied with attacks on their superiors, but also staged extensive riots in Istanbul and other cities, killing and maiming civilians especially among Jews and Christians, and pillaging their homes and stores. Such losses of life and property intensified the dis-

organization of family life and often greatly interfered with
the normal processes of population increase. So did the general insecurity of roads and sea-lanes. Highway robbery and
piracy on the seas, murder of travelers and seizure of goods
by hired waggoners and ship crews were almost daily occurrences. They caused extensive loss of life or long-term bondage, once again the minorities being chosen targets.[17]

Equally serious were the natural forces of destruction. Many
Ottoman areas suffered from recurrent earthquakes. We are
particularly well informed about the destructive effects of these
elemental forces on Palestinian cities, including Jerusalem and
Safed. But some earthquakes took in much larger areas and
caused many more casualties. Another constant threat to life
and property came from fires. Reference has already been
made to destructive conflagrations which laid to ashes entire
quarters in Istanbul and Salonica. One of the most devastating
fires started in Salonica on a Monday night, July 13, 1545,
caused by the negligence of a local druggist. Sandwiched in
between two attacks of the plague, which found many Jewish
inhabitants "wandering aimlessly to and fro because of the fear
of the Lord," it spread quickly through the entire quarter,
causing the loss of 200 lives, 8,000 houses, and 18 synagogues
with their scrolls of law. It was followed by a renewed onslaught of the plague, which so terrified the populace that
many persons, "young and old, boys and girls, lay down on
the streets naked with no shame." The contemporary chronicler Joseph ha-Kohen ends his graphic recital of that devastating epidemic by declaring that ultimately even "the grave dig-
gers were exhausted . . . and Israel sank very low." This event
had wide repercussions in Jewish letters for several generations. In general, the effects of frequently recurrent and long-
lasting plagues were most catastrophic. The origin of the Black
Death in Asia and its destructive march through the Middle
East and Europe have already been mentioned. But human
mortality during the lesser contagions was equally significant.
We have much evidence about Jews and others fleeing from
the cities to villages in order to escape the terrifying exposure
to epidemics. However, the countryside often suffered as much
as the cities.[18]

Even in France, with its relatively advanced medical services, the plague, occasioned in 1720–22 by the arrival of a single ship from Syria, caused the deaths of up to 69 percent of the population in most Provençal localities regardless of their size. Despite the precautions taken by the Marseilles authorities, which impounded the entire cargo of the ship and kept crew and passengers in quarantine, the ensuing epidemic is said to have caused more than 100,000 deaths in two years. In Syria, where that ship had started its journey, the mortality rate must have been equally high or higher, because of the warmer climate. Jews suffered from these natural disasters along with their neighbors, although doubtless few of them shared the passive fatalism of the Muslim majority. According to the observations of the scholarly Austrian envoy Ogier Ghiselin de Busbecq, the Turks were particularly susceptible to infection because they carelessly used the clothing of victims of the plague for wiping their faces. They asserted that their death or survival depended wholly on God's will. Of course, pious Jews, too, saw in every pestilence a sign of the divine wrath evoked by a sinful generation. According to a story circulating among the Jews of Istanbul, R. Moses Capsali, asked by Meḥmed the Conqueror about the causes of the plague then raging in the city, replied by quoting the midrashic statement of R. Simlai that "Wherever there is widespread sexual debauchery (*zenut*), an *androlomusia* (from the Greek *androlempsia*), that is, indiscriminate punishment and death afflict the good and the bad." Capsali pointed out, in particular, that some young men, among the multitude of Jews brought by the sultan to the capital from various parts of the Empire, joined the Janissaries in sexual orgies. The rabbi advised the sultan to punish severely, but not to execute, the guilty parties; he thereby aroused the Janissaries' enmity toward the entire Jewish community. Yet, this penchant for self-accusation did not prevent the Jews from seeking medical treatment against the contagion. There was a greater availability of medical help in the Jewish quarters because of the presence there of proportionally more doctors, and the help extended to the poor by Jewish charitable organizations, some of which were principally devoted to the care of the sick. Hence the generally low differential between rich and poor victims of the plague was probably even less pronounced in the Jewish community. At the same time, Jews may have suffered disproportionate losses owing to the greater congestion in their quarters in periods of their heavy immigration.[19]

Special losses to the Jewish (and Christian) population resulted from their members' conversions to Islam without compensating gains from conversions to Judaism. According to law, any Muslim adopting another religion was subject to capital punishment, and even conversion from one minority group to another was greatly discouraged. Apostasy from Judaism to Christianity, particularly in areas of persistent Christian majorities, must have played a certain role in slowing down the population growth among Jews. However, we learn about such cases mainly from incidental references in contemporary sources. For example, in the city of Ioannina, which even under the Ottoman domination had retained its Greek character, the son of the distinguished Rabbi Benjamin adopted Greek Orthodoxy, evidently without any punitive reaction on the part of the authorities (ca. 1580). Certainly, the Jesuits who, as we recall, from Aḥmed I's reign (1603–1617) on enjoyed the effective protection of the French government and, overcoming all obstacles, indulged in missionary activities, may well have had some success in also converting both Jewish children and adults to their faith.[20]

Regrettably, our information about the process of Islamization after each conquest is extremely meager. In general, the countryside resisted conversion much more effectively than the cities. We know that Istanbul, in particular, was the scene of special efforts by Meḥmed the Conqueror to convert not only Christian houses, especially churches, into Muslim buildings but also to replace the Christians left behind after the siege by Muslim and Jewish inhabitants. This combination of governmental conversionist policies and the slower, but persistent, pressures exerted by the ruling classes on the non-Muslim masses continued and perhaps accelerated in the seventeenth century. The evolving deadlock, when the Ottoman steamroller was stopped by the Habsburgs in the West and the Persians in the East, contributed to the intensification, if not always conscious, of the missionary efforts of the Turkish authorities.[21]

On the other hand, these negative aspects were largely outweighed in the Jewish case by the continued immigration from other lands. By 1970 T. H. Hollingsworth rightly observed that "migration is becoming the most important branch of demography, just as fertility had dominated the scene for the past 80 years or so, and mortality did before that." This approach is doubly indicated in the case of the "wandering Jew" of the period. True, the mass migration set in motion by the persecutions on, and finally expulsion from, the Iberian Peninsula, ceased in the latter part of the sixteenth century. In fact, we hear more and more about Turkish Jews leaving for some Western countries, particularly Italy and the Netherlands. However, even then the continued pressure on Jews by the hostile legislation in most Western areas, as well as the idea of pilgrimage to the Holy Land, continued to bring some new settlers from abroad into the Empire. It appears, though we have no full-fledged evidence to this effect, that a trickle of new Jewish settlers continued arriving in Turkish cities even during the disturbed first quarter of the seventeenth century. Internal migration, like that of most Negropontine Jews to the capital, helped to swell the number and size of Jewish settlements, particularly in economically more favored areas. We also recall the forcible transplantation of Jews by government fiat after the conquests of Istanbul and probably Cyprus. The effects of such relocations on population growth were far from insignificant. While some individuals benefited economically by becoming, for the first time, owners of dwellings, many others lost the property they had in their old habitats and were converted into governmental tenants, subject to bureaucratic whims for years thereafter. Quite a few of these uprooted individuals or families clandestinely returned to their old homes or to some locations in their vicinity. Experiences of this kind, or their mere anticipation, unavoidably had deleterious effects on family stability. In short, there were both positive and negative factors of great force which accounted for the general increase or decrease of the Jewish population in the Empire.[22]

POPULATION ESTIMATES

Perhaps the time has come seriously to calculate the size of the Jewish population in a number of Ottoman cities during the early modern period. The publication during the last several decades of many *defters* and their analyses by Ömer Lutfi Barkan, his disciples, Bernard Lewis, and others have opened up some such new possibilities. Leila Erder does not exaggerate when she contends that "their [the *defters*] early date, some from before the conquest of Istanbul, their meticulous preparation, repeated collation and standardized form, make them a unique find not only for the history of the Middle East but for historical demography in general." However, the expectation of reaching dependable general conclusions for the whole Ottoman Empire has thus far proved quite illusory. Nikolaj Todorov, who made considerable use of the Turkish censuses in analyzing the conditions in several Bulgarian cities, has rightly argued that, because of the insufficiency of sources, it is not yet possible to reconstruct all demographic aspects of the Balkan cities of the period, except, perhaps, Dubrovnik. Certainly, the evidence hitherto available enables us to cover only a limited number of specific areas for relatively short periods of time. While we ought to be grateful even for such fragmentary information, which, because of its solidity based upon careful contemporary enumerations, stands out against the largely conjectural demographic estimates of most other countries, we must beware of unwarranted generalizations. Such caution is doubly indicated in the case of minorities, including Jews, where the enumerators faced additional handicaps.[23]

Many uncertainties have come to the fore even with respect to the most intensively investigated history of the population of Istanbul. We recall the various ups and downs of the Byzantine capital in the Late Middle Ages. Although it seems consistently to have retained its place as the largest city in medieval Europe, its size varied from generation to generation. Its Jewish community, too, affected as it was by the aforementioned four edicts of forced conversion, the attacks by Crusaders, and the general decline of Byzantine power and wealth, had been greatly reduced before the onset of the Ottoman regime. However, its numbers, further decimated during the siege, were speedily replenished by Meḥmed the Conqueror. The first Ottoman census, conducted in the city as early as 1478, showed that there were 1,647 Jewish households in a total of 16,326 hearths in the city. This figure marked a substantial increase in the Jewish population paralleling that of the Muslims who, within the quarter century since the conquest, became the majority of the population. They embraced 9,517 households, while the former Christian majority had dwindled to 5,162 households, or a little more than one-third of the total.[24]

According to Barkan's computation, in its continued upsurge after 1478, Istanbul's population increased by the 1520s to some 400,000 persons and in the following half a century to some 700,000. However, Barkan himself indicated the questionable nature of these estimates. They were based on the assumption that in Istanbul, even more than elsewhere, the *defters* did not cover the entire population because the enumerators failed to include the nontaxpayers. The Istanbul total was to be increased, therefore, according to Barkan, by 20 percent and that of other cities by 10 percent. This assumption seems to underestimate the number of those who were not reached by the census takers. Suffice it to mention that, according to the report of Marc'Antonio Pigafetta of Vicenza, Selim II's court alone included 40,000 persons. To these tax-exempt individuals one had to add the numerous other functionaries of state and Mosque, as well as some of the clergy of the minorities and the various classes of the population like the indigent, the infirm, and others mentioned above. They must easily have exceeded the ratio of 20 percent. This would have been doubly the case if the population as a whole had risen to some 700,000. On the other hand, Robert Mantran, after quoting Evliya Čelebi's and other contemporary computations, reviewed the population of the capital on the basis of the quarters surveyed in Murad IV's 1638 census: they included 9,990 Muslim, 657 Jewish, 304 Greek, 27 Armenian, and 17 Frankish quarters. Mantran thus found that the resulting figures raised his estimate of the city's total population to approximately 1,000,000 inhabitants, of which only about 10 percent were non-Muslims. But after analyzing other sources, he concluded that both the total figure and the relative proportion were erroneous. Quoting further data from two manuscripts, he reached the conclusion that in 1690–91 the city's population ranged between 600,000 and 750,000. Using another computation, based upon Istanbul's total area which, according to different travelers, extended to between 10 and 16 miles within the walled city, Traian Stoianovich decided that even in 1650 the city's population could not have exceeded 400,000 persons, rising to some 500,000 by 1800. However, Stoianovich did not include in this estimate the areas outside the city wall, among them not only such suburbs as Pera-Galata but also settlements across the Bosporus which were legitimately counted as part of the metropolitan area. In any case, in the sixteenth and seventeenth centuries Istanbul still was the most populous city in the entire Mediterranean Basin.[25]

In Istanbul the Jewish population increased even more rapidly than its neighbors. If in 1478 its total membership seems not to have exceeded 10,000 persons, during Suleiman's Golden Age of the sixteenth century it embraced more than 40,000 inhabitants. As early as the middle of the sixteenth century Hans Dernschwam found in the city no less than 40 Jewish communal groups. Later observers increased that number to 42 or 44, a fact confirmed by extant seventeenth-century communal records. Among them was a sizable group of Karaites who, from the standpoint of the official enumerators, were counted as Jews. During the sixteenth century the individual congregations increased their membership without further major splits into new congregational bodies. After 1650, however, there set in a sizable emigration of Jews from the Ottoman Empire to the Western countries, although the number of immigrants probably still exceeded that of émigrés. In any case, the Jewish community of the Ottoman capital far exceeded in size any contemporary community in or outside the Ottoman Empire.[26]

The second largest Jewish community arose in Salonica. Because of the disturbances of the early fifteenth century, with changing sovereignties, Byzantine, Venetian, and Ottoman, the number of Jews must have greatly diminished. It was further depleted by the forced or voluntary transplantation of many Salonican Jews to the newly conquered capital by Meḥmed II after 1453. However, Barkan's assertion that in 1478 there was "not a single Jew" in Salonica is indubitably unfounded. It merely means that no Jews were recorded in the register of the census of that year, a fact confirmed by Bernard Lewis on the basis of registers which had more recently come to light. Yet it is more likely that whatever Jews remained in the great harbor city after the official "deportation" to the capital had gone into hiding and probably were still evading the enumerators in 1478. Be this as it may, the community grew by leaps and bounds in the following decades. In the 1520s the official records indicated that out of a total of 4,863 households counted in the city, 1,229 were Muslim and 989 Christian. Both denominations were greatly outnumbered by the existing 2,645 Jewish households. Hence the aforementioned statement by R. Samuel de Medina that the majority of the population of the city was Jewish was borne out by the census. While the community's continued growth was impeded by the catastrophic fire of 1545 and other calamities, the Jews seem to have preserved their majority status uninterruptedly until World War I. We shall see that this numerical strength also contributed significantly to the occupational stratification of Salonican Jewry in a way unrivaled elsewhere during the early modern period.[27]

Other Balkan cities lagged far behind. Even the third largest, Adrianople-Edirne, which in the 1520s had a population of 6,351 hearths and a total of over 35,000 persons, according to the census, embraced only 201 Jewish and 522 Christian taxpaying families. Another register of 1519 listed 231 Jewish families and 7 bachelors. Half a century later (1570–71) their number increased to 336 families and 146 bachelors. These fairly substantial numbers are doubly remarkable, since after 1453 many Jews seem to have voluntarily departed or been forcibly evacuated from the old to the new capital. However, when in the 1550s Nicholas de Nicholay reported to have found in the city "an infinite number of Jews, very rich and very great traders in both merchandise and money," he was evidently misled by meeting a few wealthy Jews and noticing

many others whose ubiquity in the bazaars and other important meeting places gave him the impression of large numbers. At the same time the relatively small town of Trikkala
embraced 181 Jewish families, practically rivaling that of Adrianople. The rest of the population was much smaller, however; it consisted of only 343 Christian and 301 Muslim hearths
in the total of 825 families. The town, which still had but a
Muslim minority, thus had a Jewry amounting to more than
one-fifth of the population. In contrast, comparable cities like
Sofia or Skoplje included only 12 and 34 Jewish families, respectively. Even the two somewhat larger cities of Nicopolis,
with a recorded population of 1,343 families, and Sarajevo with
its 1,024 hearths, at that time enumerated no Jews in their
midst at all.[28]

To be sure, these figures are by no means definitive. Sofia,
for example, recorded 32 Jewish families in 1546, there being
no reason why its Jewish community should have more than
doubled in size during the intervening twenty years; it may
merely have been the result of a more effective recording.
Similarly, Larissa, which had quite a noteworthy Jewish history
in the Middle Ages, probably was not completely devoid of
Jews in the early sixteenth century. Nicopolis, whose destruction by the Walachian Michael the Brave had greatly reduced
the population, recovered speedily enough to regain its former size. From the Hebrew records of the time, we have also
learned about the reconstitution of the Jewish community after
the Walachian war. Sarajevo actually gained in size, reaching
before long the population of more than 23,000 in 1571–80.
Its Jewish community, however, as we recall, had only started
developing in the sixteenth century and its members may, indeed, not yet have been counted as such among the city's residents in the 1520s. As late as 1672, Bishop Olivier found there
only 100 Jews, as well as 100 Roman Catholics, along with 2,000
Greek Orthodox and 10,000 Muslims. Subsequently, most of
these cities grew considerably, though the lack of precise documentation leaves many questions open. The seventeenth-
century estimates of some Moldavian cities, discussed by Al-
exandru Ligor, likewise show wide discrepancies. Various calculations derived from the number of houses appearing in the

records of the years 1623–43, and ranging from 9,600 to 15,000 buildings, yielded approximate totals between 60,470 and 100,202 inhabitants. Clearly, we need not be misled by the precision offered by these figures. Similarly, in Belgrade of the mid-seventeenth century the population, estimated by the generally well-informed Evliya Čelebi at 90,000 and by another Turkish writer at 100,000, is given by a Venetian observer as amounting to only 50,000. Regrettably, for this period no contemporary *defters* have thus far offered more solid information.[29]

Of interest in this connection also is Nikolaj Todorov's effort to estimate the value of the respective houses in Sofia, Vidin, and Ruse (in Turkish, Ruschuk). Presumably, the respective Jewish dwellings in these cities were of approximately equal size and value. Citing documents of the eighteenth century Todorov shows that a large majority, ranging from 73–80 percent of the houses in the three cities, were valued at only 1,000 grush. Another 20 percent or more consisted of housing worth between 1,000 and 5,000 grush, whereas a tiny minority of less than 1 percent owned houses costing more than 20,000 grush. These conditions in the Bulgarian cities may not have been typical of other Ottoman or even Balkan cities, however. We recall how different a situation arose in Buda, as a result of its propinquity to Austria and Transylvania. Here appeared a particularly sharp demographic contrast between the Jews and the Christians. According to Lajos Fekete, the city's general population of some 8,000 in 1500 was reduced in 1546, five years after the Turkish conquest, to a total of 390 taxpaying families, that is probably to less than half its former number. The diminution of the Christian sector was further accelerated: from 318 families in 1546 to 223 families in 1559, to 140 in 1590, and to a tiny minority of 14 families in 1633. In contrast, the Jews who, at first, also had been reduced from 72 families in 1546 to 63 families in 1580, recovered to embrace 104 families ten years later. The main gainers were, of course, the Muslims who quickly became the majority of the population owing to both conversion of a great many local inhabitants and the immigration of "Turks" from other parts of the Empire.[30]

Much less is known about the size of Jewish populations in the Asian and African provinces. The original heartland of the Empire, Anatolia, almost rivaled in size and population the Balkan possessions up to the Danube frontier, but the number of Jews living there remained limited. According to Barkan's computations, the various districts of Asia Minor embraced in the 1520s a total of 474,447 households; this number increased to 672,512 households in the 1570s. At the same time the recorded Jewish population almost doubled, from 271 to 534 households, but it was mentioned in only 5 of the 17 districts. Curiously, such an important district as that of Ankara registered only 33 Jewish families in the 1520s and 61 in the 1570s. The largest aggregation of Jews appears to have lived, as could be expected, in Brusa, Anatolia's greatest administrative and commercial center. According to data supplied by the records of the office of the local qadhis, early modern Jewry reached there its apogee of 504 families or about 2,500 persons in 1583, to diminish gradually to 270 families and *ca.* 1,350 persons in 1618–19, and to decline to only 141 families or some 700 persons in 1696–97. More remarkable was the early growth of the Jewish community in the *liva* of Khodavendkiar, where its membership had increased during the half century of 1520–70, from 117 families or some 600 persons to 308 households of *ca.* 1,500 persons. Between them these two communities thus embraced the large majority of all registered Anatolian Jews.[31]

Remarkably, the city of Izmir (Smyrna), which was rapidly becoming an important center of Jewish life and culture, is not mentioned in Barkan's tables. Yet, without the aid of the censuses, Abraham Galanté was able, on the basis of the published records, to ascertain the presence of a number of Jewish communities throughout the peninsula before, during, and after that period.[32]

More important from the Jewish point of view were the newly acquired Mameluke and Persian provinces. They included Palestine, with its crucial role in the life and thought of the Jewish people, and Iraq-Babylonia with its great memories of the Babylonian Exile and the talmudic-geonic period. After the conquest of Syria and Egypt by Selim II in 1517 the

Ottoman hold over these provinces was still rather tenuous. Quite early the new governor general of Egypt, Aḥmed Pasha (1522–24), dreamed of establishing an independent monarchy in that province which, despite the last decades of Mameluke mismanagement, was still richly endowed with human and natural resources. It required the personal intervention of Grand Vizier Ibrahim Pasha, at the head of a large Ottoman army, to suppress the rebellion. Ibrahim stayed on for another year to reestablish order and to issue several decrees which laid the foundation for the new Ottoman administration. The first comprehensive Syro-Egyptian census was, therefore, delayed until 1525. As elsewhere it was followed by similar enumerations in the succeeding decades, but it became quite irregular in the seventeenth century. Even less firm, as we recall, was the Ottoman control over the Babylonian possessions, with their old Jewish communities in Baghdad, Mosul, Basra, and others. Though conquered by Suleiman the Magnificent in 1535, they did not become a permanent part of the Empire until 1638. According to a foreign traveler's report, Murad IV's powerful Turkish army of 150,000 men during the 1638 campaign was said to have included 10,000 Jewish soldiers— an incredibly large figure, since otherwise relatively few Jews appear among the Turkish combatants away from home. On the other hand, there may have been many Jewish victims among the 30,000 "Shi'ite Persian" residents of Baghdad, allegedly slain during its conquest by the Turks (December 24– 25, 1638). It should be mentioned, however, that in 1632 the traveler Jean Baptiste Tavernier claimed to have found the sizable number of 15,000 Jews in the province. This figure is quite plausible, since two registers of the last quarter of the sixteenth century listed, respectively, in Mosul alone the presence of 79 Jewish families (and 3 bachelors), and 145 Jewish families, as members of the Jewish community.[33]

Remarkably, in contrast to the other newly conquered areas except Hungary, the Syrian cities at first sustained serious demographic losses. Aleppo witnessed a reduction from 67,344 hearths in 1519 to 56,881 in the following decade and to 45,331 in the 1570s. Damascus, which had 57,326 households in the 1520s, registered only 42,779 in 1595. Of course, part of that diminution was owing to the negligence of enumerators or to the intervening impoverishment of many families who had to be dropped from the taxpayers' rolls. The Jewish population in both cities, on the contrary, seems to have increased in strength, largely as a result of the continued Sephardic immigration.[34]

During the same period Palestine grew by leaps and bounds in the first decades of the sixteenth century: Jerusalem and Safed, especially, attracted numerous Jewish immigrants. We recall that toward the end of the Mameluke regime the Holy City's Jewish community had been reduced from 250 families in 1481 to 76 families in 1488, according to the admittedly none-too-reliable estimates recorded by the visitors Meshullam da Volterra and Obadiah di Bertinoro. After the Ottoman occupation the census of 1525–26 revealed the presence of 199 Jewish families, compared with 119 Christian and 616 Muslim families. Their number increased to 224 families and 19 bachelors according to the census of 1538–39, to 324 families and 13 bachelors in 1553–54, though it fell back to 237 families and 12 bachelors in 1562–63. Even more pronounced was the growth of the new great center of Judaism in Safed. From a total of 233 Jewish families and 40 bachelors in 1525–26 (compared with 693 Muslim families and 40 bachelors) there was a rapid increase to 719 Jewish families and 63 bachelors (against 1,093 Muslim families and 222 bachelors) in 1555–56, and to 945 Jewish families and 12 bachelors (compared with 986 Muslim families and 306 bachelors) in 1567–68. Even the often-cited larger figure of 15,000 Jews inhabiting Safed during the mid-sixteenth century may not have been as exaggerated as it appears, since a great many recent immigrants may have eluded registration during all these censuses. For reasons explained elsewhere the Jewish community rapidly declined at the turn from the sixteenth to the seventeenth century. The third large city, Gaza, which finally even outstripped Jerusalem in its total population, underscored the general demographic fluctuations of the area. The respective censuses reveal the presence of 95 Jewish families in 1525–26 (in addition to 25 Samaritan families), 98 (plus 15) in 1538–39, 115 and 5 bachelors (plus 18 and 2) in 1548–49, but only 81 (plus 18) in

1556–57, and 73 (plus 8) in 1596–97. This Jewish decline was proportionately smaller, however, than that of the general tax-paying population from its apex of 2,224 families and 187 bachelors in 1548–49 to but 1,073 families and 113 bachelors in 1596–97.[35]

Even less is known about the population of Egypt and the other North African possessions of the Ottoman Empire. There is no question that Jews played a considerable role in Cairo, Alexandria, Tunis, Algiers, and other communities. However, unlike Morocco, these areas have preserved few specific demographic estimates concerning Jews. True, as we recall, on their visits in 1481 and 1488, Meshullam da Volterra and Obadiah di Bertinoro indicated the presence of approximately 5,000 Jews (including Karaites) in the Egyptian metropolis. They must have substantially increased during the great Spanish and Portuguese immigration after 1492, but no detailed data are available. We learn only from the Crimean Karaite Samuel b. David Yemsel, who visited Cairo in 1541, that the Rabbanite community alone worshiped in 31 synagogues. In addition there was at least one house of worship each of Karaites and Samaritans. This fact reaffirms the intervening increase in the numerical strength of the Jewish community, although not to the extent indicated by some travelers. Certainly, the estimate mentioned by Jacques Savary, after his visit to Egypt in 1465, that Cairo included 200,000 Jews in a population of 4,000,000–5,000,000 inhabitants, or the claim by Henri Castela in 1603 that it embraced 3,000,000 men in addition to women and children (he did not specify the number of Jews) are enormously exaggerated. Much more acceptable are the approximations suggested by Marcel Clerget in 1934 and André Raymond in 1976. According to Clerget, Cairo reached the acme of its population of 500,000–600,000 under the reign of An-Naṣir ad-Din (1294–1340, with two interruptions). It dropped sharply after the Black Death and the devastation by Timur (Tamerlane). It continued with various ups and downs until the Ottoman conquest in 1517, reaching some 385,000 or even 450,000 by 1550, to drop again to below 250,000 in 1798. Using a new method and emphasizing, particularly, the rapid sequence of epidemics in the city, Raymond suggested

250,000 inhabitants before 1348, 150,000 in 1410–20, 200,000 in 1517, 390,000 in 1700, and 250,000 in 1798. Jews must have shared many of these vicissitudes and probably before the twentieth century they never exceeded the total of 10,000 persons. On the other hand, the figure of 3,000 Jews (alongside 10,000 Copts, 5,000 Syrian Christians, and 5,000 Greeks) among the population of Cairo, mentioned in the census of 1798, may have been too low.[36]

What was the total population in the Ottoman Empire? Unfortunately, there are no reliable estimates even for the general population of the Empire during that period. Some eighty years ago Karl Julius Beloch published his classical study of "Europe's Population during the Renaissance" and followed it up with a more detailed examination of Italy's demographic history. His estimates, though preliminary, have largely been accepted by such successors as Fernand Braudel and Ömer Lutfi Barkan. Their interest, however, lay mainly in contrasting the numerical strength of the Christian powers of the western Mediterranean with that of the Islamic countries, chiefly the Ottoman Empire. Finally, in part because of their growing demographic strength, magnified by that of the Holy Roman Empire, Poland, and Muscovy—which were to play an increasing role in first stemming, and later rolling back, the Ottoman advance—the preponderance of the Christian West proved irresistible. For the Ottoman Jewish population we have a vague estimate of its increase in European Turkey, including the Aegean Islands, from about 30,000 in the year 1500 to about 150,000 in 1600. In the following half a century we may postulate a slow growth to perhaps 200,000. No such approximation can be validly presented for the total Jewish population in the Asian and African provinces. Yet it may not be too rash to assume that their total before 1650 did not exceed 100,000–150,000 persons. In short, despite their much greater dispersion over the vast domains of the Ottoman Empire, the total Jewish population of some 300,000–350,000 did not quite reach the size of the approximately 450,000 of its coreligionists in Poland-Lithuania in 1648. Nevertheless, with their combined strength of some 750,000–800,000 persons the Polish and Turkish Jews numerically far outstripped the rest of world

Jewry. If we may assume, as it is likely, that the global Jewish population probably lagged behind the total of 1,000,000 souls, it is clear that these two countries were demographically, as well as culturally, the leading centers of Judaism.[37]

ERRATIC ECONOMIC MOVEMENTS

As elsewhere in the western Mediterranean world, the sixteenth-century population explosion in the Ottoman Empire was accompanied by a similar economic upsurge. In our earlier chapters we had numerous occasions to refer to economic developments in the respective areas. Moreover, many lines of economic evolution in both the former Mameluke and Byzantine Empires continued in some force under the Ottoman regime. Hence, we need not concern ourselves with these aspects, but rather supplement our earlier treatment with a general review of the basic economic trends which accompanied the rise and subsequent decline of the Ottoman Empire.

A major overall description of the imperial economy may perhaps be formulated in terms of modified state capitalism. The absolute monarchical power directing much of the economic endeavor was delimited only by the force of local traditions and the actions of local and regional authorities, whether juridically justified or wholly arbitrary and self-seeking. The general idea that what was good for the state, as personified by the sultan, was also good for society at large, was the firm foundation on which rested much of the economic, as well as political, theory of the country. While the Turkish sultans refrained from running as many state monopolies as did their Mameluke predecessors in Syria and Egypt, and while both rulers and subjects often realized that the country's prosperity depended to a large extent on the enterprising spirit and profit motives of the private sector, the monarch's will proved decisive at many critical moments.

As we recall, the sultan could and did expropriate at will the possessions of any subject, particularly after his or her demise. Some of the leading statesmen, even grand viziers—who were able to amass great fortunes through their high salaries, royal gifts, and legitimate offerings by foreign envoys and merchants, as well as through clandestine or overt mercantile operations of their own—were never certain that they would transmit their property to members of their families. Even the powerful grand viziers Rustem Pasha and Meḥmed Sokolli, who helped to guide the destinies of the Empire through most of Suleiman the Magnificent's reign and beyond, were not immune to a wholesale postmortem confiscation of their estates. The old islamic evasion of such contingencies by rich landowners and merchants through establishing mosques or academies of learning in their lifetimes or through converting large parts of their property into *waqf*s (charitable institutions of various kinds), may have left much of such property to the control of the donors' descendants. But as a rule such families enjoyed only the power of initially providing how such philanthropies should be run and of subsequently helping to determine specific expenditures by these institutions, while they themselves could only indirectly derive some income from these sources. The situation is somewhat similar to the American system of heavy estate taxes, federal, as well as state, with the possibility of bequeathing large amounts to philanthropic institutions or to newly created tax-exempt foundations. The Turkish system, however, had the additional weaknesses of whimsical decisions by central and local bureaucracies and even many clearly unlawful acts by a variety of public officials which could not be fully counteracted by court action and only in rare cases could be remedied by a direct appeal to the Porte. It is not surprising, therefore, that, to quote an old American adage, the duration of family fortunes lasted only from "shirt sleeve to shirt sleeve" over three or four generations. In this respect, the Ottoman regime differed only by degree from that of the Mameluke Burji dynasty, where even the association of Karimi merchants, which as such lasted in the Mameluke Empire for a relatively long time, did not guarantee the continued enjoyment of a fortune by a single family for an extended period of time.[38]

These adverse factors operated with redoubled strength against the Jews. Apart from having no chance to be appointed to high state office, with its incomparably better opportunities to amass great fortunes—as private citizens they could at best serve as close advisers and intermediaries to Muslim dignitaries—their large majority was frequently subject to arbitrary acts of government or direct extortions. In many cases their Muslim counterparts could persuasively argue for their rights under the general islamic *shari'a*. Redress under the provisions of the *millet* system or of specific privileges granted to a few leading families was far more dependent on frequently impulsive decisions by some high officials. Establishing a charitable foundation (a *heqdesh*) did not guarantee any continued control over the disposition of that foundation's revenue even by the original donor, and still less by his descendants. The foundation became part of the communal structure controlled either by a society, a congregation, or the community at large, which often held views diametrically opposed to the founding family's wishes.

Even a charitable bequest for a yeshivah in Safed or for the poor of Jerusalem, though greatly appealing to almost every Jew, could nevertheless be questioned by some communal leaders, harassed by the presence of a local indigent population whom they were obliged to support. These leaders readily invoked the old talmudic provision that when it comes to philanthropic assistance, "the poor of thy city have precedence over those of another city." The controversy in the small community of Tiria over the legacy for the Safed yeshivah left by one of the Jewish merchants may not have been typical, however. The Holy Land, and especially the academy of Safed, with the glorious intellectual achievements of its sixteenth-century leaders, must have struck a particularly responsive chord in all Diaspora communities. Joseph di Trani, the rabbi who ultimately decided in favor of the academy, had actually come to Istanbul from Safed but a few years before and still must have had some sentimental attachment to that old Palestinian city. We must also bear in mind that, despite numerous variations in economic conditions and practices among the different parts of the Empire, there grew up many common traits owing to the constant mercantile and intellectual exchanges between them and to their increasingly sharing the common destinies of the Ottoman Empire. True of most segments of the population, such a community of interest was particularly manifest among the Jewish communities which so greatly depended on the well-being of the general Ottoman society and the good will of its rulers.[39]

More disadvantageous was the growing Ottoman neglect of contemporary technological advances, in part nurtured by the euphoria caused by the Empire's spectacular expansion during the fifteenth and sixteenth centuries. At first the gifted and dedicated sultans and their advisers were eager to embrace Western methods of warfare and to improve their own equipment for successful campaigns. During the great transition from heavy armor to gunpowder and ultimately to heavy artillery, the Turks made great efforts to secure the manufacture of new weapons and to teach the armies to use them to best advantage. It was partly on this score that the sultans were glad to admit Jewish exiles from Spain, Portugal, and Sicily, some of whom were known to be experts in the manufacture of new arms. When in 1492, the citizens of Palermo objected to Ferdinand and Isabella's decree of expulsion of Jews from all Spanish possessions, they emphasized that the departing Jews would leave behind them a void in general craftsmanship and particularly in the production of weapons. Some eighty years later the Venetian statesman Jacopo Soranzo pleaded with the Venetian Council of Ten against the decree banishing the Jews from the city on the ground that such a measure would only help the Turks to increase their military strength through the arrival of new experts in the production of "cannons, bows, crude shooting engines, swords, shields and spears." Christian voices blaming Jews for the Ottoman victories in Europe had frequently been heard before. The contemporary world hardly realized, however, the extent to which, for example, the speedy occupation of the entire Mameluke Empire by Selim I in 1516–17 was owing to the Turkish superiority in armaments, especially canons. The Mamelukes were so convinced of the value of their old methods of warfare—which had, indeed, enabled them successfully to resist the repeated Mongolian invasions from Hulagu to Timur in the thirteenth through the fifteenth centuries—that they refused to adopt the new weapons at that time effectively utilized by the Turks. They thus rapidly went into a total eclipse within little more than a year. The situation was reversed in the following centuries, when the misguided feeling of superiority was to prove an Achilles heel of the Turkish armies.[40]

While the era of European feudalism was drawing to an end and the rising modern states began increasingly relying on mercenary troops, and later on national standing armies, the Turks were slow in adjusting to these new conditions. They continued to place their trust in the traditional combination of the Janissary elite corps and the soldiers of the imperial household, supported by detachments of *sipahis* furnished and headed by the feudal lords from among their peons in the *timars*. But this situation deteriorated in the "period of troubles" after Selim II, when the Janissaries grew in number but declined in loyalty, and the *sipahis* often failed to make their appearance altogether. Nor was the Treasury always solvent enough to supply the necessary funds for paying the Janissaries' overdue regular wages. The resulting Janissary uprisings even led to the assassination of Sultans Osman II (1622) and Ibrahim (1648)—regicides theretofore unprecedented in the Osmanli dynasty. This even though Islamic law had not emphasized the "divine right of kings," as the Western Europeans did, even after the Osmanli sultans had also become caliphs, that is, Mohammed's successors as spiritual leaders of the whole Islamic world. Certainly, the practice of legalized fratricide of all sons of a deceased monarch except the one chosen to be his successor (to prevent subsequent civil wars between various pretenders to the throne) made the life of the surviving successful candidate to the throne appear less holy and inviolate.[41]

Not surprisingly, therefore, the relatively small Republic of Venice, could, with the help of a well-built and well-manned navy, militarily resist the encroachments of the awesome Turkish power. Similarly, Portugal, with a population which early in the sixteenth century barely exceeded 1,000,000 persons, could, even after Selim I, continue its domination over the Indian Ocean by frustrating all Turkish attempts to win direct access to India from the sea. Remarkably, this Ottoman weakness on the Indian Ocean and the gradual shift of the world trade's center of gravity to the Atlantic countries did not escape the attention of far-sighted Turkish thinkers. In 1625 'Omer Ṭalib pointed out to his compatriots that the Europeans had vastly increased their knowledge of the world and that "they send their ships everywhere and seize important ports." He therefore warned his government that "the Ottoman Empire must seize the shores of Yemen and the trade passing that way; otherwise before very long the Europeans will rule over the lands of Islam." However, the administration was then controlled by feeble advisers of the still adolescent Murad IV and it had neither the means nor the will to follow that advice.[42]

Needless to say, neither Ṭalib, nor Kuchu Bey, nor any other critic of the existing conditions were economists in the modern meaning of this term. They analyzed economic phenomena principally from their political, legal, or theological angles. Even Ibn Khaldun, whom a recent writer, Jean D. C. Boulakia, called "a fourteenth-century economist," did not deserve this designation despite his noteworthy innovative sociopolitical approaches. Boulakia himself admitted that the great North African historian was, with respect to economics, "an accident of history . . . without predecessors and without successors." The example of economic teachings, cited by this author, namely that Ibn Khaldun, long before Adam Smith, had advocated the division of labor, is unfortunate. The observation that "the power of the individual human being is not sufficient for him to obtain [the food] he needs" and that hence "he cannot do without the combination of many powers from among his fellow beings," happened to be a long-accepted assumption among thinkers before the fourteenth century. For one example, Maimonides, in arguing for the need of cooperation under managerial guidance, wrote:

For the food which man requires for his subsistence demands much work and preparation, which can only be accomplished by reflection and planning, by the utilization of many utensils, and by the employment of numerous individuals, each performing a particular function.

Yet, without being economists both the sage of Fusṭaṭ and Ibn Khaldun made many acute observations on economic matters. It is from such general views and individual actions that Halil

Inalcik could attempt to reconstruct something approximating an Ottoman consensus on certain economic principles.[43]

The government's failure to continue utilizing Jews and other minorities in advancing Turkish technology was even more significant in the private sector. In the aforementioned petition to the Spanish monarchs to revoke the decree of expulsion of the Jews from Sicily, the writers emphasized that

> in this realm almost all the artisans are Jews. If all of them will suddenly depart there will be a shortage of many commodities, for the Christians are accustomed to receive from them many mechanical objects, particularly iron works needed for the shoeing of animals and for cultivating the soil; also the necessary supplies for ships, galleys, and other maritime vessels.

Jews coming from the West were undoubtedly familiar with the use made of mechanical instruments propelled by natural forces such as windmills and flour mills, the absence of which in most parts of the Ottoman Empire has been noted by travelers. To be sure, irrigation of arid lands had for millennia been an accepted practice in many Ottoman provinces. Egypt's civilization to a large extent depended on the annual inundations of the Nile. Below average floods caused visible failures in crops with aftereffects felt for years. However, for instance, in Palestine the Turks continued the dismal practice of the earlier Arab conquerors of cutting down trees without replanting them. The result of this neglect was a growing deforestation of the country, followed by the erosion of the black soil on many slopes unprotected by trees against the desert winds. Moreover, the soil, thus washed down into the valleys, created numerous marshes which, useless for agriculture, became breeding grounds for various diseases, and erected serious obstacles to communications. These deficiencies were not fully remedied even in the nineteenth and early twentieth centuries. It may also be noted that upon explaining most social developments principally by economic factors, some Marxist historians in France have, beginning in 1964, introduced the concept of an "Asiatic Mode of Production" which was supposed to differ fundamentally from the European method. This difference was said to have been responsible for the sharp decline of Ottoman productivity, when compared with that of the West. Such generalization has rightly been rejected by Y. Seitel and others who pointed out, among other matters, that one could not apply any single model to the complicated Turkish economy which greatly differed in various parts of so vast an Empire. Yet, the mere conservative adherence to methods, long perfectly valid and successful, while other nations were making increasingly rapid technological advances, combined with the abuses of the soil, faulty fiscal policies, and declining social controls, would by themselves suffice to explain why the Ottoman economy gradually fell behind that of the speedily advancing Western countries in the era of the Commercial and Industrial Revolutions.[44]

The conditions on the Turkish money markets well illustrated the existing administrative chaos and in many cases the inability of the Turkish central authorities to hold their far-flung Empire together, except through military power. From the outset the Empire had a concurrent circulation of foreign and domestic coins, the accumulation of which was often considered the best method of acquiring wealth. The main difficulties arose when their number, enormous variety, and differing qualities increased greatly in the course of time. On the whole, foreign coins maintained their stability much better than those produced in the country; they were therefore much in demand. It was particularly the Venetian ducat which, ever since 1526, maintained its steady weight of 3.49 grams of gold during the following two-and-a-half centuries. Its reputation was so great that its holder could often get an agio of 10 percent by exchanging it for the local gold coin of exactly the same weight. However, as elsewhere, Gresham's Law—attributed to Thomas Gresham of the sixteenth century, but fully anticipated by Johannes de Strygis, an agent of the house of Gonzaga, who in 1472 warned his employer in Mantua that *la cattiva cazarà via la bona* (the bad [coin] will chase away the good one)—operated in Turkey, too. It quickly displaced, at least numerically, the superior coins with others of lesser intrinsic value. In fact, gold was used less and less in business transactions, being replaced by various silver coins and even by calculations based upon the Turkish aspers (akçes) and the Egyptian *para*s. Their number became so large and so diversified that substantial international contracts and many local exchanges were made on the basis of a fictitious currency such as "purses" of copper coins. These represented a value of 25,000 small aspers which were not meant to be handed from buyer to seller but merely represented a certain total sum payable in whatever other currency was available. This procedure became particularly necessary in international trade when, for example, in the late seventeenth century, Marseilles traders alone paid annually 1,000,000–3,000,000 French livres for coffee and spices to Alexandrian merchants. These amounts represented a value of *ca.* 16,600,000–50,000,000 medins (half-dirhems) in silver currency.[45]

In general, the European nations paid to the Mid-Eastern trade centers more gold and silver than they received in return for their exports. On their part, the Mid-Eastern states had to pay out substantial amounts in precious metals to Persia, India, and other places of origin of the silk, spices, and other Oriental goods in demand in the West. The difference between these mutual payments often did not suffice to cover the Turkish trade deficit, and the merchants had to supplement their foreign exchange earnings by Turkish coins. These were made from metals mined in their own lands (such as the silver mines in Serbia) or brought in by caravans of Muslim pilgrims or by merchants from Africa and Asia. We hear at least of one case where Egyptian Jews supplied gold they had obtained from the Moroccan pilgrims arriving in Egypt. The Turkish mints continued their operations through the centuries, though their products often left something to be desired. Since, like the Mameluke rulers, the Porte often resorted to the depreciation of currency by reducing the silver content of many coins through increasing the share of alloys, the mints had much leeway in going beyond the prescribed ratios of alloy to silver. Such manipulations were recorded, for example, in Egypt where a *wali* (governor-general or viceroy), though well provided for by an annual salary of 1,135,000 paras and numerous fringe benefits, conspired with the directors of the Cairo mint in increasing the percentage of alloys in coins produced there and dividing the ensuing profits. It is small wonder that there was considerable uncertainty about the actual

value of coins handled by nonprofessionals. Even under somewhat more stable conditions of twelfth-century Egypt, Maimonides had already declared that "the banker alone knows
the coin, its deficiency and its monetary value."[46]

The resulting confusion in all business transactions involving the exchange of coins affected with greatest severity the
masses of unaware farmers and artisans who were easily victimized by receiving inferior or clipped coins, or even full-
fledged counterfeits, for their products. We recall the sharp
rabbinic warnings against Jews indulging in these prohibited,
but highly tempting, practices. Certainly, the confusion arising
from the frequent official depreciations of the currency, combined with the enormous diversity of coins in circulation,
proved to be a major obstacle to orderly financial transactions.
This situation, in large measure created by the government's
ruthless fiscal policies had, even in the days of Meḥmed the
Conqueror, led to an enforced decennial exchange of all aspers in circulation at a rate of 10 new aspers replacing 12 old
ones of higher quality. According to Theodorus Spanduginus,
the well-informed near-contemporary (fl. in 1538), this operation yielded each time a profit of 800,000 ducats to the
Treasury. This was a major item in the imperial budget, since,
according to the contemporary testimony of Cardinal Johannes Bessarion, the Treasury's annual revenue amounted to only
2,000,000 ducats. This budgetary advantage was far outweighed, however, by its serious undermining of the country's
economic stability, the spread of black markets, and private
coin clipping by both Turks and members of other ethnic
groups. These machinations could not be wholly suppressed
by the severe government prohibitions against tampering with
coins, under the sanction of physical mutilation or execution
of the culprits.[47]

Among Jews the additional outlawry of these transgressions
by rabbinic authorities did not completely stop certain individuals from directly or indirectly contributing to such monetary
disorders. From a responsum by R. Abraham de Boton we
learn that, sometime after 1594, a Jewish moneychanger continued receiving his regular deliveries of clipped coins from a
Turkish supplier, even after the Turk had his arm cut off by

an executioner. De Boton does not mention what, if any, penalty was inflicted on the Jewish collaborator. Like any one else, the Turkish rabbis were often confused about resolving conflicting claims of various parties concerning the amounts due them under the rapidly changing currency values. For instance, R. Yeḥiel Basan took the position that in general a borrower ought to repay his loan in a sum equivalent to the weight in silver of the original loan. On the other hand, the Safed rabbinate in desperation decided that, since a Damascus Jewish woman's marriage contract had stipulated that she be paid in gold ducats and interveningly the value of the ducat had dropped from 100 to 80 aspers, she ought to be paid at the compromise rate of 90 aspers per ducat. In fact, even in the very Golden Age, we are told, the same silver dirhem which in Lepanto fetched 55 aspers was worth only 48 aspers in some neighboring cities.[48]

Notwithstanding these adverse circumstances the Ottoman peoples, for the most part, continued to maintain a tolerable standard of life. This condition resulted less from government action, which went through alternating periods of marked successes and dismal failures, than to the blessings of a beneficial climate, an abundantly fertile soil, and the persistent toil of millions of workers on farms or in crafts as well as to gifted merchants and entrepreneurs who kept the wheels of agriculture, industry, and commerce rolling. There were, of course, major and minor crises. But somehow society at large showed sufficient recuperative powers to continue living on a more or less even keel. This did not, however, prevent the Ottoman Empire from losing its original expansive momentum and from increasingly falling behind the Western powers, which went through the dynamic expansion of the Commercial Revolution.[49]

AGRICULTURE AND INDUSTRY

According to an enthusiastic seventeenth-century writer, the monetary yellow and white metals were the nerve of every government, "its pulse, movement, spirit; they are its being and life itself." At the same time agricultural production was the real foundation of the Ottoman Empire, and its economic structure. The large majority of the Ottoman population derived its livelihood from the cultivation of the soil and such related activities as cattle raising, the production of wool and linen, and so forth. Intimate interrelations between all these activities came to the fore in every aspect of daily life as well as in the recurrent emergency periods. Unavoidably, the population and monetary explosions of the sixteenth century deeply affected the country's agriculture, too. If, for example, according to François Simiand the circulation of money in the Mediterranean world doubled in amount between 1500 and 1520, and again from 1520 to 1550, and quadrupled in the following half a century, the pressure on prices of agricultural products was enormous. Moreover, this impact was not unilinear but rapidly changed from year to year or even within each year, dependent on the amount of agricultural produce and the sums of money available for their purchase to satisfy the needs of both the Empire's population and its extended export trade.[50]

Factors operating within agricultural production itself were no less far-reaching. To begin with, neither the increase in cultivable land nor the productivity of agricultural labor kept pace with the population increase. In fact, the early modern period coincided with the progressive deterioration of the *timar* system under which most of the land was tilled. Because of the growing pressure on the fellahin and their steady land flight the vitality of the Middle East rapidly declined. Generally held in low esteem, many peasants settled in neighboring cities looking for new employment. Unskilled for urban pursuits, however, these internal immigrants often joined the ranks of the unemployed, swelling the masses of discontented who furnished much manpower to the recurrent revolts. While the government felt it incumbent upon itself to assure the necessary supplies of foodstuffs for Istanbul, it was less intent upon preserving the markets of the smaller cities and hamlets.

The urban population suffered, therefore, not only from the general rise in prices, with which the wages could not always keep pace, but also from their great instability and unexpected oscillations. Suffice it to refer to the example of

Egypt's price evolution in the latter part of the seventeenth and throughout the eighteenth centuries. According to a careful study published by André Raymond, the average and the maximum prices for an *ardab* (5.619 U.S. bushels) of wheat ranged from 34–41 paras in 1661, to 51–80 in 1663, and 60–80 in 1664. Even sharper discrepancies were observed in the 1670s. While in 1675 both the average and maximum prices had declined to 31 paras, a year later they went up to 37 and 42 respectively, to jump in 1677 to 93 and 126, in 1678 to 76 and 252, to fall back in 1679 to 84 each, and in 1681 to drop to 25 and 30, respectively. Similar extremes were shown in the average prices on a decennial basis. Using, as in the previous compilation, prices calculated in constant monetary value, Raymond has shown that the index of the average cost of wheat went up from 332 paras in the 1620s to 405 in the 1630s, but fell back to 304 in 1643 and to as little as 119 in 1650. That low was not repeated in any following decade but, with various ups and downs, the index reached a high of 420 in 1696. This range was maintained through most of the eighteenth century except that during the last two decades it suddenly increased to 715 in 1784 and to 745 in 1792, although it fell considerably in later years. Equally variable were the prices in Syria and other provinces, where from time immemorial the price fluctuations greatly differed from those prevailing simultaneously in Egypt.[51]

Jews seem to have taken little part in the production of agricultural goods and, most remarkably, there is little evidence for their playing any significant role in the marketing thereof. To be sure, we have practically no source material pertaining to these aspects of Ottoman Jewry's economic activities. That the large immigration of Jews into the Empire did not lead to any significant increase in the number of Jewish farmers is understandable. Even in the Mameluke Empire, as we recall, the share of Jews in agricultural endeavor had been rather small. The mere operation of the feudal system, where one could either be the landlord, one of his assistants, or a lowly and despised peasant, did not encourage the new Jewish arrivals to settle on land. As non-Muslims they rarely could become *timariots*, that is, members of the landowning class, as did one of the relatively few Albanian Jews, nor were they attracted to the life of peons. Unlike the European countries, and especially Poland-Lithuania, none of the provinces of the Ottoman Empire seems to have developed a class of Jewish advisers and administrators of the extended possessions of some landlords. Perhaps because a *timar* was not only an agricultural but also a military entity non-Muslims could play a significant role in them only after conversion to Islam. Of course, the long-established Christian population, whether in Rumelia or in Egypt and Syria, for the most part (despite the land flight of some) continued to live on their forefathers' lands even if they were controlled by Muslim masters. Moreover, the theory of the law that all land belonged to the sultan and that even great landowners held their possessions only at the sultan's discretion—there were indeed many changes of ownership by decrees issued by the Porte—must have discouraged non-Muslim newcomers from settling in villages. While it stands to reason that Jews had to acquire cattle and fowl for the production of kosher meat and very likely some Jews also engaged in the preparation of dairy products, particularly cheese, we have little documentary evidence to sustain these facts and still less to ascertain their frequency and locales. Only in North Africa did the Turkish conquerors find a sizable Jewish population living in rural areas and deriving much of its livelihood from agricultural pursuits.[52]

Very likely, however, some Jews living in small towns could own vegetable gardens and orchards and even occasionally maintain a cow, a goat, and chickens without disturbing the public order. Such domestic occupations were not alien even in many European townships where the difference between city and village was far more pronounced. Jews may have had a particular incentive to cultivate vegetables for, according to at least one writer, the preference of Jews for a vegetable diet—reminiscent already of the ancient Hellenistic attribution to Jews of a special liking for onions and garlic—aroused the ridicule of their Muslim neighbors.[53]

Much more, though still not enough, is known about Jews in Ottoman industry. Our sources of information, primarily the Hebrew responsa and some legislative acts of government, are rather one-sided in their respective ways. They furnish us considerable data on certain legal aspects of the industry but they fail to inform us about many other vital details, such as the number of Jews engaged in particular branches of production, its technological aspects, the methods of training new workers, relationships between employers and employees, the wage scales in different periods, or their financial effects on sales, profits, or losses. Even I. S. Emmanuel, to whom we owe a substantial monograph on the important Jewish textile industry in Salonica, admitted that "we are very little informed about these crafts and the methods in which they were exercised." In fact, his monograph is more concerned with the required fiscal payments in kind to the government than with the actual production and ordinary merchandizing of such goods. Some information is also available about the Jewish membership in guilds. It is not surprising, therefore, that even André Raymond, who wrote his excellent study about the craftsmen and merchants in Cairo in the seventeenth and eighteenth centuries—regrettably there is no comparably detailed work on the preceding century of Turkish domination—had more to say about commerce than about industry. His emphasis is more on guild organization and other external forms of industrial production and its exploitation by the authorities for fiscal purposes, than on the technical methods employed in its various branches of production and the economic aspects of supply and demand, the quality and quantity of the output, presence of any forms of class struggle, and the like.[54]

On the whole, it appears that Jews were not hindered, in fact rather encouraged, by the Turkish rulers, to enter various crafts. In the sixteenth century, particularly—when numerous Jewish immigrants arrived from the Iberian Peninsula and southern Italy where they had played a considerable role in certain industrial branches and had been able, as we recall, occasionally to form guilds of their own—their special skills were much in demand. Ironically, in seventeenth-century Brusa, Jewish butchers, whose trade had distinctively Jewish ritualistic requirements, belonged to a general butchers' guild. They seem to have been gladly admitted to membership, paying the usual dues. Once, two Jewish members who had failed to pay were billed by the guild authorities until they brought, as witnesses, some shopkeepers from the Jewish market who testified that they had changed their occupation two years before. In contrast, there existed in Brusa not only a special Jewish guild of cheese and yogurt producers, who had to observe certain Jewish religious rules, but also similar separate Jewish organizations of dyers and belt makers, whose occupations were of a purely secular character. Both entrepreneurs and workers were stimulated by the authorities to furnish industrial goods not only to the public at large but also to the army and the court. Remarkably, Jews could play some role even in mining, although the Ottoman Empire was not very productive in exploiting its rich natural resources and had to import much of the metals, including gold and silver. In a somewhat exceptional case, the French visitor Pierre Belon observed in 1547 that a mine in the vicinity of Salonica supplied the Turks with a "large quantity of gold and silver." In this connection he also referred to Jews:

They have multiplied to such an extent [among the workers] that they made the Spanish language the common means of exchange. They speak to each other in no other language. What the Grand Turk receives from that mine . . . amounts to the sum of 18,000 ducats a month, sometimes 30,000 ducats. . . . These metals are subsequently refined by the labor of Albanese, Greeks and Jews, as well as Turks. . . . They [the Jews] have a habit of working only during the week beginning on Monday and ending before Friday evening for Jews do not work on Saturdays.

In this connection Belon also mentioned that a Jewish owner of a mine was forced to abandon it because of the interference of the *daemon metallicus*. The Jewish share was even greater in the importation of precious metals, particularly from the Sudan, through the "Jewish routes," established already in the medieval period. They also played an outstanding role as goldsmiths and silversmiths, as well as in the related jewelry trade in its various branches. In Brusa Jews actively participated in refining silver and converting it into salable objects. As elsewhere they were also active in dyeing silk and producing silk thread frequently sewn into garments. Some also acquired an expertise in appraising the varying qualities of the dyes used on a particular shipment of goods. According to Robert Mantran, some Istanbul Jewish artisans also engaged in diamond cutting, "although there is no clear evidence to that effect," and in the manufacture of parchment and turbans.[55]

While facing few obstacles in entering any craft, Jews were especially attracted to certain branches of the Turkish industry. Their choice was often determined by the existing needs of Turkish society, as well as by certain ritualistic requirements of Jewish law, or by their prior acquisition of pertinent skills in the countries of their origin. An outstanding example of such a Jewish contribution to Ottoman crafts was the printing trade. Coming from Portugal, a family Gedaliah opened the first Hebrew printing press in Istanbul in 1512, more than two centuries before similar presses began putting out books in Arabic script. Until 1737, it appears, no Muslim seems to have been eager to publish his work in print, while Jews and Christians were forbidden by law to issue works in the Arabic alphabet. The Gedaliahs were followed by the famous Italian Jewish family Soncino and other Jewish printers. Before long the Hebrew presses in Istanbul and Salonica offered serious competition to the predominance of Venice, and later Amsterdam, as centers of Hebrew printing. To be sure, the paper used in Turkey had to be largely imported from Italy, and because of the very high prices fetched by its better grades, it was usually of inferior quality than that used in the works published by Daniel Bomberg, the Bragadinis, and the Giustinianis of the City of the Lagoons. At first the Turkish Jewish presses actually required financial subsidies from their communities or from some wealthy patrons, such as Gracia Mendes and her daughter Reyna Nasi.[56]

Other industrial occupations influenced by cultural-religious traditions included butcher shops. Not only were Jews restricted to the use of kosher meats, but their slaughterhouses usually produced also meat ritually unfit for Jewish consumption either because, after the slaughtering, it was discovered that the animal concerned had a disqualifying blemish, because of some accident in the slaughtering process, or because the local community did not have in its midst a skilled deveiner able to remove a forbidden sinew from an otherwise to be rejected hind part of the animal. In such cases, the Jewish butchers had to look for some non-Jews willing to purchase the non-kosher meat, usually at bargain prices. Naturally, the kosher butchers passed on the increased costs to their Jewish customers. While this procedure ran counter to the Muslim doctrine of *hisba* (just price), the authorities usually overlooked "transgressions" of this type. In Cairo, we are told, Jews regularly acquired with impunity fruits of better than average quality by paying higher than the controlled prices. Jewish cheese makers had to process their wares under strict rabbinic supervision and understandably formed workers' groups apart from other producers for the general market. To some extent the same ritualistic taboos operated to create separate groups of Jewish and Christian producers of wine and other alcoholic beverages forbidden to Muslims. With such production often went the keeping of taverns. In Brusa, for instance, the relatively small Jewish community included 6 of the 20 tavern keepers in 1670. While in some areas the Muslim authorities refrained from taxing such forbidden foods, in Cairo and many other places they raised the tax rates on them precisely because they supposedly were consumed only by infidels. We know, however, that in many parts of early and medieval Islam wine was a very popular drink among the Muslim majority, too. We recall that, since the quality of wine often depended on taste, certain wines produced by Jews of Rhodes or Chios enjoyed a higher reputation than similar products emanating from other areas.[57]

The most important branch of industry where Jewish participation was traditionally influenced by the commandments of Mosaic law was the textile industry and such of its offshoots as tailoring. From time immemorial Jewish workers in woolen goods had to be aware of the ritual prohibition against mixing them with linen threads in any form. Many craftsmen also devoted themselves to the highly skilled operation of dyeing. A rabbinic responsum by R. Samuel de Medina offers a description of the process employed by the Salonican Jewish textile workers in the delicate procedures connected with the drying of the woolen cloth before it was subjected to the coloring process. These occupations pursued by Jews in the Byzantine as well as Mameluke Empires continued in high gear under the Turkish domination. R. Joseph Ibn Leb was but slightly exaggerating when, referring to the Salonican textile industry and particularly urging landlords to tolerate unpleasant odors emanating from the dyeing of cloth in neighboring courtyards, he pointed out that "the entire livelihood of the city's [community's] residents depends on the manufacture of clothing." Some of the cloth produced by the Turkish Jews was highly praised by such outsiders as Esprit Marie Cousinéry. Writing in 1785 this French visitor contended:

Jews are in control of the manufacture of carpets; they produce them in all sizes from the most beautiful qualities down to those of the more common kind. Their use all over European Turkey does injustice to the carpets of Smyrna. The latter are velvety and more expensive, while those made in Salonica which imitate the rare velours, are cheaper but have a much shorter life.

In view of the preponderant use of textiles in the furnishing of Turkish offices and homes the entire population was made extremely conscious of the quality and prices of these products. On some occasions recipients of money due them preferred to get such goods instead of coins, since the value of textiles was much more stable than that of the currency. It is a matter of record that when the English developed their great export of woolens to the Middle East, they obtained spices and other Eastern products by paying three-quarters of the price through barter with textiles and only one-quarter in cash.[58]

In many respects the Jewish community was as protective of the interests of its craftsmen as was, on a much larger scale, the government of all artisans. In the strong regulatory climate of the contemporary world, both in the West and East, governments issued numerous decrees designed to stem competition and to preserve markets for the producers. In the expanding periods of the Empire they also tried to establish new industries, if need be by forcing trained craftsmen from newly conquered areas to move to the capital and other emporia. For example, after his victory at Chaldaran over Shah Isma'il in 1514, Selim I forcibly transplanted 700 artisan families from Tabriz to Istanbul in order to promote the manufacture of ceramics there. Such promotion of industry and commerce also played a role in the forcible deportation of Jews and other residents by Meḥmed II to Istanbul and in the attempted transplantation of Jews from Safed to Cyprus. Generally, too, the qadhis and the *muḥtasibs*, the officials supervising the operations of guilds, often tried to limit the competition between various groups, to prevent encroachments of outsiders in fields of activity reserved for special individuals, to help regulate prices, and so forth. On its part, the Jewish community, too, endeavored to control the entry of new members into existing trades and to protect those working in a certain area from "interlopers." Although the general *ḥezqat ha-yishub* (the acquired settlement right) was not as fully developed in the Middle East as in medieval and early modern Europe, existing "rights" were often protected by communal ordinances. At times they even went beyond the geographic boundaries of their towns. As a noteworthy example of such protective regulations one may cite the Salonican enactment (about 1534) of a ban, signed by fifteen local rabbis and elders, forbidding the export of wool and indigo to any locality within a radius of three days journey from the city. To reinforce this ordinance, these leaders inserted into their proclamation a number of invocations and curses imploring not only God but also certain angels and satanic powers severely to punish transgressors. Such a proclamation, when solemnly recited in all local synagogues, must have inspired more awe and trepidation in the large majority of the then generally credulous listeners than did the announcement of any governmental regulation.[59]

As elsewhere, however, such excessive controls at times boomeranged. To prevent undue competition among Jewish textile producers, the Salonican elders and rabbis, followed by those of Larissa and Trikkala, ordained early in the sixteenth century that no Jew be allowed to outbid another in seeking to acquire the needed raw wool from the neighboring villagers. They also provided that such purchases be made only on credit, so as to protect the would-be buyers who were short of cash. The result was that the owners of sheep raised their prices to safeguard themselves against risks inherent in credit transactions and, in 1565, this ordinance had to be rescinded.[60]

Even more serious in the long run, however, was this excessive regulatory conservatism of the Ottoman public, including its craftsmen. After the Golden Age it stifled the spirit of industrial innovation which had characterized the Turkish economy at the time of the Jewish mass immigration. Even the conquest of Cyprus in 1571, of Baghdad in 1638, and of Crete in 1669 failed to bring new creative forces into the country. In fact, in its fiscal penury and financial short-sightedness, the government actually welcomed the flood of Frankish imports, because by paying the required customs duties these foreign merchants helped supply some cash to the Treasury, even if it accrued to the detriment of the domestic production of finished goods.

One regulatory action of the Salonican Jewish community, enacted by it with the best intentions of promoting its crafts, brought it to the brink of disaster. Because of the high quality of the fabrics produced by the Jewish craftsmen, the Turkish authorities, sometime before 1535, arranged with the Jewish community that, in lieu of a new tax, its craftsmen should deliver to the government in Istanbul 1,000 blue and 200 red pieces of fabric each between 22 and 24 pics long (the equivalent of 14.08 and 15.36 meters in length) to be sewn into uniforms for the Janissaries. So insistent was the government on receiving these precious fabrics that it obtained a guarantee for their regular supply from the Salonican Jewish community as a whole; it even considered this obligation a lien on the property of every Salonican Jew. During the stable reign of Suleiman the Magnificent this arrangement worked out very well for both sides. However, in the period of troubles which followed Selim II's regime, the constant depreciation of the currency and some apparent difficulties in securing the necessary woolens and manpower after the fires and plagues which had ravaged Salonica, made such deliveries extremely burdensome for the Jews. Yet, because of the growth of the Janissary corps and their own lack of funds, the Turkish authorities became increasingly demanding; they gradually raised the quota of free deliveries from 1,200 pieces to 2,400, 3,500, and finally, to 4,000 pieces, allegedly valued at 5,520,000 aspers or some 46,000 ducats. The blue Salonican fabrics now had to help satisfy the needs of 80,000 Janissaries. For this purpose, the government established in Istanbul a special depot which, in the seventeenth century, required the services of 150 employees recruited from among the elite corps itself. They celebrated a festive annual gathering on the holy "Night of Power" (*kadir gecesi,* on the 27th of Ramadhan) in the presence of the highest Janissary officials, during which each commander of the 162 Istanbul barracks (*odas*) received 10 *arşins* (*ca.* 90 yards) of the material.[61]

As a result of this intolerable situation the Salonican Jewish community decided in 1636 to dispatch a delegation headed by R. Yehudah Covo to Istanbul. The delegates were to beg the sultan for forgiveness of the arrears in the required quantity of shipments which had accumulated over the preceding two years. They also were to renegotiate the agreement by greatly reducing the required quota and by converting it into a monetary tax. Unfortunately for the delegates, the then reigning sultan, Murad IV, was a man of ruthless disposition who had concentrated on rebuilding his own financial resources with all means at his disposal. He is reputed to have ultimately accumulated savings of 30,000,000 ducats, the highest monetary reserve ever assembled by an Ottoman sultan. Hence he not only roundly refused the Jewish request but he angrily ordered Covo's execution, purportedly because the cloth delivered by the delegation was of inferior quality. The rabbi was hanged on a Sabbath, September 5, 1637, and the other delegates were arrested. They seem to have been released only after the payment of a fine of 300,000 aspers. This tragedy contributed to the general decline of the great Salonican community, a decline from which it took generations to recover. Ultimately, however, the Salonican quota was reduced to the original 1,200 pieces a year, but otherwise the tax was maintained with varying success into the nineteenth century. Fortunately for Ottoman Jewry, none of its other communities carried on its shoulders such an obligation which, because of lack of foresight, perpetuated a tax in kind when a regular monetary impost would have proved to be much more flexible in the following generations.[62]

Needless to say, many other Turkish cities had a number of

skilled Jewish artisans working in the production of textiles, dyeing, tailoring, and so forth. Most remarkably, even Safed, in the sixteenth century the city of great rabbis, kabbalists, and messianic dreamers, also developed a substantial Jewish textile industry of its own. As early as 1521 Moses Bassola observed "four good crafts in all of Palestine: weavers, metal forgers, saddlers, and tanners. . . . A tailor likewise makes a living." Fourteen years later the Italian Jewish immigrant to Safed, David de' Rossi, wrote about the textile industry's increasing prosperity from day to day.

They say that more than 15,000 carisets [pieces of coarse canvas] have been produced this year in Safed, apart from refined vestments [begadim gevohim for festive occasions]. Some of them make fabrics of as good quality as those of Venice. Any man or woman pursuing a calling connected with woolens earns a good living. . . . I have bought some carisets and clothing for resale and have made a good profit.

However, here too governmental mismangement and oppressive taxation, combined with Druse and Bedouin attacks and natural disturbances, all but eliminated this industry, together with most of Safed Jewry, by the beginning of the seventeenth century.[63]

The few documents available mention no organized guilds of Jewish workers in Palestine. Nonetheless, it may be assumed that a few existed (for instance, in Safed) and, like that of the Salonican textile workers, they may have been exposed to governmental attempts to collect special payments in kind. Our ignorance of such important facets illustrates how little we know about the Jewish role in the Turkish guild system. Despite the considerable literature which has accumulated in recent years about the diverse craft associations operating in various provinces of the Ottoman Empire, there still are many lacunae in our information about them and the picture as a whole appears rather blurred. Clearly, the Ottoman guild system greatly differed from its predecessors under medieval Islam. It began to flourish soon after the conquest of Constantinople, but from the outset Meḥmed II incorporated it into the centralized Turkish governmental system. Unlike their counterparts in medieval and modern Europe, the Turkish guilds had few political aspirations. While in Europe many guilds sought to dominate the municipal councils, the Turkish corporations were sharply controlled by government functionaries appointed as part of the Empire's bureaucratic system. Yet, in all major cities, like Istanbul or Cairo, they embraced the large majority of craftsmen. If we are to accept Evliya Čelebi's figures, evidently based upon an official compilation, there were in the capital no less than 57 groups embracing about 1,100 corporations. They had no substantial control over the quantity of goods to be produced or the setting of prices. Nor did they play the decisive role in the training of apprentices; these were usually taken from among the children of members. Yet, because of their numbers and large membership, they were a significant segment of society and, however indirectly, affected also the economy at large.[64]

The Jewish part in that corporate structure is still controversial. Gabriel Baer, a specialist on the history and operations of Turkish guilds, has consistently argued that the Turkish guilds were essentially divided along ethnoreligious lines and that, wherever their number was sufficiently large, the Jewish craftsmen usually formed their own guilds. On the other hand, Louis Massignon, the Western pioneer in this field, and more recently Robert Mantran and André Raymond have regularly treated Jews as members of general guilds. There is little question that at least some guilds had Jewish members. Among the unresolved questions is how Jewish craftsmen reconciled themselves to attendance at meetings of associations, which had Muslim patron saints, usually selected from Mohammed's family or even from some pre-Islamic pagan leaders. Nor do we know what they did when, as was the rule, each assembly started with a recitation of Muslim prayers, often performed under the guidance of a special official charged with the supervision of such ritual functions. Did they absent themselves during the prayer periods? Were they reciting Hebrew prayers of their own either quietly or in separate assemblies? No answers seem to be given by the existing sources. This issue was somehow circumvented in the case of all "infidel" or "heretical" members, since full membership meetings seem to have been very infrequent. The main business of the association was conducted by their officials in charge under the strict control of the local qadhi and *muḥtasib* (market supervisor). Wherever separate Jewish guilds operated, such questions did not arise. But the documents thus far examined have given us little indication of their daily operations. All of which did not prevent, however, the rise of a large class of Jewish workmen in various branches of industry.[65]

INTERNATIONAL COMMERCE

Our information about the role of the Jews in Ottoman commerce is even less satisfactory than that concerning Jewish participation in industry. To begin with commercial pursuits had many diverse aspects and innumerable subdivisions. Next to the growing and later declining international trade, we have to consider the Jewish part in the trade between the various provinces in the Empire, between cities within the same province, and purely local trade like shopkeeping. In addition, there were many crosscurrents. A large number of craftsmen also engaged in direct sales to their customers, while they themselves appeared as purchasers of raw materials or semifinished products from wholesalers or retailers. Many businessmen often also dealt in money changing or lending on the side. Much of the trade was conducted by family members, with or without assistance of unrelated employees. At the same time slaves seem to have played a very minor role in Jewish business enterprises. A good deal of commerce, moreover, depended on intermediaries. Jewish agents, frequently also serving as interpreters (dragomans) for Jewish and non-Jewish firms as well as in diplomatic exchanges, were sometimes more important in bringing about successful transactions than the entrepreneurs themselves.

Regrettably, the records available for international and domestic trade in the Ottoman Empire are far from satisfactory. Despite the recently growing interest of scholars in quantitative history and related investigations in the generally more easily measurable economic sphere, which has led to the vast intensification of archival research into Western economic history of the early modern period, relatively little has been achieved in clarifying the corresponding Ottoman economic developments. Even the extant extensive Turkish archival sources, which have proved so helpful to all students of the Empire's demographic history, have thus far been less well utilized for reaching statistically dependable conclusions about various aspects of Turkish business history outside the predominantly revenue-oriented governmental interests. Nor have the rich records of the local qadhi offices been sufficiently used for the reconstruction of Ottoman commercial history. In the special case of Jewish trade only a few studies—like those presented by Bistra Cvetkova, Robert Mantran, Nicolai Svoronos, André Raymond, Ronald Jennings, and Haim Gerber—have proved to be truly helpful to me. Even in Salonica, where from the sixteenth century on Jewish merchants played a prominent role in both the domestic and international trade, our more detailed information is derived mainly from the reports of the French and other foreign consuls established in the eighteenth century. These reports are understandably concerned mainly with Jews who had secured French protection under the system of capitulations, or played the game of seeking English, Dutch, or Tuscan protection against the French and/or one another in order to secure from them more favorable conditions. The eighteenth-century situation reflects, therefore, so many novel elements that it contributes relatively few dependable data on the conditions prevailing in the preceding two or three centuries. On the other hand, Turkish taxation has shed much light on the official attitudes to commerce, and the records of the collection of customs duties have proved very helpful in reconstructing many individual transactions in the Empire's import and export business. But they have supplied much less information on the extensive domestic trade. Even European archives which, for example, through the publications of Henry de Castries's monumental collection have yielded so many data concerning the Moroccan economy of the period, have been much less productive for researchers of Ottoman economic history. In the case of Jews the nearly total disappearance of their first-hand communal records throughout the Empire has made itself doubly felt because of the extensive Jewish self-government, as a result of which many

Jewish business deals were originally reflected only in the largely unrecorded internal Jewish administration.[66]

A partial remedy for this lack of archival material is offered by the extensive rabbinic literature produced by the Mid-Eastern Jewish sages. The responsa literature in particular has offered a considerable amount of detailed information concerning Jewish business transactions in various parts of the Empire. However, by their very nature, responsa were concerned with legal rather than purely economic aspects. More importantly, the overwhelming majority of business exchanges never led to legal disputes. Most of those which were brought to the attention of local rabbis were usually disposed of quickly by them without leaving any records about the details of the disputes or their ultimate settlement. Those which were reviewed by higher Jewish authorities—either because the local judges hesitated to pass judgments on certain fine points of the law or because they held divergent opinions—for the most part were submitted to recognized leaders of the rabbinic profession in the form of brief inquiries describing the main legal points at issue. But the questioners usually left out the economically significant pecuniary and other details of the underlying transactions. Moreover, the inquiries and replies, now as a rule available only in their highly condensed form prepared for publication, are usually undated, omit the names of persons and localities involved, and remain silent about most juridically "irrelevant" data.

For one example, one of the most prolific authors of the Hebrew responsa of the time was R. David Ibn abi Zimra, reputed to have written more than 3,000 responsa in the course of his long life (1479–1573). Apart from the seven volumes of published responsa, there exist at least three additional manuscript collections in Jerusalem, Vienna, and New York, of which only a few selected items have thus far been printed. Probably most of these replies were written during David's forty-year stay in Egypt (1513–54), rather than in Palestine where he spent his early and declining years. Although shortly after his arrival in Egypt the country was incorporated by Selim I in the Ottoman Empire, the province was left with much autonomy in internal affairs and was able to preserve its unbroken continuity in the operation of its economic system. Bordering on state capitalism, this system had, in varying degrees, characterized Egyptian life from antiquity through the Mameluke regime. For this reason Ibn abi Zimra's responsa may have reflected conditions existing in Egypt and Syria under both Mamelukes and Turks rather than those prevailing in other parts of the Empire. To be sure, if the responsa were addressed to inquirers from other provinces or even such a foreign country as Italy, the replies must also be examined from the standpoint of possible divergences in the evaluation of the pertinent economic facts between inquirer and author. With all possible exploitation of these sources, therefore, we cannot use them as full-fledged substitutes for contracts, wills, account books, and other documents which would offer more decisive data for the reconstruction of Jewish commerce. Notwithstanding these serious difficulties, however, the responsa of Turkish rabbis of the fifteenth, sixteenth, and seventeenth centuries, especially those of R. Samuel de Medina of Salonica, have preserved a mine of information on all aspects of Turkish Jewry's life including its economic endeavors.[67]

Nor are the occasional comments by foreign visitors or diplomatic representatives located in the Middle East truly helpful before the full flowering of the capitulations system in the late seventeenth and eighteenth centuries. For the most part they offer some generalizations which, even if partially correct, contribute little to the accurate knowledge of specific conditions existing either in a particular locality or in the country at large. We recall, for example, that the generally well-informed French visitor Nicholas Nicholay reported in 1551 that, on his arrival in Adrianople, he had found there "an infinite number of very rich Jews who are great traders in both merchandise and money; for the latter they charge excessive usury." This observation is demonstrably exaggerated. As we recall, after 1453 most Adrianople Jews seem to have been evacuated to Istanbul and the remaining community, though gradually recovering, never achieved again its pristine glory. Even when on another occasion Nicholay became more outspoken and at some length discussed the Jewish share in Istanbul's commerce, he still adhered to generalities and offered no detailed illustrations or statistical approximations. After discussing the Jewish role as intermediaries and agents (see below), he asserted:

Besides, this detestable nation of the Iewes, are men ful of all malice, fraude, deceit, and subtill dealing, exercising execrabl vsuries amongst the Christians and other nations without any consciences or reprehension, but haue free licence, paying the tribute: a thing whiche is great ruine untoo the countries and people where they are conuersant. They are maruelous obstinate and stubborne in their infidelitie attending daily their Messiahs promised; they have the vale [!] of Moses so knit before their eyes of their vnderstanding, that they will not by any manner or meanes can [!] see, or acknowledge the brightness and light of Iesus Christ.[68]

Similarly another Frenchman, Jean Chesneau, describing the journcy of the French ambassador, Gabriel de Lutz d'Aramon, whom he had accompanied, contended that he had found in Istanbul that "most of the shops were owned by Jews." This was clearly untrue even if he should have referred only to a particular quarter of the city or to the foreign settlement in Pera-Galata. However, in 1612 the generally level-headed Venetian baïlo, Simeone Contarini, likewise reported home that "the largest part of the commission houses [*fascende*] are in the hands of Jews," and demanded that the Jews pay their share in the land tax [*cottimo de terra*], although they apparently did not own the land. He went to a further extreme in asserting that "otherwise there is a serious danger that our entire trade will get into the hands of the Jews." At the time when this dispatch was written Jewish business was actually declining and most Jewish merchants were having a hard time in meeting the exactions of the bureaucracy. These were but some of the usual stereotypes relating to Jews, also exemplified by the eighteenth-century visitor who, in discussing one of numerous devaluations of the Turkish currency—a practice indulged in by governments in the entire area under both the Mameluke and Ottoman sultans—blamed it entirely on the depreciation of the aspers by a number of provincial pashas, who, "with the aid of Jews," circulated defective coins produced by them. Yet while in these cases Jews played their traditional role of chosen scapegoats, such observations, when cautiously culled from the large multilingual literature of Ottoman chroniclers, foreign consuls, pilgrims, and businessmen, however biased or misinformed, add a little color and occasional substance to the meager information otherwise available on these subjects.[69]

A variety of other man-made and natural difficulties confronted the Levantine trade which remarkably continued to flourish during the sixteenth and seventeenth centuries even though some of its mediating functions between Europe and the Far East were increasingly taken over by Iberian, French, English, and Dutch traders during the West-European colonial expansion. The Ottoman traders suffered, first of all, from the insufficiency of communications. The land routes through the Balkans, Western Asia, and North Africa, though well established already in ancient times, were both inadequate and insecure. Although some sultans like Suleiman the Magnificent made efforts to keep the roads open and in good shape, most other rulers, constantly pinched for money, allowed them to decay under the impact of stormy winters or devastating desert winds. Partly for that reason the Eastern Mediterranean land transport was conducted almost entirely on the backs of animals—particularly camels in the East, mules in the West, and donkeys throughout the Empire. Horses were infrequently used because they were needed by the army. Camels, which made few demands on their owners, were very useful in arid and sandy areas, where they proceeded patiently and enduringly for long periods of time. Travel at night was always extremely dangerous because of the frequent assaults by highwaymen. Travelers could not even be sure of the probity of innkeepers with whom they had to stay during their nightly intermissions. We have references to innkeepers mixing sleeping drugs into the food they offered their guests in order to appropriate their possessions. In addition, in periods of the frequent local disturbances some rioters, such as the Croatian Uscocchi or the North African corsairs, considered it a patriotic duty to attack traveling merchants whom they considered their sworn enemies. Only a few major emporia maintained large ḥans, or *funduq*s (from which stemmed the Italian *fondachi;* in Egypt they were often called *waqalas*), to accommodate passengers, at times for longer periods, especially during the fairs. Certainly, the famed Cairo fairs, which attracted up to 150,000 visitors, required special accommodations for strangers arriving from both Muslim and Christian lands. Some Jewish communities, too, maintained hostelries (*heqdeshim*, often serving also as hospitals), especially for poorer transients. But at best, long-distance land journeys, even in large groups forming caravans, involved severe hardships. Nevertheless, thousands of merchants or their agents, as well as pilgrims (including Jews of all these categories) generally succeeded in overcoming all obstacles and safely reaching their destinations.[70]

Remarkably, wheels—which had become such an eminent tool in transporting passengers and goods in Europe—were rarely used in the Balkans and the Middle East; naturally their absence greatly slowed down traffic. Another major obstacle to landlocked traffic consisted in the general lack in the Empire of large navigable rivers, except for the Danube in the Balkans, and the Nile in Egypt. Even here travelers faced numerous natural obstacles, such as protruding rock formations or cataracts. As a result in many places, especially on the Danube, passengers had to leave their ships together with their belongings and board other vessels in the middle of the journey. Needless to say, during warlike disturbances Jews and other minorities were not only exposed to attacks by enemies, but they were not even secure against depradations by their own country's soldiers marching to the front. What the French consul in Salonica, De Joinville, described in 1744 applied generally to inhabitants living close to the scenes of battle. Illustrating the conditions in the environs of Salonica during the Austro-Turkish wars, he stated that "the Greeks and the Jews of the countryside lock up their money and do not dare to purchase clothing apparel out of fear of thereby arousing the appetites for pillage among the Turkish soldiers passing through their area."[71]

It is small wonder, then, that most of the traffic was conducted by sea through the Mediterranean, the Red Sea, and the Indian Ocean. The same factors—a long coastline endowed with numerous fine harbors, the large forests supplying wood for shipbuilding, and the availability of trained seamen—which made the sixteenth-century Ottoman navy a dominant power in the Mediterranean, also promoted the growth of a maritime civilian fleet. It was augmented by the presence of a great many foreign vessels, which carried passengers and cargo in both directions. Not that these sea routes were devoid of hazards. Shipwrecks were very frequent because even the large transport ships, which sometimes accommodated four hundred or more passengers, were of relatively fragile construction unable to withstand severe storms. Seeking shelter in one of the smaller harbors was not only technically difficult but depended on the goodwill of the authorities on shore. Time and again, ships were seized by the local leaders and held for ransom. In a case recorded in a Genizah paper the Egyptian governor himself confiscated a ship which was to sail from Alexandria, transported all the cargo to Cairo, held the passengers up for ransom—under the threat of their being sold into slavery—and subsequently forced them to redeem their merchandise at a high price. Nor were Jewish passengers safe against theft and robbery by the crews of the ships on which they traveled. A particularly drastic case is recorded in two responsa by R. Samuel de Medina. A ship belonging to the famous Mount Athos monastery once included among its passengers 55 Jews. Before reaching their destination the rapacious captain and sailors threw all of them overboard, and appropriated their goods. One man managed to survive because the sailors erroneously assumed that he could not swim to a distant shore. After telling his story to the Jewish court in Salonica, he was able to help identify the ship when, on a later occasion, it landed in that city, leading to its seizure by the Turkish authorities. Even more frequently such adventures befell passengers and cargoes on the open seas. Piracy was flourishing not only as a private enterprise but also as one cultivated by various governments as hostile acts against "enemies." Although after the cessation of the crusading movements such ideological justification for attacks on foreign ships lost much of its religious coloring, it was easily replaced by the almost incessant warfare between the Ottoman Empire and one or another Christian power. We recall the great historic role played by North African corsairs such as Khair adh-Dhin Barbarossa. Under these circumstances private business depended greatly on the protection of friendly governments. Jews, having no country of their own to negotiate for them with other states, had to seek the protection of their local or foreign rulers. Under the system of capitulations which fully developed in the seventeenth and eighteenth centuries, the French, English, and other nations concluded such treaties with the Porte. Some Jews actually secured such protection under the umbrella of one or another of the treaty powers as had, we remember, the medieval "white Venetians" in Istanbul and other Eastern areas.[72]

The only remedy of a more general nature consisted in securing some sort of prepaid insurance for cargoes, especially if they were not accompanied by their owners. Understandably, even in periods of peace maritime insurance was very expensive wherever piracy flourished. In wartime it became quite prohibitive. In certain instances during the eighteenth century owners paid premiums of 30 percent of the value of the cargo. Clearly, compared with the days of Justinian, this ratio was enormous. In addition some pietists among both Muslims and Jews expressed serious reservations about the insurance system as such, since either the insurer received payments without returning the full amount to the owners or, if the insurance fell due, he paid out more than he had received. The result was a form of usurious gain by either party. As late as 1712, moreover, when Western cultural and economic patterns began to be emulated in their Empire, some Turks still argued (to quote the French consul, Le Maire) that to take out insurance is "tantamount to losing confidence in Providence." As a result, after a shipwreck, or a ship's capture by pirates, many an owner or shipper was totally ruined. While most Jews may have been less restrained on this score than the more fatalistic Muslims, some of them may have placed their expectation in divine grace rather than paying the high cost of insurance, a system generally little developed in the Middle East. It may also be noted that pirates often indiscriminately attacked very large as well as tiny ships. In one recorded case of the 1740s the English corsairs captured a two-ton ship carrying arms. At the end, after six years, the courts allotted to the captain and crew a total of 30 francs for the booty, whereas

the lengthy proceedings had cost them 140 francs. On the
other hand, about the same time (during the war with France
in 1744) two English pirates captured two French ships on the
Atlantic Ocean. One of the passengers, the governor of the
Spanish province of Peru, was carrying with him cash and
goods valued at 26,000,000 francs. As a result the captains
ultimately received 92,000 francs and the rest of the crew
12,000 francs each. No such extremes are recorded among the
mutual assailants of the Christian and Muslim fleets in the
Mediterranean, but piracy remained a permanent plague which
greatly complicated peaceful navigation and shipping of goods.
Nevertheless, the maritime traffic seemed both more reliable
and less expensive than that over land. It appears that some
three-quarters of the goods internationally exchanged, and
even most of those carried to and from the African, Asian,
and European provinces of the Empire itself, were transported on sea or river vessels.[73]

The Jews were in a particularly good strategic situation actively to participate in the expanding Mediterranean trade.
Through their extensive migrations and their settlement,
whether as professing or secret Jews, in various Muslim and
Christian countries, they were in a position to familiarize
themselves with conditions in various lands and to communicate in several languages. They could also profitably use whatever capital and know-how they may have salvaged from their
native lands. The advantages enjoyed by Jewish physicians,
mentioned by Nicholas de Nicholay, applied with particular
force also to the Jewish role in international trade. The generally unsympathetic Frenchman explained the presence of
many Jewish doctors "skilful in theoretica and experimented
in practice" by the fact that "they commonly exceede all other
nations [in] the knowledge which they haue in the languages
and letters, Greeke, Arabian, Chaldee, and Hebrew" in which
most medical works were written. Particularly true in the mid-
sixteenth century, at the height of the Jewish immigration to
Turkey, this polyglot qualification continued to be helpful to
many Jewish businessmen in the following generations.[74]

Because of their own almost exclusive relations with non-
Muslim traders, many foreign visitors believed, as did William

Lithgow, a Scot traveler who spent many years in the Middle East, that

the whole commerce of all commodities in Turkey is in the hands of Jewes and Christians, to wit Ragusans, Venetians, English, French, and Flamingo who so warily manage their business that they enjoyed the most profits of any trading there, disappointing the Turks owne subjects of their due, and ordinary traficke.

Outsiders were particularly prone to exaggerate the indubitably existing contacts between the Jews of Salonica, Istanbul, Smyrna, and Alexandria with Venice, and to a lesser extent with Ancona and the rapidly rising Jewish communities of Amsterdam and Leghorn. These contacts were often reinforced by close personal, even family ties, across the boundaries of the various states. We recall the French diplomat's (perhaps Ambassador de Beaurepas') report of 1618 emphasizing the influential role played by the burgeoning Jewish community in Amsterdam, "because they are equally attentive to foreign news and to commerce. . . . In both matters they obtain their information from the other Jewish communities with which they are in close contact. The most important of these is that of Venice, . . . because it unites the West with the East and the South through the community of Salonica, which is the leading center for these other parts of the world." In this connection the French diplomat reported to his king about secret sessions allegedly held every Sunday in the home of the local rabbi by the Jewish businessmen of Amsterdam with Jewish envoys from Venice and Salonica. Here the representatives of the Jewries residing in three leading centers of the Levant and Atlantic trade allegedly exchanged their information about the latest events and trends affecting business in their respective areas so that they could take early action in the markets of the three cities, ahead of their Christian and Muslim competitors. Both these reports were premature because Amsterdam Jewry had just begun taking its place within the business community of the Dutch metropolis and the need of more reliable information about the general trade between Amsterdam and the Ottoman Empire arose only after the first Ottoman–Dutch treaty of 1612. The role of the Jews, both as individuals, and as members of the Dutch Levant Company founded in 1625, was still very limited throughout the first half of the seventeenth century. Similarly, the slowly developing trade between Hamburg Jewry and Salonica or Smyrna also was but a minor factor in the imports and exports of the Ottoman Empire. When as early as 1615 an Istanbul "Hakham" Bensur sought to obtain a shipment of arms through a relative in Hamburg, the German emperor forbade such assistance to an enemy power.[75]

Exchanges with Venice, however, were very ramified and profitable to both cities. According to contemporary information, the Republic of the Lagoons kept no less than 4,000 representatives in the Turkish possessions during the second half of the seventeenth century. At the same time the nascent Jewish and Marrano community of Venice maintained numerous personal relations with its coreligionists in the leading centers of Ottoman commerce, especially Salonica. Their role in Venice itself was so great that, when on July 8, 1550 the Venetian Senate voted by a large majority to expel all Marranos, it elicited sharp protests from among the leading merchants of the city. Remarkably, despite the strong pro-business orientation of the Venetian ruling class, these protests were officially disregarded, but they probably helped to reduce the effectiveness of the decree's implementation. Once again the irate Venetian patricians responded, as we recall, to the Cyprus war with Turkey, at least in part initiated by Don Joseph Nasi, by attempting not only to expel all professing Jews but also to confiscate the vast holdings of goods by Turkish Jewish merchants located in Venice. At that time, the Salonican leaders tried to secure the intervention of an apparently highly influential Jewish agent, Ḥayyim Ibn Saruk, in Venice to obtain the release of their goods in return for a very profitable commission of 50 percent of their value. This time the implementation of the decree was delayed long enough for the peace treaty concluded by the two powers with the direct participation of Solomon Ashkenazi to cause the Venetian authorities to change their minds. Thenceforth the business relations between the two cities and the other emporia on both sides continued unhindered by major anti-Jewish actions of the Venetian authorities.[76]

Nevertheless, the total amount of the Turco-Venetian trade

was in constant decline as a result of both the political disorders in the Empire and the general rise of the West-European powers. The retreat of the Italian merchants in their competition with the French, English, and Dutch traders was accelerated after 1650. This retrogression is well illustrated by the following statistical compilations of the export and import data for 1687 and 1710. They show that in 1687 Venice still had the largest imports from Turkey, then valued at 283,200 piasters, but its exports to the Empire had fallen to second place with merchandise estimated at 366,900 piasters. Twenty-three years later the City of the Lagoons sank to fifth place with its exports of £246,000 sterling (no estimates are given for the 1710 imports). At the same time England, which in 1687 had held the third place with exports totaling 302,743 piasters and played but a minor role with a value of a mere 10,000 piasters in imports, in 1710 climbed to first place with exports estimated at £4,184,000 sterling. In other words Venice, which for generations had been the leader in Western exports to the Ottoman Empire, now shipped goods valued at but 6 percent of those exported by England. It was also outstripped by Holland, France, and even Leghorn, a relative newcomer among the great Mediterranean emporia.[77]

In the meantime, some Ottoman Jews were able to participate also in the resuscitation of the Ottoman trade with the Indian subcontinent. To be sure, the old Jewish role in the trade with India, especially from Egypt (about which we expect to learn more from the vast amount of the pertinent Genizah material assembled by S. D. Goitein in his eagerly awaited and long-delayed publication) could not be repeated particularly after the Turks' two unsuccessful sieges of Diu in 1538 and 1545, where in 1509 a Mameluke fleet had been defeated by the Portuguese admiral Francisco de Almeida. Yet there still were some opportunities open for an exchange of goods by Jewish, Arab, and Indian traders, who brought their wares to the Persian Gulf, where the city of Ormuz, then under Portuguese domination, embraced a substantial Jewish community. From a responsum by R. David Ibn abi Zimra we also learn of direct contacts between Syro-Egyptian Jews and the exotic Cochin Jewish community.[78]

Needless to say, much international trade was conducted by

Ottoman Jews also with other countries. We recall the important influence exerted upon Polish-Turkish commerce by Joseph Nasi and his representatives in Lwów. Although the declining prestige of Don Joseph at the Porte after the death of his friend, Selim II, and the apparent mismanagement of his firm's affairs in the Lwów office, caused that enterprise to end in failure, the Poles still entertained some expectations of benefits accruing from the mediation of Sephardic Jewish settlers from the Balkans. The Polish invitation to Turkish Jews to settle in Zamość opened up new vistas for an expansion of the commercial relations between the two countries. But the time was no longer propitious in view of the incipient decline in the political and military power of both countries. Exchanges with Austria, on the other hand, suffered from the absence of populous Jewish communities on the Austrian side while the almost constant wars between the Osmanlis and the Habsburgs interfered with whatever commercial exchanges existed between the two empires. Similarly the few Jews returning to Marseilles in the seventeenth century began participating in the Levant trade only on a minor scale. At the same time the flourishing Franco-Turkish trade of the sixteenth and seventeenth centuries required many local intermediaries on the Turkish side, since even in 1698 the total number of Frenchmen living in Salonica amounted to only three individuals, including a consul. Hence, when as far back as the year 1500 three French ships brought cargoes of textiles to the city, they evidently used local merchants, especially Jews, as distributors of these wares. In return, after the establishment, in 1680, of a French consulate in Salonica many Jews enjoyed French "protection" under the "capitulation" system while others secured English, Dutch, or Tuscan protection.[79]

DOMESTIC TRADE

No less significant, though less spectacular and hence less frequently recorded in contemporary consular dispatches and travelogues, was the domestic trade within the Empire. Some of it was interregional and interurban. Even in the trade between Cairo-Alexandria and Aleppo, Istanbul, or Salonica, shipment of passengers and cargoes was usually made by sea, since the cost of transporting cargo from Egypt to the Balkans or northern Syria by ship was sometimes as low as 10 percent of that on camel back. In local trade Jews and Christians excelled in certain specialties. Certainly the sale of wines and other liquors such as *arrack* (usually made of dates) was monopolized by non-Muslims because of the Islamic taboo. We recall the occasional preponderance of Jewish vintners and wine merchants in parts of North Africa, the islands of Rhodes, Chios, and Naxos, and in the Turkish exports to Poland. With the wine trade frequently also went ownership of taverns, although it appears that most innkeepers, especially outside the big cities, were either Greeks, Armenians, or Turks. Because of ritualistic needs Jewish occupations often included, particularly, the management of butcher shops which, at times, also played a considerable role in supplying meats for Istanbul's general population in behalf of the government. The traditional Jewish trade in precious metals and jewelry was symbolized by the propinquity in the capital of the bazaars dealing in these objects to the Jewish quarter (*harat al-Yahud*). In passing, one may mention also the presence of Jewish peddlers in the various provinces of the Empire.[80]

In contrast to modern times, however, the real estate business, in which nineteenth- and twentieth-century Jews excelled in many lands, played but a minor role in Turkish Jewish commerce. Of course, like most other inhabitants, Jews for the most part lived in their own houses or those owned by coreligionists. However, sales and exchanges of houses were made very difficult not only by the denominational segregation of most quarters in the larger cities (only in some of which, like Plevna, are Jews recorded as proprietors of houses in non-Jewish quarters), but also by the strict controls exercised by the Jewish communities for the protection of both owners and tenants against competition by outsiders. We recall a few of the regulations enacted to this effect by the joint action of the various Jewish congregations in Salonica. Based upon the old principle of "acquired rights" (*hazzaqah*) of the existing owners and tenants, the rabbis sharply interfered with the free trade in housing. For one example, a lengthy ordinance, dated Elul

19 [August 26], 1584 and issued by several leading rabbis (Samuel de Medina, Jacob b. Samuel Ṭaiṭaṣaq, Solomon ha-Kohen, David b. Nehemias, and Joseph b. Peraḥiah ha-Kohen), read:

We have noted the great outcry of the proprietors of the *ḥazzaqot* in [leasing] houses, courtyards, and shops about the men who tried to "remove their boundaries" and set their eyes on buying their houses, courtyards, and stalls from the owners; they believe that they did no wrong for they were ready to pay the possessors of these rights an appropriate [compensation for the] value of these rights as indicated by the appraisers. . . . [This violation of the established rights is particularly flagrant] during these days when one cannot turn right or left to rent houses and courtyards. As a result, any displaced person deprived of his acquired right becomes a "fugitive and wanderer" in the land without finding a home. We have decided, therefore, . . . that no Jew, man, woman, adult, or minor, should be allowed to acquire, in whatever form, from either a Christian or a Muslim owner, any house, courtyard, or shop held by a Jew as a *ḥazzaqah* either from inheritance or through the adjudication of a court.

Any violator of that ordinance was to be excommunicated and prevented from occupying such premises at any time in the future. Ordinances of this type were enacted in many communities and clearly hindered any extensive real estate transactions under a free market. The frequencies of fires and plagues causing a mass flight of the population must likewise have discouraged large-scale investment in houses which could suddenly be destroyed or emptied of their inhabitants by such unforeseeable catastrophes. Moreover, the general theory that all land belonged to the sultan opened the gate to much bureaucratic interference. This was particularly the case if an owner died without leaving easily identifiable heirs. According to R. Samuel de Medina, "it is known in this country that if a man dies without children and other [recognized] heirs . . . the royal official in charge immediately after his demise claims that such 'heirless' possessions belong to the monarch; and who is able to argue with such an overpowering claimant?"[81]

The relatively few Jewish speculators with large sums at their disposal had other, more rewarding, opportunities to make quick gains. Although shady business practices like "cornering the market" were from time immemorial frowned upon by the rabbis, direct interventions by the Jewish authorities with such antisocial speculations are rarely recorded. For example, when a Salonican Jew, Yehudah Benveniste, purchased an entire shipload of paper which had arrived from Flanders—evidently in order to sell these goods to the very literate Jewish public at high prices—this transaction must have been particularly galling to the rabbinical writers, such as R. Samuel de Medina. But in his pertinent responsum the rabbi suggested no effective communal reaction nor any request to Turkish authorities to nullify this transaction as a clear violation of the Muslim principle of *hisba* (equivalent of the Western "just price"). Clearly, only a few wealthy Jewish merchants could make such large investments, which contrasted with the very limited funds available to the large majority of Jewish traders—petty shopkeepers, vendors in stalls, or peddlers.[82]

Large investments were also needed in interurban, and particularly in international, trade because of the length of time usually required for delivery, the perilous nature of most long-distance shipments, and the general instability in the circulation of coins. A considerable amount of cash was also required for travel expenses, since many leading merchants personally journeyed from time to time on both purchasing and selling missions. The entire realm was open to Jewish travelers, except for the Arabian peninsula; only large Muslim coffee merchants of Cairo sometimes made several trips to Hedjaz annually. But certain difficulties must have arisen when Jews or Christians were looking for lodging in localities where few, if any, of their coreligionists resided. The *hans* (*funduq*s or *waqala*s) or caravansaries, insofar as they were not preempted by foreign merchants, were apparently open to travelers of all faiths, although some tensions probably arose from time to time among the occupants, about which, however, we learn next to nothing from the sources. For the most part, it appears, Jewish travelers, even if recognized as such—we recall that in North Africa many were not easily identified—probably found some way to stay overnight. It may have been more difficult to escape detection on a lengthy journey on shipboard, or as a member of a caravan, particularly if it consisted primarily of pilgrims to Mecca.[83]

Similar complications may have arisen for Jewish visitors to fairs, which for the most part lasted from eight to fifteen days. Some were held annually for as many as twenty to forty days. At times these lengthy fairs, held in the early autumn, coincided with the Jewish High Holiday season, making it extremely inconvenient for the Jewish traders to be away from their homes. On one such occasion, the Jewish visitors to the large regional fair held annually during the Jewish month of Tishre at Istruma in the district of Kosovo, Serbia, decided to try to induce the managers of the fair to change its traditional date. On Elul 21 (September 9), 1582 they adopted a binding resolution reading:

We the undersigned have noted the great danger arising from coming to the fair of Istrona, particularly since in most years it is held during the period of the New Year, Day of Atonement, and the Feast of Tabernacles. Because of our sinfulness we very often desecrate these holidays, willingly or unwillingly. We have therefore decided that no [Jewish] inhabitant of Monastir, Belgrade or any other locality shall for the next three years from today come [to the fair] unless they assure our persons and goods [of better conditions not specified here] and give us back the shops which we now hold.

This agreement apparently continued beyond the original date. But in 1586 some merchants complained that the boycott was very injurious to them and wished to revoke it. Their change of mind was authorized by R. Samuel de Medina over the objections of the Belgrade rabbi Abraham Soscul. In general, the large international fairs, such as those annually meeting in Cairo, which attracted huge cosmopolitan crowds, were indulgent enough to provide sleeping accommodations, as well as space for displaying merchandise, for non-Muslim arrivals. All such long-range enterprises were quite costly, however. They often required a substantial investment of capital in high-priced merchandise, its transportation over long distances, and the living expenses of the merchants before purchasers were found who, in many cases, may not have paid the full purchase price in cash.[84]

Accumulation of large sums of money by individual Jews and other minorities was handicapped by the extortionist fiscal policies and the invasions into business by an often corrupt bureaucracy. Total confiscation of wealth even if accumulated by high dignitaries, not to speak of members of the tolerated minorities, was far from infrequent. On a more regular basis the confusing variety of governmental imposts, often increased by extralegal payments to the local market police and toll collectors, made accumulation of savings for major investments very difficult. Hence, to secure larger investment capital or to divide the risks, many enterprises were conducted by partnerships which, for the most part, consisted of only two to four partners. As usual, such collaboration often ended in discord and even led to litigation. For this reason we now have the benefit of their having been recorded in one or another inquiry from a rabbinic authority. The same handicaps affected, of course, not only the Greeks and Armenians, the two other leading trading peoples, but also the Arabs, Slavs, and Turks engaged in commerce. Regrettably, all these aspects have rarely been recorded in the extant sources and have even less frequently been as fully investigated as was done, for example, by Robert Mantran for Istanbul in the seventeenth century and by André Raymond for Cairo in the eighteenth.[85]

Another obstacle in the pursuit of profitable business consisted in the frequently sharp competition between the merchants. Intergroup relations, as we have seen in other connections, often left much to be desired. Armenians, Greeks, Slavs, and Jews often resented one another more than they did their Turkish masters. Similar discord existed between the native merchants of various faiths and the European "intruders." While theoretically foreigners were supposed to enjoy fewer rights than the native "protected subjects" (at times they had, indeed, to pay higher customs duties than the *dhimmis*), the spread of capitulations from the late sixteenth century on turned many aliens into members of privileged groups; in some respects, they were better off than even most native Muslims. Being subject to a large extent to the jurisdiction of their respective consuls stemming from their own countries and classes, they possessed in them influential natural protectors whose major business consisted in facilitating their commercial undertakings. In cases of conflict with the native merchants the consuls often served as advocates for their compatriots regardless of the merits of the individual cases. At one point, we learn with amazement, some French merchants, claiming that they were misled by local Jews, suggested to their consul that he persuade the sultan to issue a general decree of expulsion of the Jews from the Empire. Of course, this was mere wishful thinking. At the same time, the presence of a multilingual native population, which included a considerable number of men with expertise in commercial and legal affairs, often proved very helpful to foreign visitors in whatever dealings they engaged in with the local merchants and authorities. In some respects the special legislation, traditionally extended by Islam to the "peoples of the book," became an important tool of international commerce as well, and had a great impact on the mercantile exchanges and even international political relations between the two major sectors of the Mediterranean world.[86]

BANKING, BROKERAGE, AND PROFESSIONS

Moneylending was undoubtedly an important facet of Jewish commercial activity. An unfriendly observer, the Capuchin friar Michel Febvre, who in the latter part of the seventeenth century had spent eighteen years in Turkey, placed banking at the top of the Jewish occupations which he described with considerable venom:

Their [the Jews'] ordinary callings consist in being bankers, changing coins, which they clip and falsify, and lending money on usury. They interweave silk with gold, purchase old goods and sell them as new after having repaired them, serve at customs, or as factors, that is intermediaries in markets; also as physicians, druggists, or interpreters. They do not exercise any other occupations because these are most lucrative and least fatiguing.

Yet, when it comes to detailed knowledge of how their banking business was conducted, we are reduced to a few occasional hints in the available sources. No regular well organized and consistently used ledgers of any Jewish bank in Istanbul or Salonica seem to have been preserved, if they ever were kept by medieval and early modern Turkish Jews. Such relative neglect obviously arose from the general prohibition of charging interest on loans, in which, as we recall, Islamic law went much further even than that of the Jews or Christians.

Hence all sorts of subterfuges had to be used to mask an interest-bearing transaction. For the most part a loan or a sale of merchandise on credit was concealed through entering into the contract an amount larger than was borrowed; it included the interest computed in advance for the duration of the loan. On its expiration the debtor usually paid his creditor a "fee" for its renewal, not construed as an interest payment. Another evasion used by Muslims and Christians, as well as Jews, consisted in forming a purported partnership between the borrower and the lender in which the former guaranteed his partner a certain "profit" from the transaction. The Jewish practice was so prevalent in the West that it became customary for many a pious borrower to mark the bill of exchange with the standard acronym *AŞHI* (*'al şad heter 'isqa*) standing for the formula: "On the basis of the permission of a silent partnership." There also were other methods of evasion to which reference is rarely made in the existing sources.[87]

Nevertheless the need for credit in the relatively complex economy of the Ottoman Empire was undeniable. That is why the various edicts issued by the Porte, even if they were reviewed before their promulgation by the Sheikh al-Islam (the chief ecclesiastical officer of the Muslim population and a member of the royal Council), did not intend to curtail whatever business along these lines was conducted in the capital and in the various provinces. The government realized that capital formation was to be promoted and its fruits made available for productive purposes in industry and commerce. Even agricultural loans were often needed to improve the productivity of the land and of the labor on it. That is why charitable *waqf*s often engaged in moneylending on interest under the usual disguises. Such practices of cash-rich charitable foundations (some were from the outset established by currency donations which often served the donors' convenience and occasionally even profit) could lead to controversies among scholars concerning their ethical aspects. But these usually ended with the *waqf*s continuing with their theoretically sinful proceedings. This situation resembled in many ways the conditions in contemporary Poland, where numerous Catholic churches and monasteries invested their surplus funds in interest-bearing loans to Jewish communities. Under the ever-growing fiscal pressure of the government, the *kahal*s very frequently were forced to keep on renewing these loans in ever larger sums over decades and generations, creating serious problems to both Jews and governments long after the partitions of Poland. On the other hand, in a city like Jerusalem, where there were relatively few other ways of making a living, Jews are recorded to have been major lenders to the proliferating Christian monastic orders, especially the Franciscans.[88]

Because all loans on interest were theoretically forbiddden, there was no official distinction between terms designating excessive and moderate rates of interest—all were called usury: It stands to reason that in periods of rampant inflation or rapid deterioration of the currency the risks for the lenders increased termendously, so that credit was available only at compensatory high rates. But even in ordinary times such rates doubtless varied with the credit worthiness of the borrower, the urgency of his needs, and other economic and psychological factors. On the whole, the recorded rates, mostly entered with Muslim creditors, ranged between 11½ and 12 percent, but they often rose to 15, or 20, and in some cases even to 30, 40, and more percent, charged as parts of normal business transactions. According to Dubrovnik archival documents of 1573, some local Jews borrowed money from Egyptian coreligionists on short-term loans of one to four months at the rate of 40 percent. In Syria Venetian merchants were in 1596 indebted to local Turks for loans contracted at rates ranging from 30 to 40 percent. It is noteworthy that nowhere do we hear of any protests against overcharges by Jewish debtors after the event. Certainly in the numerous published responsa of the Turkish rabbis we find no demand for the nullification of a contract because of the excessive rates of interest charged, be it in outright loans or in sales on credit. More remarkably, in contracts officially recorded by Turkish qadhis in Anatolia, the very heartland of Turkish ethnic concentration, the rates charged are mentioned without much ado. Pertinent archival materials (covering 130 months in 1605–1625) from the Anatolian city of Kayseri were carefully examined by Ronald C. Jennings. They revealed the absence of any compunction on the part of the *shari'a* courts to record the actual rates of interest charged on each loan. They have also shown that:

1. The use of credit was widespread among all elements of the urban and rural society. 2. The supply of capital available for credit was fairly abundant and hence not the monopoly of any small clique of big money lenders. 3. Loans and credit were very much the domain of the Muslim Turkish inhabitants of Kayseri, not the preserve of the local Greek or Armenian Christians. 4. Interest was regularly charged on credit in accordance with the sharia and kanun, with the consent and approval of the kadi's court, the Ulema, and the sultan. 5. A "commercial" or "mercantile" mentality and profit motive permeated all the elements of Kayseri society, not just the people of the bazaars but the rural agas, the Ottoman military class, and the Ulema as well.

The same observation may be made concerning such other Anatolian cities as Karaman, Amasya, and Trebizond. If Jews are not mentioned in this connection, this is probably owing to their very small number in the population of these cities. In Brusa, on the other hand, the locale of a fairly large Jewish community, interest charges may have been camouflaged by proportionately raising the price of an object sold on credit. This procedure may well have applied to an unusual long-term contract between an Armenian seller and a Jewish purchaser. The Jew acquired a quantity of Persian silk for 600 grush by promising to make ten annual payments of 60 grush each to his Persian seller, who presumably resided in Brusa. Percentagewise, however, the Jews probably outnumbered their Christian and Muslim counterparts in extending loans on interest for whatever purpose and under whatever formal disguise, or without it.[89]

Needless to say, some credit was also extended free of charge. This was frequently done by relatives or close friends to help out a person in distress or to help him or her to conclude some profitable business arrangement, to provide a dowry, acquire a house, or to meet a payment due. Sometimes sellers of merchandise were prepared to accept part-payment on the price set by them because the purchaser could or would not pay the full amount. This must have been a common occurrence at fairs, or on other occasions, when deliveries had to be postponed. On still other occasions capitalists extended interest-free loans to dignitaries or even lower officials merely in order to captivate their benevolence, expecting that the particular official's good will might prove useful to them at a later time. We recall examples of such Jewish relationships with Turkish dignitaries in the sixteenth century. Two centuries later we learn from a French consular dispatch (dated Cairo, September 11, 1747) that the Jewish magnate Abraham Serrano, "the richest merchant in Cairo," held at that time bad loans in the amount of 12,500,000 paras owed him by beys who had been killed or had fled during the "recent revolution" [of 1740]. On the other hand, we also hear of 18 Jewish traders in the Egyptian capital who, in 1732, owed 668,951 medins (silver coins) to two French merchants, the brothers Dou. This sum was more than a quarter of all the loans the firm had extended to Cairene debtors who also included seven Syrian Christians, three Armenians, and several Muslims.

Some such unproductive loans were also granted to diplomatic envoys or consuls of foreign powers by Jews and others. Quite possibly some such "loans" were not expected to be repaid—a clandestine form of bribery. In the case of Jewish diplomats like Don Joseph Nasi, interest-free loans even to kings may have been a part of a diplomatic-commercial design. Probably only on such grounds could the kinds of France have obtained loans totaling 150,000 écus from the House of Mendes, resulting in their unwillingness or inability to repay the capital. Their refusal to pay embroiled, as we recall, the two otherwise allied governments in a serious diplomatic controversy. On the other hand, even rich Venice did not always provide its representatives in Istanbul with sufficient funds for carrying on their diplomatic or consular activities. These officials often had to have recourse to moneylenders which led to their subsequent grievances in their reports home. On one occasion the Venetian Baïlo Giacomo Soranzo even complained that the Jews of Pera-Galata refused to pay their *cottimo* (housing tax) for the privilege of securing the Venetian protection against Turkish authorities. However, such moneylending fell outside the domain of purely economic activity and was part of personal or political relations which may merely have complicated the life of those who lent money for profit.[90]

SOCIOECONOMIC TRANSFORMATIONS 257

In any case, there seem to have been few Jewish or other bankers whose business consisted exclusively in extending loans. They usually combined with it some other banking activities such as money changing, accepting and guarding deposits, and the like. By far the majority, moreover, consisted of merchants who combined moneylending with salesmanship, with the regular sales often much more rewarding financially than the possible gains through loans.

Far more numerous was the class of Jewish brokers and agents. These terms cover a wide range of activities in which Jews helped their coreligionists or non-Jews in various pursuits. To them belongs also the large class of dragomans who originally consisted of interpreters equipped with the knowledge of several languages. According to Pierre Belon, "Jews living in Turkey are usually able to speak in four or five languages; many of them know ten or more." They were also familiar with the mores, business usages, and administrative procedures and politics of the country. Before long the foreigners began using the dragomans also as their representatives in conducting commercial or even diplomatic negotiations. To quote their unfriendly observer Michel Febvre again, one notes the undertone of envy in his statement that

they [the Jews] are so adroit and diligent that they make themselves indispensable to everybody. One cannot find any well-to-do family among Turks and foreign merchants which does not employ a Jew in its service be it for appraising merchandise and its quality, for serving as an interpreter, or for giving advice on any other occurrence. They know how to give detailed information about anything that happens in the city, as well as about the location of any particular object, its quality and quantity available for sale or purchase; thus one cannot obtain accurate commercial data except through them. The other Oriental nationalities like the Greeks, Armenians, and so forth, do not possess the same talents and cannot equal their skill. This circumstance forces the merchants to make use of their services no matter how much they may be averse to doing it.

A similar observation was made with reference to the English trade by Dudley North (considered a forerunner of Adam Smith) who commented that "the merchant can no more shake off his Jew than his skin . . . [he] cannot be without a Jew nor change that he hath . . . for they [the Jews] serve in the qual-

ity of universal brokers, as well for small as great things."
North, an informed observer, who spent almost nineteen years
(1662–80) in Turkey and, in contrast to most of his compatriots, mastered the Turkish language, further explained that,
because of the internal Jewish solidarity, no other Jewish broker would accept an assignment from a Frankish merchant, so
long as the first Jew (often accepted by the foreigner by mere
chance) was available. On the other hand, we must bear in
mind that the brokers' remuneration was quite modest. They
often received a fee of but 1 percent of the value of the goods
and one-quarter of one percent of the cash they handled.[91]

The most prestigious among the various types of agents were
the dragomans when they began serving as intermediaries in
negotiations with foreign powers. At first they merely accompanied diplomatic envoys or were sent as messengers trans-
mitting memoranda and other communications to other capitals. For the most part, they had no power to make decisions
on their own but had to refer all matters to higher authorities
at home. In time, however, some of them assumed broader
responsibilities. Certainly when, in 1580, after several years of
negotiations, the dragoman Harem Bey signed in behalf of
Philip II an outline of the Spanish-Turkish armistice, while
Solomon Ashkenazi attached to it his signature in the name of
Murad III, they both thus documented the important role intermediaries had played in the preceding years of protracted
negotiations which had led to the conclusion of that treaty.
Moreover, attending, as they did, in their capacity of interpreters, some of the secret conversations among influential
dignitaries, the dragomans gathered not only interesting gossip but often also vital information which, in all probability,
they could use to their own advantage on later occasions. While
we have no direct evidence of their "leaks," whether given out
with the knowledge of their superiors or as a means of entry
to other influential persons, they began playing a significant
role in the diplomacy of the Middle East. To be sure, we have
no records of Jewish dragomans playing a role similar to those
assumed by David Mavrogonato of Crete in his four missions
to Istanbul during the siege by Meḥmed the Conqueror, the
Jewish diplomats of Suleiman, Selim II, and Murad III in the

sixteenth century, or by the Greeks, Alexander Mavrocordato and the family of Phanariots in the latter part of the seventeenth century. Yet, some of them doubtless contributed greatly to the complicated exchanges and mutual intrigues in the diplomatic corps of Istanbul and elsewhere. At times, however, they may have run into diplomats who were unwilling to listen to their informed advice. For example, Cornelius Haga, the first Dutch envoy after the establishment of close diplomatic relations between the Netherlands and the Ottoman Empire in 1612, in his general parsimony, actually resented the advice of his Jewish broker that he give more expensive gifts to certain Turkish officials. Although the local Jews undoubtedly were better informed about the customs prevailing in the Ottoman capital, the Dutchman rejected the advice given. The English agents, beginning with William Harborne, were for the most part much more flexible, although as we recall Harborne's successor, Edward Barton, was quite inimical to the Jewish advisers of the sultan, an attitude which temporarily accrued to England's disadvantage.[92]

It would lead us too far afield to discuss in any detail the numerous areas of activity in which Jewish agents were engaged. By learning the intricacies of certain commercial usages and noting opportunities opening to themselves, some of them became merchants in their own right, without necessarily abandoning their factorial services. Others, probably the majority, were rather simple intermediaries aiding in minor purchases or sales. At times they served some families of dignitaries by sparing the ladies the necessity of shopping for themselves—which some considered undignified—but rather bringing the goods to their customers for inspection and eventual purchase. We remember that it was this type of intermediation which secured for Esther Kyra the first entry to the sultan's harem and opened for her the opportunities for an influential diplomatic career, although, because of the ever changing constellations at the Court, it ultimately ended in her execution. Generally, however, we know very little about these agents as individuals. Only here and there is one of them referred to by name. For instance, Isaac Cormano, Alvaro Mendes' cousin, mentioned above in connection with a diplomatic mission from Alvaro to England, was also a confidant of Grand Vizier Naṣuḥa for whom he established certain contacts with the Spanish viceroy of Naples, Pedro Tellez y Giron, duke of Ossuna. When Cormano, after completing one of his missions, which included also the ransom of prisoners from corsairs, returned to Istanbul, he found that his patron had been executed (December 28, 1614). Cormano saved himself by going into hiding. Most other agents, mentioned only by name, included the Jew Ephraim who served Grand Vizier Khalil Pasha. Equally unfamiliar to us are the identities of Moshe Eyrusalmista, Emmanuel Pimentel, and the brothers Joseph and Israel Čelebi Alamanogli (Ashkenazi) mentioned in connection with the Dutch embassy. Most remarkably, we also know very little about the details of the agents' remuneration and other financial aspects of their trade. For instance, we are not told whether their commission of only 1 percent of the cost of the merchandise acquired or sold was imposed on both the seller and the purchaser. Occasionally a higher commission of 2½ percent is mentioned. But it is quite possible that the brokers found ways of increasing their revenue at least in more perilous, complicated, or very time-consuming transactions. It also appears that gradually the Jewish agents were losing out in their competition not only with Armenians and Greeks but also with Muslims. Curiously, very frequently it was a Turkish or a Palestinian Muslim who served as a broker in Cairo, whereas men of Egyptian descent appear less frequently in the sources.[93]

Jewish professionals, like their Muslim and Christian counterparts, belonged to two major categories. Some performed functions directly related to their religious and communal life. Not only rabbis, but also cantors and other synagogue officials, as well as writers, poets, and scribes (a profession which included copyists and letter writers), constituted a part of communal officialdom. Many references to them have already been made in the course of our earlier presentation, but the fuller analysis of their functions and socioeconomic standing must be relegated to future chapters dealing with Jewish communal and intellectual life. On the other hand, there were also some professional groups functioning on an interdenominational basis, some of which even formed corporations with a membership of diverse ethnic and religious backgrounds. Most important among them was the medical profession which, in its broader sense, included physicians, surgeons, pharmacists, midwives, and numerous other persons performing health services.

We generally have more information about doctors than about other professionals. In Istanbul, for example, we learn from Evliya Čelebi of the presence of two major groups of physicians in the mid-seventeenth century. One association consisted of 1,000 doctors occupying 700 offices (shops); another counted 700 surgeons with 400 offices. These associations were open to Jews and Christians but only that of the surgeons admitted foreign members. Fuller information is available from some archival documents, especially those analyzed by Ahmed Refik in his comprehensive work on the life of Istanbul. One document dating from the middle of June 1700 gives fairly detailed data about 25 doctors and 28 surgeons. The physicians included 5 Muslims (the official head of doctors among them), 5 Greeks, 1 Armenian, and no less than 13 Jews (one each stemming from the Netherlands and Venice). In other words the Jewish doctors formed a majority. Among the 28 surgeons, on the other hand, there were only 8 Jews as against 4 Muslims, 12 Greeks, 1 Armenian, 1 Frenchman, and 1 Englishman. We have had occasion to refer to some outstanding Jewish doctors in the capital such as Ya'qub of Gaëta, Moses Hamon, Solomon Ashkenazi, and even such ladies as Ashkenazi's wife, Bela. Of course, we have much more information about these leaders, because they played a role also in diplomacy and finance, whereas most other practitioners are completely forgotten. Our general information about the doctors' training, the examinations they had to pass, and their way of securing licenses from the authorities leaves much to be desired. To be sure, there existed in Istanbul an academy—one of seven connected with the Suleimaniye Mosque—which, according to a contemporary record, was devoted "to the noble science of medicine." It is possible that such an academy also admitted non-Muslim students. In general, however, it appears that most doctors and surgeons received their training from older professionals, sometimes their own fathers or other relatives, who may have taught them their profession in hospitals or in private practice. Even the licensing procedure on the part of the government is not quite clear, although it seems to have resembled the long-established practices in the Byzantine and Mameluke Empires. The Ottoman administration was generally very conservative. In a decree of June 1704 the government actually prohibited the prescription of any "new remedies" and the employment of Frankish physicians. Needless to say this prohibition was not always observed by anxious patients and physicians; we have clear evidence for the importation of a variety of drugs from Venice. One may mention here also some Jewish professionals in the entertainment world. They included story tellers, musicians, magicians, and others. As a rule they appeared at Jewish weddings and other festive occasions, but they were also well seen in some Muslim circles, even at the sultan's court. Needless to say, they appealed to different tastes. One such quintet of Jewish artists is graphically described by Stephan Gerlach: "These musicians have already appeared twenty-two times before the sultan. Each time they received sixty ducats. This is almost the best music heard by the monarch."[94]

Nevertheless staunch adherence to tradition, shared by the public at large and aided by the general fatalism of the Muslim majority, must have proved to be a serious obstacle to medical progress such as was taking place in the contemporary Western world. In time Turkish medicine fell considerably behind the Western medical expertise. With the cessation of the large-scale Jewish immigration from the Western lands and the partial reversal to Jewish emigration from the Empire in the seventeenth and eighteenth centuries, the contribution of Jewish physicians greatly diminished. The same undoubtedly held true also for the allied occupations including that of the apothecaries.

TAXATION

Beginning with the crisis of the late sixteenth century, the once prosperous economy of the Ottoman Empire suffered severely from the ever-increasing burden of taxes and a variety of other imposts. To be sure, unlike the situation in the declining Mameluke Empire we cannot speak of an Ottoman "fiscal jungle." The handling of the complicated imperial and provincial revenues and expenditures was on the whole distinguished by its detailed and fairly accurate recording. Its bookkeeping was "conducted in form and technique so clearly that one may contend that the level of its tax accounting did not lag behind anything prevailing in our own time" (C. Lyerer). This statement is borne out by some extant ledgers such as were found in Budapest and carefully edited by Lajos Fckete and Gyula Káldy-Nagy. To be sure, most of such records have suffered from the ravages of time and are irretrievable. Mishaps such as occurred in 1931, when the Turkish Ministry of Finance, ever overburdened and penurious, sold a load of documents to Bulgaria for a pittance (this error was early rectified when the administration realized its enormity) must have passed unnoticed in many other cases. Nevertheless there is a vast amount of material still extant in the Ottoman archives, parts of which have already been subjected to worthwhile imperial and regional studies.[95]

The general rise and fall of the Ottoman economy naturally affected the extent of the fiscal pressures on the population. As long as the Ottoman armies were victorious and expanded the imperial frontiers into newly conquered areas, the campaigns, however costly, largely maintained themselves at the expense of the conquered populations. Quite apart from paying off the soldiers participating in the victorious battles, the booty brought home actually alleviated the general burdens of the Treasury. While domestic affairs required ever-greater expenditures by the central organs, these could more or less easily be covered by the revenues collected from the constantly advancing economy. By the end of the sixteenth century, however, the great Ottoman steamroller was checked in the West and gained little financial profit from advances in the East into the scorched lands abandoned by Persia, while retreats were as a rule very costly. The maintenance of the ever-increasing court personnel, lay and military, as well as of the provincial and local bureaucracy, combined with the growing quest for luxuries imported from the West, could be met only by tightening the screws on the tax-paying population. The frequent domestic disturbances, whether man-made or caused by fires or plagues, likewise caused recurrent fiscal shortages which led to searches for new sources of revenue, the collection of which was often costly in itself and prone to be less and less productive in the long run. These untoward developments were further aggravated by the extralegal or downright illegal actions of both the military and bureaucratic apparatus of the government. We recall the numerous acts of oppression from which Palestinian and other Jewries suffered, along with their fellow citizens of other faiths, at the hands of ruthless and corrupt officials. The taxes were often imposed with no consideration for the taxpayers' ability to pay, but rather in proportion to the weakness of their resistance to the intensity of the governmental pressures.[96]

The increasing variety and unpredictability of new imposts was further aggravated by questions raised about their legality. Some pietists actually argued that only "canonical" taxes—that is, those established in the early Islamic tradition of the Qur'an and *hadith*—were legally valid. All subsequent innovations, like other *bid'ah*s, were illegal and represented an uncalled-for exploitation of the weak public. Such scruples were actually shoved aside in practice, as they were in the case of the *devshirme* institution with respect to the forcible conversion of child prisoners. It was clear to most thinking persons that an empire run under the primitive taxation system of the first centuries of the Muslim calendar could not last very long. But there still remained significant differences between the spirit and letter of the published laws by the *qanunname*s promulgated by Meḥmed the Conqueror or Suleiman the Lawgiver, and their actual application. Frequently the tax collectors gave the provisions of these laws the broadest possible interpretation. Even if occasionally overruled by the qadhis acting on petitions by injured parties, such interpretations often become established precedents for future action. As far as the minorities were concerned the greatest danger loomed from the local fiscal administrators who ruthlessly grabbed as much revenue as they could beyond the limitations of the existing laws.

The bureaucratic excesses are well illustrated by Aḥmed I's "Justice Decree" of 1609 which tried to pacify the spreading popular malaise. The sultan scolded the Anatolian and Rumelian military commanders and judges:

You are not making the rounds of your provinces doing your duties. Instead you are going around taking money from the people unlawfully. And it has been brought to my attention that during these so-called "patrols" which you are making for this purpose accompanied by unnecessary numbers of cavalrymen you are committing the following abuses: If somebody falls out of a tree you make this out to be a murder, you go to a village, settle down, and in order to rout out the supposed killer you harass the people by putting them in irons and beating them. Finally besides taking hundreds of gold or silver pieces as "blood money," you collect from the villagers free of charge as a so-called "requisition" horses, mules, slaves, barley, straw, wood, hay, sheep, lambs, chickens, oil, honey and other things to eat.

While these censures applied primarily to the collectors' overweening behavior in villages, they also indirectly illustrated the frequent abuses in towns and cities. The situation was doubtless even more intolerable in such distant provinces as semi-independent Algeria, where the controls of the central government were very weak. According to the personal observations of the local Jewish chronicler, Abraham Gavison (Gabishon), the local despots of Mustaganem and Tlemcen, "slaves of slaves of the Turks," selected two or three Jewish leaders at their pleasure and forced them to exact an enormous variety of payments beyond the possible endurance of their communities.[97]

Research into the operations of the Ottoman fiscal system is also impeded by its great diversity, both territorially and chronologically. Because of its reverence for tradition, the Ottoman regime often respected the existing methods of taxation in the various areas occupied by its troops. It imposed upon them only its basic, though often superficial, uniformity demanded by its overall administrative centralization. Egypt, for example, which had inherited from ancient times a peculiar kind of state capitalism, retained many earlier procedures even after the Ottoman conquest of 1517 and the reforms introduced seven years later by its viceroy, Grand Vizier Ibrahim. As a result the Egyptian wali enjoyed many prerogatives denied to the beglerbegs in other provinces. On the other hand, the Balkan *sanjak*s inherited much of their fiscal system from the Byzantine Empire. On its part, Iraq continued to employ some methods established by its former Il-Khan and other Persian rulers. Anatolia, the cradle of the Ottoman Empire, as well as Syria and Hungary, among its youngest provinces, followed somewhat more closely the general centralized patterns, although here, too, many former practices were maintained under the new rulers. For modern research this diversity is further complicated by the concentration of modern historians, in both the successor states of the Empire and in the West, on only certain geographic areas. As a result, Egypt, which was also blessed by the better preservation of its archival resources and a certain stability brought about by the long absence of foreign invaders, benefited from more intensive interest by scholars than other provinces. Among the Balkan countries, modern Bulgarian scholarship has particularly excelled in gathering documentary evidence and publishing many archival collections and valuable analytical studies. Hungary, too, has evinced a sustained interest in its century and a half of Turkish domination and produced a number of penetrating investigations of great value not only for that relatively small Turkish province but also for the entire Ottoman Empire. Above all, understandably, scholarly interest has often been focused on Istanbul with its large population, its imperial court and centralized offices of administration, and its rich archival collections. It is only to be regretted that the periods most intensively studied were those after 1650, leaving the most vital era of Ottoman rise and decline of 1453 to 1650—which is of main interest to our presentation—to play but a secondary role in modern research in the fiscal and economic history.[98]

As far as the minorities were concerned, the Jews, Armenians, and Greeks were particularly concerned about taxes collected in urban areas. At the same time the mass of Slavs, Hungarians, Anatolian Turks, and Syro-Egyptian Arabs happened to be affected most by the rural taxation. While we often speak of Ottoman feudalism, a term emphasized particularly by Marxist scholars, its differences from Western feudalism must not be overlooked. To begin with the feudal landlords enjoyed much less independence from the central power than their European counterparts, who often behaved like sovereigns of the territories under their control. Nor were the Ottoman peasants in any way "serfs" of the type prevailing among European villagers who were attached to the soil without freedom of movement. In fact, some of the greatest Ottoman demographic changes, also resulting in major economic and political transformations, originated from the excessive immigration of peasants into cities throughout the Empire. However, as long as they lived in their villages they were subject to larger payments in cash and in kind to their immediate lords than they might have been while facing the imperial tax collector. Corvée labor was also performed for the landlord rather than for the central regime. Even the recruitment of the peasants for military service was conducted under the guidance of the landlords, the *sipahi*s. Jews seem to have played a minor role in the rural fiscal systems, except indirectly as artisans or peddlers supplying goods to both masters and villagers. Occasionally they also served as advisers to the lords of the *timar*s. The urban imposts, on the other hand, deeply affected the Jews, Greeks, and Armenians particularly through their enormous variety and general efficiency in collections. For example, the Turkish *muḥtasib,* the official who was at first functioning merely as supervisor of morals and then became the chief superintendent of markets, had under his control in Istanbul no less than six different categories of imposts, as analyzed by Robert Mantran. These imposts represented, however, only a fraction of the taxes collected from the urban population. For example, there was a curious tax *tefavlet* (differential) which consisted of the reduction of payments owed to merchants and others by the government to the tune of 1 asper out of 41, or almost 2½ percent of the amount due. One is astounded by the ingenuity of the Turkish fiscal authorities in inventing ever-new sources of revenue, an ingenuity undoubtedly matched by the tax farmers who became the main governmental arm for securing the actual collections. During the great financial crisis which began around 1590 and the disorders generated by the governmental weakness in the face of soldiers' rebellions, the fiscal authorities became ever-more convinced of the advantages to them of the *iltizam* system, that is by entrusting the collection of special imposts to financially gifted individuals—mostly Christians or Jews—against the payment of an annual agreed-upon lump sum. Of course, this arrangement opened the gate to many abuses on the part of the tax farmers and their subordinates. Although generally these *mültezims* were able to collect more than their due and thus make a substantial profit, there were some years, especially following some catastrophic events like plagues or fires, during which the receipts fell below their own stipulated payments. In such cases many a tax farmer, threatened by severe penalties for nondelivery (sometimes torture or even decapitation), would ask for a rebate or, if refused, for a loan from the government. This was a no less risky expedient, for failure to repay the loan on time likewise entailed severe penalties.[99]

Most of these taxes were of a general nature and were officially imposed upon all subjects alike. In some cases, however, where religion played a part, there undoubtedly were opportunities for discrimination against the *dhimmi*s. For example, the special tax collected from funerals, as it was practiced with respect to Jews in Palestine, was subject to willful discrimination and frequent abuses of power. According to the existing regulations each family was supposed to report without delay the demise of its head. Thereupon either a Treasury official or the tax farmer appeared on the scene, tried to collect information about the entire estate left behind by the deceased and, in the absence of direct descendants, tried to confiscate as much of the property as possible. These investigators often completely disregarded the long-established regulation that relatives, however distant, and in their absence the religious community to which the deceased had belonged, were the legitimate heirs of the entire estate. As we recall, R. Samuel de Medina observed, "it is known in this realm that if a man has no children or designated heirs . . . the government officials of the pertinent office immediately after his death insist that his property belongs to the sultan, for the estate is heirless; and who can argue with so powerful an opponent?" Another set of taxes relating to non-Muslims only was imposed on the manufacture and sale of arrack (a rum-like drink mostly made of dates). Since intoxicating drinks were forbidden to the Muslims, the government considered it improper to collect revenue from that "sinful" trade, if engaged in by Muslims. The size of this impost, thus limited to Christians and Jews, was likely to be raised arbitrarily by both legislation and excessive collections. In the eighteenth century, the Egyptian Janissaries alone collected annually 3,500,000 paras from this source.[100]

Most important and permanent among the special imposts on the religious minorities was the capitation tax (*jizya* or *jeliya*). Going back to the very beginnings of Islam and included in 'Umar I's treaty with the surrendering Christians in Jerusalem in 636 C.E., this tax was one of the most enduring accompaniments of Jewish and Christian life in Islamic countries. The original law attributed to 'Umar, which set a tax of four gold dinars for the rich taxpayers, two dinars for the middle class, and one dinar for the poor (with numerous exemptions), remained basically intact in various countries through the Middle Ages and early modern times. In general, this tax was uniformly imposed upon all *dhimmi*s, but as usual there were frequent exceptions. For instance, in the province of Damascus, the corresponding computation of gold coins into aspers was increased by an additional 5 aspers for Christians and 10 aspers for Jews. The pertinent sixteenth-century regulation (*qanunname*) does not mention the occasion on which this discriminatory treatment was first introduced. In the Ottoman Empire the *jizya* was originally intended to be used primarily for pious purposes, such as pensions to be paid to religious or meditating Muslim persons. It thus relieved the Treasury from financial burdens, since before the mass conversions to Islam, its yield must have contributed a good deal to public finance. In Egypt, it was still considered in Ibrahim's reform in 1524–25 as sufficiently promising for him to provide that, after covering the expenditures for pensions, the balance should be paid to the Treasury for general purposes. Before very long, however, it turned out that this tax yielded less than was necessary for the pensions, creating annual deficits which ranged from 194,522 paras in 964 A.H. (1556–57 C.E.) to 336,000 paras fourteen years later. Such deficiencies doubtless continued in the following decades, although the budget of 1039–40/1630–31 showed that the imperial revenue from the *jizya* collected in the European provinces (Rumelia), Cyprus, Moldavia, Walachia, and Anatolia had reached the large sum of 15,760,385 aspers or over 5.6 percent of the total revenue. In general, such deficits had to be covered by the Treasury. Indirectly perhaps the tax collectors were able to persuade the religious leaders in charge of collecting the *jizya* from the taxpayers to make up for these deficits out of their communal treasuries. As we shall see, these communities had a taxation system for their own needs in which the three classes of taxpayers were less mechanically divided by their tax assessors. They eliminated some poor taxpayers altogether and distributed the entire amount due among the better situated members through individual assessments. A complete revision of the *jizya* system was introduced by Grand Vizier Köprülü Zâde Pasha in 1694 and gradually implemented in the various provinces; in Egypt as late as 1734.[101]

There were certain peculiarities with the capitation tax which differed from all other imposts. From the outset this tax was considered as being more of a ransom for the right given to each individual to live as an "infidel" in the Muslim world, rather than a mere tax arbitrarily imposed by a government which could be revoked or modified at will. Its purpose, too, was intended to be kept outside the normal boundaries of the fiscal administration. It was paid to a special official, emin-i Jevali (a term borrowed from the concept of "wanderer") and destined to be used mainly for the aforementioned charitable pensions, and later expanded to include also orphans and widows, and even other poor. To be sure, the term "poor" was much more rigidly applied in both East and West in early modern times than it is in the United States today, with the relatively high "poverty levels" established by law. On the basis of the American criteria, even if computed by the respective purchasing power of their currencies, one would have had to place more than 90 percent of the Ottoman population in the category of "poor." The adherence to the original scale of one to four gold pieces must also have played havoc with the orderly disbursement of the charitable donations because of the changing values of the *sultanyas* or the Venetian ducats in relation to the aspers or paras in which the general taxation was computed in Rumelia or Egypt. On the other hand, the government enjoyed here the unusual cooperation of the taxpayers themselves, inasmuch as the religious minorities often felt, and were repeatedly told so by the Muslim leaders, that it was only owing to their payment of that regular impost that they enjoyed the toleration by any Muslim regime. The Mameluke system, however, of issuing to each taxpayer receipts attesting that he had paid the tax, and the threat of instantaneous arrest of a person failing to show his certificate on the demand of the authorities, seems not to have been continued even in Egypt under Ottoman rule. Incidentally, in view of the force of tradition the *jizya* did not materially change in size, except for the adjustments caused by the fluctuation of the currencies. It is possible in this way even to measure the various ups and downs in the prosperity of a Jewish community and its general decline in the seventeenth century. For instance, in Brusa in 1568–89, among Jewish payers of the capitation tax, 48 percent were assessed at the highest rate, 31 percent were in the middle bracket, and only 21 percent paid the minimum. More than a century later (in 1688–89) the respective ratios were 11, 54, and 38. It is, of course, possible that this discrepancy was partially the result of less efficient collections, or more successful tax evasion by the rich. But although we hear in Brusa more complaints about tax evasions than about excessive taxation (which may not be true of other communities), it does reveal the deterioration of the Jewish status, also reflected in the general diminution of the Jewish population.[102]

Independently important was the wide range of customs duties imposed on all imports not only from foreign countries but frequently also from one province to another. They were at times collected successively by several cities or customs stations often located at short distances from one another. They thus resembled medieval and modern excise taxes imposed in Europe by local legislation, although here they were part of the imperial system intended to benefit the central Treasury at large or a particular provincial administration such as that of the Egyptian *wali* (viceroy). In fact, such an important customs station as that of Suez, where most of the duties on spices and other goods brought from India and other eastern lands were collected, was not run by officials residing in that city. They had to be called in from Cairo upon the arrival of the ships or caravans, including large ones consisting of up to 2,000 mules or camels. One can readily imagine the inconvenience to travelers and importers who had to wait for the arrival of the Cairo collectors who appraised the incoming goods and assessed their value and duty. Subsequently the cargoes were reloaded for shipment to Cairo and time and again transferred to other vehicles before they reached their ultimate destination. Such a procedure was not only costly in time and repeated tolls, but also depended on the various collectors' whims. The size of the duties, too, differed from period to period and from one station to another, although all of them were supposedly centralized under the Istanbul Treasury. In addition the Janissaries and other leaseholders (*mültezim*s) secured further payments from a "protection tax" they forced upon the owners and their goods. Jews, like the other minorities, were on the whole subjected to higher duties than the Muslim subjects. Taking over the scale recorded in the Mameluke Empire, Suleiman the Magnificent provided for the following differentials: Muslims were to pay 3 percent *ad valorem,* native Christians and Jews 5 percent, and foreigners up to 10 percent. This scale was not rigidly adhered to, however; it also was easily subject to evasion. Foreign exporters often shipped their merchandise under the names of Turkish Muslims, Jews, or Christians. In the seventeenth and eighteenth centuries the Dutch and English traders, especially, used their contacts with Leghorn, a major center of Jewish participation in the Levant trade, to register their shipments under the name of a Turkish Jewish merchant, often a relative of their Leghornese Jewish correspondents. Moreover, as most collectors of customs duties throughout the ages, these officials often faced importers trying to undervalue their dutiable merchandise. We even know of a Jewish community which compromised with the local customs collectors so that its members would pay 2 (instead of the required 5) percent in return for a guaranteed *honest* declaration of the value of the articles imported.[103]

We hear relatively few complaints of anti-*dhimmi* discrimination in the collection of customs duties. In this area Jews to some extent enjoyed a privileged position. The prevailing road toll charge was 8 aspers for Christians, 6 aspers for Jews, while Muslims paid less or nothing at all. Customs duties naturally varied, according to the objects imported, but in Bernard Lewis's summary:

There were basically three rates—the lowest for the Muslims; the intermediate rate for dhimmis . . . and the highest for *harbis*, i.e. foreign non-Muslims coming from the *Dār al-Ḥarb*. . . . It would seem that in Ottoman practice Muslims and Jews enjoyed the benefits of the lower or intermediate rates irrespective of whether they were Ottoman subjects or not. Christians paid the intermediate rates if they were Ottoman subjects, and the highest if they were foreigners.

Foreign Jewish importers (doubtless a small minority) were apparently treated in this respect like their Christian counterparts. However, this procedure underwent great changes after the spread of the system of capitulations, when in accordance with the respective treaties, "protected" foreigners often enjoyed preferential treatment. In contrast, in the most important emporia, such as Salonica, Istanbul, Smyrna, Alexandria, and Cairo, the actual collection of the duties was for the most part entrusted to Jews, Copts, or other Christians. This was accounted for by the very nature of the customs' administration. Originally intending to channel most of their receipts to the central Treasury, the Porte early realized that it could not handle the orderly collection of the complex duties over the Empire's far-flung boundaries as well as at the various customs stations within the country. In their general liberality the sultans sometimes transferred the entire collection of duties in a particular district as a feudal *timar* to a high official in recognition of the services he had rendered to the Crown. More frequently, many such stations were given over to a powerful recipient (or a group) in the form of an *iltizam* (tax farm), which meant that the leaseholder in charge of the station collected all duties under the condition that he pay a fixed amount to the Treasury. Ultimately, despite the constant increase in tolls—that on the growingly significant import of coffee rose in the latter half of the seventeenth century to 14 and, later at times even to 18 percent of their value—the Treasury received no more than between one-sixth and one-quarter of that revenue.[104]

In Egypt, according to Stanford J. Shaw, the general imperial system underwent some major changes in 1608–1609. To satisfy the viceroy the entire administration of the customs was given him as an *iltizam* in order to supplement his revenues from other sources. He in turn handed over the actual management to Jewish or Christian tax farmers. In 1671–72 the entire revenue from customs was seized by the Janissaries who paid only a fixed amount to both the *wali* and the Treasury. However, "Jewish traders continued to administer the customs for the Janissaries as *mu'allem*s until 'Ali Bey's rise to power in 1763, when they were for the most part supplanted by Copts." (This has been but a part of 'Ali Bey's ruthless anti-Jewish policy.) The Janissaries were thus able to maintain their control through most of the seventeenth and eighteenth centuries because of the general fear, in Cairo as well as in Istanbul and other major cities, of their bloody uprisings. The agas of the Janissaries or parallel military commanders of other troops, however, were seldom fit to administer the necessary financial operations, which required an extensive knowledge of the great variety of imported goods, as well as of the coins used for the payment of duties. They usually handed the actual exercise of that power to Jewish and, to a lesser extent, to Christian entrepreneurs. A curious illustration is offered by the dispatch sent on January 22, 1742, by Everard Fawkener, the English resident in Istanbul, to the Foreign Office. We are told that the servant of one such agent, called Bazargan Bashi, had once been seized by the vizier's men for some transgression he committed with respect to his attire. He was immediately removed from the vizier's control, however, on the order of the aga of the Janissaries. Thereupon the matter was dropped because "it is not easy to imagine the credit this Jew Agent of the Janissaries has in that body. He disposes of all Offices, and applications are made by the pretenders to him." The agent simultaneously held also the position of "Honorary British

Druggoman." The great power thus acquired by the Jewish agents of the Janissaries accrued directly to the advantage of the Jewish communities at large by providing a livelihood to many of their coreligionists serving as their employees. Yet it made them all wholly dependent on the good will and whims of the Janissary agas and their military associates. At the same time this system also evoked much envy and resentment among the masses of taxpayers and consumers who felt oppressed and overcharged by the Jewish collectors rather than by their Muslim masters. Sometimes one or another Jewish merchant lost his life because of some differences of opinion with his superiors. For instance, in 1697 Yusuf al-Yahudi, "the all-powerful customs farmer" (called Leon Zaphir in French consular dispatches) was arrested and, without trial, executed. More remarkably, in 1712 the entire Jewish community of Alexandria was fined 5,000,000 paras because of the alleged transgressions of some of its tax-farming members.[105]

MILLET SYSTEM

Jewish self-government and its relation to the Muslim state have frequently been referred to in our previous chapters. On the other hand, the internal operations of the Jewish communities will have to be further elaborated in the next volume in connection with our treatment of the Jewish community organization and its institutions throughout the Jewish world of the period. Hence, we must limit ourselves here to a few highlights of the developments during the Ottoman expansion in the fifteenth and sixteenth centuries, as well as of the incipient manifestations of external and internal deterioration in the critical decades of 1590 to 1650.

In its treatment of minorities the Ottoman Empire inherited many existing traditions and institutions from its predecessors, particularly the Byzantine and Mameluke empires. The Muslim rulers were also bound by the basic legislation in the *shari'a* going back to the Qur'an and the *hadith*. However much the medieval Muslim states adjusted the fundamental Islamic law to the imperatives of changing circumstances, they could not abandon the principle itself not only of tolerating Jews and

Christians, but also of granting them a considerable measure of self-determination in matters relating to their faiths and the observance of their rituals. On the whole, while conquering various provinces from Byzantium and other countries, they generally maintained the status quo of the ethnoreligious groups then living in these areas. Perhaps mindful of the Qur'anic saying: "And we have made you into peoples and tribes," the Turks accepted the presence of a variety of religious and ethnic attitudes as a fact of life.[106]

There were, however, major modifications imposed by the requirements of the new regime. The pressure to establish a comprehensive system of dealing with the masses of the non-Muslim populations became quite urgent after the conquest of Constantinople in 1453. Meḥmed the Conqueror drastically converted his newly depopulated capital into a predominantly Muslim city and attracted many non-Muslim settlers, extending to them a large measure of self-determination. In the new capital, now increasingly known by its Turkish designation, Istanbul, he thus quickly replaced the former inhabitants, who had been killed, taken captive, or put to flight during the siege, by a deliberate repopulation, both voluntary and forcible. His policy of Islamization and Turkicization of the capital greatly reduced the size of the Greek population, whose fidelity the sultan doubted (although there were many Greeks who soon learned to prefer the orderly Ottoman administration to the decaying Byzantine regime) and brought in as many Muslims as possible. To increase the number of new settlers, as we recall, Meḥmed also transplanted a great many Jews from the previously Byzantine areas into the capital. He did not hesitate for this purpose to uproot entire Jewish (including Karaite) communities from both Anatolia and Rumelia. He combined, however, the carrot with the stick and extended to the settlers in his new capital and, indirectly also in his other possessions, many self-governmental privileges. He and his early successors realized that in their vast and growing domain the Turks still were but a small minority living in a sea of Greek, Slavonic, Armenian and Jewish populations. Nor could they view complacently the presence of some Islamic minorities. The Shi'ites, especially, inhabiting many regions along the eastern border, could become a major obstacle to the Empire's pursuit of its eastern expansion into predominantly Shi'ite Kurdistan, and other areas of the Persian Empire, the Ottoman's hereditary enemy. Among all the various minorities the Jews could be considered the most steadfastly loyal to the regime, despite their initial feelings of despondency over being uprooted from their long-inhabited places of settlement and perhaps also because of a certain residual loyalty to the Byzantine Empire and their various regional rulers.[107]

For Meḥmed the most important non-Muslim ethnoreligious group were the Christians. Far-sighted statesman that he was, he realized that the greatest danger to the fidelity of his Christian subjects consisted in the possibility of a reunification of the Greek Orthodox and the Roman Catholic Churches. The idea of their reunion was actively propagated by the Papacy and the Ecumenical Council of Ferrara-Florence in 1438–45, which had concluded its deliberations only eight years before the fall of Constantinople. On the political level the ruling classes of the declining Byzantine Empire saw their salvation in the military intervention of the Western powers which would have been facilitated by such a reunion. The masses of the Byzantine population, however, and the Orthodox clergy consistently favored their cherished ecclesiastical independence from Rome. To nurture that anti-Roman spirit Meḥmed II appointed, as we recall, the anti-unionist cleric Gennadios as patriarch of Constantinople and thus, to all intents and purposes, made him the supreme ecclesiastical chief of all the Greek Orthodox believers. This appointment actually represented an enhancement in the patriarch's stature, since before the fall of Byzantium he had been but a second-ranking official of the Church, which was permanently headed by the Byzantine emperor. Now there was no emperor to interfere—at least not until the rise of the Russian Orthodox Church with the absolutist tsar towering over both the Moscovite patriarch and synod. Further to enlarge Gennadios' authority Meḥmed enthroned him in a spectacular ceremony and extended to him a broad privilege which became the foundation stone of the Greek Orthodox *millet* (a term designating a non-Muslim ethnoreligious group apparently derived from the Aramaic *milta*

= word). In 1461 the sultan extended the same treatment to the Armenians and revived some of their older privileges specifically exempting them from military service and from the payment of ransom for their unbelief in the form of a capitation tax. Before long, as we recall, he also installed a chief rabbi in the person of Moses b. Elijah Capsali. Although Capsali's authority extended formally only over the Romaniot community in Istanbul, his propinquity to the throne and his good personal connections with many of the sultan's advisers secured for him considerable influence over the destinies of all Jewish communities in the Empire.[108]

One could actually contend that the autonomous rights granted to Jews and Christians went further than were those extended to the predominantly Muslim municipalities or to residents and visitors stemming from foreign countries. Turkish municipalities were not governed by elected officials but by *qadhi*s and other bureaucrats appointed by the rulers of the state. Only in larger cities, especially in Istanbul, were the citizens able to pursue semi-independent activities through their numerous corporations acting under the close supervision of governmental officials. Foreigners, too, long enjoyed but limited rights, unless their home countries secured (usually through the threat or use of force) special privileges from the sultans or their Byzantine predecessors, as did the Venetians and Genoese. These privileges often included clauses guaranteeing a measure of self-government to such foreign "colonies." We recall that in the Byzantine Empire even native-born subjects, including Jews, could secure some such rights as so-called "white" Venetians. At the same time the Genoese went even further and indiscriminately admitted natives of their choice to full-fledged Genoese citizenship. Thus the inhabitants of an entire township of "infidels" like Pera-Galata could control their own municipal affairs more freely than their Muslim confreres in the other quarters of Istanbul. Later on under the Turkish regime the system of "capitulations" extended to an ever increasing number of foreign residents the right to have many of their internal affairs administered by their mercantile associations under the laws of their home countries and the direction of their foreign consuls. Ultimately even some native Jews and Christians found the protective laws under the "capitulations" more advantageous in theory, and still more in actual practice, than those of their religious autonomy. At that time many a wealthy and influential Ottoman Christian or Jew lived, indeed, under the protection of both a foreign power and of his particular *millet*.[109]

Unlike the Muslims, the Orthodox, and the Armenians, however, the Jewish minority did not have a centralized ecclesiastical establishment. To be sure, some chief rabbis of Istanbul like Moses Capsali (1453–97), Elijah Mizrahi (1498–1526), and Joseph b. Moses di Trani (Mitrani, 1604–1639), held considerable sway over the Jewish communities throughout the Empire. But they certainly did not have a status comparable to those of the Sheikh al-Islam, the Orthodox or Armenian patriarchs, or even of their own Egyptian *nagid,* an office held by members of the Maimonidean family down to the Ottoman conquest of 1517. The power of the Istanbul chief rabbis derived more from their personal prestige as scholars and leaders than from their office. From the second half of the sixteenth century they also faced the competition of the famed Salonican scholars including Rabbis Samuel de Medina and Joseph Ṭaiṭaṣaq as well as of those residing in Safed and Jerusalem.[110]

For a moment it actually looked as if the Palestinian rabbis would take over the leadership not only of all Ottoman Jewry but also of the Jews throughout the world. R. Jacob Berab, in his day the leading rabbi of Safed, the great center of mystical and halahkic learning, conceived the notion that, in view of the disarray caused by the expulsions of the Jews from western and central Europe and the ensuing scattering of Jewish settlements in the Mediterranean basin, the time had come for resuscitation of the ancient Sanhedrin as a focus of both learning and jurisdiction for world Jewry. As we recall, that institution of seventy (or seventy-one) members had functioned alongside the Second Temple of Jerusalem and, a long time after its fall, served as the supreme tribunal and the highest academy of learning for Jews in the Holy Land as well as in the dispersion. But in the subsequent decline of Palestine as a center of Jewish life, the weakened autonomous Jewish community had to abandon even the practice of the ancient form of ordination. Although Judaism never had sacraments of the kind of observed in the Catholic Church, it attached to the ordination conferred by one ordained person on another from generation to generation (adopted as the "Apostolic succession" by canon law) a semi-sacramental character endowed with some special grace divine. Since membership in the Sanhedrin depended on one's previous ordination, the entire institution went out of existence. It even appeared that, once the succession had been broken, there was no way to restore it. However, Berab and his associates believed that, in the light of the high prestige enjoyed by the authorities of Safed, a change of succession could be reestablished by his being "ordained" formally through a consensus of his colleagues. He subsequently ordained some of his outstanding disciples including R. Joseph Karo, author of what was to become the leading code of Jewish law, the Shulḥan 'Arukh. The pupils were in turn to ordain other scholars of great distinction until the number of ordained rabbis would reach the required number of seventy (or seventy-one), whereupon a new Sanhedrin could be convoked. That institution would subsequently serve as the final court of appeals and as a substitute legislative body for the dispersed Jewish communities the world over. This scheme, if brought to a successful conclusion might in many ways have altered the course of Jewish history in the following centuries. However, the entire undertaking was quashed by the rabbinate of Jerusalem, led by R. Levi Ibn Ḥabib, partly because of serious legalistic objections and partly because of personal and interurban rivalries between Jerusalem and Safed. Remarkably, the chief rabbinate of Istanbul did not even play any role in this controversy, simply because the prestige of its occupants hardly equaled that of these two protagonists and their associates. Similarly the position of the chief rabbi versus the throne largely depended on the individuals concerned. The assumption, often repeated in the historical literature, that every occupant of the Istanbul chief rabbinate automatically held a seat in the imperial Diwan (the royal cabinet), according to some chroniclers even ahead of the Orthodox Patriarch, is not sustained by any reliable Turkish or other historical evidence.[111]

In contrast with the more thoroughly organized Churches, the Jewish communities laid their main stress on the individual unit, the congregation. In fact, going beyond the practice established in the other Diaspora communities, including the Byzantine and Mameluke empires, the basic autonomy related to the congregation rather than to the community at large. For a long time Turkish Jewry actually applied to individual synagogue groups the talmudic dictum that one town ought not to dictate to another. This departure from long-standing precedents in Jewish law and practice stemmed from the large number of new congregations established during the Sephardic mass migrations of the sixteenth century. These congregations for the most part hailed from different regions of the Iberian Peninsula in addition to some groups established from time to time by Hungarian and other Ashkenazic Jews. Since each of these regions had developed certain specific practices, rituals, and had introduced some minor liturgical variations into their prayer books, their offshoots preferred to continue life in the Middle East along their peculiar traditional lines.

Nonetheless, in everyday life they also had many interests in common. Certainly, in their dealings with the Ottoman authorities their negotiators carried much more weight if they represented an entire community rather than its individual subgroups. At times even a large community like that of Salonica had to dispatch delegations to the capital to deal with the central authorities. Their success or failure often depended on the help they could obtain from highly placed coreligionists in Istanbul, as was shown by the aforementioned felicitous mission of Moses Almosnino in the sixteenth century and the tragic outcome of the Salonican delegation's quest to obtain some relief from the increasingly unsustainable "garment tax" in the seventeenth century. There also were economic problems requiring united action. We recall the ordinances issued by the Salonican and other communities to prevent Jews from overbidding one another in the renting of dwellings or in securing brokerage employment from either the government or major tax farmers. To be at all effective such ordinances had to be issued by the leaders of all, or most, local congregations in a joint proclamation and to be backed up by sanctions, spiritual or financial, enforced by them on a community-wide basis. Of course, at times some interested minorities objected to such joint decisions. But public opinion generally agreed with R. Samuel de Medina's statement (issued in connection with the location of a hostelry for poor transients to be built in Patras):

It is my judgment that once the majority of the men of the town agreed upon the selection of a place, all others must abide by their decision. . . . The great halahkists such as Maimonides, Ibn Adret, and the Rosh [R. Asher b. Yeḥiel] have all agreed on the principle that, when the majority of members of a community enact ordinances pertaining to communal affairs, the dissenting minority must accept their decision. For, unless we adhere to this principle no community would ever agree on any action.

R. Samuel went even so far as to insist that the majority had the right to enforce its will—if necessary by appealing to non-Jewish courts. Needless to say, it often depended on the prestige of the ordaining leaders, particularly the rabbis, whether the minorities yielded and whether the ordinances thus enacted had a long-lasting life. In more far-reaching undertakings, on the other hand, when agreements among many communities were needed, common action could more easily be impeded by a determined dissenting group. We recall how, for example, the ambitious 1555 boycott of Ancona and other papal possessions in retaliation for the burning of twenty-three Marranos, initiated by Gracia Mendes in cooperation with many rabbinic and lay leaders, was frustrated by the sharp dissent of a faction headed by R. Joshua Soncino of Istanbul. Over a long period, however, there was a gradual amalgamation of the respective congregations; it proceeded far enough for the original topographical divisions to lose ground and to leave the large, as well as the smaller, communities divided mainly along such major lines as Romaniot, Sephardic, and Ashkenazic Jews (in addition to the Karaite and Samaritan groups), with the Sephardim gradually achieving an undisputed hegemony over the entire Jewish communal life.[112]

Unity of action was sometimes determined by the institutional structure of the community itself. In the aforementioned example of the hostelry in Patras no one argued in favor of separate hostelries being established by each of the four congregations of the city, a procedure which a community of Patras' size could not possibly afford. Even the much larger and wealthier community of Salonica found that united action of all congregations was imposed by its very growth. The larger the Jewish majority in the city became and the more residential space it required, the more awkward became the talmudic prohibitions of carrying objects on a Sabbath from private into public property and vice versa. To facilitate the inhabitants' mobility, the Talmud itself had established the institution of 'erub, a symbolic act, such as stringing wire over many streets to maintain the fiction that the whole city was controlled by the united community. Hence negotiations were conducted with the governmental authorities in behalf of all congregations and the pertinent contract was signed in the name of them all. More importantly, the community early found it more opportune to establish a joint Talmud Torah school, an institution which later achieved great fame through its distinguished library and its fine educational program.[113]

Needless to say, these Salonican agreements did not prevent many individual synagogues from setting aside certain chambers open for study groups of adults or for any of their rabbis leading a yeshivah (a school of higher learning) of his own. But as we shall see in another connection many broad educational regulations were adopted, for the most part, for an entire city or even province. In matters of taxation, too, both united governmental and communal actions were often indicated. Certainly, all congregations wished to persuade the authorities to grant their rabbis, and even nonprofessional scholars devoting all their time to study, an exemption from the capitation tax. This privilege was to parallel that granted to the often state- or waqf-supported Muslim full-time devotees to "meditation." Otherwise the communities sometimes made up the arising deficiency in the state's revenues from their own funds. They did the same for the very poor members from whom some exacting tax farmers sought to collect the minimal poll tax of a gold piece required by law. On the other hand, we shall also see that charities which were left in the domain of the religious groups were often administered by the individual congregations or by some of the philanthropic societies under their control. In fact, R. Isaac Adarbi defined a congregation as being an organization "which has elders, a burial society, and collects philanthropic funds."[114]

In general, the democratic principle of majority rule, already preached in the Bible, had to allow for certain exceptions. For example, the theory that congregational prayers are substitutes for the regular sacrifices (*temidim*) offered at the Temple of Jerusalem, attributed to the cantors and other leaders in divine services the role of *shelihei sibbur* (representatives of the public) before God. Hence, in the election of cantors even a minority of one worshiper who rejected a particular reader as his representative had to be seriously considered. Similarly, in voting on congregational or communal budgets, especially in connection with taxes and charities based on unequal contributions and paid for diverse objectives, one had to bear in mind that the mass of noncontributing poor might use their large voting power to impose undue burdens on the taxpaying members. In a lengthy responsum, R. Samuel de Medina argued, therefore, at some length and with the support of quotations from older authorities, that some balance must be drawn. He stated:

You see that many great and noble scholars have agreed that the majority cannot force a minority [to accept a regulation] in matters involving a gain for one party and a loss for another. But even those who believe that a minority generally has to yield to a majority must admit that this rule is to be adhered to only under the condition that the majority is distinguished through wisdom, as well as through numbers, and that the regulation it wishes to enact is salutary for the public at large and would accrue to the benefit of all. Otherwise you ought to require a unanimous vote.[115]

Like the other religious minorities, Jewish settlers established certain basic institutions for the pursuit of their religious and social activities. For the most part every new Jewish community started by building a synagogue—usually after conducting divine services in homes or hired halls—as well as a cemetery. In regard to both of these institutions it was taken for granted that the government, so long as it overtly or tacitly decided to admit a particular group of immigrants, would not impede such a process but rather at times extend to it a helping hand. True, in all Muslim countries there were certain traditional restrictions inherited from the *shari'a*, as well as practical difficulties, which often limited the options available to the leaders of such new groups. We recall that, from its early beginnings, Islam had taken over from the Christian world a general prohibition against erecting new synagogues. Even if the authorities were ready to close their eyes to the unavoidable violation of that prohibition, especially by newly formed congregations, they could still insist upon some of the other traditional provisions, such as that even old synagogues should not be enlarged or raised in height beyond the original structures. In fact we are told that, upon his conquest of Constantinople, Meḥmed II allotted to the incoming Jews some of the churches abandoned by the fleeing Christians, insofar as they were not converted into mosques. In other cases Jews acquired the needed land from Muslim or Christian owners, often from *waqf*s, under peculiar conditions which in time may have turned out to be quite irksome. Yet, the Ottoman administration was generally more friendly to a synagogue than to a church (the ringing of whose bells, for instance, was generally outlawed) because of the intrinsic similarity between the synagogue and the mosque. For instance, unlike churches, neither institution was formally consecrated or considered very holy ground on which secular activities were not to be conducted. On the contrary, buildings of this type were frequently used as a combination of houses of worship and centers of communal activity even to the extent of allowing business transactions to be performed on their premises. The synagogue went even further than the mosque, however, by not requiring worshipers to take their shoes off and not having prayer meetings summoned by a muezzin from a tower. In general, a synagogue building did not differ too much in appearance or character from similar private buildings in the Jewish street. Yet, it greatly

contributed to holding the members of the congregation together. It often assigned to them certain chambers devoted to
adult study; its halls were also open to public meetings of the
members for the election of elders and for passing resolutions
governing the congregants' public and private conduct. It also
was the arena for the discussion of such mundane communal
affairs as taxation for internal needs of the community or
negotiations with the government's fiscal and other authorities.
In short, the synagogue was the focal point of Jewish communal life in secular as well as religious matters and as such
the mainstay of Jewish survival. Because of their ritualistic,
linguistic, and social differences, even some smaller Jewish
communities possessed more than one synagogue. In the
Turkish Golden Age their number in Istanbul alone had increased to forty-four. Moreover, some worshipers continued
to pray in private chapels, while maintaining their membership in their congregations.[116]

In contrast, cemeteries were not so greatly divided by reason of regional origin or diverse traditions and mores. In
smaller communities there usually was only one Jewish burial
ground which served not only several local congregations but,
at times, held its gates open for funerals from neighboring
smaller settlements. Such intercongregational solidarity was by
no means hindered, even in larger cities, by the existence of
special congregational societies, each called *Ḥevrah Qadishah*
(The Holy Society) or *Ḥevrat Qabranim* (Burial Society). These
associations consisted of pious volunteers of all classes who
performed the necessary ablutions and other preparations of
the corpses until these found their ultimate resting places in
the cemetery. Such services were usually rendered even during raging plagues, when any contact with a victim exposed
the volunteers to a serious danger of contagion. Communal
solidarity was further strengthened by difficulties which were
often encountered by Jewish funeral corteges to cemeteries
which, like the Muslim, were usually located outside city limits.
According to R. David Ibn abi Zimra, the Jews customarily
buried their dead at midnight because "during the day Gentiles would hurl insults, curses, and occasionally even throw
stones [at such processions]. This often happened even during

the early evening hours when stores were open until about 10 P.M." We remember that similar disturbances were not infrequent also in the Christian world during the Middle Ages and early modern times. Nor were the Jewish dead left in peace after their interment. While in Europe most of the attacks on cemeteries were the result of vandalism, a circumstance which induced the twelfth-century popes and their successors to insert into their traditional *constitutio de judaeis* a special clause forbidding such brutality, in the Muslim lands these provocations were mostly motivated by greed. Muslim neighbors learned quite early, especially in Egypt, that some Jewish families long after a burial dug up the grave of a relative in order to fulfill his wish to have his remains reburied in the Holy Land, a wish which also animated many Jewish individuals from remote Western Europe, Persia, or Yemen. A great many were convinced, as succinctly stated by R. Samuel de Medina, that "even if one dies in another country, it is a great privilege for him to be buried in the Land of Israel." Partly it was the belief that, on the Day of Resurrection after the advent of the Messiah, such remains would escape the underground journey to Palestine. Some also had the notion, according to a legend spread by credulous souls, that a body interred in Palestine would be immune from destruction by vermin. Hence, after the ensuing exhumation, the tombstone previously erected on such a grave lost its importance and, after the erasure of its inscription, could be sold to another bereaved Jewish family. The rabbis actually permitted such purchases, but they forbade the acquisition of tombstones stolen while the grave was still intact. Other difficulties arose; for example, in Istanbul, when a plot of land purchased by the Jewish community from a *waqf* for use as a cemetery was located in the vicinity of Muslim dwellings. At times, the Muslim owners encroached upon the land assigned to the cemetery, and tried to incorporate a piece into their own possessions. These conditions often led to litigations in which Muslim courts, for the most part, sided with the injured party. But there were also cases of their favoring the Muslim wrongdoers. Ultimately, Sultan Murad III himself had to step in and issue several decrees forbidding such encroachments (1583–87). It may be stated, however, that such incidents are rarely recorded in the Ottoman sources and that in general the Jewish communities found effective ways to protect their communal burial grounds.[117]

Most significant was the frequent practice of Turkish Jewry to repair to state courts rather than to their own tribunals. Occasionally we hear of protests echoing the Jewish communities' old insistence dating back to the days of the pre-Christian Roman Empire that, in their litigations with fellow Jews, their members should submit their differences exclusively to Jewish judges. As a rule, this principle was adhered to in Christian Europe throughout the Middle Ages and early modern times and the rabbinical authorities guarded it with great devotion. Under the Ottoman Empire, on the other hand, most Jews appeared before the state courts not only to settle juridical conflicts but also to have their deeds registered under governmental authority. This was particularly true with respect to real estate transactions, since all land was supposed to be the property of the sultan. According to R. David Ibn abi Zimra, "even land which is deeded to the Jewish community as *Heqdesh* is executed in their [the Muslim] courts. . . . This has become an established custom since the days of the early negidim." Ibn abi Zimra also stated, more broadly, that "the public has been accustomed to deal with all kinds of deeds in Gentile courts except for writs of divorce for women or deeds of emancipation for slaves." Personally, he was not quite sure that such a procedure was justified and, in another responsum, he declared:

Deeds [prepared by Gentile authorities] are not valid except if they relate to contracts of sales and the like. But . . . deeds concerning gifts, divorces of women, and liberation of slaves, if written before their courts, have no validity whatsoever. For our law, agreeing with Mar Samuel's dictum that the "law of the kingdom is law," applies only to proceedings in which the king has a direct interest, such as taxes or corvée labor and other aspects of public law, but in civil matters between one person and another the royal law is not really legal.

In support Ibn Zimra quoted a similar statement by R. Jacob b. Asher in the name of his father, R. Asher b. Yeḥiel, forgetting that both these fourteenth-century sages had lived in Christian Spain under entirely different conditions. In the

Muslim world, however, one could frequently see Jews repairing to non-Jewish tribunals and even Ibn abi Zimra had to admit the validity of what had become a *minhag* (custom) and that in all cases where the law of the country demanded action by governmental courts Jews had to obey that law. We also remember that, upon their early march of conquest, the Ottoman Turks annexed one province after another mainly from the Byzantines. There, as we recall, the Roman imperial legislation had followed the principle, first proclaimed in 398 c.e. and then included in the Theodosian Code, which had declared that Jewish courts were mere courts of arbitration; Jews might voluntarily submit to them, but these had no official standing in public law. The government helped to execute the judgments of such courts, if the parties concerned agreed in advance to accept them. Byzantine Jewry had thus long been accustomed to use governmental notaries and registries and to apply to regular courts in most civil matters. There was even less hesitation to recognize the superior authority of the governmental courts in criminal proceedings which fell into the domain of maintaining public order and could far more effectively be enforced by the Turkish judicial and police power.[118]

In time, however, the preponderance of Sephardic and Ashkenazic rabbis coming from the Western countries—where the authority of the Jewish judiciary in most civil affairs and particularly in family matters, inheritances, and the like had long been firmly established—produced a counterbalance to the Byzantine traditions. It was especially a Salonican ordinance of 1552, signed by the leading rabbis Joseph Ṭaiṭaṣaq, Samuel de Medina, and others, which provided that

no person of the Children of Israel, man or woman, shall, either in person or through somebody else, take any actions in matters of inheritance or a marriage contract . . . except on the basis of the teachings of the Torah and its scholarly interpreters and deal with them only in accordance with the conditions described in it. Anyone breaking this rule . . . shall be excommunicated before God and humanity. The same ban shall apply to the witnesses who will testify in these matters contrary to the provisions of our faith and its exponents. They and the plaintiffs will be counted among the "informers" against Israel [considered by Jewish law a cardinal sin and crime] and its enemies.

To reinforce their proclamation the signers ordered its monthly public recitation in all Salonican synagogues and sent copies to Istanbul and other cities. In specific cases, too, the Salonican rabbis tried to enforce their insistence on Jews repairing to Jewish courts exclusively in their intracommunal disputes. For example, R. Samuel de Medina once went so far as to declare suing a fellow Jew before Gentile authorities an even greater sin than violating the Sabbath rest commandment. Referring to a litigation between a houseowner and his tenant, he cited Maimonides' statement that "it is forbidden to place a Jew or his possessions in the hands of non-Jewish authorities even if he is a wicked person and is guilty of having violated the Jewish laws or having caused serious troubles to another Jew." Pursuing with that insistence in many areas of life, the Turkish Jewish leaders established a measure of hegemony of the Jewish judiciary in many communities, particularly those more recently founded or reconstituted, such as Izmir. As late as the mid-nineteenth century, the Izmir rabbi Hayyim Palagi emphatically asserted that he had "never seen nor heard of any local Jew repairing to a general Turkish court to claim inheritance rights at variance with the provisions of our holy Torah." On the whole, sufficient authority still remained in the hands of the Turkish rabbinate for the civil provisions, as summarized in the *Ḥoshen Mishpaṭ* and similar works of Jewish jurisprudence, to enjoy wide application throughout the Ottoman Empire. Needless to say, the Jewish public and its rabbinic leaders freely adhered to the more ritualistic sections of their Jewish law books from the Mishnah to the Talmud and Maimonides and down to the interpretation of the codes by a host of contemporary rabbis.[119]

CREATIVE COEXISTENCE AND NATIONALIST DISRUPTIONS

Impressed by the deteriorating conditions during the last two centuries of the weakened Ottoman Empire, Western observers were prone to denigrate its sociopolitical and cultural achievements and to join in its condemnation by Otto von Bismarck as "the sick man of Europe." They were inclined to denounce particularly its lack of creativity, an assertion which they readily extended even to its Golden Age. True, when it came to the Industrial Revolution of the eighteenth and nineteenth centuries the Turks no longer were able to keep up with the great technological changes which entirely altered the life and image of the West-European societies. In the sixteenth century, however, the Empire, and particularly its major cities—Istanbul, Salonica, Aleppo, Alexandria, and Cairo—could favorably compare themselves with any of their counterparts in the West. It certainly demanded much creative imagination to build up an empire of its size, as was achieved by the Ottomans in the fifteenth and sixteenth centuries, to reorganize it according to their own plans and, despite its inherent heterogeneity, to lend it a cohesiveness which for many generations outlasted all the blows and misfortunes inflicted upon its inhabitants by a world of enemies and their own internal discords. At first even those centrifugal tendencies were minimized by the regime's wise policy of toleration of the ethnoreligious disparities. A keen, even if somewhat erratic, observer like Guillaume Postel, who spent a long time in the Ottoman Empire, as emissary of the king of France in charge of collecting books and manuscripts for French libraries, could claim that a Turk (who prefers to be called an Ottoman) "will either demand nothing or merely rob some property from a Christian or a Jew, but would put a fellow Turk to death in a most cruel fashion he can imagine."[120]

It was indeed a masterly achievement of Meḥmed II and his early successors to rebuild Istanbul from its decaying conditions under the late Byzantine Empire and its further depopulation during the Ottoman siege and conquest, and to raise it to the status of a metropolis much larger and more dynamic than any other in Europe or the Mediterranean world of their time. Adorned by beautiful buildings, particularly mosques and palaces of grandees built under the guidance of master architects like Sinan (1489–1578); provided with gardens of great beauty and variety; accommodating a cosmopolitan population of some three-quarter million; running its own economic and social affairs through a network of some 1,100 corporations; all living more or less peacefully together under the central direction of gifted sultans and their brilliant advisers—the capital's management and regeneration required indeed a great deal of foresight and profound creativity. It was small wonder, then, that the imperial rulers were able to instill in their subjects a considerable sense of achievement. As Robert Mantran rightly commented:

In the course of the sixteenth century the city enjoyed unprecedented prosperity; in it was reflected the glory of Empire and the high prestige of its sultans. Its inhabitants, whether Turks, Greeks, or Jews, conceived therefrom a feeling of pride which distinguished them and lent them an attitude of superiority.

To be sure, that feeling could in later generations appear quite misplaced; it was, indeed, considered obnoxious by latter-day visitors from the rapidly advancing civilization of France, Holland, or England. But during the Golden Age it greatly helped to overcome whatever difficulties would have normally arisen from the presence of numerous minorities, each of which cultivated its own traditions and mode of living. We certainly must not underestimate the difficulties of a bureaucracy confronting these diverse cultures and yet possessing much leeway in its operations and maintaining a certain basic element of solidarity and love for their common fatherland.[121]

One must bear in mind, however, that in their aggregate these minorities constituted the majority of the imperial population. The Turks themselves, even if reinforced by the renegades from many faiths whom they succeeded in integrating into their own ethnic body, always remained a minority ruling over a conglomeration of Greeks, Hungarians, Serbs, Bulgarians, as well as Syro-Egyptian Arabs and North African Arab-Berber mixtures. Yet by insisting that neither territorial nor linguistic divisions really mattered but that the main differences between the populations essentially consisted in their diverse faiths the Turks could claim that the overriding religious group was Muslim, while Christian sects and the Jews were only religious minorities. A living illustration is offered, for example, by the Bosnian Muslims who today still number some 40 percent of the population of Bosnia and Hercegovina and who, before the spread of modern nationalism, were considered as part of the Muslim ethnic majority, rather than as Serbs or Croats, although they have continued speaking Serbian or Croatian to the present day. Moreover, not all Christians regarded themselves as belonging entirely to the same faith. Even the Armenians were often looked upon by the Balkan Christians as being members of a different religious denomination, governed by another patriarch who was also the ecclesiastical representative of such diverse groups as the Copts and old Syrian Christians. Yet the Armenians, at least before the massacres of 1855, could feel much more at home under the Ottoman rule than under that of fellow-Christians in Russia. An Armenian leader epitomized their grievances by exclaiming: "The Turk takes the body, the Russian takes the soul."[122]

For most Turkish Jews the contrast between the tolerant Ottoman regime and that of the Western Christian powers, from whose lands their ancestors had fled or been expelled, remained a permanent recollection. It nurtured a sense of patriotism and allegiance to the sultan such as was frequently expressed in the responsa literature and the homilies of many Turkish rabbis. In his aforementioned typical declaration R. Samuel de Medina wrote: "He who is not concerned with honoring our king, the great and pious sultan, may his majesty be glorified, would be better off if he had not come into the world, for it is an obligation . . . to pay fearful heed to his utterances and to obey his orders and enactments as it is an obligation to obey the orders and commandments of the King of the World." The only difficulty, however, remained that under the *millet* system each of these religious entities lived for the most part segregated from the others, not only geographically, but also mentally; each knew very little about the internal life of its neighbors. As a reviewer of Sir Harry Luke's *The Making of Modern Turkey* expressed it: "Turkey was less like a country than like a block of flats inhabited by a number of families which met only on the stairs."[123]

Such a self-imposed separation, which carried with it no deprecatory connotations, could only prove helpful to the preservation of Jewish culture. In time the various languages spoken by the Jews were submerged in a new tongue which, largely based upon the Castilian dialect of Spanish, brought with them by the first Sephardic settlers, absorbed a strong admixture of Slavic, Turkish, and particularly Hebraic elements. This amalgam became the new language of Ladino which, preserving its Castillian ingredients in greater purity than did the Spanish of the inhabitants of the Iberian homeland, nevertheless adopted much of the Hebrew syntax and the use of Hebraic abstract and learned terms. It was also, for the most part, written in Hebrew script. It was in this language that the majority of the occupants of the Jewish quarters conversed with one another, transacted their business deals, and recorded their private and communal documents insofar as they were not altogether written in Hebrew. A great many Jews could live out their lives in some major communities with few, more or less casual, contacts with non-Jews. Their intellectuals produced a significant Hebrew literature of learned rabbinic works as well as some Ladino folk literature. To be sure, as a result of the self-imposed mutual segregation even the descendants of the former Spanish, Portuguese, or Italian savants lost most of their interest in general arts and sciences. But within the narrower confines of Jewish letters their contribution to world Jewry for a long time paralleled that of the Polish Jewish communities within the Ashkenazic world.

It was only the general decline of Ottoman power, interlocked with the rise of Western capitalism, science, and fervid nationalism which undermined the forces of cohesion of these segregated ethnoreligious groups within the Empire. With the penetration of modern nationalist doctrines—with secularization accentuating linguistic rather than denominational differences, and the growing quest for national self-determination by the various ethnic and linguistic groups within the Empire—their originally harmonious coexistence was destroyed. Beginning with the Greek War of National Liberation in 1821–29, one Balkan nationality after another began striving for, and finally achieved, complete national independence—a movement which during the First World War brought about the total dissolution of the Empire into its component parts. This development generally augured badly for the Jewish

communities, which were increasingly subject to diverse nationalist pressures for total assimilation and to being gradually
reduced in numbers and influence in these lands of their
forefathers.

PERSIA—IRAN

ERSIA (since 1935 officially known as Iran) had been a
focus of Jewish life long before the period here under
review. The origins of the Jewish settlements in that area
probably antedate the First Fall of Jerusalem in 586 B.C.E. and
may actually go back to the Assyrian deportations following
the fall of Northern Israel in 721 B.C.E. According to the biblical record: "In the ninth year of Hoshea, the king of Assyria
took Samaria and carried Israel away unto Assyria, and placed
them in Halah, and in Habor, on the river of Gozan, and in
the cities of the Medes." Of course, the Medes, inhabiting parts
of Western Iran and southern Azerbaijan, constituted an important part of the later Persian Empire. In the Late Middle
Ages a Jewish community in Azerbaijan actually claimed to
have been the heir of ancient Habor. Yaqut and other Arab
geographers and historians repeated the tradition current
among the Jews that the "Yahudiya," the Jewish section of Isfahan—which was to play a great role in the later history of
Persia—had been founded in the days of Nebukadrezzar by
Jewish exiles because its water reminded them of that in Jerusalem. Later on with the growth of the Jewish dispersion
many Jewish communities sprang up, particularly under the
tolerant Achaemenid regime. The author of the Book of Esther, which was probably written toward the end of the four-
hundred-year Persian rule over practically all of world Jewry
at the time, could put into the mouth of Haman, the reputed
anti-Jewish councillor of Ahasverus (Xerxes), the following accusation of the Jews and their religion: "There is a certain
people scattered abroad and dispersed among the peoples in
all the provinces of thy kingdom; and their laws are diverse
from those of every people; neither keep they the king's laws;
therefore it profited not the king to suffer them." These provinces numbered, according to the same biblical writer, "from
India even unto Ethiopia . . . a hundred and seven and

twenty" and formed an empire larger in area, and possibly also in population, than the Roman Empire in the days of its grandeur.[1]

These Jewish settlements continued their silent existence under the Parthian regime to the rise of the Sassanian Persian Empire. Regardless of the various storms of changing sovereignties, and even civilizations, the Jews of the area beyond Babylonia retained sufficient continuity for their Hebrew-Aramaic speech to preserve a considerable number of Persian loan-words in the form they had been used in the Achaemenid period, at a time when the Persians themselves had abandoned that usage. Such resistance to environmental influences may also be observed in early medieval Judeo-Persian. For example, Vladimir Minorsky has detected in an old Persian commentary on Ezekiel the use by the author "of a Middle Persian form of passive (*xvanihad*) entirely lost to classical Persia." This type of linguistic conservatism reminds one of the later survival of the Castilian ingredient in the Ladino speech of mid-Eastern Jewry after certain forms had disappeared from the living Castilian practice in its homeland.[2]

During the Sassanian reign (226–641 C.E.) Jews had gone through many phases from full-fledged religious toleration to regular persecutions. At first the friendly Sassanian ruler, Shapur II the Great (310–79), actually sought to increase the Jewish population on the Iranian Plateau by transplanting there numerous Jews from Armenia. According to Faustus of Byzantium, no less than 86,000 Jewish families were thus added to the existing Jewish population in the emperor's heartland. The Armenian chronicler Moses of Khorene mentions especially Armenian Jews settled in Isfahan and Susiana. But in the later more stormy periods of Sassanian history we have learned in our earlier volumes about such outbursts of intolerance as that which led to the execution of the exilarch Huna Mari in 471; it was followed by the temporary rise of an independent Jewish principality under his son, Mar Zuṭra III, which lasted only seven years (*ca.* 484–91). Jews also suffered a great deal from the rise of a Mazdakite sect which preached not only the community of possessions but also that of women—a serious threat to Jewish and Christian family life in the area. These Jewish communities also survived more or less intact the great historic conquest of the entire Persian Empire by the upsurging Arab hosts in 641. Like many of their Zoroastrian neighbors some Jews speedily adopted the Arabic speech of the conquerors, but for the most part they seem to have kept their religion. Our information is unfortunately very limited and we do not even know whether Jewish leadership shared the opinion held by such a famous Arab historian as Muḥammad aṭ-Ṭabari that Zoroaster himself had been a native of Palestine and a pupil of Baruch, prophet Jeremiah's amanuensis. In the course of time the Jews absorbed some ingredients of the Parsee religion and, as late as the ninth century, one of their teachers, Ḥivi of Balkh (now in Afghanistan), raised certain questions regarding the Hebrew Bible similar to those voiced by anti-Jewish critics from the Zoroastrian camp. They seem, however, to have played only a small role in the revival of a Persian national feeling which was combined with the renaissance of the Persian language and literature. We do not even have any evidence of Jews taking part in the *Shu'ubiya* movement whereby many Persian and other thinkers of non-Arab descent combated the Arab racialist superiority feelings. At the same time Jews were affected by the numerous sectarian trends within Islam, many of which originated on the Iranian Plateau. To be sure, Shahrastani, the distinguished student of comparative religion, whose works have also served as a major source of information for Jewish sectarianism of the period, doubtless exaggerated when he spoke of seventy-one Jewish sects. But there is no question that most of the Jewish sectarians at the end of the first millennium C.E. were of Persian-Jewish origin. They also supplied such important leaders of the Karaite movement as Benjamin ha-Nahawendi and Daniel al-Qumisi.[3]

PAUCITY OF INFORMATION

We have expatiated here on the rather well-known history of the Jews in Persia during two millennia before the Crusades and the Mongolian invasion because they had left behind them a permanent heritage which affected the destinies of the scattered Jewish communities on the Iranian Plateau and its vicinity during the turbulent centuries which followed. It was toward the end of the pre-Mongolian period that the Jewish messianic pretender, David Alroy (really Menaḥem b. Solomon) of Amadia (Amadiya), was able to form for a while a Jewish principality and defy the existing regimes (*ca.* 1120–1147). He found adherents in many Persian communities. Samau'al ibn Yaḥya al-Maghribi (d. 1175), a convert to Islam, claimed to have later "seen Persian Jewish communities in Khoi, Slamas, Tabriz, and Maragha [in northwestern Persia], who mentioned his name during their highest adoration. . . . In that city [Amadia] there is a congregation professing a faith which, they claim, emanated from the swindler, Menahem." His memory was still alive in the following centuries, and as late as the 1830s it caught the imagination of Benjamin Disraeli who wrote a historical novel with this Jewish pseudomessiah as the hero. Apart from these reminiscences there appeared to be a living testimony to the Jewish part in the various graves of biblical personalities, including Ezekiel, Ezra, Mordecai, and Esther, to which numerous Jews made pilgrimages; they also otherwise cultivated their general and specific family traditions and folkloristic practices. More prosaic, but historically more informative, were the reports by Benjamin of Tudela and, to a lesser extent, Peṭahiah of Ratisbon and Jacob, a pupil of Rabbi Yeḥiel of Paris, who, in 1228, was sent by his teacher to the Middle East to collect funds for the Parisian school, then in straitened circumstances. (His was an unusual mission, the reverse of those frequently undertaken by Palestinian messengers in the West.) R. Jacob's observations, however, on the interior of Persia were limited to a brief passage concluding with the following sentences:

Thence [from the Synagogue and tomb of Ezra] it is two days' journey to Basra and from there to Susa, the capital, six days' journey, and here is the Tower of Ahasuerus and the Palace of Queen Esther and the Tower of Haman. It is two days' journey from Susa to the place where Daniel is buried and it is fifteen days' journey from Susa to Persia and Media, where is Mordecai's Synagogue and he and Queen Esther are buried there, and outside the Synagogue are the tombs of Haggai and Zachariah.[4]

The "Mongolian Deluge" affected Persian Jews even more deeply than those of western Asia. In fact these invasions, which began with Jenghiz Khan's exploits in 1217–20 and were continued by his successors, culminating in the conquest of Baghdad by Hulagu in 1258, led to the complete destruction of the Eastern Caliphate; they resulted in a decisive turning period in Persia's general and Jewish history. Regrettably, our information about the developments in the Jewish communities in the various provinces of the Mongolian Persian subempire, whether under the reign of individual Il-Khans (1256–1336 or 1353), or later broken up into various principalities until they were reunited under the Safavid dynasty (1501–1732), is extremely limited. Persia itself left behind practically no archival records pertaining to the late medieval and early modern centuries. Here and there some vestiges of a minority community or of some charitable *waqf* have been discovered by modern scholars. Apart from the absence of authentic records emanating from governmental agencies, central, provincial, and local, students of Persian history are also handicapped, as Vladimir Minorsky has pointed out, by "the extreme scarcity of original documents having a personal character, such as private correspondence, communal documents, etc." Literary and other manuscripts of the period, too, have, for the most part, survived mainly after they had found their way into some major foreign libraries, especially the British Museum and the Bibliothèque Nationale. Nor were travelers and pilgrims from either the Christian or Muslim countries numerous and articulate enough before the sixteenth century to leave behind an extensive treasury of travelogues from which much could have been learned about the life of the country both from the point of view of its ruling caste or from that of its subject masses. To be sure, the few envoys sent by Western rulers to Tabriz or the new capital of Sultaniyeh under Il-Khan Öljeytu (1304–1317), including John de Plano Carpini and William of Rubruck, famed world travelers like Marco Polo and Abu 'Abd Muḥammad Ibn Baṭṭuṭa, in the late thirteenth and early fourteenth-century respectively, have given us useful bits of information from their direct observations. But our most important data can be culled only from the leading contemporary historians, like Juwaini, or the greatest of them all, Rashid ad-Din. They were, however, mostly concerned with the ruling houses, their military campaigns, and their administrative successes or failures.[5]

On the Jewish side we find neither travelers nor chroniclers until the Safavid period. We are also limited to a small number of literary works emanating from Persian Jewry, especially the fourteenth-century Shiraz poet Maulana Shahin. Nor were there Arabic-writing scholars of the rank of Al-Biruni, Ḥamza al-Isfahani, or Shahrastani who, in their pursuit for wide-ranging knowledge, evinced considerable interest also in the Jewish religion, biblical Scriptures, and Jewish community life. The historians of the thirteenth and fourteenth centuries, if they refer to Jews at all, usually give vent to their private biases and supply us only with very distorted pictures of what actually happened. The major exception is Rashid ad-Din who, as we shall see, grew up as a Jew until the age of thirty or more, when he adopted Islam, but who nevertheless devoted a special section to the "children of Israel" (relating to biblical history) in the framework of his great world history, the like of which was not written in either West or East during the entire Middle Ages. But his information relating to contemporary Jews is very meager. Under these circumstances, one can merely cite with confidence a few facts reported by various non-Jewish authors and reach more or less tentative conclusions on the destinies of Persian Jewry before the rise of the Safavid dynasty in the sixteenth century.[6]

IL-KHAN DYNASTY

With Hulagu (1256–65) began the regular reign of the descendants of Jenghiz Khan over Persia's fluctuating boundaries. They were called Il-Khans (substitute khans), since they acknowledged the supremacy of the Great Khans residing in Karakorum until the death in 1294 of Hulagu's elder brother, Kublai (Qubilay), founder of the Chinese Yuan dynasty, who had moved the capital to Peking. Hulagu was succeeded by his son Abaqa (1265–82), Aḥmad Tegüder (Takudar; 1282–84, assassinated after two years in office), Arghun (1284–91), Khudabanda Gaykhatu (both names having the symbolic meanings of "God's slave," the equivalents of 'Abdallah and

"Auspicious," 1291–95), and Baydu (1295). During these four decades the Mongol rulers professed in part their traditional Shamanism, though some leaned toward Buddhism, others toward Christianity or Islam. Except for the short-lived Aḥmad, none adopted Islam to the exclusion of other faiths, until Ghazan who, in 1295, became a devout Muslim and adopted the name Maḥmud. From the beginning of Jenghiz Khan's conquests until that time religious freedom and basic equality of all faiths prevailed. As Barhebraeus pointed out, "with the Mongols there is neither slave nor free man, neither believer nor pagan, neither Christian nor Jew; but they regard all men as belonging to one and the same stock."[7]

Such indifference toward religious diversity was unheard of in medieval West-Asian and European lands. As the Mongols approached East-Central Europe in 1241 a Hungarian bishop reported to the bishop of Paris that he had had occasion to interrogate some Mongol prisoners of war. Upon inquiring what religion they professed, he was informed, to his amazement, that "they believed in nothing, but that they had simply embarked on the conquest of the world. They took over the alphabet of the Jews because they had no script of their own." While the Christians saw in the sudden Mongolian expansion the arrival of Antichrist, the Jews viewed it, as they did other major critical changes in historical trends, as harbingers of the coming of the Messiah. As early as 1222 the annalist of the Marbach monastery contended:

One thing we know for certain, namely that the Jewish people had exalted in great happiness and congratulated one another, for they hoped that out of these events will arise their forthcoming liberation. That is also why they called the king of that [Mongolian] nation: the son of David.

Such rumors, increasingly embellished by popular imagination, spread all over Europe. By 1241, when the Tatars' victorious armies reached Germany, many credulous persons were ready to believe the story, reported by Matthew of Paris, that an international Jewish conference [an anticipation of the future *Protocols of Zion*], attended by leading Jews from many lands, but especially from the Holy Roman Empire, had decided to help the Tatar invaders and had even tried to smuggle to them thirty barrels of weapons, under the guise of their allegedly having been filled with poisoned wine for the detriment of the recipients.[8]

In Asia, however, religious pluralism of this kind opened many new opportunities for Jewish individuals and communities. In cities like Tabriz, which had peacefully surrendered to the conquerors and, after the discontinuance of the massacres, also in the areas taken by force, Jews enjoyed for the first time in many centuries a measure of equality of rights with the rest of the subject populations. Of course, they could not easily forget the ferocity with which the conquering hosts annihilated many populated localities. Yet within a relatively short time they must have realized that, though the damages inflicted on the occupied territories could not be readily repaired, the new situation also had some silver linings. They undoubtedly observed, as did the historian Juwaini, that "while in time of action, when attacking and assaulting, they [the Mongol armies] are like trained wild beasts out after game, in the days of peace and security they are like sheep, yielding milk, and wool, and many other useful things." For Jews this attitude opened up new prospects not only for economic prosperity, but also for a potentially greatly improved legal status. There was no *jizya*, though Jews and others were often fiscally exploited in an arbitrary fashion; no badge; and generally no discriminatory treatment specifically directed against them. Toward the end of that period, under Arghun, some Jews were even able to achieve high positions in the state administration. One of them, Sa'd al-Ṣafi ibn Ḥibbat Allah b. Moses, called ad-Daula (Support of the State), reached the highest office in the country. Apparently born in Abhar in the province of Jibal, he lived for a time in Mosul and Baghdad, where he practiced medicine. At the same time he entered the political arena, becoming a member of the governmental council. His imposing personal appearance, ability to speak Persian, Arabic, Mongolian, and Turkish, his high general qualifications as physician, statesman, and financier attracted the attention of Il-Khan Arghun who, in 1288, appointed him his court physician and a year later also vizier. Not surprisingly, Sa'd ad-Daula's administration proved to be most orderly and beneficial to the country at large. Yet he mistakenly followed the practice, widespread among his peers, of favoring members of his own family in appointments to influential positions. He conferred upon his brothers Fakhr ad-Daula and Amin ad-Daula the governorships of Baghdad and Mosul, and entrusted many other high posts to various Jewish relatives and friends. It was claimed that, were it not for two governorships, which at that time were held by Arghun's brother, Gaykhatu, and son Ghazan, the future il-khans, all highest provincial offices might have been occupied by Sa'd's Jewish appointees. Such favoritism toward members of a relatively small religious denomination aroused widespread dissatisfaction also in court circles. Utilizing Arghun's last illness in 1291, Sa'd's enemies spread the rumor that the il-khan had been poisoned by his Jewish court physician. Thereupon they arrested Sa'd at a banquet table, and executed him on the following day. They also assassinated his brothers and the populace staged regular pogroms against Jews in Tabriz and other cities.[9]

Evidently Arghun was too ill to save his friend; he died only two weeks after Sa'd. His successor Gaykhatu seems not to have cared very much about the damage caused by this cabal to the finances and the orderly administration of his Empire. He replaced Sa'd by inferior favorites who catered to his unbridled sexual desires. To cite Barhebreus again; the il-khan was concerned "with nothing except riotous living, and amusement and devotion. . . . And very many chaste women among the wives of the nobles fled from him, and others removed their sons and daughters and sent them away to remote districts." Gaykhatu was also remembered over generations for his unfortunate experiment of introducing into his country a paper currency along Chinese models. He thus hoped easily to refill the coffers of the Treasury, which had been emptied by his associates' reckless mismanagement. Yet, although the new currency was supported by a royal order to all subjects holding gold and silver coins to deliver them to his agents in exchange for the new money, under the sanction of capital punishment, the population boycotted the new currency and economic life practically came to a standstill until the old coins were reintroduced, and the then vizier decapitated.[10]

On the whole, the impact of Sa'd ad-Daula's spectacular rise to power on the well-being of Persian Jewry proved more negative than beneficial. To be sure, during the four years of his governorship and vizierate, a number of Jews were enabled to enter lucrative government service in an unprecedented fashion. The general prestige of the Jewish people likewise rose considerably and a new generation of Jews growing up for more than three decades under a system of basic equality with other imperial subjects, had become far more self-reliant and proud of its heritage. However, during the period of Sa'd's greatness opposing voices made themselves heard, especially among the Muslim majority. According to the chronicler Ibn al-Fuwaṭi,

in the year 689/1291 a document was prepared in Baghdad by respected individuals which contained libels against Sa'd ad-Daula, together with verses from the Qur'an and the history of the prophets, that stated the Jews to be a people whom Allah hath debased, and that he who would undertake to raise them would himself be made low by God.

Rumors were also spread among the Muslim masses that Sa'd had advised Arghun to attack Mecca and to convert the Kaaba, the holiest Muslim sanctuary, into a Buddhist temple. For this purpose he allegedly ordered the cutting down of old trees on the streets of Tabriz for the building of warships. Ironically the opposite was true. Even the unfriendly chronicler Vaṣṣaf admitted that Sa'd had made efforts to facilitate Muslim pilgrimages to Mecca. On one occasion three "hit men" each were sent by Sa'd's opponents to Tabriz, Baghdad, and Mosul, to assassinate him and his two brothers. True, these conspirators were apprehended and on the il-khan's orders severely punished, in contrast to the later assassins of Sa'd who were pardoned by Arghun's successor Il-Khan Gaykhatu. Moreover, immediately after the rumors about Sa'd's demise spread throughout the Empire, unruly mobs staged attacks on many Jewish communities, including that of Tabriz. In Shiraz the riot was further justified by a rumor that Jews had started a large fire, an accusation which was quite frequent in medieval and early modern Europe but was rather rare in Muslim lands. Only in Baghdad do we hear of an effective Jewish resistance.

"When they [the assailants] wanted to go into [the Jewish quarter] and plunder them the Jews rose up against them in great strength and they fought against the Arabs and killed and were killed."[11]

Although quite a few non-Muslim Mongols joined in the anti-Jewish riots, this was primarily a Muslim reaction to the regime run by Jews who had for so long been treated by the Muslim masses with much contempt. The entire evolution from Hulagu to Gaykhatu had shown the strength of the underlying power of the Muslim majority. The il-khans themselves were often vacillating in their faith, since their hereditary paganism no longer satisfied them. As often happened in history, powerful conquerors coming from underdeveloped peoples and occupying territories of superior culture were ultimately assimilated by the masses of their conquered subjects. In the East, Kublai, the great khan, became a Buddhist before he died in 1294. Before long the Mongols were generally absorbed by the deep-rooted Chinese culture. Similarly, the western il-khans vacillated between their traditional Shamanism and their individual sympathies for Buddhism, Islam, or Christianity.

Following the example set by Jenghiz Khan himself, the il-khans staged religious disputations between the representatives of the respective faiths. For political reasons, to be sure, they were attracted to Christianity because many of them aspired to conclude an alliance with the popes and Western Christian kings against the Muslim realms separating them, especially the Mameluke Empire. Between 1267 and 1277 Il-Khan Abaqa, Hulagu's seventh son, sent several envoys to Rome, Paris, and London, offering such an anti-Muslim collaboration. However, despite the warnings of Raymond Lull that the Christian world would be greatly imperiled if the Mongols were to adopt either Islam or Judaism, the Christian West was too deeply involved in its own diverse interests to enter into such an alliance. Although still professing deep faith in an all-embracing anti-Muslim crusade, it reacted to these Mongol approaches only with sweet words and occasional missions of Franciscan monks to expound the virtues of their

Christian faith. After 'Ayn-Jalut in 1260 and subsequent minor confrontations the il-khans seem to have despaired of overrunning the Mameluke Empire, while domestically the impact of Islam's popular majority proved ever stronger. At first, as we recall, the conversion to Islam of the third Persian il-khan, Aḥmad Tegüder, ended with his violent death two years after he ascended the throne. Yet, the Muslim pressure on Arghun and his brother Gaykhatu continued unabated. Finally, their successor, Arghun's son Ghazan, shortly before his coronation in October 1295 at the age of twenty-four, decided to cut the Gordian knot by adopting Islam and assuming the additional Muslim name Maḥmud.[12]

This conversion evidently was part of Ghazan's (1295–1304) planned reforms for a country which he found in a fiscal and social disarray. While still functioning as governor of the province of Khurasan, including the district of Herat, he undoubtedly realized the extent of the devastation and depopulation caused by raids of unruly vassal tribes in 1270, 1288, and 1289. In 1295, the very year of his coronation, Du'a, the Chagatai ruler, burned many villages in the province and drove 200,000 women and children into servitude. On the other hand, Ghazan must have been impressed by the relative stability existing in the Mameluke Empire. He may have decided, therefore, to follow the example of some of his subjects, embrace Islam, and introduce Muslim institutions and ways of life which, he expected, would best help him reorganize the country along stable patterns. That he was not a truly devout Muslim could easily have been noticed by observers who saw him marry one of his father's widows in defiance of an explicit prohibition in the Qur'an (4:26). The same religious ambivalence also characterized his successors Muḥammad Khudabanda Öljeytu (Uljayttu, 1304–1317) and Abu-Sa'id (1317–35). Öljeytu, in fact, was originally baptized as a child with the Christian name Nicholas, later became a Buddhist, but ultimately, like his brother Ghazan, adopted the Muslim faith. His conversion may also have taken place under the impact of a disputation, such as that which was to induce him later to change from the Sunni Ḥanafite Islam to that of the Shafi'ite school and finally to the

Shi'a, which had combatted the Sunnis for centuries but was not to become dominant in Persia until two centuries later under the Safavid dynasty.[13]

These monarchs' conversions may not have been much more deeply felt by many of their Persian subjects who followed their example. But a number of them may have joined the Old Muslims in their violent reaction to the control long exercised by non-Muslim leaders. According to the well-informed vizier-historian, Rashid ad-Din, "when the Lord of Islam, Ghazan, became a Muslim, he commanded that all the idols should be broken and all the pagodas (butkhana and atash-kada) destroyed, together with all the other temples, the presence of which in Muslim countries is forbidden by the shari'a." While this passage refers principally to Buddhist and heathen temples, Ghazan's reform entailed also the destruction of many churches and synagogues, beginning with those of the capital Tabriz. Muslim mobs went further and attacked Christian and Jewish individuals as well. According to the eloquent complaint in the continuation of Barhebraeus' Chronography,

They [the populace] destroyed all the churches which were there [in Tabriz], and there was great sorrow among the Christians in all the world. The persecutions, and disgrace, and mockings, and ignominy which the Christians suffered at this time, especially in Baghdad, words cannot describe. Behold, according to what people say, "No Christian dared to appear in the streets (or, market), but the women went out and came in and bought and sold, because they could not be distinguished from the Arab women, and could not be identified as Christians, though those who were recognized as Christians were disgraced, and slapped, and beaten, and mocked.

Jews and their synagogues seem likewise to have suffered in the same way from their ever excitable Muslim neighbors. However, Ghazan evidently allowed some Christian and Jewish sanctuaries to remain intact, and when, shortly thereafter, some overzealous assailants destroyed additional churches in Tabriz, they were severely punished.[14]

Among those new Muslims there undoubtedly were also quite a few Jews. Although the sincerity of their conversion may not have been any greater than that of their predecessors who, in 1291, after Sa'd's death, had been threatened by the anti-Jewish rioters in various cities and had saved their lives by adopting Islam. But in contrast to the earlier converts under duress who, for the most part, reverted to Judaism at the first opportunity, the apostates of 1295 and after were neither threatened by instantaneous assassination nor did they later face speedily changed situations which would induce them to return to their ancestral faith. In general, Ghazan's conversion, because of its definitive nature, turned out to have been an epochal event which altered the conditions under which millions of subjects throughout the Il-Khan Empire were to live on a permanent basis. The chances are that at least the offspring of most such converts remained regular members of the majority faith which under the Safavids became also the official religion of the state. With Ghazan's conversion went also a large-scale transformation of the governmental system which was now to a large extent based upon the *shari'a* and the practices of the Muslim caliphate. Thus were also restored the old discriminatory laws against the increasingly segregated groups of "protected subjects," consisting principally of Jews and Christians. Buddhists and Parsees were gradually excluded from the basic doctrine of religious toleration, and, as mentioned in the continuation of the above-quoted passage in Rashid ad-Din's *History*, Ghazan, noticing the hypocrisy of some of the new converts from Buddhism to Islam, told them: "My father was an idolater and died an idolater and built for himself a temple which he made into a *waqf* for that community [of idolatrous teachers]. That temple I have destroyed; go ye there and live on alms [among those ruins]."[15]

Although Christians and Jews were allowed to continue worshiping in their respective houses of prayer, they must have deeply felt the new change. Some seventy years had passed since they began to be treated as equals by the Mongol rulers; especially the younger members of their communities, who had never lived under a legally established discriminatory regime, must have found it extremely difficult to dwell amidst a society which formally excluded them from all public offices and armed services, forced them to wear garments or badges of identifying colors, and to reside in separate quarters with all marks of definite inferiority in comparison even with the lowly members of the Muslim majority. Frequent manifestations of their being treated with deep contempt by their Muslim neighbors must have been most galling to many proud young Jews who had witnessed the rise and fall of such personalities as Sa'd ad-Daula and his family.

One of the great changes under Ghazan's regime was the inability of non-Muslims to serve as high governmental officials. But there was no discrimination against converts. Among the neo-Muslims brightly shone the star of Faḍl Allah Hamadani Rashid ad-Din (ca. 1248–1318). The designation ad-Din seems to have replaced that of ad-Daula when he embraced Islam (ca. 1278). He was a man of extraordinary gifts, an outstanding physician, statesman, linguist, philosopher, theologian, and, above all, author of one of the greatest world historical works written by any man during the Middle Ages. At the same time he was a successful financier and talented administrator. It is generally accepted that Ghazan's significant reforms were largely initiated by him while he was serving as vizier. Although personally perhaps a secret Jew, he was outwardly a devout Muslim. Among his numerous buildings in various parts of the country he also established a new quarter in Tabriz named after him Rub'i Rashidi; in addition to 10,000 houses he also erected there a mosque with two minarets. On his death his estate was said to have included 4,000 villages scattered over the entire Empire, 12,000 other pieces of real estate, and a library of 50,000 to 60,000 manuscripts.[16]

Curiously, however, even in his great historical work he betrayed his pro-Jewish leanings. He not only devoted a special section to the story of the Children of Israel, in which he referred to a number of biblical terms in a way revealing his familiarity with the Hebrew language, but he also occasionally glossed over certain events which might have cast a shadow on the Jewish community. For instance, in referring to Jenghiz Khan's granting tax exemptions to the clergy of various denominations, he failed to mention that the decree had not included the rabbis. Karl Jahn rightly observed, therefore, that "had there been no other testimony for Rashid's originally belonging to the intellectual elite of Jewry, a perusal of his history of Israel would remove any shade of doubt on this score." On another occasion he was actually accused by enemies of corresponding with a Jew in a "secret script," which probably referred to a letter written in the Hebrew alphabet, a practice generally employed by Jews using that script for Persian, Arabic, or other documents or literary works. It is even possible that he wrote the entire letter in the Hebrew idiom.[17]

In his long-lasting administration of the country Rashid was even-handed and perhaps for that reason quite successful. Finding first the Treasury practically empty—it was in part totally ruined by Gaykhatu's abysmal experiment with paper money—he actually advanced funds from his considerable private fortune to bridge the gap until his own orderly fiscal administration replenished the Treasury's cash holdings. In time, he evidently accumulated a very large fortune. According to one report the il-khan offered to give him a tremendous monetary gift which was estimated by the chronicler, with considerable exaggeration, as amounting to 1,500,000 dinars. This sum was the equivalent of $6,000,000 when gold was rated at $35.00 per ounce. But Rashid is said to have asked to be given instead a grant of its equivalent in land and other real estate. At the same time, he tried to spare the population the extremely irregular and burdensome tax collections. He is reported to have pointed out to the il-khan the frequent excesses of the tax farmers, who often exacted the same tax several times a year. He also described the cruel methods often employed by the collectors:

When they went around a locality, they found some villain or other who knew the houses, and at his direction discovered the people in corners, cellars, gardens, and ruins. If they could not find the men, they seized their wives. Driving them before them like a flock of sheep, they brought them to the tax officials who had them hung up on ropes so that the wails and plaints of the women rose up to the heavens.

Rashid effectively stopped these abuses after undoubtedly arguing with the monarch, as he did in a letter to his son, Shihab ad-Din, that the Exchequer "is filled by their [the people's] good efforts and their economies. If they are ruined, the king will have no revenue." Indeed, under his regime the predominantly agricultural economy of the Il-Khan Empire made excellent progress. This is largely true also of other branches of the economy and government. In addition he effectively promoted arts and sciences. Apart from his own literary contributions and his extensive building activities in both Tabriz and the new capital, Sultaniye, he sponsored the famed Tabriz creative school of painting and supported numerous writers and scholars.[18]

Understandably, his strictness in keeping law and order antagonized a great many influential dignitaries. Many of them were undoubtedly also cognizant of his Jewish origin, which he apparently never tried to deny. However, under both Ghazan and his successor, Khudabanda Öljeytu (Uljaytu), for more than twenty years their efforts to overthrow Rashid's regime failed. They seized, however, the opportunity of Öljeytu's demise and the succession by his son Abu-Sa'id, then aged ten or twelve, to persuade the ruler that the father's death had resulted from poison administered to him by his court physician. In vain did Rashid plead before a quickly convened kangaroo court that he could not possibly have conspired against any of the il-khans, his great benefactors. He argued: "I was a simple Jew, son of an apothecary, a physician, a poor man among my fellows," from which status he had been raised by his friendly sovereigns. Rashid was speedily condemned and executed on the following day (July 17, 1318). He first had to witness the execution of one of his sons, Ibrahim, aged sixteen who, as cupbearer, had allegedly administered the poison to the ruler. By itself such a tragic end of a great career was not exceptional. Rashid merely shared the fate of all his predecessors in the Il-Khan vizierate (the first and only vizier to die a natural death, six years later, was his successor 'Ali Shah). In Rashid's case, however, the execution was aggravated by a spectacle: his head was carried through the streets of Tabriz with a crier proclaiming: "This is the head of the Jew who has dishonored the word of God, may God's curse be upon him!" Not satisfied with this degradation, even in the following century, the new ruler of western Persia and Iraq, Jalal ad-Din Miranshah (1404–1409), son of the new world conquerer, Timur (Tamerlane, 1336/1395–1405), ordered the exhumation of Rashid's body from the Muslim cemetery and its removal to that of the Jews in Tabriz. Thus ended the brilliant career of "the greatest vizier of the Il-Khan dynasty."[19]

It was of little help either to the Jews or society at large that toward the end of his reign Il-Khan Abu-Sa'id with growing maturity realized the injustice which had been committed on this most deserving servant of the Crown. He also noted that the oppression of the masses under the regime of 'Ali Shah and his other favorites caused a serious deterioration of the country's economy. He therefore appointed, in 1328, Rashid's son Ghiyath ad-Din Muḥammad to serve in his father's former position as vizier of the Empire. Ghiyath immediately restored his father's regime of law and order and brought the country back to much of its former flourishing state. He thus earned for his sovereign the praise of having been the most *rai'yat-* (people-) loving, bestowed upon him by fifteenth-century scholars. Yet, this sort of rehabilitation of Rashid's memory came too late because with Abu Sa'id's death in 1335 and the assassination of his son Arpa, together with Ghiyath, in the same year, came the end of the Il-Khan dynasty. It was followed by the dissolution of the Empire into its many component parts under the reign of various usurpers, who for the most part were fighting one another. Except for the brief reunification of the Il-Khan Empire and its incorporation into the even larger domain of Timur Lenk and again under Shah Rukh (1420–47), the fragmentation of Hulagu's original heritage into various principalities with ever fluid frontiers helped to obscure the internal evolution of the Persian people during the fifteenth century. It also almost obliterated the records of the life of the struggling Persian Jewish communities of that period.[20]

While we must be grateful to the Persian and Arab chroniclers (without corresponding Hebrew sources) for the information about the great careers of Sa'd ad-Daula, Rashid ad-Din, and his son Ghiyath, only one of whom died as a professing Jew, we learn next to nothing about the life of the Jewish masses and their intellectual and communal leaders in the Il-Khan Empire. Even the western cities—including Baghdad, Mosul, and Basra, where up to 1258 a few extant Jewish sources attest to some continuity from the days of the Great Caliphate—after the wholesale destruction caused by Hulagu's campaigns seem to have been greatly reduced. We but occasionally hear from them weak echoes of Jewish communal or intellectual activity.

This situation continued after the fall of the Il-Khan dynasty when the western provinces came under the domination of new rulers, especially of the so-called Black Horde. We have seen that Uzun Ḥasan of the Aq-Qoyunlu (White Sheep) dynasty (1453–78) for a while threatened the expansion of the Ottoman Empire. But this was a passing phenomenon and, before long, even Baghdad became part of the Turkish imperial system. As far as Persia proper is concerned our information about its Jewry in the fifteenth century is practically nil. We learn little more than the names of such leading Jewish individuals as those mentioned in fourteenth-century Baghdad as holding the position of Jewish "princes" (nesi'im). They included Sar Shalom Pinḥas (Phineas), in whose honor a contemporary Hebrew scribe Shem Ṭob b. Abraham Gaon copied a Hebrew Bible named Keter Shem Ṭob (Shem Tob's Crown), and Azariah b. Yehallel. These men apparently served as heirs of the exilarchate of the past era. At the same time the eastern provinces under the reign of various dynasties were able to maintain their flourishing Muslim intellectual activities. After reviewing the progress in exact sciences in the whole area during the Seljuk and Mongol periods and noting the significant advances made there in the foundations of mathematics, algebra, optics, and planetary theory, E. S. Kennedy concludes:

That these achievements were of a lesser order than those of Archimedes, and that their consequences were incomparably less significant than the scientific breakthrough which followed the work of Newton and Leibniz is perhaps irrelevant. The scientists of Seljuk and Mongol Iran were the best of their age.

At the same time even the Hebrew muse, which had found in fourteenth-century Shiraz a representative, Shahin—somewhat similar to, if below the rank of, Shiraz' two great Persian poets, Sa'di and Ḥafiz—fell completely silent in the fifteenth century. And yet it was that century which laid the foundations for the emergence of the Persian national state which came into the full light of history under the Safavid dynasty of the 1500s. It was under that dynasty that we begin hearing from local Jews about Jewish life, too, although this information is largely conveyed to us in connection with anti-Jewish persecutions.[21]

SAFAVID DYNASTY

From the outset the new dynasty which unified Persia pursued policies different from those of its Il-Khan and other predecessors. Its origins go back to the Ṣufi state of Ardabil, the intellectual progenitor of which was a saintly man, Isḥaq Ṣafi ad-Din (hence the name of the dynasty Safavid). Ṣafi's claim to being a descendant of 'Ali, Mohammed's son-in-law, was used by his descendants to justify their leadership of the Shi'ite sect in the area. His piety was generally recognized and he was highly praised by historians, including Rashid ad-Din. Partly for religious reasons Timur Lenk bestowed upon Ṣafi's grandson, Khozi 'Ali, the administration of the entire district of Ardabil as a pious endowment. It was out of that nucleus that Khozi's descendant Isma'il organized a fighting army of Shi'ites from his and surrounding possessions and, in 1500 at the age of thirteen, began a series of successful campaigns which led him to Baku in the West, to Persia where he became shah in 1502, to Baghdad and Mosul, as well as to Yezd (now in Afghanistan) in the South. His major reverse came when, in 1514, he was defeated by the Ottoman sultan Selim the Grim in the famous battle of Chaldaran. This defeat, which allegedly shook him so deeply that he never smiled again to the end of his life, did not hinder him from establishing a religiously oriented Persian empire under the domination of Shi'ism as a state religion. In his conquests he was aided by the Twelver Shi'ite revaluation of the old Muslim doctrine of the "holy war" (*jihad*). Some religious leaders now quoted sayings attributed to the fifth and sixth of the revered Twelve Imams that "the root of Islam is prayer, its branch is almsgiving, and the top of the hump [crown] is *jihad* for the cause of God." Imbued with the sense of such a sacred mission, Isma'il did not hesitate to use forcible means to convert Sunnis, who constituted two-thirds of the population of Tabriz and were the majority in other parts of the Empire, and make them profess Islam in its Shi'ite formulation. Symbolically, his select troops and government officials wore red caps with twelve tassels reminiscent of the twelve ancient Shi'ite saints. This select force, becoming the ruling caste of the Empire, was known under the name of *Qizil-Bash* (red-caps). Isma'il also surrounded himself with a bodyguard of Turkish and Georgian prisoners converted to Islam similar in kind to the contemporary Egyptian Mamelukes and Turkish Janissaries. Such combination of Mosque and state, established for centuries to come a "national state" of Persia, in 1935 renamed Iran.[22]

This revolutionary transformation was implemented through the relative dynastic continuity of mostly long-reigning individual shahs. In the period here under review Isma'il I reigned from 1500 (1502) to 1524. He was followed by Ṭahmasp I (1524–76), Isma'il II (1576–78), Muḥammad Khudabanda (1578–88), 'Abbas I (1588–1629), Ṣafi I (1629–42), and 'Abbas II (1642–66). Ṭahmasp proved to be a far less gifted leader than Isma'il. Confronted by a more or less permanent two-front war with the Ottomans in the West and the Uzbeks in the East, he lost many of the eastern and western possessions. Nonetheless he adhered to his father's stringent domestic policies and continued to spread Shi'ism, as did indeed most of his successors down to the eighteenth century. This ideological stance is the more noteworthy since even the Persian clergy was not sufficiently learned in theology and had to use works by Arab Shi'ite theologians in their mosques and schools. In general the intellectual level under the Isma'il and Ṭahmasp's regimes was relatively low, when compared with the great achievements of Persian science, literature, and theology in the earlier pre-Mongolian centuries. Ṭahmasp himself was often inconsistent. Under the superstitious impact of dreams, he suddenly ordered complete abstention from wine drinking and closed all shops producing or selling wine. Unlike other Muslim rulers he made no concession to his Christian and Jewish subjects, but included them in that general prohibition of liquor. Before long, however, he himself began drinking heavily and died an alcoholic in 1476 at the age of sixty-two. Regrettably, we have no information about any Jewish reaction to the outlawry of liquor which may also have affected Jewish use of sacramental wine for ritualistic purposes.[23]

Some weaknesses of this intolerant centralized regime were reduced by 'Abbas I, on whom a grateful contemporary generation and posterity conferred the designation 'Abbas the Great, the fourth monarch so honored in the long history of Persia (after the Achaemenids Cyrus and Darius I, and the Sassanian Shapur II of the days of ancient Persian grandeur). In 1623 he reconquered Iraq including the cities of Najaf and Kerbela with the tombs of their ancient martyrs 'Ali ibn abi-Ṭalib and his son Ḥusain (Mohammed's son-in-law and grandson, respectively). He also penetrated the Persian Gulf, conquering the key city of Ormuz and converting a neighboring village into a major harbor called in his name Bandar (or Bender) 'Abbas, thus opening an entry into the Indian Ocean to Persian seafarers and merchants for the following centuries. To enhance Persia's trade and industry he welcomed European traders and visitors, who now came in large numbers to the legendary Eastern country from which Europe imported some admirable textiles, especially silks, carpets, majolica, and other choice products of Persian industry and good taste. 'Abbas seems to have been particularly impressed by some English merchant-adventurers. On one occasion he actually issued an order to all Persian officials "to kindly receive and entertaine the English Frankes or Nation . . . and that you shall see them safely defended about our Coasts from any other Frank or Frankes whatssoever."[24]

In return, the Christian West welcomed the appearance of a powerful adversary of its dreaded foe, the Ottoman Empire. In 1592, early in 'Abbas' reign, Pope Clement VIII actually invited the shah to form an alliance with the Western powers against the Turks. Although no formal treaty to this effect was concluded, the Ottoman Empire often found itself forced to fight a two-front war with its then declining manpower and financial resources. In addition Europe helped Persia by bringing it some of the more advanced European methods of production. One of its most immediate contributions to the

Persian state was the work of two English merchant adventurers, Sirs Anthony and Robert Sherley, who together with a third brother formed a trio "whose wanderings and adventures outdistanced any fiction" (Alfred C. Wood). They brought with them an expert cannon caster who taught the Persians how to produce more advanced artillery with which they could effectively combat the theretofore superior Ottoman armies. Internally, too, 'Abbas the Great introduced many reforms which helped to forge the intrinsic unity of the Persian people and effectively convert the country into a "national state"—naturally without yet consciously using this concept. Uniformity of religion and mores made it possible for a long-term resident of Isfahan like Jean Chardin, later as a Huguenot refugee in London called Sir John Chardin, to make some well-informed observations. As a businessman-jeweler he had access to many classes of the population and learned the characteristics of the people around him better than many a native. He was able to describe the specific "national character" (to use a modern term) of the Persian nation in the following paragraph:

As to the spirit the Persians have as fine and excellent a spirit as their body. Their imagination is lively, quick, and facile. Their memory is easy and fertile. They have many talents for science, liberal arts and mechanical arts. They are also fully qualified for armed service. They love glory and vanity which gives them a false appearance. By nature they are pliant and simple, their spirit facile and intriguing. Their inclinations are grandiose and natural towards voluptuousness, luxury, and prodigal expense, all of which does not make them attentive to the economy and commerce. In a word they present to the world natural talents on a par with any other people but they do not transform these talents into as much as they might.

Such a nation could survive without much change a weak regime like that of 'Abbas' successor Ṣafi I and be quickly rehabilitated by 'Abbas II who successfully tried to imitate his ancestor-namesake.[25]

A major difficulty in any attempt to reconstruct the history of Safavid Persia arises from the extreme paucity of reliable documentation. As in the Il-Khan period we have few archival records preserved in the country itself and must collect bits of information about the ramified Safavid life from some chance documents and manuscripts which to a large extent found their way into European libraries. The very structure and activities of the centralized government, which were the focus of attention of both the foreign visitors and native historians, are likely to obscure the great diversities of tribal traditions and the prevailing rigid adherence of the inhabitants to their accustomed ways of life.[26]

In contrast to the early Safavid regimes of Isma'il and Ṭahmasp, that of 'Abbas I welcomed foreigners to visit, or even to reside in, the country so as to increase its trade and industry. In part emulating his Ottoman neighbors and his predecessor, Timur, 'Abbas I apparently even used forcible means to transplant desirable populations from outlying areas to the center of his empire. In one such mass deportation some 3,000 Armenians, engaged in crafts and commerce, were taken out of Armenia and resettled in the capital city, Isfahan. There the newcomers formed a semiautonomous community in the city's quarter called Julfa, after the city on the Araxes, which many of them had left. A similar transplantation of some Georgian Jews to the interior of Persia led to the establishment of a new Jewish township named Farahabad (1611). Possibly some other such attempts at transplanting active Christian and Jewish workers and merchants from outlying districts happen not to have been recorded in our meager documentation.[27]

Although early modern Persia did not have any Persian or Arab historian of the rank of Rashid ad-Din, some of the narrative sources have been used by modern scholars to good advantage in reconstructing the events and policies in the period from 'Abbas I to 'Abbas II (1588–1666). Moreover, their perennial quest for a counterweight to the rapidly expanding Ottoman Empire induced some European powers to send envoys to the Persian capital frequently, in order to secure some form of cooperation against their common enemy. Some of these envoys did not limit themselves to diplomatic negotiations with the Persian authorities but often used the opportunity to describe the existing political, military, and economic conditions in the country. In addition a number of Western Christian missionaries, especially of the Jesuit and Carmelite Orders, now pursued the Catholic mission in Persia. Foolhardy as such ef-

forts in the face of the official Shi'ite intransigence may have
appeared to some contemporary realists and later historians,
they were sufficiently serious for the Carmelites to produce
one of the best collections of historical data pertaining to the
Safavid period in general. Other European visitors pursued
more mundane aims; they included merchant adventurers of
the kind working under the guidance of the Dutch or English
East India companies, or like Jean Chardin who evinced great
curiosity about the "exotic" customs and institutions in that
far-distant country. Some foreigners, like the Frenchmen
Guillaume Postel (1510–80), or later (1670) Jean François Petit
de la Croix, were sent by Francis I and Jean Baptist Colbert
to Persia for scholarly reasons to collect manuscripts and rare
books for the home libraries as part of the promotion of the
study of Oriental languages. We must be grateful to many of
these visitors or temporary residents for leaving behind travelogues and reports which shed considerable light on the general conditions in the country. A few of them, like Chardin,
paid attention to the conditions of Persian Jewry. To them we
owe much of our information about events and ways of living
among the Jews during their rather obscure Safavid period.[28]

OUTBREAKS OF INTOLERANCE

All of these sources, however, supply us, for the most part,
merely some background and other indirect information about
Persian Jewry. Only here and there do we get a few more or
less significant details from the contemporary Persian writers
although, unlike their Turkish and Mameluke counterparts,
the historians of Iran seem not to have considered the Jewish
question significant enough to dwell on it frequently or at
length. Even casual reference to one or another Jew or a Jewish tax are quite rare in their writings. On the other hand, the
few contemporary Jewish writers were generally rather inarti-
culate about their coreligionists' sociopolitical status. The sixteenth-century poet, Imrani, followed in the footsteps of
Shahin in describing ancient events in Persian verse written in
Hebrew characters. While the appearance of a Hebrew poet
in sixteenth-century Persia is in itself a contribution to Jewish

history of that period, we cannot learn much from him about the legal and economic conditions or the daily life of his co-religionists. Of direct historical value are, therefore, only the two chronicles by Babai b. Luṭf and Babai b. Farhad, even though they describe mainly the intermittent sufferings of the Jews in 1617 to the 1660s, and in 1722 to 1725. These chronicles have often been compared to Joseph ha-Kohen's *'Emeq ha-bakha* and, to a lesser extent, to Ibn Verga's *Shebeṭ Yehudah*. Limited though they are in scope and by themselves merely a contribution to the lachrymose conception of Jewish history, they offer occasional data and insights about the ordinary life of the Jewish people also in periods of greater religious tolerance and the country's relative prosperity.[29]

The events described by Babai b. Luṭf marked indeed a turning point in the history of Persian Jewry. In their experience dating back to remote antiquity, they had never before seen under Persian rule such a far-reaching outbreak of intolerance, resulting in wholesale forced conversions. Generally rare in the annals of Islam, this outbreak reminded one of the exceptional Almohade attempt at "unification" of the entire subject population under the banner of the Crescent. Otherwise no Jewish communities of an entire Muslim country had been subjected to such protracted efforts to convert them to the ruling religion by means of a combination of extreme torture with persuasion and blandishments of high rewards, as did the Persian Jews for a number of years under the regimes of both 'Abbas I and 'Abbas II. That they survived at all as Jews was owing to their deep loyalty to their ancestral faith and their persistent living as crypto-Jews, even after formal conversion, until new opportunities were opened to them to profess their Judaism in public.[30]

Regrettably, these outbreaks are often shrouded in the mist of legends. The chief Jewish chronicler, Babai b. Luṭf, admits that "the reign of Abbas I, called the Righteous (*adil*) was [at first] a period of peace during which 'the wolves lived in amity with the sheep.' The Zoroastrian and the unbeliever, the Christian and the Jew, the Frank and the Armenian, the Georgian and all other aliens lived in mutual harmony and friendship under his rule." In 1613, at the conquest of Georgia, 'Abbas was welcomed by 200 Jews, on horseback from the community of Samum, who pledged their fidelity to him. Thereupon the shah was supposed to have pledged himself never to oppress his Jewish subjects. Allegedly, as a sign of his benevolence he transferred a number of Georgian Jews to Persia, settling them in the aforementioned new township, Farahabad. Babai exaggerates when he states—doubtless repeating a legend current among the local Jews—that 'Abbas had founded the city for the benefit of the Georgian Jews. Its foundation in 1611–12 actually preceded the king's Georgian campaigns of 1614–15 and 1616–17. But considering the thousands of Armenians thus forcibly deported to Persia, the Georgian Jews resettled in Isfahan and other places may also have consisted of a multitude of men, women, and children. While 'Abbas personally, in a speech to his people, explained the great economic benefits for the country which he expected from these transfers, before long he changed his mind and removed the Armenians from the new Julfa. He also reversed his attitude toward the Jews. As was characteristic of the contemporary historiography, particularly in such poetic accounts as produced by the two Babais, these major reversals are presented as the results of individual machinations. The first outbreak of intolerance is attributed in the sources to the internal quarrel among the Jews of Isfahan, which arose when the Jewish leaders accused a local Jewish butcher, Siman Ṭob, of cheating with his weights. In revenge Siman Ṭob abandoned Judaism and, as a Muslim, found in 'Abbas I an attentive listener to his denunciations of his former coreligionists for indulging in magic arts. He claimed, with reference to the books of "Practical Kabbalah" that Jews used their incantations to conspire against the shah. 'Abbas I, who was generally of a superstitious nature (he is said to have placed an impersonator on his throne for three days because an astrologer had predicted that the reigning monarch would be assassinated during that period), ordered the wholesale confiscation of Hebrew books. 'Abbas II, on the other hand, was allegedly persuaded by the discovery of some jewels stolen from the royal palace by its gardener in the possession of two Jewish "fences" to initiate a total suppression of the Jewish faith in Isfahan and other communities. The Jewish leaders, on their part, with their time-honored self-accusation, attributed these catastrophic developments to the divine wrath over the sins committed by the Jews of their generations.[31]

In retrospect we may somewhat better understand the underlying basic factors which directed otherwise reasonable monarchs, interested in the welfare of their people, to adopt such drastic measures. We have seen in many other connections that whenever a national state was created, whether under the shape of religious conformity or common linguistic-cultural identity, Jews were often considered an obstacle to such homogeneity and were the targets of either speedy absorption or forcible elimination. The Persian national state, formed by the Safavids, took about three centuries to achieve the desired unification under the guise of the profession of a single religious faith, namely Shi'ite Islam of the "Twelver" variety. As early as 1508–1509 Isma'il I, upon receiving a visit in Baghdad from two rulers of Khuzistan, ordered the execution of both guests because they were Shi'ites of a different sectarian coloring. In 1517–18, when the then ruler of Shirwan surrendered to Isma'il, the shah responded by sending him a representative diplomat accompanied by Persia's highest divine (ṣadr) "in order to illumine the darkness arising from certain questions of the immamite religion harbored in the heart of Sheikh-Shah." A similar procedure was employed by Ṭahmasp I with respect to Sultan Aḥmed Khan of Lahijan (d. 1533–34) who had been a Shi'ite of the "Zaidite" confession. His conversion quickly affected the subject population of that entire province. It was this singleness of purpose which, despite frequent relapses, continued throughout the Safavid period and led to the predominance of the Twelver Shi'ites, a process further facilitated by the transfer, especially by 'Abbas I, of more and more areas from what was considered state property to that of the royal domain. The property belonging to the state was usually controlled by the *walis*, or viceroys, who often enjoyed considerable autonomy and, for example, collected most of their provinces' revenue directly. The shah's special domain, on the other hand, was firmly in the hands of the central organs and was for the most part administered by shah-appointed former royal serfs, recruited, like the Mamelukes and Janissaries, primarily from captive children; in the Persian case mostly taken from Georgia, Armenia, and other neighboring territories. To be sure, the distinction between royal and state property was not clearly spelled out in Safavid Persia. In fact, as pointed out by Roger M. Savory, the Persians did not even have a term designating statehood in the Western sense, and had to substitute for it some such terms as *dawlat* (felicity). But in practice, there was a difference between the centrally administered "royal" domain and that directly controlled by the *wali*s who, though serving as royal officials, exercised many undeniably autonomous functions.[32]

It appears that the special attention paid by the two monarchs to the conversion of Jews arose not from the incidental happenings as described by the Jewish chronicler and his Armenian contemporary Arakel of Tabriz (see below), but rather from religio-political considerations connected with the changing fortunes in the frequent Turko-Persian wars. It was especially during the preparations for his attack on Iraq which resulted in the Persian conquest of Baghdad in 1623 that 'Abbas I seems to have noted the deep devotion of Iraqi Jewry to its Turkish sovereigns. The alternating controls over this important area, which had first been taken by Isma'il I in 1516, then lost to Suleiman the Magnificent in 1534, subsequently regained and lost again over a period of a century, doubtless caused the Jews of that province to evince a strong loyalty to the Ottoman Empire, which treated them consistently better than any other country of the period. The savagery which accompanied the second conquest of Baghdad in 1623, when despite the conqueror's previous promise of amnesty, many thousands of Sunnis were slain and their wives and children carried away to Persia, must also have led to the destruction of Jewish lives and property. On the other hand, according to the vastly exaggerated report by Sieur de la Boullay de Gowz, Murad IV's army, which reconquered Baghdad in 1638–39, included no fewer than 10,000 Jewish soldiers in its total of 150,000 men. Possibly it was in reaction to that Jewish fidelity to the "enemy" that 'Abbas decided to remove the Jewish group as a separate entity from Isfahan and, perhaps, the country.

At the same time he could continue more readily to tolerate Christians, who appeared to be his natural allies in the struggle against the Ottoman Empire. European Christians, especially, as the main contracting parties in Persia's international trade with the West and as likely supporters in its anti-Turkish diplomatic and military campaigns, could only be treated as friendly to 'Abbas' imperial ambitions.[33]

In the actual application of the royal orders a number of Jews were executed when they resisted to the very end. Many others accepted conversion when they faced death after prolonged tortures. According to Arakel, the Isfahan officials under 'Abbas II succeeded in converting 350 Jews out of a community originally embracing 300 families. Some others may have gone into hiding or fled to another city or country. "Some families," reports Babai, "took off under the cover of night, and emigrated to the kingdom of Caesar." This designation is taken to mean the Ottoman Empire but here may possibly refer to the Mughal Empire in India, which must have loomed large in Persian eyes since the glorious reign of Akbar the Great who died in 1605. For those who accepted conversion it often was easy enough to recite the Muslim confession of faith, "There is no God but Allah and Mohammed is the Messenger of Allah." We recall that, on similar other occasions, some insincere converts made the mental reservation that they believed in the same God as the Muslims and that Mohammed was but one of many messengers sent by God into the world. Nor did the somewhat enlarged Shi'ite Twelver Credo offer a serious obstacle. Even the crucial tests to which new converts were often submitted, namely the consumption of camel's meat cooked in milk (a practice already recorded under the Mongols and attributed again to a suggestion by Rashid ad-Din under the Il-Khan regime), could be accepted by Jews facing death, since according to talmudic law one was allowed to break all commandments, except for three prohibitions (idolatry, incest, or murder) to save one's life. To be sure, even such nominal conversions included an element of idolatry, but because Muslims shared with Jews the worship of an imageless God, the mere formal acceptance of Islam could be explained away. In fact, most such new converts seemed to have continued ad-

hering to their Jewish faith and even practiced most of its rituals in the secrecy of their homes. Persia, like other Islamic
countries, had no institution resembling the elaborate and efficient Spanish Inquisition to detect such deviations from the
road of orthodoxy. In fact, under the Shi'ite doctrine of *taqiyya*
(concealment), in the case of danger, a Muslim, too, could hide
his Shi'ite beliefs under the mask of another faith. Under these
circumstances it was relatively easy for the crypto-Jews to sustain such a disguise for some six years until 'Abbas I's death
in 1629. Subsequently, under the weak regime of Ṣafi I, general law enforcement greatly declined and neither the administration nor the public was much concerned with the implementation of the anti-Jewish orders. Many "New Muslims" were
allowed to profess Judaism in public, and, with the aid of a
court physician Daud, an influential Jew, David of Abarqu, in
central Iran, persuaded the shah to allow the Jews to stage a
procession with their scrolls of law in the state's capital. The
local Jews declared the day to serve as an annual memorial
day of that great deliverance. In general, according to the
anonymous author of *A Chronicle of the Carmelites,* the thirteen
years of Shah Ṣafi's reign (1629–42) seem to have offered the
religious minorities in Persia a respite from oppression and
persecution.[34]

During the second wave of intolerance toward Jews, which
in 1656–61 swept over Persia under Ṣafi's successor, 'Abbas II,
the Turko-Persian confrontation may likewise have played
some role. In 1638 Baghdad was retaken by the Ottomans;
this time the Ottoman rule extended over nearly three centuries to the end of World War I. On this Turkish campaign, as
we recall, the Ottoman army was rumored to have included
thousands of Jewish combatants. Possibly not only Jews from
Rumelia and western Asia but also some Iraqi coreligionists
had joined the enemies of Persia, where but a short time earlier an attempt had been made to suppress Judaism completely. It may not be too venturesome to suggest that some
exaggerated accusations of "disloyalty" of Iraqi Jews were again
spread in certain Persian circles during and after the war.

Of considerable interest also are the drastic methods employed by the Persian authorities in enforcing the mass con-

version of Jews. These cruel pressures, about which we have much contemporary information from Babai and Arakel, were initiated by the same high official, Muḥammad Beg, who had carried out the expulsion of the Armenians from their Julfa quarter in Isfahan. After assembling a strong military detachment, he went into the Jewish quarter and announced: "By order of the Shah, you Jews must all leave Isfahan and settle in its outskirts. Being non-Muslims and of an impure race you must get out of the city and live somewhere else." At the same time the government arranged that the Jewish exiles should not be admitted to any other city. The expulsion was also timed for a Friday night. The Jews were told to leave immediately; their urgent request to be given a three-day leeway was rejected. Ultimately, their quarter was pillaged, many women were raped by the soldiery, and all Jews resisting conversion were imprisoned, severely tortured, and threatened with death. At the same time the authorities combined a carrot with the stick; they tried to persuade the Jewish prisoners to adopt the state religion by a substantial gift of two tomans, the equivalent of 100 abbasis or ducats (according to Jean Chardin 'Abbas I had already paid a subsidy of 400 francs for each male and 300 for each female convert). Each *jedid al-Islam* (new convert to Islam), as he or she was officially called (they were also known under other designations), was at the same time freed from the capitation tax and promised good employment. To make sure that the converts would become good Muslims the authorities provided for them, and especially their children, instructors to teach them Islamic doctrines and rituals. They also demanded that the "New Muslims" should regularly marry Old Muslim women and that the "New Muslim" fathers should select pious Muslim husbands for their daughters. Soon thereafter the royal order was extended to other areas and, according to Arakel, all the Jews of Kashan, Qum, Ardabil, Tabriz, Qazwin, Lar, Shiraz, and Benderi-Qum were similarly converted by force. While Babai b. Luṭf gives the impression that no Persian localities were exempted, Arakel enumerates a number of towns, including Hamadan, Yezd, Kirman, the districts of Khurasan and Gilan, and the villages around Farahabad, in which the Jews escaped total conversion either by bribing the officials or by flight to some other localities in and outside the country. In Farahabad, we are told, Jews so fiercely resisted that, after three or four months, the governor gave up in despair and merely forced them to accept a distinctive badge.[35]

Many reporters, including such visitors as Chardin and Thévenot, emphasize that this mass conversion proved to be purely nominal and that a large majority of these "New Muslims" not only continued to observe the Jewish rites in secret, but even in their business dealings were said to use all sorts of evasions. For example, when a messenger of a city's governor wanted to buy some silk from a "convert" on a Sabbath, he was told to come back the next day, when he would find a much larger selection. In anticipation that some day they might be allowed to profess their ancestral faith publicly, some communities decided to be prepared to pay back to the government the stipends the "New Muslims" had received upon conversion. They also set apart annually an amount equal to the capitation tax they would have had to pay to the Treasury if they had been allowed to remain Jews. In this way they hoped more easily to persuade some future administrators to permit them to shed their masks and live as professing Jews. Outwardly, too, a "new convert to Islam" was widely suspected of being an insincere believer in his adopted faith. Even a foreigner like Jean de Thévenot rightly concluded that "despite the Muslim designation placed upon them they were always observant of the Jewish faith until the authorities finally allowed them to be good Jews, since they could not make them good Muslims."[36]

Thus ended, apparently in 1661, the two most tragic chapters in the history of early modern Persian Jewry. Except for a local episode in Kashan, where in 1722–25 some officials forced the Jews to adopt Islam, the disastrous events under 'Abbas II seem to have left behind a fairly intact number of professing Jews. It is possible, however, that some potential or actual converts had in the meantime left the country either for neighboring Turkish possessions or by emigrating to India, Turkestan, or even China. Apparently only a small minority failed to return formally to Judaism or raised its children in the new faith. This small group was quickly absorbed by the majority of Shi'ite Persians, without leaving many traces. Nonetheless, the communities which continued to struggle for survival had been greatly weakened economically as well as spiritually. Soon thereafter the spread, and failure, of the Shabbetian movement added to their perplexities. As elsewhere many downtrodden Jews were seized by their age-old dream of national independence and joined the believers of the false king-messiah. According to Chardin, some Jews refused to pay the capitation tax because, as they assured the collectors, "our liberator has come." Because their previous sufferings had turned into renewed hopes, they may have felt their disappointment even more keenly than their coreligionists in other countries.[37]

PORTUGUESE INTERLUDE

Of a different order was the area around the Persian Gulf. To begin with, the Gulf was situated between a coastline which was predominantly Arab and one mostly inhabited by Persians. Politically, too, it shared the destinies of the Safavid dynasty only beginning with the conquests of 'Abbas I. To be sure, in the Late Middle Ages the kingdom of Ormuz (Hormuz) extended beyond the island so named; yet, it long recognized the supremacy of the khans of the inland city of Lar. However, the real control was in the hands of the governors, who treated their kings as mere figureheads. According to Gaspar Corrêa, when a king died they usually elevated one of his sons, a child, to the throne. But frequently, when the royal puppet reached full maturity, they blinded him and made him incompetent to rule over his realm, though he was left for a time in the enjoyment of royal honors. Ultimately, of the ten princes reigning from 1400 to 1506, five were deposed and four assassinated. The only "king" who died a natural death was Turan-Shah (1436–1471), who lived under the constant threat of poisoning, so that he consumed only fish which he personally had caught in the Gulf waters. This situation changed completely when in 1515 the island was conquered by the Portuguese. They converted it into an emporium in the

vast international trade between East and West. Even more
than before it also became a focus of exchanges between Persia and the subcontinent of India. Correspondingly, the population was utterly mixed. Next to the Shi'ite Persians and predominantly Sunni Arabs, there were Armenians, Jews,
"Gentiles," that is, Hindus and other Asians, augmented by
some Portuguese colonists and other European traders. Under the Portuguese regime, which lasted from 1515 to 1622,
the morality of the population declined even more than before. Prostitution was rampant, there were public houses not
only of female but also of male prostitutes; some girls underwent baptism in order to mitigate the compunctions of some
Portuguese men against sexual relations with "infidels."[38]

Because of the area's intermediary position between its major neighbors, the character of the Jews living in Ormuz seems
likewise to have differed from that of the majority living
in Persia. Regrettably, we have little information about the
Jewries of the Persian Gulf's highly important geographic region. Most of our knowledge stems from the 107 years of the
Portuguese domination, about which we have reports not only
from governmental agents but also from the generally well-
informed Jesuit and other missionaries. Some extant records
attest to the presence of Jews in the Gulf region in ancient
times and again at the beginning of Islam. We are told, for
example, that in 630 C.E., still in Mohammed's lifetime, the
Jews of Bahrein repudiated his message. A number of other
Jewish communities were sporadically recorded in the area in
the following centuries. They shared the vicissitudes of their
neighbors in what is now both Iran and Iraq. We recall that a
community like Aḥwaz had a period of flowering during which
some prominent Jewish families played a considerable role in
both the economic and political life of the country. In Oman,
too, we are told by a tenth-century Arab ship captain, Buzurg
ibn Shariyar, that one Isaac had left the city for India and
thirty years later returned on a ship laden with musk, silk,
porcelain, jewels and precious metals, in addition to countless
objects of Chinese workmanship, worth some 3,000,000 dinars
or the equivalent of $12,000,000 in gold, when its value was
stabilized at $35 an ounce. Buzurg's estimates undoubtedly

were greatly inflated. But they confirmed the general opinion of the Jewish population in Baghdad of that period, as stated by Saadiah Gaon, that "everyone who goes to India gets rich." From a responsum by Hai Gaon and from Benjamin of Tudela's *Itinerary* we also learn about the presence of a Jewish community in neighboring Kish (Kais). After describing some of the natural peculiarities of that island, the famed Jewish traveler observed that

men from Shinar, El-Yemen and Persia bring hither all sorts of silk, purple and flax, cotton, hemp, worked wool, wheat, barley, millet, rye, and all sorts of food, and lentils of every description, and they trade with one another, whilst the men from India bring great quantities of spices thither. The islanders act as middlemen and earn their livelihood thereby. There are about 500 Jews there.

Benjamin further informs us that from Kish it is "a ten-days journey to Al-Katif, near Bahrein, where there are about 5,000 Jews," probably an exaggeration. For the later period, however, especially in Ormuz, we are almost entirely dependent on the information furnished by European visitors, particularly during the period of the Portuguese occupation. During the sixteenth century we also hear from a Jewish visitor, the Yemenite Zechariah b. Saadiah adh-Dhahri (or az-Zahiri), who spent about six months in Ormuz on some mission.[39]

From these bits of information we can judge that the intellectual level of the Jews was not very high. While one Jew is praised by a visitor for being well versed in the Bible, Don García de Silva y Figueroa complained that the Jews of Ormuz were Jews only by name.

They do not know any Hebrew and have no knowledge at all of the Jewish religion though they still observe some ceremonies of the ancient law, but so much changed by the mixture with the ceremonies taken from the Moors and the heathens that they are not recognizable any more.

The general atmosphere of religious toleration, concomitant with the variety of religious denominations represented by segments of the population, made it possible, as we recall, for the distinguished Jesuit missionary Gaspar Francisco Barzaeus (Berze) to preach in the local synagogue and, after a number of friendly disputations with the two local rabbis, even to expect, their conversion to Christianity. It undoubtedly was this atmosphere of mutual recognition of the rights of the various groups that attracted Rabbi Solomon, who had been trained at the distinguished Cairo Jewish academy, to settle in Ormuz, as it did a motley of immigrants from various countries. In a 1560 report sent from Goa, India, the Jesuit Ludovicus Frois asserted that Ormuz had witnessed an "influx [of Jewish arrivals] from Constantinople, Venice, Greece, Alexandria, Armenia and other lands." This aura of peace and relative prosperity did not last, however. In 1622, 'Abbas I, with the aid of the English navy, occupied the entire kingdom of Ormuz, giving rise to hopes by the agents of the East India Company that, "if the Company may have possession of Ormuz and send means to maintain it, they have gotten a key to all India." If that had happened, the Ormuz Jewish community might have avoided being drawn into the vortex of developments which led in the following years to the forced conversion of a substantial number of Persian Jews. However, the entire city of Ormuz suffered severely from the Persian occupation. Apparently disgruntled with having to deal with such a heterogeneous population as that of Ormuz, 'Abbas established a rivaling harbor in a small mainland village, Gombroon (or Gombrun), which was quickly renamed Bandar (or Bender) 'Abbas. At the same time he ordered the nearly total destruction of Ormuz. According to a report of May 30, 1624 from the English agents to the East India Company, "it is a misery to think what almost hath been and what it is now . . . scarce a stone being left upon a stone, only the castle about itself untouched." Some Jews followed, voluntarily or by governmental edict, into the new port, others doubtless were dispersed in various directions. Although later Bandar 'Abbas figured, together with Lar and Shiraz, in the decree sent by the grand vizier to the governor of Shiraz ordering the forcible conversion of the local Jews, Jean Chardin was still able to locate there 50 professing Jewish families. Thenceforth the area, insofar as it was occupied by the Persians, was increasingly assimilated to the rest of the Safavid national state, and the Jews were probably treated on a par with their coreligionists in other Persian provinces.[40]

SOME SOCIORELIGIOUS CONSEQUENCES

Intolerant outbreaks of the kind initiated by 'Abbas I and 'Abbas II were in part the result of the extremism with which the Safavid dynasty tried to forge their diverse provinces into a spiritual and cultural, as well as political, Persian unity. For this reason the Safavid monarchy allowed the Shi'ite clergy (the *mullah*s) to exercise a greater influence on public affairs than was customary in other Muslim countries. Through its direct control over the pious foundations (the *waqf*s) which owned much of the most productive land in the country (the great mosque of Ardabil, for instance, lorded over 10,000 acres of irrigated land, 40 entire villages in Azerbaijan alone, 200 houses, 8 caravansaries, and other possessions in the city of Ardabil, and so forth), the Shi'ite hierarchy dominated the economy and social life of many provinces. Its head (*ṣadr*) usually played a great role also in Persian political affairs. If 'Abbas I, more independent and powerful than other shahs, failed to appoint another ecclesiastical chief during his lifetime, his weak grandson Ṣafi quickly restored that office to its former rank in public leadership. Nor did 'Abbas himself hesitate to interfere even with internal Jewish life. On the other hand, when in the often heated polemics between Turkish and Persian theologians the Turks attempted to link the Persian Shi'ite schism with Jewish "infidelity," they had no basis in historic reality. An assertion of a Turkish mufti, "I hope also from the divine Majesty that in the Day of Judgement He will make you [the Shi'ites] serve instead of Asses to the Jews, that miserable Nation, which is the contempt of the world, may mount and trot with you to Hell," clearly deserved the extremely crude response given by the Persians.[41]

Not even the Jewish book was immune from Persia's governmental meddling. Because a disgruntled convert Siman Ṭob, wishing to take revenge on his Jewish accusers, denounced them for indulging in magic rites, at times even resulting in the death of innocent persons, 'Abbas I ordered the indiscriminate seizure and destruction of Hebrew books. They included, to be sure, some mystical writings, especially the *Sefer ha-Razim* (The Book of Secrets), a well-known classic in the practical kabbalah, which was widely used in most Jewish communities. But this kind of literature was perhaps even more intensively cultivated in the mystical environment of the Persian Shi'ites, although according to Persian law, outright sorcery, already considered a capital crime under Mongol rule, was not to be tolerated. The shah ordered, therefore, the confiscation of all such books, some of which, he was told, might be used against his own life or health through magic manipulations. But as usual the police, charged with collecting the Hebrew works, did not differentiate between those of kabbalistic and other contents. They even seized copies of the Bible or Talmud and many other works of Jewish law and liturgy and threw them into the water. Such wholesale destruction of Jewish cultural possessions, accumulated over generations, further diminished the intellectual resources of the Jewish population at large. It partly helps explain the great paucity of works of Jewish learning which have come down to us from late medieval and early modern Persia.[42]

Under the impact of the Twelver Shi'ite environment Jews intensified their traditional reverence for the reputed tombs of their ancient heroes. From time immemorial the Persian Jews revered, as we recall, the graves attributed to Mordecai and Esther in the city of Hamadan. They foregathered around those graves, especially during their celebration of Purim, and, with deep emotion, read the Scroll of Esther with its story of the danger which had once threatened their ancestors in the days of Xerxes-Ahasverus and had ended with their ultimate salvation by the intervention of the queen and her uncle. In general, the Persians so highly considered pilgrimages to Najaf, Kerbela, Meshed, and Qum, which harbored the remains of 'Ali, Hussein, and two of their Twelver descendants, that they allowed their adherents to substitute these visits for the old Islamic requirement that each pious Muslim make a pilgrimage to Mecca (hajj) at least once in his lifetime. Because of the intimate relationship between the Twelver Shi'ite faith and the Persian national feeling 'Abbas I could go so far as not only to advise his subjects not to travel to Mecca, but ultimately to forbid them to go there. According to some Ottoman opponents, the Persians even tried in this connection to switch the prescribed orientation in prayers (the *Qibla*) from Mecca to their own holy city of Ardabil. Some extremists were even accused of planning to proceed to Mecca in order to destroy Islam's generally revered old sanctuary. So deeply ingrained, indeed, did these Persian practices become that there developed a mass movement to transport bodies of deceased family members from all parts of the country for reburial in one or another of these holy places. When Iraq came under Ottoman rule, transportation to these localities raised many problems for the Turkish customs officials, particularly because it was also used by smugglers, especially of costly saffron, in order to avoid payment of the high customs duties. No such complications are recorded in the case of Jewish relatives trying to rebury the remains of persons dear to them in the Holy Land. This practice is recorded already in the Bible in the case of the patriarch Joseph whose bones were carried by Moses during the Exodus from Egypt and were ultimately reinterred in Shechem. However, such sporadic Jewish second burials never assumed the mass character vividly described by Pierre Ponafidine, a long-term Russian Consul-General in Istanbul. But pilgrimages to the graves of revered saints seem to have been more frequent among the Persian and Iraqi Jews than in any other country.[43]

No mention is made, however, during the Safavid period, of the celebrated grave of Ezekiel in Dhu'l-Kifl which, apparently since the days of Öljeytu (1310), had been appropriated by the Muslims as a tomb of one of their own saints. Most remarkably, there developed an ever-greater reverence for a tomb located in Pir Bakran, in the vicinity of Isfahan, which was attributed to a legendary lady, Serah (Sarah) bat Asher b. Ya'qub. This reputed granddaughter of Patriarch Jacob was said to have lived for several centuries and performed many miracles. Among her achievements, the Aggadah reported, was that she was able to direct the exiles from Egypt to Joseph's Egyptian grave so that they could carry his remains with them to the Holy Land. Perhaps partly because it was located in the very center of Jewish life in Safavid Persia, her grave attracted large numbers of pilgrims from all parts of the country. Among the numerous legends about Serah current among the Persian

Jews was one which attributed the termination of 'Abbas I's persecution of Jews to her ghost's miraculous intervention. Jews must have listened with relish to a storyteller describing how, on one of his hunting trips, the shah had been pursuing a gazelle. In order to capture the graceful animal, he followed it into a cave, where it was suddenly transformed into a beautiful young woman. She seized the monarch's throat and threatened to choke him to death if he did not instantaneously revoke his decree of forced conversion of his Jewish subjects. It appears that even nationalistically minded Persians did not resent the celebration by Jews of ancient heroes who not only saved their ancestors from Haman's intrigues but had taken bloody revenge on their heathen Persian enemies. In any case, we do not hear of any direct interference on the part of the authorities or the public with either the celebration of Purim or the Jewish pilgrimages to holy places.[44]

From a practical point of view, the effects of the extreme Shi'ite doctrine of purity, placed at the top of the four cardinal commandments, were far more important. Some teachers insisted that any contact with an infidel contaminated the Shi'ite with that person's native impurity. Sporadically, as we recall, such manifestations of alienation of non-Muslims appeared in other Islamic countries as well. Hence some local laws provided that, if a Jew or a Christian touched any merchandise in a Muslim shop, he or she contaminated it with impurity and was thereby immediately obligated to purchase it regardless of price. In Persia, however, such possible "contamination" was avoided in a more extreme fashion and was given as a rationale for the infidels dwelling in quarters of their own. Because such segregation was practiced also by crafts and other social groups who preferred to live together, this type of legislation encountered little resistance on the part of the Jews. It was, indeed, an exception when, arriving in Ormuz, Barzaeus noted with amazement that "the Christians lived so mingled with Moors, Turks, Jews, and gentiles (primarily Hindus) that one cannot distinguish them" from one another. This observation, of course, implied also the absence of special distinguishing marks separating the various faiths. On the other hand, the assumption of Jewish impurity easily nurtured the fertile imagination of some Muslim theologians to try to expand the segregationist provisions of the Covenant of 'Umar by adding ever new humiliating restrictions. A postulate of eighteen additional limitations of this kind was included, for instance, in the *fatwa* secured by the vengeful convert, Abu'l Ḥasan Lari. Five of these were also included in Babai's report. However, it appears that no such enactment was issued by the authorities who were engaged in the broader conversionist campaign to eliminate the Jewish minority altogether.[45]

Elsewhere in Persia the Shi'ite doctrine of purity for the most part postulated a clear outward distinction of each denomination, lest the true believers by mistake come into contact with some "infidels." Here, on the initiative of Mullah Abu'l Ḥasan Lari, the Jews were singled out for a special "mark of shame" by wearing headgear of a certain color. The Jews seem to have bitterly resented this "cap of serfdom," and they considered it an alleviation of that practice when the hat or cap was replaced by a simple badge to be worn on the outer garment. This badge consisted, as Jean Chardin observed, of a "square piece [of cloth] attached to the vest near the belly, of a color distinctly different from that of the vest." While elsewhere, too, Jews resented the badge more than the segregation in a quarter, we do not hear of any active resistance on their part or of penalties imposed upon transgressors who failed to display it. It appears that such a badge, if worn at all on journeys where it might have exposed the bearers to serious molestation, did not prevent Jews from joining caravans of predominantly Muslim travelers, which were the only safe method of transportation on roads infested with highwaymen. We learn, indeed, only of such complications as when Jews traveled long enough distances to find themselves on the road during their Sabbath. In such cases they usually made specific arrangements with the caravan leaders who provided them with special escorts. These strongmen would either accompany the Jewish patrons ahead of the caravan on Fridays or rejoin it on the following Sundays.[46]

All these chicaneries were of relatively minor importance.

Under similar circumstances Jews of many other lands learned to live with them and in time mostly forgot their origin and considered them a part of their regular lifestyle.

DEMOGRAPHIC PERPLEXITIES

Our being poorly informed about the developments of the Persian Jewish population is the less surprising, as the entire demographic structure of the Persian Empire in the period of 1200–1650 still is full of obscurities. In the nearly total absence of public archives and our great dependence on court-oriented histories and biographies, even the totals of the imperial population are subject to vague estimates. According to Sir John Malcolm, a well-informed British diplomat-historian of the early nineteenth century, even at that time half of the Empire's population consisted of nomads. Other scholars reduced that percentage to 30, at least for the end of the century, but admitted that two hundred years earlier the nomadic ratio was much higher. It was, and to a certain extent still is, in the nature of such nonsedentary tribes not to possess clear figures of their membership even on a local level, still less on a regional basis covering several provinces. Similarly, the rest of the rural population was never subjected to a census until recent times, thus leaving the field open to guesswork concerning the number and size of the farming families. Not even the cities had detailed censuses, and guesstimates of their populations, occasionally supplied by foreign visitors, ranged far and wide. Not surprisingly, therefore, even less solid information is available concerning the size of the Jewish communities. Regrettably, in the four and a half centuries here under review they were not visited by a curious Jewish traveler like Benjamin of Tudela who might have made it his business to register whatever figures had been suggested to him by direct observation or by reports from more or less well-informed members of the local communities.[47]

One conclusion appears to be fairly certain. At no time between 1200 and 1800 did the population on the Iranian Plateau reach the size it had before 1200 c.e. The Mongolian invasions had so sharply reduced the number of inhabitants of the conquered territories that for centuries thereafter the losses sustained could not be made up. Even the generally pro-Mongolian Juwaini could not suppress his horror over the devastation left behind by the eastern invaders. After describing the massacres committed by Jenghiz Khan's hosts, he asserted that "where there had been a hundred thousand people, there remained . . . not a hundred souls alive." The generally restrained Rashid ad-Din, writing at the beginning of the fourteenth century, observed:

At the time of the Mongol conquest they submitted the inhabitants of great populous cities and broad provinces to such massacres, that hardly anyone was left alive, as was the case in Balkh, Shuburqan, Ṭaliqan, Marv, Sarakhs, Herat, Turkestan, Ray, Hamadan, Qum, Isfahan, Maragheh, Ardabil, Barda'a, Ganjah, Baghdad, Irbil and the greater part of the territories belonging to these cities. . . . And one cannot describe the extent of the land laid waste in other regions as a result of the slaughter, such as the despoiled lands of Baghdad and Azarbaijan or the ruined towns and villages of Turkestan, Iran and Rum [Asia Minor], which people see with their own eyes. A general comparison shows that not a tenth part of the lands is under cultivation and that all the remainder is still lying waste.

To be sure, most of these writers failed to mention the cities and their surrounding areas which voluntarily surrendered to the conquerors and were generally spared. However, for example, Tabriz, which largely escaped the Mongolian devastation, became the subject of massacres and forcible evacuation during the frequent Turko-Perisan wars of the fifteenth to the seventeenth centuries. If in his anti-Shi'ite fervor Sultan Selim the Grim is said to have caused the slaying of 40,000 of the 70,000 Shi'ites living in his dominion, many like-minded generals under his successors during the later campaigns must have evinced little compassion for the Shi'ites of the West-Persian provinces. Conversely, 'Abbas I, during his conquest of Baghdad in 1623, caused the massacre of 40,000 predominantly Sunni inhabitants. These figures are rather suspect, for the number "forty" was frequently used in the Middle East as a round number, similar to our "hundred" or "thousand," merely conveying the idea of a large total. But there is no question that almost every conquest and retreat in the Turko-Persian hostilities was accompanied by large-scale slaughter among both combatants and civilians.[48]

In addition, the population sustained great losses during the numerous earthquakes, plagues, and famines. As late as 1811–12 a general drought in the country brought about a 10 percent decline in the Persian population. While famines and plagues were quite frequent and usually extended over large areas, earthquakes, though often localized, were more destructive. For example, the city of Nishapur and its environs—where Jewish settlements existed in early Islamic times and, according to local traditions, had been established there much earlier—were the scene of numerous quakes in the medieval and early modern periods. Six major catastrophes of this kind were recorded between 1251 and 1405. One of October 1270 is said to have destroyed more than 10,000 lives. Another of 1405 allegedly inflicted 30,000 fatalities. The same helplessness of the population in the face of elementary catastrophes was again illustrated in 1721 when an earthquake caused 80,000 deaths (Krushinsky) and in 1750 when the city lost 40,000 inhabitants. Remarkably, the population, far from discouraged, succeeded each time in quickly rebuilding its towns and villages. The frequent alternation between demolition and rehabilitation in the city of Nishapur evoked Lord Curzon's observation that "from the twelfth century onwards it may be said that if 'Nishapur was only destroyed in order that it might be rebuilt,' it was no sooner rebuilt than it was again destroyed." The perseverance of the Persians in rebuilding their lives after such recurrent catastrophes also had made possible the return of some sort of normality to the nation under the Il-Khan regime. Yet, Ḥamd Allah Mustaufi Qazwini was but partly wrong when, some thirty years after Rashid ad-Din, he predicted that "even if for a thousand years to come no evil befalls the country, yet will it not be possible completely to repair the damage, and bring back the land to the state in which it was formerly." Certainly, the demographic losses were not made up even during the nineteenth century when, according to Charles Issawi, Persia's population doubled from 5,000,000 to 10,000,000. It is definitely only in the twentieth century, before the end of which Persia is likely to quadruple its population to some 40,000,000, that the demographic damage inflicted by the Mongols will be more than made good.[49]

Factual information about Persian-Jewish demography under the Il-Khan and Safavid dynasties, if available at all, is even less dependable than that of the general population. In the pre-Mongolian period, too, the data furnished by Benjamin of Tudela concerning Persian Jewry are far less reliable than his estimates of the size of communities he had observed before he reached the Iranian Plateau. Not only did he personally visit only a few of the widely scattered communities established long before the twelfth century east of what is now Iraq, but he apparently knew most Persian cities mentioned in his *Itinerary* mainly from hearsay. Certainly, the figures mentioned by him such as Hamadan's 30,000, Samarkand's 50,000, and Ghazni's 80,000 Jews, were decidedly overstated even if they referred to persons, rather than families or taxpayers as is usually implied in his earlier treatment. Equally unreliable are the round estimates of 40,000 in Ghazni and 40,000 more in the rest of Khurasan, mentioned by Abraham ibn Ezra, Benjamin's older contemporary. Though a great traveler, Ibn Ezra never reached the vicinity of Persia. More reasonable appear to be Benjamin's numbers of 10,000 Jews allegedly residing in Basra (Bassorah) or Shiraz and the 15,000 Jews attributed to Isfahan. But whatever one thinks about these figures, they offer little guidance to the conditions existing after the Mongol flood.[50]

If we should assume with John Masson Smith that the ultimate demographic effect of the century of Mongolian invasions was the reduction of Persia's general population to about 10 percent of its former size, the Jewish losses may actually have been even greater. To begin with, there is no record of any Jewish mass immigration similar to that of the new Mongolian and Turkoman settlers, a movement which at least partially replaced the multitudes killed, starved out, or put to flight outside the country. The subsequent great Spanish-Portuguese migrations did not significantly extend into areas east of the Ottoman Empire. In addition the wide geographic dispersion of the Persian Jews militated against their concentration in major communities. Even the relatively large Jewish community of Ormuz was estimated by Pedro Teixeira, who had spent four years in the city (1593–97), as embracing only 150 households. Of Jewish descent and probably considered by some Portuguese contemporaries as belonging to the "New Christian" category, Teixeira must have evinced some interest in the local Jews, and probably offered a plausible estimate. In 1606 a Carmelite monk mentioned the presence of 200 Jewish inhabitants. These figures testify to the growing erosion of the Jewish settlement in Ormuz even before its conquest by 'Abbas I in 1622, despite its unusual combination of commercial opportunities and considerable toleration of religious diversity. Under these circumstances the statement of Muḥammad Ṭahir Wahid, the main biographer of 'Abbas II, that when the shah's decree concerning the gifts to be given to the new converts became known throughout Persia "nearly 20,000 families of those [Jewish] communities became honored with the honor of Islam" is decidedly exaggerated. Since, as we know, a number of communities resisted conversion, many individuals escaped or went into hiding, a total of some 100,000 Jews thus converted was probably given by the historian merely in an effort to magnify the shah's success. The figure of 100,000 Jews, probably a round total for the Jewish population, was assumed by some contemporaries to have lived in all of Persia at the apogee of Jewish life in the early years of 'Abbas I's reign. It is also mentioned later by a Carmelite monk in 1657, evidently from hearsay. This was undoubtedly an exaggeration even for the years 1623–38, when the Safavid Empire included the Iraqi areas with their Jewish population of 15,000 or more. More acceptable is the estimate given by Pedro Teixeira of some 8,000 to 10,000 Jewish families or some 40,000 to 50,000 persons living in the country around 1600 C.E. This number was doubtless reduced during the great persecutions under 'Abbas I and II and the ensuing flight of many Jews. Hence more acceptable is the estimate given by Jean Chardin of some 30,000 to 35,000 Jews living in the Empire around 1670. If these estimates were more or less correct, Chardin's figure confirms the impression that during the four years since 'Abbas II's death the majority of Jewish "new converts to Islam" had publicly reverted to Judaism. More generally Chardin attests that "The race of Jews is dispersed in Media, Hyrcania, in the land of Parhes, in the two Caramanians along the Persian Gulf and in some other localities."[51]

Equally frustrating is our nearly total lack of knowledge of the Jewish natality and mortality rates or, connected with them, the average size of the Jewish family. Such data would enable us more exactly to interpret the occasional references in the sources to Jewish households, or taxpayers. If we learn, for example, from incidental mention in Rashid ad-Din's correspondence that he had at least sixteen sons and four daughters, we realize that we deal here with an exceptional case. Not only was Rashid a convert to Islam, who may well have had the permitted number of four wives in addition to concubines, but he also was a man of enormous financial resources for whom the maintenance of a large family presented no financial burden. Professing Jews may well have been, as in other Islamic lands, almost exclusively monogamous and, since their overwhelming majority consisted of petty merchants and artisans, few were in a position to maintain large households.[52]

Here and there, moreover, we hear that Jews were particularly careful in selecting localities with a healthy climate. We are told, for example, by the fourteenth-century historian-geographer Ḥamd Allah Mustaufi Qazwini that in Abarqu or Abarquyah (Fars province) Jews stayed alive for only forty days because they could not endure the local climate. This myth seems to be contradicted by the residence there of the aforementioned David, who won some influence at the court of Shah Ṣafi I. Another difficulty consisted in frequent shifts of economic centers of gravity even in the same region. For example, in the Persian Gulf area Siraf first served as the most important harbor for international trade. It was succeeded by Lar, which in turn gave way to the socioeconomic and demographic concentration, including that of Jews, in Ormuz. During the century of Portuguese domination the Ormuz Jewish community grew in numbers and influence despite the sharpening anti-Jewish trends in the rest of Persia. However, this situation changed again in 1622 when the newly established harbor of Bandar 'Abbas took over many of the commercial

activities of Ormuz and the latter's Jewish population greatly
shrank without fully compensating this loss by its rise in 'Abbas' privileged harbor. We must also bear in mind that if, because of both warlike and domestic disturbances, the general
population did not grow significantly under the Safavid domination, the Jewish community must have felt the impact of
these adverse factors even more keenly. Certainly, the very
large nomadic segment of the population had a much higher
birthrate than that of the sedentary groups. According to close
Western observers some nomadic tribes were able to treble
their numbers within thirty to forty years. But the Jews must
have shared with the rest of the sedentary population the
influence of the existing major factors of demographic
retardation.[53]

We are relatively best informed about the city of Isfahan
which, during many periods, including that of the Safavids in
the seventeenth century, served as the capital of the Empire.
As in Tabriz under the Il-Khans, the number of inhabitants in
Isfahan increased rapidly from the moment it became the capital under 'Abbas I. The mere presence of a court, the various
governmental agencies directing the far-flung imperial bureaucracy, and the numerous soldiers of the imperial guard
and local garrison attracted a considerable number of craftsmen, merchants, and foreign visitors. It is estimated that in
little more than half a century Isfahan's population increased
from 80,000 to 600,000. Jews, too, flocked into their new-old
center. We must remember that, according to widely accepted
Muslim traditions, during the First Exile (after 586 B.C.E.) many
Jews had come to the area because its climate resembled that
of Jerusalem. Despite numerous vicissitudes in the following
centuries the Jewish community of Isfahan ranked very high
in the estimation of both Jews and Muslims. A modern scholar
has rightly observed:

It is generally believed that during the first Islamic century Isfahan
consisted of two cities separated by a small distance, sometimes given
as two miles. The two cities were the town of Jayy, referred to by
Arab geographers and historians as the Madinah and today identified with the village known as Shahristan. . . . The second town of
the pair was known as Yahudiyyah, literally the Jewish quarter. . . .
Sometime later the town of Jayy declined and the life of Isfahan was
concentrated in Yahudiyyah.

Jews were also said to have, after establishing their original settlement, repelled all attackers from the outside, introduced irrigation, and generally built up the famed city. At the same time some Arab traditions emphasized the purported role of the Isfahan Jews as the perennial enemies of Islam. The Muslim mythology concerning the future messianic age included, in part, the belief that the evil forces preceding the end of days would be led by a *dajjal*—the Muslim counterpart of Antichrist—who would appear in the Jewish quarter of Isfahan.[54]

Despite the presence of numerous foreign observers in the city, there is hardly any mention of the size of its Jewish population. The figure of only 600 Jews mentioned by Jean Chardin at the same time when he estimated their country-wide population at 50–60 times that number, may have reflected the results of 'Abbas II's forced conversion and the temporary removal of the professing Jews from the city not long before. But as we recall, most Jews were soon thereafter able to reaffirm their allegiance to their ancestral faith while continuing to live in or returning to the city. Yet, it stands to reason that, while the Jewish settlement may have increased alongside the general population it probably never reached again the number of 15,000 Jews mentioned by Benjamin in the twelfth century. Otherwise it would have embraced one-third and perhaps nearly half of the Jewish population of the entire country, and thus have further reduced the average size of the other communities existing in the latter part of the seventeenth century. If we accept Babai b. Luṭf's assertion that there were 30 organized Jewish communities in the country (probably in addition to quite a few Jewish individuals or families scattered in smaller towns and villages) and disregard the temporary upsurge of Ormuz, the average size of the Persian communities would have amounted to but 700–1,000 persons, which is possible but not very likely.[55]

ECONOMIC AMBIGUITIES

If the picture of the Jewish legal, political, and demographic situation in Persia appears rather fuzzy, that of the Jewish economic activities in the country is almost totally devoid of clarity, consistency, or concrete documentation. By the nature of things most economic data have been recorded in the older sources only when they were out of the ordinary, were subject to litigation, controversies over inheritance, related to taxation, and the like. They were usually mentioned in private correspondence, court proceedings, responsa by scholars, or accounts by fiscal administrators. Such records are almost totally absent in Persia before 1650 because few public, communal, or private archives dating from that period have been preserved.

Occasionally, a new ruler seeking popular acceptance, like Afsharid Nadir Shah (1736–47), destroyed the accumulated tax records as a demonstration of his intention to relieve the population of its oppressive fiscal burdens. The few extant Jewish sources are almost completely silent on these aspects. There are practically no responsa by contemporary Persian rabbis—elsewhere a fertile source of economic information— nor do we have business records, wills, and other documents stemming from Jewish individuals or communities. Even the private letters written by the convert Rashid ad-Din, a rarity even among the Muslim majority, which have given us so many insights into Persia's economic life at the height of its prosperity under the Il-Khan dynasty, contribute very little to our knowledge of its Jewish aspects. The historical literature, on the other hand, from which we derive most of our information about the conditions of the country and its inhabitants, is generally deficient because of its almost exclusive orientation on court and governmental affairs and its ensuing neglect of what happened among the masses, especially in the provinces. The pertinent meager information we possess stems, therefore, largely from observations of foreign visitors. But even these writers were, for the most part, either diplomats or clergymen whose interests were mostly confined to political or Muslim and Christian religious affairs, in which the Jews played a minimal role. Evidently, the Jewish minority did not seem important enough to be considered in any detail.

Hence only a visitor like Jean Chardin, himself a businessman, with a sharp eye for socioeconomic as well as political aspects of life in Isfahan, gives us some inkling about Jewish economic activity. Although not unbiased, he graphically presents the following general picture of Persian Jewry's eco-

nomic pursuits about 1670, that is, after the return to some
sort of normality among the Jewish survivors of the sharp persecutions of 1656–61:

They [the Jews] are poor and downtrodden everywhere. I have not
seen a single family whom one could call wealthy and who would not
live in a low state [*bassesse*]. A part of the people consists of artisans,
but the majority lives from machinations [*intrigues*], resales [of sec-
ond-hand clothing, furniture, and the like], usury, brokerage, sale
of wine, and procuring women. They are also frequently involved in
medicine, drugs, and magic in various places and this is the source
of their greatest gains. For their women slip into the serails [where
they sell to their foolish and naïve inmates all sorts of charms and
love potions]. . . . But to what this miserable race of men apply
themselves most is that they do not deal in good faith so that in the
end one finds oneself cheated. The Jews were once the great usurers
of the country before the arrival of the Gentile Indians who, being
richer and more accommodating, made them lose this unjust trade
which they valued more highly than any other occupation.

Prejudiced as this general description is, it appears adequately
to mirror the low standing of Persian Jewry after its emergence from the nightmare of forced conversions. Very likely,
however, its economic status was somewhat better before 'Abbas I's reversal of his friendly attitude.[56]

Any detailed study of Persian Jewish economic history is
further impeded by the prevailing self-imposed isolation and
internal diversity of Persian society at large. Symbolic of such
aloofness was the behavior of Ṭahmasp I, a long-reigning shah,
who is said to "have spent the last eleven years of his life in
voluntary solitude in his royal palace." His people did not quite
imitate the men of Kashmir who, according to Muḥammad
ibn Aḥmad Al-Biruni (973–1048), had "in former times used
to allow one or two foreigners to enter their country, particularly Jews, but at present they do not allow any Hindu whom
they do not know personally to enter, much less other people." As we shall see, Ṭahmasp rudely refused to have any
contacts with Anthony Jenkinson, the head of an English mission. On their part, the mostly poor and downtrodden Jews
were rarely in touch with their brethren in other lands. This
was in sharp contrast with the pre-Mongolian period, when
Persian Jews had continued to cultivate exchanges with the
Babylonian and Palestinian communities. Some such relation-

ships were also maintained during the short Persian occupation of Iraqi lands in the sixteenth and seventeenth centuries.
When these were annexed by the Ottoman Empire, however,
the almost constant hostilities between the two countries sty-
mied this type of rapprochement. Unlike their Muslim neighbors relatively few Jews made pilgrimages to the tombs of saints
outside their country. The great distances from the centers of
Jewish life thus made themselves deeply felt. We must remember that a Turkish army marching from Istanbul to Erzerum
on the border of Persia had to stop at 65 stations. Such distances made travel, particularly during the long and hard winters, extremely arduous. Inside Persia proper there were hardly
any regular roads, only paths, some of them through dreary
deserts, which were traversed by caravans using camels, mules,
or donkeys. Nor were there navigable rivers, except the Karun
in a small area of the south. Although organized, particularly
in the Safavid period, on the basis of royal absolutism and a
theory resembling the Western doctrine of the "divine right of
kings," the provinces represented a variety of societal structures. In fact, there existed a constant tension between the
central administration and the governors of the various provinces. There was an especially great disparity between territories inhabited predominantly by nomads, whose number was
variously estimated, we recall, as ranging from 30 to 50 percent of Persia's total population, and the sedentary rural and
urban settlements. As a small minority, Jews had to adjust
themselves to these differing environments, although we know
practically nothing about how, or even whether, they still lived
within the nomadic structures in the post-Mongolian period.
Even the few Jewish tribal villages, recorded in the vicinity of
Nishapur in the eleventh and twelfth centuries, may have disappeared during the Mongolian invasion, and we hear no more
about them after 1260.[57]

In *agriculture,* which was the mainstay of the country's economy, Jews seem to have played a very minor role. To be sure,
the manufacture of wine, prohibited to the Muslims, offered
Jews and Christians an opportunity to supply the relatively
large quantities of alcoholic beverages imbibed by numerous
Muslims, including several shahs. Some rulers became out-

right alcoholics. But this did not necessarily lead to the Jews' active participation in the cultivation of vineyards which were to be found in many areas. We also learn of Jews ordered by the king to cultivate the silkworm. We may perhaps venture to guess that some Jews of Azerbaijan and neighboring Armenia were also engaged in breeding the *kermes* (or *qirmiz*) insects which supplied the famous dye for Persia and other countries. (We still have a reminder of that dye in the English words "crimson" and "carmine.") We may perhaps assume that the three Jews of Arles, who in 1138 took over the entire output of the kermes dye in the district of Miramar from Abbot Pontius of Montmajour, came to the Provence from Persia or its vicinity. Otherwise the conditions of the farmers living under most of the autocratic Persian regimes were far from inviting for Jews to settle on land. The records pertaining to Persian agriculture are filled with complaints about the severe exploitation of the peasants, not only by their direct masters but also by the shah's officials and tax farmers. As a result very frequently the tillers of the soil completely disappeared from a village before the approach of the collectors, a practice already recorded in the Talmud as relating to some of the then numerous Jewish agriculturists in Sassanian Persia. Nor do we hear of any Jews employed by landlords for the task of collecting the produce or for selling it in urban markets. The constant growth of land held by the *waqfs* and by the religious class was likewise an impediment to Jewish participation. Certainly, nothing of the kind of administrative and financial services rendered by Jews on the Polish, Lithuanian, and Ukrainian latifundia seems to have been performed by their coreligionists in Persian lands.[58]

Somewhat better is the situation concerning the Jewish share in Persia's *industry and commerce*. To be sure, here, too, we are largely confined to generalities. We possess a few statistical data about the general trends in the Persian economy but practically none about the number of Jews engaged in either craftsmanship or domestic and international trade. Nor are we certain about the particular branches of each in which most Jews happened to be employed. A major impediment to Jewish enterprises in any field consisted in the general lack of investment capital. Such shortages are evidenced by what is known about Persian currency and the plethora of operating mints. A modern compilation has shown that more than one hundred towns in the Safavid area, at one time or another, put out a variety of coins, in addition to those brought in from other countries. Remarkably, Jews, who in earlier periods had played a considerable role in minting in both East and West, had little if any share in striking coins in Persia, although this trade was frequently entrusted to private entrepreneurs. Monetary circulation, moreover, seems to have been quite chaotic. The gold coins struck by a number of mints, including the *abbasi*s, weighing 144 grams when issued by 'Abbas I, speedily disappeared from the markets into hoards maintained by government officials, landowners, businessmen, as well as by the Treasury. By the 1670s Jean Chardin could claim that the Persians had no gold coins. In fact, the general financial policies of the Safavid regime and, to a lesser extent, that of its Il-Khan predecessors, resembled the mercantilist outlook of their Western European counterparts; they considered it advantageous for the country to export more goods than were imported, measuring its wealth by how much money could be hoarded by both the public and the government.[59]

While trade with India was uninterruptedly carried on for many centuries, exchanges with the Ottoman Empire were inhibited by the numerous years of Turko-Persian wars and a general feeling of hostility between the two countries even during the more peaceful intervals. At one point Sultan Selim I the Grim actually introduced what amounted to a blockade of Persia's shipments to the Mediterranean lands. When, in 1561, Anthony Jenkinson arrived in the Persian capital in order to establish a new channel of communication between England and Persia, he was at first received rather hospitably. But when Ṭahmasp I learned that he came for purposes of developing trade relations, the shah bluntly informed the Englishman (to quote Jenkinson's diary): "We have no need to haue friendship with unbeleuers, and so uilled me to depart." Ṭahmasp's xenophobic extremism was later moderated with respect to Muscovy. But a complete reversal came only under 'Abbas I, who was described by a Persian merchant as "a gallant soldier, very bountiful and liberal to strangers." He welcomed not only individual European businessmen but also representatives of the Dutch and English companies then newly formed to expand trade with the Middle East. Thus the Dutch East India Company, its English counterpart, and the English Levant Company were enabled to develop considerable trade relations with the Persian Empire. Possibly some of the Jewish members of the Dutch Company from among the small Jewish community of Amsterdam participated in that exchange of goods, but there is little documentary evidence to supply any details. For a time the Dutch had the advantage of both having more disposable funds and enjoying direct government support, whereas the English companies had to find their own way with occasional mild intercessions by their country's diplomatic agents. On the other hand, some English entrepreneurs, especially the brothers Anthony and Robert Sherley, played an active role as advisers to 'Abbas I on international relations. On one occasion, Robert Sherley was sent by the shah to England to negotiate with the English authorities, even though 'Abbas must have anticipated that Robert's mission would be hampered by the presence in London of an official Persian envoy and the general hostility of the English business circles to his undertaking. In Isfahan, too, the Sherleys helped the shah to improve Persia's technology, particularly for use by the army. It has long been assumed that they were responsible for teaching the Persians how effectively to construct and employ cannons and thus make up for the theretofore existing Ottoman superiority in the field. In this connection we may recall the contribution Spanish-Portuguese and Sicilian Jewish artisans had made to the early development of artillery for Ottoman use. There was no comparable influx of skilled Jewish craftsmen into Persia. To be sure, the claim by the Englishmen that they had played a decisive role in this innovation has been refuted by recent evidence of some Persian use of artillery before the Sherleys' arrival in Isfahan. But what the artisans brought with them from England may have been responsible for some improvement in the effectiveness of Persia's new cannons. Thus they may have helped the shah to overcome the resistance of many Persian officers who disliked

the deployment of that slow-moving weapon. Even later some
of them preferred speedy campaigns through the use of a mass
of cavalry which was readily available by the military training
of nomadic horsemen. This example of technological backwardness could easily be multiplied also in Persia's general agricultural and industrial pursuits.[60]

Another major difficulty consisted in the large diversity in
the economic structures and activities of the various provinces.
Because of the great distances and difficulties of communication each area was even more autonomous economically than
politically. The lack of effective guidance from the center, despite the prevailing absolutist theories, greatly contributed to
the heterogeneity of economic pursuits from one area to another. With it also went a great instability in the price structure. We need but recall Claude Cahen's reference to Sarakh-
si's comparison between the relative income levels in medieval
Baghdad and Khurasan, illustrated by the fact that an annual
income of 200 dirhems was considered below poverty level in
Baghdad, whereas in Khurasan the recipient of 50 dirhems
was viewed as a rich man. (These disparities often persisted
for centuries.) Such differences must have gravely interfered
with any kind of planning for both industrial and commercial
enterprises. Hence, there were but short periods of prosperity
like those of 1290–1330 under the Il-Khan, and 1590–1629
under the Safavid dynasties. According to Jean Chardin, when
'Abbas I "ceased to live [in 1629] Persia ceased to prosper."
This instability must have affected Jews doubly because, unlike their Ottoman coreligionists, the Persian Jews had neither
political clout nor the moderating factor of intensive connections with Jews of other lands.[61]

Nor did the Jews play a significant role in Persia's *industry,*
if we gauge from the scanty references to Jewish craftsmen in
the existing literature. Apart from the production of wine, they
may have been interested, for ritualistic reasons, in preparing
cheese and other dairy products for their own use as they did
in many other lands. Certainly, slaughtering of animals in their
traditional way, if that may be classified as a craft (together
with butcher shops), must have been part of the Jewish communal structure in most Persian cities as well. In his chronicle

Babai b. Luṭf mentions three butchers who played a part in the great tragedy. The production of silk, the most sought-for product of Persian industry, though theoretically a royal monopoly, and connected with it dyeing, carpet making, upholstering, and related activities, probably likewise offered a livelihood to a substantial number of Jews. According to J. B. Tavernier, the Jews of Lar were "famous for the manufacture of silk and especially of silk girdles." Cornelius de Bruyn, writing about the northern province of Mazandaran, stated that there "silk is fabricated by a society of Jews" and that in the southern city of Shiraz "Jews are manufacturing stuffs of gold and silk." The Jews of Yezd escaped forced conversion only because their Muslim neighbors petitioned the shah to exempt them from the decree on the grounds that the city needed the Jewish weavers and gardeners. This petition proved more successful than that of the Sicilian Christian leaders who, in 1492, had argued with Ferdinand and Isabella that the expulsion of Jews would deprive the population of irreplaceable skilled artisans producing agricultural and military equipment. Many Persian Jews undoubtedly also pursued the traditional Jewish occupations of tailoring, gold and silver smithery, manufacture of jewelry, perhaps also of glass, and the like. However, some of these assumptions are undocumented, and one must admit that the few sporadic and casual references in the extant sources do not add up to a rounded picture of Persian Jewish craftsmanship.[62]

A major question in this connection, which cannot be resolved with the documentation at hand, is the relation of Jewish craftsmen to the existing guilds. The presence of artisan guilds, as well as merchant corporations, in many Persian cities is well attested (there even was a beggars' corporation in Isfahan), although the details of their operations are far less clear than in some other Islamic countries. While the Persian guilds differed from similar organizations called *futuwwa*, with which they have often been confused, by being primarily economic rather than spiritual associations, they, too, had a definitely religious coloring. With the extreme Shi'ite doctrine of purity, some of them may have steered clear of admitting "impure infidels" to membership. On the other hand, the essential control over their operations was in the hands of officials appointed by the government rather than elected by the members, and the central regime's *raison d'état* may have regarded the participation of Armenians, Georgians, and Jews as politically and economically desirable. (This may even have been true under those monarchs who liked to display their religious piety in such extreme ways as did 'Abbas I, when he made a pilgrimage on foot to Riza's tomb in Meshed. He traversed the distance of approximately 800 miles in 28 days, averaging about 29 miles a day.) In such cases, the admission of Jewish youths as apprentices in the various crafts, and their later certification as master-artisans entitled to run their own shops, must have depended on the approval of the guilds. Together with the governmentally appointed *muḥtasib*s the guild leaders doubtless also supervised the quality of the members' work and their moral behavior. At the same time, at least in their larger communities, Jews and other religious minorities seem to have enjoyed a measure of self-government in some of these activities, at least within their own quarters. Regrettably, much of this argumentation is based upon conjecture, supported by few dependable data in the existing primary or secondary literature.[63]

Curiously, we are not better off with respect to *commerce*, international or domestic. Only relatively few Jews seem to have participated in larger undertakings of a regional or national scope. The story told by the early-eighteenth-century German antisemite Johann Andreas Eisenmenger, in his work *Entdecktes Judenthum* (published in 1700 but delayed in circulation through Jewish and imperial efforts), if true, would shed an interesting light on the Jewish part in the export of silk. According to that report, "one Eliezer, allegedly a Persian vizier, together with his brother Jacob Haya, had come to Aleppo twenty-four years ago, bringing with them 70 camels loaded with silk. From there he proceeded to Jerusalem, where he distributed a lot of money." While no price is mentioned, it stands to reason that 70 camels carried a load of some 17,000 kilograms of silk which, on the average, were worth 20–25 dinars each, or a total of some 400,000 dinars. This was a very substantial amount even if it had been handled by one of the East India Companies. We also recall the story of the Jew Isaac who several centuries earlier had brought to Ormuz or Oman a ship laden with precious ware from India worth several million dinars. While this fantastic journey dates from the pre-Mongolian period, it is not unlikely that one or another Jewish entrepreneur of Ormuz, which according to the testimony of De Silva y Figueroa and others was open to traders of all nationalities without regard to their ethnic identity, was able to handle an export or import trade of considerable size. Regrettably, the documentation even for that city, which is far more ample than for other cities (except perhaps Isfahan), does not include concrete details to illustrate such exploits.[64]

Perhaps Eisenmenger's tales merely reflected the prevailing notion in Central Europe that, like their Ottoman coreligionists, the Persian Jews, too, actively participated in their country's international trade. To be sure, during the relatively short periods when Iraq was included in the Persian possessions, the Jews of that province continued to maintain some relations with the Asian sections of the Ottoman Empire despite the discouragement of such exchanges by both regimes. It may be assumed that, through the mediation of Iraqi Jews, some of their coreligionists in other Persian provinces came into frequent contacts with West-Asian Jews, especially those of the city of Aleppo. However, as soon as the Turks recaptured Baghdad and Mosul in 1638–39 these contacts were greatly impeded. On the other hand, Persian Jewry's relations with India seem to have continued throughout the medieval period when the Arab seafarers dominated the sea-lanes on the Indian Ocean. A fuller picture of that Perso-Indian Jewish trade will undoubtedly emerge from the long-awaited publication of the Genizah materials relating to Jewish commerce on the Indian Ocean, which has been in preparation by S. D. Goitein. Although at the beginning of the modern period the Arabs were displaced by the Portuguese, and later by the Dutch and English navigators, Jews were able to reach India by land or through the mediation of Ormuz as long as it was a Portuguese colony. In all such efforts they were undoubtedly aided by the inexpensive water transport on the river Karun, which was the major waterway in that Persian region and carried much traffic from areas even beyond Khurasan.[65]

In all these matters Jews depended on some form of cooperation from the municipal authorities or even from local corporations. Many of them undoubtedly sold their wares at retail in a local bazaar, such as the grand royal bazaar of Isfahan. This remarkable institution was greatly admired by foreign visitors. According to Thomas Herbert, it was ten times the size of the largest market in Paris. It was also supposed to have been very clean, emanated aromatic odors, and was a joy to visit. Jewish merchants could naturally occupy stalls only with the permission of the authorities. It was probably there that Herbert saw the merchandise sold by Jews which he highly praised, as did John Fryer. Bazaars were, of course, not exclusive, and some wares, especially those needed for daily consumption, were probably sold closer to the customers' dwellings, including shops located inside, or very near, the Jewish quarter. In many smaller cities, too, Jews derived their livelihood from local, as well as long-distance commerce. According to Arakel, "Jews in this country were rich and opulent, many of them had booths and stalls in the bazaars where they sold fine clothes and silverware." In the small town of Karb, near Baghdad, according to Qazwini, Jews extensively traded in paper, silk, and clothes. They found, however, increasing competition from the other minorities, especially the Indians and the Armenians. Isfahan's Armenian Julfa quarter became for a time the major trading center in the city. Apparently owning more liquid capital, the Indian and Armenian merchants largely displaced the Jews even in the traditionally Jewish money trade—about the extent of which in Persia we are poorly informed—and even expanded their successful competition to Poland, for instance to the city of Zamość.[66]

Not very much more is known about Jewish *professions*. While few, if any, Jews were allowed to join the Safavid bureaucracy, some undoubtedly made a living from occupations connected with the Jewish religion. We know very little even about the Persian rabbinate, although Jewish spiritual leaders, as well as synagogue readers and sextons, existed in many communities.

We happen to learn more about scribes because their names appear on colophons of some extant Judeo-Persian manuscripts. We also come across occasional references to a Jewish doctor or midwife. For example, Pietro della Valle mentions that in Kashan he met a Jewish physician who was so greatly in demand that he refused to visit his patients. When one was too ill to come to him, he sent one of his assistants to observe the person's symptoms and then prescribed a remedy. Della Valle also complained that he could not persuade the doctor to sell him a precious Avicenna manuscript. Characteristically, we hear a good deal about Jewish entertainers: storytellers, musicians, dancers, as well as fortune tellers, and the like. Women, too, often found access to the wives of dignitaries by selling them potions designed to avert the evil influences of demons, to retain their husbands' affection, or to offer some magic healing of certain, sometimes medically uncontrollable, ailments. What we are told by a Dutch visitor, Theodor Salmon, in 1739 was undoubtedly the result of a long chain of evolution. He wrote:

The Indians [Benjanen] in Persia are superior to Jews in both trading and numbers. They have the money exchange of all of Persia in their hands and have displaced the Jews from almost all leases, exchanges, and negotiations so that the Persian Jews are a poor and despised crowd. Since they are unable to earn money through commerce, they concentrate on fortune telling and other low grade arts. Their women especially smuggle themselves into the harems and wish to help the poor women with their love potions to arouse or to maintain their husbands' amorous desires.[67]

Nor do we possess solid knowledge of any *special Jewish taxation*. The continuity of the Muslim system, which had been inherited from the Great Caliphate by its successor states, was interrupted to a large extent by the Mongolian invasions. During the first decades of the Il-Khan domination, we recall, the new rulers drew very few distinctions between the different religious communities, and the special Christian and Jewish poll tax, the *jizya*, went out of existence. If, in 1295, as the Muslim neophyte Ghazan reintroduced it into the country's fiscal system—"a monstrous and self-contradictory combination of methods introduced by the nomad conqueror . . . and ancient Iranian traditions kept up by the Abbasid caliphate"

(I. P. Petrushevsky)—he probably found the absence of records of pertinent taxpayers accumulated over the previous years so burdensome for the Treasury agents to enforce, that he himself suspended the tax after two years. It was reintroduced in 1306 by his successor, Öljeytu, but we hear very little about its actual collection in the various provinces. The operation of this fiscal branch was probably further disorganized after 1338 under the largely chaotic conditions prevailing in the respective khanates which emerged from the disintegration of the Il-Khan Empire. Neither did the imperial unity, reestablished by the Safavids, and their proclamation of the Muslim faith as the dominant factor in all public affairs necessarily reinstate an effective administration of the poll tax. In view of the great power exercised by the provincial governors, especially outside the areas covered by the crown lands, it is very likely that the local and regional authorities found simpler ways of enriching themselves at the cost of all potential taxpayers. Under the general administrative disarray most higher officials had vast opportunities to impose the annual taxes several times a year, to enforce arbitrary billets for their soldiers and functionaries, and to extract from the lower classes all sorts of other services as they saw fit. Under these circumstances it probably did not pay to have a special department in charge of taxes collectible from the tiny Jewish minority, or even from the Christian population. Moreover, a large segment of Christians consisted of tax-exempt former Georgian and Armenian captives and others serving as soldiers, or performing some other useful services for the Crown or provincial governors. At any rate, even the lesser dignitaries, as well as most individual landlords in their possessions, were able to collect needed revenue, whether it was legally prescribed or not. We have the record, for instance, of one district leader who suddenly imposed upon the local people a substantial tax for expenses connected with the marriage of his daughter. In general, the arbitrariness in the fiscal administration and its ultimate limitations are well illustrated by a saying attributed to Shah Ghazan. Addressing an assembly of his dignitaries, he is supposed to have exclaimed: "Let's rob them [the *ra'ayat* or subjects] together," but he added that in the long run there would be no *ra'ayat*. This warning that extreme fiscal exploitation would lead to total exhaustion of the population and its ensuing flight to other regions had been suggested to Ghazan by his grand vizier, Rashid ad-Din; it served as the major deterrent to total exploitation of both the peasantry and the urban masses. But such warnings were disregarded by many provincial governors and local officials in both the Il-Khan and Safavid empires. In short, it is quite possible that members of the predominantly small Jewish communities of the country escaped the additional burdens of special taxation, as was the case even in more affluent Ormuz after the Persian recapture of the district from the Portuguese.[68]

HEROIC PERSEVERANCE

According to the old adage, "Happy is the people which has no history," Persian Jewry should have been one of the happiest peoples on earth, at least during the period of 1250 to 1650. We have seen that, although one cannot literally apply here the old saying of the medieval Italian glossators, *Quod non est in actis, non est in mundo,* the extreme paucity of extant records has made it impossible for me to draw a satisfactory picture of the public and private life of the Jewish communities in Persia. Much of what has been presented here has been derived from casual remarks by travelers or occasional references in the few extant official documents. Much of that information, however, has come from different areas and periods, offering very little of comparative value. What may have been true of the Jews of Isfahan or Tabriz, when they were the respective capitals of the Empire, between themselves not fully comparable, may not have applied to any provincial community. There certainly were major differences in regard to what happened to the Jews in Iraq and those of Balkh or Herat when they all lived under Persian domination. None of them, important in their own right, have been under Persian rule in recent generations. At the moment of this writing there actually is a war going on between Iraq and Iran (curiously a war without a break in diplomatic relations!), while Balkh and Herat are parts of Afghanistan now under Soviet occupation.

Nishapur, which apparently still maintained an important Jewish community, under the Safavids, was, because of its predominantly nomadic environment, completely different in its socioeconomic pursuits than, for instance, Ormuz, whether during the century of Portuguese occupation or under Persian sovereignty. Thus, whatever we learn about the Jews on the Iranian Plateau gives us only fragmentary insights into the totality of Jewish life under the Il-Khans, Safavids, or whatever major or minor princes ruled over the Jewish communities in the century and a half between these two dynasties. Much of the effort in this chapter has therefore necessarily been based on the more familiar general conditions of the country and its diverse minorities. Hence comes also the disproportionate space given here to the general, rather than Jewishly relevant, literature, and on reasoning, conjecture, and estimates which may be disproved by future research.

One may ask, therefore, why was so much space devoted in our general historical treatment of the Jewish people as a whole to one of its relatively minor segments. Counting a population of no more than 30,000 to 50,000 persons, living in some thirty small communities, scattered over a large and diverse geographic area and, for the most part, isolated from the rest of the Jewish world; playing but a minor role in the political and economic life of their own country; and making but slight contributions to Jewish religious, literary, and artistic endeavors— it certainly was not an entity comparable in historic importance with the Jewries of many other countries located within the centers of Jewish life around the Mediterranean Basin. Yet, we must not forget that even 30,000 to 50,000 Jews were not a negligible quantity in a Jewish world population which at that time probably did not exceed 1,000,000 persons. More importantly, even these smaller communities might have exercised a great influence on world Jewry, if they had included great personalities like Rashi and his family in eleventh-century Troyes or Isaac Luria and Joseph Karo in sixteenth-century Safed. At the same time the Persian communities could look back on a very long and significant history before the Mongolian invasion, which included nearly two millennia, possibly all the way to the fall of Northern Israel in the eighth century B.C.E. Certainly, during the centuries of Achaemenid or Sassanian rule or that of the Great Caliphate, whenever the Empire included Babylonia and, for a long time, also Palestine, Persian Jewry was in the mainstream of the history of the whole people, in which the Persian civilization played a significant role.[69]

With such a millennial history behind them, the Persian Jews, after recovering from the blood bath of the Mongolian invasions revealed under the Il-Khan and Safavid dynasties a great vitality and perseverance under extremely unfavorable external conditions. In the mid-seventeenth century they even defied the two attempts by powerful despotic governments to force them to adopt Islam and thus to become completely assimilated to the Persian majority. This quiet but fierce resistance was nurtured by that great heritage to which their writers (such as the fourteenth-century poet Shahin and the two later poets-chroniclers, Babai b. Luṭf and Babai b. Farhad) looked back with much pride. The memory of their great past was also constantly revived by pious pilgrimages to the tombs of ancient prophets or the heroes of the Book of Esther. This extraordinary fortitude of a tiny minority unflinchingly retaining its identity against tremendous odds, unaided by any support it might have received from coreligionists abroad, was a testimony of an inner vitality and resilience which was often overlooked by foreign observers.

It was this vitality, moreover, which made Persian Jewry contribute to Jewish history in still another important way. We must always remember that much of what happened to the Jewish people in Central Asia, Pakistan, India, and China owed its beginnings to Persian-speaking Jews. A good deal of the early documentation found in Turkestan, Afghanistan, India, and China was written in the Judeo-Persian dialect, developed by Jews in the Persian homeland but transferred by Jewish emigrants or travelers into these lands far off the Jewish center. True, the Jewish communities in these eastern lands have always been numerically very small and made but minor contributions to world Jewish life. Yet, looking into the future, we must not forget that India and China alone now embrace a population of about one-third of all humanity, and that the story of any Jewish beginnings in these areas assumes a world significance beyond their immediate impact in the past. From this point of view, the heroic perseverance of Persian Jewry through the Mongolian Deluge and thereafter and its unbroken historic continuity to the present day has had a historic importance which cannot yet be fully assessed in world terms.

ON ISLAM'S PERIPHERY

I N THE vicinity of the Persian Empire were located the Jewish communities residing in Bukhara and Khiva whose structure, even in the period of their separation from the Empire, could be considered a simple elongation of Persian Jewish cultural patterns. Their ordinary speech was Judeo-Persian and their traditions were basically the same as those of the Jews of some northern Persian provinces. However, because of their different regimes, their outward destinies were often divergent. To some extent this is also true of Samarkand which, in the days of Timur Lenk (Tamerlane) served as the capital of another vast empire and temporarily played a certain role in the history of Asian Jewish communities at large. Of a different nature were the developments in such predominantly non-Muslim areas as Georgia and Armenia, although there, too, the Islamic influences, dating back to the Great Caliphate and the Mongolian invasions, continued to make themselves strongly felt during the long Turko-Persian confrontations. Different again was the story of the "Mountain Jews" of Caucasia, as well as of the Jews and Krimchaks in Crimea and its environs. As long as these areas were under the domination of the Mongolian states established by the descendants of Jenghiz Khan, they had little recorded Jewish history. But after their emergence as independent principalities, Jewish communities began to play an important role in the areas of the Black and Caspian Seas, while the rising star of the Muscovite Empire began casting its shadow on them, renewing some of the old influences emanating from the Byzantine Empire. Ultimately they were incorporated into the ever-expanding Russian Empire and now form an integral part of the Soviet Union.[1]

Important though the relatively long history of some of the Jewries scattered over these large territories is, it would lead us too far in our treatment of the general socioreligious history of the Jewish people as a whole to pay detailed attention to these "extraneous" groups. There is a considerable literature referring to most of these "Exiled and Redeemed" of Israel, as Itzhak Ben-Zvi called them in his pertinent study under this title. Some additional bibliography can easily be located in encyclopedias and other handbooks. An exception, however, is to be made here with respect to three countries, Ethiopia, India, and China. In the case of Ethiopia, we deal with a country which had connections with the Jewish people going back to antiquity; according to local traditions, all the way to King Solomon. Its languages have been of considerable importance in the research on the Hebrew Bible, the Apocrypha, and the Pseudepigrapha. For several centuries, moreover, there was an independent Jewish principality there which at times fired the imagination of Jews in many lands. Today the Falashas, as the Ethiopian Jews are called, still offer a great enigma about their historic role in world Jewry. Of different interest have been the communities of Bene-Israel and the "White" and "Black Jews" in Cochin, India, as well as that of Kaifeng in China. In view of the tremendous importance of these two most populous nations in the world and because their medieval and modern Jewries lived there among peoples outside the Judeo-Christian-Muslim monotheistic world, they merit special consideration.[2]

ETHIOPIA

According to deep-rooted Ethiopian traditions, the reigning Solomonid dynasty traced its descent back to King Solomon. Following the description in the *Kebra Nagast* (Glory of the Empire) which, compiled in the years 1314–22 under the reign of Amda Sion (1314–44), quickly obtained almost canonical authority. (After 1850 Ethiopia's Emperor John pleaded with the British government to return to him a manuscript of that work, since without it he could not impose his will upon his subjects.) Makeda, the Queen of Sheba, on her visit to Jerusalem, recorded in the Bible, was greatly impressed by the Israelitic religion. She reputedly exclaimed: "From now on I shall not worship the Sun, but rather the Creator of the Sun, the

God of Israel." Allegedly seduced by King Solomon, she was said to have given birth to a son who later became Emperor Menelik I of Ethiopia. Thus was founded a dynasty which became particularly prominent in the Late Middle Ages and reigned until the overthrow of the monarchy in 1974. Its legendary genealogy was reiterated in many official pronouncements throughout the centuries. As late as 1955 the new constitution adopted under the aegis of the imperial regime declared:

The Imperial dignity shall remain perpetually attached to the line of Haile Sallasie I . . . whose line descends without interruption from the dynasty of Menelik I, son of the Queen of Ethiopia, the Queen of Sheba, and King Solomon of Jerusalem [Art. 2].
By virtue of His Imperial Blood as well as by the anointing which He has received, the person of the Emperor is sacred, His dignity is inviolable and His power indisputable [Art. 4].

The very title, *negus* (king, or *negusha nagasht,* king of kings), assumed by the successive emperors, had its roots in the Hebraic term *nogesh* (he who extracts tribute). Many other Hebraic influences emanated from the Hebrew Bible which, in later generations, was circulating in Ethiopia in a Coptic translation, indebted to the Septuagint rather than to other translations underlying many Eastern and Western Christian renditions.[3]

It is possible, therefore, that, on Solomon's well-known expeditions to Ophir, whether located near the Red Sea or further east on the Indian Ocean, some Israelitic sailors landed on the western shores of the Red Sea. Of course, this possibility does not confirm the various legends current among the Falashas such as that the first Israelites to settle in the country were 12,000 men chosen by the Queen of Sheba or Menelik I when they left the land of Israel, taking with them 1,000 men chosen from each of the twelve tribes. Nor is there any evidence for Jewish settlements of refugees after the first fall of Jerusalem, especially from among the Israelites who had joined Jeremiah in his flight to Egypt or two and a half centuries later during the great commotion in the Middle East caused by the conquests of Alexander the Great.

Concerning the origin of the Jewish settlement in Ethiopia,

it has long been assumed by competent scholars that Jews may have penetrated Ethiopia from two directions. On the one hand, some may have come from the ancient Jewish groups established in southern Arabia and from among the 500 soldiers of Herod's army who had accompanied Aelius Gallus' expedition there in 24–25 B.C.E. On the other hand, inhabitants of the Jewish colonies in Upper Egypt, such as Elephantine, may also have gone beyond Nubia into the Ethiopian area. The two groups may have merged into Jewish communities especially in the period of the Byzantine-Sassanian rivalries which extended down to the Arabian peninsula. Certainly, when Judaism spread to Yemen and its vicinity and even led to the conversion of King Dhu Nuwas in the sixth century, its expansion was checked only by the Abyssinian Christians' victory over the Jewish king, initiated by Byzantine advisers. The Abyssinian conquest was in turn replaced by the occupation of the country by Persian soldiers. All those commotions doubtless strengthened the Jewish elements inside Ethiopia. Thus the early Jewish beginnings antedated the adoption of Christianity by a large part of the local population in the fourth century. It would not be at all astonishing if, as elsewhere in the Mediterranean world, the presence of Jews greatly facilitated the work of Christian missionaries in spreading their faith also among the Ethiopian natives. One may therefore agree with Hermann Norden's statement that "the most logical explanation of the enclave of Falasha is that when the major part of Abyssinia became converted to Christianity in the fourth century, they remained staunch to their ancient faith."[4]

Among the numerous tribes inhabiting the large country of Ethiopia with its fluctuating frontiers there also was a Jewish group named Falasha. This designation is often interpreted as the Ethiopic equivalent of "exilic," or a people living in the *galut*. Very likely the Falashas embraced for a long time a variety of subdivisions dependent on local conditions. In this respect they may have resembled the later development of the predominantly Muslim Gallas who, according to fairly recent estimates, embraced a population of less than 2,500,000, and yet consisted of an agglomeration of some 200 tribal units. But little is known about the Falashas as such before they aroused the curiosity of outsiders, Jewish and non-Jewish. Regrettably, little evidence has been forthcoming from their own midst. Their extant literature, largely recovered through the efforts of Western Christians and Jews, consisted of biblical and apocryphal literature, written in the Ge'ez dialect which, though no longer spoken, was considered a sacred tongue by both Christians and Jews. In fact, the texts of these sacred writings circulating among the Jewish Falashas differed but little from the same writings current among the Christian majority. These and other works may often be distinguished as Jewish only by their Jewish instead of Christological introductions. Not even all Jewish prayers, such as those first assembled by Joseph Halévy, had a pronouncedly Jewish content, although they have echoed themes from the Hebrew Bible rather than from the New Testament. In general, these writings, however enlightening they may have been with respect to their Jewish holidays, rituals, customs, and the like, have contributed little to our historical knowledge of how that separate ethnoreligious group was able to maintain its identity through the ages.[5]

From the fact that their sacred writings did not include the Books of the Maccabees and that they generally did not observe Hanukkah it has generally been assumed that their origin antedated at least the Maccabean Revolt. We are confined, however, only to some brief allusions in the midrashic literature showing that the Jews of Palestine and Babylonia were vaguely aware of the presence of coreligionists in that distant legendary African land. But neither is there any source material available which would directly contradict the possibility that some Jews penetrated Ethiopia from Egypt during these periods. In view of the extreme paucity of pertinent archaeological and documentary sources the *argumentum a silentio* definitely does not invalidate the long-lasting oral traditions that some Jews had come to Ethiopia in different periods of antiquity and early Middle Ages. Joined by a variety of native converts to Judaism these early arrivals may well have formed that distinct ethnoreligious Falasha group living at variance from most other Ethiopians. Such an amalgam would also help explain the biological facts of the different degree of blackness of skin characterizing the Falashas from the other Ethiopian tribes, as observed by a number of visitors from abroad; also the presence among the Falashas of numerous individuals with lower frequencies, than those of other Ethiopians, of the "African" chromosomes cDc and with higher frequency of CDe in their blood, suggests according to a 1962 study by A. E. Mourant, "that they are less African and more Mediterranean than the others." At the same time other Falashas revealed a greater frequency of other "African" biological characteristics—probably attesting to the historical likelihood that the Falasha ancestry included nuclei of both Jewish immigrants and native proselytes united by their common Jewish faith. The first "confirmation" of such an assumption came only in the ninth century c.e. when an unusual traveler, called Eldad ha-Dani, claiming to be himself a descendant of the tribe of Dan, appeared amidst the Jewish communities of North Africa. He told intriguing stories about his wide travels in many lands where he encountered various exotic types of Jews. He described some of their customs and religious rituals which were often at variance with the Jewish observances in the main concentrations of Jewry, and was even able to identify in each distant area descendants of each of the "Lost Ten Tribes." Some modern scholars, especially Abraham Epstein, were able to recover from under the veneer of legends with which his narratives were covered some kernels of historical reality. Even his deviations from the Orthodox halakhah were excused by the then leading Babylonian Gaon R. Ṣemaḥ b. Ḥayyim (?), through the argument that, coming from distant countries, he may indeed have known of such diverse regional practices, without being a mouthpiece for heretical teachings. Eldad's tales and reports about variant customs sufficed to arouse the curiosity of Jews in Islamic countries. They embelished the long-current legends about distant coreligionists living near a miraculous river Sambation which had the peculiarity of maintaining its usual flow six days of the week but was completely stagnant during the Sabbath day of rest. (In some legends this rumor was reversed to six days of dryness and the Sabbath-day flow.)[6]

All these legends and rumors belong, so to say, to the pre-historical phase of the Falasha people. More tangible facts begin to appear from 1270 on with the restoration of Ethiopia's Solomonid dynasty and the attested existence of an independent Jewish principality extending over a large area, especially around the fortress Simen (Semien). The name of this locality seems to have been given it by Jewish settlers arriving from Yemen (called in Hebrew: *Teiman*), although it was more suitable for a southern region like Southern Arabia than for a location in northern Ethiopia. A good deal of information may be gathered from the general Ethiopian historical records and their descriptions of military campaigns by the various rulers, campaigns in which the Falashas took an active part, either as allies or as enemies of a particular *negus*. Additional data are furnished by Arabic sources, especially those describing efforts by Muslim neighbors from either Nubia or southern Arabia to occupy parts of Ethiopia. These efforts were intensified after the conquest of Egypt, Syria, and Arabia by the Ottoman sultan, Selim I, in 1516–17. Since anything concerning the Ottoman expansion was the subject of intense interest in Christian Europe, these developments in Northeast Africa did not escape the attention of the Christian powers. For centuries past legends were current throughout Europe about a distant land ruled by a Prester John, a country which was later identified with Ethiopia. Some authentic data began being transmitted to the West by European travelers who frequently met Ethiopians in Jerusalem and elsewhere, as well as by Ethiopians who occasionally appeared in Europe.[7]

Particularly significant was the arrival of two delegates from the Ethiopian community in Jerusalem to the ecumenical council in Florence in 1441. Their presence and the subsequent settlement of some Ethiopians in Rome reinforced the older dreams of the Papacy someday to convert another Eastern "heretical" community to Catholicism. Such hopes, combined with both the expectation of finding an ally in counteracting the "Turkish menace" and the Portuguese explorations in the Indian Ocean, brought about the dispatch of Portuguese missions to Ethiopia (beginning in 1487). One, sent out in 1520, included the distinguished scholar Francisco Alvares (or Alvarez), whose "Narrative" for the first time supplied the European public with some authentic on-the-spot observations by a sympathetic foreigner. At the same time he acquainted his readers with some of the crucial legends current among the Ethiopian people. For instance, he told them about a large old book, found in a church in the capital, with an introduction in Hebrew, translated into Greek, from Greek into Chaldean (Aramaic), and finally into Abyssinian (probably Ge'ez). From it he reported the story of the Queen of Sheba's visit to Jerusalem during which King "Solomon had intercourse with her, and she became pregnant of a son, and remained in Jerusalem until she brought him forth." On returning to her country, she had left the son behind; he grew up in Jerusalem until the age of seventeen, whereupon he came back to Ethiopia, accompanied by advisers selected by his father from the twelve tribes of Israel. Alvares was also told that the Ethiopian grandees proudly asserted that they were descendants of the Israelitic "chamberlains, porters, overseers, grooms, trumpeters, chief guards, cooks and other officials," thus transplanted to Ethiopia. Before long, in 1541, a detachment of 450 Portuguese soldiers, commanded by Christopher da Gama (brother of the famous Vasco da Gama), played a disproportionately important military role in the Christian–Muslim confrontations on the Ethiopian soil. All these new developments naturally affected also the Falasha principality and raised the Falasha problem within the Jewish communities of the Middle East, particularly in Palestine.[8]

Understandably, Jews in Jerusalem and even in such communities as Ormuz evinced some curiosity about their coreligionists in that mysterious land about which some rumors had doubtless reached them from time to time. They certainly also met some Ethiopians on the streets of the Holy City and may even have had some business relations with them. One of the earliest rabbis to refer to the Falashas, Elijah of Ferrara, emphasized their wars with hostile neighbors. In 1438 he wrote a letter to his sons in Pesaro which included a brief statement about what he heard from a young Falasha about his Jewish compatriots:

[They] are their own masters, and owe no allegiance to anybody. They dwell among a great nation called Habesh (Abyssinia); they make a show of Christianity, wearing on their faces chain and filament; they are constantly at war with them and only now and again with other Jews.

These Hebrews have a language of their own. It is neither Hebrew nor Ishmaelite [Arabic]. They possess the Law and a traditional commentary upon it. They have neither our Talmud nor our codes. I have obtained information from this young Jew about several of their precepts. In some they follow our doctrine; in others they conform to the opinions of the Karaites.

Somewhat similar comments were sent home from Jerusalem half a century later (1487–90) by Obadiah Yaré di Bertinoro. In one of his celebrated epistles he wrote:

They [the Falashas] have five princes or kings, and have carried on great wars against the Johannites (Abyssinians) for more than a century, but, unfortunately, the Johannites prevailed and Ephraim was beaten. . . . Four years ago, it is said, they again made war with their neighbors, when they plundered their enemies and made many prisoners.

Conversely, Obadiah informed his correspondents, the Ethiopians had taken a number of Falasha prisoners, some of whom were ransomed by Jews and brought to the Holy City. Obadiah saw two of these captives in Jerusalem, observing that "they were black, but not as black as the Negroes. It was impossible to learn from them, whether they belonged to the Karaites or the Rabbanites. . . . They say there is no fire in their houses on the Sabbath, in other respects they seem to observe Rabbinism." [9]

While Rabbis Elijah and Obadiah calmly referred to this divergence in observances of law, it greatly worried many other Jews in Jerusalem and elsewhere. It assumed particular relevance when some legal problems emerged in connection with the treatment of individual Falashas who lived outside Ethiopia. One such case, in Jerusalem, concerned a Falasha woman who had come to the Holy City as a captive, had been sold to a Jewish master, and ultimately bore him a son. When the child grew up and wanted to marry a local Jewess the question was submitted to R. David Ibn abi Zimra for a decision whether the young man was to be treated as a full-fledged Jew and freely admitted to the Jewish community. The rabbi's reply could not fully satisfy the inquirers, since it left the basic question open. R. David argued that, generally speaking, dwelling in the dark on every Friday evening was a Karaite custom and would normally disqualify a person from membership in the Rabbanite community. But he concluded:

Those who arrive from Ethiopia, however, unquestionably belong to the tribe of Dan which did not have among them scholars familiar with the Jewish tradition. They have, therefore, adhered to the literal meaning of Scripture. If they had been taught our traditions, they surely would not have controverted the words of our teachers of blessed memory. A person of this kind is therefore like a child captured by Gentiles. One must know that [the original teachers of sectarianism] Zadok and Boethos lived during the days of the Second Temple, after the tribe of Dan had been expelled from Palestine. Therefore, if one may still maintain some doubts about the subject [of his Jewishness], one ought, nevertheless, redeem such a person from captivity because of that doubt. However, when it comes to family matters I am apprehensive that neither their marriage contracts nor their writs of divorce might be considered valid for they are not written in the form prescribed by our rabbis, since their writers are unfamiliar with our laws of marriage and divorce.[10]

This type of hesitation on the part of the majority of Jews interfered with their reception of Falasha newcomers in other lands. It may also account for a certain reserve, maintained by Jewish writers from the sixteenth to the eighteenth centuries, toward their alienated coreligionists in Ethiopia. It was only in the nineteenth century that both scholarly and national-religious interests were awakened among the Western Jews and later spread to the world Jewish community. At that time organizations like the Alliance Israélite Universelle considered it their duty to send missions to Ethiopia to investigate the conditions under which the Jews were living in that remote country. As a result, Joseph Halévy not only brought back with him a young Falasha—who was to be educated in Paris and then return to his native land in order to spread there enlightenment of the Western variety—but also a considerable number of Falasha manuscripts. Some of these he published and together with a few disciples and others thus helped to lay the foundation for truly scholarly research into the history, religion, and mores of this exotic segment of the Jewish people.[11]

FALASHA PECULIARITIES

Halévy and other students speedily discovered that the Ethiopian Jews were in many ways different from the general run of Jewry in other lands. To begin with, they physically and mentally resembled other Ethiopians more than the accepted image of Jews. The assumption, however, that they were merely Ethiopians converted to Judaism at some earlier date was staunchly contradicted by the Falashas themselves. Their claim to descent from ancient Israelites had received wider circulation in the Jewish world through the stories told by Eldad ha-Dani in the ninth century. According to his reports, it was the tribe of Dan, one of the bravest in ancient Israel, which departed early from Palestine and settled in the region which was later to be called the empire of Prester John among the Western Christians. These Danites were soon joined by the tribes of Naphtali, Gad, and Asher, who allegedly refused to get embroiled in the civil war between the northern and southern tribes after the death of King Solomon. At first they wanted to attack Egypt and conquer it for their own people. They refrained, however, when they were reminded of the Mosaic injunction, "Ye shall not continue it [Egypt] for ever." They did, however, compromise by crossing Egypt peacefully and entering Ethiopia, where, Eldad added, "they slew the men of Ethiopia, and unto this very day, they fight with the children of the kingdoms of Ethiopia." Eldad further expatiated on that theme by describing how "these four tribes have gold and silver and precious stones, much sheep and cattle and camels and asses, and they sow and they reap." Whether or not Eldad himself was a native of Ethiopia or of a neighboring land is still debatable, but he seems to have repeated a legend widely accepted not only by the Ethiopian Jews but also by their Christian, and to some extent, also by their Muslim neighbors.[12]

The fact that there was a Jewish kingdom in the world was the most astonishing and, to some extent, most important historical fact in the eyes of many downtrodden Jews in the Christian and Muslim worlds. We recall that the argument that Jews had lost their national independence because of their repudiation of Christ was playing a significant role in the Judeo-Christian controversies throughout the Middle Ages. Just as in the earlier period some Jewish controversialists had been able to point to the Khazar kingdom ruled by Jews as a contradiction of the Christian argument, they could now invoke the example of the Falasha realm to contend that Patriarch Jacob's blessing that the "sceptre shall not depart from Judah, nor the ruler's staff from between his feet, as long as men come to Shiloh" had not lost its validity with the appearance of Jesus. Discarding the legendary features, it seems likely that the Jews dominated parts of Ethiopia before the conversion of the mass of the population to Christianity in the fourth century C.E. and again at least from the ninth century on.[13]

Regrettably, our information about the early destinies of that Jewish kingdom is based upon ambivalent allusions in the limited Christian literature of those days. Only after the Solomonid dynasty came back to power in 1270 do we hear time and again of Jews in various parts of Ethiopia, but particularly in the area around Simen, acting as either enemies or allies of the emperors in the unceasing struggle for power. That the fortunes of war changed from time to time and that victory was often followed by defeat, or vice versa, was part of that story.

The first major battles, recorded in considerable detail in the Ethiopian chronicles which have come down to us, occurred under the strongly evangelizing regimes of Amda Sion (esp. 1332) and Davit I (1381–1412). They ended with the Falashas' loss of much of their territory and some individual conversions to Christianity. But the majority retained a comprehensive political self-government and the free profession of its faith. When more than a century later, Zara Ya'qob (1434–68) renewed these missionizing efforts and combined them with extensive religious reforms, he encountered a strong resistance. According to the Ethiopian chronicle of his reign, three provincial governors rose up in revolt.

After abandoning their Christian faith, they embraced the Jewish religion and caused the death of a large number of inhabitants of Amhara [province]. When the king came to the rescue [of the Christians], the rebels fought his troops, put them to flight, and burned all the churches in the area. It was thus that the Christians were ruined, when Gad Yestan [the initiator of the revolt] seized all their possessions, pillaged their homes, not leaving them even the blue ribbons [mateb, worn by all Christians]. . . . [These persecutions] extended over the entire country of Ethiopia.

Ultimately the royal forces restored the previously existing order, however, and after several decades of relative quiet the attacks on the Falashas were renewed with redoubled vigor by

Sarṣa Denghel (1563–95) and Susenyos or Susneyos (1607–1632). These battles ended with the Jewish tribe's surrender of what theretofore was their approximation of a sovereign state. But even when defeated, the Jewish fighters seemed to have filled the hearts of their opponents with admiration for their valor and particularly also for their staunch adherence to their ancient faith against tremendous odds. After the loss of their national independence Ethiopian Jewry faced unpredictably spasmodic treatment from friendliness to oppression and vice versa. It was during those centuries of warfare and subjection that Falasha life began to be the object of closer scrutiny by foreign visitors. That minority's unswerving fidelity to Judaism, even in the face of mortal danger, greatly impressed some Western missionaries, both Catholic and Protestant, who tried in vain to convert them to their religion. Their resistance exceeded that of their Monophysite compatriots who, only after a period of considerable hesitation, rejected the blandishments of the Papacy and its missionaries and refused to adopt Catholicism. Even in their military and political eclipse and in the face of numerous sufferings, as a group, the Falashas of the eighteenth to the twentieth centuries retained their dignity and pride in their heritage, whether they remained in their native land or after they emigrated to some other country.[14]

Yet, there were fundamental differences between the Falashas and the majority of world Jewry, clearly reflected in their religious doctrines, practices, and daily behavior. These differences were so great and ramified that they have been the subject of special investigations by such competent scholars as Abraham Zeev Aescoly and Wolf Leslau. It would, of course, lead us too far to examine them in detail. However, a letter addressed to Charles Singer from Addis-Ababa on July 15, 1904 by an Ethiopian scholar, Woldah Haimanot, who collected data from two informed Falashas, furnishes a sufficiently informative, though necessarily incomplete, summary of the tenets held at least by the majority of early-twentieth-century Falashas. It read in part:

1. Funeral customs just the same as Christian Abyssinians, except the body of a male Falasha is laid on the right side and that of a female on the left; any one who has touched a dead body is unclean.

2. Whenever they kill an animal for food they pronounce: "May the Lord God of Israel be blessed."

3. Phylacteries and amulets are abominations by them.

4. Priests' attire and sacrifice utensils are according to the law of the Levites, except that the vessels have short handles.

5. Priests are married and unmarried, and as the Falashas assume to be descendants of the Levites who came to Abyssinia with Menelik I, any one of them who is fit is appointed for a priest.

6. Their sacrifices, customs of food and drink are according to the law of Moses.

7. Their calendars are taken from the appearance of the moon, and their feasts are during Passion Week.

8. Marriage is performed with prayers and ceremonies; whenever the bride is not found to be a virgin she should be dismissed.

9. Circumcision is on the eighth day.

10. They do not know any history or antiquity except the Old Testament, and that they have come with Menelik I.

11. Priests are consecrated with ceremonies.

12. The women are treated well, and no divorce except for the cause of unchastity.

13. Their laws and avenging of blood are in accord with the customs of the Christian Abyssinians.

14. The manner of observing their animal foods, and all clean and unclean things, and the separation of women during child-births, etc., is exactly according to the law of Moses.

15. The day of their Atonement is in the month of November.

16. They have a hope to return to Jerusalem.

17. Except leather-tanning, which is abomination to them, they engage themselves in every other work.

18. They have no more arts or learning than the Abyssinians.

19. They have no other saints but those of the Old Testament.

20. Mohammedans are considered infidels by them, but Christians are respected.[15]

In short, the Falashas have all along tried to live up to the commandments of the Hebrew Bible as it was known among them in its Ge'ez translation which they shared with their Christian neighbors. The few apocrypha and other sacred writings in their possession offered no interpretation of the Pentateuchal laws which they therefore observed literally. Among the outstanding differences from the rest of Jewry was, especially, their literal application of the laws of purity and impurity included in the Five Books of Moses. These included the treatment of menstruating women which were given a broader application by their more rigid separation from the Gentile world. They also had a priesthood of the kind that had existed in ancient Israel but none resembling that of the ancient and medieval rabbis. To justify their election of priests, they claimed that all of them were also descendants of the ancient Levites who had originally been scattered among the twelve tribes of Israel. They also maintained a remnant of the ancient animal sacrifices by an annual paschal offering of a steer, he-goat, or ram. This practice has been discontinued, however, in recent times. Further, they had special offerings of certain types of breads, particularly those consumed on the Sabbaths in their synagogues. In emulation of their Christian neighbors, however, they continued to cultivate regular confessions to their priests. But a priest, once elected by a Falasha to serve as his confessor, could not be changed, unless either party moved away from the original locality. They did not have Torah scrolls but rather Pentateuchs, written on parchment, wherever possible by competent scribes. The language, however, was not Hebrew but Ge'ez.[16]

Their festivals likewise followed the biblical regulations. Apart from the Passover, they celebrated the Feast of Tabernacles and, in particular, also a Day of Atonement without following the calendar used by Jews, although their own was likewise based upon the lunar year. The extant sources do not refer to the New Year festival, but some fasts were observed including the Fast of Esther, which indicated their acceptance of the Book of Esther as a part of Scripture, whereas the following day of Purim was regarded as a minor holiday. Among other rituals we need but mention the practice of circumcision which, however, somewhat differed from that of the other Jews and extended also to females. The newly born girls underwent a sort of clitorectomy in emulation of similar practices among the Ethiopian Christians. Above all, they shared with the rest of Jewry the belief in the ultimate resurrection of all men and women and in rewards or punishments imposed after death. They also cherished the belief in the coming of the Messiah who would return them to the Holy Land. Even in their darkest hours they must have been consoled by such passages in the Book of Enoch, which in its Ethiopic version was part of their sacred Scriptures, and which in R. H. Charles's corresponding English version predicts the messianic age and adds:

> Then shall they rejoice with joy and be glad,
> And into the holy place shall they enter;
> And its fragrance shall be in their bones,
> And they shall live a long life on earth,
> Such as thy fathers lived:
> And in their days shall no sorrow or plague
> Or torment or calamity touch them.

To be sure, there was little Falasha emigration to Palestine. Even the appearance of Shabbetai Zevi, knowledge of which reached Ethiopia, only resulted at most in a delegation of Ethiopian Jews being sent to the pseudo-messiah. This event is questionable, however, since the unique pertinent document, reproduced by Aron Freimann, may actually refer to a delegation from India. Only in the nineteenth century, when the Falashas noted the growing interest in them on the part of the European Jews and Christians, do we hear an echo of their old yearnings to return to the land of their forefathers. At least from a letter, sent by a priest Abba Zaga to Jerusalem in behalf of Kaka Joseph, the purported chief priest of all Jews in Ethiopia (also referring to an earlier communication), we learn of a curious Falasha complaint that their people had no chief and no prophet among them. "As far as we are concerned a great agitation has captured our hearts for men of our town say that the time [for redemption] had arrived. They say: Separate yourselves from the Christians and proceed to your country, Jerusalem, and reunite there with your brethren, offering sacrifices to the God, the Lord of Israel in the Holy City."[17]

In general, however, the messianic expectations did not seem to affect deeply the religious thinking of the Ethiopian Jews. Even in the occasional disputations they had with their compatriots, as well as with the Catholic and Protestant missionaries arriving from abroad, the issue as to whether Jesus was the messiah promised by the Israelitic prophets seems to have played no significant role. Nor was it apparently stressed in the two disputations held by one Solomon son of Abraham of Vienna with Alphonso Mendes, a Portuguese Jesuit, who served as the Catholic patriarch in the 1620s, or in the Falasha discussions with the Protestant missionary Johannes Martin Flad, as reported by him in the description of his activities in Ethiopia (1855–68). Flad even went so far as to declare that "the Falashas know nothing about the hope of the coming of a future messiah. Together with the Christian Abyssinians they expect the advent of a King Theodoros."[18]

DEMOGRAPHIC AND ECONOMIC OBSCURITIES

Evidently because the Falashas' religious practices and political status attracted the main attention of both visitors and Ethiopian writers, we are much less well informed about the socioeconomic facets of their lives. It appears that until very recently even the Ethiopian government knew very little about their peculiar way of life. As late as 1900, Herbert Vivian was able to report only that

there are the Samien people about whom nothing is known. [Emperor] Menelik [II, 1889–1913] himself remarked the other day that he would be very grateful for information about them. There is also a colony of aboriginal Jews up in the mountains of Tigre. They live in pastoral fashion like the old Hebrew patriarchs, upon the produce of the flocks and herds. They have been there for centuries, perhaps even for thousands of years, and the Abyssinians confess that they have always failed to dislodge them from their inaccessible fastnesses.

Understandably, many visitors were interested in the size of the Falasha population. Clearly, reporters like Eldad ha-Dani, trying to impress the Diaspora communities with the importance of the surviving remnant in some mythical land on the shores of the miraculous river Sambation, were prone to exaggerate their number. According to some versions of his report, Eldad contended that "when they [the descendants of the four tribes] wish to go to war . . . their commanding general will start out with an army of 120 divisions bearing 120 flags, each flag representing 1,000 men." That an army of 120,000 warriors was not marshaled even by the emperor was exemplified by the aforementioned role played by a small Portuguese detachment of 450 men, and even by its remnant of 200 men in the later phases of their intervention. Such exaggerated notions of the size of the Falasha population long appealed to Europeans with their generally mythical outlook on the realm of Prester John. Even the generally cautious sixteenth-century Jewish historian, Azariah de' Rossi, often called "the father of critical Jewish historiography," quoted an anonymous "great geographer of our generation," who described the large mountains of Ethiopia and declared that, "on them lives a very large number of Jews paying tribute to the king of Ethiopia, called Prester John." Azariah found a confirmation of that statement in the then recently published *Theatrum orbis terrarum* by the contemporary Flemish scholar, Abraham Ortellius. Subsequently, most foreign visitors were able to quote far more acceptable figures, some mentioning a total of only 50,000 Falashas, which may be called a reasonable "guesstimate." To be sure, Henry Aaron Stern, a missionary, who visited Ethiopia in the mid-nineteenth century, claimed that they numbered 250,000 persons. But this clear overstatement may have been dictated by his own missionary ardor and his wish to impress his European superiors with the importance of converting the Falashas to Protestant Christianity. More moderate was the figure supplied by the famed Scottish explorer James Bruce of Kinnaird who, in 1769, arrived in Ethiopia. Combining a diplomatic mission with much personal vitality, the deep curiosity of an explorer, and the erudition of a scholar engaged in a quest for the sources of the Nile, Bruce was able to bring back to Europe not only numerous sketches and Ethiopic manuscripts, but also a vast amount of data and observations on the *realia* of Ethiopian culture which were to fructify Ethiopian studies for generations. His estimate of 100,000 Falashas may have been fairly accurate for his day. In general, their number undoubtedly differed from time to time, dependent on the fortunes of war, domestic insurrections, as well as the varying degrees of their oppression and the rates of their more or less forcible conversions to Christianity by actions of the authorities. It is very likely, therefore, that in the following generations the forces of assimilation brought about a considerable decline of the Falasha population.[19]

Needless to say, we are even less well informed about such demographic factors as birth and death rates, size of families, and the like. From the juridico-religious point of view we are told that not only were the Falashas rigidly monogamous—as were their Christian, but not their Muslim compatriots—but also that divorce was severely discouraged and that widows and widowers, as a rule, did not remarry; according to some versions, so long as there were minor children in the household. This restraint may have had some impact on the birth rate. So may have the general modicum of equality between men and women, symbolized by the severe punishments meted out for adultery by husbands (along with the mandatory divorce of unfaithful wives) and the extensive employment of women in various economic endeavors. Their funeral customs, on the other hand, were very similar to those of their Christian neighbors.[20]

In all these demographic considerations we must not overlook the usual detrimental factors of prolonged wars, pestilences, and famines, all of which exerted a decisively retarding influence on population growth. For instance, in the sixteenth and seventeenth centuries the almost constant hostilities between the monarchy and the islamized sultanates on the southeastern borders in 1529–59, the great famines of 1611, 1623, 1650–53, and the widespread epidemics of 1612, 1618–19, 1634–35, and 1653 doubtless greatly retarded any population growth, if they did not actually result in the diminution of the number of inhabitants in many regions, including Simen, which greatly suffered particularly during the epidemic of 1634–35.[21]

As a result of these uncertainties, one cannot even cite a satisfactory global figure of the Falashas living in Ethiopia during any period of the past or present. To show how unreliable the observations of visitors could be, it suffices to quote the estimates of Nahum, a rabbi sent in 1908 by the Alliance Israélite on a brief mission to Ethiopia who, upon his return, estimated the total number of Falashas in the country as amounting to only 6,000–7,000, an estimate, as patently low as H. A. Stern's was high at the other extreme of 250,000 a century earlier. Yet it seems reasonable to assume that the Falashas were constantly losing ground during the last three or four centuries after the period of frequent wars, resulting in their loss of sovereignty and becoming the oppressed subjects of the hostile majority. It is quite possible, therefore, that in the sixteenth century they may have numbered more than 100,000 persons and that their total dwindled to half that number or less three centuries later. Similarly, the number of localities which embraced Falasha communities very likely also diminished. Yet, with their staunch adherence to their faith and their own preference to live segregated from their neighbors, they were able to salvage quite a few entire Falasha villages. These settlements, however, were generally very small; they rarely exceeded 30 families. Their largest urban quarters, too, in which they lived segregated from the Gentiles, as a matter of their own choice rather than any legal decree (there are no recorded official ghettos in Ethiopia), accommodated no more than 50–60 families in Addis Ababa and 30 families in the newly founded Addis Alam. Even in the period of their flowering, it may be assumed, their communities were tiny by modern standards, although they might have appeared sizable in comparison with those of their non-Jewish compatriots in Ethiopia or even in medieval Europe. After all, we must remember the military impact on Ethiopia of the aforementioned detachment of 450 Portuguese soldiers, and, on a larger scale, what Portugal, counting no more than about 1,000,000 population, was able to achieve in a short time by establishing a far-flung empire in Africa, Asia, and South America.[22]

We are equally in the dark about the Jewish share in the Ethiopian economy. Economic statistics of any kind are generally in a bad shape for the history of Ethiopia before the twentieth century. This is doubly the case with respect to the Falashas. Their population included few, if any, prominent merchants, financiers, or physicians (such as lived in other countries), who would leave their imprint on the local society and thereby furnish some noteworthy biographical material for chroniclers and foreign observers. What is worse, in view of the paucity of archival records, one can hardly expect much improvement from specialized historical research in the near future.

From the bits of information scattered in the existing sources, it appears that probably the majority of Falashas, at least in the cities, earned a living from craftsmanship. In the middle of the nineteenth century Henry Aaron Stern, a Christian convert from Judaism and a missionary among Jews, had this general observation about the Falashas:

Exemplary in their morals, cleanly in their habits, and devout in their belief, the Falashas are also industrious in their daily pursuits and avocations of life. Husbandry and a few single trades—such as smiths, potters, and weavers—constitute the sole occupations in which they engage; commerce they unanimously repudiate as incompatible with their Mosaic Creed and it is quite a disappointment not to find a single merchant among a quarter of a million people.

They indeed generally enjoyed the reputation of being skillful masons, carpenters, blacksmiths, gold- and silversmiths, and potters, while their women excelled in all forms of weaving, including basket weaving. As late as 1771 James Bruce saw at Aduwa in Tigre province "heaps of platters and pots, that had been used by Mahometans and Jews [which] were brought thither likewise to be purified," a demonstration of both the industrial indispensability and the ritualistic segregation of the two religious minorities. Bruce also admired the roof on the royal palace in Gondar which had been built in 1736 by the Falashas "and which consisted of painted cane, split and disposed in Mosaic figures, which produce a gayer effect than it is possible to conceive." Curiously, their predilection for and high skill in crafts, serving the Falashas in good stead economically, often turned out to be a handicap in their social relations with their neighbors. The growing dispersal of the Falashas after their loss of independence was, in part, caused by forcible deportations ordered by emperors bent on introducing new crafts into localities which did not possess them. The Falashas served as chosen targets for such involuntary resettlement. In addition some neighbors who envied their skills attributed their success to the use of magic in producing goods of better quality and in less time. In fact, however, we hear very little about magic arts cultivated by the Ethiopian Jews, although a book related to practical Kabbalah was located by Carlo Conti Rossini in the collection of manuscripts brought home by Antoine d'Abbadie from his sojourn in Ethiopia. One must not overlook in this connection the generally high level of intelligence among the Ethiopians of all faiths. According to Edward Ullendorff, "everyone will agree that the Abyssinian is exceptionally intelligent, mentally agile, and extraordinarily eager to learn. His quick absorption of knowledge is at times stupefying, but profundity is not, perhaps, greatly esteemed." These characteristics were shared by most Falashas who combined them with great orderliness and personal cleanliness—some observers emphasized the great frequency of bathing among them—and a moderate lifestyle. Many visitors were, therefore, often impressed by their quick natural wit, their industry, high morality, and avoidance of drunkenness or vice. Some of the scholars have also pointed out that, perhaps because of their family cohesiveness and rigid discipline, the Falashas rarely suffered from venereal diseases which were quite widespread among the non-Jewish Ethiopians.[23]

Many Falashas also cultivated the soil. Originally, in the period of their political independence they seem to have possessed large tracts of land which they tilled with devotion and understanding. According to general Ethiopian legends, Menelik I, upon arriving from Jerusalem, divided Ethiopia's cultivable land into three sections: crown lands, those belonging to the Church, and others held by clans or individuals. This legend actually reflected the historic reality that the Church owned fully one-third of the cultivable area in the country. At a later period the Ethiopians adopted the widely held Mid-Eastern doctrine that all land belonged to the emperor. This theoretical assumption was greatly modified in Ethiopia, however, through the great power of the Church and of the provincial "kings," as well as by the prevailing practice of families maintaining their hold on the land through their respective laws of inheritance. According to Carlo Conti Rossini, a group of Ethiopian elders clarified the statement pertaining to royal ownership by asserting that it

is made in order to affirm that the earth belongs to the king in the same way as the heavens belong to God. We allude to this statement when we wish to enhance the power of the Government, but do not thereby intend to refer to the ownership of the fields. The above phrase . . . refers only to that kind of command or governmental supremacy which relates to the imposition of taxation on the soil and prevents the abuse of power and the exercise of violence. But no one can take away our lands . . . except in case of confiscation resulting from such crimes as we may commit.

In the case of the Falashas, too, we are told by Eldad ha-Dani that, in his day (ninth century), "They owned much gold and silver, cultivated flax, bred the silkworm, and produced garments." Later on, to be sure, upon their loss of independence, there was much expropriation of their lands by the Crown. "The Falashas are representatives," states Eike Haberland, "of a peasantry which under the pressure of conquerors (the Amharis) were forced to give up their free peasant status, that is, whose land had been expropriated in retaliation for their rebellion, and was assigned to Amharic colonists." Yet, many families still retained control over plots of land near their habitations and, while farming no longer played its earlier great role in their economy, it still substantially contributed to the livelihood of a large segment of the Falasha population.[24]

In contrast, commerce, the preeminent Jewish occupation in other lands, played but a minor role in Falasha circles. Some observers actually thought that they believed in a Mosaic prohibition against trade, though no record can be quoted to authenticate that assumption. Nonetheless, in fact, most of the country's commerce was in the hands of Muslims or such foreigners as Indians and Europeans. This applied not only to international trade but also to domestic exchanges. The obstacles to active Falasha participation in commercial endeavors, both objective and psychological, were indeed staggering. Before the great changes in the nineteenth and twentieth centuries, Ethiopian cities had no open shops or bazaars offering goods for sale. As was later observed by the British Vice-Consul A. H. Wylde, "an open shop would mean a temptation too great for the annexing mania of the people and the stock-in-trade would soon get spoiled, as the Abyssinians are great people for fingering articles they do not intend to buy." In the case of Falashas, with their extreme emphasis on their religious doctrine of purity, such fingering by Gentiles would immediately turn the objects impure for the merchants' own use. At the same time long-distance, especially international, trade was greatly impeded by the lack of good roads and the ensuing loss of time in traveling and transporting goods. Even in 1900, according to a British consular report, it took six weeks for a journey by donkey, mule, or camel from Addis Ababa to the relatively advanced commercial city of Harar and twenty to thirty more days to the coast. In the absence of caravanseries, for a Falasha trader to join a caravan for a long journey of this kind meant his spending many nights in Gentile houses, however hospitable, consuming whatever ritualistically questionable food was available in various localities, and running counter to some Sabbath rest commandments, all of which would have created for a pious Falasha immense conflicts with his religious conscience. Nor were the great climatic variations in the different Ethiopian regions very encouraging to business journeys. Hence even in 1899–1900, when foreigners had played a leading role in the international trade, only 3 Jews, doubtless foreign, appear in a list of principal merchants in the capital, as against 6 Arabs, 7 Armenians, 4 Frenchmen, 2 Indians, and 1 Greek. Certainly, before 1650, the Falasha share in Ethiopia's commerce appears to have been negligible.[25]

Less surprising is the apparent absence of Jewish doctors from the Falasha communities, in sharp contrast to almost all other medieval settlements. No one seems to mention even Falasha witch doctors, although the Ethiopian Jews shared to some extent with their Christian neighbors the belief in the use of some magic in medical ministrations. Nor did any Jewish authors leave behind any distinct traces in the existing Ethiopian medical writings, such as the sixteenth- or seventeenth-century *Treatise on Therapeutics,* compiled by Abba Yohannes in a mixture of Ge'ez and Amharic. However, the study of the history of Ethiopian medicine in general is much too young to allow us to draw any conclusions by an *argumentum ex silentio.* Abba Yohannes' *Treatise* itself only became fully known in scholarly circles in 1958 from copies preserved in the rich British Museum manuscript collections. Let us hope that the initial studies on these manuscripts by Polish scholars will stimulate some further discoveries in this field.[26]

Needless to say, public offices were closed to Falashas. This exclusion did not prevent the emperors from using Falasha

soldiers, generally esteemed for their valor, in special detachments fighting on their side. To be sure, their dedication to
the strict observance of the Sabbath rest commandment made
them vulnerable to enemies choosing to attack them on their
day of rest. (They were clearly unaware of the specific enactment during the Maccabean Wars permitting Jews under
certain conditions to take an active part in Sabbath battles.)
But the Falashas seemed to have secured the corresponding
permissiveness by referring to their "beautiful traditions"
recorded by Antoine d'Abbadie. According to that story, at
one time 500 Jewish soldiers fighting in the royal army were
attacked by the enemies on a Sabbath. They overcame their
aversion to break the commandment to rest by being advised
by their priests to invoke the divine name, *Ehye asher ehye* (I
am that I am; Exod. 3:14), whereupon they succeeded in de-
feating their enemies. Nor did the Falashas develop, it appears, a Jewish civil service of their own. Remarkably, despite
the great interest in the Falasha religion on the part of most
explorers and students, we know very little about the Jewish
communal organization, its institutions, and its personnel.
True, they had "priests," each called *cahen* from the Hebrew
kohen, some of whom may have claimed to be of the tribe of
Levi, which, having lived dispersed among the twelve tribes of
ancient Israel, allegedly had joined the 12,000 Israelites who
were brought into the country by Menelik I. No claim, however, was made that they were more specifically descendants
of the family of Aaron, Moses' brother, the first High Priest.
Nor is there any record of their receiving any regular salaries.
The occasional gratuities of one or two Maria Theresa thalers,
respectively, which they received for reciting the appropriate
blessings at weddings and funerals may have furnished them
some supplementary income beyond what they earned through
farming or craftsmanship. This is also true of the "High
Priests" residing in some larger communities and exercising
some supervisory functions over the regular priests. Their
"monks," too, wherever such existed, made a living from the
usual occupations on a par with their lay coreligionists. We
know even less about whatever functionaries there existed in
charge of collecting dues from members, providing services at

burials, teaching children, and so forth. Apparently with their quick intelligence and eagerness for learning quite a few laymen were able to provide such services for the community at large with little or no pay.[27]

In this connection it may also be mentioned that thus far there seems to be no detailed study of how the Ethiopian fiscal system affected the Falasha minority, especially in the Middle Ages and early modern times. It appears that with the aforementioned doctrine that all land belongs to the king, the Falasha and other farmers must have paid certain amounts, or certain shares in the crops, to the government, either under the shape of leaseholds or of a land tax. There was, moreover, a constant tug-of-war between the monarchy and the various provincial dynasties which were actually in charge of collecting the taxes and delivering a portion to the Treasury of their "king of kings." There also were frequent disputes about the billeting of soldiers and governmental officials on their movements from one locality to another. No evidence is available as to how these burdens were distributed among the various groups of the population, including the Falashas, and the extent to which they affected individual families. Here and there we hear of a capitation tax collected from some Falashas, but these references are so few and far between that one cannot assume its regular collection from "infidels," be they Falashas, Muslims, or Roman Catholics. Moreover, the religious minorities and even the Monophysite majority constantly suffered from the instability and unpredictability of tax collections. Even in the seventeenth century W. Plowden observed that "the prosperous and adverse condition of a village depends entirely upon the rapacity and moderation of its immediate chief." According to another visitor in the 1850s, there were cases when "the greater part of the people had run away from their villages" on account of the heavy imposts. Conditions were not much better in the cities. As late as the 1930s an Italian visitor observed that "perhaps a third of the Falasha produce is paid in taxes and that this was exceeded in cases when local officers imposed additional dues." Regrettably, all the economic and fiscal aspects of Ethiopian history have thus far been greatly neglected by its students who, in view of the absence of archival records, would, in any case, have faced staggering difficulties in reconstructing these aspects of past Ethiopian life. Yet, it seems that on the whole, the treatment of the Jews by the local authorities in civil affairs did not greatly differ from that of the masses of the non-Jewish population.[28]

INDIA

Equally perplexing to modern historians are the historical developments of the Jewish population in India. To begin with, India is not merely a country but a subcontinent, which now comprises three nations, India, Pakistan, and Bangladesh. But in the past it embraced a constantly varying number of principalities of all kinds with fluid frontiers; they were frequently embroiled in wars with one another. To add to the confusion, the Hebrew term *Kush,* usually denoting Ethiopia, was often used by distant Jewish writers to denote India. The same holds true for the medieval West-European Christians to whom the mythical country of Prester John could refer to either Ethiopia or India. In the Jewish case, their people's relations with India dated back, many believed, to the same King Solomon who was supposed to have been the ancestor of the ruling Ethiopian dynasty. The biblical Ophir, which was reached by the sailors of Solomon and his ally Hiram for purposes of trade, has been identified by both older and modern scholars with some location on the coast of Malabar. This identification was reinforced on zoological and philological grounds by the objects brought back by Solomon's sailors, including "ivory, and apes, and peacocks" which were indigenous to India, rather than to western Asia, while the Hebrew name for peacock, *tuqi,* appears to be related to the *tuquish* in the Tamil language. It is not surprising, therefore, that James Hornell could bluntly assert that Ophir referred to "a great mart on the west coast of India, where the produce of the gold mines of Hyderabad, of the spice lands of Malabar and of the gem-workings and pearl-fisheries of Ceylon, were collected by merchants to meet the foreign merchant-king's requirements." Of course, we hear less about relations with India after Solomon's death, when his country's division into two kingdoms, accompanied by the loss

of Israelite control over the access to the Red Sea (later resumed only for a short time under the reign of Jehoshaphat),
impeded maritime expeditions to the Indian Ocean.[29]

We are not told about any further Jewish connections with
Malabar and neighboring lands under the Achaemenide regime or even under its Hellenistic successors. However, it is
likely that some Jews participated in the developing trade between Egypt and southern Arabia on the one hand, and the
Indian emporia on the other hand in both late ancient and
early medieval times. We recall Al-Biruni's assertion that
Kashmir's xenophobic inhabitants refused to admit Indians not
known to them personally but made an exception in favor of
Jews. Similarly, the saying, frequently heard among Arabs and
Jews in Baghdad, that everyone going to India became rich—
a statement illustrated by the aforementioned tale about the
Jew Isaac who, after a long stay in India, returned to the Persian Gulf with a ship laden with precious Indian merchandise
valued at millions of gold dinars—makes it probable that some
such Jewish businessmen also remained in India. However,
there is little direct documentary evidence about Jewish settlements on the subcontinent, except for the famous copper
plates, preserved until today, in which a privilege granted by
the Rajah Bhaskara Ravi Varna provided that "to Isuppu
Irabban, prince of Ansuvannam [in Cranganore], and to his
descendants . . . Ansuvannam [is] a hereditary estate as long
as the world and the moon exist." Thus was said to have
been established a small autonomous Jewish political entity
whose rulers, according to the plates, were entitled to ride on
elephants or to be carried in litters, preceded by trumpets
signaling the inferior castes to withdraw from their path.
Opinions differ as to the date of these enactments; calculations
by scholars range from 476 to 750 and 1020 C.E. This semi-
independent Jewish state apparently survived until the Portuguese conquest of Cranganore in 1523, when most of its Jewish inhabitants seem to have moved to neighboring Cochin,
which in the preceding two centuries had played an increasing
role in international trade. It is small wonder that, in later
recollections, this autonomous Jewish entity loomed as an independent Jewish state. As late as the early eighteenth century

Alexander Hamilton, who had spent most of his adult life (1688–1723) in India and had twice visited Malabar (in 1702 and 1708), could, in his travelogue first published in 1727, report that the Jewish settlement in Cochin

of old bore the name of a kingdom and was a Republic of Jews who were once so numerous that they could reckon about 30,000 families, but at present are reduced to 4,000.

We shall see that even the smaller figure was exaggerated. But the memory of a Jewish "kingdom" allegedly established by Yussuf Rabban did not disappear from Western letters for some time.[30]

Regrettably, Benjamin of Tudela, on whose testimony we have to rely concerning many Middle-Eastern Jewish communities in the twelfth century, apparently never reached India. His brief description of the country has all the earmarks of hearsay. His informants, too, apparently supplied him with certain startling observations concerning the lifestyle of the "sun worshipers," rather than a description of the general socioeconomic or political trends affecting the population at large. Hence, what Benjamin could tell about the Indian Jews was rather vague and not too meaningful. After a lengthy description of the neighboring district of Khulam (Quilon), he observed:

And throughout the island [!], including all the towns there, live several thousand Israelites. The inhabitants are all black, and the Jews also. The latter are good and benevolent. They know the law of Moses and the prophets, and to a small extent the Talmud and Halacha.

The population estimate here given for the Jews of India is no more trustworthy than that mentioned by the traveler from Tudela concerning the city of Ibrig, often identified with Ceylon, which supposedly embraced 3,000 Jewish inhabitants. On the other hand, more and more information about the trade relations between the Egyptian and Yemenite Jews with India of that period has been forthcoming from the Genizah. Once again we may only express the hope that S. D. Goitein will be able soon to concentrate on presenting to the world the extensive Genizah materials pertaining to the Mid-Eastern Jew's relations with India, which he has assembled from the world's libraries.[31]

Essentially there were three major groups of Jews in India. One was started by immigrants into northern India, mainly coming from neighboring Persia and Central Asia, and continued through a constant admixture of Jews from western Asia and Mediterranean countries. From the sixteenth century on there was a special influx of Mediterranean Jews, particularly exiles from Spain and Portugal and their descendants. From the late eighteenth century on this group was reinforced by further immigrants from western Asia who formed another subgroup called Iraqi or Baghdadi Jews. A second group was formed by settlers calling themselves the Bene-Israel, who at an unknown date began concentrating in Bengal and especially in its capital, Bombay, but later gradually spread also into other parts of the subcontinent. A third, and best known group consisted of descendants of the long-established Jewish community of Cranganore, later transferred chiefly to Cochin.

Unfortunately, our information about the Jews in northern India during the Middle Ages is quite limited. Apart from the aforementioned testimonies by Al-Biruni, Benjamin of Tudela, and a few others before the end of the twelfth century, we know few facts except those transmitted by local traditions which cannot be satisfactorily verified from outside sources. We occasionally hear such generalizations as that from a modern Indian historian, Nuwar Muhabhat Khan, that "on the first arrival of Muslims in India, the Jews and Christians had intercourse as merchants, with most of the ports of the Dakhin . . . and others. When Mohammedans appeared Jews and Christians burned with the fire of envy and malice." From the thirteenth to the fifteenth centuries much disarray was caused by the Mongol invasions and the following fratricidal wars between the various principalities on most of the subcontinent. We hear even less about the Indian Jews than, for instance, about their coreligionists in Persia. Even Kashmir, which had been so friendly to the Jews in the earlier medieval period, seems to have preserved no records of the Jewish community or even individual Jews who lived there in the thirteenth and following centuries. True, in 1565 the distinguished traveler, François Bernier, reported:

I would be as much pleased as *Monsieur* [*Melchesedec*] *Thévenot* [an uncle of Jean frequently cited by us] himself if *Jews* were found in these mountainous regions: I mean such *Jews* as he would no doubt desire to find,—*Jews* descended from the tribes transported by *Shalmaneser:* but you may assure that gentleman that, although there seems ground for believing that some of them were formerly settled in these countries, yet the whole population is at present either *Gentile* or *Mahometan.*

But Bernier contradicted himself to some extent by contending that "there are many signs of *Judaism* to be found in the country. . . . The inhabitants of the frontier villages struck me as resembling *Jews.*" He probably wished to indicate only that they were relatively recent converts to Islam. It stands to reason, however, that Jews continued living there and perhaps even enjoyed a measure of economic prosperity, although, like the other non-Muslim inhabitants, they must have suffered from some of the discriminatory enactments by sultans of the line of Shah Mirza Swati, a Muslim adventurer, whose dynasty ruled over a large area from 1346 to 1561 (merely in the last eleven years were they considered dependent on the new Mughal regime). In fact, only under Sikandar But-shikan (Idol-Breaker; 1394–1416), who was an Orthodox Muslim patronizing the ulama, was there an outright religious persecution at least of the Hindus, many of whose temples were destroyed. Possibly in consonance with the *shariʿa,* the synagogues (about which we hear nothing) were spared, but Jews were very likely included in the ranks of taxpayers of the *jizya* proclaimed by the sultan. However, these restrictions were modified by Sikandar's successor, Zayn-al-ʿAbidin Shahi Khan, sometimes called The Great (1420–70) and by Naṣr-ad-Din Yusuf of the Ghazi Khan Chak dynasty (1579–86) described as "one of the most cultured rulers of the sultanate period." He completely abandoned the practice of both the *jizya* and corvée labor imposed upon the non-Muslim subjects and even eliminated some other oppressive taxes.[32]

MUGHAL EMPIRE

The situation changed to some extent after the establishment in 1526 of the Mughal (or Moghul) Empire by Ẓahir-ad-Din Babur, an invader from Central Asia. Himself a gifted poet and devoted Muslim, he looked down upon the masses of Hindus and other ethnic groups inhabiting his newly conquered provinces. To quote him: "Hindustan is a country of few charms. Its people have no good looks; . . . of genius capacity [there is] none; in handicraft and work there is no form or symmetry; method or quality; there are no good houses, no guard dogs; . . . no first rate fruits; . . . no good bread or cooked food in the bazaars, no hot bath, no colleges, no candles, torches or candlesticks. . . . Peasants and people of low standing go about naked." Yet he admitted that Hindustan was a very large country, distinguished by great rivers and in possession of much gold and silver.[33]

Such prejudices toward a fascinating and deep-rooted old culture by a reigning absolute monarch might have proved greatly damaging to the population. However, Babur was too intelligent a ruler to apply his own negative generalizations in practice. Moreover, his personal reign over a large area in India lasted only four years and his successors did not seem to share these preconceptions. This was particularly true of the long reign of Jalal ad-Din Akbar I the Great (1556–1605) whose empire extended over most of Northern India; it replaced the numerous smaller dynasties which in many ways contributed to the chaotic state of late medieval Indian society and political structure. Akbar is briefly characterized by Vincent A. Smith as "a born king of men, with a rightful claim to rank as one of the greatest sovereigns known to history. That claim rests securely on the basis of his extraordinary natural gifts, his original ideas, and his magnificent achievements." As a conqueror and strategist, he rivaled, or exceeded, such distinguished contemporaries, or near contemporaries, as 'Abbas the Great of Persia, Suleiman the Magnificent of the Ottoman Empire, Philip II of Spain, or Queen Elizabeth I of England.[34]

At the same time, Akbar was a man of extraordinary talents also in the cultural sphere, an indefatigable student of comparative religion, and a daring reformer. Although himself illiterate, he had such a prodigious memory that he could repeat lengthy Persian poems after hearing them recited once. Without having any theological training he revealed a remarkable ability of quickly absorbing the expositions presented to him orally by representatives of the various religions (and their respective sectarian subdivisions) among his own subjects. He thus learned a great deal about Zoroastrianism, Jainism, Hinduism, Christianity, and Judaism, as well as about the subtleties of Ṣufism and the complicated teachings separating Shiʻite from Sunnite Muslims. Remarkably, one of his greatest diversions consisted in listening to the religious debates among spokesmen of various faiths staged in his palace. He also held many private conversations with the religious leaders, evincing so much sympathy for each that the gifted Jesuit missionaries Antonio Monserrate and Rodolfo Acquaviva (nephew of a later general of the Order) were led to believe that he was almost ready to join the Christian faith. In fact, however, he was by no means inclined to make this drastic step even if the Jesuits had been prepared to compromise with him regarding certain provisions of canon law such as their insistence that he should have only one wife and consider all other women of his harem as concubines.[35]

In general, however, Akbar did not intend to favor one religion over another but he had hoped to expound a faith which would have the "great advantage of not losing what was good in any one religion, while gaining what was better in another." Ultimately, he began seeing himself as the "Just Leader" who had the authority to interpret the commandments of each religion in the way that best suited him. To eliminate the opposition from conservative Muslim quarters he persuaded in September 1580 the highest Muslim authorities to issue a covenant of a most unusual nature. Among other matters these authoritative sages wrote:

We have decreed and do decree that the rank of a just ruler is higher in the eye of God than the rank of a chief of the law; and further that the Sultan of Islam, etc., etc., Akbar, is a most just, wise, and pious king. Therefore, if there be a variance among the doctors on a question of religion, and His Majesty should give his decree for the benefit of mankind, we do agree that such a decree shall be binding upon us, and upon the whole nation. And such order (not being in opposition to the Koran) shall be imperative on all, opposition thereto being punished with damnation in the next world, excommunication and ruin in this present life.

To emphasize this new approach, the emperor appeared as the king-priest on the pulpit of the great mosque in his residence. On this occasion he recited a hymn, prepared for him by his favorite court poet, Faizi, which read:

> The Lord to me the kingdom gave,
> He made me prudent, strong, and brave,
> He guided me with right and ruth,
> Filling my heart with love of truth;
> No tongue of man can sum His state—
> *Allahu akbar!* God is great.

The last line included a conscious ambiguity, for *Allahu akbar* could also allude to Akbar personifying God. His megalomania went so far as to order a basic change in the long-established mutual greetings among the masses. Instead of the well-known phrase, "Pease be with you," to which the usual reply given was (and is to this day), "And you, too, [enjoy] peace," persons meeting each other were to begin with the exclamation, *Allahu Akbar* (God is great, possibly the allusion to Akbar) and hear in return: *Jilli jalalihu* (May His glory shine). He finally went so far as to introduce a new era beginning with his own ascension to the throne in lieu of the Muslim date of the *hejirah* and to forbid the invocation of the name of Mohammed in public prayers and in courts. At times he reached such ridiculous extremes as to alter the proper spelling of Arabic or Persian words. However, his authority was so great that whatever opposition arose in Muslim circles against his enactments and his public behavior, it led only to occasional local riots, each rebellion being quickly overcome by his troops. Above all, he thus established a basic equality of rights for all religious denominations. This attitude involved a great financial sacrifice: in 1563–64 the emperor abolished the *jizya* and the pilgrimage taxes theretofore imposed upon all non-Muslims. This was done, as Akbar's closest friend and collaborator, Abu'l Fazl i-Allami, remarked in his semi-official history of Akbar's reign, "in spite of the disapproval of statesmen and the loss of the great revenue, and of much chatter on the part of the ignorant, the sublime decree was issued." The government also relieved all foreign (including Jewish) traders from a variety of other burdensome taxes and tolls, while trying to concentrate on covering the governmental expenses from increased revenues of the land tax. In short, Akbar thus established a regime of religious toleration unknown anywhere else in the contemporary worlds of Islam and Christendom.[36]

In these great transformations some Jews seem to have played a fairly active part. They are specifically mentioned in the sources in connection with the religious disputations and with the emperor's curiosity about the holy scriptures of the various faiths. In his effort to acquaint himself with all religions in his Empire, Akbar assembled a great library of texts of sacred writings, including translations into Persian of the Pentateuch, the Psalms, and the Gospels. We have the testimony of some Jews participating in these projects, including one who helped transcribe an existing Judeo-Persian translation of parts of the Bible into one in the Persian (Arabic) alphabet. To be sure, some of the Jesuit Fathers who attended such debates claimed that Akbar was "a great enemy of the Jews." In his report of July 18, 1586 Rodolfo Acquaviva informed the general of the Jesuit Order, P. E. Mercurian, that Akbar had twice visited the Christian *oratorio* and added: "the Emperor can not stand seeing renegades or Jews, while Christians are, on the contrary, highly honored and well treated." But such observations may have been dictated by the writers' own anti-Jewish prejudice and stemmed, in part, from their wishful thinking that the great monarch might ultimately be persuaded to adopt Christianity. This delusion appears very frequently in the correspondence of Monserrate and Acquaviva, with their headquarters in Europe. Doubtless more justified was the remark of Alessandro Valignano, who later became the leading historian of the Jesuit missionary efforts in India and China. Acting as a "visitor" sent by the authorities to investigate the conditions in the Far East, Valignano mentioned in his second report (*summarium Indicum alterum*), dated Shimo, Japan, August 1580, that "there are among them [the Indian inhabitants] a large number of Gentiles [heathens] and Moors and in some parts also Jews; they all are ignorant of their own sectarian traditions."[37]

Regrettably, in none of these instances are the Jewish representatives mentioned by their names or other biographical identifications. We cannot ascertain, therefore, their origin, character, or degree of learning. Similarly, when the sources refer to "synagogues," they do not indicate their location, which might give us an insight into the existing Jewish communities in the country. The first person known to us by name is an intriguing figure appearing in the records only under Akbar's third successor, Shihab-ad-Din Shah Jihan (1628–57). No longer a professing Jew, Muḥammed Sa'id Sarmad (meaning Sa'id the Everlasting) played a considerable role at court. Himself a talented poet and wealthy merchant, Sarmad, a native of Persian Kashan, first became known widely through his *Ruba'iyat* (a collection of epigrammatic verse quatrains) which rapidly became a sort of bestseller. Before long, he was drawn into the circle of students of religion from which emerged an important work in comparative religion, entitled *Dābistān al-Madhāhib* (School of Religious Doctrines). This book, which did not become known in the West until 1787, included a chapter on Judaism, largely derived from information supplied by Sarmad, as is attested by the author's statement that he

never happened to have intercourse with learned and distinguished men among the Yahuds; and he set no value upon what he found in the books of foreigners about their religion. . . . But in the year of the Hejira 1057 (A.D. 1647), when I came to Hyderabad, I contracted friendship with Mohammed Sa'id Sarmed, who was originally from the family of learned Yahuds and of a class whom they call Rabanián [Rabbanites].

In time Sarmad gave up his business and became a dervish, publicly appearing as a naked fakir and preaching mystic ideas. He was quoted as declaring: "I obey the Qur'an, I am a Hindu priest and a monk, I am a Rabbi Jew, I am an infidel, and I am a Muslim." He also taught a like-minded Hindu, Abhi Chand, Hebrew and the Bible to such an extent that Abhi began considering himself a full-fledged Jew. Declaring, "I submit to Moses' law; I am of thy religion and a guardian of thy way; I am a rabbi of the Yahuds," Abhi finally translated the Pentateuch into classical Persian.[38]

Most important for Sarmad's career was his intimate friendship with Akbar's grandson, Crown Prince Dara Shikuh, who shared much of his grandfather's outlook and maintained close association with Brahmins, Zoroastrians, Hindus, and Christians. Unfortunately for both these men, the time for extensive religious tolerance had passed, giving way to a strong Muslim reaction which, among its other manifestations, led to the assassination of Dara Shikuh and the elevation of his brother, Muḥyi-ad-Din Awrangzib 'Alamgir I to the imperial throne (1658–1707). Awrangzib restored the traditional Islamic legal system including the collection of the *jizya* and the other discriminatory regulations affecting "unbelievers." Under such a regime there was no room for an agnostic like Sarmad and, under the excuse that he had refused to recite the full Muslim credo, but really because of his close association with Dara Shikuh, he was executed in 1661. Thus ended the remarkable career of a prominent former Jew, the only man thus far somewhat better known to us from among the shadowy Jewish personalities occasionally referred to in the early sources of the Mughal Empire.[39]

We are slightly better off with respect to the Jews of Goa and its environs. In addition to some earlier settlers, they largely consisted of Marranos who arrived on the subcontinent together with other Portuguese officials and merchants. Some are mentioned by name because of their prominence or because of certain functions they performed for the Portuguese rulers. One of them was Gaspar da Gama, whose memorable services for Vasco da Gama and his successors were frequently recorded in contemporary reports and letters. Another was the *converso* scientist Garcia d'Orta who escaped the clutches of the Inquisition established in Goa in 1560 only through his premature demise, while his surviving sister was burned at the stake. Much of this tragic history has been told here in an earlier volume in connection with the general Portuguese colonial expansion and it need not be repeated in the present context. However, there also were professing Jews, possibly even among recent Sephardic immigrants, whose New Christian antecedents escaped the attention of the Inquisitors, and who joined the existing older communities, about which, unfortunately, we have little documentary information.[40]

Neither the province of Goa nor any other Portuguese possession in India became a truly Christian land. Despite vigorous missionary efforts, fully supported by the colonial authorities, often with the use of force and other pressures, most natives adhered to their traditional faith and general class system. On the other hand, the Mughal Empire could not be classified as a full-fledged Muslim state, although it was politically and economically dominated by Muslim rulers. Even under the regime of the intolerant Awrangzib, when conversionist Muslim pressures were highly intensified, the imperial society remained, in its majority, divided both denominationally and by class structure as it had been before Babur. Certainly, the ostensibly egalitarian orientation of the *shari'a* had no room in the Mughal administrative system.[41]

BENE-ISRAEL

Quite different from the Jewish population in the Mughal Empire were the Bene-Israel. This group, which seems never to have greatly exceeded the 10,000 members counted at the beginning of the twentieth century, offers more puzzling problems than perhaps any other segment of world Jewry. Regrettably, although existing for many centuries in Bombay and the Bombay province, it left behind no early written records elucidating its origin and early history. We must rely entirely on its own oral traditions, which vaguely claim descent from the ancient Israelites of the First Commonwealth. One basic legend assures us that in remote antiquity an Israelitic group coming "from the North" (usually identified as Northern Israel) had approached India by ship. The fleet suffered shipwreck, however, in the vicinity of the Kennery and Henney Islands some six miles south of Bombay; only seven males and seven females allegedly succeeded in swimming to shore. Subsequently, some of the corpses were recovered from the sea and buried in two adjoining mounds, one each for men and women. These mounds have served through the ages as centers for pilgrimages. The seven pairs of survivors, we are told, later multiplied and in time were joined by arrivals from West-Central Asia. It is unfortunate that a similar legend was preserved also by a neighboring Chipavan Brahmin group, curiously revealing certain facial similarities to the Bene-Israel, and thus far, at least, no one could satisfactorily explain which legend had historic priority. Moreover, whatever one thinks about the Phoenician-Israelite expansion in India, there is no question about the incorporation of parts of the subcontinent into the vast empire established by Alexander the Great. Even after its divisions in the Diadoch period, Alexander's conquests created an expanding Hellenistic civilization which brought India into the orbit of a commercially and intellectually interwoven world extending from Italy to India. Such contacts continued also in the Roman period despite the obstacles placed in these relationships by the Parthians and later the Persians. Jews residing in most of the great centers of the Mediterranean civilization, particularly in Egypt, Palestine, and Babylonia, may well have played a certain role in these exchanges.[42]

In any case, there appears to be a kernel of truth in the contention that the foundations of that community reached back to the ancient period. Their antiquity seems also to be attested by their religious observances. While strictly adhering to their religious rituals and observing the Jewish holidays very much in accordance with normative Judaism, they seem never to have celebrated the festival of Ḥanukkah which followed the victorious Maccabean Revolt. To be sure, here as in Ethiopia, that festival may not have been adopted because of a certain resistance in some Diaspora circles. We recall that as late as 126 B.C.E., that is, almost two decades after the establishment of the sovereign Maccabean state under Simon the Hasmonean, the sages of Jerusalem felt impelled to address a special message to Egyptian Jewry demanding the observances of the Ḥanukkah festival. Perhaps because of the divided opinions even in ancient Palestine about the sociopolitical benefits of the Maccabean regime and growing internal dissensions between the Sadducees and Pharisees, the Jerusalem authorities emphasized the religious aspects of the holiday, celebrating the miraculous nature of the rededication of the Temple rather than the political struggle for independence. It is quite possible, therefore, that similar messages, if sent at all to the remote Jewish settlements of Ethiopia and India, evoked no echo in these communities, which never introduced that eight-day celebration into their calendar.[43]

This argument is weakened, however, to some extent by the fact that Shavuot (the Feast of Weeks), although clearly enjoined in the Pentateuchal legislation, seems likewise to have been forgotten in the Bene-Israel community. Certainly, whether it was originally celebrated primarily as a festival of the first fruits brought to the Temple in Jerusalem, or as a memorial for God's revealing the Torah to Moses on Sinai, it would not have aroused any serious opposition in whatever Jewish circles it had been observed before. It simply may have been some historical accident brought about by a lapse of memory, similar to that which caused a difference of two weeks in the date of the Sukkot (Feast of Tabernacles) celebration as observed by the Bene-Israel at variance from that ordered by the Bible and generally adhered to among Jews in the rest of the world. Some other deviations from customs prevailing elsewhere, as well as the strict enforcement of certain fast days in the form recorded first only in the tannaitic literature, have induced some modern scholars to postulate the origin of the Bene-Israel group as dating back to some time between 200 B.C.E. and 200 C.E., although some other scholars attributed these changes to a religious reform introduced by one David Rahabi, a shadowy figure mentioned in later traditions of the people. In short, despite diligent efforts of many Christian missionaries and students of Indian history, as well as of western Jewish leaders interested in the presence of that noteworthy branch of Judaism, the history of the Bene-Israel before the early modern period is still covered by impenetrable darkness. We shall see that, like their better known brethren of Cochin, they have felt the impact of those historical riddles not only in theory but also in some very vital aspects of the application to them of the halakhic requirements, especially after the rise of the new State of Israel. Yet, in the fall of 1951, as a matter of principle the Israeli Chief Rabbinate, after the immigration of 6,000 Bene-Israel to the State of Israel, proclaimed a fundamental decision that there was "no question about the Jewishness of the 'Bene-Israel' who from an early period have been accepted as being of Jewish descent. . . . Hence, there is no reason to forbid their marriages with other Jews." Investigations in individual cases were to relate, therefore, only to the immediate ancestry of the applicants. As a result of the final recognition of the Bene-Israel as full-fledged Jews, the emigration to Israel increased by leaps and bounds. Their population in India, which is said to have doubled in the half century before 1948 from 10,000 to 20,000 persons—apparently the all-time peak—declined rapidly. Today, we are told, "more than 25,000 Bene Israel live in Israel."[44]

COCHIN

The most important and best-known Jewish community in medieval and early modern India inhabited Cochin. The city had played some role in the trade with western Asia and China in ancient times but it became a major emporium only after a torrential flood greatly enlarged its harbor in 1341. From that time on, it was regarded by many Europeans as the best and most secure port in India. Mentioned under somewhat different names by Muslim and Western travelers, it became a dependency of the ruler of Zamorin, but it was directly governed by the rajah of Cochin. It attracted a variety of immigrants, although it suffered, like the rest of the subcontinent, from the extremely rigid caste system. To quote George Philips's English summary of Ma Huan's description of the seaport:

There are five classes of men in this kingdom. The Nayars rank with the king. In the first class are those who shave their heads, and have a thread or string hanging over their shoulders; these are looked upon as belonging to the noblest families. In the second are the Mahommedans; in the third the Chittis, who are capitalists; in the fourth the Kolings, who act as commission agents; in the fifth the Mukwas, who are the lowest and poorest of all. The Mukwas live in houses which are forbidden by the Government to be more than three feet high, and they are not allowed to wear long garments; when abroad, if they happen to meet a Nayar or a Chitti, they at once prostrate themselves on the ground and dare not rise until they have passed by; these Mukwas get their living by fishing and carrying burdens.

These differences continued over generations because social mobility, especially in overcoming the caste differences, was extremely limited by both law and social prejudice. The outward distinctions, such as those indicated here in the case of the Nayars, were strictly observed and any display of a distinctive shape of attire by an unauthorized person was severely punished. Not surprisingly, these caste distinctions affected also the Jewish community which in almost all other countries was internally rather egalitarian in both law and prevailing practice.[45]

Characteristically, in the above enumeration of the castes only the Muslim community is distinguished as one of the five special classes. This was undoubtedly owing to the numerous rulers and considerable groups of the native population, especially in western India, professing Islam. In contrast, the Christians were a permanent minority even in the areas which they had inhabited from time immemorial. According to a legend current among the "Syrian Christians," their history reached back to the New Testament age. They believed that Apostle Thomas had come to India in 52 c.e. to proclaim the new Gospel to its inhabitants and that he had succeeded in establishing the first community of so-called St. Thomas Christians. This sect, understandably, was of great interest to the sixteenth- and seventeenth-century Christian missionaries. In addition there was a variety of medieval Christian settlers from Egypt, Syria, Iraq, and Persia, as well as Old and New Christian arrivals from the Iberian Peninsula. They were all joined by local converts and together founded ever new Christian communities. The Western settlers were often named "Portugalls," regardless of their country of origin. Because of their great Catholic zeal some of the Jesuit missionaries had tried to convert even the Eastern Christians to their brand of Christianity. On one occasion, Alessandro Valignano, the contemporary historian of the Jesuit Order, mentions finding in Cochin in 1557 a group of more than twenty New Christians who were "most sinfully involved in Jewish ceremonies and superstitions." Ultimately, they fell into the hands of the Portuguese Inquisition, sent back to Portugal, tried by the Holy Office, and condemned either to burning on the stake or to wearing the sanbenito. Complicated by the work of rivaling Franciscans, Dominicans, and Capucins, and later by the arrival of Protestant missionaries, the situation of the Christian population, still only a small minority, was quite fluid and subject to various ups and downs.[46]

Some such uncertainties, on a far lesser scale, bedeviled also the Jews residing in Cochin and its environs. This despite the availability of many more local and foreign sources, including a few Hebrew statements dating from different centuries. We recall Benjamin of Tudela's brief reference to India, evidently referring to the area of "Qimlon," not far from Cochin and Cranganore. No less an authority than Maimonides likewise contributed observations on the Cochin Jews. Although he doubtless heard a good deal about them from Jewish India traders in Egypt (among them his own brother David who was finally shipwrecked and drowned on one such trip), the contrast he drew between the Yemenite and the Indian Jews is not particularly enlightening and, perhaps, not even quite correct for his time. While censoring even the Yemenite Jews for their limited study of the Talmud and their excessive reliance on the aggadic interpretation of the Bible, he claimed that Indian Jews "do not know the written law. They have nothing of religion except that they rest on Sabbath and perform circumcision on the eighth day."[47]

More meaningful were some later rabbinic responsa to inquiries concerning the position of the Cochin Jews in Jewish law. The earliest and in some respects the most important, though not unequivocal, decisions on this question were rendered by the sixteenth century rabbis David Ibn abi Zimra and his pupil, Jacob b. Abraham Castro (d. 1610). Because of the basic importance of marriage laws in Judaism the question whether the Cochin Jews, as well as the Bene-Israel, were to be allowed freely to marry other Jews or Jewesses and thus be qualified for full-fledged admission to the broader Jewish communities in time became a burning issue. It was heatedly debated in connection with the Law of Return which was enacted by Israel immediately after its emergence as an independent state and which opened the gate for the admission of a wide variety of Jews from many lands. Incidentally, some of the rabbinic responsa, while dealing mainly with legal technicalities, have often included significant factual information concerning the demographic and other social aspects of Cochin Jewish life.[48]

In early modern times we also hear more and more about

Cochin from Western Christian and Jewish visitors. The six-teenth-century Yemenite poet-traveler, R. Zechariah b. Saa-diah adh-Dhahri (az-Zahiri) who, as we remember, had visited Ormuz, left behind a brief record of his observations during his sojourn of several months in Cochin, too. Long known in manuscript, his *Sefer ha-Musar* (Book of Moral Conduct) is now available in Y. Ratzaby's edition. More important was the del-egation sent in 1686 by the Amsterdam Jewish community to investigate the conditions of the Indian coreligionists on the spot. It consisted of Mosseh Pereira de Paiva as chairman, Isaac Irgas, Isaac Moscat, and Abraham Vort. In his *Notisias dos Ju-deos de Cochin,* published in Amsterdam in 1687 (and subse-quently republished by Moses Amzalak in Lisbon, 1923), Pe-reira not only described the general situation and the specific Jewish condition in the city of Cochin and its environs, but he also offered a partial listing of names of the leading Jewish citizens who had not long before settled in Cochin; he also indicated their places of origin. His other data, such as those concerning the nine Jewish congregations in the region (three in Cochin, two in Angicaimal, one each in Parur, Paluk, Che-notta, and Muttancheri, together embracing 480 families), have also helped enrich our knowledge of the local situation more than anything offered by his predecessors. Such visits multi-plied in the nineteenth century and we owe a good deal in particular to David D'Beth-Hillel, and the world travelers Is-rael Joseph Benjamin, often called Benjamin II, and Jacob Sa-phir. Nor are we completely devoid of some local documen-tation in Hebrew. One such Hebrew manuscript, included in the Sassoon library, has been utilized to good advantage by David Bar Giyora, especially for his analysis of the long-raging intercommunal strife in Cochin.[49]

From another angle, but equally important, have been the observations by non-Jewish visitors and Company officials. Apart from the itineraries of such famous travelers as Marco Polo and Ibn Baṭṭuṭa (containing a few incidental remarks on Indian Jewish life which, because of the extreme paucity of medieval sources, are more significant than they appear at first glance) we have the reports sent home by Jesuit and other missionaries, and by Portuguese, French, Dutch, and English officials and merchants. Though rarely mentioning Jews by name, these observations in their sum total furnish us a valuable body of information. Some of these sources have already been mentioned in connection with the history of Ormuz, the Mughal Empire, and the Portuguese, Dutch, English, and French colonial expansion. In addition we have some equally casual remarks of native Indian writers. Yet, it must be admitted, that after using all these primary sources, together with a host of secondary writings that have accumulated over the years, we are able to obtain only a rather blurred picture of the historical evolution of this relatively small, but highly intriguing, segment of world Jewry.[50]

An outstanding feature of the Cochin community was its pronounced caste divisions in emulation of the system prevailing in the Indian environment from time immemorial. The inquiry to Ibn abi Zimra, addressed by an unknown writer in India, described the Cochin community as having "about 900 families, a hundred of them consisting of original Jews called the *meyuḥasim* (well born) and the rest embraces children of male and female slaves who include rich and philanthropic Jews. The *meyuḥasim* do not intermarry with them and call them slaves. Hence there are endless quarrels and controversies." The two classes were also largely distinguished by the color of their skin, the former being known as "White" Jews, whereas the *meshuḥrarim* (liberated slaves) were as a rule black, or rather deeply tanned. The latter coloring has often been compared with that of the southern Mediterranean peoples of Italy or Spain. In between there was a group called the Malabar "brown" Jews who, however, did not form a community apart. Despite these internal caste distinctions, to outsiders they all formed a single group known principally by their Jewish religion. Mosseh Pereyra de Paiva—who collected detailed data with the aid of a questionnaire which included forty-six pertinent queries apparently answered by many well-informed local leaders—had this to say about the *meyuḥasim*:

All these people are very well disposed and of gentle character; [they embrace] very prominent *bahale Torah* [men, learned in the Torah], and no less famous merchants. Their colour is brown, caused no doubt by the climate, for they are entirely separated from the Malabari (Jews) of rank because it is a great disgrace to intermarry with them. They do not eat of what the Malabari Jews kill, nor do they celebrate minyan [a quorum for divine services] in their company. They allege that the Malabaris are sons of slaves and are mixed with guerim [proselytes from among], kenahanitas [Canaanites or heathen], and Ismaelim [Muslims]. But in all things the two groups observe the same rites and ceremonies.

Such social separation, though less sharp than that between the Brahmins and pariahs in Indian society, was very far-reaching. Even within the synagogue precincts, where officially all Jews were treated as equals, in Cochin there was a sharp line of demarcation. As late as 1860 a Western visitor, R. Jacob Saphir, described the discriminatory treatment of the "black" majority as follows:

If a black man comes to a white man's house he will not allow him to sit in his house but must stand up as a slave before his master. Similarly if he should once come into the synagogue of the whites they will not allow him to sit down on a chair but he must remain seated on the ground near the door on a par with slaves. He will not be called to the Torah nor counted in the quorum for any sacred ceremony, nor will he be permitted to put on the Talit and tefillin [phylacteries] in the white man's presence, as is the case with a gentile slave. Neither shall they intermarry with them under any condition. It is easier for the whites to liberate their female slaves and marry them, rather than marry the daughters of such slaves. The hatred has been so deep-rooted that they consider such intermarriage as highly dangerous.

Saphir explains this Jewish caste system historically by the black Jews being essentially descendants of local women with whom the Jewish arrivals had had children. Yet, concluded Saphir, "there is no doubt that they are Jewish offspring from the paternal side, they serve the God of their Fathers and let us beware of excluding them from the House of Israel."[51]

These testimonies coming from different generations confirm the persistence of the local social system in the face of great historical changes in India's general and Jewish society, occasioned by such epochal transformations as the partial occupation of the coastal areas by the Portuguese (1500–1663); their replacement by the Dutch conquerors (1663–1795), and finally the occupation of the whole country and its unification under the British aegis after 1795. Just as these manifold regimes failed to change the caste structure in general Indian society, so did they leave the disparity between the white and black Jews basically untouched until the twentieth century. Hence the testimony of the relatively few extant sources, though stemming from different periods, may be used for the reconstruction of a general picture of the entire Jewish community. Remarkably, however, the great separation between Sephardim and Ashkenazim which, in the modern period, reached a climax in England and Holland, was not taken over by the settlers of the two groups in Cochin. Their mutual accommodation was well illustrated by the prevailing practice in the white synagogue called Paradesi (of foreigners). If during the Sabbath services an Ashkenazic Jew led the morning prayers, he was immediately followed in the Musaf service by a Sephardic reader, and vice versa. Naturally the respective readers could use their particular prayer books, notwithstanding the numerous differences in their respective texts.[52]

Demographically, it appears, there was a steady decline in the Jewish population in the area. While in the 1160s Benjamin of Tudela wrote broadly of thousands of Jews residing in that area, and in the mid-sixteenth century Ibn abi Zimra's correspondent still referred to 900 families living there, which was the equivalent of more than 4,000 persons, later estimates show a steady decline. From about 460 or 422 families counting some 2,200 or 2,000 persons, respectively, as mentioned by Pereyra de Paiva in 1687 and by the Dutch Governor Adriaan Mones in 1781, the total declined to 1,039 in 1839. This diminution is the more remarkable, as before 1687, there had been an influx into Cochin of Jews from various lands. In his own partial enumeration of the "white" Jewish families then living in the Cochin districts, Pereyra mentioned four families which came from Aleppo, two each from Jerusalem, Germany, and Persia, and one each from Damascus, Safed, Algiers, Castile, "Baliel" (Baghdad?), and Berberia (North Africa). It doubtless was this continued Jewish immigration, particularly of the so-called Baghdadi or Iraqi Jews who, in the course of the nineteenth century, formed the aforementioned additional communal groupings in Bombay, Calcutta, Poona, and other cities; these arrivals helped the total Cochin

Jewish population to increase to 1,790 persons by 1857. Yet the generally adverse socioeconomic and cultural factors which have caused a continued shrinking of India's total Jewish population to less than 5,000 persons since the country's independence in 1947—this in the midst of a general population explosion—also operated on the local level in the preceding generations, when the total number of Jews in Cochin ranged only from 1,137 to 1,451 persons in the years 1891–1931. Curiously, even in these four decades the ratio of "white" Jews declined from 180 to 144 persons, while that of the black increased from 957 to 1,307. Such disparity was undoubtedly even greater in the earlier periods, since we have evidence for the practice of some white Jews discharging their non-Jewish slaves, or of suddenly departing and leaving them behind, without a formal writ of emancipation. In such cases the stranded individuals usually joined the black Jewish community. It is to be assumed that the British outlawry of slavery had put an end to this particular contribution to the demographic growth of the black community.[53]

The long prevailing view that the majority of black Jews in Cochin had originated from the conversion of native Hindustanis to Judaism and that the community grew mainly through liberated slaves and others from the same native population was reinforced by biological tests. Taken by Dr. E. J. W. Macfarlane in the mid-1930s, these tests showed that 62 percent of the white Jews had blood group A. In contrast, 73.6 percent of the black Jews had blood group O, similar to that of the majority of Cochin Hindus. Apparently, the differences between the Bene-Israel and either Cochin group were even more far reaching, although little is really known about the Bene-Israel in Cochin. Whatever individuals may have settled there in the course of time seem to have joined either community without leaving traces of their own. Moreover, the Bombay Bene-Israel predominantly spoke the Marathi language, while the Cochin Jews used the Malayalam Indian dialect. It may be noted that in this respect the Cochin Jews also differed from the general population which mostly used the general Hindustani vernacular. As emphasized by Prime Minister Indira Gandhi in her address at the 400th anniversary celebration of the Cochin synagogue in December 1968, the Cochin Jews, while generally but a small minority in the population, constituted a majority of the Malayalam-speaking group. This point had frequently been stressed also by S. S. Koder, the leader of the Jewish community of Cochin in recent years.[54]

We have little information about the occupational distribution of the Cochin Jews. In the sixteenth century the white Jews, at least, seemed to have been quite prosperous, deriving most of their livelihood from commerce. The Dutch official John Huyghen van Linschoten, who spent more than five years (1583–89) in India, observed that some Cochin Jews "built very fair stone houses, and are rich merchants, and of the king of Cochin's nearest Counsellers. . . . There are manie of them that came out of the country of Palestina and Jeruselem thether, and speake over all the Exchange [verie perfect and] good Spanish." Other visitors likewise referred to rich Jews without clarifying how they amassed their fortunes. Among the relatively few Jewish converts to Christianity in Malacca the Jesuit, Ruy Gonsalves de Caminha, reported home on January 30, 1548 the death of a Jew who left behind 6,000 or 7,000 pardaos; this man's two sons had adopted Christianity and were expected to leave for Italy. Of special interest is the comment by the Dutch Governor Adriaan Mones in his memorandum of 1781 which read:

One does not notice in these Jews the acuteness, the activity, and still less, that cheating, which is usually ascribed to the Jews of our times. On the contrary, I have found them to be honest men who would feel ashamed to cheat a Christian, a heathen or a Moor purposely. It may also be said of them that they are not, by far, so dirty and slovenly as are, by common imputation, the Jews of our day. . . . But the Jews here, without distinction down to the lowest and the poorest, are as clean in their houses and bodies, their table and their bed, as we; so that you can hardly tell that they are Jews and Jewesses, if they were not recognizable through being distinguished from other nations by a peculiar sort of dress and by physical peculiarities.

This observation doubtless held true also for the preceding centuries.[55]

Here and there we also learn about Jewish intermediaries and factors. Probably mostly recruited from Sephardic and other Western arrivals, these men resembled the dragomans of the Ottoman Empire, serving as both interpreters and business agents. Some may also have served Western diplomats and merchants as aides in their negotiations with the local authorities. Regrettably, the existing sources do not give details about such Jewish functionaries. Only occasionally do we read a report about an agent of the kind encountered by François Pyrard de Laval sometime between 1602 and 1607. This particular individual happened to be a man without conscience whom Pyrard designated as "the greatest scoundrel in the world." In command of many languages including Hindi, Arabic, and English, he attached himself to an English general who was pursuing trade in pepper. This general "went to Batan in Java, where this Jew robbed him of twelve or fifteen hundred pieces of forty sols Spanish, and made his escape. With the English he was of their religion; with the Mahometans, of theirs; whereas he was all the while a Jew. He married a wife wherever he happened to be, and thus he had four or five wives in India." Undoubtedly, however, this confidence man was an exception, since we hear of no other such unsavory Jewish characters in the reports of the various East India Companies and other contemporary sources.[56]

In general, however, it appears that Jews never played a significant role in Indian commerce, domestic or international. They actually seem to have lost some additional ground in the course of the eighteenth and nineteenth centuries when most of the trade was conducted by gifted Indian merchants, as well as by foreign traders from various lands. Of course, there were some exceptions; among them the outstanding Jewish intermediaries and merchants like Abraham Navarro in the late seventeenth, Ezekiel Rahabi in the eighteenth, and the Sassoon family (who had come from Baghdad) in the nineteenth centuries. But these were relative newcomers who did not typify the long-established Jewries of the subcontinent. In Cochin specifically one gets the impression (no more than that can be derived from the existing documentation) that in such towns as Cochin and Ernakulam or in their neighboring villages, Jews earned their living in ways similar to those of the corresponding classes among the majority of the inhabitants.[57]

Otherwise the sociopolitical status of the Cochin Jews was rather favorable. Not only did they possess with great pride the old copper plates describing their privileges—the community still keeps these plates as their cherished possession in the Paradesi synagogue—but in practice, too, they enjoyed considerable rights. The fact that their chief synagogue, built first in 1565 and rebuilt after the establishment of the Dutch regime in 1665, was located in the immediate proximity of the ruler's palace and temple so that the religious services of either denomination were easily heard in the other's sanctuary without causing any disputes, reflected a considerable degree of religious toleration. The rajah also often had Jewish councilors and, like his major antagonist, the king of neighboring Zamorin, employed Jewish soldiers. In 1550, when an alliance of Portuguese and Cochin armies battled against the rajah of Vatakkenkur, the rajah of Cochin objected to an attack on Saturday, because the Jews, "the best warriors he had raised," refused to fight on their Sabbath. It is small wonder that some outsiders styled him the "king of Jews." Such Jewish participation in Indian armed services, also as officers of various ranks, continued under the later British regime. It ceased only when a new caste law provided that, for more egalitarian treatment, officers be appointed to army units consisting to a large extent of members of their own caste—a provision which could not apply to a small minority like the Jews.[58]

In their internal affairs, too, the Cochin Jews (like most other castes) enjoyed a large measure of self-government. The first known *mudeliar*, Baruch Joseph Levi, officiated in the mid-fifteenth century. He was followed by his son, Joseph Levi. According to a charter issued in 1683, which undoubtedly reflected conditions prevailing for a long time in the community, Shemṭob Castilien was appointed *mudeliar* of the White Jews in Cochin. He was in charge of all communal affairs and exercised full judiciary authority in criminal and civil proceedings affecting his coreligionists. Only capital sentences needed the rajah's confirmation. Subsequently, this office became hereditary in the Castilien family. Needless to say, the synagogues ran their own affairs without outside interference. According to Menasseh ben Israel, in his petition to Oliver

Cromwell, there were four such institutions in Cochin in the 1650s. Their number increased to seven in the following generations, but some rapidly declined when the Jewish population diminished. Jewish autonomy extended also to Ernakulam, the second important community in the Cochin area, as is attested by the charter issued by the rajah in 1711. In short, combined with the general religious toleration of the Cochin rajahs, the position of the Jews in the course of time was sufficiently favorable for them to be subject to ever greater assimilatory pressures. This condition also helps explain in part the decline of the Jewish population in the last two centuries, although their community from time to time was reinforced by some immigration from Western lands.[59]

Of course, there was also some emigration. To be sure, settling in other Jewish communities often raised some legal difficulties for the Cochin "black" Jews. While the *meyuḥasim* generally had little difficulty in being accepted by their coreligionists abroad, the *meshuḥrarim* frequently were subject to questioning concerning the purity of their descent. In this respect Cochin's black Jews were in a worse position than the Bene-Israel, who were generally, as we recall, recognized as Jews as a matter of principle. As to the Cochin blacks, however, the problem was more complicated. According to a rigid interpretation of the old rabbinic law, only slaves, duly emancipated with a formal writ of liberation by their owners, and their descendants could readily be admitted to the Jewish community. It was widely known, however, that, in many cases, Cochin slaveholders, even if informally treating their slaves as free persons, often failed to hand them the prescribed deeds. The same held true in the case of divorces, which could legally be performed only with pedantically formulated writs of divorce. Any failure to live up to this requirement made the children of an "illegally" remarried divorcee technically *mamzerim* (bastards in a narrower sense), whose progeny was not to be admitted to the Jewish community even many generations later. Since the Cochin Jews were not sufficiently familiar with the detailed provisions of Jewish laws of divorce and slave emancipation, some rigorists of other lands took the hard line of excluding such new arrivals from marrying into

the Jewish community. Generation after generation, therefore, such questions were raised with rabbis of various communities; the answers often depended on diverse interpretations given the application of these laws by individual rabbis.[60]

This question became a burning issue after the rise of the
State of Israel. The new state generally welcomed the influx
of Jews from all lands and indeed, under the constitutional
Law of Return, received members of all communities from East
and West with open arms. Before long the rabbinate of Jerusalem was confronted with a decision about the legal status of
the arrivals from India. Under the general structure of the
country, the law inherited from Turkish and British times left
the main jurisdiction over personal laws concerning marriage,
divorce, and inheritance in the hands of the ecclesiastical leadership of the respective denominations. Hence, the decisions
of the rabbinical tribunals were, as a rule, binding also on the
secular authorities. As a result, some disgruntled Indian immigrants returned to their native land. On a lesser scale such
complications arose also in other Jewish communities to the
dismay of secular nationalists and many humanitarians. Senti-
mentally, too, large segments of the Jewish public were prepared to share their destinies with these long-alienated fragments of their people.[61]

CHINA

The history of the Jews in China greatly resembles that of
their coreligionists in India; there, too, the documentary evidence for most periods and geographic areas is extremely
scarce. We are somewhat better informed only about one community, that of Kaifeng, the capital of Honan Province. The
rich Chinese literature produced over the centuries has thus
far contributed very little to our knowledge of the evolution
of even that extraordinary community. To be sure, in the last
few generations Chinese gazetteers and journals have mentioned a number of Jewish individuals who achieved a certain
distinction in one or another profession or in public service.
But usually they fail to refer to the person's Jewish activities
or concerns. Before the eighteenth century, moreover, even

such brief allusions are very sparse and contribute very little to our knowledge of Jewish life in the country. Most importantly, except for a few allusions in Hebrew letters during the Middle Ages and early modern times, we learn very little from the existing Hebrew sources about the developments in that large, highly civilized, and in some periods wealthy country which, it has been estimated, by 1705 already embraced some 300,000,000 and in 1800 about 400,000,000 inhabitants. These totals surpassed the entire population of Europe and the Americas combined, and probably amounted to two hundred times the number of their Jewish, and double that of their Christian contemporaries in the world.[62]

As in India and Ethiopia the oral traditions of the Chinese Jews claimed their descent from ancient Palestinian exiles. True, a curious passage in the book of Isaiah, referring to the return of the exiles, states: "Behold, these shall come from far; . . . and these from the land of Sinim" (49:2). This verse has often been taken as an allusion to China and its Israelite inhabitants, but, in fact, it may not refer to China at all. Nevertheless, the tradition persisted that at some remote period in antiquity Israelitic exiles, particularly from the "Lost Ten Tribes," found their way into the Far East, probably following the general immigration into China, overland from Persia-Khurasan-Turkestan or by sea around India and the Malayan archipelago to the Chinese port of Canton and others. This, indeed, was what the Jesuit missionaries of the seventeenth and eighteenth centuries persistently heard from the Kaifeng Jews. Summarizing in 1754 or 1757 his predecessors' reports Abbé Gabriel Brotier wrote:

Let us now turn to the question of the time when these Jews entered China. They have constantly asserted to all the missionaries that they came here under the family of the Han, and their records say the same thing. The Han Dynasty began in the year 206 B.C. It was therefore about that time that the Jews penetrated to China; they may have gone thither before the downfall of their empire, but it is more natural to believe that it was not until after the terrible catastrophe of Jerusalem that, scattered in all directions, those of Korassan and of the Transoxane spread into China. This supposition becomes practically a certainty when it is recalled that several of these Jews asserted that they arrived during the reign of Ming Ti. This

Prince ascended the throne in the year 56 A.D., and died in 78. The dates could not better agree with the destruction of Jerusalem, which was in the year 70.

During the Han dynasty's regime, which extended to 220 C.E., a vigorous trade developed between the Roman Empire and China. It was particularly the "silk route" which brought much silk from China to the Western Empire whose aristocracy was greatly enamored of silk clothing. It stands to reason that some Jews, particularly from Egypt, took part in that trade. But all this is merely a surmise unsupported by any documentary evidence or even by such informed reports as given by Pliny and other Roman writers.[63]

We are on somewhat safer ground for the period of the T'ang and Sung dynasties (618–906, 960–1279). We need but recall the report of Postmaster General Ibn Khurdadhbah of 846 C.E., describing the four routes taken by the Jewish "Rhadanites" which connected Western Europe with the Far East. This well-informed official specifically mentioned China as one of the destinations of the Western travelers. We also remember the report of the Arab trader "Sulayman" in China of 851 which, together with its commentator, Abu Zaid al-Ḥasan as-Sirafi (ca. 916), specifically referred to Jews among the 120,000 victims massacred by a revolutionary leader at the occupation of Canton in 878. Certainly, the four waves of expulsion or forced conversion of the Jews in the Byzantine Empire, in each of the four centuries from the seventh to the tenth, must have set in motion a considerable number of Jewish refugees who escaped these persecutions by fleeing to other lands, possibly including China. The fact that we hear less about these Far-Eastern Jews even from Eldad ha-Dani and Benjamin of Tudela (their comments are definitely too vague and unreliable) may only have been a testimony to the quick absorption of such Jewish settlers by the Chinese majority. China was indeed a country famous for assimilating any number of foreign rulers, and ruling castes such as the Mongols, who in time were so completely submerged by the Chinese majority that their traces in the contemporary population have almost completely vanished. This factor also operated against the Christians, whose two periods of flowering in certain

Chinese communities in the seventh through the ninth and the fourteenth through the fifteenth centuries seem to have been followed by their nearly total disappearance. More fortunate were the Muslims, whose presence in substantial and increasing numbers is attested to by many contemporary records, the study of which has made considerable progress only in the twentieth century.[64]

Nor can we tell with complete assurance from which country most of the Jews arrived during the Sung dynasty. According to their own traditions most of them had come from India. This contention is partly confirmed by their preferred designation of themselves as Iseloye (Chinese for Israel), reminiscent of the Bene-Israel of India. In contrast, in the few references to them in official Chinese documents they are for the most part called *Djuhud, Yuhud,* or some related designation of "Jew," an evident borrowing from Persian and Arabic. The motivation here, as in India, may have been the Jews' preference to refer to themselves by their biblical name because of the high esteem in which the Hebrew Bible was held by their Muslim neighbors, whereas the official designation may have been adopted by the Yüan dynasty (1260–1368), when the large Mongolian Empire embraced both China and Persian-Arab territories in central and western Asia. It was, indeed, in 1280 that Kublai Khan (1259–94) specifically forbade both Jews and Muslims to slaughter sheep through their own ritual methods. We recall that a similar law was issued by the Mongolian rulers of Persia, who at that time were still recognizing the superior authority of the great khan, now residing in China. In 1329 Kublai's successors also introduced the special taxes imposed upon the religious minorities, including Jews, in Muslim countries, a practice likewise reintroduced about that time in the western provinces. These discriminatory ordinances were followed by the prohibition in 1340 of levirate marriages as practiced by Jews and Muslims, and in 1354 by the summons to Peking of the leaders of the two communities to announce to them the inclusion of their members in the obligatory army service. We shall see that both Jews and Muslims in China were later often attracted to military careers. The internal evidence of the extant Jewish sources concerning the religious practices of the Chinese Jews likewise reveal strong Persian influences, whether these were transmitted by direct immigrants from Persia or else were brought in by some Jews settled in India where Judeo-Persian rituals had long played a great role. In any case, the Jews must have been constant participants in the Indian–Chinese trade largely conducted on Arab ships throughout the Middle Ages. It was no accident that whatever mention of Jews occurs in the Chinese sources refers to cities which were great centers of maritime trade. Apart from Canton, specified by "Sulayman," we learn about the presence of Jews in Nanking, Ch'üan-chou (Tsinkiang), Ningpo (in Portuguese called Lampo), and Yangchow (Yüanchow), all of them important ports on the Pacific Ocean, except for Yangchow which served as a port on the Yangtse River, but was also easily reached from the ocean. In fact, Marco Polo started his return journey from that harbor, which he called Cinghian. On the other hand, we hear only of one city located in Inner Mongolia (or northwest China) which was more easily approached through the land route from Khurasan and Kwarizm, namely Ninghsia (Ningsia). But as far as Jews are concerned, at the present state of our knowledge, all these Jewries are but shadow communities about whose origin and history we know next to nothing.[65]

KAIFENG

Chinese Jewish history in the period from 1200 to 1650 here under review is almost synonymous with that of the community of Kaifeng. This city, located in central China some 370 miles south-southwest of Peking, long served as a capital of the Empire under the Five Dynasties (907–960) and the northern Sung Dynasty (960–1127). It continued as the capital of Honan province under the Mongol rulers (1280–1368) and remained an important center of commerce and cultural life to the present. The Jews settled in Kaifeng, as they claimed, under the Sung Dynasty, and continued living there until the twentieth century. They were of a different type than either the Bene-Israel, the Cochin Jews, or the Falashas. From all the testimonies we have in the available sources, they looked and acted like other Chinese, spoke Chinese, rather than any Jewish dialect, and were only distinguished from their neighbors by their religion and its rituals. Remarkably, their outstanding feature, noticed by non-Jews, was that they were "the people who cut out the sinews" after slaughtering an animal. Such deveining of an animal, commemorating Patriarch Jacob's encounter with an angel which gave him and his descendants the name "Israel" (Gen. 32:25 ff.), was an important function requiring a certain expertise. The absence of such personnel has often troubled even modern Jewish communities which found themselves forced to dispose of the entire hind quarters of a ritually slaughtered animal to non-Jewish purchasers at greatly reduced prices. Probably the ritual of circumcision or the abstention from pork was less pronounced because in both these matters they resembled their far more numerous Muslim neighbors, with whom they were often identified by their Chinese compatriots. In fact, even the relatively more numerous Christians were also included in that Islamic minority of monotheistic nonprofessors of Confucianism, Buddhism, or Taoism, the faiths of the overwhelming majority.[66]

Despite the various vicissitudes, with alternating toleration and intolerance and a general welcoming of foreigners versus large-scale xenophobia, which over the centuries characterized the frequently changing attitudes of the governing circles in the Empire, the Kaifeng Jews were able to maintain their separate existence without becoming a segregated social class obviously different from the masses of the population. In fact, even the very learned *literati*, generation after generation, evinced very little interest in the small group whose numbers rarely seem to have exceeded two thousand persons. Not surprisingly, therefore, we really depend to a large extent on European visitors, and occasional longer-term residents, for our information about all matters pertaining to the Kaifeng group.

The life of the entire Kaifeng community centered around the synagogue, which also preserved most of the existing documentation of the Jews' public and private life. We have the record of Jews building a house of worship in 1173, although it may have been merely the rebuilding of a structure which had been destroyed by one of the elemental catastrophes or man-made disturbances which dominated the history of that area. The synagogue actually had to be rebuilt, wholly or partially, several times thereafter (1279, 1421, 1445, after the flood of 1461, and after a great fire sometime between 1573 and 1620). The most far-reaching destruction occurred in 1642 when the flood caused by the overflowing of the neighboring Yellow River necessitated the complete rebuilding of the synagogue from the ground up. As a result of that catastrophe many of the manuscripts and books, assembled over the previous generations, vanished without a trace. It seems, however, that the new synagogue was erected between 1653 and 1663 on the same area as its predecessors. The measurement reported, together with important drawings, by Jean Domenge (who in two visits of 1721–22 spent about a year in Kaifeng and carefully examined the synagogue's exterior and interior) were duplicated by those described about two centuries later by Bishop William Charles White of Toronto. The latter lived some twenty-five years (1909–1933) in Kaifeng as the Canadian Anglican bishop of Honan. Evidently, despite the constant decline in membership and activities during those two centuries, there was no encroachment from the outside on the land held by the Jewish community. The syngogue accommodated a library, which, however, fared less well than the land occupancy. While in the sixteenth and seventeenth centuries the congregation refused at frequent intervals even to show their sacred books to outsiders, in the following generations there was much greater apathy and readiness to part with that accumulated intellectual patrimony. Most of the synagogue's important collections have since been dispersed and found their way into numerous Western libraries.[67]

The synagogue and its services, to a larger extent than one might expect, represented traditional Judaism as it was practiced in other countries. At the same time it absorbed certain elements from the environment. Architecturally, it consisted of a beautiful complex of buildings, despite their various transformations after each destructive fire or flood. There was a main chamber for divine services and a varying number of adjoining buildings devoted to specific activities. The style was greatly influenced by Chinese-Muslim architecture but intrinsically it also followed certain traditional Jewish patterns. The descriptions by the travelers and other observers, especially when accompanied by sketches, give us a fairly accurate image of the exterior or interior of the entire synagogue complex. Remarkably, the building seems to have been open to non-Jews not only for casual visits but also for participation in the Jewish worship without conversion. At least the Jesuit Nicolò Langobardi wrote home on November 23, 1610: "I have been informed that those Christians of the Cross [referring to Nestorians], owing to the love with which they worship the same God as the Jews, go to offer their prayers in the synagogue; and the Jews allow them [to do this] because of this common reverence."[68]

It is obvious from the record, however, that the Jewish Sabbath and festivals were essentially celebrated there according to well-established Mid-Eastern rituals, in some respects resembling the Sephardic more than the Ashkenazic rites. The days of the celebrations coincided with those of the Jewish calendar, if we may judge from the records referring only to corresponding Chinese computations. However, as usual there were some relatively minor differences, which became the subjects of diverse modern interpretations. They considered, for example, the rosh-ḥodesh, the beginning of each lunar month, a more significant holiday than did the Jews of other lands. It may be noted, however, that, despite the similarity of the Chinese and the Jewish lunar calendars, we do not hear of any Jewish experts being consulted by the Chinese regimes about some astronomic details governing their calendar. This despite the fact that the Jewish calendar had been established in 359 C.E. in the days of Hillel II when the celebration by witnesses observing the appearance of a new moon had given way to a long-range astronomic computation which was used to confirm occasionally conflicting testimonies. Evidently, there was no scholar of the rank of the Jesuit father, Johann Adam Schall von Bell, a well-trained mathematician, who could advise the Chinese government on calendar intricacies. But it appears that the majority did not resent the Jews refusing to work on the Sabbath or to eat food forbidden to them by their own law. Jewish leaders apparently were able to interpret the pertinent liturgical requirements in accordance with talmudic law, although their library, at least as it has thus far been established, seems to have included some Mishnaic but no gemara tractates. Having come for the most part from, or via, the Persian lands, they fully celebrated not only the Festival of Purim but also that of Ḥanukkah. In this respect they differed from most of their coreligionists in both Ethiopia and India. Purim seems actually to have been considered a significant holiday, since the Kaifeng Jews generally spoke with much awe about both Esther and Mordecai. Perhaps because they had come at least in part from Persian-dominated areas, they especially appreciated these biblical heroes as saviors of their people from destruction by an ancient Persian regime.[69]

On the other hand, they felt the impact of Confucianism. In part this was undoubtedly the result of outward pressure. Tolerant as some of the Chinese regimes were, they often resented any obvious denial of basic teachings of their Confucian faith which also served as the fundamental law of their country. True, among the characteristics which Max Weber detected in the rejection of "heretical" trends by the Chinese authorities was the fact that "the heretics banded together, allegedly in order to practice a virtuous life. However, they formed non-licensed associations and managed collections." Clearly, Jews fell into that category. Yet, it appears that the government, which, perhaps like the masses of the population, viewed Judaism as a sectarian branch of Islam, paid no heed to this deviation. Certainly, many statements of an ethical nature, made by Kaifeng Jewish leaders on the Chinese *liens* (vertical tablet inscriptions) hanging in the synagogue, could have been written in the Confucian spirit as well. For instance, when N'gai Ai T'ien (who as we shall see was to play a significant role in the early seventeenth century) composed the text of one of these *liens*, and when his text was supplemented on the tablet by his grandson Ai Hsien-sheng with another sentence, neither statement was likely to be resented by any pious Confucian. They read:

The Heavenly Writings [the Pentateuch] are fifty-three in number; with our mouth we recite them, and in our heart we hold them fast; praying that the Imperial Domain may be firmly established.

The Sacred Script [Hebrew] has twenty-seven letters; these we teach in our families and display on our doors; desiring that the Commonwealth may continually prosper.

Jewish interlocutors of the visiting Jesuit Jean Paul Gozani replied to his inquiry whether the Jews honored Confucius, apparently without any hesitation: "they honoured him in like manner as the heathen *literati* in China; and that they partook with them in the solemn ceremonies performed in the halls of their great men."[70]

Here Gozani touched an even more delicate nerve in Judeo-Gentile relations. Verbal homage to a great non-Jewish national hero had long been tolerated by the rabbis. But Jewish leadership elsewhere would undoubtedly have taken umbrage at the formal sacrifices and banquets staged in honor of a pagan religious teacher. Yet, this is exactly what the Kaifeng Jews did in tribute to Confucius even if they somewhat modified these ceremonies so that they would not conflict with their own law. According to Gozani, the Jews with whom he discussed these matters

added also, that in spring and autumn, they paid their ancestors the honours which are usually offered up to them in China, in the hall adjoining to their synagogues. That they indeed did not offer up swine's flesh, but that of other animals; and that, in the common ceremonies, they only presented china dishes filled with viands and sweetmeats, together with the incense; making very low bows or prostrations at the same time. I further asked them whether they kept, in their houses or in the hall of their dead, inscriptions in honour of their ancestors.

Perhaps less objectionable was the practice of holding vessels for incense in the synagogue, since incense as a part of worship was frequently mentioned in the Bible in connection with the divine services in the days of Moses and the Two Temples. In any case, we hear of no protests by Jewish visitors in the nineteenth century who probably considered all such homage paid to a long-deceased pagan leader and what they might have regarded as an excessive form of ancestor worship as a mere accommodation to the existing society and government, which carried with it no serious "idolatrous" connotations. This excuse also held true with respect to inscriptions placed in the synagogue extolling virtues of the reigning emperors. To mitigate the impression made by the display of a "foreign" matter, they placed on the top of such an inscription a tablet reading the Hebrew profession of faith, *Shema' Yisrael* (Hear, O Israel!) in Chinese translation. There certainly was among the Jews no counterpart to the *Rites Controversy* which so disturbed the Catholic ecclesiastical establishment in the seventeenth and eighteenth centuries.[71]

Nevertheless, problems of assimilation to the environmental culture increasingly bedeviled the Kaifeng community. Outwardly, the physical appearance of the Jews seems to have differed less and less from that of their Chinese neighbors. While even at the beginning of the seventeenth century the Catholic missionary Matteo Ricci stated that his Jewish visitor was recognizable as a Jew "by profession of his faith, nationality, and features," two and a half centuries later a Muslim sergeant T'aeh Ting declared to Temple A. Layton, the British Vice-Consul in Ningpo, that Jews "are quite Chinese in appearance. The women exactly resemble the Chinese women. They have all straight features like the people of the center of China." These contradictory statements may have been partially expressions of different individual judgments or biases. It is generally known that to distant Western observers many Chinese men or women look much alike, even though the latters' compatriots see the clear distinctions among them, particularly if they are based upon regional disparities. However, there is little doubt that there was a considerable amount of intermarriage between Jewish men and Muslim or heathen Chinese women. Chinese Jewesses were for a long time unable by law, and personally unwilling, to marry outside the fold, although this restraint seems to have been relaxed in more recent generations. But at times there was actually a biological disparity between the sexes. *The Chinese-Hebrew Memorial Book of the Dead,* written about 1670, which enumerated the membership of the Kaifeng Jewish community of the period, registered 453 men and 259 women. This disparity was aggravated by occasional instances of polygamy, such as that of Chang Mei, "the Handsome," who married six wives. Under such circumstances Jewish men were almost forced to look for non-Jewish mates. If we do not hear of many specific cases of

intermarriage, the reason may be that the Chinese girls usually underwent conversion before the wedlock, thus making
the union completely Jewish. This must have been particularly
the case of those girls whom their poor Chinese parents had,
in their early childhood, sold to Jews (or Muslims). In all such
instances, the racial characteristics of the mothers doubtless
played a considerable role in progressively changing the appearance of succeeding generations. Climatic and other environmental influences may also have contributed their share to
some sort of physical assimilation. Bernard Shaw's epigram that
a thousand years hence all Americans would be redskins is an
indubitable exaggeration, but it may contain a kernel of truth.
At any rate, the pictures and sketches brought with them from
China by European travelers (including those published by
Edward Isaac Ezra in 1902 and Arthur Sopher in 1926; and
by the American Jewish journalist David A. Brown after his
return from a visit to Kaifeng in 1932) frequently give the
impression of a Jewry largely consisting of Chinese-looking
men and women. This impression may have been further enhanced by the predominantly Chinese-like attire worn by the
persons so depicted, although on some festive occasions Jews
seem to have been clad in specifically Jewish holiday garments.[72]

Such assimilatory tendencies might have been strengthened
by the relatively small number of Jews inhabiting Kaifeng, a
number which led to extensive inbreeding, probably another
major factor in the gradual diminution of the Jewish population. It appears that the maximum attained by the sixteenth-
century community of some 70 clans may have reached 2,000–
2,500 persons. Then came the catastrophic flood of 1642.
While elementary catastrophes of this kind are often overcome quickly by a healthy and dynamic society, the Kaifeng
drama proved detrimental to a more or less stagnant group
like the local Jews of that period. Antoine Gaubil's description
of this catastrophe in a letter of 1725 graphically describes the
sufferings of the entire Kaifeng population. He wrote:

More than 300,000 persons perished in the waters. Among them
there was a considerable number of Christians, nearly all of whom
were drowned. The saintly Jesuit named Rodrigues Figueredo pre-

ferred to perish together with his flock rather than abandon it by saving his life. Most books of the synagogue were damaged, many of them destroyed; an infinite number of Jews died miserably and they found themselves reduced to 7 families, meaning clans, which might account for the present number of 1,000 persons.

The year 1642 thus marked a real watershed in the destinies of the Jewish community, which apparently never completely recovered from that blow. Gaubil may have known of Nicolò Langobardi's contention in 1610 that the Jews in China were surpassing the Christian population "in number, rank, and wealth." Of course, there is no question that even in 1610 Langobardi's estimate was vastly exaggerated. Some modern students have estimated the Christian population in China during that period at 13,000 inhabitants; it seems to have grown to some 300,000 a century later. In fact, after 1642 the temporary revival made possible by a few leading citizens, especially from the Li clan, helped to preserve the integrity of the community, which probably at that time consisted of only 1,000 persons or less. It declined further to 500, 200, or even 100 members in the eighteenth to the twentieth centuries.[73]

Scholars have detected two major peaks in the history of the Kaifeng community—the years 1421–1512 and 1642–1723. They referred thereby to the periods of relative prosperity of the community and the fairly favorable treatment it enjoyed from the governmental authorities. But evidently, from the standpoint of its intergroup relations with non-Jews and some major activities, they were overshadowed by the dramatic developments of the sixteenth and early seventeenth centuries. The two and a quarter centuries after 1512 became in some respects the best known in the annals of Kaifeng Jewry. We owe that more extensive information to the four major inscriptions and most of the vertical and horizontal tablets preserved in the synagogue, the *Book of the Dead,* and to Jesuit missionaries who took a deep interest in the community owing to an essential misunderstanding. It started with a visit of the Jewish leader N'gai Ai T'ien of Kaifeng to the missionary Matteo Ricci in Peking, simply because he believed that the Christian scholar represented merely a variety of Judaism. N'gai probably shared with many confreres the oppressive feeling of isolation by being cut off from the large Jewish world. At the age of sixty he used the occasion of his journey to the capital of the Empire in quest of some rewording new employment, to try to enlist Ricci's cooperation in revitalizing Jewish community life at home. This misunderstanding was further deepened when, on his arrival at the Jesuit quarters, N'gai mistook certain pictures of the Christian Holy Family and St. John the Baptist for representations of personalities from the Hebrew Bible. In complete naïveté he told Ricci: "We in China do reverence to our ancestors. This is Rebecca with her sons Jacob and Esau, but as to the other picture, why make obeisance to only four sons of Jacob, were there not twelve?" Even upon his return N'gai did not quite realize the difference between the two faiths. His mistake, doubtless shared by some of his coreligionists, had a paradoxical result. Since their old so-called rabbi (a spiritual leader without qualifications for rabbinic teachings), had passed away, they offered the post to Ricci, whom they recognized as a scholar familiar with biblical literature, although he was unable to read it in the original Hebrew. They only made the condition that Ricci abstain from eating pork. Needless to say, Ricci rejected the invitation and tried to clear up the misunderstanding by sending some missionaries into the community, perhaps hoping to use this unexpected invitation as a means of converting the Jewry of Kaifeng. This was the beginning of a major effort on the part of the Jesuit mission to get acquainted with the literature and the life of that unique Chinese community. The next century and a half saw a number of outstanding visitors from the Jesuit Order including the aforementioned fathers Langobardi, Gozani, Domenge, Gaubil, and Brotier seeking to secure fuller information about the Kaifeng Jews. The correspondence conducted by these messengers in the Far East with their European headquarters and the Papacy thus has become a major source of information for all subsequent investigators of Kaifeng Jewish history and many other aspects of Jewish life.[74]

Perhaps one may assume that the Jesuit quest for information, particularly insofar as it pertained to the Hebrew Bible kept in the ark of the Kaifeng synagogue, had a more far-reaching purpose than merely to satisfy the curiosity of scholars. Although nowhere expressed in so many words, it is not impossible that the deep Jesuit interest in part was derived from the hope of finding in the ancient Kaifeng scrolls some significant textual variants which would support the old Christian interpretations of Scripture. As we recall, the Old Testament had been a most vital instrument of Christian propaganda in the first centuries of the Common Era. The "Testimonies," supposedly proving that the Old Testament included a number of predictions of the coming of Jesus, had by the third and fourth centuries widely circulated in the circles of missionaries for the new faith. Later on, the problems connected with such predictions often played a focal role in the Judeo-Christian controversies. Christian polemists not only rejected the Jewish interpretation of the masoretic text but also accused the Jews of having "forged" certain passages in the Bible and altered the meaning of others so as to suppress the original intent of the biblical writers. Such accusations of Jewish forgeries were also shared by Muslim controversialists who tried to detect in the Old Testament predictions of the coming of Mohammed. These controversies over the centuries were familiar to the early modern Christian missionaries and they may have hoped that the ancient Scrolls, preserved in a remote corner of the Jewish world, would help prove the accuracy of their contentions.[75]

Independently, such interest in biblical and postbiblical Hebrew texts was strongly echoed in Europe because of the general impact of the Renaissance and of its attempt to revive the ancient lore of Greeks, Romans, and Hebrews. To be sure, well-informed Christian Hebraists, even when finding fault with some textual readings in the Bible, no longer believed in the myth of Jewish forgeries. Yet their growing acumen in both lower and higher criticism whetted their curiosity about possible divergent texts found anywhere in newly available copies of Scripture. Their curiosity was further sharpened by the intensifying debates on the Lost Ten Tribes of Israel, whose descendants, many felt, may well have included the Jews of Kaifeng. At the same time, the presence of such Jews in the remote Far East could be used by Menasseh ben Israel as an argument for convincing Oliver Cromwell and his revolution-

ary associates that it was England (in French called Angleterre) which was the only remaining one of the four "corners"
of the earth from which, according to the biblical predictions,
the Redeemer would foregather the Jewish remnant and thus
usher in the messianic era. In short, the small community of a
thousand Jews aroused a disproportionately intense interest,
at least in certain circles of the West. This newly awakened
and rapidly spreading exploratory quest may also help explain
the Jesuits' apparent inadequacy in converting Chinese Jews
to Christianity, which so greatly annoyed James Finn. He insisted that

the Roman Catholic missionaries, true to their mistaken principle,
made little or no use of the written Word of God in conversation
with the Israelites. They seem to have regarded the people visited as
more properly the subjects of critical learning than of conversion to
Christianity. . . . This supposition may explain the fact, that during
the hundred and ten years of their close vicinity to the synagogue of
Kai-fung-foo, viz. from 1613 to 1723, there is no mention made of
any convert from among that congregation.

Of some minor importance may also have been the degree of
Chinese Jewry's assimilation of Confucian teachings and practices within its own faith. The Jewish example may have had
some bearing on the great "Rites Controversy" within the
Catholic Church and perhaps even on the extent to which the
Jesuit spokesmen in China were to be allowed to make concessions to the dominant faith in the large country which they
were trying to convert to Christianity.[76]

For some reason Western Jewish interest in Chinese Jews
was awakened much later than that in their Indian coreligionists. This is doubly remarkable since, as we recall, the various
groups of Indian Jews had preserved few documents and
writings in Hebrew, whereas Kaifeng Jewry had accumulated
a considerable collection of biblical writings and prayer books.
In the Chinese documents, too, there were quite a few in-
sertions of Hebrew phrases and names. There also was the
aforementioned important Chinese Hebrew *Book of the Dead,*
a *Haggadah,* a noteworthy Judeo-Persian colophon to a Pentateuch, and a variety of other fragments. It was only in the
nineteenth century that the quest for Hebrew manuscripts and

other relics of medieval and early modern Jewry has prompted some Jewish scholars to consider the Hebrew writings accumulated in the great non-Jewish libraries as worthy of research. In time, a major Jewish library, that of the Hebrew Union College of Cincinnati, succeeded in acquiring 59 Hebrew manuscripts, some of which had been provided with Judeo-Persian glosses. Evidently the Kaifeng collections were no longer so closely guarded because of the diminution and impoverishment of the Jewish community. (The story of that acquisition has been told by its then librarian Adolph S. Oko.) Nonetheless, in contrast to the Jesuit and other Christian reports from China, these Hebrew and Chinese Jewish documents have until today been relatively neglected by modern Jewish scholars. Even an important study by Adolph Neubauer of 1895–96 was stimulated by the fact that the London Society for the Promotion of Christianity Amongst Jews had in its library a substantial collection of Hebrew prayer books from Kaifeng. But his essay offered simply a listing of the texts in the liturgical works in a certain order useful to scholars. But this was by no means a searching examination into their origins, diversities from other prayer books, and various problems of form and substance.[77]

In contrast to the general theological and political concerns of most contemporary writers, we are far less well informed about the economic life, including the occupational pursuits, of the Kaifeng Jews. In an interesting report from Honan, a Jewish businessman, H. J. Solomon, wrote in 1900 that

many hundreds of years ago, there were in Kaifeng eight houses or branches bearing the names, Li, Chang, Ai, Chao, Tuh, Shih, Kao. Two of the families bore the name of Li. These clans still exist, numbering about forty houses and about 140 persons. . . . Once they were the richest and most influential people in the place, but through internal dissension they have dwindled down until now they are very poor, and, I am sorry to add, have not a very good reputation. One of them is a Buddhist priest.

This information is largely borne out by earlier Jesuit reports, the *Book of the Dead,* as well as by incidental references in the general Chinese literature of the period. Stories included in local gazetteers, dating from the Ming period (1368–1644) in particular, have shown that the road to advancement in government service was open to Jews. Those who were able to secure from a Chinese university a diploma, approximating that of an American Master's or Doctor's degree, often had access to a highly desirable public career. Referring in 1749 to the past, Antoine Gaubil asserted:

The Jews of China had been employed in high military offices. Some of them became governors of provinces, ministers of state, bachelors and doctors. Among them were owners of large tracts of land. Today they are greatly reduced and many have turned Muslim.

It appears that, like their Muslim compatriots, Jews actually preferred military to civilian careers, although, according to White's data, Jews held important posts in all fifteen provinces of the Chinese Empire. In contrast, only one visitor of 1866, W. A. P. Martin, mentions the presence of a single Jewish moneylender and money changer. Most Jews, however, eked out a meager living as craftsmen, farmers, and petty merchants. The Chinese sources of the period hardly ever mention the ordinary Jewish occupations. Only a very intensive new effort to collect the scattered information in hitherto unused Chinese publications and archives may yet help us to resolve the quantitative and qualitative aspects of Jewish contributions to China's economic and social life.[78]

EXOTIC JEWRIES

The small fragments of the Jewish people treated in the present chapter, perhaps at greater length than they deserve from the point of view of their share in world Jewish life, had certain elements in common, and others which differentiated them from one another, as well as from all other Jewish communities. They shared the destiny of having from the beginning been cut off from world Jewry. As a result, their very origins are extremely obscure and their pertinent traditions highly unreliable; they also have been the subjects of extensive controversies among modern scholars. In fact, their separation from the rest of Jewry was so great that, until the early modern period, most of their coreligionists living in Europe, western Asia, and North Africa knew of their existence only from legendary, often imaginary, tales which reached them through a few Jewish and non-Jewish travelers. Another feature in common was their small size and isolation even within their own countries. The communities recording Jewish settlements of any size were few and far between. The mountain of Simen in Ethiopia, Crangamore and Cochin in India, and Kaifeng in China were the only areas of concentration of some thousands of Jews while in their totality they formed only a minuscule percentage of their countries' population.

Another common feature was their alienation from the mass of their coreligionists by their forgetfulness of the Hebrew language and literature. Even in Kaifeng, where they maintained a library of biblical, ritualistic, and other Hebrew writings, very few members were able to read them. The rare individuals in Ethiopia, India, or China who had a superficial command of that language could hardly serve as teachers of their coreligionists. That widespread ignorance of the Jewish intellectual heritage was well exemplified in N'gai Ai T'ien's invitation to the leading Jesuit missionary Matteo Ricci to accept the post of rabbi of the Kaifeng community, if only he would not continue to eat pork. The literary creations, few in number and low in quality, left behind by these surviving communities were written in the local languages, even if here and there they included some Hebrew phrase or quotation taken from a traditional Hebrew source. Only the preservation of some Hebrew names of individuals, usually along with their local, especially Chinese, names, marked a tiny residuum of the old ties with world Judaism.

It thus was only the rituals such as the celebration of the Sabbaths and festivals, the use of Hebrew Bibles and prayer books, and the modicum of the observance of the ritual food commandments—all revealing occasional admixtures of foreign, even syncretistic, influences—preserved their identity as a Jewish minority in a sea of non-Jews. The three groups also shared in the early modern period the Western public's sudden realization of their presence and its interest in their similarities with, and dissimilarities from, its more familiar Jewries of the Christian and Muslim worlds. This awakened interest was in part the consequence of the great Age of Discovery and the European expansion in the East as well as in the West. On the other hand, while in the sixteenth and early seventeenth centuries all three groups shared, in a minor way, the advances of their European and Ottoman coreligionists, soon thereafter they entered their period of progressive decline which has become a serious menace to their survival.

At the same time there also were serious differences among these three "exotic" communities. For historical reasons the Ethiopian Falashas revealed, in both their secular and religious life, the impact of their Graeco-Roman and Byzantine background. It appears that at their inception the Ethiopian Jewish community paved the way for the spread of Christianity among the pagan population. They have ever since remained under the influence of the Eastern Churches. Conversely, it is to local and foreign churchmen that we owe much of our information about Falasha history, religion, anthropology, and sociology. In contrast, the Indian and Chinese Jewries have often betrayed some distinct features of their origin in a Persian-Muslim environment. While the Judeo-Persian dialect, with its admixture of Hebrew, was largely forgotten in the course of time, some Islamic teachings and institutions often left their traces on the Jewish community. Some such influences could further be maintained by the proximity of substantial Muslim minorities, occasionally even local majorities, and Muslim rulers in parts of India and China. Unlike the Muslim minority in Ethiopia, most of which was territorially segregated from its Jewish neighbors, Islam retained some influence on Jews in both Eastern countries. Suffice it to mention that the famed Kaifeng synagogue, before and after the flood of 1642, outwardly resembled a mosque. In fact, as we remember, many Chinese believed that the Kaifeng and other Jews represented but one of the sects within Islam. Undoubtedly in the eyes of the average man Jews also resembled Christians, although the churches and their ceremonies, as well as their belief in the Trinity and other Christian dogmas, must have revealed the difference between the two faiths to all but the least informed neighbors.

Remarkably, these three monotheistic minorities, despite their sharing a professed reverence for the Old Testament and its heroes, in contrast to the multitude of heathen cults in their environment in both India and China, showed no signs of mutual solidarity. As often happened elsewhere, the adherents of the three monotheistic faiths, though in minority positions, for the most part proved hostile to one another. To be sure, the relatively tolerant regimes in India and China—except during the periodic interludes of raging xenophobia and religious intolerance—neither really oppressed the three minorities nor used their mutual dislike for the ruling classes' advantage. The Chinese Christians, especially the missionaries, though remembering the traditional animosities toward Jews and Judaism, were more bent on converting the local Jews to Christianity than in fostering their segregation and discrimination. For specific reasons, the leaders actually evinced serious interest, for scholarly as well as missionary purposes, in the life and literature of their Jewish neighbors. The much larger Muslim group generally held itself aloof from both Christians and Jews. Needless to say, though not engaging in large-scale missionary propaganda along Christian lines, some Muslim leaders welcomed Jewish and Christian converts to their faith. However, apart from trying to prevent their coreligionists from marrying Jews, they seem not to have taken any direct action against Jews taking Muslim girls for wives or adopting Muslim, as well as heathen, children, a frequent practice in Kaifeng. In short, Jewish life in the two Asian empires proceeded rather quietly (unless it was disturbed by such elemental catastrophes as floods, fires, and plagues) without strong oppressive measures, even direct attacks, such as frequently accompanied Jewish life in most of Christendom and Islam.

The story of these splinter groups rounds out the picture of the sociopolitical life of medieval and early modern Jews from 1200 to 1650. We shall now have to turn to a description of the forces which shaped the internal evolution of the Jewish people in its communal, intellectual, and religious pursuits.

NOTES

ABBREVIATIONS

AHA	American Historical Association
AHR	American Historical Review
Annales ESC	Annales Économies, Sociétés, Civilisations
AO	Archivum Ottomanicum
AOH	Acta Orientalia Hungarica (Magyar Todományos) of the Hungarian Academy
ASI	Archivio storico italiano
b.	ben *or* bar
Bab.	Babylonian Talmud
Baer Jub. Vol.	Sefer Yobel le-Yitzhak Baer (Yitzhak Baer Jubilee Volume). Jerusalem, 1960.
BEO	Bulletin d'Études Orientales of the Institute Français de Damas
BJPES	Bulletin (*Yediot*) of the Jewish Palestine (later Israel) Exploration Society
BJRL	Bulletin of the John Rylands Library, Manchester, England
BSOAS	Bulletin of the School of Oriental and African Studies (University of London)
BZ	Byzantinische Zeitschrift
BZIH	Biuletyn of the Żydowski Instytut Historyczny, Warsaw
CHI	Cambridge History of Iran
CMRS	Cahiers du Monde Russe et Soviétique
CODOIN	Colección de documentos inéditos of the Academia de la Historia in Madrid
CT	Cahiers de Tunisie
E.'E.	Eben 'Ezer
EI	Encyclopaedia of Islam
H.M.	Ḥoshen Mishpaṭ
HUCA	Hebrew Union College Annual
IJMES	International Journal of Middle East Studies
IS	Iranian Studies
JA	Journal Asiatique
JAOS	Journal of the American Oriental Society
JC	The Jewish Community: Its History and Structure to the American Revolution by Salo W. Baron. 3 vols., Philadelphia, 1942; reprinted Westport, Conn. 1972
JEcH	Journal of Economic History

ABBREVIATIONS

JESHO	Journal of the Economic and Social History of the Orient
JQR	Jewish Quarterly Review (new series, unless otherwise stated)
JRAS	Journal of the Royal Asiatic Society
JSS	Jewish Social Studies
KS	Kirjath Sepher, Quarterly Bibliographical Review
MGH	Monumenta Germaniae Historica
MGWJ	Monatsschrift für Geschichte und Wissenschaft des Judentums
MHH	Monumenta Hungariae Historica
MHSI	Monumenta Historica Societatis Iesu
MSOS	Mitteilungen des Seminars für Orientalische Sprachen in Berlin
M.T.	Moses ben Maimon, *Mishneh Torah* (code)
O.Ḥ.	Oraḥ Ḥayyim
OLZ	Orientalische Literaturzeitung
PAAJR	Proceedings of the American Academy for Jewish Research
PG	J. P. Migne's Patrologiae cursus completus, series Graeca
REB	Revue des études byzantines
REI	Revue des études islamiques
REJ	Revue des études juives
RESEE	Revue des Études du Sud-Est Européen.
Resp.	Responsa (*She'elot u-teshubot* or *Teshubot*)
RH	Revue Historique
RRH	Revue Roumaine d'Histoire
RSI	Rivista storica italiana
RSO	Rivista di studi orientali
TJHSE	Transactions of the Jewish Historical Society of England
VSW	Vierteljahrsschrift für Sozial- und Wirtschaftsgeschichte
WZKM	Wiener Zeitschrift für die Kunde des Morgenlandes
Y.D.	Yoreh Deah
ZDMG	Zeitschrift der Deutschen Morgenländischen Gesellschaft
ZGJD	Zeitschrift für die Geschichte der Juden in Deutschland
ZfG	Zeitschrift für Geschichtswissenschaft

NOTES

CHAPTER LXXV: OTTOMAN EMPIRE

1. Because of the world importance of the rise and decline of the Ottoman Empire its history has been the subject of constant interest to the world at large. Of the vast bibliography accumulated on this subject over generations, we need but mention here the three long-time standard works written in the nineteenth and early twentieth centuries, which are still extremely useful today: J. von Hammer-Purgstall, *Geschichte des Osmanischen Reiches, grossentheils aus bisher unbenützten Handschriften,* 2d ed. rev.; J. W. Zinkeisen, *Geschichte des Osmanischen Reiches in Europa;* N. Jorga (or Iorga), *Geschichte des Osmanischen Reiches. Nach den Quellen dargestellt.* Among the more recent publications one may profitably consult the general surveys by H. Inalcik, *The Ottoman Empire: the Classical Age 1300–1600,* trans. by N. Itzkowitz and C. Imber; V. J. Parry *et al., A History of the Ottoman Empire to 1730: Chapters from The Cambridge History of Islam and The New Cambridge Modern History,* ed. with an Intro. by M. A. Cook. Of considerable assistance to students is D. E. Pitcher's *An Historical Geography of the Ottoman Empire from Earliest Times to the End of the Sixteenth Century,* with detailed maps to illustrate the Ottoman expansion. All of these works include references to primary sources and monographic literature, some of which, together with other writings, will be mentioned below.

Fuller bibliographical guidance is available in the handbook by J. D. Pearson, comp., *Index Islamicus 1906–1955: A Catalogue of Articles on Islamic Subjects in Periodicals,* with Supplements I–IV (covering the years 1956–60, 1961–65, 1966–70, 1971–75, respectively); and early additions thereto by H. G. Majer in his "Osmanische Nachträge zum Index islamicus (1906–1965)," *Südostforschungen,* XXVII, 242–91, and further comments by J. Matuz in his "À propos d'une contribution bibliographique pour servir les études ottomanes historiques," *OLZ,* LXVIII, 449–51. Independently valuable are: H. J. Kornrumpf and J. Kornrumpf, comps., *Osmanische Bibliographie, mit besonderer Berücksichtigung der Türkei in Europa,* with some supplementary data offered by A. Mumen in "Fragen der osmanischen Bibliographie," *Der Islam,* LII, 119–24; and F. Valjevec, G. Kraller-Sattler, comps., *Südosteuropa Bibliographie,* Vols. I–V, covering the years 1945–70.

Since 1975 the *Wiener Zeitschrift für die Kunde des Morgenlandes* has been issuing a parallel annual bibliography, entitled "Turkologischer Anzeiger," and ed. by G. Hazai and A. Tietze. These editors, aided by a number of specialists in various countries, have since 1977 (Vol. III), begun including American dissertations, almost all of which are available to the world at large through the service of the Xerox University Microfilms in Ann Arbor, Michigan. Previously United States dissertations had become known to the outside world principally through the *Dissertation Abstracts.* The importance of this listing need not be stressed for in this area, too, many unpublished doctoral dissertations furnish both new materials and valuable insights. Regrettably, only the German-language dissertations are listed with a fair degree of completeness in P. Kappert *et al.,* comps., "Dissertationen zur Geschichte und Kultur des osmanischen Reiches, angenommen an deutschen, österreichischen, und schweizerischen Universitäten seit

1945," *Der Islam*, XLIX, 110–19; and, more fully, K. Schwarz, comp., *Der Vordere Orient in den Hochschulschriften Deutschlands, Österreichs und der Schweiz. Eine Bibliographie von Dissertationen und Habilitationsschriften, 1885–1978* (listing 5050 titles). See, however, the surveys of the progress of Turkological research in several countries listed *infra*, nn. 5–6.

2. See, for example, A. Ducellier, "Mentalité historique et réalités politiques: L'Islam et les Musulmans vus par la Byzantine du XIIIe siècle," *Byzantinische Forschungen*, IV, 31–63, referring in particular to a document of 1246 which dismissed the Scythians (Mongols), Persians (really meaning Turks), and Arabs as "barbarian" peoples. This Byzantine writer accuses the Turks of innate cruelty, bad faith, impurity, and impiety (pp. 32, 36 f., etc.). If occasionally a visitor like Pero Tafur glowingly described the fine characteristics of the Turkish people, his praise did not reduce the apprehensions of the Western nations about their own security. See Tafur's *Travel and Adventures, 1435–1439*, trans. and ed. by M. Letts, p. 128; H. J. Kissling, "Türkenfurcht und Türkenhoffnung im 15. und 16. Jahrhundert. Zur Geschichte eines 'Komplexes'," *Südostforschungen*, XXIII, 1–16 with special reference to the Turkish conquest of Nicopolis in 1396 (p. 6). While these fears often led to exaggerations of Turkish power the later characterizations of the Ottoman Empire as the "sick man of Europe," generally attributed to Otto von Bismarck, overlooked its continued vitality which, at least until World War I, was attested in many of its encounters with the local nationalities, with the growing imperial power of Russia, and with the Western Powers. Only World War I, which climaxed the ever sharpening conflicts among the East-Central European nationalities, brought about the speedy dissolution of both the venerable Austro-Hungarian imperial structure and its Ottoman counterpart. In its aftermath World War II set in motion a similar process of disintegration among the great colonial empires.

3. See, for example, the analysis presented by a leading Turkish historian, I. H. Uzunçarşili in his *Osmanli tarihi* (Ottoman History), Vols. I–VIII, esp. I, p. xxi (emphasizing the liberation by the Turks of the Anatolian and Balkan peasant masses from the oppression by their Byzantine and Latin masters and the sultan's restoration of law and order to a society suffering from the disarray of the late Byzantine civilization). Other writers are discussed by E. Werner in his "Panturkismus und einige Tendenzen moderner türkischer Historiographie," *ZfG*, XIII, 1342–54. These exaggerations elicited sharp replies not only from historians among the formerly subjected nationalities but also from Soviet writers, such as A. S. Tveritinova in her "The Falsification of the History of Medieval Turkey in the Kemalist Historiography" (Russian), *Vizantiskii Vremenik*, VII, 9 and others, cited by E. Werner in *Die Geburt einer Grossmacht—Die Osmanen (1300–1481); Ein Beitrag zur Genesis des türkischen Feudalismus*, pp. 16 ff. These views are also expressed in the lectures delivered at the Dumbarton Oaks Symposium on "The Decline of Byzantine Civilization in Asia Minor—Eleventh to Fifteenth Century," held in Washington, D.C. in 1974 and published in the *Dumbarton Oaks Papers*, XXIX; and such other studies as S. Vryonis, Jr., *The Decline of Medieval Hellenism in Asia Minor and the Process of Islamization from the Eleventh through the Fifteenth Century*.

4. See, for instance, M. F. Köprülü's denial of any significant Byzantine heritage influencing the development of the Ottoman Commonwealth in his *Alcune osservazioni intorno all'influenza delle istituzioni bizantine sulle istituzioni ottomane;* and, in contrast thereto, B. A. Cvetkova, "Influence exercée par certaines institutions de Byzance et des Balkans du moyen âge sur le système féodale ottoman," *Byzantinobulgarica*, I, 237–

57. Of considerable interest also are such well-documented studies as Ö. L. Barkan's "Le Servage existait-il en Turquie?" *Annales ESC*, XI, 54–60 (arguing against the existence of any large-scale peasant serfdom in the Ottoman Empire similar to that developed in medieval Christian Europe); and his "Les Déportations comme méthode de peuplement et de colonisation dans l'Empire Ottoman," *Revue de la Faculté des Sciences Économiques* of the University of Istanbul, XI, 67–131 (showing how this method had been effectively used as a relatively humane instrument of Turkicization of many cities and even villages after their military conquests). See also from some other angles K. Yavuz, *Der Islam in Werken moderner türkischer Schriftsteller 1923–1950;* E. Werner, "Panturkismus," *ZfG*, XIII, 1342–54; and, more generally, A. Cevat, *Die Entwicklung des Nationalgefühls der Türken von deren Anfängen bis zur Begründung der Republik.* Diss. Munich (typescript). On the estimate of 1,080,000 nomads in thirteenth-century Anatolia, see *infra*, n. 7.

5. See D. Angelov, "Certains aspects de la conquête des peuples balkaniques par les Turcs," *Byzantinoslavica*, XVII, 220–75, esp. pp. 223 ff.; and other Balkan Slav historical writings, such as those listed in B. Narudinović, *Bibliografija jugoslovenske orientalistike, 1945–1960* (Bibliography of Yugoslav Oriental Studies, 1945–1960); B. Cvetkova, "Sources et travaux de l'orientalisme bulgare," *Annales ESC,* XVIII, 1158–82; and her more comprehensive "Bibliographie des ouvrages parus dans les pays slaves sur les aspects économiques et sociaux de la domination ottomane," *JESHO,* VI, 319–26 (includes 16 articles from her own pen, 1950–63; pp. 320 f.).

6. Some outstanding West-European and American writings in the field include P. Wittek, *The Rise of the Ottoman Empire;* new impr.; C. Cahen's penetrating researches, esp. his *Pre-Ottoman Turkey: a General Survey of the Material and Spiritual Culture and History, ca. 1071–1330,* trans. by J. Jones-Williams; F. Taeschner's succinct observations on "Der Weg des osmanischen Staates vom Glaubenskämpferbund zum islamischen Weltreich," *Welt als Geschichte,* V, 206–215, esp. p. 213; and some thought-provoking essays by A. Toynbee, C. Issawi, H. Inalcik, A. Hourani, and others, ed. by K. H. Karpat in *The Ottoman State and Its Place in World History.* Karpat's volume also includes S. J. Shaw's succinct review of "Ottoman and Turkish Studies in the United States" (pp. 118–29). A similar review for France was published by L. Bazin in "Les Activités turcologiques en France, rapport présenté à la XIIIᵉ Conference Internationale Permanente d'Études Altaïques" on June 26, 1970 in *Turcica,* II, 159–64; idem, "Les Études Turques" in "Cinquante ans d'orientalisme en France," *JA,* CCLXI, 31–295, esp. pp. 135–45. Turkish studies published during the years 1945–72 have also been reviewed by I. Gilson (for the United States); E. Tryjarski (for Poland); and A. de Groot (for the Netherlands)—all ed. by T. Halasi-Kun in the *Archivum Ottomanicum,* V. There also is a similar survey of *Fifty Years of Soviet Oriental Studies (Brief Review; 1917–1967),* Publications of the U.S.S.R. Academy of Science Institute of the Peoples of Asia which consists of 27 pamphlets including no. 5, B. Danzig's "The History, Economy and Geography of Turkey" with a listing of only 129 Russian titles (pp. 22–31); no. 15, L. P. Petrushevsky's "History of Iranian Studies"; no. 21, N. P. Šastina, "Mongolic Studies"; no. 22, I. M. Smilenskaya, "History and Economy of the Arab Countries." See also B. Fleming, "Neuere wissenschaftliche Arbeiten und Forschungsvorhaben zur Sprache, Geschichte und Kultur der vorosmanischen und osmanischen Türkei in der Bundesrepublik Deutschland seit 1968," *Turcica,* V, 131–47 (includes dissertations and works in preparation); A. Popović, "Étude de l'Empire Ottoman et l'orientalisme dans les pays balkaniques (Essai d'un répertoire bio-bibliographique et analytique de l'orientalisme yougoslave)," *ibid.,* 154–59; and *supra,* nn. 1 and 4.

7. D. J. Georgaras, *The Names of the Asia Minor Peninsula and a Register of Surviving Anatolian pre-Turkish Placenames;* O. Turan, "L'Islamisation dans la Turquie du moyen âge," *Studia islamica*, X, 137–52 (estimating that by constant Turkish immigration, rather than by forced conversion to Islam, ethnic Turks outnumbered islamized Christians in a ratio of 70:30); S. Vryonis, Jr., *The Decline of Medieval Hellenism in Asia Minor.* Oruj's praise of the Ottoman *Ghazis* is reproduced in an English translation in H. Inalcik's chapter in V. J. Parry *et al., A History,* p. 17, where the 1354 observation by Gregory Palamas about the Muslim power reflecting the will of God is likewise quoted. See also, more broadly, C. Cahen, "Le Problème ethnique en Anatolie," *Journal of World History,* II, 347–62, esp. pp. 352 ff., 360.

This speedy succession of victories by the originally small number of Osmanli Turks can be explained only by their steady reinforcement by other Turkoman nomads in Anatolia. The size of this still largely nomadic population in the late thirteenth century has been laboriously computed by the Turkish historian M. H. Yinanç in his *Türkiye tarihi* (Turkish History), p. 168, cited by E. Werner in *Die Geburt*, p. 37. According to his somewhat daring estimates, the total number of the Turkoman tribesmen amounted to 1,080,000 at that time.

8. Abu 'Abd Allah Ibn Baṭṭuṭa, *Voyages*. Ed. and trans. by C. Defrémery and B. R. Sanguinetti, and in the English trans. entitled, *Travels, A. D. 1325–1354*, ed. with Revisions and Notes by H. A. R. Gibb, esp. I, 449 f.; H. Inalcik, "Bursa and the Commerce of the Levant," *JESHO*, III, 131–47, esp. pp. 138 ff., 143 f.; *idem*, "The Conquest of Edirne (1361)," *AO*, III, 185–216; I. Beldiceanu-Steinherr, "La Conquête d'Adrianople par les Turcs: la pénétration turque en Thrace et la valeur des chroniques ottomanes," *Travaux et Mémoires* of the Centre de Recherche d'Histoire et Civilisation Byzantines, I, 439–61; *infra*, n.13; and *supra*, Vol. XVII, pp. 27, 312 f. n.31. On the "Chiones" and their conversion to Judaism, see J. Meyendorff, "Grecs, Turcs et Juifs en Asie Mineure," *Byzantinische Forschungen I-Polychorda, Festschrift Franz Dölger*, Vol. I, pp. 211–17. It appears that the Greek nationalist fervor, which had inspired the Laskarids to reconquer Constantinople in 1261, rather speedily evaporated under the burden of the internal dissensions and religious conflicts, as well as the growing feudalization of the Balkan Peninsula during the fourteenth century. See the diverse analyses from various angles by M. Angold, "Byzantine 'Nationalism' and the Nicaean Empire," *Byzantine and Modern Greek Studies,* I, 49–70; G. Vismara, "Le Relazioni dell'Impero con gli emirati selgiuchidi nel corso del secolo decimoquarto," *Byzantinische Forschungen,* III (Festschrift Franz Dölger), 210–21; I. Dujčev, "Die Krise der spätbyzantinischen Gesellschaft und die türkische Eroberung des 14. Jahrhunderts," *Jahrbücher für Geschichte Osteuropas,* XXI, 481–92.

Regrettably, we have few reliable contemporary sources for the Osman and Orkhan regimes. In her *Recherches sur les actes des règnes des sultans Osman, Orkhan et Murad I,* I. Beldiceanu-Steinherr, after carefully examining numerous documents (27 Persian, 21 Turkish, 6 Arabic, and 1 Latin) came to the conclusion that many of them were outright forgeries. (She also corrected the long-accepted date of 1326 for Orkhan's accession to the throne to 1324 by proving that Osman had died before March 17 of that year.) We are, therefore, dependent to a large extent on foreign sources, both Byzantine and West European. On the other hand, the evidence stemming from Cantacuzenus and his circle naturally offers only an opaque view of the developments. The contemporary West-European sources are mainly concerned with the incipient international reaction against the "Turkish menace." This is true especially in connection with the intervention of the Catalan mercenaries—whose occupation of Mid-Eastern cities was usually even more destructive than that by Ottoman troops—or in relation to the formation of the first anti-Turkish League in 1332–34. See D. Jacoby, "Catalans, Turcs et Vénitiens en Romanie (1303–1332): Un nouveau témoignage de Marino Sanudo Torcello," *Studi medievali*, 3d ser. XV, 217–61 (analyzing six letters of 1227–28, ed. by A. Cerlini in 1940); A. Laiou, "Marino Sanudo Torcello, Byzantium and the Turks: The Background to the Anti-Turkish League of 1332–1334," *Speculum*, XLV, 374–92, showing that, as a resident of the area for many years, Sanudo Torcello was able to supply much first-hand information.

9. See *supra*, Vols. I, pp. 170, 184, 236, 283, 377 n. 22, 393 n. 2, 401 n. 32; II, pp. 73, 165 ff., 393 f. nn. 46 ff. See also J. B. Frey, *Corpus inscriptionum judaicarum*, 2 vols.; E. R. Goodenough, *Jewish Symbols in the Greco-Roman Period;* and on the medieval period, J. Starr, *The Jews in the Byzantine Empire, 641–1204;* and Z. Ankori, *Karaites in Byzantium.* The Jewish settlement in ancient Anatolia must have been given an additional impetus before the Maccabean revolt by the recorded transplantation there of 2,000 Babylonian Jews by Antiochus III, according to Josephus' report in *Antiquities* XII, 3.41.149. See *supra*, Vol. I, pp. 216 f., 373 n. 9. It is doubtful whether at the beginning of the Osmanli expansion there were many more Jewish inhabitants in the entire peninsula.

10. J. Schiltberger, *Reisebuch*, ed. by V. Langmantel, p. 53; previously ed. by K. F. Neumann under the title, *Reisen des Johannes Schiltberger aus München 1394–1427*, from which it was trans. into English by J. B. Telfer under the title, *The Bondage and Travels . . . 1396–1427;* N. Jorga, *Geschichte des Osmanischen Reiches*, I, 204. The few records pertaining to the Jews of Anatolia in the age of Osman and Orkhan have been assembled by S. A. Rosanes in his *Dibre yeme Yisrael be Togarma* or *Qorot ha-Yehudim be-Turqiah* (A History of the Jews in the Ottoman Empire), Vols. I–III, 2d ed; IV–VI, esp. I; A. Galanté in his *Les Juifs sous la domination des Turcs seldjoukides;* and, more broadly, in his *Histoire des Juifs d'Anatolie*, with an *Appendice* thereto. Both authors had to make extensive use of sixteenth-century sources for the reconstruction of fourteenth-century conditions. Galanté's meritorious listing of eight major and some minor Turkoman marches (*beyliks*) in Anatolia, which included most of the major cities on the peninsula, often contains the remark, as in the case of Konia, that the existence of the Jewish community there—similar to that of neighboring Anṭaliya (Turkish; Adalya)—"cannot be excluded." Of course, Anṭaliya-Adalya also was an important city; it greatly impressed the visiting Ibn Baṭṭuṭa. See his *Travels, A.D. 1325–1354*, trans. by H. A. R. Gibb, II, 417 ff. See also H. Inalcik, "Bursa," *JESHO*, III, 139, 143 f.

11. See Benjamin of Tudela, *Massa'ot* (The Itinerary) ed. by N. M. Adler, pp. 17 f. (Hebrew), 14 f. (English). On the frightful earthquake of 1354 which devastated the environs of Gallipoli, put to flight many inhabitants, including Byzantine officials, of the district, and greatly weakened the city's fortifications, see N. Jorga, *Geschichte*, I, 106. Although the city of Adrianople had already embraced Jews in ancient times, we hear little about them even under Byzantine domination. It was not until later that a legend told how, warned in a dream, a local Jew once frustrated the design of a Christian neighbor to stir up his community against the Jews because of an alleged ritual murder. See J. Starr, *The Jews in the Byzantine Empire*, p. 235.

12. F. Babinger, "Von Amurath zu Amurath. Vor- und Nachspiel der Schlacht bei Varna (1444)," *Oriens*, III, 229–65; P. Wittek, "De la défaite d'Ankara à la prise de Constantinople," *REI*, XII, 1–34; and the general literature listed *supra*, n. 1. The temporary decline of Ottoman power was highlighted in 1416 by Piero Loredan's

victory over the Turkish navy at Gallipoli. The Venetian admiral boasted that the Turkish navy would not be truly dangerous to Venice for a long time to come. See Marino Sanudo, *Vitae ducum venetorum* (Milan, 1722), in L. A. Muratori, *Rerum Italicarum scriptores*, XXII, 901–909; C. Manfroni, "La Battaglia di Gallipoli e la politica veneto-turca 1381–1420," *Ateneo Veneto*, XXV, Part 2, pp. 3–34, 129–69; and on the more general impact of the battle of Ankara and its aftermath on European public opinion, see O. Intze, *Tamerlan und Bajazet in den Literaturen des Abendlandes* (Diss. Erlangen), mainly referring to belles lettres written by Christopher Marlowe and others. Fortunately for the Turks, an armistice with Venice followed in 1419 and their lifeline between Anatolia and their European possessions was never to face an equally serious threat until World War I. On the generally alternating amicable and hostile relations between Venice and the Ottoman rulers, see the literature listed *infra*, nn. 27–28.

It was Mustafa, rather than Sheikh Bedr ed-Din himself, who preached a far-reaching social revolution of all faiths. See Ducas, *Historia byzantina* or *Turco-byzantina*, xxi, ed. by I. Bekker in the *Corpus scriptorum byzantinorum*, XXI, esp. PP. 111 ff.; or in H. S. Margulias's English trans. entitled *Decline and Fall of Byzantium to the Ottoman Turks*. On the similarities with Mazdak, see *supra*, Vol. II, pp. 182 f., 231, 409 n. 7.

Not surprisingly, this aspect of the short-lived uprising aroused the interest of many modern scholars, particularly from behind the Iron Curtain. The foundation for solid research in this area was laid by F. Babinger in his "Schejch Bedr ed-Din, der Sohn des Richters von Simaw," *Der Islam*, XI, 1–106 (also reprint). He was followed by K. F. Wädekin's Leipzig dissertation, *Der Aufstand des Bürklüdsche Mustafa. Ein Beitrag zur Geschichte der Klassenkämpfe in Kleinasien im 15. Jahrhundert* (typescript); H. I. Cotsonis, "Aus der Endzeit von Byzanz. Bürklüdsche Mustafa, ein Märtyrer für die Koexistenz zwischen Islam und Christentum," *BZ*, L, 397–404 (overemphasizing the religious as against the social aspects of Mustafa's propaganda; with additional bibliography including Greek publications; p. 397 n. 1); N. Filipović's comprehensive *Princ Musa i šejh Bedreddin* (Prince Mustafa and Sheikh Bedr ed-Din). Several Turkish historians, esp. M. F. Köprülü, A. Refik, and C. Bardakçi, interpreted the same sparse documentary material largely from a non-Marxist point of view. See also E. Werner's observations in his "Häresie, Klassenkampf und religiöse Toleranz in einer islamisch-christlichen Kontaktzone, Bedr ed-Din und Bürklüce Mustafa," *ZfG*, XII, 255–76; and his *Ketzer und Weltverbesserer. Zwei Beiträge zur Geschichte Südosteuropas im 13. und 15. Jahrhundert*. None of these scholars seems to have been able to shed fuller light on the role played by Torlaq Kemal, the Jew of Magnesia in Anatolia, who, after his conversion to Islam, had become an outstanding leader of the new movement. The few known data concerning him have already been summarized a century and a half ago by J. von Hammer-Purgstall in his *Geschichte des osmanischen Reiches*, I, 181 f.

13. On the relatively few earlier records of Jewish life in the area, see J. B. Frey in his *Corpus Inscriptionum Judaicarum*, I; and other sources listed by J. Juster in *Les Juifs dans l'Empire romain, leur condition juridique, économique et sociale*, I, 187 f. (Adrianople is *not* mentioned); J. Starr, *Jews in the Byzantine Empire*, p. 235. Remarkably, the date of the final conquest of Adrianople by the Turks is still controversial. The divergent views expressed on this score by F. Babinger, I. Beldiceanu-Steinherr, and E. A. Zachariadou and their respective arguments, have been reviewed *supra*, Vol. XVII, pp. 312 f. n. 31. There is, however, a fairly general consensus that the definitive conquest of the city and its permanent incorporation in the Ottoman Empire took place in the 1360s. At least, from 1369 on Edirne, as it was now called by the Turks, was the Ottoman capital and it remained so until the Turkish conquest of Constantinople in

1453. Even thereafter many a sultan time and again spent weeks or months in Edirne's more quiet atmosphere, escaping the clamor and tensions of the great cosmopolitan metropolis.

Even less is known about the immediate impact of the Turkish occupation upon the Jews. It appears that many Jewish refugees from the siege returned after a while and rebuilt their communal life and its institutions, including the synagogue. They continued, for centuries, as a "Greek community" (*Qehillah qedoshah de Griegos*), while the later arrivals established new congregations named after their countries of origin. See S. A. Rosanes in his *Dibre yeme Yisrael*, I, 5 f.

14. See I. S. Emmanuel, *Histoire des Israélites de Salonique*, Vol. I (140 av. J. C. à 1640). Histoire sociale, économique et littéraire de la *Ville Mère en Israël*, with a Supplement, *L'Histoire de l'Industrie des Tissus des Israélites de Salonique*, esp. pp. 49 ff.; and, more generally, A. E. Vacalopoulos's succinct review of *A History of Thessaloniki*, trans. from the Greek by T. F. Carney. On the Jews in Salonica under Roman and Byzantine domination, see *supra*, the passages listed in the *Index* to Vols. I–VIII, p. 133 *s.v.* Salonica; and Vol. XVII, pp. 16 ff., 307 f. nn. 15–17.

We must bear in mind that, while most of the older Byzantine cities survived the Turkish occupation, some were peremptorily destroyed, and a number of others, newly founded by the conquerors, have not lasted to the present day. One such city, Yenice Vardar, was founded by Murad I in 1383. After 1453, it had come under the patronage of the distinguished family of Evrenos and speedily became a center of Turkish culture. It lost that status in more recent generations, and was destroyed in the war of 1912. It was repopulated by Greeks, and so almost entirely lost its Turkish character. See M. Kiel, "Yenice Vardar: a Forgotten Turkish Cultural Centre in Macedonia in the 15th and 16th Century," *Studia byzantina et neohellenica Neerlandica*, III, 300–329. On the general urban evolution in the Ottoman Empire, see *infra*, Chap. LXXVIII, nn. 25, 81.

15. G. Elezović, *Turski spomenitsi* (Turkish Documents); Michael Ducas, *Historia Byzantina*, ed. by I. Bekker, both cited by E. Werner, *Die Geburt einer Grossmacht*, pp. 155 f.; and F. Babinger, in his *Mehmed der Eroberer und seine Zeit. Weltenstürmer einer Zeitwende*, pp. 64 f. See also N. Jorga, *Geschichte des Osmanischen Reiches*, I, 361 ff., 398 ff.; and such regional histories as A. E. Vacalopoulos, *History of Macedonia 1354– 1833*, trans. by P. Megann; and I. Dujčev's "Contribution à l'histoire de la conquête turque de Thrace aux dernières décades du XIVe siècle," *Études balcaniques*, IX, Part 2, pp. 80–92, (with special reference to Démetrius Cydonius' *Correspondance*, ed. by R. J. Loenertz); and other essays in Dujčev's collection *Medioevo bizantino-slavo*, Vols. I–III.

As against these relatively moderate attitudes of prudent monarchs like Murad I and Murad II not only the self-serving *aqinji* but also the Turkish populace at large was inclined to consider the extermination of native populations and the appropriation of all their possessions as a legitimate prize of conquest. Typical of that outlook is the query of a hero in a popular romance: "We are wolves and they [the Greeks] are sheep. . . . Does a wolf ever forego the pleasure [of devouring] a sheep?" See the German trans. in H. Ethé, *Die Fahrten des Sajjid Batthâl. Ein alttürkischer Volks- und Sittenroman*, IV, 16, cited by Werner in *Die Geburt*, p. 88.

16. See N. Jorga, *Geschichte des Osmanischen Reiches*, I, 212, 22 f.; S. A. Rosanes, *Dibre yeme Yisrael*, I, 6 f.; and *supra*, Vol. XVII, pp. 102 f., 342 f. n. 71.

17. See C. Georgieva, "Certains problèmes de la structure sociale de l'Empire Ottoman aux XIVᵉ–XVIᵉ siècles (par rapport au système 'kul')," *Bulgarian Historical Review*, II, 45–57 (describing the extent of Turkish absolutism based on the theory of state ownership of all land; on the term "kul" referring to a slave boy, esp. a military slave, see C. E. Bosworth, "Kul," *EI*, 2d ed., V, 358–59); B. A. Cvetkova, "Vie économique des villes et portes balkaniques aux XVᵉ et XVIᵉ siècles," *REI*, XXXVIII, 267–355, continued as "Actes concernant la vie économique, etc.," *ibid.*, XL, 345–90; XLIII, 143–50 (analyzing, among other matters, the impact of the *qanuns* on the situation in different cities and justly complaining that many of these enactments have not yet been published; XXXVIII, 269 f.). The conflict between the secular state legislation of the *qanuns* and the Islamic religious *shari'a* has often been noted. Even contemporaries sometimes felt the need to reconcile and harmonize these main pillars of the law, although their efforts often resulted in mere evasions. See, for instance, U. Heyd, *Studies in Old Ottoman Criminal Law*, ed. by V. L. Ménage, pp. 167–207; and H. Inalcik's succinct observations in his chapter in V. J. Parry *et al.*, *A History of the Ottoman Empire*, pp. 5 f. One particular conflict of this kind is discussed *infra*, n. 20.

18. See W. C. Brice, "The Turkish Colonization of Anatolia," *BJRL*, XXXVIII, 18–44; C. Cahen, "Le Problème ethnique en Anatolie," *Journal of World History*, II, 347–62; A. Hadžibegić and A. Handžić, eds., *Oblast Brankovia opširni katastarski popis vì 1455 godine* (Detailed Register and Cadastre of the District of Vilq in 1455; Vol. II has a briefer study in English and the text in Turkish), with the comments thereon by N. Beldiceanu, "À propos d'un registre de cadastre de 1455 bürüme, günlük, lağator," *Turcica*, VIII, 272–78, esp. pp. 273 (referring to the monasteries), 275 ff. (offering detailed corrections and explaining the three terms in the title as referring to various weapons). See also, more broadly, N. Todorov, "La Situation démographique de la Peninsule balkanique au cours des XVᵉ et XVIᵉ siècles," *Godishnik* (Annual) of the University of Sofia, 5, 53, 2 ff. A major effect of this relatively tolerant policy was the constant exchange of cultural traits and the gradual emergence of a basic community of interests among the various ethnoreligious groups. See A. E. Vacalopoulos, "Traits communs du développement économique et social des peuples balcaniques et du Sud-Est Européen à l'époque ottomane," *Balkan Studies*, XVI, 154–75.

19. See G. Ostrogorski, "Byzance. État tributaire de l'Empire turc," *Sbornik* (Collected Studies) of the Institute of Byzantine Studies of the Serbian Academy of Sciences, LX, 49–56; O. Iliescu, "Le Montant du Tribut payé par Byzance à l'Empire Ottoman en 1379 et 1424," *RESEE*, IX, 427–32, esp. pp. 430 ff. See also the data furnished by N. Jorga in his *Geschichte des Osmanischen Reiches*, I, 471 f.

20. See J. A. B. Palmer, "The Origin of the Janissaries," *BJRL*, XXXV, 442–81; N. Weissmann, *Les Janissaires. Étude de l'organisation militaire des Ottomans* (Paris dissertation). The process of *devshirme*, based upon the original law which had allotted to the monarch one-fifth of all booty taken in the conquered areas, was refined by Murad II in 1438. On the intrinsic theoretical conflict between this institution and the traditional Islamic law, the *shari'a*, see *infra*, n. 50. We shall also see that the relations between the Jews and the Janissaries varied from time to time and place to place.

21. See P. Karlin-Hayter, "La Politique religieuse des conquérants ottomans dans un texte hagiographique (a. 1437)," *Byzantion*, XXXV (1965, Henri Gregoire Mem. Vol.), 353–58; Isaac Şarfati's circular in the abridged English reproduction by Franz Kobler, ed., *A Treasury of Jewish Letters: Letters from the Famous and the Humble*, I, 283–

85. The date of this noteworthy document has not yet been ascertained. The only hint given in the letter itself is the reference to the Christian law "that every Jew found on a Christian ship bound for the East shall be flung into the sea." This is evidently a reference to the sharp Christian reaction to the Jewish-Franciscan controversy in Jerusalem in 1427–28. See *supra*, Vol. X, p. 415 n. 45. Hence any date in the following decade or two would seem acceptable. Nor can we tell what, if any, influence the circular exerted on Central European Jewry. The fact that we only know of the manuscript preserved in the Paris Bibliothèque Nationale and that little had been heard about it before its Leipzig 1844 publication at the end of Eliezer b. Nathan ha-Levi's *Q̦untras Gezerot Tatnu* (The Persecutions of 1096), ed. by A. Jellinek, would rather favor the assumption that very few copies circulated immediately after its appearance. However, the sentiments expressed by Ṣarfati were undoubtedly shared by numerous contemporary arrivals from the Holy Roman Empire even before its composition in Turkey. See also *infra*, note 32.

Incidentally, the frequent assertion that many refugees from Hungary had permanently settled in the Balkans as a result of the Hungarian expulsion of 1360 probably is owing more to the penchant of modern Jewish historians to attribute most major migratory movements to decrees of expulsion or pogroms, rather than to the more permanent politicoeconomic pressures which forced many individuals over the years to change their residences. In the Hungarian case, we remember, that decree of banishment was revoked by Louis the Great in 1465 and the king actually promoted Jewish return, issuing favorable ordinances for new Jewish settlers. The chances are that, from the outset, not all Jews affected by the decree left the country and that a great many simply moved to a neighboring locality until the storm blew over. A similar occurrence in Lithuania at the end of the fifteenth century definitely did not lead to any large-scale exodus, but merely to a small temporary break in the continuity of the upbuilding of Jewish life in a country which in the subsequent generations was to play a major role in Jewish history. See *supra*, Vols. X, pp. 25 ff., 311 nn. 28–29; XVI, 317 n. 2.

22. See Matthias Döring in his Supplement to Dietrich Engelhus's *Chronica nova*, published by A. F. Riedel in his ed. of the *Codex diplomaticus Brandenburgensis*, 4th section, I, 224; and the additional German sources analyzed by J. Irmscher in his "Zeitgenössische deutsche Stimmen zum Fall von Byzantium," *Byzantinoslavica*, XIV, 109–122. Because of the tremendous impression the conquest of Constantinople made upon contemporaries and later generations, we have considerable source material as well as a plethora of secondary writings relating to this historic event. Among recent publications we need but mention J. R. M. Jones, comp. and trans., *The Siege of Constantinople, 1453. Seven Contemporary Accounts*, presenting an English trans. of passages from Giacomo Tedaldi, Leonardo of Chios, Leonikos Chalkokondylas, Michael Ducas, Cristoforo Riccherio, Zorzi Dolfin, and Angelo Giovanni Lomellino, together with that of Meḥmed's treaty with the Genoese; Georgios Sphrantzes (Phrantzes), *Chronikon*, ed. by I. Bekker in *Corpus scriptorum byzantinorum*, XXXVI; and in the annotated excerpts therefrom in *Die Letzten Tage von Konstantinopel. Der auf den Fall Konstantinopels 1453 bezügliche Teil des dem Georgios Sphranzes zugeschriebenen "Chronicon maius,"* trans. with an Intro. and Comments by E. von Ivánka; W. Röll, "Der Zweite Brief Isidors von Kiew über die Eroberung Konstantinopels," *BZ*, LXIX, 13–16 (this letter dated July 7, 1453 and addressed to the city of Bologna by the refugee clergyman from the besieged capital is published here from a Munich MS; it supplements the long-known letter written by Isidor on the following day to the Roman Curia which has been readily available in *PG*, CLIX, 953–56; also listing various similar epistles

and the literature thereon); a number of poems such as the one edited by D. Michail-idis in "Un Lamento inedito sulla caduta di Constantinopoli (Codex Alexandrinus)," *BZ*, LXV, 303–326 (also listing other poems of the same kind, *ibid.*, p. 303 n. 3).

The description of events preceding the conquest and its aftermath in the contemporary and later literature is well analyzed in a number of essays included in *Byzantinoslavica*, XIV, on the 500th anniversary of that conquest. See esp. H. Turková, "Le Siège de Constantinople d'après la Siyaḥatname d'Evliyā Čelebi," pp. 1–13; V. Grecu, "La Chute de Constantinople dans la littérature populaire roumaine," pp. 55–81; I. Dujcev, "La Conquête turque et la prise de Constantinople dans la littérature slave contemporaine," pp. 14–54, continued *ibid.*, XVI, 318–29; XVII, 276–340. The Greek reaction is best exemplified by Cardinal Bessarion's letter to Doge Francesco Foscari of July 23, 1453. In this epistle the renowned Greek humanist, who was to exert a significant influence on the progress of the Italian Renaissance, blamed principally the disunity among the Christian kings "whose hands are soiled by the blood of their brethren" for the fall of the great capital. See the quotation in E. Kafé's "Le Mythe turc et son declin dans les relations de voyage des Européens de la Renaissance," *Oriens*, XXI–XXII, 159–95, esp. p. 160. See also S. Runciman's comprehensive analysis of *The Fall of Constantinople, 1453; infra*, n. 33; and, more broadly, F. Babinger's memorable biography of *Mehmed der Eroberer und seine Zeit, Weltenstürmer einer Zeitwende*, or the recent English translation thereof.

23. Kristovoulos of Imbros, *History of Meḥmed the Conqueror*, trans. from the Greek by C. T. Riggs, p. 93. The sultan's more stringent order relating to the forcible repopulation of the city is reproduced from 'Āshikpāshāzāde in the excerpt in B. Lewis, ed. and trans. of *Islam from the Prophet Muhammad to the Capture of Constantinople*, I, 146. This drastic method was systematically used by Turkish authorities in other localities as well. See Ö. L. Barkan, "Les Déportations comme méthode de peuplement et de colonisation dans l'Empire Ottoman," *Revue de la Faculté des Sciences économiques de l'Université d'Istamboul*, XI, 67–131; Barkan's compilation of the census data for 1478 and subsequent years, in his "Essai sur les donnés statistiques des registres de recensement dans l'Empire Ottoman aux XVe et XVIe siècles," *JESHO*, I, 9–36, esp. pp. 27, 35 Table V. It is noteworthy that a contemporary judge, Muhji adh-Dhin, was able to furnish data concerning the population of Istanbul in 1477 which came very close to those compiled by Barkan from the official registers. He found that the capital included houses inhabited by roughly 9,000 Turks with additional 750 Karamanian Muslims, 3,000 Greek, 267 Crimean Christians, 1,500 Jews, and 31 Gypsies. See F. Babinger, *Mehmed der Eroberer*, p. 109; *infra*, chap. LXXVIII, nn. 23, 81–82.

24. See F. Babinger, *Mehmed der Eroberer*, p. 122; Nicolò [Niccolò] Barbaro, *Diary of the Siege of Constantinople 1453*, trans. by J. R. Jones, p. 66; D. Jacoby, "Les Quartiers juifs de Constantinople a l'époque byzantine," *Byzantion*, XXXVII, 167–227; and *supra*, Vol. XVII, pp. 18 f., 308 n. 19. It may also be noted that the generally well-informed Jewish historian, Joseph b. Joshua ha-Kohen, writing about a century later, alluded to the wholesale slaughter and pillage in the conquered city, merely adding: "And the city's population went into exile with few inhabitants left, while the women were raped and taken captive." He did not refer in this connection to any special treatment of Jews or to any substantial number of Jewish survivors. See his *Dibrei ha-Yamim le-malkhei Ṣarefat u-malkhei Bet Ottoman ha-Toger* (A History of the Frankish and Ottoman Kings: A World History) (Amsterdam, 1733), fols. 41b f. Neither does Elijah Capsali in his lengthy story of the fall of Constantinople and its effect on Jews men-

tion that Jews were a significant exception among the survivors. See *infra*, n. 25; and Chap. LXXVIII, n. 26.

25. Elijah Capsali, *Seder Eliyahu zuṭa*, ed. by A. Shmuelevitz *et al.*, pp. i, 11–12, 16, in I, 65 ff., 81, the author adding that wherever in his following conquests Meḥmed found Jews he transplanted many of them to the new capital. On the rapid increase of Istanbul's Jewish population, see *infra*, Chap. LXXVIII, n. 24.

26. See Tadi ad-Din Aḥmadi, *Iskander-Name*, written some time after 1367; E. Hocks, *Pius II. und der Halbmond*, p. 151; B. Alexandrescu-Derrea, "L'Action diplomatique et militaire de Venise pour la défense de Constantinople (1452–1453)," *RRH*, XIII, 247–67; and F. Babinger, *Mehmed der Eroberer*, pp. 67 ff. See G. L. Lewis's brief biographical sketch of "Ahmadi," in *EI*, 2d ed., I, 299–300. The Turkish Alexander legend was, of course, greatly indebted to the older tales circulating since the Hellenistic period among the various Middle Eastern peoples, including the Jews. See, for instance, M. S. Southgate's informative article, "Portrait of Alexander in Persian Alexander Romances of the Islamic Era," *JAOS*, XCVII, 278–84, discussing among other sources the anonymous *Iskandarnamuh*, a Persian text written between the twelfth and fourteenth centuries and ed. by I. Afshar. It very likely was also available to Meḥmed the Conqueror. According to Benedetto Dei, Meḥmed's Italian admirer, the sultan had a reading knowledge of five languages (Turkish, Persian, Arabic, Greek, and Slavonic) and even had some familiarity with "Chaldean," which Babinger suggests meant Hebrew, though no testimony to this effect appears in any Hebrew source. However, his linguistic prowess was doubtless limited to some more or less superficial understanding of simple texts in these languages. The same may hold true for his familiarity with Latin attributed to him by other contemporaries. See F. Babinger, "Mehmed II. der Eroberer und Italien," reprinted in his *Aufsätze und Abhandlungen zur Geschichte Süd-osteuropas und der Levante*, I, 172–200, esp. pp. 181 f.; as against C. G. Patrinelis, "Mehmed II the Conqueror and His Presumed Knowledge of Greek and Latin," *Viator, Medieval and Renaissance Studies*, II, 349–54, rather agreeing with the Greek scribes who, personally acquainted with the sultan, asserted that he did not know either language (p. 354).

27. See the general literature on Turkish history listed *supra*, n. 1; and, on the impact of the Ottoman expansion on Jews of the Aegean islands and the Black Sea, *supra*, Vol. XVII, Chap. LXXII *passim*. To the literature cited there add J. Koder, *Negroponte. Untersuchungen zur Topographie und Siedlungsgeschichte der Insel Euboia während der Zeit der Venetianerherrschaft*, esp. pp. 57, 60 ff., 86 ff. (on the Jewish quarters on the island); and E. Brockman, *The Two Sieges of Rhodes, 1480–1522*. The complicated relationships—economic, financial, political, and naval—between Venice and Turkey have often been analyzed. See, for example, F. Babinger, "Le Vicende veneziane sulla lotta contro i Turchi durante il secolo XV," in *La Civiltà Veneziana del Quattrocento*, pp. 49–73; and the more general recent review by P. Preto, *Venezia e Turchi*. Because of the extensive interrelations between the two powers as well as the fine preservation and easy accessibility of the Venetian archives, these repositories have furnished, and continue to furnish, more information about the historic evolution of the Ottoman Empire than any other collections outside the Empire itself. Nevertheless, the constant ups and downs in the Balkan wars during the fifteenth century have left behind a number of puzzling problems. See, for instance, A. E. Vacalopoulos (Bakalopulos), "Les Limites de l'Empire Byzantin depuis la fin du XIVe siècle jusqu'à son chute (1453)," *BZ*, LXV, 56–65, with the succinct comments thereon

by M. Kiel in "A Note on the History of the Frontiers of the Byzantine Empire in the 15th Century," *ibid.*, LXVI, 351–53.

28. See P. Grierson, "La Moneta veneziana nell'economia mediterranea del Trecento e Quattrocento," *La Civiltà Veneziana del Quattrocento*, pp. 75–97; F. Babinger, "Contrafazzioni ottomane dello zecchino veneziano nel XV secolo," *Annali* of the Istituto Italiano di Numismatica, II, 83–89; idem, *Mehmed der Eroberer*, esp. pp. 467 f., 489 ff.; E. Werner, *Die Geburt*, pp. 282 ff.; H. Inalcik, in V. J. Parry's *A History of the Ottoman Empire*, p. 49. Much can be learned also from the comparison with the contemporary situation in Mameluke Egypt. See A. Rangé van Genepp, "Le Ducat venitien en Égypte, son influence sur le monnayage de l'or dans ce pays au commencement du XVᵉ siècle," *Revue Numismatique*, 4th ser. I, 373–81, 494–508; J. L. Bacharach, "The Dinar versus the Ducat," *IJMES*, IV, 77–96, esp. pp. 91 Table I, and 93 ff. App. Of interest in this connection is E. Werner's "Despotie, Absolutismus oder feudale Zersplitterung? Strukturwandlungen im Osmanenreich zwischen 1566 und 1699," *Jahrbuch für Wirtschaftsgeschichte*, 1972, Part 3, pp. 107–128. Although relating to a later, much more oppressive, period in Turkish history and indirectly sounding like special pleading for the regimes behind the Iron Curtain, the author's arguments for the contrast with the weaknesses of the preceding Byzantine feudal order are particularly apposite for the reign of Meḥmed II. See also *infra*, Chap. LXXVIII, n. 96.

29. Meḥmed's major code, the *qanun-name* (which included, for instance, the extraordinary law providing for the slaying of all of a newly crowned monarch's brothers and the brothers' progeny "for the order of the world"), was later revised by Suleiman the Magnificent. A critical edition of these texts is available in F. Babinger's *Sultanische Urkunden zur Geschichte der osmanischen Wirtschafts- und Staatsverwaltung am Ausgang der Herrschaft Mehmed II., des Eroberers*, Part I (from a MS of the Bibliothèque Nationale in Paris). The more unusual codification of the customary law is discussed by N. Beldiceanu in his *Code de lois coutumières de Mehmed II*. Of course, neither code includes all the ordinances issued by the sultan; many have but recently come to light. See, for instance, M. Lefebvre, "Quinze firmans de sultan Mehmed le Conquérant," *REI*, XXXIX, 147–73, offering a French trans. of these decrees issued in 1478–80 and published by H. Inalcik in *Beleten*, XI, 693–708. Kristovoulos of Imbros' admiring, almost sycophantic, biography of the sultan is characterized by the author's dedication which, in the English trans. by C. T. Riggs entitled *History of Mehmed the Conqueror*, reads as follows: "To the Supreme Emperor, King of Kings, Mehmed, the fortunate, the victor, the winner of trophies, the triumphant, the invincible, Lord of land and sea, by the will of God, Kristovoulos, the Islander, servant of thy servants." See also G. Zoras, "Tendenze politiche in Grecia dopo la caduta di Costantinopoli," *Atti* of the VIII International Congress of Byzantine Studies, I, 11 f.

30. Lucas Notaras' much-quoted saying, reported by Michael Ducas in his *Historia byzantina*, XXXVII, ed. by I. Bekker, p. 264, or in H. J. Margulias's English trans. *Decline and Fall of Byzantium*, may have been but an irate remark provoked by the stubbornness of the Latin archbishop of Mitylene, Leonard of Chios, as suggested by S. Runciman in *The Fall of Constantinople*, p. 71. Yet, it undoubtedly verbalized a fairly widespread sentiment among the increasingly Turcophile opposition to the existing Byzantine regime among the Greeks and Slavs of the peninsula. See E. Werner, *Die Geburt*, p. 247.

31. Georgios Sphrantzes (Phrantzes), *Chronikon*, ed. by I. Bekker, III, 11, pp. 304 and 308; G. M. Thomas, "Eine Griechische Originalurkunde zur Geschichte der

anatolischen Kirche. Schreiben des griechischen Patriarchen Maximus von Constantinopel an den Dogen Giovanni Mocenigo von Venedig, Januar, 1480," *Abhandlungen* of the Bavarian Academy, Historical division, VII, 145–92, esp. pp. 182, 184 [from a Vienna manuscript]. The operations of the *millet* system, as it developed more fully in the sixteenth century, will be discussed in the next volume. On Gennadios and his relations with the regime, the legal aspects of his appointment, and the generally brief tenure of his early successors, see A. Papadakis, "Gennadius II and Mehmet the Conqueror," *Byzantion*, XLII, 88–108 (includes an English trans. of Gennadios' shorter *Expositio fidei*); G. Hering, "Das Islamische Recht und die Investitur des Gennadios Scholarios (1454)," *Balkan Studies*, II, 231–56; V. Laurent, "Les Premiers patriarches de Constantinople sous la domination turque (1454–1476). Succession et chronologie d'après un catalogue inédit," *REB*, XXVI, 229–63, esp. p. 262. Ironically, Gennadios, himself, an author of an anti-Jewish tract, *Dialogus christiani cum judaeo, sive refutatio erroris judaici et ejusdem delectus prophetiarum de Christi*, ed. by A. John and occasional remarks scattered in his other writings such as are included in his *Scripta quaedam edita et inedita*, ed. by W. Gass, became instrumental in fortifying the Jewish self-governmental structure in the Ottoman Empire. See also M. L. Pharantos, *He Theologia Gennadiou tou Scholariou* (The Theology of G. G. S.).

32. The story of the appointment of Moses b. Elijah Capsali, as reported by his grandnephew, Elijah Capsali in his chronicle, *Seder Olam zuta*, i. 16, ed. by A. Shmuelevitz *et al.*, I, 81 ff., has all the earmarks of a family legend. Yet, under the conditions of a Middle Eastern administration it may, indeed, represent some historical reality. In any case, Moses exercised his authority with considerable vigor and at times even ventured to appoint provincial chief rabbis, including Isaac Ṣarfati, the aformentioned author of the circular letter addressed to Central European Jews, who became the head of the Adrianople rabbinate. Considering that before 1453 Adrianople had been the capital of the Empire, and had at that time embraced three Jewish congregations, such an appointment doubtless required the backing of the Turkish authorities in order to become effective.

From Elijah Capsali's work written in 1522 we also learn a few details about the early administration of Istanbul's chief rabbinate and particularly about its tax collections from Jews for the benefit of both the state and the Jewish communities. But it appears likely that, from the government's point of view, the Jewish administration to some extent resembled the fiscal organization of the much larger Orthodox Church. See the well-documented work by J. Kabrda, *Le Système fiscal de l'Église orthodoxe dans l'Empire Ottoman (d'après les documents turcs)*. Otherwise we must rely principally on documents of a very much later age and try to reconstruct from them in retrospect what the status of the original chief rabbis may have been. See, for instance, the four *berats*, dated between 1842 and 1909, and reproduced in French by A. Galanté in his ed. of *Documents officiels turcs concernant les Juifs de Turquie. Recueil de 114 lois, règlements, firmans, bérats, ordres et décisions des tribunaux*, pp. 36 ff. Some rays of light are also shed by the few "Responsa and Letters by R. Moses Capsali" (Hebrew), ed. by S. Assaf in *Sinai*, III, nos. 30–31, pp. 149–58, 485–86, esp. pp. 149 ff. See also *infra*, Chap. LXXVIII, n. 108.

33. A. Danon, "The Karaites in European Turkey," *JQR*, XV, 285–360; idem, "Documents Relating to the History of the Karaites in European Turkey," *ibid.*, XVII, 165–98, 239–322; S. Assaf, "New Material to the History of the Karaites in the Orient" (Hebrew), *Zion*, I, 208–251; S. Szyszman, "Communauté karaïte d'Istamboul,"

Vetus Testamentum, VI, 309–315. On their earlier antecedents, see esp. Z. Ankori, *Karaites in Byzantium: The Formative Years, 970–1100* and the literature listed there. Karaism in Turkey will be analyzed more fully in connection with the Jewish communal and religious history in a later volume.

34. See the interesting letter, apparently written by Eliezer ha-Shimoni in 1496, published from a Prague MS by S. Assaf in his "Letters of Great Rabbis of Salonica" (Hebrew) in *Sinai*, I, nos. 1–6, pp. 32–40, 182–83 and reprinted in his *Meqorot umeḥqarim be-toledot Yisrael* (Texts and Studies in Jewish History), pp. 209–217, esp. pp. 211 f. On the writer, see the data supplied by S. A. Rosanes in his *Dibre yeme*, I, 138 ff.; II (*Qorot*), 17 f.; I. S. Emmanuel, *Maṣṣebot Saloniqi* (Precious Stones of the Jews of Salonica), I, 51 f. No. 70. Evidently at that time, which marked the onset of the Jewish mass immigration into Turkey, the chief rabbinate had not yet learned to respect the diverse customs and rites prevailing in the newly founded congregations of various geographic origins. One may also note in this connection that the study of extant tombstones as a source of history has in general been greatly neglected in Ottoman historiography, Jewish and non-Jewish. See the pertinent complaint in H. P. Laqueur's recent study, "Die Kopfbedeckung im osmanischen Reich als soziales Erkenntniszeichen, dargestellt an der Hand einiger Istanbuler Gräber des 18. und 19. Jahrhunderts," *Der Islam*, LIX, 80–92, esp. p. 80.

35. See P. Bartl, "Kryptochristentum und Formen des religiösen Synkretismus in Albanien," *Beiträge zur Kenntnis Südosteuropas und des Nahen Orients*, II, 117–27; S. Runciman, *The Great Church in Captivity*. The Marranos settling in Turkey and professing Judaism in public were, as a matter of course, counted as Jews. However, their former living as secret Jews created many legal and social problems within the Jewish community, problems which engaged the attention of its leading jurists for several generations. These aspects of their history will likewise become clearer in our later chapters. For the time being, we need but refer to H. J. Zimmels, *Die Marranen in der rabbinischen Literatur. Forschungen und Quellen zur Geschichte und Kulturgeschichte der Anussim;* idem, *Ashkenazim and Sephardim: Their Relations, Differences, and Problems as Reflected in the Rabbinical Responsa*, with a foreword by I. Brodie; and B. Netanyahu, *The Marranos of Spain. From the Late XIVth to the Early XVIth Century, According to Contemporary Hebrew Sources*, 2d ed. rev. and enlarged. See also the extensive literature listed in connection with Marrano history in other countries, *supra*, Vols. XIII–XV; and *infra*, Chap. LXXVI, n. 19.

On the contrast between the diminution in numbers of the Christian churches and the early proliferation of synagogues, see C. Patrinelis, "The Exact Time of the First Attempt of the Turks to Seize the Churches and to Convert the Christian People of Constantinople to Islam," *Actes* of the Iᵉʳ Congrès International des Études Balkanique et Sud-Est Européennes (Sofia), III, 567–72; H. Inalcik, "The Policy of Mehmed II toward the Greek Population of Istanbul and the Byzantine Buildings of the City," *Dumbarton Oaks Papers*, XXIII–XXIV, 229–49; A. Galanté, *Les Synagogues d'Istanbul*, which offers a brief survey of synagogues which had existed in Istanbul from ancient times to the 1930s. On the general Islamic laws concerning the building of new synagogues see *supra*, Vols. III, pp. 134 ff., 266 f.; and XVII, pp. 186 f., 383 n. 75. In the Ottoman Empire, too, the legal aspects of that prohibition were later often to cause much annoyance to Jewish communities trying to erect a new house of worship. These difficulties lasted well into the nineteenth century. See also *infra*, Chap. LXXVIII, n. 116.

36. See F. Babinger, *Mehmed der Eroberer*, p. 475. The priority of communal, as well as state taxes, over all other obligations of a deceased man's estate is mentioned in the Jewish case in the privilege given to Ya'qub of Gaëta, known to us from later reproductions (see below). Otherwise, Jews were submitted to an ever greater variety of imposts devised by the Ottoman and Jewish fiscal authorities, some of which are also mentioned in that privilege. Many others will be discussed *infra*, Chap. LXXVIII, nn. 95 ff., 102.

37. See T. Öz, ed., *Zwei Stiftungsurkunden des Sultans Mehmed II. Fatih*, esp. pp. 31, 33, 35, 120; A. Galanté, *Médecins juifs au service de la Turquie*, pp. 5 ff. Ya'qub of Gaëta's career, his alleged conversion, and the extent of his and his descendants' tax immunity have been analyzed by F. Babinger in "Ya'qub Pascha, ein Leibarzt Mehmeds II. Leben und Schicksale des Maestro Jacopo aus Gaeta," *RSO*, XXVI, 87–113; and by B. Lewis in "The Privilege Granted by Meḥmed II to His Physician," *BSOAS*, XIV, 550–63 (includes an English trans. of the Preamble to R. Samuel de Medina's responsum; see *infra*, n. 38). Although some specific details are still open to debate, little documentary evidence has come to light during the last quarter century to supplement the data reviewed by these two authors. The mixture of Greek, Slavic, and Turkish names in the same families, even among fathers and sons, is attested by the documents mentioned in N. Beldiceanu's "Marġarid, un timar monastique," *REB*, XXXIII, 227–55, esp. pp. 249 ff.

Needless to say, Ya'qub was not the only physician employed by Meḥmed. See, for instance, K. Kreiser, "Beşir Čelebī—Hofarzt Ibrâhim Qaramans und Vertrauter Meḥmeds II. Fatīh," *Islamkundliche Abhandlungen . . . der Universität München (Hans Joachim Kissling Jub. Vol.)*, pp. 92–103. However, from the appended documents and the author's much too brief introductory comments, it is not evident that Beşīr ever accompanied Meḥmed beyond Adrianople. In any case, Ya'qub seems to have been the sultan's most enduring, almost life-long, friend and probably also one of his most influential political and financial advisers.

38. R. Samuel b. Moses de Medina's 1571 responsum, included in his comprehensive *She'elot u-teshubot me-ha-Rashdam* (Responsa) on Ḥ. M., Salonica, 1595 ed., fols. 259b ff. It had essentially appeared in the less accurate edition of Samuel's *Pisqe* (Decisions), published in the rabbi's lifetime in two volumes (Salonica 1580–82). See II, fols. 1a ff. The preamble to this responsum (quoted here from B. Lewis's English trans. in "The Privilege," *BSOAS*, XIV, 551 ff.) not only describes the origin of the controversy and tells the story of Ya'qub and his privilege, but incidentally also offers considerable insights in regard to the legal status of the Jewish community in the middle of the fifteenth century. For instance, the above-mentioned right of the Jewish authorities to collect tax arrears from the estate of an insolvent taxpayer ahead of the wife's dowry is stated here as part of the royal legislation. It is included in the text of the privilege, which is reproduced here in a Hebrew translation with all the difficulties of rendition of a Turkish legal enactment into biblical Hebrew. It has nevertheless proved to be quite authentic with respect to its date, legal aspects, and phraseology characteristic of such imperial diplomas. See esp. Lewis's observations in *BSOAS*, XIV, 556 ff.

39. See N. Iorga, *Notes et extraits pour servir à l'histoire des croisades au XVᵉ siecle*, reprinted from the *Revue de l'Orient Latin*, II, 377, 383 f.; and the documents reproduced from Venetian archives by F. Babinger in *RSO*, XXVI, esp. pp. 106 f. As it appears from this documentation, some Venetian Jews were involved in the plot to

poison Meḥmed. They were prepared to invest money in that enterprise, hoping to obtain significant concessions from the Venetian administration. This adventure is reminiscent of the effort of several Italian Jews in 1587 to influence the election of a Polish king as a business enterprise. See *supra*, Vol. XVI, pp. 47, 337 n. 50. Considering that in 1477 Jews were not even allowed to live in Venice proper and had to dwell in Mestre, one can understand why they were not familiar with the ways in which the Signoria conducted its international diplomacy. Their information about conditions in Istanbul must have been nonexistent. In any case, neither Ya'qub nor Vlaco seems to have had any serious intention to get involved in that dangerous scheme even for the tantalizingly high rewards promised them by their would-be Venetian co-conspirators.

40. N. Beldiceanu, *Les Actes des premiers sultans*, I, 43 App. 3; H. Ahrweiler, "Une Lettre en grec du Sultan Bayezid II (1481–1512)," *Turcica*, I, 152–60; N. Jorga, *Geschichte des Osmanischen Reiches*, II, 303 n. 3; *supra*, Vol. XVII, pp. 29 f., 314 n. 35. The use of the high-sounding Greek titles *Basileos* and *Autokrator* in Bayezid's boastful preambles is doubly remarkable, as the predominantly Greek scribes in his father's chancery had rarely used the term *Basileos* for the great sultan. Apparently this usage appeared for the first time in Meḥmed II's ordinance of July 10, 1480, close to the end of his life. See A. Bombaci, "Venezia e l'impresa turca di Otranto," *RSI*, LXVI, 159–203, esp. p. 185; E. Werner, *Die Geburt*, p. 256.

The sufferings of the Constantinople Jews during the Janissary riots and Moses Capsali's rather accidental escape are described with much flourish by Elijah Capsali in his *Seder Eliyahu Zuta*, I, 35, pp. 128 ff.; and S. A. Rosanes, *Dibre yeme Yisrael*, I, 43 ff. On Bayezid's complete amnesty for the misdeeds of the Janissaries, see his early ordinance quoted in Donaldo da Lezzi's (Lese's) *Historia Turchesca (1300–1514)*, ed. with an Intro. by L. Ursu, pp. 168 f.; and, more generally, S. N. Fisher, *The Foreign Relations of Turkey 1481–1512*, esp. p. 18 n. 1.

41. The report about the numerous Jewish sailors in the Venetian navy, included in Archbishop Marco Saracho of Lepanto's communication to the Venetian government (dated July 26, 1499), was summarized in Marino Sanuto's *Diarii*, II, 1065. His exaggeration merely reflected his and other Venetian agents' concern over the newly won power of the Ottoman navy. This contribution to the Ottoman military might has rightly been considered one of Bayezid's few solid achievements. On the other hand, Venetian weakness in vigorously pursuing the war derived from the republic's reluctance to defray the high expenses connected with extended naval actions and, more fundamentally, from its general dependence both on the large revenue it collected from its Levantine trade and on its imports of Turkish grain, which were greatly reduced during the hostilities. See, for example, Marco Bembo's letter describing the grain crisis of 1483–84 and other adverse developments on the Salonican market, in F. Thiriet, "Les Lettres commerciales des Bembo et le commerce vénitien dans l'Empire Ottoman à la fin du XVe siècle," in *Studi in onore di Armando Sapori*, II, 911–33, esp. pp. 928 ff.; the letters published by I. Melikoff in her "Bayezid II et Venise. Cinq lettres imperiales (Num-i hümayün) provenant de l'Archivio di Stato di Venezia," *Turcica*, I, 123–49; Bayezid's aforementioned (n. 40) Greek letter; and H. J. Kissling, "Betrachtungen über die Flottenpolitik Sultan Bajezids II. (1481–1512)," *Saeculum*, XX, 35–43. Undoubtedly Bayezid was fully informed by his intelligence service that Venice did not even have the backing of most Italian republics. Not only did the Genoese and Florentines, Venice's old rivals, maintain their neutrality, but also the sultan could continue to cultivate friendly relations with such outsiders as Francesco

II Gonzaga. See H. J. Kissling, *Sultan Bajezids II. Beziehungen zu Markgraf Francesco II. von Gonzaga;* and his "Francesco II Gonzaga ed il sultano Bâyesîd II," *ASI*, CXXV, 34–68. On the role played by the Turkish navy in the great Ottoman expansion, see A. C. Hess's study cited *infra*, Chap. LXXVI, n. 8.

42. See *supra*, Vols. XI, Chap. L, *passim;* XII, pp. 109 f., 295 n. 45; W. H. Prescott, *History of the Reign . . . of Ferdinand and Isabella the Catholic,* II, 94 f. (implying that even other Spanish Muslims were not to depart for Turkey); Immanuel Aboab, *Nomologia, discursos legales* (an apologetical tract, posthumously published in Amsterdam, 1629; 2d ed., 1733), p. 295, Chap. ii; Samuel Usque, *Consolaçam as Tribulaçoens de Israel,* iii; English trans. by M. Cohen, *Consolation for the Tribulations of Israel,* pp. 211 f.; R. Samuel de Medina, *Resp.* on O.Ḥ. No. 88; on Y.D., Nos. 124, 181, etc. Not surprisingly, the Spaniards were increasingly concerned about their internal *converso* problem and tried to link this ever-suspect group with the Spanish Jewish exiles in the Ottoman Empire. Someone actually forged a text of "The Correspondence between the Jews of Spain and Provence and the Jews of Constantinople," in which the Jews of Istanbul were said to have advised their secret coreligionists in Iberia to remain in their old home countries and attempt, through the use of all sorts of business and political deals, to ruin their Spanish and Provençal oppressors. The spurious nature of that correspondence was demonstrated as early as 1880 by I. Loeb in "La Correspondance des Juifs d'Espagne avec ceux de Constantinople," *REJ*, XV, 262–76, esp. pp. 270 ff. (Hebrew text), 272 ff. (French trans.). See also the more recent analysis by A. Z. Aescoly, "The Correspondence between the Jews of Spain and Provence and the Jews of Constantinople, and the History of the Marranos of Provence" (Hebrew), *Zion*, X, 102–139. Needless to say, the Jewries of other European lands likewise participated in that eastward migration. On Italy, see esp. A. Milano's "Nuove luci sulla emigrazione degli Ebrei italiani nel Cinquecento verso il Levante," *Rassegna mensile di Israel,* XIX, 175–78; and, more generally, his *Storia degli Ebrei italiani nel Levante.*

43. See N. Beldiceanu, "Un Acte sur le statut de la colonie juive de Trikala," *REI*, XL, 129–38, esp. pp. 130 ff. While insisting that Jews and other settlers must not leave the country under the penalty of death, Bayezid seemingly did not go as far as did his father (at least on one occasion) in protecting Turkish Jews abroad. Such an intervention in favor of the Jews of Crete by Meḥmed II is mentioned by W. Miller in his *Essays on the Latin Orient,* pp. 361 f. On the general prohibition against Jews and others leaving the country without authorization, see Giovanni Maringhi's letter to Nicolo Micholozzi dated Pera, January 14, 1502, cited by G. R. B. Richards, ed. *Florentine Merchants in the Age of the Medici. Letters and Documents from the Selfridge Medici Manuscripts,* pp. 141 f.

44. See such local and regional histories as A. Galanté's aforementioned *Histoire des Juifs d'Istamboul;* A. Danon's "La Communauté Juive de Salonique au XVIᵉ siècle," *REJ*, XL, 206–230; XLI, 98–117, 250–65; I. S. Emmanuel, *Histoire des Israélites de Salonique,* Vol. I; J. Nehama, *Histoire des Israélites de Salonique,* Vol. I: La Communauté Romaniote—Les Sefardis et leur dispersion; II: La Communauté Sefardite, Période d'Installation (1492–1536); III: Parts 1–2: L'Age d'Or du Sefaradisme Salonicien (1536–1593); S. Mézan, *Les Juifs espagnoles en Bulgarie;* C. (B.) Roth, "A Contribution to the History of the Exiles from Sicily" (Hebrew), *Eretz-Israel,* III (M. D. U. Cassuto Mem. Vol.), 230–34, with an English summary, pp. xiv–xv. Of considerable value still are the pioneering researches by S. A. Rosanes in his *Dibre yeme Yisrael,* I, 53 ff.; the

detailed data concerning the various groups constituting Ottoman Jewry in his Apps. i–iii, pp. 203–225 (on the Romaniot Jews), and Apps. iv–xi, pp. 225–316 (on the Jews originating from other lands).

45. See Gonsalo de Illescas' observation in his *Historia pontifical y católica* (1606), cited by J. Amador de los Rios in his *Estudios históricos, políticos y literarios sobre los Judíos de España*, p. 469 n.; by H. Graetz in his *Geschichte*, IX, 10; and, more broadly, J. de Estroga, "Tradiciones españoles e las Juderías del Oriente Proximo (Reminiscencias y Apuntes)," *Sefarad*, XIV, 128–47. The development of the Ladino language and literature will be more fully discussed in a later volume.

46. Elijah Capsali, *Sefer De-be Eliyahu* in *Liqquṭim shonim*, pp. 12, 18; S. A. Rosanes, *Dibre yeme Yisrael*, I, 60 f.; H. J. Zimmels, *Ashkenazim and Sephardim*, pp. 39 ff., 288 ff. Regrettably, we have no detailed information about Ottoman Jewry's concerted activities in behalf of the Iberian and other refugees. We know of no counterpart to the recorded efforts in Candia, Crete, where in a single session on the eve of the Ninth of Ab 5253, members of the community raised 250 Venetian ducats as part of their contribution to the communal chest. Since this day fell on July 23, 1493, it is clear that that communal action was initiated in anticipation of the first anniversary of the terminal date of July 31, 1492 set by the Spanish decree for the forced departure of the exiles. See Elijah Capsali's *Liqquṭim*, p. 18. Despite the paucity of the extant records, it nevertheless would seem worthwhile to gather the scattered data which alone might enable historians to describe at least superficially these welfare activities of the small and struggling mid-eastern communities in behalf of the Spanish-Sicilian and later Portuguese and other exiles. We know little more about the ideological reactions. See, for example, H. H. Ben-Sasson's very informative essay, "The Generation of the Spanish Exiles on Its Fate" (Hebrew), *Zion*, XXVI, 23–64.

47. See S. Assaf, ed., "Responsa and Letters by R. Moses Capsali" (Hebrew), ed. from a Sassoon MS by S. Assaf in *Sinai*, III, nos. 30–31, pp. 149–58, 485–86, esp. *Resp.* Nos. 1, 2, 4; and the additional data provided by A. Obadiah in his biographical sketch of "Rabbi Eliyahu Mizraḥi" (Hebrew), *ibid.*, pp. 393–413; IV, nos. 39–44, pp. 99–110, 367–76. The provision regarding the quorum of ten adult males at each wedding (which went back to a talmudic regulation in Ketubot 8b), the subsequent neglect thereof in the medieval German communities, and the attempt by the great codifier, Joseph Karo, to reestablish this requirement as an indispensable part of a wedding ceremony, are discussed in my *JC*, I, 196; III, 46 f. n. 36 and the additional literature listed there. Karo may well have been influenced by Capsali's decision, since he himself was an Iberian refugee living first in Adrianople and later in Safed under Ottoman rule. See his *Shulḥan 'Arukh*, and Jacob b. Asher's *Ṭurim*, E.'E. 62, 4. It was also accepted by another eminent Turkish halakhist, Ḥayyin b. Israel Benveniste in his *Keneset ha-gedolah* (The Great Synagogue; a comprehensive recodification of Jewish law in the order of the *Ṭurim*), E.'E. No. 28.

Elijah Mizraḥi, Moses Capsali's younger contemporary, was far superior to him in learning. He became a renowned and prolific author despite the time and energy he had to devote to his increasingly complicated communal commitments, first as the congregational rabbi in Constantinople and then as its chief rabbi.

48. On the affair with Moses "Twenty-Four," the origin of that unusual family name, the complications caused by the intervention by R. Joseph Colon in his *Resp.*, Root 73, see the study by A. H. Freimann, "Palestine Emissaries and Pilgrims: Fif-

teenth-Century Documents from Candia" (Hebrew), *Zion*, I, 185–207; A. Yaari, *She-luḥei Ereṣ Yisrael* (Palestinian Messengers: a History of the Missions from Palestine to the Dispersion from the Destruction of the Second Temple to the Nineteenth Century), pp. 214 ff.; S. A. Rosanes, *Dibre yeme*, I, 45 ff.

49. See *supra*, Vol. XIII, pp. 170, 398 f. n. 13; A. Marx, "Hebrew Incunabula," *JQR*, XI, 98–119, esp. pp. 102 f.; idem, "Literatur über hebräische Inkunabeln," *Soncino-Blätter*, I, no. 1, pp. 159–70; and the respective facsimiles in A. Freimann's comprehensive *Thesaurus typographiae hebraicae*, Parts I–VII. See also S. A. Rosanes, *Dibre yeme*, I, 316 ff. App. xii (The First Hebrew Presses in Turkey), 322 ff. (list of Hebrew Books Printed in Turkey until 1520; enumerating 80 certain and 25 probable Constantinople prints, and 7 titles published in Salonica). Of considerable interest also are such monographs as I. Rivkind, "The Printers Jonah Ashkenazi and His Sons in Contantinople" (Hebrew), *Journal of Jewish Bibliography*, I, 50–55, 111–12 (the firm functioned in 1510–78); A. Yaari, "Three Generations of Ashkenazi Printers at Constantinople: Jonah b. Jacob Ashkenazi, His Sons and Grandsons" (Hebrew), *KS*, XIV, 238–55, 524–39; XV, 97–112, 240–57; and, more broadly, idem, *Ha-Defus ha-'ibri be-Qushta* (Hebrew Printing in Constantinople, Its History and Bibliography). A fuller story of Turkish-Jewish typography will evolve from our later general treatment of early Hebrew printing in various lands.

50. The forcible capture and conversion of Christian children could not easily be reconciled with the traditional doctrine of the *shari'a* which provided that surrendering *dhimmi*s should be subjected only to special taxes. This question has intrigued many modern scholars. Paul Wittek, in particular, came to the conclusion that the state laws, *qanun*s, enjoyed independent powers of enforcement and ran parallel to the Islamic tradition. See his "Devshirme and Shari'a," *BSOAS*, XVII, 271–78; C. Cahen, "Notes sur l'esclavage musulman et le devshirme ottoman. À propos des travaux récentes," *JESHO*, XIII, 211–18; and, more broadly, B. D. Papoulia, *Ursprung und Wesen der "Knabenlese" im Osmanischen Reich* (Diss. Munich, 1938). Reprinted in 1963 in *Südosteuropa Arbeiten*, LIX; and D. Pipes's more recent study, *Slave Soldiers and Islam: the Genesis of a Military System*, esp. pp. 159 ff.

CHAPTER LXXVI: TURKEY'S GOLDEN AGE

1. See, for example, E. Egli, *Sinan, der Baumeister osmanischer Glanzzeit;* F. Babinger's list of the buildings erected by Sinan, in *EI*, 1st ed., IV, 428–32. To be sure, as in other areas of life, on closer examination, one notices certain elements of later decay which begin to germinate in the midst of otherwise ostensibly favorable factors. Hindsight has, indeed, often revealed particularly certain sins of omission, which, unnoticed at the time, were later responsible for the unfolding of adverse developments. Such weaknesses have often been detected in Suleiman's regime as well; for example, by Subhi Labib who also emphasized the sultan's failure to take over Morocco and expand into the Atlantic world in rivalry with Spain and vigorously to oppose the Portuguese expansion into the Indian Ocean. These reflections are akin to Hans Joachim Kissling's observations on Evliya Čelebi's report about Bayezid II's refusal to listen to Columbus' proposals when, before securing Isabella's sponsorship, the great explorer urged him to promote his epochal expedition. According to Kissling, Bayezid might have varied Napoleon's regretful recollection concerning his ill treatment of the inventor of the steamship by stating: "When I showed Christopher Columbus out of my tent, I gave away the world position of the Osmanli dynasty." See S. Labib, "The Era of Suleyman the Magnificent: Crisis of Orientation," *Saeculum*, XXIX, 269–82 (or *IJMES*, X, 435–51); H. J. Kissling, "Betrachtungen über die Flottenpolitik Sultan Bajezid's II. (1481–1512)," *Saeculum*, XX, 35–43; and idem, "Die Wirtschaftliche und soziale Entwicklung der osmanischen Stadt," *Südosteuropa Jahrbuch*, IX, 1–14, esp. p. 14. Both authors overlook, however, the crucial distinction between Columbus and the Portuguese quest to reach India through the Atlantic or around Africa in order to circumvent Europe's dependence on the Muslim (now particularly Ottoman) intermediaries, and Selim I and Suleiman who, in fact, had secured direct access to the Indian subcontinent through their conquests of Iraq and the Arabian Peninsula. They thus obtained full control over the Red Sea route and easy access to that of the Persian Gulf.

2. See the general literature *supra*, Vol. XVII, pp. 299 ff. n. 1; Chap. LXXV, nn. 1 ff. On the siege of Vienna in 1529, see W. Himmelberger's detailed military analysis in his *Wiens erste Belagerung durch die Türken, 1529*. The situation in Austria and of its Jews at that time are briefly described *supra*, Vol. XIII, pp. 263 ff., 447 nn. 64–65). On the period of 1512–74 see H. Jansky, "Die Eroberung Syriens durch Sultan Selim I.," *Mitteilungen zur osmanischen Geschichte*, II, 173–241 (Diss. Vienna, 1922), and with special reference to Palestine, J. B. Evrard, "Die Statthalter Syriens im letzten halben Jahrhundert der Mamlukenherrschaft: Safad," *Islamkundliche Abhandlungen* in honor of Hans Joachim Kissling, ed. by H. G. Majer, pp. 70–83; A. C. Hess, "The Ottoman Conquest of Egypt (1517) and the Beginning of the Sixteenth-Century World War," *IJMES*, IV, 55–76, based in part on Ibn Iyas' contemporary study, *An Account of the Ottoman Conquest of Egypt in the Year A.H. 922 (A.D. 1516)*, trans. from the Third Volume of the Arabic Chronicle of . . . I. Y., an Eyewitness of the Scenes He Describes, by W. H. Salmon; G. W. F. Stripling, *The Ottoman Turks and the Arabs, 1511–1574*. For the European aspects of the sixteenth-century expansion see G. Káldy-

Nagy, "Suleimans Angriff auf Europa," *AOH*, XXVIII, 163–212; and, more broadly, W. E. D. Allen, *Problems of Turkish Power in the Sixteenth Century;* and I. Beldiceanu-Steinherr's succinct observations on "Le Règne du Selim Ier. Tournant dans la vie politique et religieuse de l'Empire Ottoman," *Turcica*, VI, 34–48. The information here given is well supplemented by the study of individual personalities such as R. B. Merriman's *Suleiman the Magnificent, 1520–1566;* H. D. Jenkins, *Ibrahim Pasha, Grand Vizir of Suleiman the Magnificent;* A. H. Lybyer, *The Government of the Ottoman Empire in the Time of Suleiman the Magnificent;* and such useful aids as J. Matuz's *Herrscherurkunden des Osmanensultans Süleymans des Prächtigen. Ein chronologisches Verzeichnis.*

3. The victory of Lepanto, which was celebrated all over Europe as a turning point in its relations with the Ottoman Empire, may not have been as important in its immediate effects as it first appeared. The Turks not only rebuilt their navy in the following year but held on to their conquest of Cyprus, a conquest which Venice had to recognize in peace negotiations, conducted on the Turkish side, to some extent, as we recall, by Solomon Ashkenazi. Yet in the long run it did adumbrate the incipient decline of Ottoman power. See A. C. Hess, "The Battle of Lepanto and Its Place in Mediterranean History," *Past and Present*, no. 57, pp. 53–73 (also citing Sokolli's boast, p. 54); and *supra*, Vol. XIV, pp. 78 f., 335 n. 6. Needless to say, the works here quoted are merely samples of various studies, both comprehensive and monographic, largely produced by Western historians. Many more can readily be found in the various bibliographical aids mentioned *supra*, Chap. LXXV, n. 1.

4. See B. Lewis, "Studies in the Ottoman Archives, I," *BSOAS*, XVI, 469–501; idem, "The Ottoman Archives as a Source for the History of the Arab Lands," *JRAS*, 1951, pp. 139–55; idem, *Notes and Documents from the Turkish Archives: a Contribution to the History of the Jews in the Ottoman Empire* (reprinted from *Oriental Notes and Studies,* III), pp. 28–34, 44–45; S. J. Shaw, "Archival Sources for Ottoman History: the Archives of Turkey," *JAOS*, LXXX, 1–12; idem, "The Ottoman Archives as a Source for Egyptian History," *ibid.*, LXXXIII, 447–52; and L. Fekete, "Über Archivalien und Archivwesen in der Türkei," *AOH*, III, 179–205. With the study of the archives went the investigation of the style of the official documents and the underlying chancery practices. See, for example, J. Matuz, *Das Kanzleiwesen Sultan Süleymans des Prächtigen;* L. Fekete, *Einführung in die Osmanisch-Türkische Diplomatik der Türkischen Botmässigkeit in Ungarn;* and particularly the comprehensive study by J. Reychman and A. Zajączkowski, *Handbook of Ottoman-Turkish Diplomatics,* rev. and expanded by A. S. Ehrenkreuz, and ed. by T. Halasi-Kun, with the review thereof (also analyzing two other works on the same subject) by J. Matuz in his "Zur osmanischen Diplomatik," *OLZ*, LXX, 118–30. Clearly, manuscripts located in libraries are of equal value. One wished that other countries would follow the German example of cataloguing all Turkish manuscripts in their possession. See B. Flemming *et al.*, *Türkische Handschriften*, Vols. I–V, in *Verzeichnis der Orientalischen Handschriften in Deutschland*, XIII. Incidentally, this valuable listing also includes in series VI 3 volumes of *Hebräische Handschriften*, ed. by H. Striedel with the cooperation of E. Roth, published beginning in 1965.

Of the numerous collections of documents preserved in other lands, we need but mention the following few examples: J. Deny, *Sommaire des archives turques du Caire;* N. Todorov, "Les Documents osmano-turks de la Bibliothèque Nationale de Sofia en tant que source démographique," *Annales de démographie historique*, 1970, pp. 123–31 (mainly useful for more recent periods); B. A. Cvetkova and A. Razboynikov, eds., *Fontes Turcici historiae bulgaricae.* Reciprocally, documents from Western archives had proved to be a boon for Turkish and other historians of the Ottoman Empire. See, for example, T. Gökgilbin, "Documents from the Period of Suleyman the Magnificent in the Collections of the Venetian State Archive" (Turkish), *Belgerel*, I, 119–220; idem, "The Collection of Turkish Documents of the Venetian State Archive and Other Documents of Interest to Us" (Turkish), *ibid.*, VII–VIII, 1–151; A. von Gévay, *Urkunden und Aktenstücke zur Geschichte der Verhältnisse zwischen Österreich-Ungarn und der Pforte im XVI. und XVII. Jahrhundert;* B. G. Spiridonakis, *Empire Ottoman: Inventaire des Mémoires et Documents aux Archives de Ministère des Affaires Étrangères de France* (listing 7,513 documents). Of considerable interest also is Z. Abrahamowicz's attempt to list documents pertaining to the history of one country and its neighbors regardless of their provenance. See his *Katalog dokumentów tureckich* (A Catalogue of Turkish Documents Pertaining to the History of Poland and Its Neighboring Countries, 1455–1672). Of course, these examples can readily be multiplied.

5. Since few Jewish archival collections and publications therefrom have survived the storms of ages, they are truly useful in the main only for the nineteenth and twentieth centuries. For the older periods we must rely, therefore, to a very large extent on legal and literary works extant in manuscripts as well as in printed form. An example of how much information may be obtained from some of these sources for Jewish and general history of various Turkish provinces is offered in the publication by E. Eskenazi and A. Hananel, eds. of *Evreiski izvori* (Jewish Sources for the Social and Economic Development of the Balkan Lands during the Sixteenth and Seventeenth Centuries). Consisting of photographic reproductions of excerpts from printed responsa by R. Samuel de Medina and other Hebrew writers with a Bulgarian translation, this two-volume publication of the Bulgarian Academy has been highly praised by such specialists in general Balkan history as Bistra A. Cvetkova in her aforementioned essay in *Annales ESC*, XVIII, 1175. See also other literature listed in S. Israel's thoughtful review of "État actuel, problèmes et perspectives de l'historiographie judéo-balkanique," *Études balkaniques*, 1971, no. 2, pp. 120–134. Details of this type of documentation will become manifest in our forthcoming notes.

Long regretful over the persistent neglect by Jewish historians of the vast Hebrew homiletical literature as a source for the social history of Ottoman and other Jewries, I was delighted, while proofreading the present volume, to have received the lengthy essay by M. Benayahu, "The Sermons of R. Yosef b. Meir Garson as a Source for the History of the Expulsion from Spain and the Sephardic Diaspora" (Hebrew), *Michael*, VII, 42–205, based on the Gaster MS No. 762, now in the British Museum. See also *infra*, n. 33.

6. See R. Mantran, "Bagdad à l'époque ottomane," *Arabica*, IX, 311–24, esp. p. 316; Ö. L. Barkan, "Research on the Ottoman Fiscal Surveys," in M. A. Cook, ed., *Studies in the Economic History of the Middle East*, pp. 163–71, esp. p. 171 Table 4; J. B. Tavernier, *Les Six Voyages qu'il a fait en Turquie, en Perse et aux Indes*, Paris, 1881 ed., I, 237. Even if we assume that some of the figures given in the official Ottoman registers understated the size of the Jewish population (see *infra*, Chap. LXXVIII, n. 38), they offer us the best approximations. The paucity of extant documentation concerning the Jews of Iraq-Babylonia in the Late Middle Ages and early modern times is well illustrated by the careful analysis presented by A. Ben Jacob in his *Yehudei Babel* (A History of the Jews in Iraq. From the End of the Gaonic Period [1038 C.E.] to the Present Time); and the two monographs by D. S. Sassoon, *The History of the Jews of Baghdad*, esp. p. 101; and "The History of the Jews in Baṣra," *JQR*, XVII, 407–469. On Baghdad's Jewish population in the days of Benjamin, see Vol. III. pp. 276 f. n. 32. See also the supplementary early data furnished by Ben Jacob in his new volume,

Yehudei Babel ba-tekufot ha-aḥronot (Jews in Iraq in the Recent Periods), mainly dealing with the last two centuries. The Jews under the Safavid domination are treated *infra*, Chap. LXXIX.

After the Ottoman annexation of Iraq in 1534, the formerly intensive relationships between its Jewish communities and those of Palestine and the other centers of Jewish life in the eastern Mediterranean were greatly impeded by the difficulties of travel and correspondence. For example, after 1580 the Jewish traveler Zechariah b. Saadiah adh-Dhahri spent forty days on his journey from the Persian Gulf's commercial center of Harun to Basra, and another forty days from Basra to Baghdad, where, incidentally, he found and described the still existing large synagogue which had survived the community's vicissitudes in the preceding centuries. See Zechariah Adh-Dhahri's travelogue, cited in an English trans. from a Sassoon Library MS by D. S. Sassoon in his *A History of the Jew in Baghdad*, p. 101. It is now available in the ed. of Adh-Dhahri's *Sefer ha-Musar* (Book of Moral Conduct) by V. Ratzaby. See *supra*, Vol. XV, pp. 544 f. n. 111.

7. See H. A. R. Gibb and H. Bowen, *Islamic Society and the West. A Study of the Impact of Western Civilization on Moslem Culture in the Near East*. Vol. 1: Islamic Society in the Eighteenth Century, Part 2, pp. 207 ff., 217 f. Internationally, as well as domestically, the *pax turcica* secured for the inhabitants of the vast empire (except for the frontier areas), was of enduring significance. True, there was continued threat of a simultaneous attack from the West by the Christian powers and from the East by the Persian Shi'ites. Hence from the early fifteenth century on European statesmen tried to enlist the cooperation of Persia in fighting the Ottomans in a two-front war. See esp. V. F. Minorsky, *La Perse au XVᵉ siècle entre la Turquie et la Venise;* B. von Palombini, *Bündniswerben abendländischer Mächte um Persien 1453–1600* (Diss. Freiburg i. B.); and *infra,* Chap. LXXIX, n. 23. Internally, too, the presence of a militarily strong Shi'ite monarchy in the proximity of Anatolia, the center of Turkish power, increased the ever-present menace of civil strife. Especially the agitation of numerous itinerant dervishes, often animated by utopian and antisocial ideals, became a perennial source of subversion which threatened, especially after the rise of the Safavid dynasty, the preservation of the existing order. See H. Sohrweide, "Der Sieg der Ṣafawiden in Persien und seine Rückwirkung auf die Schi'iten Anatoliens im 16. Jahrhundert," *Der Islam*, XLI, 95–223, esp. pp. 164 ff., 183 ff.

8. Selim's conquests and their praise by contemporaries are described by A. C. Hess in "The Evolution of the Ottoman Seaborne Empire in the Age of the Oceanic Discoveries, 1450–1525," *AHR*, LXXV, 1892–1919. According to H. A. R. Gibb, "Luṭfi Paşa on the Ottoman Caliphate," *Oriens*, XV, 287–95, the Turkish statesman eloquently controverted 'Umar an-Nasafi's original assertion that "the Imam is of Quraiṣ, and may not be of other than Quraiṣ," and insisted that Suleiman was in fact "the lieutenant of the Apostle [Mohammed] maintaining the Faith in the requisite manner over all the peoples subject to him." See also N. Ahmet Asrar, "The Myth about the Transfer of the Caliphate to the Ottomans," *Journal of Regional Cultural History*, V, 111–20.

9. See A. Ballagi, *Buda és Pest a vilagirodalomban* (Buda and Pest; a bibliography), I, 162 ff.; and other sources cited in F. Grünvald and S. (A.) Scheiber, comps., *Magyar-Zsido Oklevéltár* (Monumenta Hungariae Judaica), V, Part 1, 162 ff. Nos. 330 ff., esp. No. 333; Joseph b. Joshua ha-Kohen, *Dibre ha-Yamim le-malkhe Ṣarefat u-malkhe bet Ottoman*, fol. 76a; N. Katzburg, "Contributions to the History of the Jews in Hungary

in the Period of Ottoman Domination" (Hebrew), *Sinai*, XVI, nos. 189–94, pp. 339–52; nos. 195–200, pp. 78–82. See also J. von Hammer-Purgstall, *Geschichte des osmanischen Reiches*, III, 62 ff.; *MHH*, II, 3, 26; Sultan 'Abd al-'Aziz' decree of July 25, 1865 in A. Galanté's French trans. in his compilation of *Documents officiels concernant les Juifs de Turquie*, pp. 166 ff.; and, more generally, J. Bergl's old and rather too superficial survey, *Geschichte der ungarischen Juden. Nach den besten Quellen bearbeitet*, esp. pp. 58 f.

10. See G. Fehér, Jr., "Recent Data of the Turkish Campaign of 1543," *Studia turcica*, ed. by L. Ligeti, pp. 161–68. On the intended deportation of Jews from Safed to Cyprus, see *infra*, n. 76; Chap. LXXVII, n. 41.

Of special interest also are the transfers effected after the conquest of Buda. The number of 2,500 Jewish deportees is borne out by the Turkish sources quoted by Hammer, although the Jewish historian David b. Solomon Gans merely indicates that Suleiman did no harm to the Buda Jews. See his *Sefer Ṣemaḥ David* (The Scion of David; a World Chronicle), Prague, 1592 ed., fols. 102b f., 104b f., 110b f.; Frankfort, 1692 ed., fols. 68b f., 70, 74a. This historian, writing in Prague some years after the event, probably wished to intimate that this "deportation" was largely accomplished with the consent of the deportees. Nevertheless, some Jews undoubtedly remained behind and established active commercial relations with their coreligionists and others in the rest of the Empire. Similarly, Jews from Salonica and other cities frequently visited Buda on business. These mutual visits offered some unfriendly Hungarian observers an opportunity to accuse the Jews of helping the Turkish intelligence service. For example, in his report to the government Szerémi György wrote: "Turkish Jews have been coming here to the Buda Jews and what they heard from them or else learned here, they quickly brought back to Constantinople and in their jargon faithfully informed the Sultan. They also imported manifold wares from Turkey, causing some Hungarian simpletons to wonder how such goods could have arrived." *MHH*, I, 1, 49. Without being an explicit accusation of spying, Szerémi's assertion bore overtones to that effect. He must also have realized that on that date the Jews of Buda had already been for some time subjects of the sultan and thus were obliged to reveal to him whatever he might have wished to know.

Remarkably, even the Hungarians and the German Szeklers residing in Transylvania, which was a semi-independent state under Turkish overlordship, were expected by the Ottomans to assist them in their military expeditions against the Habsburg-dominated western part of Hungary—an expectation which the vassal Transylvanian King John Zapolya could not deny but merely sought to evade by delaying its implementation. See I. Matei, "Quelques problèmes concernant le régime de la domination ottomane dans les pays roumains (concernant particulièrement la Valachie)," *RESEE*, X, 65–81, esp. p. 72. See also A. Scheiber, "Jüdische Grabsteine in Ofen zur Türkenzeit," *Acta Orientalia Hungarica*, XXV, 465–74, esp. p. 472; further details to be culled from L. Fekete, "The Commerce of the City of Buda in the Second Half of the Sixteenth Century under Turkish Domination," *Fontes Orientales*, ed. by A. S. Tveritinova, I, 91–118; idem and G. Káldy-Nagy, *Rechnungsbücher Türkischer Finanzstellen in Buda (Ofen) 1550–1580; Türkischer Text*; E. Vass, "Eléments pour completer l'histoire de l'administration des finances du vilayet de Buda au XVIe siècle," *Studia turcica*, ed. by L. Ligeti, 1971, pp. 483–90; and, more generally, W. Björkman, *Ofen zur Türkenzeit*; A. Lefaivre, *Les Magyars pendant la domination ottomane en Hongrie, 1526–1722*; G. Müller, *Die Türkenherrschaft in Siebenbürgen. Verfassungsrechtliches Verhältniss Siebenbürgens zu der Pforte, 1541–1688*.

11. See Don Isaac b. Yehudah Abravanel, *Ma'ayene ha-Yeshu'ah* (Springs of Salvation, on the Book of Daniel; a messianic tract), Intro.; *supra*, Vols. XI, pp. 213 ff., 406 f. nn. 64 and 68; XIII, pp. 115 ff.; XVII, pp. 20 f., 309 n. 22; S. A. Rosanes, *Dibre yeme Yisrael*, I, 119 n. 7. The pioneering computation of the 1471 data by this meritorious historian of Ottoman Jewry, though leaving some open questions, gives us a fair approximation of reality. This and other related demographic problems will be more fully discussed *infra*, Chapter LXXVIII.

12. See Samuel b. Moses de Medina, *She'elot u-teshubot* or *Pesaqim* (Responsa; organized in the order of Jacob b. Asher's *Ṭurim* and Joseph Karo's *Shulḥan 'Arukh*), H.M. No. 124; Meshullam da Volterra, *Massa'*, pp. 71 f. (emphasizing the presence of a Jewish minority of 250 against 10,000 Muslim families. The resulting figure of some 50,000 Muslim inhabitants is very likely exaggerated); Obadiah Bertinoro's *Iggeret* in A. Yaari's *Iggerot Ereṣ Yisrael*, pp. 127 f.; Moses Bassola, *Massa'ot Ereṣ Yisrael* (A Pilgrimage to Palestine), ed. by I. Ben-Zevi, pp. 61 f. (finding in 1552 in Jerusalem not only 300 Jewish families but also more than 500 widows "who make a comfortable living because they pay no taxes or other imposts, and whose property, if heirless, is subsequently inherited by the community").

Of the plethora of monographic studies concerning Ottoman Palestine published in fairly recent years we need but mention the following: E. Ashtor, "Jerusalem in the Late Middle Ages" (Hebrew), *Yerushalayim, Review for Eretz-Israel Research*, II-V, 71-116; B. Lewis, "Jaffa in the 16th Century, according to the Ottoman Tahrir Registers," *Necati Legal Armağani*, pp. 435–46; his "Nazareth in the Sixteenth Century, according to the Ottoman Tapu Registers," *Arabic and Islamic Studies in Honor of Hamilton A. R. Gibb*, ed. by G. (J.) al-Makdisi, pp. 416–25, esp. p. 421; his "The Population and Tax Revenue of Ereṣ Yisrael in the Sixteenth Century according to Turkish Documents" (Hebrew), *Yerushalayim, Review*, I, 133–37; his "Cities in Ereṣ-Yisrael in the XVIth Century c.e. according to Documents from Ottoman Archives, I: Jerusalem" (Hebrew), *ibid.*, II-V, 117–27; U. Heyd, "Turkish Documents from Ottoman Archives Concerning Safed Jews in the Sixteenth Century c.e." (Hebrew), *ibid.*, II-V, 128–35; idem, "The Jews of Ereṣ Yisrael in the Late Seventeenth Century according to the Turkish Registers of the Poll Tax" (Hebrew), *ibid.*, I, 173–84; idem, *Ottoman Documents on Palestine 1552–1615: a Study of the Firmans according to the Mühimme Defteri;* several pertinent essays included in J. Braslavski's *Le-Ḥeqer Arṣenu* (Contributions to the Study of Our Country: Its Past and Monuments); and in I. Ben-Zvi's *Kitbe* (Collected Writings). See also the comprehensive works by him, *Eretz-Yisrael ve-Yishuvah bime ha-shilṭon ha-'ottomani* (Eretz-Yisrael under Ottoman Rule: Four Centuries of History), esp. pp. 141 ff.; and by A. Cohen and B. Lewis, *Population and Revenue in the Towns of Palestine in the Sixteenth Century.*

Of considerable interest also is M. Ish-Shalom's *Massa'ei Noṣrim le-Ereṣ-Yisrael* (Christian Travels in the Holy Land: Descriptions and Sources on the History of the Jews in Palestine), esp. pp. 279 ff. The enormous older literature is easily ascertainable from the seven volumes of P. Thomsen's *Die Palästina-Literatur. Eine Internationale Bibliographie in systematischer Ordnung mit Autoren und Sachregister* (covering publications up to the year 1945); and S. A. Udin, ed., *Palestine and Zionism: an Author and Subject Index to Books, Pamphlets and Periodicals* (for the years 1946–53). On Baghdad, see Pedro Teixeira, *The Travels* (1604), pp. 65 ff.; Jean Baptiste Tavernier, *Les Six Voyages*, I, 1676 ed., or in the English trans. by V. Bell entitled *Travels to India*, with a Biographical Sketch of the author, Notes and Appendices; 2d ed. by W. Crooke; and *supra*, n. 6. See also, more generally, A. Ben Jacob, *Yehudei Babel*, esp. p. 86.

13. Bab. Talmud, Yebamot 13b reinterpreting Deut. 14:1; Joseph b. David Ibn Leb, *Resp.*, new ed. (Amsterdam, 1726), together with his *Ḥiddushim* (Novellae), II, fol. 32b No. 72; Samuel de Medina, *Resp.* Y.D., fol. 10cd No. 139; and other sources summarized by I. S. Emmanuel in his *Histoire des Israélites de Salonique*, I, 144 ff. Even a special communal ordinance, signed by the Salonican rabbis in 1525 and threatening violators with excommunication, proved ineffectual. It read in part: "No individual or group, has the right to register in another synagogue [*Mahallah*] . . . ; nor is a synagogue, large or small, entitled to divide itself in order to found another congregation and thus increase the number of synagogues already existing in this city [Salonica]." Quoted by Isaac b. Samuel Adarbi in his *Sefer Dibre ribot* (Controversial Matters; responsa), Salonica, 1582 ed., No. 59.

14. R. Samuel de Medina's *Resp.*, Ḥ.M. fol. 75ab No. 507; Rashi, Commentary on the aforementioned passage (*supra*, n. 13) in Yebamot 13b *s.v. Lo ta'asu agudot;* A. Lutzky, "The 'Francos' and the Effect of the Capitulations on the Jews in Aleppo (from 1673 till the time of the French Revolution)" (Hebrew), *Zion*, VI, 46–72; A. J. Brawer, "Jewish Enjoyment of the Privileges of the Capitulations in Palestine" (Hebrew), *ibid.*, V, 161–69.

15. See F. (Y.) Baer, *Die Juden im christlichen Spanien*, Part I: *Urkunden und Regesten*, I, 216 ff. No. 175, esp. p. 220; II, 263 ff. No. 275, esp. p. 268; other passages listed *ibid.*, *s.v.* Freizügigkeit (I, 1163; II, 589). On the operation of *ḥezqat* or *ḥerem ha-yishub* see *supra*, Vols. IV, pp. 71, 330 f. n. 45; V, pp. 68 f.; my *JC*, I, 348 f.; and the studies listed *ibid.*, III, 98 ff. nn. 2 and 4, especially those by L. I. Rabinowitz, "The Talmudic Basis of the *Ḥerem ha-yishub*," *JQR*, XXVIII, 217–23; "The Medieval Jewish Counterpart to the Gild Merchant," *Economic History Review*, VIII, 180–85; and his comprehensive study on *The Ḥerem Ha-yishub; a Contribution to the Medieval Economic History of the Jews*.

16. See R. Samuel de Medina's aforementioned *Resp.*, Ḥ.M. fol. 75ab No. 407, here quoted from the English trans. by M. S. Goodblatt in *Jewish Life in Turkey in the XVIth Century as Reflected in the Legal Writing of Samuel de Medina*, pp. 187 f. App. 18. This highly important aspect of Jewish communal self-government and its variations in different countries and periods will be more fully clarified in the next volume.

17. See E. Rivlin and Y. Y. Rivlin, "Contribution to the History of the Jews in Damascus in the Fourth Century of the Sixth Millennium [1541–1640]," (Hebrew), *Reshumot*, IV, 77–119, esp. pp. 88 ff.; Moses B. Ḥayyim Alshekh, *Sefer Torat Mosheh* (The Law of Moses; homilies on the Pentateuch), Venice, 1601 or Amsterdam, 1710, No. 59. "On the Power Struggle in the Jewish Community of Patras in the Sixteenth Century," see the pertinent Hebrew article by L. Bornstein-Makovetski in *Michael*, VII, 3–41.

18. See Benjamin b. Mattathiah, *Sefer Binyamin Ze'ev* (Responsa), Venice, 1539 ed. No. 203; Isaac b. Sheshet Perfet, *Resp.*, No. 11; Joseph b. Solomon Ṭaiṭaṣaq and R. Ṣemaḥ Gaon quoted by Samuel de Medina in *Resp.*, Ḥ.M. fols. 47d f. No. 327; E.'E. fols. 55d f. No. 112; and other sources cited by M. S. Goodblatt in *Jewish Life in Turkey*, esp. pp. 111 ff., 213 f.

19. See *Sefer Ḥayyat qaneh* (A Story of His Visions) attributed to Solomon Molkho, and ed. by Abraham b. Joseph Rothenburg, Amsterdam, 1648, and again by A. Z.

Aescoly, in 1938 (it is quoted at length in H. Graetz's *Geschichte der Juden*, 4th ed., IX, 522 App. V); and on Molkho's involvement in David Reubeni's diplomatic adventure, the *Sippur David Reubeni* (Reubeni's Story), ed. by A. Z. Aescoly, pp. 27–64, 140–83; and *supra*, Vol. XIII, pp. 109 ff., 364 f. nn. 53 ff. Molkho's role in the Jewish messianic movements will be discussed here in a later volume. The conflicting decisions in Pisa and Leghorn are cited by S. Assaf in "The Spanish and Portuguese Marranos in the Responsa Literature" (Hebrew), *Zion*, V, 19–60, reprinted in his *Be-Ohole Ya'aqob* (In the Tents of Jacob: Chapters in the Cultural Life of the Jews in the Middle Ages), pp. 145–80, esp. p. 152. On the varying attitudes of the Jewish communal leaders to Marrano arrivals, see Joseph Ibn Leb, *Resp.*, II, fols. 13bc No. 23, 31d f. No. 72; or Samuel de Medina, *Resp.*, H.M. fol. 74ab No. 402; and, more generally, C. Roth, *A History of the Marranos*, esp. pp. 199 f.; idem, "The Religion of the Marranos," *JQR*, XXII, 1–33; H. J. Zimmels, *Die Marranen in der rabbinischen Literatur: Forschungen und Quellen zur Geschichte und Kulturgeschichte der Anussim;* B. Netanyahu, *The Marranos of Spain from the Late XIVth to the Early XVIth Century, According to Contemporary Hebrew Sources*, 2d ed., rev. and enlarged. See also *supra*, Vol. XIII, pp. 143 ff., 384 ff. nn. 86–97.

20. See Samuel de Medina's *Resp.*, E.'E. fol. 95ab No. 110; Joseph Taitasaq's statement quoted *supra*, n. 16. See also I. S. Emmanuel, *Histoire des Israélites de Salonique*, p. 135; J. Nehama, *Histoire des Israélites de Salonique*, esp. II, 82. Despite these differences of opinion, however, in an emergency the community as a whole acted in favor of the Marranos. For example, when in 1550 Venice decided to expel its New Christians, and some 40 families were forced to leave the Republic immediately, the Salonican elders invited them to come to their community. "Come here on a trial basis," they wrote, "if you will be pleased to stay with us and you will find that your affairs will succeed here, you may remain. Otherwise you may depart without owing us any taxes for the entire period of your experimentation." Nehama, III, 39; and, more generally, D. Kaufmann, "Die Vertreibung der Marranen aus Venedig im Jahre 1550," *JQR*, [o.s.] XIII, 520–32; and C. Roth, "Les Marranes à Venise," *REJ*, LXXXIX, 201–223.

21. See S. A. Rosanes, *Dibre yeme Yisrael*, I, 173 f.; the enactment of 1568 published by A. Danon in "La Communauté juive de Salonique au XVIe siècle," *REJ*, XL, 206–230; XLI, 98–117, 250–65, esp. pp. 256 f. No. 16; the Fez ordinances, reproduced in Abraham b. Mordecai, ed., *Sefer Kerem hemer* (A Vineyard of Foaming Wine; a collection of halakhic texts), II, 2 ff.; A. I. Laredo, "Las Taqanot de los expulsados de Castilla en Marruecos y su regimen," *Sefarad*, VIII, 245–76; and *JC*, III, 46 f. n. 36. See also, more generally, A. H. Freimann, *Seder qiddushin ve-nissuin* (The Order of Betrothals and Marriages since the Completion of the Talmud); and L. M. Epstein, *Marriage Laws in the Bible and Talmud, passim.*

22. See Mishnah Qiddushin, II, 6; Bab. 50b; Rashi's Commentary thereon *s.v.* Hosheshim; Joseph Ibn Leb, *Resp.*, I, fols. 9 f. No. 17; II, fol. 22bc No. 43; Elijah b. Abraham Mizrahi, *Teshubot She'elot* (Responsa), Constantinople, 1560 ed., reprinted Jerusalem, 1946, fols. 49a ff. Nos. 18–19.

23. See *supra*, n. 22; R. Samuel de Medina, *Resp.* E.'E. fols. 7d ff. Nos. 14–15; Tam [or Jacob] b. Yahya, *Tummat yesharim* (Simplicity of the Righteous; a collection of rabbinic texts), Venice, 1622; S. A. Rosanes, *Dibre yeme Yisrael*, I, *passim;* Joseph Karo and Moses Isserles, *Shulhan 'Arukh*, E.'E. cxxxiv, with E. G. Alinson's comments thereon in

his "Refusal to Give a Writ of Divorce" (Hebrew), *Sinai*, XXXV, nos. 417–18, pp. 134–58. The rabbis were particularly indulgent with husbands whose wives remained barren for ten years or more and who ardently wished to fulfill the commandment of procreation. A levir, too, who, though married, wished to marry his widowed sister-in-law, rather than give her the prescribed *ḥaliṣah* in a mutually repulsive ceremony, was occasionally allowed to do so. R. Isaac b. Samuel Adarbi cited to this effect a series of distinguished medieval jurists down to R. Elijah Mizraḥi who taught that "the commandment of levirate marriage has precedence over that of *ḥaliṣah*, and one does not force a levir to perform the *ḥaliṣah*." See Adarbi's *Dibre ribot*, fol. 17b No. 13; and other sources, cited by M. S. Goodblatt in his *Jewish Life in Turkey*, p. 210 n. 40; and H. J. Zimmels, *Ashkenazim and Sephardim*, pp. 166 ff., 333 ff. Adarbi actually claimed that such unions occurred "from day to day" in Salonica with no one objecting. According to R. Samuel de Medina, even two German Jews whose wives had deserted them had secured licenses to remarry. See his *Resp.*, E.'E., fol. 58cd No. 120. See also an interesting betrothal contract written in Sofia in 1582, reproduced by Goodblatt, p. 208 n. 15; and, more generally, L. M. Epstein, *The Jewish Marriage Contract; a Study in the Status of Woman in Jewish Law*.

24. See E. and Y. Y. Rivlin, "Contribution . . . Jews in Damascus" (Hebrew), *Reshumot*, IV, pp. 84 ff.; Israel of Perugia, "Two Epistles (1517–23)" (Hebrew), reproduced in A. Yaari, ed., *Iggerot Ereṣ-Yisrael*, pp. 166–78, esp. p. 170; *supra*, n. 17. It is quite possible that in Syria Jews could secure from the local Turkish officials (usually with the aid of douceurs) more effective protection, or retribution for crimes committed against them, than in the other Turkish provinces. It is known that, although they were fellow Muslims and the chief heirs of the venerable Islamic traditions, the Arabs were generally held in contempt by the Turkish bureaucracy. See G. W. F. Stripling, *The Ottoman Turks and the Arabs, 1511–1574*, esp. pp. 102 ff.

25. See Joseph b. Ephraim Karo, *Sefer Bet Yosef* (House of Joseph; a Commentary on Jacob b. Asher's *Ṭurim*), Y.D. No. 39; R. Samuel de Medina, *Resp.*, Ḥ.M., fol. 30bd No. 281; R. David b. Ḥayyim ha-Kohen, *Teshubot* (Responsa), Constantinople, 1538, No. 91; R. Joseph Ibn Leb, *Resp.*, I, fol. 44bd No. 77. The waiting period of three years after the departure of the original Jewish tenant naturally created a great hardship for the landlord and, in some respect, also for new settlers or newlyweds in search of dwellings. What probably happened in practice was that a would-be new resident paid some compensation (today often called "key-money" in Israel) to the old inhabitant for his "right" (*ḥazzaqah*) and was allowed to move in during that vacancy. This restriction seems to have been a necessary safeguard against any landlord's possible chicaneries to force an existing tenant out in favor of a higher bidder. See also *infra*, n. 26.

26. R. Samuel de Medina, *Resp.*, Ḥ.M. No. 296; Y.D. No. 117; R. David Ibn abi Zimra, *Resp.*, II, 644. The various ordinances enacted by the Salonica congregations, jointly or separately, over the years have been the subject of intensive study by S. A. Rosanes, J. Nehama, and I. S. Emmanuel in their respective histories. See also the brief survey by M. Molho, "The Ordinance Concerning the Acquired Rights in Houses, Courtyards, and Shops in Salonica" (Hebrew), *Sinai*, XIV, nos. 165–70, pp. 296–314. On the contrast with the last stages of Byzantine rule, see M. Molho's brief sketch, "The Salonican Community in the Early Generations," *ibid.*, XIV, nos. 159–64, pp. 89–103.

27. R. Isaac Adarbi, *Dibre ribot*, fols. 29d ff. Nos. 56, 59; S. A. Rosanes, *Dibre yeme (Qorot)*, II, 61; and the compact of the seven congregations analyzed by I. S. Emmanuel in his *Histoire*, I, 167 f. An interesting inquiry addressed to R. Samuel de Medina raised the question of a new resident who, after living in his new locality for twelve months, contributed to all charitable and communal funds on a par with the other residents. However, his former compatriots continued to bill him for his part in their imposts, claiming that in communal taxes a person's intention was the decisive factor. Since he had left his previous residence under some unspecified non-Jewish military pressure and really intended to return to their city, they insisted that he ought to contribute his share to the continued operations of their community. This contention was not completely devoid of merit, because in rabbinic law the subjective will to own a certain property has been considered an integral part of that ownership. See the analysis of the rabbinic doctrine of private ownership in my "Economic Views of Maimonides" in *Essays on Maimonides*, ed. by me, pp. 145 ff., reprinted in my *Ancient and Medieval Jewish History*, pp. 159 ff., 453 ff. nn. 40 ff. Nevertheless R. Samuel rejected that reasoning. He pointed out that the general rabbinic rule that a temporary resident must observe the more stringent ritualistic requirements of both localities did not apply to civil transactions. The rabbi even denied the former community's demand that the contributor in question deny under oath that he intended to return to his earlier residence. See De Medina's *Resp.*, H.M. fol. 62cd No. 369, rendered into English by M. S. Goodblatt in his *Jewish Life in Turkey*, pp. 182 ff. App. 17.

28. Rosanes, *Dibre yeme*, II, 241–78, App. ii; R. J. Z. Werblowsky, *Joseph Karo, Lawyer and Mystic*. On similar changes of residence among Muslim scholars, see S. Faroghi (Faroqhi), "Social Mobility among the Ottoman 'Ulemâ in the Late Sixteenth Century," *IJMES*, IV, 204–218; and, more broadly, the essays ed. by G. Baer, in *The 'Ulema' in Modern History and Problems of Religion in the Muslim World*.

29. See Tam ibn Yahya, *Ohole Tam* (Tam's Tents; Resp. and Notes on Alfasi), Nos. 103, 194; Rosanes, *Dibre yeme (Qorot)*, II, 74. Curiously non-Jewish historiography seems not to have referred to any such outbreaks against the Jews of Nicopolis or to the Salonican delegation sent to the Porte. However, dealing with a predominantly Greek and Slavonic population, long accustomed to blaming Jews for allegedly usurious transactions, while being prone to overlook similar acts by their own or by Armenian or Turkish moneylenders, makes these reports from Jewish sources quite credible.

30. On the Blood Accusations in the Ottoman Empire, see Joseph ha-Kohen, *'Emeq ha-bakha*, pp. 105 f.; and more broadly, U. Heyd's careful analysis of three official documents, especially No. 3, dated in 1603, in his "Ritual Murder Accusations in 15th and 16th Century Turkey" (Hebrew), *Sefunot*, V (*Isaiah Sonne Mem. Vol.*), 135–50, with an English summary, pp. 7 f. Although not completely unexpected, the appearance of the ritual murder accusation in Amasia in Turkey's Anatolian heartland (probably in 1553) and its initiation not by Greeks but by Armenians is of some significance. The encyclicals of the Greek Orthodox patriarchs Anthimos, Joachim, and Constantin, issued in the years 1873–98, are reproduced in the Greek originals and a French translation in A. Galanté's *Documents officiels turcs*, pp. 223 ff. The contrast between these guarded utterances and the outspoken repudiations of the Blood Accusation by a number of Roman popes may easily be gleaned from M. Stern's anonymous publication of *Die Päpstlichen Bullen über die Blutbeschuldigung*. Only a few strongly anti-

Jewish popes, such as Paul IV, intimated any kind of acceptance of the ritual murder myth. See esp. the brief survey, *supra*, Vol. XI, pp. 146 ff., 358 ff. nn. 31 ff.

31. See S. A. Rosanes, *Dibre yeme* (*Qorot*), II, 74 f., 173 ff. App. ii. The author reproduces here the brief matter-of-fact account by Joseph ha-Kohen in his *Dibre ha-Yamim le-Malkhe Ṣarefat*, II, as well as the more picturesque descriptions by Joseph Sambari in his chronicle *Dibre Yosef*, I, 147 f. (from a Paris MS); and by an unknown author of a modern Adrianople manuscript. Both Sambari and the Adrianople anonym describe Ibrahim Pasha's downfall in a legendary form and in a style imitative of the Book of Esther.

32. See the two major studies by H. Gross, "La Famille juive des Hamon. Contribution à l'histoire des Juifs en Turquie," *REJ*, LVI, 1–26; LVII, 55–78 (chiefly based upon rabbinic sources which understandably offer data mainly on the role played by the Hamons in Jewish communal affairs); and by U. Heyd, "Moses Hamon, Chief Jewish Physician to Sultan Süleymān the Magnifixent," *Oriens*, XVI, 152–70 (with valuable information derived from official Turkish registers preserved in the Istanbul archives). We do not hear much about the international ramifications of the influence of the Hamon medical family in Istanbul. Apart from whatever assistance Moses may have extended to Gracia Mendes in her effort to reach the Ottoman Empire (see below), he probably played some role in promoting the peace treaty concluded by Venice with the sultan after their two-year war in 1540. At least we learn from a contemporary record that he and his son Joseph were beneficiaries of 1,000 and 500 ducats, respectively, in gifts donated by the *Signoria* to the sultan's court personnel. On that peace treaty see T. F. Jones, "The Turco-Venetian Treaty of 1540," *AHA Annual Report for 1914*, I, 159–67; W. Lehmann's Bonn diss. *Der Friedensvertrag zwischen Venedig und der Türkei vom 2. Oktober 1540. Nach dem türkischen Original herausgegeben und erläutert.*

33. The rumor about Joseph Hamon's role in the poisoning of Bayezid II is mentioned by Giovanni Sagredo in his *Memorie istoriche de monarchi ottomani*, Venice, 1673, and in later eds.; while Joseph b. Meir Garson's address is included in his *Porat Yosef* (Joseph's Winepress; homilies), quoted from a Gaster manuscript (now in the British Museum) by H. Gross in "La Famille juive des Hamon," *REJ*, LVI, 8 ff.; and by H. H. Ben Sasson in "The Generation of the Spanish Exiles" (Hebrew), *Zion*, XXVI, 27 f. n. 21, also emphasizing that Joseph Hamon the Elder had "stood in the breach to save Jews from great dangers." Nor do any Turkish sources seem to connect Joseph with the assassination of the then reigning sultan. See U. Heyd's comments in *Oriens*, XVI, 155 f. On Garson's sermons, see also *supra*, n. 5.

34. See *supra*, Vol. VIII, pp. 245 f., 396 n. 32; F. Babinger, ed., *Hans Dernschwam's Tagebuch*, p. 113; Nicolas de Nicolay, *Navigations et pérégrinations et voyages faites en Turquie*, Antwerp, 1556, pp. 259 f.; and other data analyzed in the essays cited *supra*, n. 33. See also A. Terzieglu, "Eine bisher unbekannte türkische Abhandlung über die Zahnheilkunde des Moses Hamon aus dem Anfang des 16. Jahrhunderts," *Sudhof's Archiv-Zeitschrift für Wissenschaftsgeschichte*, LVIII, 276–82. It appears that Moses Hamon was not the only Turkish Jewish medical author of the time. See, for example, U. Heyd, "An Unknown Turkish Treatise by a Jewish Physician under Süleymān the Magnificent," *Eretz Israel*, VII (1964—*L. A. Mayer Mem. Vol.*), 48[+]–53[+], suggesting that the writer may have been identical with Don Manuel Brudo, called Brudus Lusitanus. See the biographical data assembled by H. Friedenwald, *The Jews and Medicine, Essays,*

pp. 460–67; and C. Roth, "The Middle Period of Anglo-Jewish History (1290–1655) Reconsidered," *TJHSE*, XIX, 1–12, esp. pp. 4 ff. On other Jewish doctors active in the Ottoman Empire see the brief biographical summaries in A. Galanté's essay, *Médecins juifs au service de la Turquie;* and, more generally, in S. Krauss's *Geschichte der jüdischen Ärzte.*

35. Samuel Usque, *Consolaçam as Tribulaçoens de Ysrael,* ii. 37 in M. A. Cohen's English trans. *Consolation for the Tribulations of Israel,* pp. 37, 230. Gracia's activities are here described at considerable length; they are considered the sixth of eight "Consolations" which, according to the author, God had prepared for his anguished people after the numerous persecutions and "tribulations" from which it had suffered, as described earlier in his volume. The impact of this book on Marranos in the dispersion was immediate. See, for example, the attitude of the members of the burgeoning Marrano community of London, cited *supra*, Vol. XV, pp. 126, 432 n. 62. A similarly glowing dedication was offered to Gracia by the publishers of the remarkable "Ferrara Bible." This Spanish translation was issued in two editions, one aimed at the Christian public and another for use by Jews whose earlier Spanish version underlay the new edition. See the citation of that dedication by C. Roth in *The House of Nasi: Doña Gracia,* p. 74.

The rumor about Moses Hamon's expectation that his son would marry the heiress Reyna, Gracia's daughter, was reported in a dispatch by the French ambassador to Venice De Morvilliers, cited *ibid.,* p. 58 from E. Charrière, *Négociations de la France dans le Levant, ou Correspondances, Mémoires et Actes diplomatiques* (in the *Collection de documents inédits sur l'histoire de France*), I, 101 n. 1 (July 1549). This report, based upon gossip current in Venice, is not likely to be true. Not only did Joseph Hamon fail to marry Reyna when she arrived in Istanbul a few years later, but Doña Gracia, who had rejected a number of marriage offers for her daughter from high Christian aristocrats (we recall her firm resistance to pressures exercised on her by Queen Maria of the Netherlands in behalf of a scion of the House of Aragon; *supra*, Vol. XIII, pp. 123, 371 f. n. 67), must have had in mind the union between her nephew João Miguez and her daughter long before she could realize that plan after his arrival in Istanbul in 1553. Undoubtedly, their determination to hold the fortune of the House of Mendes together, and to administer it with the aid of that nephew, received priority over all other concerns for both mother and daughter. Moreover, Moses Hamon who, like his ancestors, had always professed Judaism in public (he was a young child when his father reached Turkey in 1493, one year after the fall of Granada and the issuance of the decree of expulsion) may have had some compunctions about admitting to their orthodox family circle a young woman who had grown up as a New Christian and had had few opportunities to acquire any familiarity with the numerous Jewish religious observances. On the growing tensions between the older professing Jews and the former Marranos, see the data supplied by H. H. Ben Sasson in "The Generation," *Zion*, XXVI, 34 ff.; and *supra*, n. 18.

36. The dramatic story of the Mendes family's sojourn in Venice and Ferrara; the repeatedly impending threat of the confiscation of its entire fortune by the Venetian or French authorities; the alleged romantic interlude of João's abduction of Brianda's daughter Beatrice *la chica,* and the Venetian price set on his head have all been graphically narrated by P. Grunebaum-Ballin after noteworthy, assiduous research in Venetian and other archives. See his *Joseph Naci duc de Naxos,* pp. 45 ff. Additional details may be gleaned from C. Roth, *Doña Gracia,* Chaps. III and IV; and particularly from C. H. Rose's "New Information on the Life of Joseph Nasi Duke of Naxos: the

Venetian Phase," *JQR*, LX, 330–44. See also the extensive older literature on Don Joseph Nasi quoted in the forthcoming notes.

37. See *supra*, Vol. XIV, pp. 32 ff., 317 ff. nn. 30 ff.; Joshua Soncino's *Naḥlah li-Yehoshu'a* (Joshua's Heritage; responsa), Constantinople, 1731, Nos. 12 and 39. Ironically, despite the persistent papal efforts to undermine the growing commercial exchanges between Christian Europe and the Ottoman Empire and thus help to stem the Empire's rapid expansion, Ancona's share in the trade with the Turkish Levant proved economically and fiscally quite beneficial to the States of the Church themselves from the Late Middle Ages on. See E. Ashtor, "Il Commercio levantino di Ancona nel basso medioevo," *Rivista storica italiana*, LXXXVIII, 213–53, pointing out that even the fall of Constantinople in 1453 caused no more than a temporary diminution of these commercial exchanges (pp. 235 ff.).

38. The story of these conflicts is well reflected in a number of rabbinic responsa. There, according to an old usage, the names of the parties are given under the accepted pseudonyms of the sons or wives of Patriarch Jacob: Reuben, Simon, Leah, and so forth, akin to the English usage of John and Jane Doe. However, students of the much-discussed Mendes family, beginning in 1839 with M. A. Levy (in his *Don Joseph Nasi, Herzog von Naxos, seine Familie und zwei jüdische Diplomaten seiner Zeit. Eine Biographie nach neuen Quellen dargestelt*, esp. pp. 18, 50 n. 62), long ago detected the true names of the persons who were the principals in these controversies. See esp. the responsa by R. Joshua Soncino in his *Naḥlah li-Yehoshu'a*, Nos. 12, 20, 39. (These responsa are written in an elegant Hebrew style current in contemporary Renaissance Hebrew letters; R. Joshua himself once expressed regret that a great German scholar like R. Moses Menz was unable to dress his deep and erudite thoughts in a proper Hebrew garb.) See also R. Samuel de Medina's *Resp.* on Ḥ.M. Nos. 327 ff.; R. Joseph Ibn Leb's *Resp.*, II, No. 23; and R. Joseph Karo's *Abqat Rokhel* (A Peddler's Spice-Box; Responsa), Nos. 80–81, all summarized by J. H. Zimmels in *Die Marranen in der rabbinischen Literatur*, pp. 107 ff., 129 ff.; and in S. Assaf's essay in *Be-Ohole Ya'aqob*, pp. 172 ff. Ibn Leb asserted that "such matters were submitted to me many times in Salonica and I have decided in the same vein. Nor have I ever heard or seen anyone expressing an opposing view."

Like other merchants, the Mendes firm also sustained losses on account of the general insecurity of travel. On one occasion, in 1564, six of Gracia's agents, after visiting Belgrade on business, left for Vidin. As a precaution, before their departure they registered with the Belgrade authorities. When their ship landed none of the six were found among the passengers; evidently they were murdered by the ship's captain and crew who appropriated their possessions. On learning of their disappearance Gracia obtained an order from the sultan to the beg of Smederevo (Semendria) and the qadhi of Belgrade (dated Jan. 20, 1565) thoroughly to investigate and severely to punish the culprits according to the laws of the *shari'a*. See A. Galanté, "Deux nouveaux documents sur Doña Gracia Nassy," *REJ*, LXV, 151–54.

39. See H. H. Ben Sasson, "The Generation," *Zion*, XXVI, 28 ff.; Samuel de Medina, *Resp.* on Y.D., No. 99; Moses b. Baruch Almosnino, *Sefer Me'ammeṣ Koaḥ* (Increasing Strength; homilies: with reference to Prov. 24:5), Venice, 1588, fols. 64a, 134a; C. Roth, *Doña Gracia*, pp. 182 ff.; and *infra*, n. 73. On Esther Kyra and other influential Jewish ladies see *infra*, Chap. LXXVII, nn. 13–14.

40. See M. Bataillon, "Alonso Nuñez de Reinoso et les Marranes portugais en Italie," *Revista* of the Facultade de Lettras of Lisbon, III (= *Miscelánea de estudos in*

honor of Hernani Cidade), 1–21, esp. p. 11; C. H. Rose, *Alonso Nuñez de Reinoso: the Lament of a Sixteenth-Century Exile*, esp. pp. 33, 44 ff., 49 ff., 100 ff., 160 ff. (trying to reconstruct from the novels and poems of this apparent *converso* some aspects of the Mendes family life in Italy, although apart from the financial support which Alonso evidently received from both Gracia and Joseph, we learn relatively little about their own behavior and outlook); the correspondence between Maximilian and Anton Veranchich (Verantius), reproduced in *MHH*, 2d ser., V, 24, 50, 183, 186, 191, 235 (Sept. 11, 1567 [or 1568]); IX, 225 (May 28, 1568); 5th ser. VI; analyzed by S. Kohn in his "Österreichisch-ungarische Gesandtschaftsberichte über Don Joseph Nasi," *MGWJ*, XXVIII, 113–21; the correspondence between Charles V and his sister Marie, preserved in the Belgian National Archive, extensively quoted by E. Ginsburger, "Marie de Hongrie, Charles-Quint, les veuves Mendès et les Néo-Chrétiens," *REJ*, LXXXIX, 179–92 (see *supra*, Vol. XIII, p. 371 n. 67); and, together with other archival sources, by J. Reznik in *Le Duc de Naxos. Contribution à l'histoire juive du XVI siècle;* or in the revised Hebrew version, entitled *Don Yosef Nasi* and published by the author under his Hebrew name, Harozin.

Curiously, despite the extensive researches into Don Joseph's and his family's early career, the date of his birth has not yet been ascertained. The best approximation is given in the anonymous document, published by V. Meysztowicz (quoted *infra*, n. 47). According to this letter, tentatively dated by the editor in 1570, but possibly written in 1567 or earlier (see *ibid.*), Joseph was at that time "approximately 56 years old," which places his birth at *ca.* 1514, or even 1510. If either of these dates is to be accepted, it would appear more likely that Doña Gracia, his aunt, was several years older and hence born before 1510, the date usually assumed. See also the additional data supplied from various archives by C. H. Rose in her "New Information on the Life of Joseph Nasi, Duke of Naxos, the Venetian Phase," *JQR*, IX, 330–44; and particularly by P. Grunebaum-Ballin, *Joseph Naci*, pp. 27 ff., whose archival documentation has been particularly helpful to me. See also *supra*, Vol. XIII, pp. 119 ff., 368 ff. nn. 62–69; XV, pp. 7 ff., 379 n. 1, etc; and more generally, A. von Gévay, *Urkunden und Aktenstücke*. In general Austria, though a close neighbor and from time to time at war with the Ottoman Empire, seems to have had fewer channels of communication with the Porte than did either Venice, Genoa, or France. Probably because it was under the reign of Ferdinand, Charles V's brother, and his descendents, the Turks harbored suspicions toward the occasional special envoys sent by the Austrian regime to Constantinople.

41. See Andrés de Laguna, *Viaje de Turquia*, originally attributed to Cristóbal de Villalón by its first editor, M. Serrano y Sanz in his collection *Autobiográfias y Memorias*, pp. 1–149, but identified as the work of Laguna, known as the translator of Dioscorides' Book on Drugs, by M. Bataillon in "Nouvelles recherches sur Viaje de Turquia," *Romance Philology*, V, 77–97; here cited in the English trans. of that passage in C. Roth's *The House of Nasi: the Duke of Naxos*, p. 8; the dispatch of March 18, 1553 by the Austrian ambassador to Venice, Dominik de Gaztelu, summarized from an Austrian archival document by P. Grunewald-Ballin, *Joseph Naci*, pp. 47, 52 f. (see also *ibid.*, pp. 67 ff.); and C. Sauzé, ed., *Correspondance politique de M. de Lansac* (Louis de Saint Gelais) = *Archives historiques de Poitou*, XXXIII, pp. 254 f. dated October 26, 1553.

42. The intriguing story of Don Joseph's alleged first marriage to his cousin Beatrice the Younger still awaits fuller elucidation. Our main source of information comes from Dominik de Gaztelu, Austrian ambassador to Venice, who wrote about it to his

government clearly from hearsay. See his aforementioned dispatch (*supra*, n. 41) of March 18, 1553, summarized from an Austrian archival document by P. Grunewald-Ballin in his *Joseph Naci*, pp. 47, 52 f., 67 ff. The Austrian diplomat may have repeated a rumor intentionally spread by the family Mendes in support of Joseph's claim for the return to him of both his "wife's" and his property. In that romantic age full of adventure such a rumor would have been quite persuasive and occasionally effective. However, the greed of the respective governments to keep possession of whatever parts of the Mendes fortune they held probably would have made them resist returning the confiscated property even if the Papacy had formally recognized João's marriage to Beatrice. On the attitude of the Turkish Sephardim to plural marriages and the nonvalidity of Marrano unions celebrated according to non-Jewish rites on the Iberian Peninsula after the expulsion, see *supra*, nn. 20 ff.

43. See H. Inalcik, "Capital Formation in the Ottoman Empire," *Journal of Economic History*, XXIX, 97–140; R. C. Jennings, "Loans and Credit in Early 17th Century Ottoman Judicial Records: the Shari'a Court of Anatolian Kayseri," *JESHO*, XVI, 168–216 (this dichotomy between legal theory and practice must have been doubly strong in the great and flourishing emporia of the sixteenth century); and, on Michael Cantacuzenus, Stephan Gerlach the Elder, *Tage-Buch*, pp. xxii ff., with the comments thereon by J. W. Zinkeisen, *Geschichte des osmanischen Reiches in Europa*, III, 366 ff.; and S. Runciman, *The Great Church in Captivity: A Study of the Patriarchate of Constantinople from the Eve of the Turkish Conquest to the Greek War of Independence*, p. 197. On the medieval antecedents of the varying attitudes toward, and the ambiguous role played by certain religious doctrines of Islam in the evolution of some protocapitalist forms of economic activity in the Middle East, see W. Björkmann's judicious analysis of "Kapitalentstehung und -anlage im Islam," *MSOS*, XXXII, Part 2, pp. 80–98.

Rustem Pasha, a Serb converted to Islam, who was characterized by the Austrian envoy Augier Ghislain de Busbecq (in his *Lettres*, French trans. by Abbé du Foy, I, 26 f.) as *tristis et atrox* (withdrawn and crude) and was disliked also by other foreign envoys, nevertheless befriended the Mendes family. He was grand vizier in 1544–61 (with a brief break in 1554–55). He was able to exercise considerable influence on all Turkish affairs—particularly since he was aided and abetted by his wife, one of Suleiman's daughters, and his alliance with Khurrem-Roxelana, the sultan's favorite wife. Probably Gracia and Joseph knew how to placate him with precious gifts. Upon his demise, he left behind a great fortune which included 2,000 slaves. His widow, as we shall see, was able to maintain and even to increase these possessions in the following fifteen years. See J. von Hammer-Purgstall, *Geschichte*, III, 384 ff. In any case, Rustem's passing in 1561 found the Mendes family sufficiently well established to weather less friendly feelings from the new grand viziers, even before Selim II's succession to the throne.

44. See *supra*, Vol. XVI, pp. 47 ff., 231 f., 337 ff. nn. 51 ff., 426 n. 21 (with information on the international importance of the Polish exports of wax); A. Galanté, "Nouveaux documents sur Joseph Nassy, Duc de Naxos," *REJ*, LXIV, 236–43, esp. p. 240 App. iv; idem, *Don Joseph Nassi Duc de Naxos d'après des nouveaux documents;* M. Balaban, *Żydzi lwowscy na przelomie XVIgo i XVIIgo wieku* (The Jews in Lwów at the Turn from the Sixteenth to the Seventeenth Century), including its fine documentary appendix. On the causes of the ultimate failure of Don Joseph's export business in Poland, see also Z. Świtalski, "The Reasons for the Withdrawal of the Turkish Jews, Refugees from Spain, from the Levant Trade of the Polish Commonwealth in the Last Years of the Sixteenth Century" (Polish), *Biuletyn* of the Żydowski Instytut His-

toryczny Warsaw (*BZIH*), no. 37, pp. 59–65, with an English summary, pp. 109–110; and other sources listed *supra*, Vol. XVI. Hans Dernschwam's dislike of the Turkish wines, expressed in several passages of his diary, is quoted and interpreted by H. P. Laqueur in his "Einige Anmerkungen zur Weinbereitung im Osmanischen Reich im 16. Jahrhundert," *Islamkundliche Abhandlungen . . . Hans Joachim Kissling . . . gewidmet*, pp. 127–29. On the political aspects connected with these business relationships, see also K. Beydilli's dissertation, *Die Machtpolitik der Osmanen in der zweiten Hälfte des 16. Jahrhunderts am Beispiel der polnischen Königswahlen von 1573 und 1575*.

Notwithstanding his numerous vicissitudes with the Venetian regime, Don Joseph apparently continued to participate in the intensive Turko-Venetian commercial exchanges. True, the revocation of the Venetian resolution about the price set on his head may not have completely reassured him about his safety when personally visiting the Republic, but through agents he could continue his business there undisturbed. His brother, Bernardo-Samuel, for example, had no difficulty in journeying to Venice on a safe-conduct. See, in general, the extensive documentation published by C. Villain-Gandossi in her "Contribution à l'étude des relations diplomatiques et commerciales entre Venise et la Porte ottomane au XVIᵉ siècle," *Südost-Forschungen*, XXVI, 22–45; XXVIII, 13–47; XXIX, 290–301 (also reprint), esp. p. 290 No. 1; and by M. Lesure in his "Notes et documents sur les relations véneto-ottomanes, 1570–1573," *Turcica*, IV, 134–64.

45. Like most other travelers Pierre Belon was not an unbiased observer. This is revealed also in the passage quoted here. See his *Les Observations de plusieurs singularitez et choses mémorables trouvées en Grèce, Asie, Judée, Égypte, Arabie et autres pays estranges*, Paris, 1553, fols. 180 f. (appeared also in a Latin ed., Antwerp, 1589, and in an English trans.). While we are not sure of the exact date of his visit to the Ottoman Empire, the tenor of his "observations" indicates that it took place not many years before the publication of the book, the preface of which was signed in 1553, that is, shortly before Joseph's arrival in Istanbul. Belon's comments are often very acute and have frequently been quoted by modern historians.

46. See E. Charrière, ed., *Négociations de la France dans le Levant*, 1st ser. XV, Vol. II, 415 ff.; A. Arce, "Espionaje y última aventura de José Nasi (1569–1574)," *Sefarad*, XIII, 257–86. How anxious the Western powers were to have at least sporadic representatives at the center of the Ottoman Empire may be seen from the efforts of the Papacy, notwithstanding its almost incessant preachment of an anti-Turkish Crusade, to keep up its diplomatic relations with the Porte. See L. Biskupski, *L'Origine et l'historique de la représentation officielle du Saint-Siège en Turquie (1204–1967)*; and K. M. Setton, *The Papacy and the Levant (1204–1571)*, Vol. I: The Thirteenth and Fourteenth Centuries.

47. See *supra*, n. 40; Vol. XV, pp. 48 f., 399 f. n. 57. Regrettably, we are not fully informed about the numerous agents and associates employed by Don Joseph at home and abroad. Some names are revealed incidentally on special occasions; for instance, in litigations over claims and counter-claims such as those with Agostino Enriquez (Abraham Benveniste) and Duarte Gómez mentioned *supra*, n. 38. We owe it to a recent discovery in the Spanish archive of Simancas by a Polish scholar Valerian Meysztowicz, that a document, probably written in 1570, and listing a number of Don Joseph's business employees in Istanbul has been published. An interesting feature of this list is the description of facial and other personal characteristics of these employees. Evidently, it was intended for its recipients the more readily to identify one or

another of them, if they should be found in a Western country under an assumed name. This method was used, for example, by Joachim von Sinzendorf, Emperor Rudolph II's envoy to the Porte, in his dispatch home of September 17, 1580, warning the imperial authorities of the forthcoming arrival in Germany of Gabriel Defrens (or de Bourgoigne, after his conversion to Islam named Maḥmud 'Abdullah Frenk) whom the sultan sent on a diplomatic mission to Queen Elizabeth. Sinzendorf suspected that Defrens, under the pretext of buying clocks and other objects, intended to spy on all the Christian rulers who had allied themselves against Turkey. See the excerpt from his dispatch, published from an Austrian archival document by S. A. Skilliter in "The Sultan's Messenger, Gabriel Defrens, an Ottoman Master-Spy of the Sixteenth Century," *WZKM*, LXVIII, 47–59, esp. pp. 48 f. (English), 56 f. App. i (German).

The names of these associates are reproduced here with their descriptions in translation from that anonymous Italian document, so that interested scholars, having access to the Turkish archives, may more readily be able to identify them. See V. Meysztowicz, *Documenta Polonica ex archivo generali Hispaniae in Simancas* (Elementa ad fontium editiones, VIII, published by the Institutum Historicum Polonicum in Rome), I, 169 ff. No. 133. After describing, with some inaccuracies, Don Joseph's earlier career (without mentioning his dukedom of Naxos, which may perhaps be a reason for dating the entire document in 1567 or earlier), the writer briefly noted the Jewish diplomat's important services to the Porte. According to him, Giovanni Miches, then approximately 56 years of age, was in correspondence with "Marranos and renegades of whom there are many in Italy." The writer then gives the following description of Joseph's favorite assistants.

—

Chesa, from Cracow, a relative of one Jacob residing in Prague, aged 44–45; of fine presence, tall with a long red beard, who directly visits the imperial court under the pretext of selling sables.

Joseph Padovano, a Jew aged 28, distributor of lemons and oranges.

Abraham Saboc, aged 54, with a short gray beard, a tall and slender man.

Joseph Saboc, aged 50, with a black-gray beard, pale and not very tall.

Joseph Sarfatello, aged 46, small, with a gray beard.

Salomon Giemnero, close relative, aged 40, tall, slender, with a long and distinguished beard and sparse hair; he is employed in Candia and other maritime localities under the guise of a contractor for dams [*dighe*].

Vida Levi, aged 34, of average height, with [*resigna*] a ruddy countenance and a round face.

Salomon Albano, aged 52, tall, corpulent, with a large head and a round gray beard.

Joseph Zio, aged 36–38, with a round face, medium height, and a short black beard.

He [Miches], uses as a secretary one Judah Cohen, aged about 32, pale, with a long black beard, lean and of the right height. [See *infra*, n. 69 where he is called Joseph.]

He [Miches] also uses non-suspect methods to send letters [to persons] living in different parts of Poland who are his beneficiaries for many years. Their names are as follows: Salomon Phedico, Salomon Candida, Caim Coen, Salomon Gige, Abraham Mocia.

Judah Bensura who had recently come from Lwów.

Abraham de Vide, a Portuguese, aged 42–44.

The above mentioned have the duty to send letters to Constantinople and to receive them, so that letters arriving from Caminis [Kamieniec or Kamenets Podolski] to Lwów, are placed in the hands of Jews who forward them to Lublin; they are delivered to

Calimas [Kalman] the Printer, who sends them on to Cracow and, when necessary, from Cracow to Lwów.

The above mentioned are Marranos and renegade Christians; they know many languages and, dependent on the localities, appear as Jews, or Christians, and [as natives] of various lands. They also change their attire.

He [Miches] also employs one David Cabi, his cousin, aged about 52, of medium size, fat, with a divided red beard which begins graying. He makes the profession of . . . [word blotted] located throughout Italy.

Also one Zacaeia, son of Filosegia, a shipping agent from Lwów [condottore del Lipolto] of Polish wax, who had sworn loyalty to Mahomed Pasha [Sokolli], also in the name of his father Felice. On account of that oath they both hold out much promise.

This Giovanni Miches keeps for these purposes an agent named Abraham Maimon in Cutin [Chocim?], a locality in Bogodano (?), who is aged about 38, small, with a chestnut-colored beard. He travels with the letters or sends them on to Chieli [doubtless referring to Kilia, a port on the Danube delta] and from there they are dispatched to Constantinople along the ordinary route [la scala ordinaria é questa]. From Vienna to Cracow, from Cracow to Lublin, from Lublin to Lwów, from Lwów to Caminies, from Caminies to Cutin (?), from there to Chieli, and from Chieli to Constantinople. In return when they leave Constantinople they take the same route in reverse. The traveling Jews are as follows: Diodato Nolano of Bologna, aged about 22, of medium size, dark, with a short black beard, clad in Italian fashion; Jacob Brasighella of Ferrara, aged about 26, tall, white with a small blond beard.

An inscription on the reverse side of the documents reads: "The spies and correspondents kept by Juan Micas in various parts and provinces of Christianity." On the trade and trade route indicated in this document, see P. P. Panaitescu, *La Route commerciale de Pologne à la Mer Noire au moyen âge;* G. Cvetana, "Les Rapports des commerce entre l'Empire Ottoman et la Pologne et les terres bulgares au XVIe siècle," *Bulgarian Historical Review,* VI, no. 3, pp. 38–51; and, more generally, G. I. Bratianu, *La Mer Noire. Des origines à la conquête ottomanes.* Not surprisingly, the Italian informer, a copy of whose communication was forwarded to Madrid, seems to have stressed data of special interest to Poland. He was prone to believe anything that was told him. Certainly, the figure of 700,000 ducats, which Reyna was supposed to have received as a dowry when she married Joseph, was highly inflated. From later records we know that it amounted to only 90,000. See *infra,* n. 61. Nonetheless, a careful examination of this report may yield interesting results.

48. See Stephan Gerlach's *Tage-Buch,* pp. 247 f. (also mentioning the intervention of a Jewish doctor); N. Jorga, *Geschichte,* III, 200 ff.; S. Runciman, *The Great Church,* esp. pp. 198 ff. Almosnino's description of the patriarch's visit, included in the original Ladino version of his *Extremos y Grandezas de Constantinopla,* was omitted in the printed Spanish edition by Jacob Cansino, Madrid, 1638, probably because of Cansino's tenuous position in Madrid. See M. Lattes, *Notizie e documenti di letterature e storia giudaica,* pp. 18 f., cited by C. Roth in *The Duke of Naxos,* pp. 45, 235 n. 2; and *supra,* Vol. XV, pp. 221 f., 480 f. n. 69. In this transaction, it may be assumed, Don Joseph must also have feared that a possible refusal by the sultan to confirm a properly conducted election of an ecclesiastical chief by a religious minority might establish an undesirable precedent for similar confirmations of Jewish officials. These elections and the government's role in them will be discussed in the next volume.

It may be mentioned in this connection that Almosnino's friendship with the Nasi family lasted beyond Don Joseph's lifetime. In his tract on Abraham Ibn Ezra's commentary the author noted that this study was written "in the house of the Dignitary and Great Man in Israel Don Joseph of blessed memory in the year [5]342 [1582]," that is some three years after the duke's demise. See N. Ben-Menachem's "Rabbi Moses Almosnino's Additional Observations on R. Abraham Ibn Ezra's Commentary on the Pentateuch" (Hebrew), *Sinai*, X, nos. 7–12, pp. 136–71, reproducing the text of Almosnino's tract from an Oxford MS, esp. p. 138 n. Evidently the palace of Belvedere, still inhabited by the widowed Duchess Reyna, hospitably accommodated a number of Jewish scholars. See *infra*, n. 61.

49. See Fabiano Strada, *De bello belgico, decas prima et secunda*, I, 170 f.; *supra*, Vols. XIII, pp. 50 f., 349 f. nn. 53–54; XV, pp. 4 ff., 18 f., 305 f. n. 21; XVI, pp. 34 ff., 332 f. nn. 38–39; E. Charrière, *Négociations*, II, 715 f.; III, 63 ff.; C. Barnate, "La Missione de Sampiero Corso a Constantinopoli (Documenti)," *Archivo Storico di Corsica*, XV, 472–502, esp. pp. 480, 498 ff. No. xvii; P. Grunebaum-Ballin, *Joseph Naci*, pp. 83, 107, 130 f., 140, and the sources listed there. To be sure, Joseph's anti-Spanish stance was not necessarily consistent. Under the ever-changing power constellations in the Mediterranean world, his policies had to be flexible enough to promote whatever the Ottoman national interest called for at the moment. In this sense N. Rosenblatt may be right in discussing some aspects of "Joseph Nasi, Friend of Spain," *Studies in Honor of M. F. Benardete* (Essays in Hispanic and Sephardic Culture), ed. by I. A. Langas and B. Sholod, pp. 323–32. Otherwise he places too much faith in the documents published by A. Arce and his biased interpretation. See *infra*, nn. 50–51. However, we cannot tell whether Joseph's heart was in whatever duty of that kind he performed to meet the exigencies of the moment or whether some of these moves may merely have been stratagems in the complicated diplomatic game characteristic of the international relations of that period. If so, they would offer but another example of the then growing acceptance of the *raison d'état* as the guiding principle for action by every sovereign state.

50. See Philip II's letter of October 26, 1569, in part reproduced from a Simancas archival document by A. Arce in his colored description of the "Espionaje e última aventura de José Nasi," *Sefarad*, XIII, esp. pp. 259 ff., 276 ff. Docs. 1–2. It is noteworthy that the Orthodox patriarch Metrophanes III was expected to participate in these subversive activities against his own country and perhaps also to aid in the kidnaping or slaying of his likely benefactor, the duke of Naxos. See *supra*, n. 48; and *infra*, n. 61.

51. See the pertinent documents, reproduced by A. Arce, in *Sefarad*, XIII; R. Mantran, "L'Echo de la bataille de Lepante à Constantinople," *Annales ESC*, XXVIII, 396–405; other literature listed *supra*, Chap. LXXV, n. 22; and, more generally, P. Herre, *Europäische Politik im Cyprischen Krieg (1570–1573), mit Vorgeschichte und Vorverhandlungen*. On Selim's threat to Sokolli, see H. Inalcik, "The Origin of the Ottoman Russian Rivalry and the Don-Volga Canal" (Turkish), *Belleten* of Türk Tarih Kurumu (Turkish Historical Society), 1948, pp. 47–100, esp. p. 44, cited by W. E. D. Allen in his *Problems of Turkish Power in the Sixteenth Century*, p. 28. The likelihood that Joseph's alleged memorandum in cipher was an outright forgery is discussed, *infra*, n. 60.

52. Count de Monteagudo's letter to Philip II, dated Spires, Oct. 10, 1570, in *Colección de documentos inéditos para la historia de España* (CODOIN), ed. by M. Fernandez Marquis de Fuentes *et al.*, CXI, 84 (see also J. Paz Espeso's valuable *Catálogo* to that

extensive collection, published Madrid, 1930–31); De Chatoney's letters to Philip II, dated Vienna, May 23, 1567 and February 16, and 28, 1568, *ibid.*, CI, 314, 375, 379 f.; and other sources cited by N. Rosenblatt in *Studies in Honor of M. J. Benardete*, pp. 327 ff.; *supra*, n. 49. Even the documents published by Arce in *Sefarad*, XIII, however, reveal Philip's suspicion of the veracity of Agostín Manuel's testimony and his mere willingness to explore, in every indirect way, the possibilities of achieving a truce with the Ottoman Empire. This desire was ultimately to be fulfilled in 1580 and the following years. On the diplomatic vagaries and often tortuous methods used in these long-lasting pourparlers which included, for example, the 1576 offer by Claude du Bourg, the former French envoy in Istanbul, to secure an armistice for Spain for a remuneration of 100,000 ducats, see F. Braudel's analysis in *La Mediterranée*, 2d ed., II, 431 ff. See also *infra*, n. 61.

Joseph's possible temporary loss of self-control would have been fully understandable, if he listened to some of his friends and acquaintances in the diplomatic corps who, among themselves, doubtless aired the views most of them held, about the dim outlook for the Ottoman navy to be quickly reconstructed. For example, the generally knowledgeable French ambassador, François de Noailles, bishop of Dax, in the extensive memoir he wrote to King Charles IX as late as March 1572, stated unequivocally that he was looking forward to a decline of Turkish power. He doubted, in particular, whether Selim, "the most imbecile prince ever to rule this state," would be able speedily to take the necessary measures "to halt the downfall of his empire." See his interesting lengthy memoir reproduced in I. von Testa's ed., *Recueil des traités de la Porte Ottomane avec les Puissances étrangères depuis le premier traité conclu en 1536 [1535] entre Suleyman I et François I, jusqu'à nos jours*, I, 99 ff., esp. item vi. Certainly, Joseph could no more foresee at the end of 1571 than did the bishop several months later that by the early summer of 1572 the Ottoman shipyards, feverishly working over the winter and spring months, would place at the sultan's disposal a new powerful fleet of some 250 warships.

53. See H. K. G. Gelzer, *Geistliches und Weltliches aus dem türkisch-griechischen Orient; selbsterlebtes und selbstgesehenes*, p. 179; H. G. Majer's broader study of *Herkunft and Volkszugehörigkeit muslimischer Amtsträger als historisches Problem in der Osmanistik, Ethnogenese und Staatsbildung in Osteuropa;* H. Gross, "La Famille juive des Hamon," *REJ*, LVI, 8 f. In general there was no need to clarify the constitutional status of the new duke of Naxos. Without being a regular "vassal" as were the Danubian voivodes, he was evidently something else than a mere official in the Turkish administration. Don Joseph doubtless shared with the vassals a position somewhat akin to that existing between the *dar al-Islam* and the *dar al-ḥarb*. Vaguely defined as an *ahdname* (treaty area), the status of such intermediary entities had already been controversial in the classical age of Arab jurisprudence and political philosophy. See I. Matei's pertinent observations in his "Quelques problèmes concernant le régime de la domination ottomane dans les pays roumaines (concernant particulièrement la Valachie)," *RESEE*, X, 65–81, esp. p. 68. It may also be noted that, theoretically, pressured conversions for careerist reasons ran counter to the long-established traditions of both the Muslim theologians and rabbis. This theory was also accepted by the sultans. See F. Babinger, "Grossherrliche Schutzvorschrift gegen nutzniesslichen Glaubenswechsel," *Der Orient in Forschung, Festschrift für Otto Spies*, ed. by W. Hoenebach, pp. 1–8. Yet the imperative need to employ highly qualified persons in the supreme office of grand vizier overruled whatever compunctions individual monarchs may have felt about inducing desirable candidates to change their faith.

54. Moses b. Baruch Almosnino, *Extremos e grandezas de Constantinopla*, Spanish ed., from an unpublished Ladino MS of 1565 by Jacob Cansino, Madrid, 1638, pp. 77 f.; the sultan's order of November 24, 1567, reproduced in a French translation by A. Galanté in his comp. of *Documents officiels turcs concernant les Juifs de Turquie. Recueil de 114 lois, règlements, firmans, bérats, ordres et décisions de tribunaux*, trans. with historical summaries, notes and 7 additional documents, pp. 188 f. Nos. ii–iii; idem, *Histoire des Juifs de Rhodes, Chio, Cos, etc.*, pp. 158 f.; and, more generally, idem, *Don Joseph Nassi Duc de Naxos d'après des nouveaux documents*, supplemented by his "Nouveaux documents sur Joseph Nassy, Duc de Naxos," *REJ*, LXIV, 236–43. On the twenty-one dukes of Naxos before 1566, see the data mentioned in K. M. Setton's *The Papacy and the Levant*, pp. 18 f. n. 78.

It was easier for the sultans to confer a title like *mutafarik*, the equivalent to that of a nobleman-courtier in the Western countries. We recall Selim's 1562 letter to the Polish king thus designating Don Joseph, *supra*, n. 44. Because of the increasing frequency with which that title was conferred for a price, rather than on the basis of merit, it did not carry much weight in Ottoman society. A contemporary Ottoman chronicler actually denigrated the new nobility as consisting of "vagabonds, highwaymen, gypsies, Jews, Lasis, Russians, *gens des villes*." See B. A. Cvetkova, "L'Evolution du régime féodal turc de la fin du XVIe siècle jusqu'au milieu du XVIIIe siècle," *Études historiques à l'occasion du XIe Congrès International des Sciences Historiques*, held in Stockholm in August 1960 and published by the Bulgarian Academy of Sciences, I, 184 f. See also pp. 158, 188. Such venality in conferring titles was not much worse than that prevailing in France and other Western countries in the seventeenth century. It was actually easier for the sultans than for the Western kings to engage in such practices since the Sublime Porte was not controlled by the aristocracy of descent. Many a Western observer was disconcerted by being told, as was Augier Ghislain de Busbecq (Busbeck), Flemish scholar and Austrian ambassador at the Porte (1554–62), that in their own harems sultans preferred to keep slave girls than the daughters of the Byzantine aristocracy. See E. Kafé, "Le Mythe turc et son déclin dans les relations de voyage des Européens de la Renaissance," *Oriens*, XXI–XXII, 159–95, esp. p. 170.

55. See the text of Marco Belogna's nomination published, along with other Coronello papers, by M. Curtius in his *Naxos*, and translated into French by P. Grunebaum-Ballin, in *Joseph Naci*, p. 96. This document evidently carries a mistaken date of November 8, 1631, since Joseph had died in 1579. From the context it appears that it was really dated in 1571, in the early years of his administration. Equally galling to the native population must have been the public investiture in 1572 (1577?) of Marino D'Argenta, the eldest son of Nicolo d'Argenta of the island of Santorin, into a feudal fief which had belonged to his uncle. This ceremony was conducted by Coronello in the duke's name in the traditional medieval forms of a lord conferring a feudal benefice upon a vassal "in accordance with the laws of the Romania Empire." See *ibid.*, p. 97. It is also noteworthy that the 6,000 ducats annually contributed by Joseph to the Ottoman Treasury in behalf of his duchy, although forming but a tiny part of the imperial budget, was considered a worthwhile item of revenue. Suffice it to compare it with the tribute of only 3,000 ducats paid every year by Venice to stave off Turkish attacks on the large island of Cyprus. When the sultan asked for a raise to 4,000 ducats, the Republic's refusal became one of the immediate causes for the outbreak of the Turco-Venetian War of 1570–73.

56. See J. C. Sauzé, ed., *Correspondance politique de M. de Lansac*, pp. 254 f. No. 136 (*supra*, n. 41); Gabriel de Lutz d'Aramon, *Le Voyage . . . d'Aramon, ambassadeur pour le*

Roy en Levant. Escript par noble homme Jean Chesneau l'un de secrétaires dudict seigneur ambassadeur, ed. and annotated by C. Schefer, p. 48 n. 1 (reprinted Paris, 1970); and the brief description of "L'Affaire d'Alexandrie," largely on the basis of reports of the French, Italian, and Austrian ambassadors, by P. Grunebaum-Ballin in *Joseph Naci,* pp. 119 ff.

57. See *supra,* Vol. XII, pp. 109 f., 295 n. 45; E. Charrière, *Négociations,* III, 70 f., 820; and the dispatches sent by the Venetian *bailo* Marcantonio Barbaro and the Austrian envoys, Adam de Franchi and Albert von Wyss to their respective governments cited by P. Grunebaum-Ballin in *Joseph Naci,* pp. 121 ff.

58. See Charrière, *Négociations,* III, 87; *Articles accordez par le Grand Seigneur en faveur du Roy et de ses Subjects à Messire Claude du Bourg chevalier sieur de Guerines, Conseiller du Roy et trésorier de France pour la liberté et sureté due trafficq commerce et passage ès pairs et mers du Levant,* cited from a rare copy in the Paris Bibliothèque Nationale by Grunebaum-Ballin in *Joseph Naci,* p. 124. In his quest for data about Joseph's role in the Franco-Turkish negotiations leading up to the historic treaty of 1569, Jacob Reznik found in the Foreign Office Archive in Paris a mysterious document which caused quite a stir in the Jewish scholarly world. Dated November 12, 1782, this text was part of a collection assembled by Count François Emmanuel de St. Priest, French ambassador to the Porte, in preparation for the writing of a history of the French embassy in Istanbul. (This study was later to appear under the title, *Mémoires de l'ambassade de France en Turquie et sur le commerce des Français dans le Lévant, suivis du texte des traductions originales des capitulations et des traités conclus avec la Sublime Porte Ottomane;* see esp. pp. 79–268, 345–537 dealing with the history of the embassy in the period of 1535–1792.) The document in the St. Priest collection is described in an accompanying French note which reads: "Translated from the original Hebrew by Domenico Oliveri, the king's interpreter and literally copied by Mr. Gautier in 1783."

This entry is followed by the French translation of the 1569 treaty in 18 paragraphs. Reznik assumed that the underlying Hebrew text represented the original prepared in the chancery of the duke of Naxos on which were based the Turkish and French texts signed by the two powers. This assumption was widely heralded in the Jewish press and accepted by scholars like Joseph Klausner and Salomon Abraham Rosanes. See J. Reznik's *Le Duc de Naxos: Contributions à l'histoire du XVIe siècle;* repeated in his Hebrew essay, "Don Joseph Nasi, the Builder of Tiberias," *Sinai,* XV, nos. 177–82, pp. 295–317, esp. pp. 300 f.; and his Hebrew biography of *Don Joseph Nasi;* J. Klausner, *Ke-she-ummah nilḥemet 'al ḥerutah* (When a People Fights for Its Liberation), 3d ed., pp. 267–75; and S. A. Rosanes, *Dibre yeme (Qorot),* II, 321.

These authors would have been even more enthusiastic about that alleged Hebrew draft had they known, as was soon thereafter proved by Gaston Zeller, that it was the 1569 treaty, and not the mere proposals submitted in 1535 by the French and never agreed upon by the Porte, which laid the firm foundation for the later system of capitulations. See Zeller, "Une Légende qui a la vie dure: les capitulations de 1535," *Revue d'histoire moderne et contemporaine,* II, 127–32 (pointing out that a suggestion along these lines had been made by Nicolas Iorga as early as 1925); and J. Billoud's comments thereon in his "Capitulations et histoire du commerce à propos de l'étude de M. Gaston Zeller," *ibid.,* pp. 312–15, also showing that, as a result of that treaty, French shipping to the Levant increased greatly.

Reznik's theory is very dubious, however. Quite apart from the absence of the original Hebrew text and its French translation (reference to which is extant only in this copy of the French rendition) as well as the late date of this entry, the need for an intermediate Hebrew version between the Turkish and French originals has not been explained. There is no evidence that someone in Joseph's chancery prepared the original draft in Hebrew—although this language was quite popular in non-Jewish circles during the Renaissance—for use in the final French and Turkish versions. Moreover, if the French version of the preamble, as published in I. von Testa's *Recueil des traités,* I, 90 ff., was part of the original agreement, it could not possibly have emanated from Joseph's office. Here Selim, after the introductory paragraph, which is even more than usually boastful, rather humbly apologized for the seizure of the French ships in Alexandria to satisfy Joseph's claims. He expostulated that Joseph's deep indebtedness to various creditors made it impossible to exact from him any compensation for the damages caused by that confiscation to the owners of the seized cargoes and promised not to allow any such proceedings in the future. It is not inconceivable, however, that the Hebrew text stemmed from Solomon Ashkenazi. A recent arrival (see below), he was certainly not yet able to advise Sokolli on a Turkish text, so he might have prepared such a memorandum in Hebrew translation for his own use. More likely, it was a Jewish dragoman who, at some later date, rendered the long-accepted Turkish or French text into Hebrew, perhaps for use by a Jewish client wishing to invoke some of its provisions. The document might somehow have aroused the curiosity of a French ambassador who had it translated and sent on to Paris. The final resolution of this problem must await further documentary discoveries.

59. See E. Albéri, ed., *Relazioni degli ambasciatori veneti,* XIX, 182; and, more generally, Giampietro Contarini, *Historia delle case successe dal principio della guerra mossa da Selim ottomano ai Venetiani,* Venice, 1572; A. Dragonetti de Torres, *La Lega di Lepanto nel carteggio diplomatico inedito di Don Luis de Torres;* P. Herre, *Europäische Politik im cyprischen Krieg (1570–1573), mit Vorgeschichte und Vorverhandlungen;* M. Lesure, "Notes et documents," *Turcica,* IV, 134–64. Of considerable interest still is the description of *Cyprus under the Turks 1571–1878: a Record Based on the Archives of the English Consulate in Cyprus under the Levant Company and After* by H. C. Luke, including his lengthy translation of passages (pp. 19 ff.) from the eighteenth-century work by Archimandrite Kyprianos, *Istoria chronologiké tes nesou Kyprou* (The Chronological History of the Island of Cyprus).

60. The early Ottoman efforts to colonize Cyprus with Jews as analyzed by B. Lewis, U. Heyd, and others are more fully discussed *infra,* n. 75. On the Jewish community under Turkish domination in Cyprus and the Turkish colonization of the island in general, see S. Marcus, "The History of the Jews of Cyprus in the Days of the Turks and Greeks" (Hebrew), *Oṣar Yehude Sefarad* (Tesoro de los judíos sefardíes), VI, 84–101; and, more generally, C. Orhonlu, "The Ottoman Turks Settle in Cyprus (1570–1580)," *Turkologischer Anzeiger,* II, 257–61; H. Inalcik, "Ottoman Policy and Administration in Cyprus after the Conquest," *ibid.,* pp. 119–36; G. F. Hill, *A History of Cyprus,* Vols. I–IV. Regrettably, we know very little about the attitude of the previously established small and struggling Cypriot Jewish community to the Turkish invasion. On its condition at that time see *supra,* Vol. XVII, pp. 77 ff., 331 f. nn. 38–40; and particularly B. Arbel, "The Jews of Cyprus: New Evidence from the Venetian Period," *JSS,* XLI, 23–40. How anxious the Turkish authorities were, from the beginning of their occupation of Cyprus, to convert the local population, particularly its upper classes, to Islam, may be seen from C. P. Kyrris's "L'Importance sociale de la conversion à

l'Islam (volontaire ou non) d'une section des classes dirigeantes de Chypre pendant les premiers siècles de l'occupation turque (1570–fin du XVIIe siècle)," *Actes* of the First Congrès International des études balkaniques et sud-est européennes, III, 437–62.

61. See *supra*, nn. 48–51; Vol. XIV, pp. 77 ff., 335 n. 6 with the sources quoted there; Don Joseph's 1571 purported letter to Philip II published by A. Arce in his "Espionaje," *Sefarad*, XIII, 280 f. No. 4; E. Charrière, *Négociations*, III, 808, 931; I. von Testa, *Recueil des traités de la Porte Ottomane avec les Puissances étrangères*, I, 126 item xii. As mentioned above, the problem of Joseph's memorandum is still unsolved. To begin with, Arce, who reproduced this memorandum from a Simancas document, gives only the vague date of 1571 as that of its writing. It is improbable that a letter written to a powerful monarch like Philip II should have been scribbled without a specific date. If indeed it was submitted in 1571, it would be important to know whether it was composed before or after the Battle of Lepanto. Since news about the Turkish defeat did not reach Istanbul before the middle of October 1571, Joseph must have written it, if indeed he did, in reaction to indubitably exaggerated reports. This means that either Joseph became so panicky as to lose all control over his actions or, possibly, that he anticipated the need for a truce between the two leading Mediterranean powers, such as was to lead to their hesitant negotiations in the later 1570s. An armistice was indeed concluded in 1580 and renewed twice in the following five years. However, his alleged offer to return to Spain as a professing Christian appears to be either spurious or consciously misleading.

Joseph's continued high standing even after Selim's death in 1574 is attested, as late as 1578, a year before his death, by his role in the negotiations initiated by Francesco de' Medici of Tuscany. The grand duke's father, the famous Cosimo I, had already evinced interest in pourparlers with the Ottoman regime in 1569 and 1574. Probably remembering some encouragement on the part of the duke of Naxos to these early attempts, Francesco sent his envoy Giovanni Bonfigliazzi directly to him. The Tuscan diplomat stayed in the Belvedere palace for two days before having an audience with the sultan. During the following few days he still kept in close communication with the duke, receiving some briefings concerning items in the negotiations. Suddenly Bonfigliazzi's visits stopped. As it turned out, Sokolli tried to undercut his competitor and advised the envoy to stay away from the duke. This may have been one of several disappointments for Joseph who was perhaps in ill health at that time. See Joseph's letter to the grand duke dated November 7, 1578; Francesco's rather cool reply; and the dispatches of the Austrian ambassador Joachim von Sinzendorf of July 14, and November 15, 1578, cited from MSS in the Medicean Archive in Florence and the Austrian Staatsarchiv by P. Grunebaum-Ballin in *Joseph Naci*, pp. 162 f. On Cosimo's Florentine relations with Solomon Ashkenazi, see *infra*, n. 65.

62. See *supra*, Vols. XV, pp. 132 ff., 435 ff. nn. 69–71; XVI, pp. 34 ff., 332 f. nn. 38–39. To the bibliography in Vol. XV add H. Sinsheimer, *Shylock: the History of a Character*, which is the English version of an enlarged German essay cited there, XV, 435 ff. n. 70.

63. Saadiah b. Abraham Longo, *Sefer Seder zemanim* (Order of Festivals, poems), Vol. I, Salonica, 1594; Moses b. Baruch Almosnino, *Tratado de los sueños*, a section of his widely read *Regimento della vida* (*Sefer Hanhagot ha-Ḥayyim*), published first in Hebrew characters in Salonica, 1564, and later in the Latin alphabet in Amsterdam, 1729, and reprinted frequently thereafter (this section was translated into English by

L. Elmaleh and published under the title, *Dreams, Their Origin and True Nature;* see esp. pp. 43 f.); idem, *Sefer Me'ammeṣ koaḥ* (Increasing Strength; homilies), Venice, 1588; and Don Joseph Nasi and Isaac Onqeneira's *Ben Porat Yosef* (Joseph Is a Fruitful Vine; a polemical tract), Constantinople, 1577. As an example of the several dedications of Hebrew volumes to Don Joseph one may mention the *Sefer Yosef leqaḥ* (Increase in Learning: a commentary on the Book of Esther), by the distinguished scholar Eliezer b. Elijah Ashkenazi, Cremona, 1576. See also other relevant data cited by C. Roth in *The Duke of Naxos,* Chaps. VII–VIII, esp. pp. 180 f.; and in his "Immanuel Aboab's Proselytization of the Marranos. From an Unpublished Letter," *JQR,* XXIII, 121–62, esp. p. 137. Characteristic of Don Joseph's realistic approach also to scientific problems was his utter repudiation of astrology and the use of astronomic observations for predictions on the future course of human developments. In his purported debate with a Christian theologian, reflected in his *Ben Porat Yosef,* he was particularly happy to cite the ancient talmudic doctrine that Israel had nothing to fear from the changing celestial constellations and exclaimed, "I bless the Lord for having brought me into Israel, His people and congregation and I am not afraid of the heavenly stars." Quoted by S. A. Rosanes in his *Dibre yeme (Qorot),* III, 2 f.

These occasional Hebrew references to Don Joseph and his mother-in-law would nevertheless have left us in the dark about most of his life and work. Even if supplemented by such imprecise data as are included in imaginative poems, such as Manoli Blessi's *Al Signor Zan Miches, ditto Giosuf Ebreo* and *Dialogo di Selin con Giosuf Hebreo,* both published in Venice in 1572, and by the few Turkish documents which have thus far come to light (some of which are available in A. Galanté's French translations), we would still know very little about his ramified activities. We are mainly dependent, therefore, on the frequent and extensive references to him in the Venetian, French, and Austrian ambassadorial dispatches. Of course, these foreign envoys were not only biased observers and special pleaders for the national interests of their countries, but also limited their observations to matters of special interest to their home offices. That is why we are so much better informed about Don Joseph's international role in the power politics of the 1560s and 1570s than we are even about his business dealings, although he probably spent more time on his mercantile than on his diplomatic activities. Don Joseph's internal contributions to Jewish culture and community life were of practically no concern to the foreign ambassadors, except if they happened to be Renaissance scholars. It is also for this reason that, although our presentation generally avoids extensive biographical treatment, more than the usual amount of space has been allotted to a description of the unusual career of a Marrano turned lay Jewish leader, international banker, and diplomat—a career which indirectly sheds much light on otherwise obscure areas of Jewish history during the early modern period.

64. See Guillaume le Granteir de Grandchamp's reports of October 3 and 30, 1569 in E. Charrière's *Négociations,* III, 80 ff.; and on Daud's testimony and ban, S. A. Rosanes's data in his *Dibre yeme (Qorot),* II, 98; III, 6 ff., 32 f. See also T. Bertile, *Il Palazzo degli ambasciatori di Venezia a Constantinopoli e le sue antiche memorie* (esp. p. 137 n. 84, mentioning the Jewish merchant Aron Segura's large monetary claim because of an unlawful seizure of his property); as well as the following notes; and *infra,* Chap. LXXVII, n. 22, airing the possibility of David's identity with David Passi.

65. See Joseph ha-Kohen, *'Emeq ha-bakha,* pp. 153 f., 168 f.; N. Jorga, *Geschichte des Osmanischen Reiches,* III, 156 f.; and other literature emntioned *supra,* Vols. XIV, pp. 77 ff., 335 n. 6; XVI, pp. 24 ff., 336 f. nn. 48–49. Of interest also is Ashkenazi's

correspondence with Grand Duke Francesco of Tuscany. See I. Zoller (Zolli), "Una Lettera di Salomone Ashkenazi al Granduca di Toscana," *Rivista israelitica*, VI, 145–51. Solomon seems to have spent some time in Venice before his appearance at the Council, if we may take a cue from the colophon written by the printer of the Venice, 1574 edition of Joseph Karo's code, the *Shulḥan 'Arukh*, Ḥ.M. Here the typographer thanked God for having enabled him to complete the printing on Tammuz 10, 5734 (June 30, 1574) during the presence in the city of Solomon Ashkenazi as ambassador of the great Sultan Selim II, an event "such as had not been seen since the separation of Judah from Ephraim [ancient Northern Israel], namely the great dignity and honor with which he [Ashkenazi] was treated by our rulers here, a distinction the like of which had not been granted to any Hebrew since the destruction of our Temple." Moreover, in addition to whatever presents they may have given the Turkish envoy, the Venetian authorities undertook to provide for the higher education of Solomon's three sons Nathan, Samuel, and Obadiah, at their expense. See S. A. Rosanes, *Dibre yeme (Qorot)*, III, 349 ff. App. i; and *infra*, Chap. LXXVII n. 11.

66. Soranzo's speech quoted from Ha-Kohen stems from the pen of the "proof-reader" (*ha-maggiah*) who brought the chronicle up to 1605, about a quarter century after the author's death (pp. 155 ff.). On this proofreader who successfully emulated Ha-Kohen's style see, for instance, M. Shulvass, "To Which of R. Joseph ha-Kohen's Works Had the 'Proof-Reader' written His Continuation?" (Hebrew), *Zion*, X, 78–79. This speech is also available in a German translation by M. Wiener in his *Emek ha-bacha*, p. 121; and in the recent English translation (which differs from the rendition in the text) by H. S. May entitled *The Vale of Tears (Emek Habacha)*, trans. and with Critical Commentary, pp. 114 f. On the literary device à la Livy, widespread in Renaissance historiography, see the brief remarks in my twin essays on Ha-Kohen's contemporary, "Azariah de' Rossi's Attitude to Life" in *Jewish Studies in Memory of Israel Abrahams*, pp. 12–52; and "La Méthode historique d'Azaria de' Rossi," *REJ*, LXXXVI, 151–75; LXXXVII, 43–78, both reprinted (the latter in an English translation entitled "Azariah de'Rossi's Historical Method") in my *History and Jewish Historians*, pp. 174–204, 406–422, 205–239, 422–42, esp. p. 214. Although we do not have any direct evidence for Ha-Kohen's or his anonymous proofreader's indebtedness to the ancient Roman historian, there is little doubt that, like most of their contemporaries, they shared Azariah's great admiration for Livy. In one passage De' Rossi called Livy a writer who "had no equal among the Gentile nations either before or after him until the present day." See his *Sefer Me'or 'Eynaim* (The Light of the Eyes; historical essays), ed. by A. Benjacob, I, 254; ed. by D. Cassel, p. 264.

Yet, whatever one thinks of the authenticity of Soranzo's speech, there were, of course, fundamental forces in Venetian society which induced the Senate first to vote for and then to revoke the decree of expulsion. See now B. C. L. Ravid's "The Socio-economic Background of the Expulsion and Readmission of the Venetian Jews, 1571–1573" in *Essays in Modern Jewish History: a Tribute to Benjamin Halpern*, ed. by F. Malino and P. C. Albert, pp. 29–55.

67. See George Sandys, *A Relation of a Journey Begun A.D. 1610*, III, 148; R. B. Davis, *George Sandys, Poet-Adventurer*, pp. 68 ff., 76 f.; D. Tamar, "The Expectation of Redemption to Come in the Year 5335 [1575]" (Hebrew), *Sefunot*, II, 61–88, esp. pp. 62 ff. During her sojourn in Italy, Gracia must have been well acquainted with her counterparts, Samuel and Benvenida Abravanel, son and daughter-in-law respectively of Don Isaac Abravanel, the great diplomat and scholar. She must have heard about that author's works on Jewish messianism, particularly his Commentary on the Book

of Daniel, which enjoyed a great reputation among both Jewish and Christian intellectuals. See B. Netanyahu, *Don Isaac Abravanel Statesman and Philosopher*, 2d ed. esp. pp. 82 ff., 195 ff. She doubtless also learned a good deal about the fantastic Reubeni-Molkho episode which in part took place in Venice but a few years before her arrival there. See *supra*, Vol. XIII, pp. 109 ff., 364 ff. nn. 53–58. Gracia may further have been told about the then prevailing Jewish messianic expectations from her protégé, Samuel Usque, who had dedicated his major work to her. In her contacts with the distinguished doctor Amatus Lusitanus, both friend and physician of the Nasi family, especially after his settlement in Salonica, she must have heard from him about various Jewish individuals who had medical problems because of their messianic involvement—one might call them messianic complexes today—described in his classical medical work, *Centuriae*, V (which in 1559 he dedicated to Joseph Nasi). See the facsimile of the dedication, reproduced in C. Roth, *The Duke of Naxos* (facing p. 178). See also, more generally, A. H. Silver, *A History of Messianic Speculation in Israel from the First to the Seventeenth Centuries* (reprinted in New York, 1959), pp. 120 ff. The impact on the messianic expectations in Palestine and the diverse interpretations of the duty of that generation to prepare itself for that momentous event—a phase of which resulted in the earlier renowned "Controversy on the Semikhah (Ordination) between R. Jacob Beirab and R. Levi Ibn Habib." See, for instance, J. Katz's pertinent Hebrew article in *Zion*, XVI, 28–45—will be analyzed *infra*, Chap. LXXVIII, n. 111; and more fully in a later volume. Under these circumstances it was almost impossible for a lady with her devotion to the Jewish religion during her stormy career not to have been affected by these mystical trends in her Jewish environment.

68. On the ancient messianic connections with Tiberias, see Bab. Talmud, Rosh ha-Shanah, 31b (invoking the allusion to Isa. 52:2 because of Tiberias' location 695 feet below sea level); Maimonides, *M.T.* Sanhedrin, xiv, 12; the document of June 15, 1560 published by U. Heyd in his *Ottoman Documents on Palestine 1552–1615; a Study of the Firman according to the* Mühimme Defteri, pp. XV–XVIII, 3 ff.; and again in the Turkish original with a Hebrew translation in his "Turkish Documents concerning the Reconstruction of Tiberias in the Sixteenth Century" (Hebrew), *Sefunot*, X, 193–210, esp. pp. 202 f. On the earlier history of the Jews of Tiberias see the numerous references in Vols. II, III, V, and VI listed in the Index to Vols. I–VIII, *s.v.;* and for the early modern period J. Braslawski's introductory remarks to his "Jewish Settlement in Tiberias from Don Joseph Nasi to Ibn Ya'ish" (Hebrew) *Zion*, V, 45–72, reprinted with other essays, in his *Le-heqer Arṣenu* (On the Study of Our Land), pp. 191–215; and the various references in I. Ben-Zvi's *Eretz-Yisrael ve-yishubah* (Eretz-Israel under Ottoman Rule: Four Centuries of History), Index, *s.v.* The relatively few comments by Christian pilgrims and other travelers are, for the most part, well reproduced in a Hebrew translation with comments by M. Ish-Shalom in his *Massa'ei Noṣrim le-Ereṣ Yisrael* (Christian Travels in the Holy Land: Description and Sources on the History of the Jews in Palestine), Index, p. 856, *s.v.* Tveryah.

69. Joseph ha-Kohen, *'Emeq ha-bakha*, pp. 127 ff.; in M. Wiener's German trans., pp. 104 f.; and in H. S. May's (different) English rendition in *The Vale of Tears*, pp. 100 f. A suggestion made by Cecil Roth (in *The Duke of Naxos*, pp. 112, 234 n. 5) that the Ibn Arduṭ mentioned in Joseph ha-Kohen's Chronicle may be identical with the duke's secretary Joseph Cohen who signed the aforementioned order concerning the monastery D'Annunciata (*supra*, n. 55) seems unlikely. Certainly, the name Cohen would more pertinently be used in a Hebrew text like the chronicle here quoted than in an official governmental decree for Naxos, originally written in Turkish. Moreover,

this decree was actually issued by Samuel Cohen, who appears to have been Joseph Cohen's superior. Otherwise nothing else seems to be known about this new official receiving a governmental salary for work in Jewish Tiberias. On the scale of salaries for court physicians see the data assembled by U. Heyd, cited *supra*, n. 47.

70. See E. Charrière, *Négociations*, II, 738. The phrase used by De Pétrémol has been taken seriously by a number of Jewish scholars. See in particular, J. Reznik and J. Klausner in their studies mentioned *supra*, n. 57. However, the majority of scholars rejected these high-sounding implications of a much more moderate approach on the part of Joseph Nasi. De Pétrémol's exaggerating phrase was no more meaningful than when some nineteenth-century antisemites attributed to the Rothschilds the desire to become "kings of the Jews." It was to such rumors that, for one example, Isaac M. Wise replied in 1876 (partly out of his anti-Zionist bias) that "no European country to-day would give permission to the Jews to emigrate with their wealth or even without it, and the European Jews have as little an idea to go as the Rothschilds want to purchase Palestine, or be Kings of the Jews." See his "The Jews Return to Palestine," *The American Israelite*, XXVII, no. 11, p. 5; XXVIII, no. 3, pp. 2, 4, cited in J. M. Baron and S. W. Baron, "Palestinian Messengers in America, 1849–79: a Record of Four Journeys," *JSS*, V, 115–62, 225–92, esp. p. 265; reprinted in my *Steeled by Adversity: Essays and Addresses on American Jewish Life*, ed. by J. M. Baron, pp. 241, 624 n. 92. A well-known antisemitic work by Antoine de Toussenel, very popular in the mid-1840s bore the characteristic title, *Les Juifs, rois de l'époque. Histoire de la féodalité financière*, referring to the great power of Jewish capitalists. None of these attributions were meant to be taken literally.

71. Of course, Gracia's initial application for a tiny colony, opening its gates to Jewish refugees from persecution and enjoying a modicum of autonomy to develop its members' economic and cultural creativity, did not preclude the realization of some higher goals conceived in Don Joseph's fertile mind. If successful, such a nuclear development might indeed have led to a Jewish establishment of greater dimensions in Palestine. But as we shall presently see, even the original modest expectations were not to be fulfilled.

72. See Pantaleõa de Aveiro, *Itinerario da Terra Sancta e suas particularidades*, ed. with an Intro. by A. Baião, pp. 105, 471 f.; Guillaume Postel, *De la Republique des Turcs*, Part 2, p. 23; Eugene Roger, *La Terre Sainte*, Paris, 1664, p. 70; and on the considerable tensions prevailing between the Turkish ruling group and the local Arab majority, G. W. F. Stripling in *The Ottoman Turks and the Arabs*, pp. 102 ff. See also *infra*, n. 76. While Roger refers to a synagogue in Tiberias, apparently none had existed there during the earlier visit of De Aveiro, who mentions only one he had visited in Venice. There he had heard some Jews predicting the coming of the Messiah within six or seven years.

The aversion of orthodox Jews to pray in churches or mosques while they were functioning as houses of worship for other faiths is well known. There is some ambivalence, however, about whether it is permissible to convert an abandoned or otherwise unused church into a synagogue. This matter became of great importance particularly in the United States during the rising tide of Jewish immigration in the nineteenth century. Owing to the general mobility of the American population, groups of Jews, especially in New York City, often replaced an earlier ethnic group in certain quarters. When the Irish, German, and other Christian residents moved out, they usually left behind them some churches which had lost most of their worshipers. Because of the general housing shortage, it was mutually convenient for the Christians to sell their churches to new Jewish arrivals who had found that, with relatively little remodeling, they could be made serviceable for Jewish communal purposes. To overcome the compunctions of many Jewish worshipers, two American Orthodox rabbis inquired from authoritative confreres in Europe whether under Jewish law their congregation could hold divine services in such newly converted synagogues. In reply Rabbi Joseph Saul Nathanson of Lwów argued that, since the biblical messianic prophesies foretold that at the end of days all nations would worship the God of Israel, this promise presupposed the wholesale conversion of all other sanctuaries into synagogues. See Nathanson's responsum, cited in the English translation by M. Silber in his *America in Hebrew Literature*, pp. 92 f.; and my *Steeled by Adversity*, pp. 388 f., 667 n. 142. Yet no such argument seems to have been heard among sixteenth-century Jewish pilgrims to Palestine.

73. Joseph ha-Kohen, *'Emeq ha-bakha* (see n. 63); and particularly the Turkish documents presented by Uriel Heyd in *Sefunot*, II, 104 ff. Nos. 2–7. These data also help identify four of the seven villages which were included in Suleiman's grant to Joseph, as well as the protective measures taken to quell the Arab boycott and to prevent thieves from stealing the belongings of the new arrivals. For a while, it appears, the pasha of Damascus kept a few Janissaries as permanent guards on the new settlement. As given by both Ha-Kohen and the Turkish source, the wall had a circumference of some 1,500 ells, probably of about three-quarters of a meter each, making a total of about 1,200 meters. To be sure Roger, who visited Tiberias about 1630, gives the smaller measurement of but 600–700 "paces." It is not to be assumed that in the intervening sixty years the wall was allowed to shrink in size. Probably the French visitor offered but a general approximation. On Doña Gracia's last years, see *supra*, n. 39.

74. See P. de Aveiro, *Itinerario da Terra Sancta*, p. 474 (describing how he had met a Jew who made a living from fishing in the Sea of Galilee; hospitably entertained at dinner, he was served fresh fish from the Jew's catch); U. Heyd, *Ottoman Documents*, p. 141 (adding sugar cane to the agricultural production of Tiberias); Joseph ha-Kohen, *'Emeq ha-bakha; supra*, Vol. XIV, pp. 32 ff., 43 ff. with the notes thereon. The noteworthy letter from the community of Cori was published by D. Kaufmann in "Don Joseph Nasi, Founder of Colonies in the Holy Land, and the Community of Cori in the Campagna," *JQR*, [o.s.] II, 291–310; it has since been extensively quoted by scholars. Because of its wordiness, translations into Western languages could not be literal. An adequate abridgement in English has been included in C. Roth, *The Duke of Naxos*, pp. 126 ff. from which the passages cited in the text are quoted. The aftermath of the papal decree of expulsion of 1569 has likewise been illumined by the documents first published by D. Kaufmann in "A Letter from the Community of Pesaro to Don Joseph Nasi," *JQR*, [o.s.] IV, 509–512; and in his "Contributions à l'histoire des Juifs en Italie, V: La Quète pour les Expulsés de Pesaro," *REJ*, XX, 34–72, esp. pp. 46 f., 70 ff. App. xi–xiii. See also the other sources, cited in the Hebrew publications by M. A. Shulvass in his *Roma vi-Yerushalayim* (Rome and Jerusalem: a History of the Attitudes of the Jews of Italy toward Palestine), pp. 74 ff.; and by I. Sonne in his *Mi-Pavlo ha-rebi'i 'ad Pius ha-ḥamishi* (From Paul IV to Pius V), esp. pp. 204 ff.

Undoubtedly because of the tension between the Ottoman Empire and Venice during the war of 1570–73, particularly after the defeat of the Turkish navy at Lepanto, the Hospitallers of Malta and other Christian corsairs were free to roam the Adriatic

Sea and the eastern Mediterranean with greater than the usual impunity. Among the sufferers were some of the Jews of Pesaro who tried to move to Turkey. The "proof-reader" of Ha-Kohen's '*Emeq* graphically describes the sufferings of the Jews captured by the Maltese and sold into slavery, especially those serving as galley slaves whose life expectancy was, as a rule, very short. See '*Emeq ha-bakha*, pp. 140 f.; in M. Wiener's German trans., pp. 114 f., 214; in H. S. May's English trans., pp. 109 f. See also, more generally, C. Roth, "The Jews of Malta," *Transactions* of the Jewish Historical Society of England, XII, 187–251 (also reprint), esp. pp. 212 ff.

75. See the documents published by B. Lewis in his *Notes and Documents*, pp. 28 ff., 33 ff. Nos. i–iii (Turkish and English); by U. Heyd in his *Ottoman Documents on Palestine*, esp. pp. 121 f. No. 71, 164 ff. Nos. 109–115 (English), Plates XV–XVI, "Documents 109, 111, 113–14 (Turkish); and his analytical Hebrew study of "Turkish Documents from Ottoman Archives Concerning Safed Jews in the Sixteenth Century C.E.," *Yerushalayim, Review*, II–V, 125–35 (includes facsimiles of 5 Turkish documents and their Hebrew translation). The flimsy nature of some of the ploys used by officials to extort payments from Safed Jews is well illustrated by the complaint of one individual that "Mohammed, the beg of Safed, alleged that I had committed fornication with a Jewess and without [securing] a legal proof or confession took 150 florins of mine [for himself] and [another] 50 florins of mine were spent [as bribes?] at his Porte." This and other complaints elicited an imperial order of July 26, 1576 to the beglerbeg and qadhi of Damascus to investigate these grievances and, if they proved justified, to order the return of the wrongly exacted fines to the falsely accused party. See Heyd, *Ottoman Documents*, pp. 104 ff. No. 109 (English), Plate XV No. 109 (Turkish). See also *supra*, n. 60.

76. See Eugène Roger, *La Terre Sainte ou Description topographique très particulière des saintes lieux et de la Terre de Promission*, Paris, 1664, p. 70; and *infra*, Chap. LXXVIII, nn. 124–27. Roger's observations in 1629–34 have given rise to varying interpretations by modern scholars. See esp. I. Ben-Zvi's "Palestine Settlement in the Seventeenth Century" (Hebrew), *Zion*, VII, 156–71, with the comments thereon by A. J. Brawer in his "Roger's Book as a Source of Information Regarding Jews and Economics in Palestine during the Seventeenth Century" (Hebrew), *ibid.*, VIII, 157–61 (pointing out, in particular, twelve localities which theretofore had had no recorded Jewish settlements); I. Press, "Roger's Book as a Source of Information Regarding Jews and Economics in Palestine" (Hebrew), *ibid.*, pp. 162–63; and Ben-Zvi's "Reply," *ibid.*, p. 163. See also M. Ish-Shalom, *Massa'ei Noṣrim*, pp. 121 ff., 330 ff. (includes facsimile of the title page of Roger's work). Some of the eighteenth-century developments, which need not be elaborated here, are discussed, for instance, in my "On the History of the Jewish Settlement in Tiberias in 1742–44" (Hebrew), *Sefer ha-Yobel* (A Tribute to) *Professor Alexander Marx*, ed. by D. Fränkel, pp. 79–88, with the sources cited there.

Tiberias' adversities were also owing to the sharp decline of Ottoman power, economic as well as political, after the deaths in 1574 and 1579 of Selim II and Sokolli, about which more anon. See, in particular, also S. Schwarzfuchs, "La Décadence de la Galilée juive du XVIᵉ siècle et la crise du textile du Proche-Orient," *REJ*, CXXI, 169–79; and O. Avissar's comprehensive study, *Sefer Tveriah* (The Book of Tiberias: Geography, History and Folklore of Tiberias and Its Region, with Special Reference to the History of the Jewish Community during the Ottoman Period).

77. R. Samuel de Medina, *Resp.*, II No. 124; and other passages quoted by M. S. Goodblatt in his *Jewish Life in Turkey*, pp. 118 ff., 214 ff.

CHAPTER LXXVII: INCIPIENT STAGNATION

1. The dating of the beginning of the Ottoman crisis with the succession of Murad III in 1574, rather than the widely accepted end of the Ottoman Golden Age at the death of Suleiman the Magnificent in 1566, is somewhat arbitrary, as are all such precise datings for changes requiring years, even decades, to come to the fore. However, others, too, have felt that, at least politically, the power of the Empire continued to the death of Meḥmed Sokolli in 1579. See R. Lewis, *Everyday Life in Ottoman Turkey;* and F. David's comments thereon in his review of that work in *AO*, V, 324–27. However, during the last five years of his life the grand vizier lost much of his influence under the ever suspicious controls of Selim II's son and successor. See also the general literature on Ottoman history listed *supra*, Chap. LXXV, n. 1; and some of the monographs cited in the previous and forthcoming notes.

There is occasional confusion with regard to the dates of the respective reigns of individual sultans of that period. The obscurities have largely been resolved as a result of the assiduous work of a number of scholars, especially S. Lane-Poole in *The Mohammaden Dynasties: Chronological and Genealogical Tables with Historical Introductions;* and E. von Zambaur, *Manuel de généalogie et de chronologie pour l'histoire de l'Islam,* which also lists the grand viziers from the reign of Murad I (pp. 101 ff.), the pashas of Egypt from Selim I (pp. 160 ff.), and so forth. For quick and more up-to-date reference one may conveniently use C. E. Bosworth, *The Islamic Dynasties: a Chronological and Genealogical Handbook.* In view of the sultans' greatly concentrated power their activity or neglect largely determined the course of public affairs. Hence individual biographies of the monarchs are also very helpful. Suffice it to mention the overall lively review by N. Barber, *The Lords of the Golden Horn from Suleiman the Magnificent to Kamal Ataturk.*

2. Ḥasan al-Kafi (or al-Kiafi) Aḥizari's missive, entitled *Usul al-hikem fi nizam ul-ālam* (Philosophic Principles Concerning the World Order), is available in his own Turkish rendition of 1597 and in modern French and German translations by G. de Tassy in his "Principe de Sagesse touchant l'art de gouverner," *JA*, IV, 213–76, 283–90; and by L. Thallóczy in his and E. J. Karácson's "Eine Staatsschrift des bosnischen Mahommedaners Mulla Hassan Elkjafi über die Art und Weise des Regierens," *Archiv für slavische Philologie,* XXXII, 139–58. See the general bio-bibliographical data on both men in F. Babinger, *Die Geschichtsschreiber der Osmanen,* with a supplement on *Osmanische Zeitrechnungen* by Joachim Mayr, esp. pp. 144 f., 184, 414 f.; and the meaningful analysis by Mustafa A. Mehmed, "La Crise Ottomane dans la vision de Hasan Kiafi Akhizari (1544–1616)," *RESEE,* XIII, 385–402, esp. pp. 393 ff. Mustafa Kochu Bey's tract, also known simply as a *risala* (missive), was translated into German by W. F. A. Behrnauer in his "Koǧagbeg's Abhandlung über den Verfall des osmanischen Staatsgebäudes seit Sultan Suleiman dem Grossen. Nach Wiener und St. Petersburger Handschriften," *ZDMG,* XV, 272–332, with about a dozen corrections, suggested by Baron Schlechta-Wssehrel and published by H. L. Fleischer in his "Nachträgliche Bemerkungen," *ibid.,* XVI, 271–72. The varying French appraisals are noted by C. D. Rouillard in *The Turk in French History, Thought and Literature (1520–1660),* which includes a bibliography of French pamphlets relating to Turkey published between 1520 and 1660 (pp. 646–65). Among more recent studies, see, for instance, B. Lewis's "Some

Reflections on the Decline of the Ottoman Empire," *Studia islamica*, IX, 111–27. See also *infra*, n. 28.

3. See Martin Crusius, *Turcogreciae libri octo*, Basel, 1584, p. 505. On the gradual alienation of Moldavia and Walachia, see the brief remarks by N. Jorga in his *Geschichte*, III, 302 ff. For the rather speedy emancipation of the begs of Tunisia and Algeria from Turkish tutelage while they still paid homage to Ottoman suzerainty, and their establishment of semi-monarchical systems along hereditary lines see, J. M. Abu-Nasr, "The Beylicate in Seventeenth-Century Tunisia," *IJMES*, VI, 70–93; and *infra*, nn. 44, 70. Such semi-independence enabled these North African officials to maintain separate diplomatic correspondence with foreign powers like France. See the twin publications by E. Plantet, ed., *Correspondance des Beys de Tunis et des Consuls de France 1577–1830;* and *Correspondance des Beys d'Alger avec la Cour de France 1579–1833*. The relations between Austria and the Ottoman Empire after the Peace Treaty of 1606 are discussed by I. von Testa, in his ed. of *Recueil des Traités de la Porte Ottomane avec les Puissances étrangères depuis le premier traité conclu en 1536 entre Suleyman I et François I jusqu'à nos jours;* and many other works. See also *supra*, Chap. LXXVI, nn. 40, 44, and 52.

On the intriguing problem of why Turkey did not utilize Austria's deep involvement in the Thirty Years' War for territorial gains, see C. Rotman, "Zur Frage osmanischer Teilnahme am Dreissigjährigen Krieg (Vorabend des um 1620 Osmanischen Feldzuges gegen die Moldau)," *RESEE*, XIII, 417–24 (a contribution to the Third International Congress of Southeast European Studies, Bucharest, September 4–10, 1974); R. R. Heinisch, "Habsburg, die Pforte und der böhmische Aufstand (1618–1620)," *Südost-Forschungen*, XXXIII, 125–65; XXXIV, 79–124, esp. XXXIV, 123 f. The normalization of the relations between the two powers found its best expression in the dispatches of the Austrian envoys to Constantinople. See, for example, P. Meienberger, *Johann Rudolf Schmid zum Schwarzenhorn als kaiserlicher Resident in Konstantinopel in den Jahren 1629–1643. Ein Beitrag zur Geschichte der diplomatischen Beziehungen zwischen Österreich und der Türkei in der ersten Hälfte des 17. Jahrhunderts*. Because of this normalization of relationships the Austrian authorities were able to claim an increasing share in the protection of the Catholic population in the Ottoman Empire. See M. Lehmann's succinct observations in *Österreich und der christliche Osten. Begegnungen in Gegenwart und Vergangenheit*. We must bear in mind, however, that Charles V had already used the distinguished Orientalist, Gerhard Veltwyck, a New Christian, for diplomatic exchanges with the Ottoman authorities. Although, on his first arrival in Constantinople in July 1545 the envoy was treated "more like a prisoner than as an ambassador" and also had many other difficulties to overcome because of French intrigues, he acquitted himself of his mission so well, that in 1546 the emperor and his brother Ferdinand sent him on another such assignment to the Porte. See M. Rosenberg, *Gerhard Veltwyck, Orientalist, Theologe und Staatsmann* (Diss. Göttingen); and *supra*, Vol. XIII, pp. 368 f. n. 63.

4. See A. W. Fisher, "Moscovite-Ottoman Relations in the Seventeenth Century," *Humaniora islamica*, I, 207–217; E. Niewohner Eberhard, "Machtpolitik. Aspekte des Osmanisch-Safawidischen Kampfes um Bagdad im 16/17 Jahrhundert," *Turcica*, VI, 103–127; and the Venetian envoy Simon Contarini's laudatory characterization of 'Abbas I in his 1612 report to the Senate, reproduced in N. Barozzi and G. Berchet, eds., *Relazioni degli stati europei lette al Senato dagli ambasciatori veneti nel secolo decimoset-*

timo, I, 125 ff., esp. p. 195. See also Josef von Hammer-Purgstall, *Geschichte des osmanischen Reiches*, II, 359 f.; N. Jorga, *Geschichte*, III, 233 ff., 431 ff., and the sources listed in both these works.

5. See Stephan Gerlach, *Tage-Buch*, pp. 95 f.; A. Galanté, *Documents officiels turcs*, pp. 135 f. No. 1; Samuel de Medina, *Resp.* on Y.D. No. 124; on Ḥ.M. No. 364. An example of the decline in the payment of *kharaj* is offered by M. Bersa in his "Moldavian and Valachian Kharaj of the 15th through the 19th Centuries" (Rumanian), *Studii și articoli de Istorie Medie*, II, 7–47. The monetary crisis made itself felt with redoubled intensity in the provinces where the centralized administration of the Ottoman Empire exercised less rigid controls. For this reason, for example, such studies by Rumanian scholars about developments in Walachia or Moldavia often shed considerable additional light on the depth of the political difficulties generated by the currency depreciation. See also M. Maxim, "Considérations sur la circulation monétaire dans les pays roumains et d'Empire Ottoman dans la seconde moitié du XVIᵉ siècle," *RESEE*, XIII, 407–415 (a brief communication to the Third International Congress of Southeast European Studies, held in Bucharest September 4–10, 1974), esp. the 3 tables on pp. 409 ff.; N. Beldiceanu, "La Crise monétaire ottomane au XVIᵉ siècle et son influence sur les principautés roumaines," *Südost-Forschungen*, XVI, 70–86.

6. A. Galanté, *Documents officiels turcs*, pp. 136 f. Nos. 2–3; A. C. Schaendlinger, *Osmanische Numismatik; Von den Anfängen des Osmanischen Reiches bis zu seiner Auflösung 1922*, esp. pp. 266 ff. offering a tentative list of localities whence coins were issued; and the pertinent essays, ed. by O. Pickl in "Die Wirtschaftlichen Auswirkungen der Türkenkriege" in the Papers submitted to the First Graz International Congress on Economic and Social History of Southeastern Europe, held in Graz on October 6–10, 1970 and ed. by him.

7. Isaac b. Shem Ṭob ibn Walid, *Va-yomer Yiṣhaq* (And Isaac Said: responsa), I, No. 112; II (on Ḥ.M.), No. 154, cited by Z. (A.) Kahane in "Changes in the Value of the Currency in Jewish Law" (Hebrew), *Sinai*, XIII, nos. 147–52, pp. 129–48, esp. pp. 131 f. To be sure, in evaluating the impact of such currency depreciations on diverse groups of the population, we must bear in mind the enormous regional variations in prices, local barter trades, and standards of life. We recall Claude Cahen's reference to eleventh-century conditions, when in Iraq an annual income of 200 dirhems placed the recipient below the accepted poverty level, while a Khurasan earner of 50 dirhems a year was considered wealthy. See Cahen's "Considérations sur l'utilisation des ouvrages de droit musulman par l'historien," *Atti* of the Third Congresso di Studi Arabi e Islamici, held in Ravello, September 1–8, 1966, pp. 239–47, esp. p. 244; reprinted in his collection of essays, *Les Peuples musulmans dans l'histoire médiévale*, pp. 81–89, esp. p. 86. The same held true later for the various provinces of the Ottoman Empire. But everywhere most of their inhabitants must have suffered more or less intensely from the changing values of the currency available to them.

8. See R. Moses b. Ḥayyim Alshekh's *Resp.*, new ed. rev. with a biographical sketch of the author by Y. Ṭ. Porges, pp. 286 f. No. 129. See also *ibid.*, pp. 86 f. No. 34, 258 f. No. 116, etc. On this noteworthy scholar and communal leader, who also played a role in the renowned controversy over the attempted revival of the ancient Sanhedrin through the restoration of the ordination—Alshekh himself was ordained by R. Jacob Berab and he, in turn, ordained R. Ḥayyim Vital Calabrese—see the more ex-

tensive Hebrew biography, *Rabbi Mosheh Alshekh: le-ḥeqer shiṭṭato* (an Analysis of His Exegetical Approach and His General Views) by S. Shalem. Primarily interested in his subject's intellectual contributions Shalem excuses the meagerness of the more strictly biographical data by the paucity of pertinent sources.

9. See E. Charrière, *Négociations*, III, 918; N. Barozzi and G. Berchet, eds., *Relazioni degli stati europei lette al senato dagli ambasciatori e baili veneziani a Constantinopoli* [ser. V of 10 vol. collection], II, 83 ff.; K. Röhrborn, "Die Emanzipation der Finanzbürokratie im Osmanischen Reiche (Ende 16. Jahrhundert)," *ZDMG*, CXXII, 118–39, esp. pp. 119 f., 125; M. Maxim, "Grand Vizier Sinan Pasha and His Fabulous Riches" (Rumanian), *Magazin Istorie*, VIII, no. 10, pp. 48–53. See also the interesting characterization of Murad IV in N. Jorga's *Geschichte*, III, 447 f. The demographic and political impact of the rural pressures and the resulting peasant migrations to the overcrowded cities are analyzed, from the Marxist point of view, by E. Werner in his "Despotie, Absolutismus, oder feudale Zersplitterung? Strukturwandlungen im Osmanen Reich zwischen 1566 und 1699," *Jahrbuch für Wirtschaftsgeschichte*, 1972, no. 3, pp. 107–128. On the average yield of wheat per hectare during the earlier and later periods, see N. Kondov, "Über den wahrscheinlichen Weizenertrag auf der Balkanhalbinsel im Mittelalter," *Études balkaniques*, 1974, no. 1, pp. 97–109 with reference to the researches by N. Svoronov and others.

10. See E. Hurmuzaki, *Documente privitóaere la storia românilor* (Private Documents in Rumanian History), XII, 128, 499 No. dcccxcviii; N. Jorga, *Geschichte*, III, 410 f., 427 ff. See also the dispatch of the English ambassador in Constantinople of December 27, 1603 describing the sultan's financial stringency, reproduced in Hurmuzaki, XVI, 1 ff. No. 1. On the position of the ulema in the Ottoman Empire, see the interesting papers presented at the Jerusalem colloquium of May 1969 in memory of Uriel Heyd and ed. by G. Baer in *Ha-'Ulema u-ba'ayot dat ba-'olam ha-muslimi* (The 'Ulema and Problems of Religion in the Muslim World).

11. See I. Testa, *Recueil des traités de la Porte Ottomane*, II, 832, 893 n. 1; E. Charrière, *Négociations*, III, 832, 883 n. 1; S. A. Rosanes, *Dibre yeme* (*Qorot*), III, 9, 349 ff. excursus iii/1; and *supra*, Vols. XIV, pp. 78 f., 335 n. 6; XVI, pp. 44 ff., 336 f. nn. 48–50. Rosanes also points out that, although Polish Jewish writers were generally silent about the presence among them of the distinguished Jewish court physician from Italy, there are some brief allusions to him in connection with a marital problem of his sister-in-law in the responsa of the two greatest rabbinic luminaries in the country, Solomon b. Yeḥiel Luria and Moses b. Israel Isserles. See Luria's *Resp.*, Fürth 1768 ed., fols. 10d f., No. 21; and Isserles' *Resp.*, Cracow, 1640 ed., No. 30. In this context Rosanes mentions Eliakim Carmoly's claim to have had in his possession a manuscript describing Solomon Ashkenazi's various journeys to France, Poland, and Muscovy. However, his reference to Carmoly's *Histoire de médécins juifs, anciens et modernes*, p. 185 is incorrect. Moreover, the Belgian scholar never divulged any details about that manuscript and apparently no other specialist has ever seen it. In view of the doubts frequently expressed by Carmoly's contemporaries about some of his bibliographical assertions, one must leave the question of the authenticity of that manuscript quite open. On the skepticism, often pushed to extremes by Carmoly's confreres like Leopold Zunz and Moritz Steinschneider, see my "Moritz Steinschneider's Contributions to Jewish Historiography," *Alexander Marx Jubilee Volume*, pp. 83–148, esp. p. 115, reprinted in my *History and Jewish Historians*, pp. 276 ff., 299 f., 459 f. n. 44.

12. See the anonymous continuation [by Samuel David Luzzatto] of Joseph ha-Kohen, *'Emeq*, pp. 197 f.; in M. Wiener's German trans. pp. 145 f., 218 n. 339 (pointing out the chronological confusion in this report); in H. S. May's English trans., *The Vale of Tears*, pp. 137 f.; the Foreword to R. Moses b. Hayyim Alshekh's *Resp.* by his son in the Venice 1605–1606 ed.; and other sources quoted by S. A. Rosanes in his *Dibre yeme (Qorot)*, III, 375, excursus iii/2. As pointed out by Wiener the account in the *'Emeq* is chronologically impossible. Mehmed III died on December 22 (more correctly 16), 1603 at the age of thirty-seven. Living a life of debauchery, he may indeed have contracted the "French disease," from which he was cured by Bula in 1602. Joseph ha-Kohen's "corrector" may have been right about the date, but confused the patient with Mehmed's son, Ahmed I, "aged seventeen" (according to other sources, he was only aged fourteen) when he became sultan. See the graphic description of Mehmed's life in N. Barber's *The Lords of the Golden Horn*, pp. 74 ff., also mentioning "a Jewish woman called Chiarazzo, who regularly brought jewels to the harem for sale" (p. 76). See also Mustafa Naima's *Annals of the Turkish Empire from 1591 to 1659 of the Christian Era*, trans. by C. Fraser, Vol. I (no more published), pp. 249 ff.

13. The problem of one, two, or three Jewish *kyra*s has not yet been completely resolved. The older information about a Jewish *kyra* was summarized by H. Graetz in his *Geschichte der Juden*, 4th ed., IX, 548 ff. Note 8/11. However, in 1895 a Russian scholar, V. D. Smirnov, published an important new document which, originally found in the Museum of the Society for History and Archeology in Odessa, has since been destroyed by a fire. But his publication of a facsimile, Turkish transliteration, and Russian translation in *Vostochniie Zametki* (Oriental Notices) of the University of St. Petersburg, 1895, pp. 35 ff. has preserved its essential data. It consisted of a more or less accurate seventeenth-century copy of the original decree issued in 1548 and of its subsequent confirmations down to the reign of Osman II which clearly exempted the *kyra* and her descendants from a variety of specified imposts. It was again reproduced by J. H. Mordtman in "Die Jüdischen Kira im Serai der Sultane," *MSOS*, XXXII, 1–39. This edition offered an amended Turkish text, a German translation, and very informative notes. It also cited a rather unsatisfactory reference to this document from a French translation of another act published by N. A. Fresco (Franco ?) which appeared in the *Revue des Écoles de l'Alliance Israélite*, 1902, pp. 337–38.

Mordtman's analysis pointed out the incongruity of considering the grandmother of Kurd, that decree's adult recipient in 1548, to be identical with the same Jewish "Dame" who died in 1600, an assumption still held by A. Galanté in 1926 and S. A. Rosanes in 1938 (see the next note). However, Mordtman seems to have gone too far in postulating the existence of two other Jewish *kyra*s, who died in 1590 and 1600, respectively. His argument is based exclusively on a rather questionable report by Solomon "the Jew" (referring to either Solomon Usque, Solomon Ashkenazi, or Solomon Ibn Ya'ish, quoting a Signor Abentalon who had received the news from a high Christian ecclesiastic). This Italian report, written in 1595, is reproduced in H. G. Rosedale's *Queen Elizabeth and the Levant Company: a Diplomatic and Literary Episode of the Establishment of Our Trade with Turkey*, and cited from there by Mordtman, p. 14. But this report is too ambiguous to allow for any far-reaching conclusions. Certainly the initials B. M., which Rosedale filled in to read *Beata memoria*, may have been a mere lapsus of a pen. It certainly is not a sufficient reason to postulate on this score the existence of two distinguished Jewish court ladies living at the same time in the Turkish capital. Of interest also are Stephan Gerlach the Elder's more general observations about Jewish women who, because of their medical adroitness, often gained access to Turkish harems. See his *Tage-Buch*, Frankfort, 1674 ed., pp. 59, 381, 471.

14. See Samuel Shulam's Foreword to his ed. of Abraham Zacuto's *Sefer Yuḥasin* (Book of Genealogies; a World Chronicle), Constantinople, 1566; Joseph ha-Kohen, *'Emeq ha-bakha*, pp. 172 f.; in H. S. May's English trans., pp. 134 f.

15. John Sanderson, *The Travels in the Levant (1584–1602), with His Autobiography and Selections from His Correspondence*, new ed. by W. Forster, pp. 85 f. Further data are offered in the biography of Esther Kyra by A. Galanté, *Esther Kyra d'après de nouveaux documents* (also in a Hebrew trans. by A. Elmaleh in *Mizraḥ u-ma'arab*, II, 39–49).

16. See Public Record Office, *Calendar of State Papers*, Foreign Series, XIX, 1584–85, ed. by J. Crawford Lomas, pp. 663 f.; L. Wolf, *Jews in Elizabethan England, with Appendix of Documents*, reprinted from *TJHSE*, XI, 1–91; H. F. Brown, ed., *Calendar of State Papers and Manuscripts Venice*, VIII, *1581–1591*, esp. pp. 123 No. 291, 128 No. 301, 514 No. 994; C. Roth, *The House of Nasi: The Duke of Naxos*, pp. 204 f., 247 n. 31; and particularly the biographical sketch by S. Faroqhi (or Faroghi) in "Ein Günstling des osmanischen Sultans Murād III David Passi," *Der Islam*, XLVII, 290–97. Faroqhi used to good advantage the Sinan papers preserved in the Istanbul archives. On these documents, see her more general study, "Das Grosswesir-telḥiṣ: eine aktenkundliche Studie," *ibid.*, XLV, 96–116, itself but an excerpt from her more comprehensive Hamburg dissertation entitled *Die Vorlagen* (telḫōṣe) *des Grosswesirs Sinan Paša an Sultan Murad III*, pp. 15–254.

17. See the sources listed *supra*, n. 16. Although on the whole very helpful, some of the information submitted by the British and Venetian envoys in Istanbul to their foreign offices was biased or factually inaccurate. For example, reports which reached London before August 17, 1585 concerning David Passi's endeavors to secure for himself the duchy of Naxos, left vacant since the death of Joseph Nasi in 1579, may have been based upon a confusion of Passi with Alvaro Mendes. As we shall see (*infra*, n. 24), Mendes was indeed an aspirant to that high post, but received the duchy of Mytilene instead. However, the possibility that Passi had entertained such a notion, perhaps even before Alvaro's arrival in Istanbul, cannot be ruled out.

18. See G. Naradounghian, ed., *Recueil d'actes internationaux de l'Empire Ottoman, Traités, conventions, etc.*, I, esp. pp. 31 f. Nos. 160, 168; 35 f. Nos. 179, 186, with reference to the notices in J. von Hammer-Purgstall, *Geschichte des osmanischen Reiches*, VI, 327; VII, 44, 187; XVII, 116; P. Bartl, "Der Kosakenstaat und das Osmanische Reich im 17. und in der ersten Hälfte des 18. Jahrhunderts," *Südost-Forschungen*, XXXIII, 166–94; N. A. Smirnov, *Rossiia i Turtsiia v XVI–XVII vv.* (Russia and Turkey in the Sixteenth and Seventeenth Centuries); and T. Manteuffel *et al.*, eds., *Historia Polski* (A History of Poland), I, Part 2, pp. 210 ff., 402. For the Jewish aspects of Polish–Turkish relations of the period, see the aforementioned documentation by J. W. Hirschberg, "Joseph Nasi's Participation in the Polish-Turkish Negotiations of 1562" (Polish), *Miesięcznik Żydowski*, IV, 426–39; M. Schorr, "Zur Geschichte des Don Josef Nassi," *MGWJ*, XLI, 169–77, 228–37; *supra*, Vol. XVI, pp. 41 ff. and the literature listed in the notes thereon.

19. See Jan Zamoyski's letter to Sigismund III of May 17, 1590 and Sigismund's reply of June 14, 1590, published from the Warsaw archives with extensive comments thereon by J. Morgensztern in her "Jewish Mediation in Establishing Unofficial Diplomatic Contacts between the Polish and Turkish Sovereign Courts in 1590 (in the

Light of the Correspondence between King Sigismund III and Jan Zamoyski)" (Polish), *BZIH*, no. 40, pp. 37–49, with an English summary, pp. 89–90, esp. pp. 46 ff.; other correspondence between the Polish chancellor and his king of September 27 and October 16, 1589 as reproduced in E. Hurmuzaki, ed., *Documente privatóare la storia românilor*, Suppl. II, Part 1, ed. by E. Bogdan, pp. 296, 299. It is small wonder that both the king and Zamoyski rejoiced over the news transmitted to them through some Poles who had brought back from Istanbul the remains of the deceased Polish envoy, Rafal Uchański, that a Jew (doubtless referring to Passi) was ready to secure peace with Turkey for the relatively moderate gift of 15,000 ducats which he allegedly intended to spend on the mufti and other dignitaries with great influence at court. See Krzysztow Radziwill's letter to Zamoyski of July 1, 1590, reproduced *ibid.*, p. 315.

20. See the publications by J. Morgensztern and E. Hurmuzaki cited *supra*, n. 19; and on the misfortunes of Joseph Nasi's successors in Poland, *supra*, Vol. XVI, pp. 51 f. and 338 f. n. 55. Needless to say, after 1591 the Turco-Polish relations had their ups and downs. By 1597 they seemed close enough for Sigismund to dare to suggest to the sultan that he should voluntarily hand over Moldavia to Polish control, a suggestion which a seasoned diplomat like Passi would never have supported. Of course, Sultan Meḥmed III, though generally much weaker than his "magnificent" grandfather, roundly refused. But he renewed the old treaty. This more or less benevolent neutrality, though interrupted by the war between the two countries in 1620–21, with its high points in the Turkish victory at Cecora and the effective Polish defense of Chocim, continued through the new treaties of 1621 and later. See the literature listed *supra*, Vol. XVI, p. 396 n. 5; and G. Tahsin, "La Moldavie dans les traités de paix turco-polonais du XVIIᵉ siècle (1621–1672)," *RRH*, XII, 687–714, with its succinct review of the antecedents of these treaties. On the chief initiator of the Anglo-Turkish entente, see H. G. Rawlinson's biographical study, "The Embassy of William Harborne to Constantinople, 1583–1588," *Transactions of the Royal Historical Society*, V, 1–27; and *infra*, n. 26.

21. See H. F. Brown, ed., *Calendar of State Papers*, Venice, VIII, 123 ff. Nos. 291 and 296, 514 f. No. 994, 519 ff. Nos. 1004 and 1008, 525 No. 1015, 529 f. No. 1023, 546 f. No. 1060, 550 f. No. 1075, 552 No. 1082, 556 No. 1101; J. Morgensztern, "Jewish Mediation," *BZIH*, no. 40, *passim;* A. Galanté, *Turcs et Juifs. Étude historique, politique*, pp. 109 f.

22. The verification of this hypothesis is made doubly difficult by the uncertainty concerning the exact date of David's return from Rhodes. We merely have the brief allusion to it in R. Yehudah Algazi's pleading for the revocation of the ban of this repentant sinner that if "R. Joseph Ibn Leb and Nasi had still been alive [they died in 1580 and 1579, respectively] and they saw the man's repentance with his whole heart and soul they might have taken pity on him and tried to return him to his Father in Heaven." See Yehudah Algazi cited by S. A. Rosanes in *Dibre yeme* (*Qorot*), III, 6 ff. (erroneously mentioning R. Joseph Ibn Leb as still alive, whereas Algazi adds the usual abbreviation z[*ikhrono*] l[*i-brakhah*] = of blessed memory); R. Elijah b. Ḥayyim, *Resp.*, bound together with R. Elijah b. Abraham Mizraḥi's *Sefer Mayim 'amuqim* (Deep Waters; responsa), Venice, 1647, Nos. 54–55. After his return, openly sponsored by Ashkenazi and his faction, he may have quickly gained the confidence of Murad III and his entourage and begun to play an important role at court, following in the footsteps of his former employer, Don Joseph Nasi. David's banishment to Rhodes for some 15 years after 1566–67 may also explain the absence of his name from the

aforementioned lists of Joseph's advisers published by V. Meysztowicz; his sudden appearance in the Istanbul records of 1585, and perhaps also Sinan's choice of Rhodes for his renewed exile after his arrest. See *supra*, n. 21; and Chap. LXXVI, nn. 47, 56, and 64.

23. See L. Wolf, *Jews in Elizabethan England*, 24 ff., 71 ff., 76, and *passim*; A. Galanté, *Don Salomon Ibn Yaèche duc de Mételin*, trans. by A. Elmaleh into Hebrew under the title "Don Solomon Ibn Ya'ish Duke of Mitylene" in *Sinai*, III, nos. 32–38, pp. 459–73.

24. See E. Charrière, *Négociations*, IV, 488 n.; J. Wansbrough, "The Safe-Conduct in Muslim Chancery Practice," *BSOAS*, XXXIV, 20–35 (emphasizing in particular the theoretical conflict between the treatment of immigrants and visitors under the system of *aman* and *ahd* and that postulated by the intolerant doctrine of the *dar al-ḥarb*); S. C. Lomas, ed., *Calendar of State Papers*, Foreign, XIX (1584–85), p. 663; N. Jorga, *Geschichte des Osmanischen Reiches*, III, 276; *supra*, Vol. XV, pp. 83 f., 128 ff., 130 ff., 415 nn. 13 f., 435 nn. 62–68. Ibn Ya'ish's break with Dom Antonio is well illustrated in his long epistle of August 24, 1593, to his brother-in-law Rodrigo Lopez. In this letter, probably written in Spanish, although preserved only in the official English translation for the British Royal Council in March of that year, Alvaro calls the Pretender "Good King Anthony," but complains of the sins and the life style of that "sonn of the best prince that Portugall hath hadd & Rightest in the inheritaunce." As a result, the Pretender was consulting "a Jew traytour to his crowne and the falsest man of the world," probably referring to Passi, whose machinations may have contributed to Ibn Ya'ish's alienation from Dom Antonio. See Wolf, *Jews in Elizabethan England*, pp. 71 ff.

25. See *supra*, Vol. XV, pp. 130 ff., 435 nn. 67–68. Queen Elizabeth's letter to the sultan of March 1592, reproduced from a British Museum MS in the Latin original by L. Wolf in *Elizabethan England*, pp. 65 f., and partially quoted in his English translation, *ibid.*, p. 27, and Alvaro's Spanish reply, *ibid.*, pp. 67 f. See also S. A. Rosanes, *Dibre yeme* (Qorot), III, 556 ff. App. No. 3. The story of Alvaro's family's early emigration to Turkey has but recently emerged from Suleiman's letter of 1572 published from a Venetian archival MS in the Turkish original with an English translation in 1974 in my "Solomon ibn Ya'ish and Sultan Suleiman the Magnificent," *Joshua Finkel Festschrift*, ed. by S. B. Hoenig and L. D. Stitskin, pp. 29–36.

To be sure, the identity of Alvaro Mendes in that correspondence with Soloman ibn Ya'ish is not quite certain. That name was not uncommon in either Spain or Portugal and might conceivably refer to another person, although none is recorded as having had close contacts with the Ottoman regime. Nor do we hear of the family's actual arrival in Istanbul in 1572 or soon thereafter. Since the publication of that text in 1974 and the quotation therefrom, *supra*, Vol. XV, p. 336 n. 40, published in 1976, I have awaited possible contradictory comments from one or another specialist in Turkish history. Since none such has been forthcoming, I assume that the identification may provisionally stand. If so, it might be more understandable why Solomon encountered so many fewer obstacles in removing his possessions from the Christian West to Istanbul than did Don Joseph thirty-three years earlier. In the thirteen years after 1572, when his family may have clandestinely moved to the Turkish capital, Alvaro must have had numerous opportunities to transfer his wealth to Turkey without antagonizing his Paris or London hosts.

26. Alvaro's reports of the English victory over the Armada, his later change of mind concerning Spanish-Turkish relations, and Serfatim's mission to Spain and England are reflected in the dispatches reproduced in H. F. Brown's ed. of the *Calendar of State Papers*, Venice, VIII, 399 No. 753; and L. Wolf in *Elizabethan England*, pp. 61, 76 ff. See also Vol. XV, pp. 415 f. n. 12, 435 f. nn. 67–68, 456 n. 12.

The general Anglo-Turkish relations—which began in 1560 with the treaty between the two countries subsequently renewed and amplified over the following decades—became increasingly close after the arrival in 1579 of William Harborne as the English envoy at the Porte. See *supra*, n. 20. The reason was obvious: both countries faced a common enemy in Philip II of Spain. Even in 1589–91, after the danger of the attack by Spain's "invincible armada" had been averted, Elizabeth was bent upon maintaining close relations with the Ottoman Empire, even though she was restrained by her fear to avow publicly an alliance with a Muslim against a Christian country. It has been suggested that for this reason the pertinent passage published in 1589–90 in Hakluyt, *Principal Navigations*, was omitted, probably at the government's instigation. See P. Wittek, "The Turkish Documents in Hakluyt's 'Voyages,' " *Bulletin* of the Institute of Historical Research, XIX, 121–39. Regrettably, Professor Wittek seems to have been unable to fulfill the promise he made at the conclusion of his paper to submit a fuller analysis with additional Turkish documentation. See also, more generally, I. I. Podes, "A Contribution to the Study of Queen Elizabeth's Eastern Policy," *Mélanges d'histoire générale*, II; T. S. Willan, *Studies in Elizabethan Foreign Trade*. An anti-British Maltese, A. P. Vella, could actually speak about *An Elizabethan-Ottoman Conspiracy*.

27. See L. Wolf, *Elizabethan England*, pp. 21, 56 ff., 68, 76 ff. The two letters addressed by Judah Serfatim to the Privy Council in March 1594 and reproduced here from a British Museum MS contain a mine of information on leading personalities in Istanbul, including David Passo(!) and Moshe Benvenest. See the next note. Although far from unbiased, the data offered by Ibn Ya'ish's envoy on various individuals, including Barton, some high Turkish officials, and the two allegedly pro-Spanish Jewish diplomats, deserve more careful consideration than they have hitherto received. See also S. A. Rosanes, *Dibre yeme (Qorot)*, III, 356 ff. App. iii, 3.

28. See E. Hurmuzaki, ed., *Documente privatóare la storia românilor*, 1st ed., III, 228, XII, 112 f. No. clxxx, 193 f. No. ccxcvi; 2d ed., III, 230 f.; N. Barozzi and G. Berchet, eds., *Relazioni degli stati europei*, 5th section I, 241 f.; *MHH*, I, 13, 113; J. Bergl, *Geschichte der ungarischen Juden*, pp. 63 f.; and other sources quoted by N. Jorga in his *Geschichte des osmanischen Reiches*, III, 423 n. 4. On the Ottoman dragomans, see A. Pipidou, "Quelques dragomans de Constantinople au XVIIe siècle," *RESEE*, X, 227–35, esp. p. 229 (without mentioning Jewish names). This branch of the Jewish economy will be treated more fully in the next chapter.

29. See M. Benayahu, "Moshe Benvenest Court Physician to the Sultan and Rabbi Yehuda Zarko's Poem on His Exile to Rhodes" (Hebrew), *Sefunot*, XIV, 123–43, with an English summary, pp. 4–5 (also reprint); Jacques de Germigny's dispatch of February 1584 in E. Charrière's *Négociations*, IV, 243–48; and Judah Serfatim's aforementioned letters to the English Privy Council of 1594, reproduced by L. Wolf in *Jews in Elizabethan England*, pp. 78 ("Passo and Benvenisti are always on the look-out for finding means to serve the king of Spain"), 84 item 18 ("Passo is a Portuguese Hebrew and Mossey Benvenisti a 'turquesque' [that is, Romaniot] Hebrew").

30. See the graphic, if somewhat overdrawn, picture of Murad IV, in contrast with his immediate predecessors and successor Ibrahim, in N. Barker's chapter on "The Years of the Cage" in *The Lords of the Golden Horn*, pp. 79 ff.

31. See the dispatch of 1579 by the Venetian envoy Mafeo Venier in E. Albéri's ed., *Relazioni*, 3d ser. II, 437 ff. The exaggeration inherent in Murad III's alleged genocidal exclamation relating to Jews is also illustrated by the similar intentions attributed to Suleiman the Magnificent in 1525. Angered by a popular uprising and the assassination of two high Turkish officials in Aleppo, we are told, the sultan first reacted by wishing to destroy the city's entire population. But he was speedily placated and severely punished only the leaders of the revolt. Similarly in 1637 Murad IV allegedly intended to exterminate all Venetian citizens in the Empire in reprisal for the capture of a Turkish ship in Valona by Venetian sailors. The sultan is said to have reconsidered that drastic action when it was pointed out to him that it would entail tremendous losses to the Ottoman Treasury if, as a result of his atrocities against its citizens, Venice stopped exporting goods to the Empire. He was told that at the harbor of Split (Spalato) alone the customs duties collected annually from Venetian imports yielded at least 5,000,000 aspers. See J. M. Jouannin and J. Gaver, *Turquie*, p. 238; S. A. Rosanes, *Dibre yeme (Qorot)*, III, 191.

32. R. Joseph b. Moses di Trani, *Resp.*, I, Nos. 16 and 76; R. Samuel de Medina, *Resp.* on O.Ḥ, No. 4; other sources cited by S. A. Rosanes in his *Dibre yeme (Qorot)*, III, 10 f., 346 App. ii; and K. Röhrborn, *Untersuchungen zur osmanischen Verwaltungsgeschichte*, p. 138 (also indicating the methods of evasion). The great diversity in the generally colorful garments worn by the various groups in the population through the eighteenth century and beyond is well illustrated by the graphic material reproduced by K. Tuchelt in his ed. of *Turkische Gewänder und osmanische Gesellschaft im achtzehnten Jahrhundert*, with a facsimile of the MS "Les Portraits des differens habillemens qui sont en usage en Constantinople et dans tout[!] la Turquie" belonging to the German Archaeological Institute in Istanbul and an Intro. by R. Neumann. The ramified problems of the Jewish badge and anti-sumptuary legislation will be more fully discussed in another context.

33. A. Galanté, *Documents officiels*, pp. 60 ff. Nos. i–iii; Mustafa Naima, *Annals of the Turkish Empire*, trans. by C. Fraser, I, 144 f., 337 f.; N. Jorga, *Geschichte des osmanischen Reiches*, III, 425. The complicated problems of the ownership of non-Muslim slaves by infidels and the local divergences on this score which developed in various regions are illustrated by the studies of M. Dan and S. Belin, "À propos des esclaves dans l'Empire Ottoman. Avec quelques données relatives aux pays roumains," *Annuarul* of the Institutul de Istorie of Cluj, IV, 7–67; R. Mantran, "Règlements fiscaux ottomans: La province de Bassora (en moitié du XVIᵉ siècle)," *JESHO*, X, 224–71, esp. pp. 230 (Turkish), 256 (French); C. Cahen "Notes sur d'esclavage musulman et le devshirme ottoman," *ibid.*, XIII, 211–18.

Even more than Suleiman's code that issued by Aḥmed may serve as an object lesson for the divergence between the law prescribing what ought to be done and historical reality reflecting what actually happened. See C. Cahen's general "Considérations sur l'utilisation des ouvrages de droit musulman par l'historien," *Atti* of the III Congresso di Studi Arabi e Islamici, held in Ravello on September 1–8, 1966, pp. 239–47. This is not to deny, however, that, by using the necessary caution, one can learn much from the normative law about the existing socioeconomic and political realities. See, for example, J. Kabrda, "Les Codes (kanunname) ottomans et leur importance pour l'histoire économique et sociale de la Bulgarie," *Sbornik* in honor of N. V. Michov, pp. 163–90.

34. V. J. Parry in M. A. Cook, ed., *History of the Ottoman Empire*, p. 107; and *supra*, n. 2. Needless to say, such warnings by scholars were rarely publicized and debated in the learned circles and were paid little heed by the rulers.

35. See *supra*, Vol. XVII, pp. 182 f., 381 n. 71. The impact of the ulema on the legal practice of the Ottoman provinces was diminished by their frequently sharp differences of opinion, reinforced by different regional traditions. Quite apart from the deeply rooted diversities represented by the traditional four schools of Muslim jurisprudence, there was an abundance of divergent views espoused even by scholars of the same localities and periods. These differences made themselves felt particularly in the fields of penal, fiscal, and public law—traditional Muslim jurisprudence did not divide the law according to these categories—but even in the more intimate domain of family laws, legal theory and practice often revealed great disparities. For example, the very important decision as to when a man reached legal maturity varied widely: some areas regarded the crucial dividing line to be age 15; others, 18; still others, 25. See R. Brunschvig, "Considérations sociologiques sur le Droit musulman," *Studia islamica*, III, 61–73, which offers many telling illustrations. There was far less disunity in these matters within the Jewish communities the world over. See also *supra*, Vol. XVII, pp. 167, 375 n. 52; and our prospective analysis of the development of Jewish law in the Late Middle Ages and early modern times in a future volume.

36. Henry Blount, *A Voyage into the Levant . . . with Particular Observations concerning the Moderne Conditions of the Turks and Other People under that Empire*, 3d ed., London, 1638, pp. 89 f. These and other acute observations made by the author immediately caught the imagination of the public and the first edition of the book in 1636 was followed by seven more editions in 1637–71. On the general impact of the multinational state on the legal status of the Jews, see *supra*, Vol. XI, pp. 198 f., 383 n. 10. Moreover, with all their temperamental outbursts the sultans felt bound by the Quranic provisions of toleration for the "protected subjects" and their elaborations through the *ḥadith* and the medieval juristic writings. In this and many other respects the Ottoman type of absolutism could not serve as a model for the European "enlightened absolutism" of the eighteenth century, as is sometimes assumed. Other arguments against this assumption are plausibly presented by E. Werner in his "Despotie, Absolutismus oder feudale Zersplitterung?" *Jahrbuch für Wirtschaftsgeschichte*, 1972, no. 3, pp. 107–128.

37. E. Hurmuzaki, ed., *Documente privatóare*, 1st ed. Suppl. I, 125 Nos. lxxv, cxc; Jorga, *Geschichte*, III, 415, reproducing the report by the French envoy, François de Gontaut baron de Salignac of 1607; Khadji-Khalifa cited by F. A. Belon in his "Essais sur l'histoire économique de la Turquie d'après les écrivains originaux," *JA*, 6th ser. III, 416–89; IV, 242–96, 301–390, 477–530; V, 127–67, esp. IV, 301 f. Another grand vizier, Ferhad, paid an even higher price than Sinan for his alleged mismanagement of the office; he was executed. Nonetheless, the office was both politically and financially so attractive that the sultans had no difficulty in finding the ablest candidates. But apparently there was a considerable dearth of a combination of talent and loyalty to the ruler in that period of troubles.

38. The Russian "Tale of the Appearance of the Miraculous Icon of Our Lady, the Virgin Mary," published in *Tvoreniia svinteiskogo Germogena Patriarkha Moskovskogo i*

vseiia Rossii (The Works of St. Hermogenes, the Patriarch of Moscow and All of Russia), pp. 1–16, esp. p. 16 excerpted in an English rendition by J. Pelinski in his "Muscovite Imperial Claims to the Kazan Khanate," *Slavic Review,* XXVI, 573 (describing the vision of the Virgin's assistance in the conquest of Kazan). See also E. L. Keenan, Jr., "Muscovy and Kazan. Some Introductory Remarks to the Pattern of Steppe Diplomacy," *ibid.,* pp. 548–68; and A. W. Fisher, "Muscovite-Ottoman Relations," *Humaniora islamica,* I, 209 f.; *supra,* n. 4.

The reorientation of Ottoman policy away from the Mediterranean basin and the parallel evolution in Spain during the last years of Philip II has been suggested by F. Braudel in *La Méditerrannée,* 2d ed., II, 431 ff.; and accepted, with minor variations concerning an earlier date, by W. E. D. Allen in his *Problems of Turkish Power in the Sixteenth Century,* esp. pp. 10 ff., 29 ff. On the inherent threat to the northern lifeline, see esp. H. Carrières d'Encosse, "Les Routes commerciales de l'Asie Centrale et les tentatives de reconquête d'Astrakhan d'après les registres des 'Affaires Importantes' des Archives ottomanes," *CMRS,* XI, 391–422. We have seen that, soon after the battle of Lepanto, Don Joseph Nasi was caught in the web of this gradual change of orientation which was reflected in his somewhat erratic behavior in the early 1570s. See *supra,* Chap. LXXVI, nn. 51–52.

39. Understandably, the growing sense of insecurity in the country affected even Jewish family life. We learn, for example, from a rabbinic responsum, about a marital difficulty of a Jewish couple in Adrianople and Kavalla in southern Thrace. According to the husband, he had arranged with the representative of his fiancée Dinah's father that, after the wedding, she would move to his residence in Kavalla. However, the bride staunchly refused to go there not only because Kavalla was a much smaller town than Adrianople but also because "it has unhealthy water, has a high mortality rate, and suffers from armed bands which often come there for pillage." After a lengthy explanation, R. Moses Alshekh decided that Dinah was right. See his *Resp.,* pp. 114 ff. No. 55.

40. See J. Zinkeisen, *Geschichte des osmanischen Reiches,* IV, 100 ff. Regrettably, we know almost nothing about how Fakhr ad-Din's semiautonomous administration affected the local Jews. He seems to have been rather friendly to the Maronite Christians, perhaps because he tried to secure some support for his ambitious schemes from the Christian West. See, for instance, K. S. Salibi's incidental data in "The Sayfās and the Eyalet of Tripoli (1579–1640)," *Arabica,* XX, 25–52, esp. pp. 28 ff.

The story of the various uprisings fills many pages in the contemporary Turkish chronicles and modern historical writings. Particularly the *Jalaliyam* rebellion has engaged the attention of Turkish historians. While most scholars have discarded its biased designation as a revolt of "bandits," their explanations of its fundamental and immediate causes have greatly varied. See, for instance, the brief discussion in Ö. L. Barkan's "The Price Revolution of the Sixteenth Century: a Turning Point in the Economic History of the Near East," *IJMES,* VI, 3–28. On the simultaneous unrest in the European provinces during that period, see S. Fischer-Galati, "Revolutionary Activity in the Balkans from Lepanto to Kuchuk Kainardgi," *Südost-Forschungen,* XXI, 194–213.

41. The disturbance of 1589 in Istanbul made a tremendous impression in the country and abroad. Two contemporary French pamphlets, quickly distributed in Paris, described these events in graphic detail. They saw in them signs of the divine wrath and portents of the approaching ruin of the Ottoman Empire. See C. D. Rouillard,

The Turk in French History, pp. 76 f.; E. Charrière, *Négociations,* IV, 720 f. See also the vivid description of these events in Henry (Harrie) Cavendish's *Journey to and from Constantinople, 1589 by Fox His Servant,* ed. by A. C. Wood, p. 16. On the Jewish sufferings in Safed, see Israel b. Moses Najara's wordy rather than enlightening description of these hostile acts, cited and analyzed together with other sources by S. A. Rosanes in *Dibre yeme (Qorot),* III, 422 ff. App. xiii; Aquilante Rocchetta, *Peregrinationes di Terra Santa ed altre provincie,* Palermo, 1630, fol. 100a, reproduced in P. A. Arce, ed., *Documentos y textos para la historia de Tierra Santa y sus santuarios, 1600–1700, . . . Textos impresos rares y viaje de Tierra Santa,* ed. with Intro. and Notes, I, 1600–1622, pp. 56 ff. See also, more broadly, M. Ish-Shalom, *Mass'ei ha-Noṣrim,* pp. 125 ff.; J. Braslawsky, "The Jewish Settlement in Tiberias" (Hebrew), *Zion,* V, 45–72, reprinted in his *Le-Ḥeqer Arṣenu,* pp. 180 ff.; and I. Ben-Zvi, *Eretz-Israel,* pp. 205 ff., 211 ff.

42. See Ö. L. Barkan, "Price Revolutic   *JMES,* VI, 20 ff. Table 4; E. Hurmuzaki, ed., *Documente,* 2d ed., IV, 195 no. clv; N. Jorga, *Geschichte,* III, 418.

43. See E. Fawkener's report, cited by R. W. Olson in his "Jews, Janissaries, Esnaf and the Revolt of 1740 in Istanbul: Social Upheaval and Political Realignment in the Ottoman Empire," *JESHO,* XX, 185–207. See also Olson's related study, "Jews in the Ottoman Empire in Light of New Documents," *JSS,* XLI, 75–88. Although both essays deal with mid-eighteenth-century conditions, they well illustrate situations and trends in Ottoman society, resembling those debilitating forces which had so greatly undermined the Empire's power in the early seventeenth century. Changes in the structure and the operation of the *timars* have been widely discussed in the modern historical literature, both Turkish and foreign. Suffice it to refer here to the Czech scholar, Josef Kabrda, who considers these changes far-reaching enough to justify the division of the history of Turkish feudalism into three periods, the first ending about 1600, the second extending over a period from 1600 to 1800, and the third involving its nineteenth-century revaluation. It was the second period which so greatly contributed to the speedy decline from the peak of Ottoman power reached under Suleiman the Magnificent. See Kabrda's "Les Problèmes de l'étude de l'histoire de la Bulgarie à l'époque de la domination turque," *Byzantinoslavica,* XV, 173–208. What is said here about Bulgaria applied also, with minor modifications, to other provinces of the Empire. Everywhere the deficiencies of the new system affected also all other walks of life.

44. See the lists compiled by E. von Zambaur in his *Manuel de Chronologie,* pp. 162 ff., 168 ff.; R. Y. Ebied and M. J. L. Young, "A List of Ottoman Governors of Aleppo A.H. 1002–1168 (1594–1755)," *Annali* of the Istituto Orientale in Naples, XXXIV (n.s. XXIV), 102–108; P. Bayer, "Alger en 1645, d'après les notes de R. B. Herault (Introduction à la publication de ce dernier)," *Revue de l'Occident Musulman,* XVII, 19–41 (was to be continued); A. von Gévay, "Versuch eines chronologischen Verzeichnisses der türkischen Stadthalter von Ofen," *Der Österreichische Geschichtsforscher,* ed. by J. von Chmel, II, 56–90; G. Jacob, ed., "Türkisches aus Ungarn, I: Eine unverwertete Liste der Bejlerbejs von Ofen," *Der Islam,* VIII, 237–51; with F. Babinger's succinct note thereon in "Die Osmanischen Stadthalter von Ofen," *ibid.,* XII, 233; and *supra,* Vol. I, pp. 264, 410 f. n. 20. Clearly, so quick a turnover in the personnel of the leading provincial administrators necessarily also adversely affected their efficacy and contributed much to the weakening of all central controls. See, for instance, in the case of the Egyptian governors-general, S. J. Shaw, *The Financial and*

Administrative Organization and Development of Ottoman Egypt, 1517–1798, esp. pp. 338 ff., supplying rich data on the fiscal structure, rather than the individuals in charge.

45. See S. A. Rosanes, *Dibre yeme (Qorot),* III, 266 f., 315 f., 417 ff. App. xii, 432 f. App. xiii; I. Ben-Zvi, *Ereṣ Yisrael,* pp. 220 ff. In their brief reviews of the Jerusalem developments Rosanes and Ben Zvi have principally summarized the tract *Ḥorbot Yerushalayim* (Epistle on Jerusalem's Ruin). This tract, originally signed by 7 Jerusalem and 5 Italian rabbis, including such well-known figures as Leon (Yehudah Aryeh) di Modena and Azariah Piccio, was first published in Venice soon after the events in 1636. It was later republished with comments by E. Rivlin in Jerusalem, 1928. While describing the sufferings of a single Jewish community, it has served as a graphic illustration of what could happen to any group of Ottoman Jews under the arbitrary administration of a local potentate. It is only astonishing that the Jerusalem Jews waited that long before they sought redress against Ibn Farukh's excesses first from the provincial governor in Damascus and later from the Porte.

Without wishing to minimize the importance of the right of petition, the exercise of which generated a number of legal precedents and imperial acts widely publicized by rumor and laudatory description in chronicles, it is difficult to accept the sweeping designation of the Empire as a "law and welfare state" given it by J. Matuz in *Das Kanzleiwesen Sultan Süleymans des Prächtigen,* p. 8. He himself admitted that the general orderliness of the Ottoman administration declined under Suleiman's successors. The Polish parallel is discussed *supra,* Vol. XVI, pp. 265 ff., 443 ff. nn. 61 ff., esp. n. 74. On Joseph di Trani's apparently unsuccessful intervention at the Porte in 1599–1600 and his ultimate departure in 1604 for the capital, where he was to play a leading role in the Jewish community, see his *Resp.,* Intro. and I, No. 29; S. A. Rosanes, *Dibre yeme (Qorot),* III, 95 ff.

46. See the royal memorandum intended to serve as instructions to Denis de la Hay Vantelay, dated August 22, 1665 and reproduced by P. Duparc, comp., in his *Recueil des instructions données aux ambassadeurs et ministres de France depuis les Traités de Westphalie jusqu'à la Revolution Française,* Vol. XXIX: Turquie, pp. 25 ff., esp. p. 45. In an earlier passage (p. 19) the king admitted that some Frenchmen had given advice to Turkish officials aimed at ruining other traders, and yet complained that these men had been exposed "to the avarice of all the pashas and lower officials and to the usury of all the Jews and Turks." On the proposal of the Aleppo Frenchman in 1632, see N. Steensgaard, "Consuls and Nations in the Levant from 1570 to 1650," *Scandinavian Historical Review,* XV, 13–35, esp. p. 23 (citing a Marseilles archival document). No less antagonistic to Jews was, for example, the eminent Venetian *bailo* Simeone Contarini. In his dispatch of 1612 he attacked the Turkish Jews "who control most of the business." He demanded that they be made to pay the *Cottimo di terra* (land tax). Otherwise, he contended, "very soon our entire trade will get into the hands of the Jews." See N. Barozzi and G. Berchet, *Le Relazioni,* I, 240 ff.

47. See Ḥayyim Joseph David Azulai, *Sefer Shem ha-Gedolim* (The Fame of the Great; a bio-bibliographical dictionary), ed. and rearranged by Y. E. Benjacob with notes by him and A. Fuld and a biography of Azulai by E. Carmoly, fols. 28 ff., *s.v.* Ḥayyim Vital; M. Benayahu, "R. Ḥayyim Vital in Jerusalem" (Hebrew), *Sinai,* XV, nos. 177–82, pp. 65–75; Israel b. Moses Najara, *Meimei Yisrael* (Israel's Waters; poems and letters), Venice, 1599–1600 ed., Part 4 (called *Mei ha-Maṣor* [Waves of Oppression]), fols. 149 f.; S. A. Rosanes, *Dibre yeme,* III, 229 f., 242 f. The incidents recorded here are but a small selection from the sources quoted by Rosanes in Vols. III and IV. The

reason why the Holy Land figures so prominently in this tale of woe is not necessarily because of the greater severity of the Palestine administration, but rather because of the greater articulateness of its numerous rabbinic leaders and the more intensive interest of modern scholars in anything that happened to Palestinian Jews in past centuries.

48. Ö. L. Barkan, "The Price Revolution," *IJMES*, VI, 12, 15 Graph 1, etc. On the impact of the discovery of America on the inflationary trends of the sixteenth century in Spain and other countries, see the debates initiated especially by E. J. Hamilton in his *American Treasure and the Price Revolution in Spain, 1502–1510;* and other works analyzed *supra*, Vols. XV, pp. 177 f., 458 f. n. 20; XVI, pp. 369 f. n. 40, etc. A good illustration of the nearly chaotic conditions created by the monetary disarray in the Empire is offered by M. Maxim's succinct review of valuable Turkish archival documents in his "Considérations sur la circulation monétaire dans les pays roumains et d'Empire Ottoman dans la seconde moitié du XVIe siècle," *RESEE*, XIII, 407–415, esp. pp. 409 f. with its three noteworthy tables concerning the Moldavian monetary circulation in 1543–92, that of Walachia in 1543–89, and the values of the respective coins during those periods. The fuller story of the decline of the Turkish currency and the price increases in Turkey and of their impact on the economic life of Turkish Jewry will unfold, in the context of the Empire's general economic evolution, in the next chapter.

49. See R. Joshua Ḥandali, *Pne Yehosh'a* (Joshua's Face; responsa), published together with R. Elijah Qobo's (Qovo's) *Aderet Eliyahu* (Elijah's Coat; responsa) and Isaac Almeda's *Ḥiddushin* (Novellae), under the title *Shne ha-Me'orot ha-gedolim* (Two Great Luminaries; responsa), Constantinople, 1739, Part 2, No. 61; R. Solomon b. Abraham ha-Kohen, *Resp.*, 3 parts, Salonica and Venice, 1586–94, Part 2, No. 31, all cited by S. A. Rosanes in his *Dibre yeme*, III, 52 f.

50. See the aforementioned *Ḥorbot Yerushalayim;* and some additional data presented by J. Schwarz in his well-known Palestinological work, *Tebu'ot ha-Areṣ* (The Country's Produce), reed. by A. M. Luncz, Period IV, fol. 42; *supra*, n. 45. Probably Ibn Farukh's Jewish advisers were also able to inform him about a number of Jews fleeing from the city in disregard of his general prohibition of such unauthorized departures. He may also have received advance notice about Jewish funerals which involved transporting corpses outside the city walls. Possibly it was the Jewish informers' recollection of the famous story about R. Johanan b. Zakkai's escape during Vespasian's siege of Jerusalem which aroused their suspicion about the use of caskets for smuggling such endangered individuals out of the city. On Ibn Farukh's order, guards at the gates were piercing each casket with spears to make sure that it carried a dead body. See S. A. Rosanes, *Dibre yeme*, III, 266 ff.

51. R. Jacob b. Abraham Castro, *Ohole Ya'aqob* (Tents of Jacob; responsa), Leghorn, 1774, No. 662; S. A. Rosanes, *Dibre yeme (Qorot)*, III, 251; R. Moses Alshekh, *Resp.*, ed. by Y. Ṭ. Porges, pp. 60 f. No. 26. It may be noted that no one raised the problem of bigamy in this affair. Such silence is quite explainable because the Sephardim, though infrequently practicing polygamy, insisted on their right to disregard the pertinent ban of R. Gershom the Light of the Exile which their ancestors had never recognized. The only formal safeguard against a husband wedding another woman consisted in the monogamy pledge inserted in many marriage contracts at the bride's insistence—a practice more frequently recorded in North-African Jewish communities

than in the Middle East—though the power of custom supported by public opinion seems to have reduced multiple marriages also among the Ottoman Sephardic families to a minimum. See *supra*, Vol. VI, pp. 135 ff., 393 ff. nn. 156 ff.; and other passages listed in the *Index to Vols. I–VIII*, pp. 99 *s.v.* Monogamy, 118 *s.v.* Polygamy. To the sources listed there see the additional documentation offered by S. Lowy in "The Extent of Jewish Polygamy in Talmudic Times," *Journal of Jewish Studies*, IX, 120–24; the Genizah documents published by M. A. Friedman in his Hebrew essays, "Polygamy: New Information from the Genizah," *Tarbiz*, XL, 329–59; and additional "Notes" thereon, *ibid.*, XLIII, 166–98; and more broadly, S. D. Goitein, *The Mediterranean Society*.

52. R. Ḥayyim Shabbetai, *Sefer Torat Ḥayyim* (Living Torah; responsa, arranged in the order of the *Shulḥan 'Arukh*), on Ḥ.M. fol. 80, published together with Solomon b. Joseph Amarillo's *'Ollelot Shlomoh* (Solomon's Gleanings: responsa omitted from Amarillo's own collection), Salonica, 1713–22. On the continued Rabbanite immigration from Italy, see *supra*, Vol. XIV, pp. 45 ff., 57 ff., 72 ff., and the notes thereon.

53. R. Joseph b. Moses di Trani, *Resp.*, No. 7; S. A. Rosanes, *Dibre yeme (Qorot)*, III, 99. Such interventions of a Muslim pasha in safeguarding religious conformity also among the minority faiths were not rare. The German traveler, Salomon Schweigger, who visited the Ottoman lands in 1576–81, saw a Jew severely punished for "blaspheming" against Christ. See his *Eine neue Reysebeschreibung aus Teutschland nach Konstantinopel und Jerusalem*, Graz, 1864 ed., p. 175.

54. See the document published by D. S. Richard in his "Arabic Documents from the Karaite Community in Cairo," *JESHO*, XV 105–162, esp. pp. 144 f. No. xxii. On the attitudes of the Istanbul Rabbanites to their Karaite neighbors, see S. Assaf, "New Material on the History of the Karaites in the Orient" (Hebrew), *Zion*, I, 208–251, esp. pp. 218 ff. These sporadic illustrations of the intergroup relations between the Jews and their own sectarians as well as the other religious minorities will be more fully elaborated in a later chapter.

55. See B. McGowan, "Food Supply and Taxation on the Middle Danube (1568–1579)," *AO*, I, 138–96, esp. pp. 164 f.; Muḥammad b. Aḥmed al-Sarakhsi, *K. al-Mabsut* (written between 1073 and 1084 C.E.), cited by C. Cahen in his "Considérations sur l'ultilisation des ouvrages de droit musulman par l'historien," *Atti* of the Congresso di Studi arabi e islamici, held in Ravello, September 1–8, 1966, pp. 239–47, esp. p. 244. See also the fuller details supplied by E. Ashtor in his *Histoire des prix et des salaires dans l'Orient médiéval, passim*. These differences are the more significant as economic integration of a country and the overcoming of economic differentials between regions usually depended on variables in the cost of transportation of certain goods more than on ethnoreligious diversities. However, even here, too, ingrained habits of consumption may have affected prices to a major extent. But the general leveling down of such differences by living together under the same regime for generations tended to become more pronounced as time went on. On the Ottoman Empire, see A. E. Vacalopoulos, "Traits communs du développement économique et social des peuples balcaniques et du Sud-Est européen à l'époque ottomane," *Balkan Studies*, XVI, 154–75; and the next note.

56. See M. Maxim, "L'Autonomie de la Moldavie et de la Valachie dans les actes officiels de la Porte au cours de la seconde moitié du XVIᵉ siècle," *RESEE*, XV, 207–

232, esp. p. 207 n. 1 (announcing future publications relating to the autonomy of the khanate of Crimea, the Georgian principalities, and the islands of Chios, Naxos, and others); M. I. Kunt, "Ethnic-Regional (*Cins*) Solidarity in the Seventeenth-Century Ottoman Establishment," *IJMES*, V, 233–39. On Dubrovnik, see *supra*, Vol. XVII, pp. 106 ff., 345 ff. nn. 77–86.

57. Henry Blount, *A Voyage into the Levant*, 3d ed., p. 111. In general see, for example, C. P. Kyrris's monographic study, "L'Importance sociale de la conversion à l'Islam (volontaire ou non) d'une section des classes dirigeantes de Chypre pendant les premiers siècles de l'occupation turque (1570–fin du XVIIᵉ siècle)," *Actes* of the Iᵉʳ Congrès International des Études Balkaniques et Sud-Est Européennes, III (Sofia, 1969), 437–62. Such conversionist attempts were even more pronounced in the earlier period of the Ottoman expansion stimulated, in part, by the Turkish warriors' great enthusiasm for the holy war against the infidels. See O. Turan, "L'Islamisation dans la Turquie du moyen âge," *Studia Islamica*, X, 137–52 (argues that of the later preponderantly Muslim population of Anatolia only 30 percent stemmed from converted non-Muslims, whereas 70 percent had Turkish origins). On Islam's often irresistible appeal to enterprising and talented careerists, see H. G. Majer, *Herkunft und Volkzugehörigkeit muslimischer Amtsträger als historisches Problem in der Osmanistik: Ethnogenese und Staatsbildung in Osteuropa*. See also S. Vrionis, Jr., "Nomadization and Islamization in Asia Minor," *Dumbarton Oaks Papers*, XXIX, 43–71. The appropriation of churches by the conquering Turks and their combination of religious toleration with subtle pressure for conversion are discussed by H. Hanson in his "Konstantinopels Kirchen und die Moscheen Istanbuls. Antlitz und Schicksal der Stadt am Goldenen Horn im Spiegel der Baukunst," in *Istanbul. Geschichte und Entwicklung der Stadt*, ed. by K. Bachteler (*Festschrift Kurt Albrecht*), pp. 89–130, 191–266 (does not refer to synagogues); and R. F. Kreutel, "Ein Kirchenraub in Selānīk," *WZKM*, LXIX, 73–90. See also L. Hadrovics, "L'Église serbe sous la domination turque," *Archives d'histoire du droit oriental*, III, 411–72; and *infra*, Chap. LXXVIII, nn. 20–21.

58. See H. Scheel, *Die Staatsrechtliche Stellung der ökumenischen Kirchenfürsten in der alten Turkei;* J. Koder, "Zur Frage der slawischen Siedlungsgebiete im mittelalterlichen Griechenland," *BZ*, LXXI, 313–31; B. Grafenauer, *Die Ethnische Gliederung und geschichtliche Rolle der westlichen Slawen im Mittelalter*. Report to the I. Balkanological Congress in Sofia, August 26–September 1, 1966. On the hellenizing efforts of the Greek Orthodox hierarchy among their Slavic coreligionists and the resistance thereto by the Serbo-Bulgarian masses, aided by the Turkish administration, see J. Kabrda, "Les Problèmes de l'étude de l'histoire de la Bulgarie à l'époque de la domination turque," *Byzantinoslavica*, XV, 173–208, esp. pp. 174 ff., 196 f. Of interest also is such an occasional expression of goodwill, on the part of even so "grim" a sultan as Selim I, toward his Slav subjects as is illustrated by B. O. Unbegani's ed. of "Four Writings of the Turkish Sultan Selim I. in the Serbian Language" (Serbian), in *Xenia slavica*, Papers Presented to Gojko Ružičić, pp. 221–28. See also, more generally, S. Runciman's *The Great Church in Captivity: a Study of the Patriarchate of Constantinople from the Eve of the Turkish Conquest to the Greek War of Independence*.

59. See Shabbetai Ḥayyim, *Torat ḥayyim* (Ḥayyim's Lore; reponsa), arranged in the order of Joseph Karo's code and published, together with *'Ollelot ha-Kerem* (Fruit of Vineyards; responsa) which appeared as supplements to Solomon B. Joseph Amarillo's *Kerem Shlomoh* (Solomon's Vineyard; responsa), Salonica, 1713, II, No. 9; S. A. Rosanes, *Qorot*, III, 201. Many other such ritualistic differences have been noted *su-*

pra, Chap. LXXVI; and, more generally, in Vol. VII, pp. 105 ff., 151 ff.; and I. El-bogen, *Der Jüdische Gottesdienst in seiner geschichtlichen Entwicklung*, 3d ed.

60. See *supra*, Vol. XVII, pp. 72 ff., 329 ff. nn. 33–37; A. Galanté, *Histoire des Juifs de Rhodes, Chio, Cos, etc.*, pp. 13 f. This extraordinarily favorable decree may perhaps be attributed to the desire of the Turkish rulers to enlist the assistance of Jews in administering and economically utilizing the resources of the rich island theretofore ruled by inimical Hospitalers. It was, indeed, under the Turkish administration that the Rhodes Jewish community enjoyed periods of relative affluence and extensive cultural creativity.

61. See *supra*, Chap. LXXVI, nn. 44 ff.; Vols. XIV, pp. 20 f., 316 n. 26; XVII, pp. 77 ff., 369 ff. nn. 38–40; Joseph b. Moses di Trani, *Resp.*, I, Nos. 40–41; S. A. Ro-sanes, *Qorot*, III, 216; B. Arbel, "The Jews in Cyprus: New Evidence from the Vene-tian Period," *JSS*, XLI, 23–40, esp. pp. 29 f.

62. I. Meyendorff, "Grecs, Turcs et Juifs en Asie Mineure au XIVe siècle," *Poly-chordia Festschrift Franz Dölger*, I (1966 = *Byzantinische Forschungen*, I), 211–17; W. C. Brice, "The Turkish Colonisation of Anatolia," *BJRL*, XXXVIII, 18–44; and, more broadly, H. Gerber, "Jews in the Economic life of the Anatolian City of Bursa [or Brusa] in the Seventeenth Century: Notes and Documents" (Hebrew), *Sefunot*, XVI (n.s. I), 235–72, with an English summary, pp. xxi–xxii, esp. pp. 236 ff. (based on the qadhi records of that city); H. Inalchik, "Bursa and the Commerce of the Levant," *JESHO*, III, 131–47; C. Cahen, "Le Problème ethnique en Anatolie," *Journal of World History*, II, 347–62; and S. Vryonis, Jr.'s twin studies, "Patterns of Population Move-ment in Byzantine Asia Minor 1071–1261," *Report* to the XVe Congrès International d'Études Byzantines, held in Athens, 1976, Vol. I; and *The Decline of Medieval Hellen-ism in Asia Minor and the Process of Islamization from the Eleventh through the Fifteenth Century*. On the Jews of Anatolia see the scattered data, primarily from rabbinic sources, offered by S. A. Rosanes in his *Qorot*, III, 204 ff.; and, more fully, by A. Galanté in *Histoire des Juifs d'Anatolie;* with an *Appendice* thereto; and other literature mentioned *supra*, Chap. LXXVI, nn. 10, etc. The projected volume on Izmir (Smyrna) by Galanté seems never to have seen the light of day, however. Its ancient history is illustrated by the few inscriptions recorded in J. B. Frey's *Corpus inscriptionum judaicarum*, II, 9–12; and such monographs as those by S. Werses in his "From the Life of the Jewish Community in Izmir" (Hebrew), *Yavneh*, III, 93–111 (mainly discussing the Jews' use of Muslim courts and their taxes); A. Yaari in his "Hebrew Printing in Izmir" (He-brew), *Areshet*, I, 97–222 (beginning in 1658, there were four major periods of fruitful activity resulting in the aggregate appearance of 415 Hebrew books, here listed). See also the interesting documentation on the small town of Tiria offered by M. Bena-yahu in his "Concerning the History of Jews of Tiria" (Hebrew), *Zion*, XII, 37–48. Among the rabbinic documents summarized by Rosanes we find no less than three references to substantial bequests left by wealthy Anatolian Jews for the benefit of the Safed yeshivah. At least in one case, as often elsewhere, some objectors raised the question whether such privileged treatment of a Palestinian academy did not run counter to the talmudic regulation that "the poor of one's own community should have precedence over those of other cities." This was but part of the numerous com-plexities of the "Communal Support of the Poor" as practiced in the various medieval and early modern Jewish communities, summarized in *JC*, II, 319 ff.

63. See H. Ritter, *Ṭūrōyo. Die Volkssprache der syrischen Christen des Tur-Abdin* A. Texte, Vol I; J. Braslavsky, *Le-ḥeqer Arṣenu: 'Avar u-seridim* (Studies in Our Country: Its Past

and Remains), esp. pp. 172 ff. (denying the widely accepted ancient origin of the Peki'in settlement); B. Lewis, *Notes and Documents*, pp. 9, 20 f. Regrettably, we have no comprehensive history of Syria under Ottoman rule similar to those published by Maurice Gaudefroy-Demembynes and Claude Cahen for the medieval period. But some special studies on individual phases have appeared in recent years, among others, by J. C. David, "Alep, dégradation et tentatives actuelles de réadaptation des structures urbaines traditionelles," *BEO*, XXVIII, 19–50; A. K. Rafeq, "Les Registres des tribunaux de Damas comme source pour l'histoire de la Syrie," *ibid.*, XXVI, 219–26; M. Markhit, *The Ottoman Province of Damascus in the Sixteenth Century* (unpublished London diss.); and for Iraq, R. Mantran, "Bagdād à l'époque Ottoman," *Arabica*, IX, 311–24.

64. See S. J. Shaw's succinct summary "The Political Structure and Development of Ottoman Egypt (1517–1798)" in his *Financial and Administrative Organization and Development of Ottoman Egypt*, pp. 1 ff. The constant tensions between the large Arab majority and the Turkish ruling minority are well documented by G. W. F. Stripling in *The Ottoman Turks and the Arabs, 1511–1574*. The Turks had to contend, moreover, with the permanent threat of incursions by the Bedouins on the desert fringes of their Asian possessions. As the royal firman of 1578 emphasized: "The province of Damascus is the borderland of the desert and the frontier of the rebellious Bedouins." See U. Heyd, ed., *Ottoman Documents on Palestine*, p. 40. The sultans felt obliged to protect not only their subjects settled in the towns and villages, but also the thousands of Muslim pilgrims annually traversing that area on their way to Mecca and Medina. See M. Sharon, "The Political Role of the Bedouins in Palestine" (Hebrew), in M. Ma'oz, ed., *Studies in Palestine during the Ottoman Period*, pp. 11–30.

65. See G. Scholem, "The Cabbalist Rabbi Abraham ben Eliezer Halevi" (Hebrew), *KS*, II, 101–141, 269–73; VII, 149–65, 440–65; A. L. Frumkin and E. Rivlin, *Toledot ḥakhmei Yerushalayim* (A History of the Jerusalem Sages), II, 269. On Reubeni and Molkho see *supra*, Vol. XIII, pp. 109 ff., 364 ff. nn. 53–58.

66. See the brief summary of these events in I. Ben Zvi's *Ereṣ-Yisrael ve-yishubah*, pp. 155 ff.; and the sources listed there. R. Levi Ibn Ḥabib later reminisced with pride about his role during the messianic excitement. He claimed that he had succeeded, through his soft-spoken and yet persuasive arguments in controverting the "fool's tidings" reaching Jerusalem and thus had saved the Jewish community of the Holy City from nearly total extinction. See his *Resp.*, Venice, 1565 ed., fol. 298a, reproducing his *Quntras 'al 'Inyanei ha-Semikhah* (Tract on Matters Relating to Ordination). On Ibn Ḥabib and his opponent Jacob Berab, see the succinct biographical data in M. D. Gaon, *Yehudei ha-mizraḥ be-Ereṣ Yisrael be-'avar u-ba-hoveh* (Oriental Jews in Palestine in the Past and Present), II, 144 ff., 239 ff. The controversy concerning the ordination will be discussed *infra*, Chap. LXXVIII, n. 111; and more fully in a later volume.

67. I. Ben Zvi, *Ereṣ Yisrael*, pp. 34 ff.; J. Hacker, *Megoreshei ve-ṣeṣaehem ba-Imperiah ha-'Otomanit ba-me'ah ha-shesh-'esreh* (Spanish Exiles and Their Descendants in the Ottoman Empire in the Sixteenth Century [Salonica, Istanbul and Their Environs]), pp. 267 ff.

68. S. J. Shaw, *The Financial and Administrative Organization and Development of Ottoman Egypt 1517–1798*, pp. 323 f., 334; E. Combe, *L'Égypte Ottoman de la conquête par Selim (1517) à l'arrivée de Bonaparte (1798)*; P. M. Holt, *Egypt and the Fertile Crescent*,

1516–1922: a Political History. It was part of the nationalistic atmosphere prevailing in the Middle East during the early postwar period that G. Wiet spoke of "L'Agonie de la domination ottomane en Égypte," *Cahiers d'histoire égyptienne,* II, 494–519. Compared with the general improvement in Egypt's economic life and the removal of much of the oppressive Mameluke regime, which ended in 1517, the situation of the peasant masses, craftsmen, and businessmen and particularly that of the Copts, Jews, and other ethnoreligious minorities was greatly ameliorated under the relative orderliness of the Turkish administration. Israel of Perugia, a relatively recent arrival in Palestine, succinctly described the state of mind of the masses of the local population. In his letter to a friend in Perugia written shortly after Selim the Grim's occupation of Palestine in 1516, he depicted the sufferings of the inhabitants occasioned by the war and particularly by the enormous rise in prices and the general cost of living. But he added pithily: "And yet despite its destruction and desolation, the country is full of glee and rejoicing." See the second epistle he addressed to his benefactor Abraham in Perugia, sometime between 1517 and 1522, reproduced in A. Yaari's *Iggerot Ereṣ Yisrael,* pp. 166 ff., 177. Admittedly, conditions worsened with the general decline of the Ottoman Empire in the early seventeenth century. But even in the eighteenth and nineteenth centuries they never quite reached the low point of the maladministration under the "Circassian" Mameluke dynasty.

69. See the story of Ibn Velisseir told by Joseph Sambari in his *Dibre Yosef* (Joseph's Words: a Chronicle) and quoted from the unpublished part of that work, fol. 222 by S. A. Rosanes in his *Qorot,* III, 316 f. The Ḥusain Pasha mentioned is probably identical with the governor whose exactions of gifts from the Cairo merchants for holidays in 1636 are referred to by A. Raymond in his *Artisans et commerçants au Caire au XVIIIe siècle,* II, 704. The vicissitudes of Ibn Velisseir (*ca.* 1580–1635) are typical for the speedy rise and fall of leading Jewish financiers in both Istanbul and Cairo. We shall see (*infra,* Chap. LXXVIII, nn. 91–93) how greatly even the petty Jewish dragomans influenced the operations of the administration of the Ottoman monopolies and the import-export business conducted by foreign merchants in Istanbul and Cairo.

70. The observation by the Danish secretary is quoted from C. F. Wandel, *Danmark og Barbareskerne, 1746,* p. 4 by H. Z. (J. W.) Hirschberg in his *Toledot ha-Yehudim be-Afriqah ha-ṣefonit* (The History of the Jews in North Africa), II, 41. See also, more generally, S. Rang and F. Denis, *Fondation de la Régence d'Alger: Histoire de Barberousse;* J. M. Haddey, *Le Livre d'or des Israélites algériens; recueil des resseignements inédits et authentiques sur les principaux négociants juifs d'Alger pendant la période turque;* J. M. Abu Nasr, "The Beylicate in Seventeenth-Century Tunisia," *IJMES,* VI, 70–93; T. Bachrouch, "Fondements de l'autonomie de la Régence de Tunis au XVIIe siècle," *Revue Tunisienne de Sciences Sociales,* XII, nos. 40–43, pp. 163–84.

71. See *supra,* n. 56.

CHAPTER LXXVIII: SOCIOECONOMIC TRANSFORMATIONS

1. See H. Inalcik, "The Foundations of the Ottoman Economic-Social System in Cities," *Studia Balcanica*, III, 17–24; B. McGowan, "Food Supply and Taxation on the Middle Danube (1568–1579)," *AO*, I, 138–96, esp. pp. 141 ff.; J. Káldy-Nagy, "The Administration of the Sanjak Registration in Hungary," *AOH*, XXI, 181–223; and J. Perényi, "Villes hongroises sous la domination ottomane aux XVIᵉ–XVIIᵉ s. Les chefs-lieux de l'administration ottomane," *Studia Balcanica*, III, 25–31; idem, "Trois villes hongroises sous la domination ottomane au XVIIᵉ siècle," *Actes* of the I Congrès International des Études Balkaniques et Sud-Est Européenes, III, 581–91 (referring to Buda, Pest, and Pecs). It is truly remarkable how long these local differences persisted. After three centuries of Ottoman domination such neighboring cities as Sofia, Vidin, and Ruse (Ruschuk), in Bulgaria, still showed noteworthy dissimilarities reflected in the cases administered by the local qadhis. See N. Todorov, "La Différenciation de la population urbaine au XVIIIᵉ s. d'après des registres du cadis de Vidin, Sofia et Ruse," *Studia Balcanica*, III, 45–62.

2. See the *Nasthatname* (Counseling Handbook) in the passage quoted in English by H. Inalcik in the "Foundations," *Studia Balcanica*, III, 21; *supra*, Vol. XVII, pp. 207 ff. This favorable attitude to commerce prevailed throughout the Empire, including even Egypt, despite its deeply rooted state controls over the entire economy. Of course, there were great differences from province to province. The analysis presented by E. Burke in "Morocco and the Near East: Reflections on Some Basic Differences," *European Journal of Sociology* (*Archives Européens de Sociologie*), X, 70–94, applies not only to Morocco which, on the whole, retained its sovereignty throughout the modern period, but also to the other North African lands which became more or less regular Ottoman pashaliks. In some respects close parallels found in areas of diverse origin are often more instructive than those between localities with similar backgrounds. As Marc Bloch observed, most conspicuous service is rendered by "many similarities which, when closely examined, prove not to be explicable in terms of imitation." See his "A Contribution towards a Comparative History of European Societies" (1928), reproduced in his *Land and Work in Mediaeval Europe: Selected Papers*, trans. by J. E. Anderson, pp. 44–81, esp. p. 54. Incidentally, this remark may also be relevant with respect to certain developments within the Jewish community when they show unintentional similarities with those of other ethnoreligious groups, especially in cases where the Jewish leadership had made a special effort to prevent the imitation of neighbors' mores. On the speedy growth of the Sephardic population of the Empire see H. J. Zimmels, *Ashkenazim and Sephardim, passim;* and *supra*, particularly Chap. LXXVI.

3. L. Henry, "Historical Demography," *Daedalus*, XCVII (Part 2: Historical Population Studies, Spring 1968), 385–96, esp. p. 395; idem, *Manuel de Démographie Historique.* Much of the information about the Turkish census records, their gradual discovery, and their utilization has been made available over the last several decades by Ömer Lutfi Barkan, the Turkish pioneer in historical demographic research in his

country. See esp. his "Les Grands recensements de la population et du territoire de l'empire ottoman et les registres impériaux de statistique," *Revue de la Faculté des Sciences Économiques [Iktisat Fakültytesi]* of the University of Istanbul, II, 1–40, 168–78 and the Turkish section [Documents], *ibid.*, pp. 20–59, 214–47; his "Essai sur les données statistiques de registres de recensement dans l'Empire Ottoman au XVᵉ et XVIᵉ siècles," *JESHO*, I, 9–36, esp. pp. 27, 35 (regarding Muslim, Christian, and Jewish hearths in 1578); and his "Research on the Ottoman Fiscal Surveys," in M. A. Cook, ed., *Studies in the Economic History of the Middle East*, pp. 163–71, with reference to some of his more detailed investigations published in Turkish. Among Western scholars we need but mention Bernard Lewis's significant contributions, "The Ottoman Archives as a Source for the History of the Arab Lands," *JRAS*, 1951, 139–55; "An Arabic Account of the Province of Safed," *BSOAS*, XV, 477–88; "The Population and Tax Revenue of Eretz-Israel in the Sixteenth Century according to Turkish Documents" (Hebrew), *Yerushalayim* (Review), I, 133–37; "Cities in Ereṣ-Israel in the XVIIth Century according to Documents from Ottoman Archives" (Hebrew), *ibid.*, II–V, 117–27; "Nazareth in the Sixteenth Century according to the Ottoman *Taḥrir* Registers" in George Makdisi, ed., *Arabic and Islamic Studies in Honor of Hamilton A. R. Gibb*, pp. 416–25; "Jaffa in the Sixteenth Century according to the Ottoman *Tahrir* Registers" in *Necati Lugar Armağani*, 1968, pp. 435–46; and particularly Amnon Cohen and his recent comprehensive study on *Population and Revenue in the Towns of Palestine in the Sixteenth Century*. Of course, although dealing with Palestine's population at large, these contributions are of special interest to the history of the Jewish people. Many other Western studies in the demographic field appeared from the pens of Greek, Bulgarian, Serbian, and Hungarian historians whose countries had been part of the Ottoman Empire, wholly or partially, during the early modern period. Some of their publications and those of many other scholars will be quoted in the following notes.

4. See T. H. Hollingsworth, "The Importance of the Quality of the Data in Historical Demography," *Daedalus*, XCVII (Spring, 1968), 415–32; the hereditary exemption of the family of Ya'qub of Gaëta and others cited *supra*, Chap. LXXV, nn. 37–38. Among the most important problems in the quantitative computations is the extent to which the households listed in the Turkish records reflect the total number of their members. This question cannot be fully answered by the internal evidence. Internationally, as it has been shown, families have very frequently differed in their average numerical strength. See P. Laslett, "International Comparison in the Size and Structure of the Household Over Time," *Colloque International de Démographie Historique*, Florence, October 1971 (mimeographed).

5. 'Abd al-Mu'in Muḥammad Luṭfi Pasha, *Āṣaf-nāme*, ed. according to 3 MSS and trans. into German by R. Tschudi, pp. 41 f. (Turkish), 33 f. (German); Ö. L. Barkan, "Essai," *JESHO*, I, 11. Some variations in the methods of keeping *defters*, however, did arise from the different origins of regulations issued through the chancery of the Grand Vizier and those stemming from the chief fiscal official of the Empire, the *defterdar*. There also existed regional differences. See, for instance, M. H. Biegman, "Some Peculiarities of Firmans Issued by the Ottoman Treasury in the Sixteenth Century," *AO*, I, 9–13, largely based on his *The Turco-Ragusan Relationship, According to the Firmans of Murad III (1575–1595) Extant in the State Archives of Dubrovnik*. Biegman's publications include materials derived from other archival sources such as the records of customs houses. Even more directly based upon registers of the collections of customs duties is the significant edition by L. Fekete and G. Káldy-Nagy, *Rechnungsbücher türkischer Finanzstellen in Buda (Ofen), 1550–1580*, referring particularly to the registers

of 1571, 1573, and 1580. The data yielded by these documents are helpful also in the interpretation of the figures presented by the population *defters*. On the medieval antecedents of the Turkish census and other registers, see the brief remarks by B. Lewis in his "Daftar," *EI*, 2d ed., II, 77–81.

6. See, for instance, P. Goubert, "Registres paroissiaux et démographie dans la France du XVIe siècle," *Annales de Démographie Historique* (Études et chroniques), II, 43–48; F. Lebrun, "Registres paroissiaux et démographie en Anjou au XVIe siècle," *ibid.*, pp. 49–50; other studies discussed *supra*, Vols. XII, pp. 4 ff., 243 ff.; and XVI, pp. 192 f., 405 f. n. 32. On the sporadic references to lists of births and deaths in the Mameluke and Ottoman Empire, see H. Rabie, *The Financial System of Egypt A.H. 564– 741/A.D. 1169–1341*, esp. pp. 135 f.; S. J. Shaw, *The Financial and Administrative Organization and Development of Ottoman Egypt*, pp. 151 ff.; R. Mantran, "Règlements fiscaux ottomans. La province de Bassore (La moitié du XVIe s.)," *JESHO*, X, 224–77, esp. pp. 268 f.; and *supra*, Vol. XVII, pp. 225 ff., 401 nn. 123–24.

The strengths and weaknesses of the methods used in the compilation of the registers have often been analyzed in the literature mentioned in our earlier notes, such as the latest remarks by Amnon Cohen and B. Lewis in their *Population and Revenue . . . of Palestine*, pp. 3 ff. Because of the incompleteness of the extant documentation many registers can only be used as "samples" for their respective areas. However, in each case we must examine to what extent these samples are truly representative of the regions as a whole—a promising procedure only if sufficient pertinent material is available. This method has been extensively used, for example, by Josiah Cox Russell, a leading student of medieval historical demography in Western Europe. See his publications quoted *supra*, Vols. II, p. 394; III, p. 276; IV, p. 277, etc. Even then there will necessarily remain a certain element of doubt. In the case of the ethnoreligious minorities the difficulties are aggravated by the varying demographic features characteristic of each. See, for example, U. O. Schmelz's analysis, "Some Demographic Peculiarities of the Jews in Jerusalem in the Nineteenth Century" in M. Ma'oz, ed., *Studies on Palestine during the Ottoman Period*, pp. 119–41.

7. See K. Lamprecht, *Deutsche Geschichte;* idem, "Zur Sozialstatistik der deutschen Städte im Mittelalter," *Archiv für Soziale Gesetzgebung und Statistik*, I; I. Ben Zvi, "Jewish Settlements in Palestine in the Seventeenth Century" (Hebrew), *Zion*, VII, 156–71; VIII, 183. See also *infra*, n. 35.

In the Turkish case we also must bear in mind the ever changing names of villages quoted in the sources. Quite apart from the obvious divergences when localities are cited in their Greek, Arabic, Slav, or Hungarian names or in those given them by the Turkish conquerors, quite a number of localities covered different areas from time to time. Some were so depopulated that their names were quickly forgotten. See K. Kreiser, *Die Ortsnamen der europäischen Türkei nach "ämtlichen" Verzeichnissen in Kartenwerken*. As far as Jews are concerned, we only have such detailed researches concerning settlements in the Holy Land. See I. Ben Zvi's data in *Zion*, VII–VIII; Y. Kaniel, ed., *Reshimat ha-yishuvim ha-yehudiim ba-mizraḥ u-ba-negev* (A List of Jewish Settlements in the East and the South [of Palestine] at the Zenith of the Ottoman Empire); J. Hacker, ed., *Shalem: Meḥqarim be-toledot Eretz-Yisrael ve-yishuvah* (Studies in the History of the Jews in Eretz Israel and Its Population). Although these studies understandably deal for the most part with the nineteenth and twentieth centuries, they shed much light on the earlier period as well. See also, more generally, W. D. Hütteroth and K. Abdalfatah, *Historical Geography of Palestine, Transjordan and Southern Syria in the Late Sixteenth Century*. On the criticism of both the sample and settlement criteria, as well as of the conversion of death taxes into death rates for older population research see G. Ohlin, "No Safety in Numbers: Some Pitfalls in Historical Research," *Industrialization in Two Systems: Essays in Honor of Alexander Gerschenkron,* ed. by H. Rosofsky, pp. 68–90.

8. See, for example, E. Grozdanova, "Das Kadiamt und die Selbstverwaltung der bulgarischen Gemeinden im 15. bis 16. Jahrhundert," *Études historiques* (Sofia), VII, 147–59; H. W. Duda, ed., *Die Protokollbücher des Kadiamtes Sofia,* arranged by G. D. Galabov; J. Kabrda, "Les Anciens registres turcs des cadis de Sofia et de Vidin et leur importance pour l'histoire de la Bulgarie," *Archiv Orientální,* XIX, 329–81; 'A. K. Rafeq, "Les Registres des tribunaux de Damas comme source pour l'histoire de la Syrie," *BEO,* XXVI, 219–76; and particularly R. C. Jennings's twin essays (based on his more comprehensive UCLA dissertation), "Urban Population in Anatolia in the Sixteenth Century: a Study of Kayseri, Karaman, Amasya, Trabyzon and Erzurum," *IJMES,* VII, 21–57 and "Kadi, Court, and Legal Proceedings in 17th Century Ottoman Kayseri (1590–1630) as a Source of Ottoman History," *Studia Islamica,* XLVII, 133–72. The qadhi records have also preserved much valuable information concerning Ottoman Jews. Partly because of the widespread Jewish practice of repairing to Muslim courts even in their civil litigations with fellow Jews, and partly on account of the Turkish fiscal authorities' interest in the estates left behind by Jews, along with those of other inhabitants, the qadhi offices have preserved many detailed data about local Jewish families, their possessions, occupations, and a variety of other aspects. Regrettably this source of information has hitherto been but scantily exploited. An excellent example of the information available in such records was offered by H. Gerber in his Hebrew dissertation, *Ha-'Ir ha-Anatolit Bursa ba-me'ah ha-17* (The Anatolian City of Bursa in the Seventeenth Century), submitted in 1976 to the Hebrew University in Jerusalem. See his essay, based thereon, "The Jews in the Economic Life of the Anatolian City of Bursa in the Seventeenth Century; Notes and Documents" (Hebrew), *Sefunot,* XVI (n.s. I), 235–72 (with 10 valuable excerpts in Arabic with a Hebrew trans., pp. 255 ff., from the archival documents). See also *supra,* Chaps. LXXV, n. 10; and LXXVII, n. 62.

The complementary Jewish sources, largely consisting in responsa, are of course far less detailed. Yet, they have proved very useful for the reconstruction of many aspects of Jewish history, including some of its demographic phases, and they have frequently been mentioned in our earlier chapters. However, systematic research on the facts recorded in them have thus far been limited to works of individual rabbis, such as David Ibn abi Zimra and Samuel de Medina. Much of this vast literature is still available only in the original editions, for the most part conveniently listed in Boaz Cohen's *Quntras ha-Teshuvot* (Bibliography of the Responsa. With an Intro. about Their Value for the History of the Halakhah and the Evolution of the Hebrew Law), reprinted from the periodical *Ha-Ṣofeh le-Ḥokhmat Yisrael.* Of considerable assistance to future research promises to be the work now in progress at Bar Ilan University in Israel in indexing the responsa of R. Isaac Adarbi and others. In this connection one ought to bear in mind, however, the issues raised in connection with the parallel notarial documents in the West by M. Robine in "Les Archives notariales complément des registres paroissiaux. Étude sur de la distribution statistique de délai entre contrat de marriage aux XVIIe, XVIIIe et XIXe siècles dans un village de Bazadais," *Annales de Démographie Historique,* VIII, 59–97.

9. See the numerous travelogues and diplomatic reports mentioned in the preceding three chapters and in our earlier volumes. To these we might add: the older but

still very useful Polish collection by J. I. Kraszewski, ed. by K. J. Turowski, *Podróże i poselstwa polskie do Turcyi* (Polish Voyages and Missions to Turkey, namely: The Voyages by E. Otwinowski, 1557; Jędrzej Taranowski, the Canon of His Royal Majesty, 1569; and the Diplomatic Mission of Piotr Zborowski, 1568); L. Tardy and I. Vásáry, "Andrzej Taranowskis Bericht über seine Gesandtschaftsreise in der Tartarei (1569)," *AOH*, XXVIII, 213–52; J. Zuallart, *Le Très dévot voyage de Jerusalem;* E. Browne, *A Brief Account of Some Travels in Divers Parts of Europe, viz. Hungaria, Servia, Bulgaria, Macedonia, Thessaly, Austria, Styria, Carinthia, Carniola, and Friuli. . . . With Some Observations on the Gold, Silver, Copper, Quick Silver Mines, the Berths and Mineral Waters in These Parts* [1669]; and the other Jewish and non-Jewish travelers whose writings are reproduced or analyzed in E. N. Adler's *Jewish Travellers: a Treasury of Travelogues from 9 Centuries,* ed. with an Introduction, 2d ed.; or in the Hebrew works by J. D. Eisenstein, *Oṣar Massa'ot; a Collection of Itineraries by Jewish Travelers to Palestine, Syria, Egypt and Other Countries. Pilgrimage to Holy Tombs and Sepulchres;* A. Yaari, ed., *Massa'ot Ereṣ-Yisrael* (Travels to Palestine); M. Ish-Shalom, *Massa'ei Noṣrim le-Ereṣ-Yisrael* (Christian Travels in the Holy Land: Descriptions and Sources on the History of the Jews in Palestine). On the diplomatic correspondence, especially the dispatches by the Venetian, French, and British envoys see *supra,* Chaps. LXXV, LXXVI, and LXXVII; and Vol. XVII, *passim.* The rather confusing succession of European diplomats in Istanbul has largely been unraveled by B. Spuler in his "Europäische Diplomaten in Konstantinopel bis zum Frieden von Belgrad (1739)," *Jahrbücher für Kultur und Geschichte der Slaven,* 1935, pp. 53–115, 171–222, 313–66; continued in that journal, renamed *Jahrbücher für Geschichte Osteuropas,* I, 229–62, 383–440.

Much information can also be obtained from private correspondence by businessmen, pilgrims, missionaries, or tourists addressed to their home countries. To that mentioned in previous chapters, such as the Jewish letters from Palestine readily available in A. Yaari's collection of *Iggerot Ereṣ Yisrael* (Letters from Palestine), and such less sophisticated six "Yiddish and Hebrew Private Letters of 1533" written by male and female members of a Polish Jewish immigrant family from Bulgaria and published with comments in Yiddish by D. Ginsberg, in *YIVO Bleter,* XIII, 325–44; we need but add Lady Mary Wortley Montagu's *The Complete Letters,* ed. by R. Halsband. Although mostly written in the first half of the eighteenth century, the Montagu letters illustrate Turkish life in the earlier two centuries as well.

It stands to reason that most of the demographic information received from the travelers and envoys was derived from oral communications by officials or other more or less informed local persons. These in turn may have heard about the size of the population from the census takers or, with respect to events and trends in the past, from oral transmission over generations. On the value of such oral traditions, especially in the Middle East, see the literature cited *supra,* Vol. I, pp. 304 f. n. 10; and the numerous other references listed in the *Index to Volumes I–VIII,* pp. 109 *s.v.* Oral Law and 154 *s.v.* Transmission Oral, etc.; to which add J. Vansina's *De la tradition orale; essai de méthode historique,* esp. pp. 24 ff., 69 ff., 83 ff., 92 ff., 118 ff., and 153 ff.; or in the corresponding passages in the English trans. by H. M. Wright, entitled, *Oral Tradition: a Study of Historical Methodology.* See also Chap. LXXX, n. 6.

10. A cautious attempt at using aspects of the topographical method for estimating the population of localities was used by me as early as 1928 in a Hebrew essay in the *Chajes Memorial Volume,* cited at the end of this note. This method has more recently been applied, with reference to the Ottoman Empire, by A. Ligor in his "Aspects démographiques des principales localités urbaines moldaves consignés par les voyageurs étrangers pendant le règne de Vasile Lupu 1634–1653" (Rumanian), *Revista de*

Istorie, XXIX, 63–92, with a French summary. See especially pp. 65 ff. with their statistical tables listing the number of houses alongside that of their inhabitants in Jassy and Suceava on the basis of several censuses between 1623 and 1646. E. Niewohner-Eberhard has made an interesting attempt to identify a Jewish house in Yemen on the basis of its architectural features. See "Das Jemenitisch-arabische Innenhofhaus in Sa'da, Jemen," *Der Islam*, LIV, 177–204. Some attention to the architectural aspects were also paid by Ö. L. Barkan in his "Contribution a l'étude démographique des villes balkaniques au cours des XVe–XVIe siècles," *Studia Balcanica*, III, 181–82. However, the relationship between the location of the great mosques, hospitals, etc. and residences in general and their bearing on the number of inhabitants was not sufficiently clarified. See also, more generally, G. Goodwin, *A History of Ottoman Architecture*.

On examples of the density of the mid-Eastern cities in both ancient times and in the 1920s, see my preliminary observations in "The Israelitic Population under the Kings" reproduced in an English translation (from a Hebrew essay written in 1928 for the *Abhandlungen zur Erinnerung an Hirsch Perez Chajes*, pp. 76–130), in my *Ancient and Medieval Jewish History: Essays*, ed. by L. A. Feldman, pp. 23–73, 380–99, esp. pp. 50 ff., 66 ff., 390 ff. Research along these lines, which is probably even more arduous than that based on data recorded in written documents, still is in its infancy.

11. See T. H. Hollingsworth's and G. Ohlin's essays, cited *supra*, nn. 4 and 7; and, more generally, L. Lehr, "The Determinant Factors in the Demographic Evolution of Turkish Rumania in the Seventeenth Century" (Rumanian), *Studii și Articole de istorie medie*, VII, 161–207; and my general observations on medieval Jewish West-European and Polish-Lithuanian demography, *supra*, Vols. XII, pp. 4 ff., 243 ff.; XVI, pp. 192 ff., 405 ff.

12. See B. McGowan's noteworthy attempt to utilize the advanced American measurements of the relationship between the available food supply and the size of population. Understandably, there is no unanimity in such estimates but they open new vistas by relating the impact, for example, of the quantity of vegetables and barley compared with that of a kilogram of wheat. Using the experiences of the United States Department of Agriculture in studying world conditions, McGowan applies their lessons to the available records of four Hungarian-Turkish *sanjaks*; two of them largely Hungarian and one each with strong Slav and Vlach minorities. He also considers the relation between the prevailing food prices and the size of the population in the Ottoman Empire as a whole. See his "Food Supply and Taxation on the Middle Danube (1568–79)," *AO*, I, 141, 155 f., 159 f. See also, more generally, M. K. Bennett, *The World's Food*.

We must also bear in mind, of course, the influence of external circumstances, often differing in time and place, such as a decline in harvests or a breakdown in communications. See, for example, the chapter on the food crisis of 1483–84 and its impact on the Salonican market discussed by F. Thiriet in "Les Lettres commerciales des Bembo et le commerce vénitien dans l'Empire Ottoman à la fin du XVe siècle," *Studi in onore di Armando Sapori*, II, 911–33, esp. pp. 925 ff. The general assumption among demographers that countries exporting grain have as a rule a slower population growth than countries importing it applies only to Western Europe. It evidently did not hold true for the United States or Canada in the periods of their greatest population expansion. Nor does it seem to be useful in the study of Turkish demography. As a whole, the Ottoman Empire was an exporting country during the sixteenth century, when the population grew substantially, whereas the decline in grain exports at the end of the century and beyond was caused by changing conditions in the Western markets rather than by the demographic trends in the Empire itself.

13. See C. Cahen, "Du Nouveau sur les frontaliers dans l'Islam médiéval," *JESHO*, II, 333–35, with reference to V. Minorsky's *A History of Sharwān and Derbend.*

14. Bab. Talmud Yebamot 62a, 63b; N. Hines, *A Medical History of Contraception;* J. T. Noonan, Jr., "Intellectual and Demographic History," *Daedalus*, XCVII, 463–85. The question of whether polygamy permitted by Muslim law and its rare occurrence among Jews had any effect on population growth has been rather controversial. Ö. L. Barkan's claim that Muslim polygamy increased the birth rate is not supported by detailed evidence. The few cases recorded of monarchs with large harems begetting many children are counterbalanced by the numerous eunuchs which every harem employed and which diminished the number of reproductive men in society. Similarly, the numerous bachelors recorded in the *defters* doubtless were deprived of potential wives through the plural marriages of others. Their deficiency was not fully made up by any surplus in the importation of female slaves over their male counterparts, particularly in the period when *devshirme* was widely used. At the same time we must bear in mind that polygamy was not as widespread in the Ottoman Empire as is usually imagined. Examining the qadhi records in a typical Turkish town like Kayseri, R. C. Jennings found that of over 2,000 estates left by male Muslims only 20 belonged to families with two or more wives. On the other hand, birth control was rarely practiced; D. Kirk observed that "empirically Islam has been a more effective barrier to the diffusion of family planning than Catholicism." See Jennings, "Women in Early 17th Century Ottoman Judicial Records, the Shari'a Court of Anatolian Kayseri," *JESHO*, XVIII, 53–114; and D. Kirk, "Factors Affecting Moslem Natality," in D. Berelson's *Family Planning and Population Programs*, esp. p. 296. See also H. Gerber's more general study of the "Social and Economic Position of Women in an Ottoman City, Bursa, 1600–1700," *IJMES*, XII, 231–44. On the differences, as well as similarities, in the Muslim and Jewish marriage laws, see S. Bialoblocki, *Materialien zum islamischen und jüdischen Eherecht, mit einer Einleitung über die jüdischen Einflüsse auf den Hadīth.*

Compared with these biological factors, intermarriage seems to have played but a minor role. Legally, this was a one-way street. To cite an English visitor of 1589, "No Chrystyan [or Jewish] man may have to do wythe a Turkyshe woman, but he shall dye for yt be known, but a Turk may have as many Chrystyan women as he wyll." See *Mr. Harrie Cavendish his Journey to and from Constantinople 1589 by Fox his servant*, ed. by A. C. Wood, pp. 24 f. Needless to say, marriage with a Muslim often involved the woman's conversion to Islam, although some husbands seem to have allowed their Christian wives quietly to practice their own faith. But we hear very little about Jewish demographic losses on this score.

15. See H. Inalcik, "The Rise of the Ottoman Empire" in V. J. Parry *et al.*, eds., *A History of the Ottoman Empire*, pp. 35 ff.; idem, "Ottoman Methods of Conquest," *Studia Islamica*, II, 103–130.

16. See G. Káldy-Nagy, "Suleimans Angriff auf Europa," *AOH*, XXVIII, 163–212, esp. p. 212; J. Perényi, "Villes hongroises sous la domination ottomane aux XVIe– XVIIes. Les chefs-lieux de l'administration ottomane," *Studia Balcanica*, III, 25–31; L. Fekete, *Buda and Pest under Turkish Rule* (a revised, though abridged, version of his *Budapest a törökkorban*), pp. 13 ff.; G. David, "Some Aspects of 16th Century Depop-

ulation in the Sanjak of Simontonya," *AOH*, XXVIII, 63–74. A subsidiary cause for population decline was a large number of both soldiers and civilians carried away into captivity by the victors. While many prisoners were ransomed, sometimes by the payment of fairly large amounts, their protracted absence from home and likely physical injuries must have contributed to the disorganization of their family lives. On the sufferings of such captives see, for example, the treatment record of the Turkish qadhi in 1599 and of a wealthy Jew in 1663 as described by W. Schmucker in "Die Maltesischen Gefangenschaftserinnerungen eines türkischen Kadi von 1599," *AO*, II, 191–251; and by C. Roth in "The Jews of Malta," *TJHSE*, XII, 187–251. Because of the relatively high position of the qadhi the Maltese ruler demanded 1,000 gold pieces for his ransom, while negotiators for the qadhi offered only 200 gold pieces. This large amount was overshadowed when Kara 'Ali, who was both a Janissary and a merchant, dared to demand as indemnity for his kidnapped slave the huge amount of 3,422 ducats, which he later raised further by 900 ducats allegedly due him for his intervening expenses. Needless to say, that demand was rejected, particularly since after the peace treaty of Karlowitz (Velka Karlovici) of 1699 the Turkish clout was greatly reduced. However, the usual going rate ranged from 200 to 400 gurush per slave girl and up to 600 gurush for prospective galley slaves. See K. Jahn, "Zum Loskauf christlicher und türkischer Gefangener und Sklaven im 18. Jahrhundert," *ZDMG*, CXI, 63–85, esp. pp. 75 ff. Partly because of their high prices the number of slaves in the Ottoman Empire became increasingly limited and probably carried little weight as a demographic factor, especially since the birth rate in slave families was very much lower than among free laborers. See also E. Bashan's comprehensive study, *Shebiah u-fedut ba-ḥebrah ha-yehudit* (Captivity and Ransom in Mediterranean Jewish Society).

17. See G. Baer, "Popular Revolts in Ottoman Cairo," *Der Islam*, LIV, 213–42 (mainly with reference to the eighteenth century); *supra*, Chaps. LXXV, nn. 12 and 20; LXXVII, n. 14.

18. The grave effects of Palestinian earthquakes had already caused the early biblical prophet Amos to date events as having happened "two years before the earthquake" (1:1). According to one calculation there had been no less than 33 major outbreaks of this kind recorded in the Holy Land from antiquity to the beginning of the twentieth century. However, an earthquake in Jerusalem was not necessarily deeply felt in Safed and vice versa. See N. Shalem, "Earthquakes in Jerusalem" (Hebrew), *Yerushalayim Quarterly*, II, 22–54. See also *supra*, Chaps. LXXVI and LXXVII; Vol. VII, p. 167 (a poem describing the earthquake of 1033), and so forth. In connection with this factor we may also mention D. Ashbel's study, "The Jerusalem Climate" (Hebrew), *ibid.*, III, 1–19. Ashbel offers a good review of rainfall and other climatic elements and insists that, contrary to popular opinion, there, indeed, have been some climatic changes since ancient times. On the great fires in Istanbul and Salonica see Joseph ha-Kohen's description of the 1545 fire in his *'Emeq ha-bakha*, p. 121; in H. S. May's English trans., pp. 82 f.; and other sources cited by S. A. Rosanes in his *Qorot*, II, 296 f. App. V.

19. See *The Turkish Letters of Ogier Ghiselin de Busbecq (1554–1562)*, trans. from the [Latin] Elzevier ed. of 1633 by E. S. Forster, pp. 188 f., also mentioning the estimate of some attendants of the well-informed Grand Vizier 'Ali Rustem Pasha that 1,200 lives were lost daily in Istanbul during the plague of 1550. The story of R. Moses Capsali's conversation with Meḥmed II is told in graphic detail in Elijah Capsali's *Seder*

Eliyahu Zuta, ed. by A. Shmuelevitz *et al.,* I, 82, quoting Gen. rabbah 26,10. It is also repeated in a Ladino chronicle, cited by S. A. Rosanes in his *Dibre yeme Yisrael be-Togarma,* I, 40. On the term *Androlomusia* and its Greek etymology, see S. Kraus, *Griechische und lateinische Lehnwörter im Talmud, Midrasch und Targum mit Bemerkungen bei I. Löw,* II, 65. The small differential between rich and poor in the death rates from plagues is briefly discussed and documented, mainly from Western sources, by C. M. Cipolla and D. E. Zanetti in their "Peste et mortalité différentielle," *Annales de Démographie Historique,* 1972, pp. 197–202.

The arrival of the Syrian ship *St. Grand Antoine* from Syria in Marseilles on May 25, 1720, which started the epidemic, cost the lives of 39,334 persons or 43.7 percent of that harbor city's total population alone. See C. Carrière *et al., Marseille ville morte. La peste de 1720;* with the remarks thereon by J. N. Biraben, "La Peste en 1720 à Marseille à propos d'un livre récent," *RH,* CCXLVII, 407–426; idem, "Certain Demographic Characteristics of the Plague Epidemic in France, 1720–22," *Daedalus,* XCVII, 536–45. We can readily imagine the devastation caused by the plague at the ship's point of origin in Syria. One characteristic of the early modern epidemics, compared with the Black Death of 1348, was their longer duration. For example, in Smyrna one attack lasted from September 1713 to December 1716; another from June 1744 to June 1747; and the longest from December 1772 to June 1778, fully five and a half years. See D. Panzac, "La Peste à Smyrna au XVIIIe siècle," *Annales ESC,* XXVIII, 1071–91. Similarly, among the thirteen plagues analyzed by A. Raymond in his "Les Grandes épidémies de peste au Caire aux XVIIe et XVIIIe siècles," *BEO,* XXV, 203–210, one lasted from August 1601 to September 1603, another from November 1642 to March 1644, and so forth. According to Raymond, some of these plague-caused losses of 25–33 percent of the population and, even assuming a very high 10 percent rate of growth annually during the recovery periods, it would have required 29 years to make up for these losses. See his "La Population du Caire de Maqrizi à la Description de l'Égypte," *BEO,* XXVIII, 201–215, esp. p. 213. See also, more generally, J. N. Biraben's comprehensive history of and the people's reaction to large-scale pestilences in his *Les Hommes et la peste en France et dans les pays européens et méditerranéens.*

No effort has been made in this study to consider the extent to which hereditary genetic factors, including the possible greater or lesser frequency of certain diseases among Ottoman Jews, when compared with their non-Jewish neighbors, may have affected the growth of Ottoman Jewry. Although studies of this kind have been pursued by a number of competent scholars for many years, the demographic effects of these factors on Jews (see, for instance, A. E. Mourant et al., *The Genetics of the Jews,* esp. pp. 33 ff.; and the literature listed there) are not yet sufficiently clarified to serve as a basis for comparing them with those of their compatriots in any period before the nineteenth century.

Nor were the Jews, especially their immigrants and pilgrims, spared the accusation that they had spread the plague. We recall the story circulating in North Africa at the turn from the fifteenth to the sixteenth century that the new Jewish arrivals had brought with them the "French disease" (syphilis) which was then ravaging the Middle East. Similarly, we hear of the Muslim authorities of Jerusalem in 1556 claiming that the Jewish pilgrims came from infested localities; they were also supposed to have caused famine in the country, a claim used by a writer as a means of extorting from them "much money." See the Jews' complaint and the sultan's decision in their favor of May 1556, reproduced by Amnon Cohen in his *Yehudei Yerushalayim ba-me'ah ha-shesh-esreh* (Ottoman Documents on the Jewish Community of Jerusalem in the Sixteenth Century), Doc. 20, pp. 59 f. (Hebrew), 92 f. (Turkish); *supra,* Chap. LXXVI, nn. 13 ff. and Vol. XVII, pp. 164 f., 373 n. 48.

20. See Samuel b. Moses Kala'i, *Mishpeṭei Shemuel* (Samuel's Sentences; responsa), Venice, 1599, No. 68; S. A. Rosanes, *Qorot*, III, 7 n. 6. On intergroup conversions within the minorities themselves see, for instance, G. Nešov, "La Propagande catholique dans les turcs bulgares au XVIIᵉ siècle et le développement historique du Sud-Est Européen," *Bulgarian Historical Review*, III, no. 3, 43–52; and G. de Mun, "L'Établissement des Jésuites à Constantinople sous le règne d'Ahmet Iᵉʳ (1603–1617)," *Revue des Questions Historiques*, LXXIV, 163–72. It may be assumed that the conversion of a Greek Orthodox to Catholicism was less objectionable to the powers that were than the conversion of a Jew to Christianity. However, some such conversions to any non-Muslim faith seem to have had little impact on the demographic strength of the respective groups. There certainly were but few conversions to Judaism, except for Marranos whose public return to their ancestral faith can hardly be called a conversion. However, more careful studies in this area, with partial aid of the *defters*, would be highly desirable.

21. See C. Patrinelis, "The Exact Time of the First Attempt of the Turks to Seize the Churches and to Convert the Christian People of Constantinople to Islam," *Actes de the Iᵉʳ Congrès International des Études Balkaniques et Sud-Est Européens* held in Sofia, 1969, III, 567–72; H. Inalcik, "The Policy of Mehmed II toward the Greek Population of Istanbul and the Byzantine Buildings in the City," *Dumbarton Oaks Papers*, XXIII–XXIV, 229–49. The role of the Turkish religious authorities in converting non-Muslims is discussed by H. Kaleshi in "Das Türkische Vordringen auf dem Balkan und die Islamisierung—Faktoren für die Erhaltung der ethnischen und nationalen Existenz des albanischen Volkes," *Südosteuropa unter dem Halbmond . . . Georg Stadtmüller gewidmet*, pp. 125–38; R. W. Bulliet's brief study, "The Sheikh al-Islam and the Evolution of Islamic Society," *Studia Islamica*, XXXV, 53–67; and, more generally, in his *Conversion to Islam in the Middle Ages: an Essay in Quantitative History; supra*, Chap. LXXVII, n. 57; and *infra*, n. 29.

22. See T. H. Hollingsworth, "Historical Studies of Migration," *Annales de Démographie Historique*, 1970, pp. 87–96, esp. p. 96; M. A. Cook, *Population Pressure in Rural Anatolia 1450–1600* (analyzing in part the continued infiltration of Turkic groups from the East); M. Sharon, "The Political Role of the Bedouins in Palestine in the Sixteenth and Seventeenth Centuries" in M. Ma'oz, ed., *Studies in Palestine during the Ottoman Period*, pp. 11–30; and E. Pittora, "Les Peuples que les Turcs ont ammenés dans les Balkans," *REB*, I, 533–38. On the Jewish mass immigration into the Balkans during its peak period in the sixteenth century, see *supra*, Chap. LXXVI, nn. 9 f. The legal consequences of the mass transplantations, which in many cases converted free individuals into persons attached to their new locations somewhat akin to the *glebae adscripti* Western villeins, are described in N. Beldiceanu, *Recherche sur la ville Ottomane au XVᵉ siècle. Étude et actes*, pp. 36 ff., 121 f., 136. Of the vast array of recent studies on human migrations in general, we need but mention here the papers submitted in April 1976 to the Conference sponsored by the Mideast Center of the Academy of Arts and Sciences and Indiana University in New Harmony, Indiana and ed. by W. H. McNeill and R. S. Adam under the title, *Human Migrations: Patterns and Policies*. This whole area of Jewish migrations, into and out of the Ottoman Empire, ought to be the subject of numerous detailed inquiries.

23. See L. Erder, "The Measurement of Preindustrial Population Changes: The Ottoman Empire from the 15th to the 17th Century," *Middle Eastern Studies*, XI, 284–301, esp. p. 290; N. Todorov, in the discussion on papers submitted to the Confér-

ence sur les villes balcaniques (XVe–XVIIIe s.) held in Moscow on March 29–30, 1969, as summarized in *Studia Balcanica*, III, 183–97. Even some of Barkan's seemingly definitive computations have, upon closer scrutiny, proved to be incorrect. Immediately upon the publication of his article in *JESHO*, I, Charles Issawi rightly pointed out that Barkan's figure of only 944 Christian households, or 1.5 percent of the total population, in an area roughly corresponding to what are now Syria, Lebanon, Israel, and Jordan, was in glaring contrast with the more reliable censuses of the 1930s, which showed that in this region the Christian share amounted to 16.4 percent. Issawi argued that, if anything, the Christian population must have had a still higher percentage in the 1520s, while the growth of the Muslim population postulated by Barkan was exaggerated. See Issawi's "Comment on Professor Barkan's Estimate of the Population of the Ottoman Empire in 1520–1530," *JESHO*, I, 329–31. His arguments have largely retained their validity after Barkan's defense of his thesis, *ibid.*, pp. 331–33. See also Amnon Cohen and B. Lewis's reservations in the introductory chapter, "The Taḥir Registers of Palestine," in their *Population and Revenue in the Towns of Palestine in the Sixteenth Century*, pp. 3–18, supplemented by such additional data as supplied, for instance, by B. Lewis's succinct study of "Acre in the Sixteenth Century According to the Ottoman *Tapu* Registers," *Mémorial Ömer Lûtfi Barkan* (Bibliothèque de l'Institut Français d'Études Anatoliens d'Istanbul, XXVIII), 135–39.

24. See Ö. L. Barkan's "Les Déportations comme méthode de peuplement et de colonisation dans l'Empire Ottoman," *Revue de la Faculté des Sciences Économiques de l'Université d'Istanbul*, XI, 67, 131; Elijah Capsali, *Seder Eliyahu Zuta*, xvi, ed. by A. Shmuelevitz *et al.*, I, 81. On the population in Istanbul in 1478, see Barkan's data in his "Essai," *JESHO*, I, 27 and 35; and *infra*, n. 27. In all these computations we depend greatly on which multiple is given to the listed number of hearths or families— a matter of controversy for many years. In fact, the average size of families has often differed from locality to locality and period to period. In his various studies Barkan usually assumes a multiple of 5. This assumption may perhaps offer the best general approximation, although we have seen that in some Western communities Jewish families often came closer to consisting of 7 members on the average. See *supra*, Vol. XII, pp. 4 ff., 243 ff. See also L. Erder's observations in "The Measurement of Preindustrial Population Changes," in *Middle Eastern Studies*, XI, esp. pp. 294 f.; and, more generally, P. Laslett, "International Comparison in the Size and Structure of the Household Over Time," *Colloque International de Démographie Historique, Florence, October 1971* (mimeographed).

25. See Ö. L. Barkan, "Essai," *JESHO*, I, 20 ff.; R. Mantran, "La Police des marchés de Stamboul au début du XVIe siècle," *Cahiers de Tunisie*, XIV, 213–41, esp. pp. 236, 238; idem, *Istanbul dans la seconde moitié du XVIIe siècle. Essai d'histoire institutionelle, économique et sociale*, esp. pp. 46 f., 57 f. Using still another method, that of housing, Mantran estimates that about 1550 there were 60,000 Muslim, 40,000 Christian, and 4,000 Jewish houses in the city of Istanbul and some 10,000 (including 1,697 Jewish) houses in Galata (*ibid.*, pp. 41 f.). These figures would indicate a total of at least 500,000 inhabitants including some 30,000 Jews. The estimate of 700,000 population for late-sixteenth-century Istanbul, first mentioned by Giovanni Botero in his *Relationi universali*, Brescia, 1599, was widely accepted by scholars. On that basis Fernand Braudel attributed to Istanbul a population twice the size of that of Paris, two and a half times that of the then largest Italian city of Naples, five times that of Venice, seven and a half times that of Rome, and about twenty times that of Marseilles. See his *La Méditerranée et le monde méditerranéen*, I, 255, 316. Traian Stoianovich's objections are based

upon the records of the size of the city (within its walls) given by the travelers Jean de Thévenot (10 miles), G. d'Aramon (13–15 miles), Constantino Garzoni (16 miles). See his "Model and Mirror of the Premodern Balkan City," *Studia Balcanica*, III, 83–110, esp. p. 90 n. 1 (also mentioning Marc'Antonio Pigafetta's estimate of 40,000 courtiers serving Selim II, p. 88).

26. See Hans Dernschwam's *Tagebuch*, p. 90; Stephan Gerlach, *Tage-Buch;* and U. Heyd's careful analysis of "The Jewish Communities of Istanbul in the Seventeenth Century," *Oriens*, VI, 299–314, esp. pp. 300 f., 309 ff. Doc. No. 3661, dated 1691–92, listing the 21 quarters of the city which embraced over 5,000 Jewish taxpayers. To their number is to be added that of the Karaite community which, although rapidly declining from the high level of its cultural achievements during the fifteenth and early sixteenth centuries, still was numerically and economically a sizable entity. See S. Szyszman, "Communauté Karaïte d'Istamboul," *Vetus Testamentum*, VI, 309–315. See also R. Mantran's *Istanbul dans la seconde moitié du XVIIᵉ siècle;* and, more generally, the essays, ed. by K. Bachteler in the *Festschrift* in honor of Kurt Albrecht entitled *Istanbul. Geschichte und Entwicklung der Stadt*, including four essays relating to the Ottoman period; pp. 166 ff.

27. See Ö. L. Barkan's emphatic assertion: "In 1478, not a single Jew lived yet in Salonica," in his "Research on the Ottoman Fiscal Surveys," in M. A. Cook, ed., *Studies in the Economic History of the Middle East from the Rise of Islam to the Present Day*, pp. 163–71, esp. p. 171. The absence of Jews from still another register of 1478 is confirmed by B. Lewis in his "Judaeo-Islamica," in the forthcoming *Simon Rawidowicz Mem. Vol.* From Jewish sources, however, we learn that, in spite of their great sufferings during the early decades of the century they did not completely disappear from the city. See I. S. Emmanuel, *Histoire des Israélites de Salonique*, Vol. I: 140 B.C. to 1640 C.E.; J. Nehama, *Histoire des Israélites de Salonique*. See also the widely divergent estimates of the Jewish population in Salonica during the eighteenth century, cited by N. G. Svoronos in his richly documented *Le Commerce de Salonique au XVIIIᵉ siècle*, with a Preface by E. Labrousse (a thesis presented to the École Pratique des Hautes Études in 1949), p. 10 n. 2. The author also mentions in this connection the number of Doenmehs (Dönmes), descendants of some Jewish followers of Shabbetai Zevi who in 1666, like their leader, had adopted Islam, but were generally suspected of professing Judaism in secret. Their number is given here as ranging between 500 families and 5,000 persons. *Ibid.* n. 4. Of interest also is Svoronos's earlier publication *Salonique et Cavalla (1686–1792). Inventaire des correspondances des consuls de France au Levant conservées aux Archives Nationales*. Certainly, the Jewish population of Salonica for the decades preceding 1478 calls for further detailed investigation. See also N. Beldiceanu's informative review of M. A. Epstein's *The Ottoman Jewish Communities (infra*, n. 106) in *Der Islam*, LVIII, 370–73, which mentions that, according to the Tapu registers, the Jewish majority in Salonica amounted to 56 percent in 1519, dropped to 52 percent in 1530–31, but rose to 68 percent in 1619 (p. 371).

28. See Ö. L. Barkan, "Essai," *JESHO*, I, 27 Table 4 and 33 ff. Table 5; idem, "Quelques observations sur l'organisation économique et sociale des villes ottomanes des XVIᵉ et XVIIᵉ siècles," *Recueils de la Société Jean Bodin*, Vol. VII: La Ville, II, 289–311; Nicolas de Nicolay, *Navigations, Pérégrinations et Voyages*, p. 265; K. Kreiser, *Edirne im 17. Jahrhundert nach Evliya Čelebi*, pp. 136 ff. (admitting that he "could not do justice to the Jewish streets"; p. 139); N. Beldiceanu, "Un Acte sur le statut de la com-

munauté juive de Trikala," *REI*, XL, 129–38; idem, *Recherche sur la ville ottomane au XVe siècle. Études et actes*, esp. pp. 29 ff.

29. See A. Ligor, "Aspects démographiques des principales localités urbaines moldaves" (Rumanian), *Revista de Istorie*, XXIX, 63–92; S. Stefanescu, *Demografia, dimensioni a istorii* (Demography: Historical Dimensions), pp. 118–41; R. Samardžić, "Belgrade," *Studia Balcanica*, III, 33–44; Ö. L. Barkan, "Essai," *JESHO*, I, 27, Table 4; *supra*, n. 10. On the rapid growth of the Muslim and the relative paucity of the Jewish population in Sarajevo, see the figures cited by A. Sučeska in "Die Rechtsstellung der Bevölkerung in den Städten Bosniens und der Herzegowina unter den Osmanen," *Südosteuropa-Jahrbuch*, VIII, 84–99, esp. p. 90. Because of the selectivity of the *defters*, Barkan's figure of 23,000 inhabitants in the 1570s and Sučeska's computation that after 1580 Sarajevo's population consisted of 30,000 persons inhabiting 4,000 houses on 104 streets are not necessarily contradictory.

Somewhat different was the situation in the Black Sea area after the Turkish conquest of the former Venetian and Genoese colonies. See N. Beldiceanu, "Kilia et Cetatea-Albá à travers les documents ottomans," *REI*, XXXVI, 215–62; also in his *Recherche sur la ville ottomane*, pp. 121 ff.

30. See N. Todorov, "La Différentiation de la population urbaine au XVIIIe s. d'après des registres du cadis de Vidin, Sofia et Ruse," *Studia Balcanica*, III, 45–62; and on the noteworthy changes in Buda, L. Fekete, *Buda and Pest under Turkish Rule*, pp. 12 ff. Needless to say, the frequent numerical preponderance of the Muslim residents in many Balkan cities within a generation or two after their occupation by the Turkish armies was owing largely to the conscious Islamization efforts of the governmental authorities. While only in the case of captives used for the *devshirme* (recruitment for the army) or of women taken into Turkish harems were forcible means employed in a wholesale fashion, more subtle methods of persuasion and the lure of economic and social advancement as a rule sufficed to convert a large number of newly acquired subjects. See, for example, the study, based particularly on Albanian data presented by H. Kaleshi in "Das Türkische Vordringen auf dem Balkan," *Südosteuropa unter dem Halbmond . . . Georg Stadtmüller gewidmet*, pp. 125–38. Of some demographic interest also are the observations, however often imprecise, of foreign visitors, like the physician Edward Brown who described Belgrade as a city one-half or one-third the size of Salonica, and one-tenth that of Istanbul. See his *A Brief Account of Some Travels in Hungary, Servia, Belgrade, Macedonia, Thessaly, Austria, Styria, Carinthia, Carniola, Trieste*, London, 1667, esp. pp. 39 f. On Bulgarian cities see, for instance, the analyses by M. Leo, *La Bulgarie et son peuple sous la domination ottomane, tels que les ont vus les voyageurs anglo-saxons (1586–1878); découvert d'une nationalité;* and M. Bur, "Berichte aus dem XVII. Jahrhundert über bulgarische Städte aus Tagebüchern ungarischer Reisenden," *Studia Balcanica*, III, 165–68.

31. Ö. L. Barkan, "Essai," *JESHO*, I, pp. 20 Table 1, 29 f. Table 5. Brusa, the old Anatolian capital of the early Osmanli rulers, continued to play an important role in international trade and registered 117 Jewish and 69 Christian families in a total of 6,351 hearths. See H. Gerber, "The Jews in the Economic Life of the Anatolian City of Bursa" (Hebrew), *Sefunot*, XVI, 236 ff.; and *supra*, Chap. LXXV, n. 62. No Jews, however, are mentioned in Iznik, the ancient Nicaea. Yet, here as elsewhere, such silence in the *defters* may have been accidental. See J. Raby, "A Seventeenth-Century Description of Iznik-Nicaea," *Istanbuler Mitteilungen*, XXVI, 141–80; and, more generally, M. A. Cook, *Population Pressure in Rural Anatolia 1450–1600*.

32. Ö. L. Barkan, "Essai," *JESHO*, I, 30 Table 5; A. Galanté, *Histoire des Juifs d'Anatolie, passim.*

33. See S. J. Shaw's succinct Introduction to his *The Financial and Administrative Organization and Development of Ottoman Egypt 1517–1789*, p. 4; idem, "Cairo's Archives and the History of Ottoman Egypt," *Report on Current Research*, Spring, 1956; idem, "Archival Sources for the Study of Ottoman History: The Archives of Turkey," *JAOS*, LXXX, 1–12; and other literature, particularly in Turkish, listed by him in these publications. On Iraq, see N. Barozzi and G. Berchet, eds., *Relazioni*, I, 347, 425; *Les Voyages et les observations du Sieur de la Boullay el-Gowz*, p. 325; J. W. Zinkeisen, *Geschichte des osmanischen Reiches in Europa*, IV, 169 ff.; N. Jorga, *Geschichte*, III, 474 ff.; J. B. Tavernier's *Les Six Voyages*, or in the English trans., *Six Voyages through Turkey into Asia*, p. 237; B. Lewis, "Judaeo-Osmanica," in the forthcoming *Rawidowicz Mem. Vol.*; A. Ben-Jacob, *Yehudei Babel*, p. 88. The paucity of information concerning the number of Jewish inhabitants in Iraq is the less surprising as the early studies in modern Iraqi (as well as Egyptian) demography in general have lagged far behind those concerning European Turkey and Palestine.

34. Ö. L. Barkan, "Essai," *JESHO*, I, 33 f. Table 5; J. C. David, "Alep, dégradation et tentatives actuelles de réadaptation des structures urbaines traditionelles," *BEO*, XXVIII, 19–50; H. Guys, *Statistiques du Pashalek d'Alep;* M. Bakhit, *The Ottoman Province of Damascus in the Sixteenth Century* (unpublished London dissertation). Of related interest are some of the financial and fiscal data analyzed by R. Mantran in "Règlements fiscaux ottomans. La province de Bassore (2ᵉ moitié du XVI s.)," *JESHO*, X, 224–77; and by A. K. Rafeq in "Les Registres des tribunaux de Damas comme source pour l'histoire de la Syrie," *BEO*, XXVI, 219–76.

35. See Amnon Cohen and B. Lewis, *Population and Revenue in the Towns of Palestine in the Sixteenth Century*, esp. pp. 92 ff. Table 1, 161 ff. Table 6; C. Issawi's aforementioned observations on Barkan's study in *JESHO*, I, 329 ff.; B. Lewis's earlier studies, especially his Hebrew essay "Eretz-Israel in the First Fifty Years of Ottoman Rule according to the Registers of the Ottoman Cadaster," *Eretz Israel*, IV (1956= *Isaac Ben Zvi Jub. Vol.*), 170–87; his "Studies in the Ottoman Archives, I," *BSOAS*, XVI, 469–501; and his *Notes and Documents from the Turkish Archives*, esp. pp. 5 ff. and 25 ff. with the notes thereon; and *supra*, Vol. XVII, pp. 164, 373 n. 47. See also, more generally, Amnon Cohen's *Yehudei Yerushalayim ba-me'ah ha-shesh-esreh* (Ottoman Documents on the Jewish Community of Jerusalem in the Sixteenth Century, with an extensive English summary); and idem, *Palestine in the 18th Century: Patterns of Government and Administration*. This volume sheds much light also upon the conditions in the Holy Land in the preceding two centuries. Of considerable interest also is the recent *Historical Geography of Palestine, Transjordan and Southern Syria in the Late 16th century*, ed. by W. D. Hütteroth and K. Abdalfatah.

The decline of Safed Jewry reached its nadir in the middle of the seventeenth century during the civil war between the Druze chieftain Takhr ad-Din and the pasha of Damascus. By 1655 the Jewish remnant evacuated Safed altogether; Jews returned there only three years later. Some additional material on this episode has been supplied by M. Benayahu through his publication of five letters written by the Italian rabbis Samuel Aboab and Moses Zacuto in his "Documents from Italy Relating to the Temporary Abandonment of Safed by the Jews (1655–1658)" (Hebrew), *Eretz-Israel*, III (1954 = *M. D. U. Cassuto Mem. Vol.*), 244–48.

36. See Samuel b. David Yemsel's Hebrew travelogue (*Massa‘*), published by J. Ḥ. Gurland in his collection *Ginze Yisrael be-Sanct-Petersburg* (Jewish Treasures in St. Petersburg), and republished in J. D. Eisenstein's *Ozar Massaot* (A Collection of Itineraries), pp. 188–205, esp. p. 191; and in the English trans. by E. N. Adler in his *Jewish Travellers*, pp. 329–44, esp. p. 340 (Eisenstein's suggestion that Yemsel was not the voyager's name, but rather an acronym for *Yanuaḥ ‘al mishkabo shalom* [May he rest in peace] is more ingenious than probable). The various estimates mentioned in the text were given by Jacques Savary in his widely read and discussed work (it was republished six times within 38 years) *Le Parfait Negociant; ou Instruction generale pour ce qui regarde le commerce de toute sorte de marchandise, tant de France, que des pays estrangers,* Paris 1675; H. Castela, *Le Sainct Voyage de Hierusalem et Sinai,* 2d ed., Paris, 1612; M. Clerget, *Le Caire. Étude de géographie urbaine et d'histoire économique,* esp. I, 174 ff., 215 ff., 238 ff.; II, 21 ff.; A. Raymond, "La Population du Caire de Maqrizi à la Description de l'Égypte," *BEO,* XXVIII, 201–215, esp. pp. 213 f. One may also mention another traveler, Grettin Affagart who, in his *Relation de Terre Sainte (1533–34),* ed. with an Intro. and Notes by J. Chavanou, refers to the presence of 20,000 Jews in Cairo, probably an exaggeration. On the conflicting calculations of the total population of Cairo according to the census of 1798, ranging between 263,000 and 300,000, see E. F. Jomard, "Description abrégée de la Ville et Citadelle du Kaire" in *Description de l'Égypte, État moderne,* II, Part 2, pp. 579–764, esp. pp. 586, 694; and M. de Chabrol, "Essai sur les moers des habitants modernes de l'Égypte," *ibid.,* pp. 361–524, esp. pp. 364 f.; and, based thereon, A. Raymond, *Artisans et commerçants au Caire au XVIIIe siècle,* I, 204 Table 28; II, 459 ff. Jomard and his associates themselves expressed doubts about the accuracy of the 3,000 figure for Jews. The estimate of 5,000 Jewish inhabitants in Cairo early in the nineteenth century, mentioned by Y. W. Lane in *An Account of the Manners and Customs of the Modern Egyptians,* 5th ed. by E. S. Poole, I, 26 ff., 303 ff. is probably too low.

37. K. J. Beloch, "Die Bevölkerung Europas zur Zeit der Renaissance," *Zeitschrift für Socialwissenschaft,* III, 405–423, esp. his listing of population estimates of eight West European countries totaling 53,000,000 (p. 420); idem, *Bevölkerungsgeschichte Italiens;* Ö. L. Barkan, "Essai," *JESHO,* I, 20 Table 1; and his "Quelques observations," *Recueils de la Société Jean Bodin,* VII, 289 f.; and F. Braudel, *La Méditerranée,* I, 361 ff. and *passim.* In general, Barkan and other scholars have been on safer ground when they sought to ascertain the population of a single city or district than when they tried to extrapolate from such findings the population of an entire region or of a country as a whole. It should be noted that the Ottoman Empire of the period had not yet fully felt the impact of the mass movement of the rural population to the cities (and later to the rapidly expanding metropolitan areas) and that, hence, most municipalities throughout the Empire had relatively small populations of 10,000 persons or less. One certainly could not compare the population density of the Turkish cities other than Istanbul with that of the numerous city-states of the Apennine Peninsula. Apart from Naples, the largest city, Italy could boast of several other urban centers exceeding 100,000 inhabitants before 1650. On the general problem of the then incipient gradual metropolitanization of Western Europe see K. Olbricht's observations in his "Die Vergrossstädterung des Abendlandes zu Beginn des Dreissigjärhigen Krieges," *Petermanns Geographische Mitteilungen,* 1900. In this connection, Olbricht's estimate of only 6,000,000 population for European Turkey in the late sixteenth century (p. 349) is somewhat more persuasive than Barkan's 8,000,000. As far as Jews are concerned such global figures are almost unobtainable. However, the figure of 150,000–200,000

Jews of European Turkey in 1650 seems to be the closest "guestimate" one can make. Nor is the estimate of some 100,000 more for the rest of the Empire too venturesome.

38. See E. Ashtor, "The Karimi Merchants," *JRAS*, 1956, pp. 45–56. Regrettably, despite the availability of a plethora of archival and other sources, the study of the economic history of the Ottoman Empire has lagged behind, even in Turkey. To be sure, a good beginning in that direction was made back in 1864 when F. A. Belin published his "Essai sur l'histoire économique de la Turquie, d'après les écrivains originaux," *JA*, 6th ser. III, 416–89; IV, 242–96, 301–390, 477–530; V, 127–67. Writing in 1955, however, Claude Cahen has rightly complained that most of the available published material had been written by missionaries, diplomats, businessmen, and other persons without the necessary linguistic and historical training. The pointed remark quoted by another leading authority, Bernard Lewis, about the history of the Arabs, that (until recently) it was "written in Europe chiefly by historians who knew no Arabic and by Arabists who knew no history," essentially applied also to Turkish history. In the case of economic history even professional historians often lacked the prerequisites for more specialized evaluations of economic trends. It was not surprising, therefore, that as late as the interwar period the first edition of the *Encyclopaedia of Islam*, prepared by the leading experts in this field, contributed but little to the knowledge of economic movements and statistical details. See C. Cahen, "L'Histoire économique et sociale de l'Orient musulman médiéval," *Studia islamica*, III, 93–115, esp. pp. 96 ff.; and B. Lewis, "Islam," in *Orientalism and History*, ed. by D. Sinor, 2d ed., pp. 16–34, esp. p. 16. Of course, in the last several decades preoccupation with all phases of economic history has grown rapidly not only in countries with a preeminently Marxist outlook but also among the "quantitative" and other schools of Western historians. Yet, as of now, one need but mention a Turkish work by M. Akdağ, *Türkiyenin Ikdisadi* (Histoire économique et sociale de la Turquie); and a relatively brief general survey of this much-promising field in a Western language by Z. Y. Hershlag, *Introduction to the Modern Economic History of the Middle East* (also in a Hebrew edition) which devotes but a brief introductory chapter to the developments before the nineteenth century. Even the recently published Turkish work by Aydin Yelçin, *Türkiye Iktisat Tarihi* (Economic History of Turkey) has but partially filled this historiographic lacuna.

A number of meritorious more specialized studies, however, particularly referring to the Empire's successor states, have appeared in recent years. To mention only a few: N. Todorov's "Certains problèmes du développement économique et social dans les provinces balkaniques de l'Empire Ottoman aux XVIe–XIXe siècles," *Bulletin* of the Association Internationale d'Études du Sud-Est Européen, XII, 43–58; M. Todorova, "Istanbul à la jonction des cultures balcaniques, méditerranéennes, slaves et orientales, XVIe–XIXe siècles," *Études Balcaniques*, X, no. 1, pp. 138–41; B. A. Cvetkova, "Vie économique des villes et ports balkaniques au XVe et XVIe siècles," *REI*, XXXVIII, 267–355; continued with extensive documentation thereto in "Actes concernant la vie économique de villes et ports balkaniques au XVe et XVIe siècles," *ibid.*, XL, 345–90; XLIII, 143–80; numerous other studies (including 16 of her own publications of 1950–63), listed in her "Bibliographie des ouvrages parus dans les pays slaves sur les aspects économiques et sociaux de la domination ottomane," *JESHO*, VI, 319–26, esp. pp. 320 f.; P. Cernovodeanu, "Les Échanges économiques dans l'évolution des relations roumano-turques (XVe–XVIIIe siècle)," *RESEE*, XVI, 81–90; C. M. Kortepeter, "Ottoman Imperial Policy and the Economy of the Black Sea Region in the Sixteenth Century," *JAOS*, LXXXVI, 86–113 (includes an interesting table of "Resources of the Black Sea Litloral by Region," p. 110). Needless to say much can be learned from studies on the earlier conditions in parts of the empire such as E. Ashtor's review of *A Social and Economic History of the Near East in the Middle Ages.*

Of interest also are some more theoretical studies such as S. N. Haider Naqvi's "Islamic 'Economic System': Fundamental Issues," *Islamic Studies*, XV, 327–46 (emphasizing in particular the conflict between the traditional teachings of Islam related to individual creativity and the modern stress on social action); Ö. L. Barkan, "The Social Consequences of Economic Crisis in Later Seventeenth Century Turkey," *Social Aspects of Economic Development:* A Report submitted to the International Conference on Social Aspects . . . held at Istanbul on August 4–24, 1963, pp. 17–36; H. Inalcik, "Capital Formation in the Ottoman Empire," *JEcH*, XXIX, 97–140; his "The Ottoman Economic Mind and Aspects of Ottoman Economy," in M. A. Cook, ed., *Studies in the Economic History of the Middle East*, pp. 207–218; and particularly M. Rodinson's "Histoire économique et histoire des classes sociales dans le Monde Musulman," *ibid.*, pp. 139–55; and his searching, though somewhat doctrinaire, analysis of the relationship between *Islam and Capitalism*, trans. from the French by B. Pearce.

39. Bab. Talmud, Baba Meṣiah, fol. 71a with reference to Exod. 22:24; Joseph b. Moses di Trani, *Resp.*, E.'E. No. 35; S. A. Rosanes, *Qorot*, III, 213. On the growing integration of the imperial population, see the two studies, independently written and published in the same year, by J. G. Da Silva, "Traits communs du développement économique et social: le capitalisme marchand et les économies méditerranéennes et balkaniques, XVᵉ–XVIIIᵉ siècles," *Études Balcaniques*, XI, 114–22; and A. E. Vacalopoulos, "Traits communs du développement économique et social des peuples balkaniques et du Sud-Est européen à l'époque ottoman," *Balkan Studies*, XVI, 154–75. Since Jews played a significant role in many branches of the Ottoman economy, we must more particularly regret the paucity of detailed studies of Turkish Jewish economic history. Even so noteworthy a collection of essays as that ed. by M. Ma'oz in *Studies on Palestine during the Ottoman Period* includes no chapter pertaining to the economic evolution of that Turkish province, although a good deal can be learned even from the data incidentally mentioned in the responsa of Turkish rabbis. See, for example, the succinct references to such data in E. Bashan's "The Political and Economic Crisis in the Ottoman Empire from the End of the Sixteenth Century as Reflected in the Responsa Literature" (Hebrew), *Proceedings* of the VI World Congress of Jewish Studies held in Jerusalem on 16–19, August 1973, ed. by A. Shinan and M. Jagendorf, II, 107–115, with an English summary, p. 417.

40. See *supra*, Chaps. LXXVI, nn. 24 ff.; LXXVII, nn. 2 ff.; and Vols. XI, pp. 255 f., 413 n. 79; XII, pp. 51, 269 n. 50; XIV, pp. 77 ff., 335 n. 6. The speech by Jacopo Soranzo, as reported by Joseph ha-Kohen in his *'Emeq ha-bakha*, pp. 168 f.; and in the English trans. by H. S. May, pp. 114 f., need not be considered an accurate rendering of his actual oration in Venice. But its general meaning is undoubtedly well reproduced. Curiously, the excessive appreciation of the role of the "hero" prevailing in Renaissance historiography so blinded even the generally level-headed thinker Jean Bodin that he attributed Selim's spectacular victories to that sultan's reading about Julius Caesar's exploits in Gaul and his wish to emulate the ancient Roman conqueror. See Bodin's *Methodus ad facilem historiarum cognitionem* (1566), Strasbourg, 1607 ed., or in the English trans. by B. Reynolds, *Method for the Easy Comprehension of History* (Records of Civilization, Records and Studies, XXXVII).

41. See V. J. Parry *et al.* in M. A. Cook, ed., *A History of the Ottoman Empire to 1730*, esp. pp. 127 ff., 137, 139 ff., and 155; *supra*, Chap. LXXVII, n. 9.

42. Omer Ṭalib's eloquent pamphlet failed in his day to arouse Ottoman public opinion, and was hardly mentioned in the subsequent Turkish literature. It was first published by A. Zeki Velidi Togan (2d ed., 1947, esp. I, 127). It is here quoted from the English trans. in B. Lewis's "Some Reflections on the Decline of the Ottoman Empire," *Studia Islamica*, IX, 111–27, esp. p. 118. In this connection Lewis also refers to earlier warnings sounded by a writer in 1580. On other criticisms, voiced during those years, see *supra*, Chap. LXXVI.

43. J. D. C. Boulakia, "Ibn Khaldun, a Fourteenth Century Economist," *Journal of Political Economy*, LXXIX, 1105–1118, esp. pp. 1107 f.; 'Abd ar-Raḥman b. Muhammad Ibn Khaldun, *K. al-Muqaddima*, in F. Rosenthal's English trans. *The Muqaddimah: an Introduction to History*, I, 89 f.; II, 271 f.; Maimonides, *Guide for the Perplexed*, I, 72; III, 45; in I. Friedlander's English trans., cited in my "The Economic Views of Maimonides" in *Essays on Maimonides*, ed. by me, pp. 134 ff., 136 n. 21, 144 f.; reprinted in my *Ancient and Medieval History: Essays*, pp. 153 ff., 158 f., 447 n. 21, 453 n. 38; H. Inalcik, "The Ottoman Economic Mind and Aspects of the Ottoman Economy," in *Studies on the Economic History of the Middle East*, ed. by M. A. Cook, pp. 207–218. In view of the great similarity in phrasing and argumentation between Ibn Khaldun's and Maimonides' observations, one might be tempted to assume that it was not wholly coincidental. Maimonides' *Guide* was fairly well known in the Muslim intellectual circles in fourteenth-century North Africa, the ambiance within which Ibn Khaldun developed his own fundamental outlook on life. See, for instance, *supra*, Vol. VIII, p. 307 n. 17. However, it is more likely that both thinkers were influenced by some earlier Arabic writings, including the Arabic translation of the Hellenistic tract *Oikonomikos* by Bryson. See M. Plessner's ed., *Der Oikonomikos des Neupythagoräers "Bryson" und sein Einfluss auf die islamische Wissenschaft*; and the brief sketch of early Islamic economic thought in S. Mahmassani's *Les Idées économiques d'Ibn Khaldoun*.

44. See *supra*, Vol. XII, p. 51, where a somewhat fuller quotation from the Sicilian petition is given. The significant changes in Turkish feudalism in the seventeenth century are well analyzed by B. A. Cvetkova in "L'Évolution du régime féodal turc de la fin du XVIe siècle jusq'au milieu du XVIIIe siècle," *Études historiques*, published in Sofia on the occasion of the International Congress of Historical Sciences, Stockholm, August 1960, I, 171–206, esp. pp. 188 f. The impact of the *timar* system, which originally was beneficial to the power of the Turkish army, turned into a calamity when the landholdings ceased to be reserved for lords distinguished through their services to the state, particularly in the military field, and began to be used as mere sources of revenue, by being handed over by the authorities to the highest bidders without regard to class. These new landlords often tried to recoup their investment as speedily as possible to the detriment of the land's fertility and of the well-being of the peasantry. See, for example, G. Káldy-Nagy, "The Effect of the Timār-System on Agricultural Production in Hungary," *Studia turcica*, ed. by L. Ligeti, 1971, pp. 241–48; and, more generally, B. A. Cvetkova, "Vie économique des villes et ports balcaniques aux XVe et XVIe siècles," *REI*, XXXVIII, 267–355; and Ali Faik Bey, *Volkswirtschaftspolitik der Türkei im 16. und 17. Jahrhundert. Agrarverfassung, Lehnsystem, Finanzpolitik unter dem Lehnsystem und Geldpolitik*, Diss. Kiel, 1921. On the debate concerning the so-called Asiatic Mode of Production, see Č. Keyder, "The Dissolution of the Asiatic Mode of Production," *Economies et sociologie*, V, 179–96; and Y. Seitel, "Le Concept de 'mode de production asiatique' et les interprétations de l'histoire ottomane," *Persie*, 186, pp. 77–92, both published in 1976. The various aspects of Ottoman agricultural production and the Jewish role therein are more fully discussed *infra*, nn. 50 ff.

45. Johannes de Strygis' letter to the Duke of Gonzaga, dated June 6, 1472, is cited from a Mantuan archival document by F. Braudel in *La Méditerranée*, I, 355. On the value of the Marseilles-Alexandrian exchanges, see A. Raymond, *Artisans et commerçants au Caire*, I, 18.

46. Maimonides, *Commentary* on the Mishnah Baba Meşia IV, 6; *M.T.* Mekhirah XII, 8–12; and other data on Muslim and Jewish minters and moneychangers discussed in my "The Economic Views of Maimonides," in *Essays on Maimonides*, ed. by me, pp. 127–264, esp. pp. 194 f. (reprinted in my *Ancient and Medieval Jewish History: Essays*, esp. pp. 189 f., 474 f. n. 124); S. J. Shaw, *The Financial and Administrative Organization and Development of Ottoman Egypt, 1517–1798*, p. 323. Maimonides' observations, though mainly relating to medieval Islam, applied also, perhaps even with greater force, under the Ottoman domination. "The Turks," rightly observed Robert Paris, "were much less expert than the Westerners in appreciating the grade of precious metal free of alloys. The use of the touchstone, especially, was far less extensive in the Ottoman Empire than in Europe. That is why the mass of the population attributed the price of coins more to their appearance than to their nominal value." See his ed. of Vol. V of the *Histoire du Commerce de la Ville de Marseille*, under the general editorship of G. Rambert, p. 324.

47. See Meḥmed II's decennial operations and Theodorus Spanduginus' estimate of their yield in his *Petit Traité de l'origine des Turqz*, ed. with Notes by C. Shefer and cited by F. A. (M.) Belin in his "Essai," *JA*, 6th ser. IV, 270 ff.; Cardinal Johannes Bessarion's observation, cited by N. Jorga in his *Geschichte des osmanischen Reiches*, II, 217 f. Here Jorga also quotes other estimates of the Treasury's annual revenue in the days of Meḥmed II.

48. See R. Yeḥiel Basan, *Resp.*, Constantinople, 1737, Nos. 58, 61, 68; R. Abraham Ḥiyya b. Moses de Boton, *Leḥem rab* (Great Dispute; responsa), Smyrna, 1660, No. 103; the Safed rabbinate's decision, cited from a Mantuan MS by E. Bashan in his aforementioned (n. 39) Hebrew communication in *Proceedings* of the VI World Congress of Jewish Studies, pp. 113 ff. In his essay, Bashan also quotes, from a Jerusalem MS, R. David b. Shushan's report of a Salonican rabbinical ordinance sharply enjoining the Jews to adhere closely to Murad III's 1590 decree which had set the value of the Turkish gold coin at 70 aspers. R. David's assertion, however, that "from that time until today all business has been conducted on that basis," is open to doubt.

The general confusion created by the large variety of coins, both good and bad, foreign and local, which circulated in the Empire has often been described. See esp. R. Mantran's *Istanbul dans la seconde moitié du XVIIe siècle*, pp. 233 ff., 248 ff.; and A. Raymond's *Artisans et commerçants au Caire au XVIIIe siècle*, I, 17 ff. Although both these works deal with the later period, they describe conditions which were basically similar in the early seventeenth century and, to a lesser extent, in the sixteenth century.

49. We must also realize that the economies of all Mediterranean states were gradually declining during the seventeenth century and that there was a general shift of the economic, as well as political, center of gravity from the Mediterranean to the Atlantic area. Even the enormously rich and well-managed economy of Venice, which still maintained its major role as the cultural and commercial mediator between East and West, was slowly but uninterruptedly sinking on the scale of international trade. See H. G. Beck *et al.*, eds., *Venezia centro di mediazione tra Oriente e Ocidente (secoli XV–XVI). Aspetti e problemi* (papers submitted to the II Convegno internazionale di storia

della civiltà veneziana held in Venice on October 3–6, 1973); together with the papers presented at an earlier *Convegno* held in Venice on June 27–July 2, 1957 and published as *Aspetti e cause della decadenza economica veneziana nel secolo XVII*, in *Civiltà Veneziana, Studi*, IX, which includes the pertinent brief essay by Ö. L. Barkan, "Le Déclin de Venise dans ses rapports avec la décadence économique de l'Empire Ottoman," pp. 275–79. Needless to say, the nearly constant wars in which the Ottoman Empire was engaged were one of the principal deleterious factors in the Ottoman decline. It is a pity, therefore, that we have no Turkey-oriented counterpart to the aforementioned study by O. Pickl, ed., *Die Wirtschaftlichen Auswirkungen der Türkenkriege*, which deals exclusively with the effects of these wars on the Christian countries. See also, more generally, the comparative study by A. Despaux, *Les Dévaluations monétaires dans l'histoire*, dealing with France and other European countries.

50. See the unnamed enthusiastic writer, cited by F. Braudel, *La Méditerranée*, I, 420; and, more broadly, F. J. C. Simiand, *Recherches anciennes et nouvelles sur le mouvement général des prix du XVIe au XIXe siècle*. An analysis of the recurrent monetary crises, followed by intervening periods of stability, and their impact on the general price level is offered by A. Raymond in his *Artisans*, I, 40 ff. It includes numerous noteworthy tables, such as Table 1 (p. 42) illustrating the changing value of the para year by year from 1670 to 1798 when compared with its value during the stable period of 1681–88; and Table 2 (p. 50) offering a comparison of the respective values of the Ottoman asper and the Egyptian para in relation to the gold coin *bunduqi* during the years 1664 to 1797. See also *infra*, n. 51. No such detailed examination seems to be available for the period before 1650. However, similar oscillations had also taken place in the decades following the Golden Age.

51. See A. Raymond, *Artisans*, I, 56 ff., esp. Tables 3–4; F. J. C. Simiand, *Cours d'économie politique*, I, 128; M. Verner, "Periodical Water-Volume Fluctuation of the Nile," *Archiv Orientálni*, XL, 105–123 (concluding with the aid of computers and other modern techniques that, during the period of 1200 to 1450, Egypt had predominantly suffered from drought, while in 1450–1700 the floods were generally more ample, though various local shortages were not infrequent); S. J. Shaw, "The Land Law of the Ottoman Egypt 960/1533: a Contribution to the Study of Landholdings in the Early Years of the Ottoman Rule in Egypt," *Der Islam*, XXXVIII, 106–137 (offering the text in Turkish [pp. 118 ff.] and in English trans. [pp. 126 ff.]); I. El-Mouelhy, "Nouveaux documents sur le fallah et le régime des terres sous les Ottomans," *Annales Islamologiques*, XI (*Gaston Wiet Mem. Vol.*), 252–61, esp. pp. 256 ff. On the great price differentials between Egypt and neighboring Syria in the Mameluke and earlier periods, see the data assembled by E. Ashtor in his *Histoire des prix et des salaires dans l'Orient médiéval*, esp. pp. 77 ff., 124 ff., 242 ff., 282 ff., 392 ff. The *timar* and the related *'iqta* systems, their origins in both the Byzantine and Mameluke environments, their developments under the early Turkish regimes, and their gradual deterioration have been discussed *supra*, n. 42; Vol. XVII, pp. 196 ff., 387 f. nn. 87–90. See also *infra*, n. 57; the succinct general review by Z. Haque, "Origin and Development of Ottoman Timar System," *Islamic Studies*, XV, 123–34; and G. Káldy-Nagy, "The Effect of the Timār System," *Studia turcica*, ed. by L. Ligeti, 1971, pp. 241–48.

Of course, these transformations were part of the first developing, and subsequently declining, Middle Eastern feudalism. We have seen in other contexts that the feudal order developing there in the twelfth and thirteenth centuries in many ways differed from the patterns of European feudalism. As far as agriculture was concerned the fellah, despite the oppressive nature of his master's control, was not legally a "serf" attached to the soil like his Western counterpart. Whether he appeared as a soldier under the command of the lord of his *timar*, or whether he quietly attended to his rather primitive methods of tilling the soil, he was essentially a free individual who could leave his village without committing an offense against the law. Many peasants, indeed, availed themselves of these opportunities, at times causing serious depopulation of their villages. Clearly, the weakening of the feudal regime, notwithstanding manifold attempts at reforming it, greatly facilitated such movements and contributed to an overall decline of agricultural productivity. These developments had their antecedents already in the Mameluke period, as described by M. Chapoutot-Remadi in "L'Agriculture dans l'empire mamlouk en moyen-âge d'après al-Nuwayri," *Cahiers de Tunisie*, XXII, nos. 85–86, pp. 23–45, showing how in periods of drought (for instance, in 1294–96) there was an increased land flight of the peasants or numerous local uprisings which were usually suppressed by the authorities with great severity. See also E. Ashtor's *A Social and Economic History of the Near East in the Middle Ages*, pp. 281 ff. On the major reforms initiated by Meḥmed II which, however, did not prove to be enduring, see B. A. Cvetkova, "Sur certaines réformes du régime foncier au temps de Méhemed II," *JESHO*, VI, 104–120. Another generally aggravating factor in the decline was the interrelated rapidly changing prices of most agricultural products in various periods, which have been carefully investigated by A. Ashtor in *Histoire des prix;* and by A. Raymond in his *Artisans et Commerçants*, esp. I, 53 ff., Tables 3–4, etc. See also, more generally, C. Cahen, "Notes pour une histoire de l'agriculture dans les pays musulmans médiévaux," *JESHO*, XIV, 63–68; B. A. Cvetkova's study "L'Évolution du régime féodal turc," *Études historiques*, I, 171–206; and, more generally, the aforementioned Kiel dissertation by Ali Faik Bey, *Volkswirtschaftspolitik der Türkei*. See *supra*, n. 44.

52. See *supra*, Vol. XVII, pp. 196 ff., 280 ff., 386 nn. 86–90, and 428 n. 63. Our evidence for Jewish farming in the areas included in the Ottoman Empire date rather from earlier periods, particularly from that of the Faṭimid caliphs and their immediate successors. See esp. S. D. Goitein, *A Mediterranean Society: the Jewish Communities of the Arab World . . . in Cairo Genizah*, I, 116 ff., 425 ff.; H. Z. Hirschberg, *Toledot ha-Yehudim be-Afriqah ha-Ṣefonit*, I, 196 ff., 371 f. nn. 22–26; also in the English trans., *A History of the Jews in North Africa*, I, 262 ff. However, after the Almohade and Mongolian floods, as well as the repeatedly enforced conversion of Jews in the Byzantine Empire, the number of Jewish tillers of the soil must have greatly diminished. European travelers mainly paid attention to the cities they visited rather than the countryside, the major exception being Leo Africanus, whose reports on North African Jews of the sixteenth century contain, as we recall, much information even about Jewish preagricultural settlements near the Sahara. Unfortunately, the story of the Middle Eastern Muslim and Christian peasants in the Late Middle Ages and early modern times—who formed the majority of the population—has not yet been told in full and illuminating detail except for some limited areas in the Balkans. See, for instance, the more general survey of S. Faroqhi, "Rural Society in Anatolia and the Balkans during the Sixteenth Century, I," *Turcica*, I, 161–95.

53. See G. Salmon, "Sur quelques noms de plantes en arabe et en berbère," *Archives Marocaines*, VIII, 1–98, esp. p. 70, cited by R. Le Tourneau, *Fès avant le protectorat*, p. 390 n. 8. Some scattered data may also be gleaned from the comprehensive, though mainly philologically oriented, work by I. Löw, *Die Flora der Juden;* and his numerous pertinent essays listed in E. Frenkel's "Bibliographie der Schriften Immanuel Löws" in the special jubilee issue in his honor of the *MGWJ*, LXXVIII, 236–55; and con-

tinued in the later *Semitic Studies in Memory of Immanuel Loew,* ed. by A. Scheiber, pp. 6–11.

54. See I. S. Emmanuel, *Historire de l'industrie des tissues des Isréalites de Salonique;* idem, *Histoire des Israélites de Salonique,* I, 237. See also the biographical data assembled by him in his *Maṣṣebot Saloniqi* (Precious Stones of the Jews of Salonica, together with the Biographies of Its Great Communal Leaders). On the guilds and the Jewish participation therein, see *infra,* nn. 64 f.

55. Pierre Belon, *Les Observations des plusiers singularitez et choses mémorables trouvées en Grèce, Asie, Judée, Égypte, Arabie et autres pays estrangers,* Paris, 1553, fols., 44b f.; R. Mantran, *Istanbul,* p. 419; H. Gerber, "Guilds in Seventeenth Century Anatolian Bursa," *Asian and African Studies,* XI, 59–86, esp. p. 61; idem, "Jews in the Economic Life of . . . Bursa," *Sefunot,* XVI, 245, 260, pointing out that silver trade often required investment of much capital; for instance, when a Jewish partnership with a Muslim had come to an end, the remaining partner owed the other the substantial sum of 6,000 grush. Evidently, the manufacture of silk thread and related activities by Jews and non-Jews in Brusa depended, in part, on the degree of friendly Ottoman–Persian relationships. This situation is well illustrated by the size of the customs receipts from silk imports in the city. While they totaled between 120,000 gold ducats in 1487 and 130,000 in 1512, they dropped after the decisive 1514 battle at Chaldaran between Selim I and Isma'il I to but 40,000 ducats in 1521. See M. Çizakça's "A Short History of the Bursa Silk Industry (1500–1900)," *JESHO,* XXIII, 142–52, esp. p. 144. In evaluating Belon's statement we must bear in mind that he was by no means a friend of Jews. We have had several occasions to quote him in other contexts where his anti-Jewish animus came clearly to the fore. See also, more generally, R. Anhegger, *Beiträge zur Geschichte des Bergbaus im Osmanischen Reich* (Diss. Zurich, 1945). One wished that the considerable amount of information available in the Turkish and other primary sources relating to mining in the Ottoman Empire, including the role played therein by Jews and other ethnic minorities, would become the subject of fuller investigation by competent scholars.

56. See *supra,* Chaps. LXXV, n. 49; LXXVII, n. 62. The story of Jewish pioneering in the printing trade, part of the intellectual as well as economic history of the Jews, will be more fully treated in a later volume. For the time being we need but refer to the data supplied by S. A. Rosanes in his *Qorot,* I, 85 ff., 231 ff.; II, 195 ff.; III, 258 ff.; A. Yaari in *Ha-Defus ha-'ibri be-Qushta* (Hebrew Printing in Constantinople from the Beginning to the Outbreak of World War II) including a list of Hebrew books printed there, of which 252 appeared between 1504 and 1650 (pp. 59–274, Nos. 1–758); idem, *Ha-Defus ha-'ibri be-arṣot ha-mizraḥ* (Hebrew Printing in Mid-Eastern Countries); A. Freimann, "Die Soncinatendrucke in Salonichi und Konstantinopel (1526–1547)," *Zeitschrift für hebräische Bibliographie,* IX, 21–25; and his more comprehensive *Gazetteer of Hebrew Printing* (reprinted from the *Bulletin* of the New York Public Library); and I. Sonne's very informative article "Druckwesen," in the *Encyclopaedia Judaica* (German), VI, 39–81, with an extensive bibliography. Postponement of printing books in Arabic script was facilitated by the lack of differentiation between the printed and handwritten characters. In fact the Arab, Persian, Turkish, and other Arabic scribes had early developed a craft of gifted calligraphers who were in great demand and belonged to the highest paid artisans. While we do not learn of Jewish calligraphers producing documents or manuscripts in Arabic script, there was enough of a market for them in Hebrew writings not only in such official documents as mar-

riage contracts or writs of divorce but also in books (including those written in Judeo-Arabic or Ladino), for Jewish scribes to become an important branch of Jewish communal officialdom.

57. See R. Mantran, *Istanbul,* pp. 419, 446 f.; A. Raymond, *Artisans,* II, 524 f., 597; H. Gerber, "The Jews in the Economic Life," *Sefunot,* XVI, 251. In some respects the Muslim authorities had to pay special attention to Jewish butchers because in Istanbul they were held responsible in part for supplying food needed by its large cosmopolitan population. It is not surprising, therefore, that between 1566 and 1587 no less than eight decrees were issued concerning the supply of meat to the capital. To pay for such goods the first of these decrees ordered a collection of 10,000 florins from the Ashkenazic, Sicilian, Geronese, and Karaite congregations in addition to supplementary imposts demanded from twenty individual Jews. These special taxpayers resented being thus singled out for the tax and argued with the authorities that "apart from us there exists an infinite number of rich Jews" in the city. Eight days after that decree, another ordinance imposed upon the Jews the obligation to deliver mutton to the sultan's palace and the kitchens for the poor. See the texts reproduced by A. Galanté in his *Documents officiels turcs,* pp. 140 ff.; and, more generally, W. Hahn, *Die Verpflegung Konstantinopels durch staatliche Zwangswirtschaft nach türkischen Urkunden des 16. Jahrhunderts* (Diss. Kiel, 1921), pointing out how the government exploited suppliers from the provinces extending from Kaffa to Egypt for the benefit of the consumers in the capital. See also L. Gücer, "Le Problème d'approvisionnement d'Istanbul en céréales vers le milieu du XVIIIᵉ siècle," *Revue de l'Institut des Sciences Économiques de l'Université d'Istanbul,* XI, 153–62.

The sale of wine to Muslims by Jews or Christians doubtless aroused much resentment among pious Muslims. At times even Jewish leaders tried to interfere with this lucrative trade. On one occasion the chief of the Jewish community of Damascus denounced a coreligionist to the Muslim court for producing wine and selling it to a Muslim. See the document, dated December 23, 1707, mentioned by A. K. Rafeq in "Les Registres des Tribunaux de Damas," *BEO,* XXV, 226.

58. R. Samuel de Medina, *Resp.,* on Ḥ.M., No. 45; R. Joseph Ibn Leb, *Resp.,* III, No. 33; E. M. Cousinéry, *Voyage dans la Macédoine,* cited by I. S. Emmanuel in his *Histoire de l'industrie des tissues,* p. 49; and M. S. Goodblatt's brief summary of some other pertinent responsa by R. Samuel in his *Jewish Life in Turkey,* pp. 54 ff. On the earlier conditions in Egypt and Palestine, see *supra,* Vol. XVII, pp. 203 f., 389 ff. nn. 96–97. To the literature cited there, and the more recent comprehensive study by M. Lombard, *Les Textiles dans le monde musulman du VIIᵉ au XIIᵉ siècle. Études d'économie médiévale.* On the rapidly expanding English trade with the Mid-Eastern countries and the role of barter therein, see R. Hakluyt, *The Principal Navigations, Voyages, Traffiques and Discoveries of the English Nation,* II, 246 f., cited by F. Braudcl in *La Méditerranée,* I, 424. See also A. C. Wood, *A History of the Levant Company.* This Company, bearing a semi-official character and often commanding armed forces of its own, for a long time dominated all Anglo-Turkish commercial exchanges and even played a major role in the diplomatic relations between the two countries.

59. See G. Migeon and A. B. Sakisian, "Les Faïences d'Asie Mineure en XIIIᵉ [XVᵉ] au XVIᵉ [XVIIIᵉ] siècle," *Revue de l'Art Ancien et Moderne,* XLIII, 241–52, 353–64; XLIV, 125–41; A. Danon, "La Communauté juive de Salonique au XVIᵉ siècle," *REJ,* XL, 206–230; XLI, 98–117, 250–65, esp. pp. 252 f. No. 12; reproduced in its Hebrew original and French trans. in I. S. Emmanuel, *L'Histoire de l'industrie,* pp. 31 ff. This

curious document, copied from a later transcript without the usual date, was probably first written around 1534, when two of the fifteen signatories are recorded in other contemporary sources as active in congregational affairs.

60. See R. Samuel de Medina's *Resp.* on Y.D. Nos. 117–18; R. Joseph Ibn Leb, *Resp.*, I, No. 47; R. Isaac Adarbi, *Dibre Ribot*, No. 138; M. S. Goodblatt, *Jewish Life in Turkey*, pp. 56 f. A similar reversal occurred in the case of the Salonican Jewish butchers. The frequent contradictions inherent in the issuance of such *ad hoc* decisions were aggravated by the inability of the rabbinic regulators to foretell the vagaries of the government's financial and fiscal policies and of the generally adverse international trends beyond the control of them all.

61. The developments connected with the fabrics produced by the Jewish textile workers in Salonica, and the Draconian methods used by the authorities in extorting ever-greater deliveries of these materials needed for the uniforms of the increasingly rebellious Janissaries, is told with adequate documentation (largely from the rabbinic writings of the period) by I. S. Emmanuel in his *Histoire de l'industrie des tissus des Israélites de Salonique*, esp. pp. 41 ff. On the special Janissary depot for the blue fabrics from Salonica, see I. H. Uzunçarşili, *Osmanli devleti* (Institutions of the Ottoman State), I, 276, cited by R. Mantran in his *Istanbul*, p. 403.

62. The tragic story of the Jewish delegation of 1636 and the execution of its leader R. Yehudah Covo is told by R. Hayyim Shabbetai, who was soon thereafter to serve as chief rabbi of Salonica, in his *Torat Hayyim* (The Living Torah; responsa), Part 1, fols. 145 ff.; it is summarized by S.A. Rosanes in his *Quorot*, III, 396 f., App. VIII/7; and by I. S. Emmanuel in his *Histoire de l'industrie*, pp. 49 f. See also idem, *Gedolei Saloniqi le-dorotam* (Salonica's Great Scholars through the Generations), Vol. I, pp. 294 ff. No. 446.

63. Moses Bassola, *Massa'ot Ereṣ Yisrael* (A Pilgrimage to Palestine), ed. by I. Ben-Zevi, p. 44; David de' Rossi's letter of 1535, reproduced in A. Yaari's ed. of *Iggerot Ereṣ Yisrael*, pp. 184, 186 f. De' Rossi's emphasis on the manufacture of "refined vestments" is understandable in the light of the great variety of colorful garments worn by the Ottoman upper classes as well as by the participants in the numerous ethnic folk festivities. See K. Tuchelt's aforementioned *Türkische Gewänder und osmanische Gesellschaft im achtzehnten Jahrhundert*, with the comments thereon by Z. Abrahamowicz in *Der Islam*, LII, 132–40, cited *supra*, Chap. LXXVII, n. 32. The data and illustrations here offered largely apply also to conditions in the preceding two centuries.

In the case of Safed, it is possible that its new Jewish community's relative youth and main concentration on idealistic rather than material pursuits made the members less able to weather the great pressures of an unfriendly bureaucracy and untoward external developments. See *supra*, Chap. LXXVI, nn. 75 f.; and, more specifically, Y. Kenaani, "Economic Life in Safed and Its Surroundings during the Sixteenth and the First Half of the Seventeenth Centuries" (Hebrew), *Siyyon*, VI, 172–217, esp. pp. 195 ff.; S. Schwarzfuchs, "La Décadence de la Galilée juive du XVIᵉ siècle et la crise du textile au Proche Orient," *REJ*, CXXI, 169–79.

64. See Evliya Čelebi's *Seyaḥatname*, pp. 507 ff., 511 f.; R. Mantran, *Istanbul*, pp. 351 f.; A. Raymond, *Artisans*, II, 503 ff., 587 ff.; and H. Gerber, "Guilds in Seventeenth-Century Anatolian Bursa," *Asian and African Studies*, XI, 59–86. Mantran rechecked Evliya's compilation and, according to his detailed enumeration, actually found 1,109

corporations operating in Istanbul. This staggering figure seems excessive even for a
population counting at its maximum 750,000 persons. However, this is the best figure
one can give under the existing circumstances. One must also bear in mind that Evliya's listing does not seem to cover all crafts practiced in the capital. He does not
mention any glass workers, for example. Much glassware, to be sure, was imported
from Venice. But there must have been a considerable need for glaziers to install and
to repair windows in the numerous houses of worship, as well as in private dwellings.
This lacuna is doubly important in the case of Jews, since from time immemorial their
community had embraced some members of that craft. In fact, in Europe skilled
Jewish glaziers often were in such demand that they were permitted to ply their craft
even where other Jewish artisans were excluded under the pressure of the monopolistic Christian guilds. See *supra*, Vol. XII, pp. 57 f., 272 f. n. 57. Nor is any reference
made in this connection to mosques, in whose yards skilled workers often contributed
their share to the city's industrial output, just as the Salonican Jewish educational
Talmud Torah Society derived some of its funds from sponsoring textile production
and sales. On this important institution of learning, see H. Bentov's interesting analysis of the "Methods of Study of Talmud in the Yeshivot of Salonica and Turkey
After the Expulsion from Spain" (Hebrew), *Sefunot*, XIII, 5–102, with an English
summary pp. 7–9, esp. pp. 39 f. Not to speak of the vast amount of sewing, weaving,
and other chores performed in private houses by nonprofessional family members,
especially wives and daughters. See B. Hrabak, "La Verrerie dans les villes et aux
demeures des fonctionnaires et de grands propriéters turciens dans les pays balkaniques (1480–1600)," submitted to the Conference on Medieval Glass in the Balkans
from the Fifth to the Fifteenth Century held in Belgrade on April 22–26, 1974, pp.
225–36; and Ö. L. Barkan, "L'Organisation de travail dans les chantiers d'une grande
mosquée à Istanbul au XVIe siècle," *Annales ESC*, 1961, pp. 1092–1106; R. Samuel de
Medina, *Resp.* Ḥ.M., No. 472; I. S. Emmanuel, *Histoire de l'Industrie*, p. 21.

65. In his *Egyptian Guilds in Modern Times*, G. Baer made the outright statement
that "with few exceptions, members of a guild belonged to the same religious or ethnic community" (p. 29). In another study he summarized his general views that
professional associations emerged in the fifteenth century and that by the seventeenth
and eighteenth centuries they were "moulded into an all-embracing system which
served as an administrative link between the government and the urban population."
See his "Monopolies and Restrictive Practices of Turkish Guilds," *JESHO*, XIII, 145–
65, 336, esp. p. 145; and his "The Administrative, Economic, and Social Function of
Turkish Guilds," *IJMES*, I, 28–50. On the opposing side one may mention L. Massignon's "Les Corps de métiers et la cité islamique," *Revue internationale de Sociologie*,
XXVIII, 473–89; reprinted in his *Opera minore*, I, 369–84; and the more general
works by R. Mantran and A. Raymond. Among the Turkish scholars interested in the
subject of mercantile and artisan corporations we need but mention Osman Nuri, who
summarized his pertinent researches in his French study, "L'Organisation et les sources
de *Fütjüvvet* [the name of a benevolent society] dans les pays musulmans et turcs,"
Revue des Sciences économiques de l'Université d'Istanbul, XI, nos. 1–4, pp. 5–49. Additional studies, mentioned by these authors, have shown how keen an interest has been
aroused in recent years by the problem of the Turkish guilds. See also the earlier
analysis by V. Gordlevskii in his "The Corporations in Constantinople" (Russian), *Mémoires* (*Contributions*) of the Leningrad Academy of Science, 1926, no. 8; 1927, no. 1,
with the comments thereon by G. Vajda in his "Les Corps de métiers en Turquie
d'après publications de V. Gordlevskij," *REI*, VIII, 79–88; and the brief summaries

by W. Taeschner in his "Das Zunftwesen in der Türkei," *Leipziger Vierteljahrsschrift für Südosteuropa,* V, 772–88; his more recent article, "Futuwwa," in *EI,* 2d ed., II, 965–69; and his comprehensive documentary collection, *Zünfte und Bruderschaften im Islam. Texte zur Geschichte der Futuwwa.* The fact that many important issues have remained unresolved, especially with respect to the behavior of the Christian and Jewish members of mixed guilds in regard to Muslim prayers and festivals, shows how much more is to be learned about the operation of those guilds which, though quite secularized in form, must have retained a preponderantly Muslim coloring.

66. See B. Lewis, "Sources for the Economic History of the Middle East," in M. A. Cook, ed., *Studies in the Economic History of the Middle East,* pp. 78–92; H. R. Roemer, "Vorschläge für die Sammlung von Urkunden zur islamischen Geschichte Persiens," *ZDMG,* CIV, 362–70 (largely applies also to Ottoman documents). On the role played by Jewish merchants in eighteenth-century Salonica, see N. G. Svoronos's *Le Commerce de Salonique,* pp. 8 ff., 187 ff. and more than fifty other pages listed in the Index, p. 410 *s.v.* Juifs. However, we must not forget that, mainly from data preserved in the Paris Archives Nationales, Svoronos offers a somewhat distorted picture in favor of Jewish and other merchants enjoying foreign, especially French, "protection," which played a smaller role before 1650.

Of course, the need for documentary materials concerning international and domestic commerce, along with other aspects of public and private life in the Ottoman Empire, has long been felt. One of the Western pioneers in the historical research of the Empire, Joseph von Hammer-Purgstall, a century and a half ago appended to the ninth volume of his *Geschichte des Osmanischen Reiches* a lengthy "List of Four Thousand Ottoman State and Business Writings, Diplomas, and Other Documents Culled from Epistolary Collections and State Archives" (pp. 335–680). Much additional material has come to light, particularly in recent decades, owing to the intensive research especially by Turkish scholars and their counterparts in the other successor states of the Ottoman Empire. Some of these collections, including notarial documents referring to colonies in the Black Sea, have been mentioned *supra,* vol. XVII, pp. 98 f., 340 f. n. 66. However, the time may be approaching when perhaps a major international effort would be undertaken to collect all the documentary material available in the Western and Central European archives concerning the relations between the respective countries and the various provinces of the Ottoman Empire, along the lines adopted by Henry de Castries and his associates for the Western archival materials pertaining to Morocco. Needless to say, with modern computer techniques such a task relating to Turkey, though in itself much larger and more complicated, would be greatly facilitated.

A similar gigantic effort, perhaps also made with the international cooperation of experts from various lands, including those residing in the successor states of the Ottoman Empire, ought to be made in the cataloguing and selective publication of the enormous archival collections in the central depositories of Turkey. We must not forget that the Başvekalet Archive in Istanbul alone is estimated to contain no less than 3,000,000 documents. Further progress must also be made with the fuller utilization of surviving inscriptions and the large historical Turkish literature. Nor must we neglect, as Andreas Tietze has pointed out, such other sources of historical information as have come down to us in the shape of

oral narratives; legal traditions; the physical remnants such as buildings, bridges, fountains, etc., drastically reduced by the destructions of earlier times but now to some extent protected by a new mentality and the interest in tourism; the linguistic heritage which in recent times has attracted more attention; the toponymy, an area in which we still lack the most elementary research; and so forth.

See Tietze's stimulating survey, "The Balkans and Ottoman Sources—Ottoman Sources and the Balkans" in *Aspects of the Balkans: Continuity and Change. Contributions to the International Balkan Conference* held at UCLA, October 23–28, 1969, ed. by H. Birnbaum and S. Vryonis, Jr., pp. 285–97, esp. pp. 286 f., 291. This succinct survey of the existing resources and the possibilities of their fuller utilization, though limited to the Balkan area, apply with some modifications also to the other provinces of the vast Ottoman Empire at its height.

67. The selection from the 3,000 responsa written by R. David Ibn abi Zimra (according to Ḥayyim Joseph David Azulai in his *Shem ha-Gedolim,* ed. by Y. E. Benjacob, I, 44 f. No. 16) appeared in the several volumes begun in Leghorn in 1562 and was reprinted in the comprehensive seven-volume edition in Warsaw, 1882. Additional texts were edited by A. Marx in his "Contribution à l'histoire des Juifs de Cochin," *REJ,* LXXXIX, 293–304, esp. pp. 297 ff. (referring to an interesting inquiry concerning the Jewish character of that Indian Jewish community and Ibn abi Zimra's affirmative answer thereto); and Simha Assaf in his "From the Rare Collections of the Jerusalem Library" (Hebrew), *Minḥah le-David (David Yellin Jub. Vol.),* pp. 221–37, esp. pp. 228–33 (reproducing Ibn abi Zimra's responsum regarding penalties to be imposed upon a person who publicly accuses a fellow Jew of being a heretic). See also the two biographies of that author by H. J. Zimmels, *Rabbi David ibn Abi Simra I: Leben und Lebenswerk;* I. M. Goldman, *The Life and Times of Rabbi David Ibn Abi Zimra: A Social, Economic and Cultural Study of Jewish Life in the Ottoman Empire in the 15th and 16th Centuries as Reflected in the Responsa of the RDBZ.* Neither biographer undertook the difficult task of ascertaining the dates of some of the respona parallel to the effort made by A. M. Hershman in his *Rabbi Isaac Ben Sheshet Perfet and His Times.* Certainly, there is no way of telling which of Ibn abi Zimra's responsa were written in Egypt and which emanated from his school in either Jerusalem or Safed. Unlike Perfet's career and ambiance, which was radically altered after his emigration from Aragon to Algiers, David's life-style was but slightly affected by the Turkish conquest of Palestine, Syria, and Egypt in 1516–17. That is why the data found in his responsa doubtless illustrate the commercial life of the Jews in these countries under either the Mameluke and Ottoman domination. We may, therefore, rather safely use them in connection with the developments under both empires, as described *supra,* Vol. XVII, esp. pp. 207 ff.; and in the present volume.

68. See Nicholas Nicholay, *The Navigations, Peregrinations and Voyages made into Turkie . . . Deuided into four Bookes, with threescore figures . . . ,* trans. from the French by T. Washington the Younger, London, 1585, fol. 131a. On this author and his general anti-Jewish bias, see *supra,* Chap. LXXVI, n. 34.

69. See J. Chesneau's *Le Voyage de B. Monsieur d'Aramon ambassadeur pour le Roy en Levant. Escript par . . . J. Ch. l'un des secretaires dudict seigneur l'ambassadeur,* ed. by C. Schefer, pp. 31 f.; Simeone Contarini's 1612 report, reproduced in N. Barozzi and G. Berchet, eds., *Le Relazioni degli stati europei,* ser. V, esp. I, 218 f., 240 ff. The accusation that Jews participated actively in the production and distribution of the debased coinage sounded plausible enough to the masses familiar with the extensive Jewish activities in the money trade and in general commerce. The facts, however, seem to

be different. Insofar as one can see through the fog of the few and often obscure records many more Jews suffered from the manipulation of the currency by the governments, both Mameluke and Turkish, whereas the few profiteers faced in addition to the governmental penalties many retributions threatened by Jewish law. Some leading rabbis actually issued special ordinances against such transgressions and placed them under the sanction of severe human and divine retributions. See *supra*, Vol. XVII, pp. 216 ff., 396 ff. nn. 112–14.

The frequent generalizations, heard particularly from casual Western visitors, about the dominant role played by Jews in Ottoman commerce is, to a minor extent, justified with respect to Istanbul, Salonica, and some other major cities. In provincial towns, even such as Belgrade or Buda, the relatively small number of Jews (see above) by itself precluded any kind of preeminence; it was mainly their generally higher visibility which often misled casual observers. Suffice it to mention the example of these two cities about which we happen to have considerable documentary evidence which shows that in 1570 the large majority of merchants were Muslims, even if many of them were either converts or offspring of converts, or else had been brought in by the government from other areas after the occupation of Belgrade in 1521 and that of Buda in 1541. See A. Z. Hertz, "Muslims, Christians and Jews in Sixteenth Century Ottoman Belgrade," in A. Ascher *et al.* eds., *The Mutual Effects*, pp. 149–64, esp. pp. 152 f. Of a special nature were the commercial relations with such semi-independent vassal states as Walachia and Moldavia, which were more deeply affected by the changing political and military developments. See, for instance, P. Cernovodeanu, "Les Echanges économiques dans l'évolution des relations roumano-turques," *RESEE*, XVI, 81–90; and *infra*, n. 98.

70. See A. Mehlan, "Die Handelsstrassen des Balkans während der Türkenzeit," *Südostdeutsche Forschungen*, IV, 249–96, describing in particular four major routes traversing the peninsula from Belgrade to the Black Sea. The utter neglect of river traffic by the riparian authorities is well illustrated by their frequent failures for years on end to remove trees felled by storms into the rivers. *Ibid.*, pp. 270 f. Such neglect was particularly pronounced in the case of smaller rivers such as the Pruth, Sava, or Morava. On the other hand, in "The Ottoman Turks and the Routes of Oriental Trade," *English Historical Review*, XXX, 577–88, written about a quarter of a century earlier, A. H. Lybyer dealt mainly with the broader effects of the transportation by land from the Persian Gulf to the Balkans or Egypt and the interference with it by the expanding Portuguese, and later Dutch and English, ships traveling around the Cape of Good Hope. It turned out that, despite the great differences in the distances covered by such transports, the costs seem to have been about equal, according to P. Masson's calculation in his *Histoire du commerce français dans le Levant au XVIIe siècle*, p. 543 and *passim*. See also the continuation in his *Histoire du commerce français dans le Levant au XVIIIe siècle;* H. Inalcik's brief survey in his "International Trade Routes and the Ottoman Empire" in the *Papers of the Fifth International Congress of Economic History*, held in Leningrad in 1970 (published in Moscow, 1976), VI, 294–302.

71. See A. Mehlan, "Die Handelsstrassen des Balkans," *Südostdeutsche Forschungen*, IV, esp. pp. 262, 269, 277; L. Berov, "Transport Costs and Their Role in the Balkan Lands in the 16th-19th Centuries," *Bulgarian Historical Review*, III, no. 4, pp. 74–98; De Joinville's unpublished "Memoire sur le commerce des Français et des protégés de France à Salonique" dated May 10, 1744 and cited by N. G. Svoronos in *Le Commerce de Salonique*, p. 123. On the navigation on the Nile, see for the Faṭimid period S. D. Goitein, *A Mediterranean Society*, I, 295 ff., 475 ff.; and on the eighteenth century, A.

Raymond, *Artisans et commerçants*, I, 243 f., 246 ff. Although we have less extensive information on the Nile transportation during the early modern period, it may be assumed that the changes from the previous periods were not very great. See also *supra*, Vol. XVII, pp. 207 ff.

72. See S. J. Shaw, "Selim III and the Ottoman Navy," *Turcica*, I, 212–41; R. Samuel de Medina, *Resp.*, on E.ʿE. (III), No. 168; on Ḥ.M. (IV), No. 100; I. S. Emmanuel, *Histoire de l'industrie de tissus*, p. 6; D. A. Zakythinos, *Corsairs et pirates dans les mers grecques au temps de la domination turque;* G. Fisher, *Barbary Legends: War, Trade and Piracy in North Africa, 1415–1830;* and the somewhat older but still very useful study by O. Eck, *Seeräuberei im Mittelmeer. Dunkle Blätter europäischer Geschichte*, 2d ed.; and the literature listed *supra*, Vol. XVII, pp. 29 f., 314 n. 35 (including a reference to Sultan Bayezid II's complaint to Doge Leonardo Loredan).

In some respects Jews ran smaller risks when they were captured by pirates than did members of other denominations. It was generally known, and frequently commented upon by outsiders, that Jews were not likely to remain in captivity very long. To cite only the testimony of Pierre Belon de Mans who observed that, while Christians and Jews were forbidden by Ottoman law to own Muslim slaves, "Christians could keep a Jewish slave. But Jews are so closely knit and full of finesse that they will never allow one of their nation to be a slave. For whether he is taken captive on the sea or land, during war or peace, they put so much effort to redeem him that he will never remain in slavery for lack of funds." See his *Observations des plusieurs singularitez*, p. 195. See also *supra*, n. 55.

73. See O. Eck, *Unfreiheit der Meere: Dunkle Blätter der Seekriegsgeschichte* (a continuation of his *Seeräuberei*); M. de Gemigny, *Les Brigandages maritimes de l'Angleterre*. Le Maire's assertion is quoted by A. Raymond in his *Artisans and Commerçants*, I, 298, from Venture de Paradis' *Detail sur l'état actuel de l'Égypte*, preserved in a MS in the Archives Nationales of Paris. See also M. Sley's brief survey of "Insurance among the Jewish Merchants in the Provinces of the Ottoman Empire in the Seventeenth and Eighteenth Centuries" (Hebrew), *Ha-Me'assef*, III, 385–92.

74. Nicholas Nicholay, *The Navigations, Peregrinations and Voyages*, fols. 93 f. On the close contacts between the Sephardic communities in the West and those which were rising in the Ottoman Empire, see *supra*, Chap. LXXV, n. 74; and my *JC*, I, 308 f.; III, 73 n. 20, with special reference to international relief activities.

75. See William Lithgow, *The Totall Discourse of the Rare Adventures and Painfull Peregrinations of long Nineteen Years Travayles from Scotland to the Most Famous Kingdoms in Europe, Asia and Africa*, published in 1632 and reprinted, among others, in Glasgow, 1906, esp. p. 148; L. Vignols, "Le Commerce hollandais et les associations juives à la fin du XVIIᵉ siècle," *RH*, XLIV, 327–30; and other sources, mentioned *supra*, Vol. XV, pp. 48 f., 399 f. n. 57; H. I. Bloom, *The Economic Activities of the Jews of Amsterdam in the Seventeenth and Eighteenth Centuries*, pp. 82 ff. On a Ḥakham Bensur who, in cooperation with the Turkish admiralty, wished to obtain from Hamburg some war materials but was prevented from doing so by an imperial prohibition, see H. Kellenbenz, *Sephardim an der unteren Elbe, ihre wirtschaftliche und politische Bedeutung vom Ende des 16. bis zum Beginn des 18. Jahrhunderts*, pp. 136 f.

Kellenbenz also mentions that the trade between the Netherlands and Turkey was greatly interfered with by the operations of the Algerian corsairs. We have records of the period of 1617–25 when no less than 206 Dutch as well as 56 German ships were captured by pirates on the Mediterranean. As a result, there was not only a considerable loss of property but the Dutch, aided by Jews, were busily redeeming captives. Hamburg's maritime operations in the Mediterranean were further impeded by the absence in Algeria of diplomatic representation from a hundred Hanseatic cities; they were mostly represented by the Dutch consuls there. One intervention by a Raby Josep, who in 1620 had come from Hamburg to Algiers for the purpose of ransoming captives, is mentioned in a communication of the Dutch consul to his Istanbul counterpart, Haga. See L. Beutin, *Der Deutsche Seehandel im Mittelmeergebiet bis zu den Napoleonischen Kriegen,* esp. pp. 37 ff., 173; K. Heeringa, *Bronnen tot de Geschiedenis van den Levantischen Handel,* I: 1650–1660, p. 842 (indeed the bulk of this volume deals with Dutch–Turkish relations and the Levant trade, pp. 153–423, 426–627); and Eck, *Seeräuberei,* 1st ed., pp. 148, 263.

76. See D. Kaufmann, "Die Vertreibung der Marranen aus Venedig im Jahre 1550," *JQR,* [o.s.] XIII, 520–32, esp. pp. 529 f.; R. Samuel de Medina, *Resp.* Ḥ.M., Nos. 70, 80, 99, 118; I. S. Emmanuel, *Histoire des Israélites,* I, 228 f. On the importance of the Levantine Jews for the Venetian trade with the Middle East, especially during the economic crisis after the Turco-Venetian war of 1570–73, and the resulting change of Venetian policy toward the settlement of Ottoman Jews in Venice under very favorable conditions, see B. C. L. Ravid's recent publication, *Economics and Toleration in Seventeenth Century Venice: the Background and Context of the* Discorso *of Simone Luzzatto;* it includes a valuable documentary appendix, reproducing four texts of charters or their reconfirmations in 1624–36 (pp. 99–126) and extensive bibliographical notes. It also refers to R. Maestro's unpublished 1935 Venetian dissertation, *L'Attività commerciale svolta in Venezia dagli Ebrei levantini e ponentini dall'anno 1550 al 1700.* This favorable treatment of the Levantine Jews is even more noteworthy when it is compared with that of the Levantine Greeks, Turkish Jewry's major business competitors. It appears that most Greeks settling in Venice did not consist of members of the mercantile class. On their pursuit of a variety of other occupations, see G. Plumidis's "Considerazioni sulla popolazione greca a Venezia nella seconda metà del '500," *Studi Veneziani,* XIV, 219–26, esp. p. 223. Only 1 Greek is listed here as a "merchant," compared with 88 galley personnel and other mariners, 3 shipowners, 5 barbers, 16 members of the clergy, male and female, and so forth.

77. See F. Fouqueville, *Mémoire historique et diplomatique sur le commerce et les établissements français au Levant,* p. 62; P. Cernovodeanu, *England's Trade Policy in the Levant and Her Exchange of Goods with the Romanian Countries under the Latter Stuarts (1669–1714);* and, more generally, *Aspetti e cause della decadenza economica veneziana nel secolo XVII,* Atti of the Convegno of June 27–July 2, 1957 in *Civiltà Veneziana, Studi,* IX which includes Ö. L. Barkan's "Le Déclin de Venise ses rapports avec la décadence économique de l'Empire Ottoman" (pp. 275–79). See also G. Campos, "Il Commercio esterno veneziano della seconda metà del '700 secondo le statistiche ufficiali," *Archivio Veneto,* 5th ser. XIX, 145–83; and R. Mantran, "Venise et ses concurrents en Méditerranée orientale aux XVIIᵉ et XVIIIᵉ siècles," *Mediterraneo e Oceano Indiano* (Florence, 1970).

78. G. W. F. Stripling, *The Ottoman Turks and the Arabs, 1511–1574,* esp. pp. 95 ff.; E. Sancau, "Uma Narrativa do expedição portuguesa de 1541 ao Mar Roxo," *Studia* of the Centro de Estudos Históricos Ultramarinos, XI, 199–234; and other literature listed *supra,* Vol. XV, pp. 543 f. nn. 108–109. On the Jews in the Indian trade of that period see, for the time being, S. D. Goitein's "From the Mediterranean to India.

Documents on Trade to India, South Arabia and East Africa from the Eleventh and Twelfth Centuries," *Speculum*, XXIX, 181–97; A. Marx's comments on the responsum by R. David Ibn abi Zimra relating to Cochin Jewry in *REJ*, LXXXIX, 293–304; and *infra*, Chap. LXXX. Turkish Jews traveling to Persia and India are occasionally mentioned in the responsa by R. Yeḥiel Basan, No. 100; and by R. Joseph di Trani (Mitrani) on E.'E. No. 30 (referring to one David Toby, who, together with his son, traveled to India while leaving his wife Tamar behind in Istanbul). On the Portuguese colony of Ormuz and its Jewish community there, see W. J. Fischel, "New Sources for the History of the Jewish Diaspora in Asia in the 16th Century," *JQR*, XL, 379–99; and the additional material, particularly from Jesuit sources, analyzed *supra*, Vol. XV, pp. 356 ff., 543 n. 109. See also N. A. Ziadeh's succinct observations on "Changes of Trade Centres in the Persian Gulf of the Middle Ages," *Studies in Asian History. Proceedings* of the Asian History Congress held in New Delhi in 1961, pp. 297–301. The history of the Jews of India from 1200 to 1650 will be treated more generally *infra*, Chap. LXXX.

79. See P. Masson, *Histoire du commerce français dans le Levant au XVIIᵉ siècle*, pp. 288, 438; N. G. Svoronos, *Le Commerce de Salonique*, pp. 141 ff., 150 ff.; *supra*, Vol. XVI, pp. 47 ff., 240, 337 ff. nn. 51 ff., 430 nn. 31 f.; Z. Świtalski, "The Reasons for the Withdrawal of the Turkish Jews, Refugees from Spain, from the Levant Trade of the Polish Commonwealth in the Last Years of the Sixteenth Century" (Polish), *BZIH*, no. 37, pp. 59–65, with an English summary, pp. 109–110; A. Raymond, *Artisans et commerçants*, I, 80. On the revival of the trade between Marseilles and the Middle East see, for instance, Jonas Weyl, "Les Juifs protégés français aux Échelles du Levant et en Barbarie sous le règne de Louis XIV et de Louis XV d'après des documents inédits des Archives de la Chambre du Commerce de Marseille," *REJ*, XII, 267–82; XIII, 277–94; discussed *supra*, Vol. XVII, pp. 285 f., 430 n. 70; and the more general data presented by L. Bergasse and G. Rambert in *Histoire du commerce de Marseille*, Vol. IV: 1559–1789; and by R. Paris, *ibid.*, Vol. V, 1660–1789, both published in the collection issued under Rambert's general editorship for the Marseilles municipality.

80. See S. D. Goitein, *A Mediterranean Society*, I, 156 ff. (referring to "itinerant merchants," rather than peddlers who probably had few occasions to write business letters); A. Raymond, *Artisans et commerçants*, I, 381 (peddlers counted among the low-class "populace"); R. David Ibn abi Zimra, *Resp.*, III, fol. 435d; Walter Hahn, *Die Verpflegung Konstantinopels durch staatliche Zwangswirtschaft*. Regrettably, our information about Jewish peddlers like that about itinerant artisans is extremely limited. See *supra*, Vol. XVII, pp. 289, 432 n. 76. Generally, peddling was not a widespread occupation in Ottoman lands during the sixteenth and seventeenth centuries. The numerous bazaars, open shops, and stalls in the cities offered most customers sufficient means to acquire the necessary goods, while rural peddling was quite perilous and individual travel even over short distances was usually limited, compared with group journeys.

81. A. Danon, "La Communauté israélite de Salonique," *REJ*, XLI, 226, 259; the more detailed analysis of one such ordinance by M. Molkho in his "The Ordinance Concerning Acquired Rights in Houses, Courtyards, and Shops in Salonica" (Hebrew), *Sinai*, XIV, nos. 165–70, pp. 296–314 (mentioning that the text of the original enactment had been preserved in Salonica until 1890 when it fell victim to a fire). The severity of the Salonican excommunication is well illustrated by the text of a similar proclamation issued by the local rabbinate in connection with the violation of a marital regulation. See Danon, *REJ*, XLI, 255 No. 14.

In time, however, the problems of the *ḥazzaqah* in housing became increasingly complicated. The rabbis themselves were not quite sure how to treat a contractual sale of such a Jewish acquired right to a Gentile. The influential R. Salomon of "the House of Levi" decided that in general such a sale was not valid because the non-Jewish purchaser could not take over the acquired right which, according to the ordinance, was to apply exclusively to Jewish owners of such holdings. However, he admitted that, if the Jewish proprietor made it clear in his contract that he wished to divest himself completely of any rights in that property, a non-Jewish purchaser might really be considered its true owner. "There is some hesitation [*gimgum*] in this matter." The impetus to the ultimate decision favoring the Gentile owner was given by the consideration that the Jewish holder of the *ḥazzaqah* owed the Gentile money and that, without the sale, would have to face default entailing serious consequences. See Danon's lengthy documents in *REJ*, XLI, 257 ff. Nos. 17–18.

The impact of the frequent Salonican fires on house ownership is well illustrated by the great conflagrations of 1633 and 1660, which so thoroughly devastated the homes and synagogue of the Romaniot community that, unable to rebuild their ruins, they gradually mingled with the Sephardic majority which thenceforth wholly dominated Jewish communal life in the city; only the Ashkenazic and Karaite communities retained their independent functions. See R. Mantran, *Istanbul*, p. 58; and *supra*, Chap. LXXV, nn. 9 ff. See also the generally interesting data on the sales of houses in Sofia in G. D. Galabov, comp., *Die Protokollbücher des Kadiamtes Sofia*, ed. by H. W. Duda; and the comments thereon by Z. Pljakov in his "Über das soziale Gepräge der bulgarischen Stadt im XV. bis zur Mitte des XVII. Jahrhunderts," *Byzantinobulgarica*, III, 231–44.

82. On Yehudah Benveniste's speculation, see R. Samuel de Medina's *Resp.* Ḥ.M. No. 116. The identity of this speculator is not readily ascertainable. Chronologically it is very unlikely that he was the person mentioned by I. S. Emmanuel in his thoroughgoing study of *Maṣṣebot Saloniqi* (Precious Stones of the Jews of Salonica), see his Index, II, 927 *s.v.* Since the large Benveniste family played a significant role in the history of the community for several generations, it doubtless included several members named Yehudah. Our speculator may either have died elsewhere or, even if he was buried in Salonica, may not have been recorded on any extant tombstone. At any rate, the Benvenistes seem not to have maintained a family grave, as did a number of other prominent Jewish families. See Emmanuel, *Maṣṣebot*, I, 11 f.

83. See J. Sauvaget, "Les Caravansérails syriens du moyen âge," *Ars Islamica*, VI, 48–55; VII, 1–19; A. Raymond, *Artisans et commerçants*, I, 131 ff., 251 ff.; *supra*, Vol. XVII, pp. 291, 433 n. 78. Swelled by the hosts of pilgrims fulfilling their religious duty of visiting Mecca at least once during their lifetime, the fairs conducted on the occasion of such a mass influx to Islam's holiest city belonged to the largest held in the Muslim world. According to the French consul Benoit de Maillet, who served in Cairo some sixteen years (1692–1708), "during the short period of time [when the fairs were held] they counted the turnover of merchandise coming from India at several million [francs?]; this was in addition to coffee, myrrh, incense, and other products of the country itself." Cited by Raymond, I, 127. It stands to reason that these estimates would have been even higher during the period of greatest flowering of the Levant trade in the sixteenth century. See also the next note.

84. See H. J. Kissling, *Beiträge zur Kenntnis Thrakiens im 17. Jahrhundert*, p. 18; T. Stoianovich, "Model and Mirror of the Premodern Balkan City," *Studia balcanica*, 1970,

no. 3, pp. 83–110, esp. p. 110; A. Mehlan, "Die Grossen Balkanmessen in der Tür-kenzeit," *VSW*, XXXI, 10–49, esp. pp. 29 f.; the numerous monographs cited in my earlier notes concerning the intensive commercial exchanges within the Empire, es-pecially with Ragusa and within Bulgaria, to which one might add the comprehensive literature listed in N. V. Michoff, *Contributions à l'histoire du commerce bulgare. Documents officiels et rapports consulaires;* A. Raymond, *Artisans et commerçants,* I, 251 ff. On the ordinance pertaining to the Serbian fair and its revocation, see R. Samuel de Medina, *Resp.,* Y.D. No. 155; and A. S. Rosanes, *Qorot,* III, 167 f., 172. This incident well illustrates the readiness of the leading Turkish rabbis to adjust their ordinances to the changing needs of each period. It is also an illustration of how economic realities, when in conflict even with deeply felt religious scruples, often prevailed and forced reconsideration of established patterns.

Although since the early Middle Ages Jews were known intensively to participate in local and international fairs, and they undoubtedly did the same in the Ottoman Em-pire, our direct evidence thereon is very limited. Possibly the commercial exchanges performed at fairs and the contracts concluded there not only among Jews but also between Jews and Muslims or Christians led to relatively few differences of opinion between the parties; they were probably adjusted on the spot by the fair supervisors. Only a few found their way into the rabbinic courts and still fewer gave occasion to inquiries from higher authorities mentioned in the Hebrew responsa literature.

85. See, for the earlier periods, S. D. Goitein, *A Mediterranean Society,* I, 169 ff., and the numerous other references in the Index, p. 544 *s.v.* Partnership; R. Mantran, "La Police des marchés de Stamboul au début du XVIe siècle," *Cahiers de Tunisie,* no. 14, 213–41, esp. pp. 230, 238; idem, *Istanbul,* pp. 427 ff. Understandably, there also ex-isted larger partnerships, especially when one wished to invest in a fair-sized ship and its cargo. We hear of a French partnership of six entrepreneurs who in 1576 jointly acquired the share of one karat, or $1/24$ ownership of a barque sailing to Syria. See M. Boulant, *Letters de négocians marseillais: les Frères Hermites (1570–1612),* with a Foreword by F. Braudel, pp. 27 f. nn. 27–29. On the other hand, we recall the case of the Ragusan Jew and a local priest each of whom owned a larger share than was actually permitted by the existing regulations. See *supra,* Vol. XVII, pp. 112 f., 347 n. 85. The relatively meager resources of the majority of merchants in the Ottoman Empire are well illustrated by the materials assembled by A. Raymond for late-eighteenth-century Egypt. His findings show that in the period of 1776 to 1798, 300 of the 347 traders whose financial resources are recorded in the Maḥkama archives had at their disposal an average capital of but 35,288 paras. While this amount was higher than the aver-age of the 152 artisans, whose resources averaged only 25,993 paras, this was very little indeed in actual monetary value or purchasing power. Raymond himself has shown that a para, which in the days of Suleiman the Magnificent had weighed 1.289 grams of silver and was worth 2 aspers, two centuries later had a silver content of a mere 0.225 gram, justifying Samuel-Bernard's comment that "this singular coin was lighter than a sheet of paper." See Raymond, I, 34 f., 296 ff., 301 ff.

It must be borne in mind, however, that apart from capital needed for commercial transactions there were family pressures to accumulate funds. In the Jewish case, the impetus to save, sometimes over many years, was given by the need to provide dow-ries, especially for daughters. See M. Glazer, "The Dowry as Capital Accumulation among the Sephardic Jews of Istanbul, Turkey," *IJMES,* X, 373–80. Among the po-lygamous Muslims, on the other hand, there was the opposite urge for many fathers to have ready cash for the purchase of brides for their sons.

86. N. Steengaard, "Consuls and Nations in the Levant from 1570 to 1650," *Scandinavian Economic History Review*, XV, 13–55, esp. pp. 18, 23; A. Mehlan, "Der Einfluss der Raja-Privilegierung auf die Balkanwirtschaft zur Türkenzeit," *Leipziger Vierteljahrsschrift für Südosteuropa*, VI (1941).

87. Michel Febvre, *Thèâtre de la Turquie, où sont représentées les choses les plus remarquables qui s'y passent aujourd'hui*, Paris, 1682; Neş'et Çağatay, "Riba and Interest Concept and Banking in the Ottoman Empire" (Turkish), *Vakiféar dergèsé*, IX, 51–56; M. 'Uzair, "Some Conceptual and Practical Aspects of Interest-Free Banking," *Islamic Studies*, XV, 247–69, with a critical letter thereon by M. A. Khan, *ibid.*, XVI, 151–53, who calls 'Uzair's arguments "wishful thinking"; other sources listed in the article "Riba" by J. Schacht in *EI*, 1st cd., III, 1148 50; and for Jewish practices, E. Bashan (Sternberg), "A Document of 1624 Concerning a Dispute over Lending Money to Christians in Jerusalem" (Hebrew) in *Peraqim le-toledot ha-Yishuv bi-Yerushalayim* (Chapters in the History of the Jewish Settlement in Jerusalem), II, 77–96, with an English summary, p. ix; and, more generally, N. Schur, "The Jewish Community in Jerusalem in the 16th to the 18th Centuries According to Christian Chronicles and Travel Descriptions" (Hebrew) in Amnon Cohen, ed., *Peraqim be-toledot Yerushalayim* (Jerusalem in the Early Ottoman Period), esp. pp. 378 f.; and H. Gerber, "Jews in Money-Lending in the Ottoman Empire," *JQR*, LXXII, 100–120, esp. pp. 101 f.; *supra*, Chap. LXVI, n. 12. Such evasions were both very old and widespread. For example, the second-century teacher R. 'Aqiba had frequently asserted that "the shop is open and the shopkeeper gives credit" (M. Abot, III, 17). Maimonides' decision was in line with the general recognition of the necessity of making concessions to inescapable economic realities. Hence, though generally opposed to usury in any form, he encouraged, at least indirectly, the subterfuge via a pretended silent partnership as both riskless and profitable. See his *Resp.*, ed. by J. Blau, I, 88 f. No. 53; my "Economic Views of Maimonides," in *Essays on Maimonides*, ed. by me, pp. 199 ff., 213 ff., also in my *Ancient and Medieval Jewish History: Essays*, cd. by L. A. Feldman, pp. 192 ff., 201 ff., 477 ff. nn. 129 ff.; 481 ff. nn. 148 ff.; and, more generally, *supra*, Vols. IV, pp. 197 ff., 338 ff. nn. 60 ff.; XII, Chap. LIII; XVII, pp. 217 f., 397 f. nn. 114–15; and *infra*, n. 89.

88. J. E. Mandaville, "Usurious Piety: The Cash Waqf Controversy in the Ottoman Empire," *IJMES*, X, 289–308; A. Udovich, "Credit as a Means of Investment in Medieval Islamic Trade," *JAOS*, LXXXVII, 260–64; and, on the general methods of obtaining capital formation in medieval Islam as well as in the Ottoman Empire, W. Björkman, "Kapitalentstchung und anlage im Islam," *MSOS*, XXXII, Part 2, pp. 80–98; H. Inalcik, "Capital Formation in the Ottoman Empire," *JEcH*, XXIX, 97–140, esp. pp. 97 f., 99. On the Polish churches and monasteries and their often century-old loans to the country's Jewish communities (and somewhat similar occurrences in France and elsewhere), see *supra*, Vol. XVI, pp. 220 ff., 421 f. nn. 8–9; and *JC*, II, 268 ff.; III, 190 ff. nn. 31–32.

None of this prevented discontented borrowers from denouncing the Jews to the government. In 1525, for example, some Christian inhabitants of three Bulgarian cities complained to Suleiman the Magnificent about the injurious effects of Jewish usury as well as the offensiveness of the new Sephardic immigrants excessively displaying costly garments and jewelry. See Z. Pljakov, "Über das soziale Gepräge der bulgarischen Stadt," *Byzantinobulgarica*, III, 241. We do not know of any effective remedies adopted on this occasion by the distinguished "lawgiver" to stem either excessive charges for loans or luxury in attire, but such complaints were repeatedly heard about the behavior of wealthy Jews. In the days of Murad IV, we remember, the appearance of a wealthy Jewess wearing jewelry allegedly worth over 40,000 dinars placed the entire Jewish community of the Empire in grave jeopardy. See *supra*, Chap. LXXVII, n. 31. We shall see that even parallel efforts by the Jewish leaders themselves did not stem the love for display of wealth by rich Jewish men or women. See also, more generally, M. Rodinson's *Islam and Capitalism*.

89. R. C. Jennings, "Loans and Credit in Early 17th Century Ottoman Judicial Records," *JESHO*, XVI, 168–216; H. Gerber, "The Jews in the Economic Life of . . . Bursa" (Hebrew), *Sefunot*, XVI, 240; F. Braudel, *La Méditerranée*, I, 423. On the earlier rates of interest see E. Ashtor, "Le Taux d'interêt dans l'Orient médiéval," *Fatti e idee di storia economica nel secolo XII–XX* in honor of Franco Borlando, pp. 197–213. Remarkably, according to Jennings, fully one-third of the 30,000 inhabitants of Kayseri are recorded as having borrowed money. This very high percentage is doubly meaningful as the 10,000 borrowers, evidently almost all of them adults, constituted much more than one-third of the city's adult population.

90. See A. Raymond, *Artisans*, I, 200 n. 1; II, 462 n. 22, 484 (citing the French consular dispatch of March 24, 1732 from the Consular Archives now in the custody of the Archives Nationales in Paris); R. Mantran, *Istanbul*, p. 525, citing Giacomo Soranzo's dispatch of July 12, 1646 from an archival document; J.-B. Tavernier, *Les Six voyages qu'il a faits en Turquie, en Perse et aux Indes*, I, 270. Soranzo's complaint merely underscored the fact that the Istanbul Jews, in contrast to their predecessors in the Byzantine period, could get along without Venetian protection. On the Jewish "white Venetians," see *supra*, Vol. XVII, pp. 84 ff., 334 f. nn. 48–51.

91. Pierre Belon, *Les Observations*, p. 118; Michel Febvre, *Théâtre de la Turquie*; Dudley North, *Discourse upon Trade*, London, 1691; R. North, *Lives of the Norths*, III, 53 f.; cited by A. C. Wood, *History of the Levant Company*, pp. 214 f. See also the kindred observations by Lady Montagu-Wortley in her *Letters, Written during Her Travels into Europe, Asia and Africa*, III, 125. These comments undoubtedly reflected also the business practices prevailing in Istanbul before 1650. The anti-Jewish bias of these foreign observers is evident in such comments as Febvre's (*supra*, n. 87) description of the ordinary Jewish occupations. Similarly North could not refrain from adding to his comment on the "unshakable" Jew by saying: "He sticks like a burr and whether well-used or ill-used will be at every turn in with him [the merchant] and no remedy." Few were, indeed, the foreigners who were inclined to express their appreciation for the valuable services rendered by the Jewish factors to them and their compatriots as well as to the Turkish economy at large.

92. E. Charrière, ed., *Négociations de la France dans le Levant*, III, 832; N. Camariano, *Alexandre Mavrocordato le Grand Drogman. Son activité diplomatique, 1673–1709;* A. Pippidi, "Quelques drogmans de Constantinople au XVIIe siècle," *RESEE*, X, 227–55 (describing the life and activities of the family Bruti and other Italians); J. Matuz, "Die Pforten Dolmetscher zur Herrschaftszeit Suleymans des Prächtigen," *Südost-Forschungen*, XXXIV, 26–60 (offering brief biographical sketches of some Greek, German, and Hungarian dragomans, for the most part renegades); A. H. De Groot, *The Ottoman Empire and the Dutch Republic: a History of the Earliest Diplomatic Relations 1610–1630*, esp. pp. 111 f., 134 ff., 154, 196 f., 222. On the preliminaries of the Turco-Spanish armistice of 1581, see F. Braudel, *La Méditerranée*, I, 432 ff., 439 f.; S. A.

Skilliter, "The Hispanic-Ottoman Armistice of 1581," *Iran and Islam,* pp. 491–515; and *supra,* Vol. XVII, pp. 50 f., 321 n. 5. See also, more generally, the succinct analysis by C. Orhonlu, "The Institution of the Dragoman in the Ottoman Empire" (Turkish), *Ataturk Konferenslaki* (Ankara), V, 13–23.

93. See De Groot, cited in n. 92. In some cases, a fixed commission was agreed upon in advance. For instance, a wealthy Istanbul merchant, Yom Ṭob b. Abraham Ibn Ya'ish, through his agent Solomon Pardo, amassed a huge profit in selling a large collection of precious jewels he had acquired from a Turkish pasha. The principal and his agent agreed in advance that the intermediary would receive a commission of 500 ducats which, upon completion of the transaction, was duly paid him. Ten years later, however, Pardo regretted having accepted that amount and demanded additional payment. But his arguments were rejected by the rabbinical court in Istanbul. See the interesting data relating to the disposal of these jewels, cited in R. Joseph b. Moses di Trani's *Resp.,* III, Nos. 18–19; and summarized by S. A. Rosanes in his *Qorot,* III, 85.

94. See R. Mantran, *Istanbul,* pp. 493 ff.; A. Raymond, *Artisans,* II, 260 n. 3, 531, 538; Evliyah Čelebi, *Seyaḥatname* (Narrative of Travels), pp. 531 ff.; A. Refik, *Istanbul hayati* (Istanbul Life), esp. pp. 28 ff. No. 40, 37 f. No. 57; and H. Hines, *Medical History of Constantinople.* The Jewish role in that history is briefly sketched in A. Galanté's *Médecins juifs au service de la Turquie;* M. Perlmann's "Notes on the Position of Jewish Physicians in Medieval Muslim Countries," *Israel Oriental Studies,* II (1972 = *Samuel M. Stern Mem. Vol.*), pp. 315–19; and, more generally, in H. Friedenwald, *The Jews and Medicine: Essays,* esp. I, 460–67; and S. Krauss's *Die Geschichte der jüdischen Ärtze vom frühesten Mittelalter bis zur Gleichberechtigung,* ed. by I. Fischer. See also *supra,* Vol. XVII, 220 f., 398 f. n. 117; Chaps. LXXV, n. 35; LXXVI, nn. 31 f. and the literature listed there, as well as in R. V. Ebied's *Bibliography of Mediaeval Arab and Jewish Medicine and Allied Sciences* with a Foreword by A. M. Honeyman. On the Muslim and Jewish share in pharmacology and the drug trade, see S. Hamarneh, "Pharmacy in Medieval Islam and the History of Drug Addiction," *Medical History,* XVI, 226–37; and M. Meyerhoff, "Der Basar der Drogen und Wohlgerüche in Kairo," *Archiv für Wirtschaftsforschung im Orient,* IV, no. 3. On the Istanbul entertainers, see Stephan Gerlach's *Tage-Buch,* pp. 402 and 449; and J. W. Zinkeisen, *Geschichte des-Osmanischen Reiches in Europa,* III, 369 f. These diverse professions will be more fully discussed in their respective contexts in Jewish communal and intellectual life of the period in later volumes.

95. C. Lyerer, "Die Verrechnung von Steuern im islamischen Ägypten; Vorbericht nach Papyri," *ZDMG,* CIII, pp. 40–69, esp. p. 53; L. Fekete and G. Káldy-Nagy, *Rechnungsbücher türkischer Finanzstellen in Buda (Ofen) 1550–1580: Türkischer Text;* G. Káldy-Nagy, *Baranya megyo XVI. szazds-tòrök adromeiorásai* (The Turkish Tax Computations for the District of Baranya in the XVIth Century); E. Vass, "Éléments pour compléter l'histoire de l'administration des finances du vilayet du Buda au XVIᵉ siècle," *Studia turcica,* ed. by C. Ligeti, 1971, pp. 483–90. These Hungarian studies reflect, of course, certain peculiarities of that province which differed in many respects from other areas of the Empire. See *infra,* n. 98; and Ö. L. Barkan's more general observations on "Research on the Ottoman Fiscal Surveys," in M. A. Cook, ed., *Studies in the Economic History of the Middle East,* pp. 163–71.

96. The enormous variety of Ottoman taxes is well illustrated by the extant original surveys of taxes assessed on the population from time to time. See, for example, the

good editions, with English translations, published by S. J. Shaw in *The Budget of Ottoman Egypt 1005–1006/1596–1597*, No. 12 (pp. 22–83, transcription of the Turkish document; pp. 84–207, English translation with extensive notes; also includes a useful "Concordance of the Coptic Financial Year Used in Ottoman Egypt with the Muslim Hegira and Christian Calendars, 1572–1597"; p. 208); B. W. McGowan, *Defter i-Mufassal-i-Liva-i-Sirem: an Ottoman Revenue Survey dating from the Reign of Selim II* (Turkish Text with an English introduction), Diss. Columbia University; H. G. Majer, "Ein Osmanisches Budget aus der Zeit Meḥmeds des Eroberers," *Der Islam*, LIX, 40–63; and *infra*, n. 98.

Assessments were based on the enormous amount of regulation emanating from the Treasury and judicial departments through the centuries, only a small part of which has thus far been published. Much of it was derived from the *qanunname*s of sultans Meḥmed III, Suleiman the Magnificent (in Turkish usually called the Lawgiver), Meḥmed IV, and others. See, for example, the chronological list compiled by J. Matuz, *Herrscherurkunden des Osmanensultans Suleyman des Prächtigen. Ein chronologisches Verzeichnis*. See also such detailed studies as T. Bachrouch's careful analysis of a document dating from 1087 A.H. (1676–77) in "La Fiscalité muradite. Présentation d'une source et des premiers resultats d'une enquête en cours," *CT* XX, nos. 79–80, pp. 125–46. Investigators of such documents must be constantly aware, however, of the frequent legal inconsistencies favoring the Treasury. Not only did it demand from the taxpayers payments in good, as a rule in silver, currency—a demand which probably was not always complied with—but it also differentiated between revenues which were computed by solar years, while most expenditures were recorded along the lines of the eleven-days-shorter lunar year. For a discussion on how this type of accounting was reconciled, see H. Sahillağlu, "Sivig Year Crises in the Ottoman Empire," in M. A. Cook, ed., *Studies in the Economic History of the Middle East*, pp. 230–52.

97. See P. Wittek, "Devshirme and Shari'a," *BSOAS*, XVII, 271–78 (pointing out the conflict between traditional law and existing practices without attempting to offer a definitive answer to these inherent contradictions); Abraham b. Jacob Gavison (Gabishon), *'Omer ha-Shikḥah* (Forgotten Sheaf: Commentary on the Book of Proverbs), Leghorn, 1748; new ed. with an Intro. and Notes by R. S. Sirat, fol. 73d, cited with additional comments by the editor in "La Vie des Juifs en Alger au XVIᵉ siècle d'après *'Omer Hašikḥa* ('O.Š.). Commentaire sur les Proverbes d'A. Gabišon," in *Mélanges André Neher*, pp. 317–29, esp. pp. 321 f.; H. Inalcik, "The Ottoman Decline and Its Effects upon the *Reaya*," in H. Birnbaum and S. Vryonis, Jr., eds., *Aspects of the Balkans Continuity and Change; Contributions to the International Balkan Conference Held at UCLA, October 23–28, 1969*, pp. 338–54, esp. p. 344; *Slavistic Printings and Reprintings*, ed. by C. H. Van Schooneveld, No. 270. The liberties taken by the fiscal officials, often in deviation from the existing law and in disobedience to the directives given by the central government, are curiously treated by K. Röhrborn as "Die Emanzipation der Finanzbürokratie im Osmanischen Reich (Ende 16. Jahrhunderts)," *ZDMG*, CXXII, 118–39, emphasizing, above all, the independence of the fiscal administrators, mostly of Turkish origin, from the viziers, who were largely recruited from the slaves of Greek ancestry. See also his more comprehensive *Untersuchungen zur osmanischen Verwaltungsgeschichte*.

98. Going back to H. Rabie's *The Financial System of Egypt A.H. 564–741/A.D. 1169–1341*, and other studies of the early Ottoman administration, S. J. Shaw has produced a very detailed examination of *The Financial and Administrative Organization and Development of Ottoman Egypt 1517–1798*; and the aforementioned *Budget of Ottoman Egypt*

1005–1006/1596–1597. He was followed by an equally searching investigation by A. Raymond in his *Artisans et Commerçants,* esp. pp. 587–658. Independently, R. Mantran has devoted several important chapters of his *Istanbul* to the financial and fiscal administration of the Ottoman capital. These major contributions dealing with the period after 1650 have quite a few flashbacks to earlier developments. They also have a good deal to say about the role played by the religious minorities, especially Jews. Of course, sporadic references of this type do not add up to any comprehensive picture of the Jewish role in the Ottoman fiscal structure, as both taxpayers and collectors, during the Golden Age and the initial stages of the financial crisis in the first half of the seventeenth century. On the other hand, the special analysis in A. Danon's "Étude historique sur les impôts directs et indirects des communautés israélites en Turquie," *REJ,* XXXV, 52–61, esp. pp. 57 f.: "Impots payée à l'état," offers but a few general references to some of the oppressive taxes which deeply affected Jewish and general life in the Empire.

Other regional studies of considerable importance include: R. Mantran's "Règlements fiscaux ottomans: la province de Bassore (au moitié du XVIe s.)," *JESHO,* X, 224–77 (publishing the text of a decree of 1574 in a Turkish facsimile, transliteration, and French trans.); and his and J. Sauvaget's *Règlements fiscaux ottomans, les provinces syriennes.* Quite different, of course, was the fiscal situation in such political dependencies as Moldavia and Walachia, which were not formally annexed to the Empire. For instance, 81.1 percent of Brašov's foreign trade was handled in 1554 by Walachian merchants. See M. Bersa, "Moldavian and Walachian Kharaz of the 15th through the 19th Centuries" (Rumanian), *Studi și articole de Istorie Medie,* II, 7–47; and M. Cazacu, "L'Impact ottoman sur les Pays roumains et ses incidences monétaires (1452–1504)," *RRH,* XII, no. 1, 159–92, esp. p. 192. Unfortunately, taxation in the important commercial center of Salonica, doubly significant for the history of the Jews who constituted the majority of both population and taxpayers, has hitherto not been studied in depth from either the general or Jewish point of view. The relatively few pages devoted to this subject in I. S. Emmanuel's *Histoire des Israélites de Salonique,* pp. 210 ff., and N. G. Svoronos's more general study of *Le Commerce de Salonique au XVIIIe siècle,* merely scratch the surface. A complete study of the Jews and the fiscal system of the Empire both as agents for the administration and as direct or indirect taxpayers is a major historical desideratum.

99. See R. Mantran, *Istanbul,* esp. pp. 310 ff. In the vast variety of imposts those on almost all victuals were most burdensome. That on wine and arrack, especially, mainly affected non-Muslim producers and traders. Yet we hear of relatively few complaints about this particular tax. In general, however, the burdens on the Jewish masses far outweighed the benefits derived by the numerous Jewish tax farmers and their employees. The dread of failure to meet a governmental claim on time is also reflected in the contemporary rabbinic writings. For example, Ibn abi Zimra stated succinctly: "there is no greater crime than a deficit in tax collections" and "all debts owed to the sultan, whether consisting in payments of capitation or land taxes, or in funds owed on *iltizam*s, or on merchandise purchased, enjoy priority over all other claims." See his *Resp.,* I, Nos. 96, 128–29, 136, 417; I. Goldman, *The Life of . . . Ibn abi Zimra,* pp. 152 f.

100. S. J. Shaw, *The Financial . . . Organization,* p. 140; A. Raymond, *Artisans,* II, 649; Joshua b. Hananiah, "Taxes and Hardships at Funerals in Jerusalem" (Hebrew), *Yerushalaym* (Quarterly), I, 43–46; with comments thereon by M. Benayahu in his "Some More about the Funeral Taxes in Jerusalem" (Hebrew), *ibid.,* pp. 46–49; and

by J. Prawer, "On the Problem of the Funeral Taxes in Jerusalem" (Hebrew), *ibid.*, II, 101–102. The tax collectors' abuses after the death of a head of a family and their appropriation of a whole or part of his estate are discussed by R. Samuel de Medina in his *Resp.* Ḥ.M. No. 336, and with comments thereon by M. S. Goodblatt in his *Jewish Life in Turkey*, pp. 121, 214 nn. 17–18. See also, more generally, S. J. Shaw, *Financial . . . Organization*, pp. 171 f.

In connection with these excesses one may also mention the difficulties encountered by Jews living in quarters of their own after the discovery there of a corpse whose murderers could not be traced. In such cases the law provided that a fine (*geremet* = blood money) be imposed on the inhabitants of the quarter. Because of the severity of that penalty—one imposed in 1574 amounted to 600 ducats—the Muslims of an imperiled quarter, upon such a discovery, clandestinely threw the body into the Jewish Street, making the Jews responsible for the fine. After one such occurrence in Salonica, we are told, Jews tried to dispose of the corpse by throwing it into the sea, for which they were even more severely penalized. The Salonican community decided to pay the fine rather than be subject to prosecution. See J. Petit de La Croix, *Relation . . . État général de l'Empire Ottoman*, I, 200; Stephan Gerlach, *Tage-Buch*, p. 449; I. S. Emmanuel, *Histoire des Israélites*, pp. 123 f. De La Croix also mentions that the French considered the blood money so disagreeable that, in 1673, they demanded that a clause in the Franco-Turkish capitulations provide for an exemption from it for French citizens (p. 427). By that time the fine had been reduced to the still sizable amount of 40,000 aspers. See Sieur de Vignau, *L'État présent de la puissance ottomane*, p. 115. See also the brief statement in Joseph Ibn Leb's *Resp.*, I, fol. 67a.

101. See esp. the data analyzed by S. J. Shaw in *The Financial and Administrative Organization*, pp. 151 ff.; idem, *The Budget*, p. 154; and R. Mantran in *Istanbul*, p. 281; idem and J. Sauvaget, eds., *Règlements fiscaux ottomans, les provinces syriennes*, p. 32; Amnon Cohen and B. Lewis, *Population and Revenues*, pp. 11 n. 40, and 71. The literature on the *jizya* paid in the Ottoman Empire, though quite extensive, is largely limited to certain provinces. Apart from the material included in Shaw's studies on Egypt, see B. C. Nedkoff, *Die Gizje (Kopfsteuer) im Osmanischen Reich, mit besonderer Berücksichtigung von Bulgarien* (Diss. Berlin, 1941); Ö. L. Barkan, "The Sum Total Concerning the Collection of the Capitation Tax for the Year 864 (1488–89)" (Turkish), *Bergeler*, I, no. 1; E. Grozdanova, "The Collection of the Djizya Tax in Bulgarian Areas in the XVII and XVIII Centuries" (Bulgarian), *Istorichekski Preglad*, XXVI, no. 5, pp. 75–90, esp. the Table on p. 84 (listing the data from five districts in 1651–52 and of one each from 1681); E. Eškenazi, "On the Method of Collecting Some Taxes in Western Bulgaria before the Liberation in the Nineteenth Century" (Bulgarian), *Izvestiya* of the Historical Institute in Sofia, XVI–XVII, 333–45; H. Hadžibegić, "Jizya or Ḥaraj," *Prilozi* (Contributions to Oriental Philology and the History of the Yugoslav Nation under Turkish Domination), V, 43–102; idem, *Glavarina u Osmanskoj državi* (The Capitation Tax in the Ottoman Empire). Of course, references to that tax are found in many other studies, especially in those relating to the various regions. Because of the antiquity of this impost one may also consult the literature referring to its modifications under Islam cited in our earlier volumes, esp. Vol. XVII, pp. 221 f., 399 f. nn. 118–19.

In this connection one must also bear in mind the inequalities created by the sultans in granting a totally tax-exempt status to families of individuals who had rendered signal services to the state or to them personally. At times such privileges were granted in a hereditary fashion to entire groups in the population for certain useful services they were performing for the government. For example, large segments of the sizable

Gypsy and Vlad population of Belgrade were officially freed from paying governmental imposts in return for work they were regularly performing as blacksmiths on the imperial fleet and as guards at the imperial powder magazines, respectively. See B. Djurdjev, "Belgrade," *EI,* new ed., I, 1163–65.

102. See H. Gerber, "The Jews in the Economic Life . . . Bursa" (Hebrew), *Sefunot,* XVI, 241 f., 251; and the literature listed *supra,* n. 101; and Vol. XVII, pp. 222 f., 400 n. 119. The question as to whether the *jizya* was principally a tax on a subject population or a ransom for sparing the lives of the "infidels" by grace of the Muslim tradition, is analyzed by A. Abel in his "La Djizya: Tribut ou rançon?" *Studia Islamica,* XXXII, 5–19, referring to speculations on this score going back to Al-Jaḥiz (ninth century). This tax has, in fact, retained some of the characteristics of both in the minds of many Muslim observers. On the various categories of "poor" throughout the Middle Ages and early modern times in both the Christian and Muslim worlds, see M. Mollat, *Les Pauvres au moyen âge: étude sociale;* idem, *Études sur l'histoire de la pauvreté (Moyen âge, XVIe siècle).* It may also be noted that the Muslim concept and treatment of the poor, like that prevailing in Christian Europe, were much indebted to Jewish prototypes and even terminology. See J. Leclercq, "Aux origines bibliques du vocabulaire de la pauvreté," *Byzantion,* XLV, 35–43. In proclaiming "charity" to be one of the five principal commandments of Islam, its adherents gave it the name *sedaqa,* very likely a borrowing from the corresponding Hebrew term in its more contemporary Jewish, rather than biblical meaning.

103. See Samuel de Medina's *Resp.* Y.D. Nos. 138, 235; other sources cited by M. S. Goodblatt in *Jewish Life in Turkey,* esp. pp. 50 f., 76 f. Once again Egypt has supplied us with the relatively fullest material for the functioning of the customs services during the Muslim period. It was already in operation during the Mameluke regime, which had inherited it largely from its Faṭimid and Seljuk predecessors. See Vol. XVII, pp. 224 f., 401 n. 121. It was greatly altered after the Turkish occupation especially under the administration of Viceroy Ibrahim through his reforms of 1524–25. A good and well-documented analysis is offered by A. Raymond in his *Artisans,* esp. II, 496 ff. and 618 ff. See also S. J. Shaw, *Financial Organization,* pp. 103 ff. To be sure, there were great changes in the seventeenth century, particularly in its second half. Nevertheless, apart from the transfer of the direction of the customs houses from government officials to the Janissaries and their appointees, the daily operations of the individual houses in Alexandria, Rosetta, Damietta, and Cairo-Bulaq seem not to have undergone any major alterations. Despite its complications it has been estimated that the duties collected at the Suez station alone amounted to some 60,000,000 paras annually. See Raymond, II, 623 f.; S. J. Shaw, *Financial Organization,* pp. 106 ff.

104. See B. Lewis, "Judeo-Osmanica" in *Rawidowicz Mem. Vol.* pp. 9–16; A. Raymond, *Artisans,* p. 614. In fact, of the approximately 60,000,000 paras collected annually at Suez, only 4,000,000–5,000,000, that is one-fifteenth to one-twelfth, reached Istanbul. See *supra,* n. 103. We must bear in mind, however, that the collected amounts were recorded as received, whereas the funds sent to the Treasury were computed after deducting the costs of the complicated administration, which frequently included two or three tiers of agents and their employees.

105. See Everard Fawkener's dispatch, excerpts from which were published by R. W. Olsen in his "Jews in the Ottoman Empire in Light of New Documents," *JSS,* XLI, 75–88, esp. p. 85 App. iii; A. Raymond, *Artisans,* I, 87 f.; II, 462 n. 5; I. Wolfenson

(Ben Ze'ev), " 'Ali bey Alkabir and the Jews of Egypt" (Hebrew), *Zion*, IV, 237–49, with an English summary, p. iii. In some of these customs houses the Jewish control was so great that at times operations were wholly suspended on Saturday. See Raymond, II, 625. According to S. J. Shaw (*The Financial and Administrative Organization*, p. 125), the Jewish collectors "paid small Ja'ize fees to the *Valis* in return for the confirmation of their appointment." This kind of control, exercised through hard work, combined with an available working capital, held doubly true in Salonica where the Jews greatly outnumbered the Muslims and Christians in manpower and wealth. See on the general operations of that harbor, A. Stojanovski, "Some Laws about the Market Taxes and Customs Duties in Salonica in the Sixteenth Century" (Serbo-Croatian), *Jugoslovenski Jstorijski Časopis*, 1969, no. 3, pp. 3–8, with a French summary.

106. *Qur'an*, 49:18. The situation in the countries occupied during the fourteenth to the sixteenth centuries has been discussed in such studies as I. Dujčev's "Die Krise der spätbyzantinischen Gesellschaft und die türkische Eroberung des 14. Jahrhunderts," *Jahrbuch für Geschichte Osteuropas*, n.s. XXI, 481–92; other essays in his *Medioevo bizantino-slavo;* D. Angelov, "Die Stadt im mittelalterlichen Bulgarien," *Zeitschrift für Geschichtswissenschaft*, X, 405–416, esp. pp. 408 f.; N. Todorov, "Quelques aspects de la structure ethnique de la ville médiévale balkanique," *Actes* of the Colloque international de civilisations balkaniques, held in Sinaia, 1962, pp. 39–45; and other literature listed here in the earlier chapters. In many ways different were the conditions in the previously Muslim provinces. See the story of the largest and oldest ethnoreligious minority in Egypt described in considerable detail by M. Roncaglia, in his *Histoire de l'église Copte*. See also O. Meinardus, "The Attitude of the Orthodox Copts towards the Islamic State," *Ostkirchliche Studien*, XIII, 153–70. On the conditions of the Jewish minority, see especially the comprehensive analysis by S. D. Goitein in *The Mediterranean Society*, Vol. II; E. Strauss (Ashtor), *Toledot ha-Yehudim be-Miṣraim* (A History of the Jews in Egypt and Syria under Mameluke Rule), *passim;* and *supra*, Vol. XVII, esp. Chap. LXXIII. See also, more generally, B. Lewis's judicious overall survey, "L'Islam et les non-musulmans," *Annales ESC*, XXXV, 784–800, a problem discussed in this and our earlier volumes in different contexts. To the literature listed there add such more recent publications as M. R. Cohen, *Jewish Self-Government in Medieval Egypt: the Origins of the Office of the Head of the Jews, ca. 1065–1126;* N. A. Stillman, *The Jews in Arab Lands: a History and a Source Book;* and M. A. Epstein, *The Ottoman Jewish Communities and Their Role in the Fifteenth and Sixteenth Centuries*.

107. See, for example, C. H. Imber, "The Persecution of the Ottoman Shi'ites according to the Mühimme Defterleri, 1565–1585," *Der Islam*, LVI, 245–73; and *infra*, Chap. LXXIX.

108. H. Inalcik, "The Policy of Mehmed II toward the Greek Population of Istanbul and the Byzantine Buildings of the City," *Dumbarton Oaks Papers*, XXIII–XXIV, 1969–70, pp. 229–49; H. Hanson, "Konstantinopels Kirchen und die Moscheen Istanbuls. Antlitz und Schicksal der Stadt am Goldenen Horn im Spiegel der Baukunst," *Istanbul, Geschichte und Entwicklung der Stadt*, ed. by K. Bachteler (*Festschrift für Kurt Albrecht*), pp. 89–130, 191–266; S. Runciman, "The Greek Church under the Ottoman Turks," *Studies in Church History*, II, 38–53; and, more fully, in his *The Great Church in Captivity: a Study of the Patriarchate of Constantinople from the Eve of the Turkish Conquest to the Greek War of Independence*. Of considerable interest also are such detailed documentary and regional studies as A. Rabbath, *Documents inédits pour servir à l'histoire du christianisme en Orient;* V. Laurent, "Les Chrétiens sous les sultans (1553–1592), un

recueil de documents turcs," *Échos d'Orient*, XXVIII, 398–406; T. Haardt, *Die Lage der bulgarischen Kirche im Osmanischen Reich bis zur Zeit der Tanzimat*, Diss. Vienna, 1949 (typescript); L. Hadrovics, "L'Église serbe sous la domination turque," *Archives d'histoire du droit oriental*, III, 411–72; M. Ormanian, *The Church of Armenia, Her History, Doctrine, Rule, Discipline, Liturgy, Literature and Existing Condition*, trans. from the French by M. Gregory, with an Intro. by J. E. C. Weldon. See also the useful reference work by E. von Ivánka, J. Tyciak, and P. Wirth, eds., *Handbuch der Ostkirchenkunde*.

On the term *millet* and its application, see L. Massignon, "L' 'Umma et ses synonymes. Notions de 'communauté sociale' en Islam" (1946), reprinted in his *Opera minora*, I, 97–103, esp. p. 99; H. A. R. Gibb and H. Bowen, *Islamic Society and the West*, Vol. I: Islamic Society in the Eighteenth Century. The limited self-government of the Muslim and Jewish corporations is discussed *supra*, nn. 54 ff., 59.

109. The numerous changes which took place in the treatment of foreigners in Muslim countries and the new forms taken by the system of "capitulations" in the sixteenth century, with their medieval antecedents, have been treated, among others, in the following studies: W. Heffening, *Das Islamische Fremdenrecht bis zu den islamisch-fränkischen Staatsverträgen. Eine rechtshistorische Studie zum Fiqh;* L. Böttger, *Die Entwicklung des Fremdenrechts in der Türkei bis in die Gegenwart;* F. P. Rey, *De la protection diplomatique et consulaire dans les Échelles du Levant et de Barbarie*, Paris thesis, 1899; V. L. Ménage, "The English Capitulation of 1580: a Review Article," *IJMES*, XII, 373–83, mainly based on S. A. Skilliter's documentary study of *William Harborne and the Trade with Turkey, 1578–1582*. We recall that France's influence on the status of its nationals in the Ottoman possessions sometimes took the curious form of direct exchanges between the French court and the beys of Algeria and Tunisia, rather than exclusively with the central authorities in Istanbul. See E. Plantet, ed., *Correspondance des Beys d'Alger avec la Cour de France, 1579–1833;* idem, *Correspondance des Beys de Tunis et des Consuls de France, 1577–1830.* See also the literature listed *supra*, Chap. LXXV, n. 103; Vol. XVII, pp. 85 ff., 334 f. nn. 49–51; and some additional documents reproduced by J. C. Hurewitz in his *Diplomacy in the Near and Middle East.*

110. See R. W. Bulliet, "The Shaikh al-Islam and the Evolution of Islamic Society," *Studia islamica*, XXXV, 53–67; H. Scheel, *Die Staatsrechtliche Stellung der ökumenischen Kirchenfürsten in der alten Türkei. Ein Beitrag zur türkischen Verfassung und Verwaltung.* On the office of the Egyptian *nagid*, see *supra*, Vol. V, pp. 40 ff., 309 f. nn. 47 ff.; and such additional literature as S. D. Goitein, "The Title and Office of Nagid: a Reexamination," *JQR*, LIII, 93–119; idem, "New Sources Concerning the Nagids of Qairawan" (Hebrew), *Zion*, XXVII, 11–23. See also J. Bernay, "The Status of the Chief Rabbinate in Jerusalem during the Ottoman Period" (Hebrew), *Cathedra*, XIII, 47–69.

111. The historic controversy over the revival of the ancient ordination is adequately documented by the writings of the two protagonists, Jacob Berab and Levi Ibn Ḥabib. It has been extensively analyzed by modern scholars including J. Katz in his "The Controversy on the Semikhah between Rabbi Jacob Beirab and the Ralbaḥ" (Hebrew), *Zion*, XVI, 27–45; Meir Benayahu, in "The Revival of Ordination in Safed" (Hebrew), *Baer Jub. Vol.*, pp. 248–69, with an English summary, pp. xvii–xviii; C. Z. Dimitrovsky in his "Two New Documents Regarding the Semicha Controversy in Safed" (Hebrew), *Sefunot*, X, 113–92. We shall have to revert to the subject of the *semikhah*, its underlying motivations, and its impact upon the Jewish community of Palestine in our general review of Jewish self-government in the next volume.

The myth of the high governmental position held by the chief rabbi of Istanbul, nurtured by the reports of Elijah Capsali, a nephew of the first chief rabbi, Moses Capsali, in his *Seder 'Olam Zuṭa,* and further elaborated by Joseph Sambari in his early-eighteenth-century chronicle *Dibre Yosef, Liqqutim,* selections from which were published by A. Neubauer in his *Mediaeval Jewish Chronicles,* I, 115–62, was exploded in 1931 by A. Galanté's publication of his *Documents officiels Turcs* in French translation, esp. pp. 32 ff. Here Galanté reproduced the sultan's decree of October 19, 1837, appointing the then chief rabbi to an honorary position with a special decoration (*pelisse*). Thenceforth the chief rabbis of the capital did indeed enjoy some control over the Jewish communities of the Empire until the First World War. In this connection the government's official journal describing the ceremony made it perfectly clear that "the chief rabbis had heretofore been elected by themselves [the Jewish community] without the custom of according them the decoration." All along, however, the Jewish community had to pay a special tax (*rav-aktchesi*) for the permission to have this ecclesiastical chief. This was parallel to the Greek Orthodox patriarchate's annual payment, a circumstance somehow overlooked by R. Mantran in his *Istanbul,* p. 227 n. 2. Some such special taxes were also recorded in connection with the official confirmation of the appointment of local rabbis. See B. Lewis, *Notes and Documents,* pp. 27, 43 n. 1; and H. Gerber, "The Jews in the Economic Life . . . Bursa" (Hebrew), *Sefunot,* XVI, 241.

112. See Moses b. Baruch Almosnino, *Extremos y grandezas de Constantinopla.* Spanish ed. from an unpublished Ladino MS of 1565 by Jacob Cansino, *passim;* R. Yehudah Covo's tragic mission to Istanbul, described *supra,* n. 62; R. Samuel de Medina's *Resp.* I, on O.Ḥ. No. 20 (cited here from the English translation in M. S. Goodblatt's *Jewish Life in Turkey,* pp. 134 ff. App. 2, esp. pp. 136 f.; and other sources listed *ibid.,* pp. 72 ff.); I. S. Emmanuel's *Histoire des Israélites,* pp. 211 ff.; and idem, *Histoire de l'industrie du tissus,* pp. 49 ff.

113. See R. Samuel de Medina, *Resp.,* Ḥ.M. No. 372; and other sources cited by M. S. Goodblatt in *Jewish Life,* pp. 20 f., 193 nn. 69 ff. De Medina did not exaggerate when, in another context, he declared that "the great prestige and holiness of the Talmud Torah society in this city of Salonica is well known to us. There is none superior to it in quantity or quality in the Jewish dispersion." His contemporary, Isaac Adarbi, asserted that "even the inhabitants of far-off lands have their eyes and hearts turned toward it [the Talmud Torah society]." See his *Dibre ribot* (Matters of Controversy; responsa), p. 68 No. 223. See also the references to this famous Salonican institution in S. Assaf's *Meqorot le-toledot ha-ḥinukh be-Yisrael* (Sources for the History of Jewish Education; from the Beginning of the Middle Ages to the Haskalah Period), III, 37 ff. Nos. 31, 32; and H. Bentov's aforementioned (n. 64) Hebrew essay on "Methods of Study of Talmud in the Yeshivot of Salonica and Turkey," *Sefunot,* XIII, 5–102. On the institution of the *'erub,* derived from the biblical hint that on a Sabbath "abide ye every man in his place" (Exod. 16:29) and the ensuing negotiations between the representative Jewish leaders of Salonica and the Gentile authorities, see J. Nehama, *Histoire des Israélites de Salonique.*

114. R. Isaac Adarbi, *Dibre ribot,* No. 139; R. Samuel de Medina, *Resp.* on Ḥ.M. No. 369 (trans. into English by S. M. Goodblatt in *Jewish Life,* pp. 182 ff. App. 17). The numerous Jewish charitable societies characterizing the Jewish communities in the Middle Ages and modern times will likewise be analyzed in the next volume. For the time being, see the chapter on "Social Welfare" in *JC,* II, 290–350; III, 197–219.

115. See R. Samuel de Medina, *Resp.* on O.Ḥ. No. 36. This long-winded responsum reveals the relative embarrassment with which the rabbi argued against the unrestrained dominance of a majority. The problem of egalitarianism in voting for communal expenditure was particularly irksome in regard to the amounts a community was to pay to the government in behalf of those who could not afford to make any payments even for the capitation tax required by law. There also was a problem of up to what maximum the tax could be imposed upon very wealthy members. In both Salonica and Istanbul there was an accepted principle that no member, however rich, should be forced to pay more than 300,000 aspers as his share in the communal tax. This "custom" was upheld, for example, by R. Isaac Adarbi in his *Dibre ribot*, No. 139. (With growing inflation this maximum was raised to 400,000 aspers in the early eighteenth century; see I. S. Emmanuel, *Histoire des Israélites*, p. 131.) The two responsa quoted in this note are also reproduced in the comprehensive collection, ed. by J. Hacker in his *Megoreshe Sefarad veṣeṣa'ehem ba-Imperiah ha-Otomanit ba-me'ah ha-ṭ"z* (The Spanish Exiles and Their Offspring in the Sixteenth Century: Salonica, Istanbul, and Their Environs), esp. pp. 16 ff., 23 ff. This conflict of full equality vs. expediency and a measure of social balance preoccupied Jewish communal leadership in both East and West for many centuries. See *JC*, II, 27 f.; III, 109 n. 22.

116. See U. Heyd's detailed analysis of "The Jewish Communities of Istanbul in the Seventeenth Century," *Oriens*, VI, 299–316; I. S. Emmanuel, *Histoire des Israélites*, pp. 308 ff.; M. S. Goodblatt, *Jewish Life in Turkey*, esp. p. 65; J. Pinkerfeld, *Bate ha-knesiot be-Ereṣ Yisrael* (Jewish Synagogues in Palestine from the Geonic Period to the Ḥasidic Immigration); J. M. Toledano, "Ancient Synagogues in Alexandria and Its Environs" (Hebrew), *HUCA*, XII–XIII, 701–714. The Islamic restrictions on synagogues were strictly enforced in the Ottoman Empire well into the nineteenth century and beyond. As late as April 8, 1837 a special *firman* by the sultan described in considerable detail the government's elaborate proceedings before granting the Jewish community the license to rebuild a synagogue destroyed by fire. After consultation with the ecclesiastical chief of Islam the sultan permitted the Jews to repair their house of worship "under the condition that it should not exceed its former size by even a palm or a finger in length, height, or width." See the text in French translation in A. Galanté's *Documents officiels Turcs*, pp. 52 ff. It took the community of Sarajevo nearly twenty years (1794–1813) of constant negotiations before it received a permit to replace its burned synagogue. See Moritz Levy, *Die Sephardim in Bosnien. Ein Beitrag zur Geschichte der Juden auf der Balkan-Halbinsel*, pp. 112 ff.

117. See R. David Ibn abi Zimra, *Resp.*, I, No. 484; II, No. 741; and the MS responsum, all cited by I. M. Goldman in *The Life and Times of Rabbi David Ibn Abi Zimra*, pp. 125 f.; R. Isaac Adarbi, *Dibre ribot*, Nos. 60, 125; R. Samuel de Medina, *Resp.* on Y.D. (II), Nos. 173, 203; A. Galanté, *Documents officiels Turcs*, pp. 60 ff. (reproducing four governmental decrees from 1583 to 1587); and the aforementioned Hebrew essay by Joshua ben Hananiah, "Taxation and Burial Difficulties in Jerusalem," with the discussion thereon in *Yerusualayim* (Quarterly), I, 43–49; II, 101–102.

Theft of Jewish tombstones for resale is the less astonishing as, according to Stephan Gerlach, some wealthy Turkish-Jewish families spent 80 or 90 ducats on placing such a monument on the grave of a deceased relative. See Gerlach's *Tage-Buch*, p. 342. The location of the Jewish (and Muslim) cemeteries outside the Turkish towns impressed foreigners like the Venetian envoy, Mattei Venier. See his 1579 report, reproduced in E. Albéri, ed., *Relazioni*, 3d ser. I, 456. See also the succinct introductory sketch by I. S. Emmanuel to his *Maṣṣebot Saloniqi* (Precious Stones of the Jews of

Salonica), I, 11 ff. Regrettably, this work is one of but very few relating to Jewish cemeteries and their tombstones preserved from the Ottoman regime. The internal aspects of the cemetery administration, funeral customs, and the like will be more fully treated in the next volume.

118. See R. David Ibn abi Zimra, *Resp.*, I, Nos. 67 and 541; II, Nos. 219 and 634; and other data analyzed by I. M. Goldman in *The Life and Times of . . . Zimra*, pp. 153 ff. There were also cases of Jews repairing to Muslim courts even in matters fully reserved to denominational laws, such as marital affairs. We have records of individuals who, either to spite the Jewish authorities or to circumvent their jurisdiction— for instance, when a man wished to marry a second wife during his first wife's lifetime or when a Kohen (a descendant of the ancient Israelitic priesthood) desired to wed a divorcée and could find no officiating rabbi to perform the marriage ceremony—the party appealed to a Muslim judge who had no such compunctions. In such cases the Jewish leaders often found it inappropriate, or even dangerous, to deny the validity of such a Muslim ceremony. See S. A. Rosanes, *Qorot*, I, 157. On the Byzantine heritage of Jews repairing to Gentile courts, see *supra*, Vol. XVII, pp. 23 f., 310 f. nn. 26– 28. It appears that when the Osmanlis first conquered the Byzantine cities in Anatolia, they retained the existing judiciary practices among the local Jews. We have evidence that in such cities as Brusa, these continued to be observed in the early modern period despite the changed patterns developed in the meantime in other areas of the Empire. See H. Gerber, "The Jews in the Economic Life of . . . Bursa" (Hebrew), *Sefunot*, XVI, 259 ff. Nos. 5, 9–10. See also *supra*, n. 8; and Vol. XVII, pp. 167 f., 375 f. nn. 52–53.

119. See the text of the noteworthy Salonican ordinance of 1552, reproduced by A. Danon in "La Communauté juive de Salonique au XVIᵉ siècle," *REJ*, XLI, 112 ff.; and again by S. Assaf in his *Bate ha-Din ve-sidrehem* (The Organization of the Jewish Courts after the Conclusion of the Talmud), pp. 111 f.; R. Samuel de Medina, *Resp.* in M. S. Goodblatt's trans. in his *Jewish Life in Turkey*, pp. 131 ff. In his *Bate ha-Din*, pp. 20 ff., Assaf also offers a brief description of the struggle of the Turkish rabbinate against the proclivities of some Balkan Jews to repair to Turkish courts in their litigations over estates left behind by relatives and the like. Assaf's suggestion, however, that this phenomenon resulted from the immigration of numerous Iberian Marranos who, after 1492, had no functioning Jewish courts in their home countries overlooked the long-established practices of this kind among the Romaniot communities since the decree of 398 C.E. On the ramified problems of Jewish judicial autonomy, see *JC*, II–III, Chap. XIV: "Law Enforcement," and Index, III, 447 ff.

At the same time both Islamic and Jewish laws, as well as that of most other denominations, generally respected the established customs. According to a talmudic adage, *minhag 'oqer din* (custom supersedes the law), rabbis often had to respect a well-established custom in their communities even if it ran counter to the letter of the codified law. By extension they also had to accept, as did Ibn abi Zimra, the habit of appealing to Muslim courts wherever such a custom existed. The prevalence of this "custom" is also evidenced by the protocols of the qadhi of Sofia, ed. by Galabov and Duda (*supra*, n. 81). See the numerous entries for the years 1550–1647, especially 1619, listed *ibid.*, Index, p. 441, *s.v.* "Jude." See also the parallel attitudes in the Greek Orthodox Church as analyzed, for example, by S. S. Bobčev in his "Quelques remarques sur le droit coutumier bulgare pendant la domination ottomane," *REB*, I, 34–45; and by C. Papastathro, "L'Église et le droit coutumier aux Balkans pendant la domination ottomane," reprinted from "Le Droit coutumier et les autonomies sur le

Balkans et dans les pays voisins" (*Recueil des travaux* of the Symposion International de Belgrade 1–2 November 1971), pp. 187–97 (with a Serbo-Croatian summary).

There were, however, also some fundamental differences between the Muslim and Jewish judiciaries based on the dichotomy between their underlying juridical approaches. Somewhat resembling the old Roman distinction between *jus* and *fas*, the Muslim law drew a sharp distinction between affairs of jurisprudence (*kaza*, related to qadhi) and matters of piety (Turkish *diyanet;* Arabic, *diyanah*), jurisdiction over which was assigned respectively to the qadhi and the mufti. On its part, Jewish law basically disregarded such differentiation. To be sure, it recognized behavior "beyond the line of duty" as transcending the strict domain of the law (*li-fnim mi-shurat ha-din*). Yet it considered both areas as being under the proper supervision of the same rabbinical authorities. See Z. Gôkalp's succinct observations in his "Religion and Law," published in English in his *Turkish Nationalism and Western Civilization: Selected Essays,* trans. and ed. with an Intro. by N. Berkes, pp. 199–202; *supra*, Vols. VI, pp. 63 ff., 121 ff., 389 ff.; XVII, pp. 310 f. n. 26. On the use of Christian notaries, see, for instance, *ibid.,* pp. 98 ff., 340 f. n. 66.

Regrettably, the widely scattered data about the authority exercised by Muslim judges upon the Jewish community and individual Jews has never yet been subjected to close scholarly scrutiny. A monograph on this subject still is an important scholarly desideratum. In the meantime much can be learned from the parallel developments among the much larger and territorially much more concentrated Christian subjects of the Porte. See S. S. Bobčev, "Coup d'oeil sur le régime juridique des Balkans sous le régime Ottoman," *REB*, I, 523–32; H. J. Kissling, *Rechtsproblematiken in den christlich-muslimischen Beziehungen vorab im Zeitalter der Türkenkriege;* F. Klebe, *Beiträge zur islamischen Rechtspraxis gegenüber Nichtmuslimen, nach türkischen Urkunden aus dem 16. Jahrhundert* (Diss. Kiel, typescript; excerpt, printed Kiel); F. Selle, *Prozessrecht des 16. Jahrhunderts im Osmanischen Reich. Auf Grund von Fetwas des Scheichulislams Ebussuud und anderen unter der Regierung des Sultans Suleiman des Prächtigen* (Diss. Cologne). See also P. Kovalevski, "La Chrétienté orientale orthodoxe et ses diverse aspects nationaux," *Revue de Psychologie des Peuples,* VIII, 85–116.

Less complicated were the problems of criminal justice, since the imposition of penalties could much more effectively be carried out by the state authorities through the uniform enforcement of state laws. See U. Heyd, *Studies in Old Ottoman Criminal Law,* ed. by V. L. Ménage. On the authority exercised by the qadhi on the self-governing minorities see E. Grozdanova, "Das Kadiamt und die Selbstverwaltung der bulgarischen Gemeinden im 15. bis 16. Jahrhundert," *Études historiques* (Sofia), VII, 147–59; and, more generally, H. Sobotta, *Das Amt des Kadi im Osmanischen Reich* (typescript, Diss. Münster); and, on some Mameluke antecedents, A. Schimmel, *Kalif und Kadi im spätmittelalterlichen Ägypten.*

120. See G. Postel, *De la Republique des Turcs:* Part II: Histoire et considération de l'origine, loy et coutume de Tartares, Persiens, Arabes, Turcs, et tous autres Ismaélites ou Muhamédiques, dicts par nous Mahométains ou Sarrazins, Poitou, 1560, p. 23.

121. R. Mantran, *Istanbul,* p. 3.

122. W. G. Lockwood, "Living Legacy of the Ottoman Empire: the Serbo-Croatian Speaking Moslems of Bosnia-Hercegovina," in *The Mutual Effects of the Islamic and Judeo-Christian Worlds: the East-European Patterns,* ed. by A. Ascher *et al.,* pp. 209–225; C. Ellcot, *Turkey in Europe,* p. 286 n. 1.

123. See R. Samuel de Medina, *Resp.*, Y.D., No. 124; Ḥ.M., No. 364, cited by M. S. Goodblatt in *Jewish Life*, p. 214 n. 2; H. Luke, *The Old Turkey and the New: From Byzantium to Ankara* (new ed. of his *The Making of Modern Turkey*), p. 8, quoting a review of that first ed. in *Tablet*.

CHAPTER LXXIX: PERSIA-IRAN

1. II Kings 17:6; Esther 3:8; W. J. Fischel, "Yahudiyah, or the Beginnings of the Jewish Settlement in Persia" (Hebrew), *Tarbiz*, VI, 523–36; and *infra*, n. 54. On the Assyrian deportations and exchanges of populations, including that of Media by Sargon II in 716–15 B.C.E., see D. D. Luckenbill, *Ancient Records of Assyria and Babylonia*, Index, *s.v.* Madai; A. Malamat, *Ha-Aramim be-Aram Naharayim* (The Aramaeans in Mesopotamia and the Rise of Their States), pp. 47 ff.; and R. Labat, "Kaštariti, Phraorte et les débuts de l'histoire mède," *JA*, CCXLIX, 1–12, esp. p. 6. On the date of the composition of the Book of Esther see *supra*, Vol. I, p. 345 n. 8, especially the works by H. Gunkel and J. Hoschander to which are to be added the more recent studies by E. J. Bickermann, *Four Strange Books of the Bible: Jonah, Daniel, Koheleth, Esther*, pp. 171–240; and H. L. Ginsberg, *The Five Megillot and Jonah*, esp. pp. 82–88. It is noteworthy that although the Book of Esther recorded an ancient conflict between the Persian population and the Jews and even mentioned the violent retribution meted out to their enemies by the Jews under the leadership of Mordecai and Esther, the medieval Jews did not mind publicly worshiping at the tombs of these two leaders who had saved their ancestors from an impending disaster. Nor did they hesitate to translate the Book of Esther into their Judeo-Persian dialect, although as in most works in that language, they used the Hebrew alphabet, making it less accessible to non-Jews, especially in the fervently nationalist Safavid period. See E. Mainz, "Esther en judéo-persan," *JA*, CCLVIII, 95–105; W. J. Fischel, "The Bible in Persian Translation," *Harvard Theological Review*, XLV, 3–45; and some of the literature listed *infra*, n. 42. Persian readers of the Jewish triumph over their foes in the days of Xerxes might have taken deep umbrage. This situation resembled that of the Passover Haggadah, apparently first composed in the third pre-Christian century in Egypt which seems to have aroused some misgivings among the local Jews about the possible negative reaction to it by their non-Jewish compatriots. See *supra*, Vol. I, p. 381 n. 30. Of course, the fact that neither most third-century B.C.E. Egyptians nor the late medieval Persians shared the faith of their ancestors in the days of the Exodus or Xerxes and that many Hellenistic Egyptians and Muslim Persians viewed their Pharaonic and Zoroastrian ancestors with much disdain served as a mitigating factor.

2. See S. Telegdi, "Essai sur la phonétique des emprunts iraniens en araméen talmudique," *JA*, CCXXVI, 177–256 (includes a glossary of 130 Persian loan words reminiscent of the usage in Achaemenid times, pp. 234 ff.); V. Minorsky, "Some Early Documents in Persian, I–II," *JRAS*, 1942, pp. 181–94; 1943, pp. 86–99; esp. 1942, p. 182, referring to D. Salesman's essay, "Zum mittelpersischen Passiv," *Bulletin* of the St. Petersburg (Leningrad) Academy of Sciences, XIII, no. 3, pp. 269–76.

3. Faustus von Byzance, *Geschichte Armeniens*, pp. 137 f.; Moses of Khorene, *Chronicle*, III, 35, ed. by P. E. Le Vaillant de Florival, III, 80 ff., with my comments thereon, *supra*, Vol. I, pp. 204, 404 f. nn. 36–37. On Zoroaster as an alleged disciple of Baruch, prophet Jeremiah's assistant, see Muḥammad aṭ-Ṭabari's *Annales*, ed. by M. J. de Goeje *et al.*, I, Part 2, pp. 648, 681; and A. V. W. Jackson, *Zoroaster, the Prophet of Ancient*

Iran, pp. 165 ff.; and the other literature listed *supra*, Vol. I, p. 341 n. 1. The persecutions of Jews in fifth-century Persia, including the execution of Huna Mari, and the rise of Mar Zuṭra III's short-lived principality are described *supra*, Vol. III, pp. 182, 399 n. 15. We shall presently see that the Mazdakite movement of the fifth century, which had caused Jews and Christians considerable difficulties (see *supra*, Vol. III, pp. 55 f., 254 f. n. 69) did not die out with the decline of Zoroastrianism and the replacement of the Sassanian by the Muslim regimes. The major complications, however, for Jews and Christians arising from the Mazdakite preachment of the community of women, seems to have been dropped by its partial adherents during the Late Middle Ages. See A. Bausani, "Religion under the Mongols," *CHI*, V, 538–49, esp. pp. 548 f.; and on the Shu'ubiyya movement and the mild Jewish reactions thereto, see my *Ancient and Medieval Jewish History: Essays*, ed. by L. A. Feldman, pp. 90, 144, 402 n. 24, 442 n. 49. To the literature listed there add: H. A. R. Gibb, "The Social Significance of the 'Shu'ubiyya,' " *Studia Orientalia Joanni Pedersen . . . dicata*, pp. 105–114; R. P. Mottahedeh, "The Shu'ubiya Controversy and the Social History of Early Islamic Iran," *IJMES*, VII, 161–82, esp. pp. 162 f., 181; D. A. Agius, "The Shu'ubiya Movement and Its Manifestations," *Islamic Quarterly*, XXIV, 76–88; and from other angles, B. Lewis's stimulating analysis of *Race and Color in Islam*, effectively arguing against the contention by the "myth makers," such as Arnold Toynbee and Malcolm X, that the Muslim societies had been free of racial discrimination.

4. See Samau'al al-Maghribi, *Ifḥam al-Yahud* (Silencing the Jews), ed. and trans. by M. Perlmann (*PAAJR*, XXXII), pp. 72 ff. (English); J. D. Eisenstein, ed., *Ozar Massaoth. A Collection of Itineraries by Jewish Travelers to Palestine, Syria, Egypt and Other Countries, Pilgrimages to Holy Tombs and Sepulchres*, pp. 65–71, esp. p. 71; in an abridged English trans. in E. N. Adler's *Jewish Travellers*, pp. 115–29, esp. p. 129; Benjamin Disraeli, *The Wondrous Tale of Alroy*. We must bear in mind, however, that R. Jacob's travelogue is of uncertain date—it may have been written more closely to the disputation, which in 1240 took place in Paris between his teacher R. Yeḥiel of Paris and Nicholas Donin and which not only led up to the burning of the Talmud but also made life for R. Yeḥiel in the French capital so difficult that he left for Palestine. See *supra*, Vol. IX, pp. 63 ff., 179 ff., 270 ff. nn. 11–16, 277 ff. nn. 30–33. Moreover, it is possible that the final paragraph beginning with the passage referring to Shiraz was not written by R. Jacob but was added by a later scribe. This passage is, indeed, missing in one of the two extant MSS. See Eisenstein's remark, p. 71 n.2.

5. See, for instance, V. Minorsky, "Some Early Documents in Persian, I–II," *JRAS*, 1942, pp. 181–94; 1943, pp. 86–99; D. N. Mac Kenzie, "An Early Jewish-Persian Document," *BSOAS*, XXXI, 249–69, dating from before 1319 and possibly even before 1021 C.E. (This tract argues that "the management of the world rests on prophethood" and that Moses' unique qualifications were confirmed by the sources.); H. R. Roemer, "Vorschläge zur Sammlung von Urkunden zur islamischen Geschichte Persiens," *ZDMG*, CIV, 363–70; B. Lewis, "Sources for the Economic History of the Middle East" in M. A. Cook, ed., *Studies on the Economic History of the Middle East*, pp. 78–92, esp. pp. 78 n. 1, 79 n. 4, 80 f. On the Persian Hebrew manuscripts available in the West see G. Margoliouth, "Persian Hebrew MSS. in the British Museum," *JQR*, [o.s.] VII, 119–20; M. Seligsohn, "The Hebrew-Persian MSS. of the British Museum," *ibid.*, XV, 278–301 (was to be continued); and those included in more comprehensive catalogues, such as E. N. Adler's *Catalogue of Hebrew Manuscripts in the Collection of E. N. A.* (now part of the vast collection of the Jewish Theological Seminary of America in New York); and D. S. Sassoon, *Ohel David* (David's Tent: a Catalogue of D. S. S.'s

Collection of Hebrew manuscripts). A large number of other important Hebrew manuscript catalogues are listed in S. Shunami's *Bibliography of Jewish Bibliographies*, 2d ed. enlarged, pp. 535–61.

Our nearly complete dependence on the Arab and Persian historians and geographers naturally limits the extent to which modern criticism can go beyond the information thus presented. Quite frequently we are not even certain about the areas which were under effective Persian domination at a particular point. The fluidity of frontiers is well illustrated by P. Schwarz's analysis in his *Iran im Mittelalter nach den arabischen Geographen;* and D. Krawulsky, *Iran—Das Reich der Ilḫane. Eine topographisch-historische Studie* (Beiträge zum Tübingen Atlas des Vorderen Orients, Reihe B, Geisteswissenschaften, XVII). Similarly, the chronicles have been carefully scrutinized on the basis of available texts—only a few in critical editions—by modern historians, particularly Hammer, D'Ohsson, Quatremère, Howorth, and Blochet, cited in Vol. XVII, pp. 365 ff. or in our forthcoming notes. For the later period, until his death in 1318, Faḍl 'Allah Hamadani Rashid ad-Din's *K. Jami' aṭ-Ṭawarikh* (Histoire des Mongols de la Perse), Vol. I, ed. with a French translation, notes, and an essay on the life and work of the author by E. Quatremère, followed by Vol. II, ed. by E. Blochet, is of extreme importance. Apart from this edition Blochet also wrote a significant *Introduction à l'histoire des Mongols de Fadl Allah Rashid Ed-Din.* Another section of that World History, ed. by A. A. Alizade, was translated into German by A. K. Arends. Of special interest to us is the section devoted to "The Children of Israel." See K. Jahn's well-documented German trans., *Die Geschichte der Kinder Israels des Rašid ad-Din (Denkschriften* of the Vienna Akademie der Wissenschaften, CXIV), with his earlier comments thereon in his "Die Erweiterung ihres Geschichtsbildes durch Raschid ad-Din und 'Die Geschichte der Kinder Israels' in der islamischen Historiographie," *Abhandlungen* of that Academy, CVII, CIX. This section reveals Rashid's familiarity with the Hebrew texts of the Bible as shown by W. J. Fischel in his biographical studies of Rashid cited *infra*, n. 13.

Among the other historical writers perhaps most informative for our purposes is Kamal ad-Din Abu'l Fadhl Ibn al-Fuwaṭi (Fuṭi), *Al-Hawadiṭ al-Jami'at* (The Comprehensive Events and Useful Experience of the Seventh Century [A.M.] in Baghdad's History), ed. by M. Jawad. The non-Muslim contemporaries include especially Gregorius Abu'l Faraj Barhebraeus, a leading ecclesiastical historian of Jewish descent but completely detached from Judaism, who offers some very enlightening data. See his *Makhtebanut zabne* (Chronicon syriacum), ed. by P. Bédjan; and the English translation entitled *The Chronography* by E. A. W. Budge (a renditioin of the first part of Barhebraeus' *Political World History*). Though less informative, the comments by Western missionaries and envoys contribute some welcome data in view of the dearth of available documentary evidence. See esp. the collection by A. van den Wyngaert, *Itinera et relationes fratrum minorum seculi XIII et XIV*, which after an informative Introduction and survey (pp. xliii–cxviii), reproduces the texts of the travelogues by John di Plano Carpini (pp. 3–130); Benedict of Poland (pp. 133–43); William of Rubruck (Vilhelm av Ruybroeck, Guillaume de Rubrouck, or de Rubruquis; pp. 147–332); and Odoricus of Portenau (pp. 381–495). See also I. de Rachewitz, *Papal Envoys to the Great Khans;* M. Komroff. *Contemporaries of Marco Polo* (includes English translations of Carpini, Rubruck, Odoricus, and Benjamin of Tudela); and L. Lockhart's general review of "Persia as Seen by the West," in *The Legacy of Persia*, ed. by A. J. Arberry, pp. 318–58. Some additional data and insights may also be obtained from incidental references in Persia's theological, political, and poetic writings, on which see E. G. Browne, *A History of Persian Literature under Tartar Dominion A.D. 1265–1502*) and idem, *A Literary History of Persia*, Vol. III. See also *infra*, n. 12.

These materials have not yet been subjected to careful scrutiny by specialists with respect to facets of Jewish history in Persia. But it appears that even if this had been done, it would have helped to fill only a few of the vast lacunae in our knowledge of Jewish history on the Iranian Plateau after the Mongolian invasions. Nor must we overlook the interrelations between the various monarchies which emerged from the division of Jenghiz Khan's world empire. Even the somewhat remote Golden Horde, which occupied much of what is Soviet territory today, from time to time intervened in the affairs of Persia and its neighbors, just as, in initial conquests, it had greatly threatened Central Europe and its Jewries. See *infra*, n. 8.

6. See W. Bacher, *Zwei jüdisch-persische Dichter—Schahin und Imrani;* K. Jahn's aforementioned translation of *Die Geschichte der Kinder Israels des Rašid ad-Din;* and, more broadly, A. Netzer, ed., *An Anthology of the Persian Poetry of the Jews of Iran;* W. J. Fischel, "Israel in Iran (A Survey of Judeo-Persian Literature)," in L. Finkelstein, ed., *The Jews: Their History, Culture and Religion,* II/3, pp. 1149–90, esp. pp. 1162 ff., 1166; idem, "The Beginnings of Judeo-Persian Literature," *Mélanges d'Orientalisme in honor of Henri Massé,* pp. 141–50; H. Mizrahi, *Toledot Yehudei Paras u-meshorrerehem* (History of the Jews of Persia and Their Poets), esp. pp. 56–67; and, more broadly, the three-volume comprehensive Persian work by Habib Lavi, *Tarikh-i Yahudan-i Iran* (History of the Jews in Iran). Of considerable interest to both Jewish and art history are the 24 miniatures reproduced and analyzed from a Tübingen MS by H. Striedl in "Die Miniaturen in der Handschrift des jüdisch-persischen Ardaschirbuch von Shāhin," in *Schriften und Bilder der Orientalischen Untersuchungen* by K. L. Janert, R. Sellheim, and H. Striedl (Verzeichnis der Orientalischen Handschriften in Deutschland, Supplementband, VII). These miniatures, probably painted by a Jewish artist, seemingly date from the seventeenth century. A fuller story of the life and work of Shahin and of another Persian Hebrew poet, Imrani, who lived in the sixteenth century, will be told here in connection with the general development of the Judeo-Persian language, literature, and art in a later volume.

Of considerable interest also is W. Bacher's ed. of *Ein Hebräisch-Persisches Wörterbuch aus dem vierzehnten Jahrhundert,* completed by Solomon b. Samuel in 1339 in the city of Urgench, located 18 miles northeast of Khiva, now in the Soviet Uzbek Republic. This distant location from the center of Jewish life in the Persian-speaking areas is not at all surprising, since some of the earliest documents in Judeo-Persian, likewise written in Hebrew script, were found in such peripheral areas as Chinese Turkestan and Malabar. See Fischel, "Israel in Iran," pp. 1155 f. It may also be assumed that the same factors which propelled the early migrations of Christians to Central Asia also led some Jews to settle in those distant territories. Certainly, Adiabene, that "nerve center of Christianity," from which many of these Christians had emigrated, also had numerous Jews, who in the first century had lived under the reign of a royal family converted to Judaism, and some of whom may have gone to Central Asia and, as in other places, they also paved the way for *The Early Spread of Christianity in Central Asia and the Far East; a New Document,* by A. Mingana in his booklet under this title. Equally enlightening is the intent and content of Solomon's dictionary. He gives in alphabetical order a large number of less familiar terms in the Bible and supplies a Judeo-Persian translation likewise in the Hebrew alphabet. Evidently, even in that distant locality there were enough Jewish students of the Bible and talmudic literature who needed assistance only with respect to more difficult and controversial terms. Basically, the same can be said about the later dictionary prepared by Moses Shirwani, also reproduced by Bacher in "Ein Hebräisch-Persisches Wörterbuch aus dem fünfzehnten Jahrhundert," *Zeitschrift für die Alttestamentliche Wissenschaft*, XVI, 201–247 (on Moses b. Aaron Shirwani's dictionary finished according to the colophon, reading: "Completed on Adar I, 14, 1771 Seleucid era" = Feb. 6, 1460 C.E.).

Regrettably, the material offered by the Cairo Genizah largely ends with the middle of the thirteenth century, in the early Mongol period of Persia. See, for example, S. D. Goitein, "Glimpses from the Cairo Geniza on Naval Warfare in the Mediterranean and on the Mongol Invasion," *Studi Orientalistici in onore di Giorgio Levi della Vida*, I, 393–408 (referring especially to the Mongol invasion of 1236 in the vicinity of Mosul). However, in view of the generally conservative leanings of the Jews of that time, one may also learn a great deal from some Genizah documents referring to conditions in Persia in the pre-Mongolian period. See the numerous entries in Goitein's *Mediterranean Society*, Indexes to Vols. I–III, *s.v.* Persia.

7. Gregorius Abu'l Faraj Barhebraeus, *The Chronography*, trans. by E. A. W. Budge, fols. 575 (Syriac), 490 (English). On the works and reliability of this author, see W. Wright, *A Short History of Syriac Literature*, pp. 265–81; G. Graf, *Geschichte der christlichen arabischen Literatur* (Studi e Testi, 118, 133, 146–47, 172), esp. II, 222–31. Among the contemporary Persian and Arab chroniclers most useful for our subject are the aforementioned (n.5) writings by Ibn al-Fuwati and Rashid ad-Din. These and other sources have been reviewed by Western scholars over a century and a half ever since C. M. D'Ohsson wrote his *Histoire des Mongols depuis Tschinguiz Khan jusqu'à Timour Bey ou Tamerlan*, followed by J. von Hammer-Purgstall, *Geschichte der Ilkhane*, and by H. H. Howorth, *History of the Mongols*. All these early standard works were updated and supplemented in the twentieth century by G. Le Strange in *The Lands of the Eastern Caliphate*; B. Spuler, *Die Mongolen in Iran. Politik, Verwaltung und Kultur der Ilchanenzeit, 1220–1350*, 3d ed. rev. and enlarged; idem, *History of the Mongols. Based on Eastern and Western Accounts of the Thirteenth and Fourteenth Centuries*, trans. from the German by H. and S. Drummond; and by J. A. Boyle, "Dynastic and Political History of the Il-Khans," in his ed. of *CHI*, Vol. V: The Saljuk and Mongol Periods, pp. 303–421.

It is to be regretted that there is no corresponding *detailed* history of the Jews in Persia—clearly a difficult undertaking in view of the paucity of available documentation. Walter J. Fischel—who pioneered in this area by his publication *Jews in the Economic and Political Life of Mediaeval Islam* (Royal Asiatic Society Monographs, XXII), or the new ed., with an additional introduction, "The Court Jew in the Islamic World," esp. pp. 90 ff., which was followed by a number of monographic studies (they will for the most part be mentioned in the following notes)—originally intended to write a comprehensive history of Persian Jewry since the rise of Islam. Unfortunately, his early demise prevented him from carrying out this undertaking. See also H. Mizrahi's Hebrew survey cited *supra*, n. 6; and the more general *Tarikh-i Yahudan-i Iran*, by Habib Lavi.

8. See Matthew of Paris, *Chronica majora*, ed. by H. R. Luard (Rerum Britannicarum medii aevi scriptores of the Public Record Office, LVII), III, 75; IV, 131; Richer of Sens, *Gesta Senonensis ecclesiae*, xx, ed. by G. Waitz, *MGH*, Scriptores, XXV, 249–348, esp. p. 310; *Annales Marbacenses* (Marbach), ed. by R. Wilmans, for the year 1222, *ibid.*, XVII, pp. 142–80, esp. pp. 174 f.; and other data succinctly analyzed by H. Bresslau in his "Juden und Mongolen," *ZGJD*, [o.s.] I, 99–102. Bresslau also cites with approval F. Zarnecke's explanation that the entire tale about the ruler of the Mongol Empire being the "son of David" had arisen from a copyist's error who had read *rex Iudeorum* instead of *rex Indorum*. See his "Der Priester Johannes, Parts I–III," *Abhandlungen* of the Sächsische Gesellschaft der Wissenschaften, XVII–XIX, esp. XIX, 22 ff.

Christians and Jews also frequently connected the sudden Mongolian invasion with the "wars of Gog and Magog" which, so vividly described in Ezekiel 38–39, had long been seen in their eschatologies as preliminary to the advent of the Redeemer or the second coming of Christ. The well-known Provençal Bible commentator, David Kimḥi (d. 1235), among others, placed the Mongols in *Paras* (Persia).

9. See 'Ala ad-Din 'Ata Malik Juwaini, *Ta'rikh-i Jāhan gushā* (The History of the World Conqueror), English trans. by J. A. Boyle, I, 50; and the data for the first time assembled by W. J. Fischel in *Jews in . . . Mediaeval Islam*, pp. 90 ff.; supplemented by some new information supplied especially by A. Ben-Jacob in his "A Hebrew Source for the History of the Jews in Babylonia and Syria in the Mongol Period" (Hebrew), *Sinai*, VIII, nos. 98–99, pp. 330–32, with some additions, *ibid*, IX, no. 105, p. 120; his "New Sources for the History of the Jews in Babylonia in the Twelfth and Thirteenth Centuries" (Hebrew), *Zion*, XV, 56–69; and in a fuller summary his *Yehudei Babel* (A History of the Jews in Iraq From the End of the Gaonic Period (1038 C.E.) to the Present Time), pp. 60 ff. See in particular the quotations from Barhebraeus' *Chronography*, trans. by Budge, fol. 576/p. 491; Ibn al-Fuwaṭi, *Al-Hawadit al-Jami'a*, p. 466. Some variants of the story are also included in the works of other chroniclers, esp. 'Abdallah Vaṣṣaf's *K. Tajziyat al-Amṣar* (In the lithographic Bombay, 1852–53 reproduction). According to the latter, who was generally unfriendly to Sa'd, no Muslims were admitted to Arghun's court during the Jewish vizier's short-lived regime. Yet, Vaṣṣaf admits that, in contrast to his predecessors, Sa'd introduced a system of law and order into the administration of the Empire, a system which fell apart shortly after his death. In this connection one may also mention the different interpretation of the then known sources by A. N. Poliak in "The Jews of the Middle East at the End of the Middle Ages (According to Arabic Sources)" (Hebrew), *Zion*, II, 256–73, III, 89–90. His conclusion, however, that Sa'd was not killed but merely changed his faith in 1291 and that he served as vizier thereafter as a Muslim was not accepted by any other scholars.

10. See J. A. Boyle's observations on Gaykhatu in his translation of the pertinent chapter of Rashid ad-Din's great history entitled *The Successors of Genghis Khan*, and in his aforementioned chapter in the *CHI*, V, 272 ff. On the luckless experiment with paper money, see esp. W. J. Fischel, "On the Iranian Paper Currency *Al-Chao* of the Mongol Persia," *JRAS*, 1939, pp. 601–603; K. Jahn's twin essays, "Das Iranische Papiergeld. Ein Beitrag zur Kultur- und Wirtschaftsgeschichte Irans in der Mongolenzeit," *Archiv Orientálni*, X, 308–339; and "Paper Currency in Iran: a Contribution to the Cultural and Economic History of Iran in the Mongol Period," *Journal of Asian History*, IV/2, pp. 101–135.

11. See Ibn al-Fuwaṭi's *Al-Hawadit al-Jami'a*, p. 466; Vaṣṣaf, *K. Tajziyat al-Amṣar*, fol. 205b, adding that despite the Jewish resistance in Baghdad "more than a hundred of the noble and wealthy Jews were slain and their property plundered." One must realize, however, that in the new and not yet fully organized Empire popular riots were quite common. Ibn al-Fuwaṭi also reports, for example, attacks by Kurds and Turkomans on both Jews and Arabs. See also Barhebraeus, *Chronography*, fol. 558/p. 476, all cited by Fischel in *Jews in . . . Mediaeval Islam*, pp. 116 f.

12. See *supra*, Vol. XVII, pp. 152 f., 367 n. 30 (including the quotation from Raymond Lull's "Petitio Raymundi pro conversione infidelium ad Coelestinum V et ad Cardinales directa" in his *Opera*, ed. by I. Sulzinger, II: Liber de quinque sapientibus,

pp. 174 f.); the reports by Giovanni di Plano Carpini, Benedict of Poland, William of Rubruck, and Odoricus of Portenau, most readily available in A. van den Wyngaert's aforementioned (n. 5) collection of *Itinera;* or in the partial English translations in C. R. Beazley, *The Texts and Versions of John de Plano Carpini and William de Rubruquis* (with reprint of Richard Hakluyt's ed., 1598); and M. Komroff, *Contemporaries of Marco Polo.* On the general relationship between the Mongolian Empires and the Western powers see I. de Rachewitz, *Papal Envoys to the Great Khan;* J. A. Boyle's succinct summary, "The Il-Khans of Persia and the Christian West," *History To-Day,* XXIII, 554–63; and L. Lockhart's study cited *supra,* n. 5.

The religious controversies between the various denominations, including the disputations frequently staged at the Il-Khan courts, facilitated by the general religious freedom prevailing under the early il-khans, are analyzed by A. Zaiyyab, "The Struggle of Religious Sects in the Court of Ilkhanids and the fate of Shi'ism in That Time," *Iran-Shinasi,* 2d ser. no. 3, pp. 103–106; and by A. Bausani, "Religion under the Mongols," *CHI,* V, 538–49; idem, "Iran, Islam e Italia nel Medioevo," *Veltro,* 141/2, pp. 29–37.

13. See Ṣaif b. Muḥammad b. Ya'qub Ṣaifi, *Tarikh Nama-yi-Harat* (History of Herat, written between 1318–1322), ed. by M. Z. Siddiqi, pp. 402, 408, 416; with the observations thereon by I. P. Petrushevsky in "The Socio-Economic Condition of Iran under the Il-Khans," in *CHI,* V, 483–537, esp. p. 489.

14. F. 'A. Rashid ad-Din, *Jami' aṭ-Ṭawarikh* (History of the Mongols), ed. by A. A. Alizade (trans. into German by A. K. Arends); Barhebraeus, *Chronography,* esp. pp. 379, 507, 596 f.; P. Bedjan, ed., *Histoire de Mar Jab-Alaha, Patriarche, et de Rabban Sauma;* or in the new ed. and English trans. by E. A. W. Budge, entitled *The Monks of Kublai Khan, Emperor of China,* esp. p. 100; with succinct comments thereon by J. Starr, "A Christian Source for Muslim History" (Hebrew), *Zion,* VI, 158–59. Starr also mentions in this connection the comment by the Alexandrian Jewish convert to Islam Sa'id ibn Ḥasan that God rewarded Ghazan for his destruction of the infidels' sanctuaries with his victory over the Mamelukes at Ḥimṣ in 1299. On Ghazan's much-discussed conversion and intolerant decrees, see H. H. Howorth, *History of the Mongols,* II, 403 ff.; and J. A. Boyle's "Dynastic and Political History," *CHI,* V, 379 ff., 493 ff. and *passim.* Some of these extremes seem to have been inspired by Ghazan's close adviser Emir Nauruz who, with the typical zeal of a neophyte, fervently propagated strict Islamic conformity. The subsequent greater moderation followed Nauruz' downfall and execution in 1297.

15. See Rashid ad-Din's *History,* section ed. by Alizade, pp. 596 f. (continuation of the passage quoted in the preceding note). See also some additional data supplied by A. Ben-Jacob in his *Yehudei Babel,* pp. 70 ff.

16. J. von Hammer-Purgstall, *Geschichte der Ilchane,* II, 186. Rashid ad-Din's meteoric rise and sudden fall has intrigued most students of Persian history under the Il-Khans. At first many scholars expressed doubt about his Jewish origin. But this metamorphosis has been cogently argued by E. Blochet in his *Introduction à l'histoire des Mongols* (Gibb Memorial Vol., XII); and more fully developed by W. J. Fischel in his *Jews . . . Mediaeval Islam,* pp. 118 ff.; and in a number of his essays, especially in his "Arabische Quellen zur Geschichte der babylonischen Judenschaft im 13. Jahrhundert," *MGWJ,* LXXIX, 302–322; "Über Raschid ad-Daulas jüdischen Ursprung," *ibid.,* LXXXI, 147–53; and "Neue Beiträge zur Geschichte der Juden im Mittelalter," *ibid.,*

pp. 416–22. This view has now been generally accepted by scholars in the field. See also *infra*, n. 17.

There is a general consensus about the validity of Howorth's appraisal of more than a century ago that Rashid ad-Din was "the greatest vizier of the Il-Khan dynasty and one of the greatest men the East has produced" (*History of the Mongols*, III, 589). He probably also was the wealthiest non-reigning individual of his time (see *infra*, n. 52). Yet, no full-length biography of this scholar, statesman, and financier has thus far been written in any language. Characteristically, some of his philosophical and theological writings—he is said to have written more than seventy tracts during a lifetime variously mentioned as lasting between 70 and 80 years—were considered by conservative Muslim theologians as bordering on heresy. But such mutual accusations by representatives of various Muslim sects and schools were quite common and for outsiders frequently confusing. It is small wonder then that Quthlugh-Shah, for a time a leading emir under Öljeytu's reign, once exclaimed that he did not understand why the Mongols had to exchange Jenghiz Khan's straightforward *Yasa* for a hundred conflicting interpretations of Muslim theology. See A. Bausani, "Religion under the Mongols," *CHI*, V, 544.

17. See the data mentioned in the literature cited *supra*, n. 16, especially also in Ben-Jacob's *Yehudei Babel*, pp. 76 f.; and K. Jahn's observations in his trans. of Rashid's *Geschichte der Kinder Israel*, p. 9. Rashid's alleged Jewish bias in not mentioning Jenghiz Khan's omission of rabbis in the tax exemption—often repeated in the literature—might in fact have come from his realization that the Jewish rabbinate was not so distinguished a class as was the clergy of the two other monotheistic denominations. In the thirteenth century there were relatively few paid Jewish religious functionaries other than the readers and sextons who served in synagogues or as teachers in schools. Not long before, Maimonides had actually fulminated against any professionalization of Jewish learning and demanded that persons teaching Judaism and performing other rabbinic functions should serve free of charge. Even in the European countries the development of a professional rabbinate occurred only in the fourteenth century and from there it spread also into the Muslim lands. See *JC*, II, 80 ff.; III, 126 f.; and the literature cited there. Perhaps it was actually a sign of Rashid's fairly intimate knowledge of the Jewish institutions that he did not mention the tax exemption for Jewish scholars, since no such exemption seems to have been granted to the numerous Muslim savants not serving as functionaries at specific mosques.

18. See Rashid ad-Din's *Jami' aṭ-Ṭawarikh*, ed. by Alizade, p. 418; his *Mukatabat-i Rashidi* (Correspondence), ed. by M. Shafi', pp. 118 f. No. 22; cited by I. P. Petrushevsky in "The Socio-Economic Conditions," *CHI*, V, 493. On Rashid's school of painting, which came to be called the Rashidiyya, and its role in the history of Islamic art, see E. de Lorey, "L'École de Tabriz. L'Islam à prise avec la Chine," *Revue des Arts Asiatiques*, IX, 27–39 (showing, on the example of several illustrations in early manuscripts of Rashid ad-Din's *World History* and of Firdausi, a remarkable synthesis of Muslim and Chinese illustrative art); and, more generally, O. Grabar, "The Visual Arts, 1050–1350," *CHI*, V, 626–658, esp. pp. 648 ff. See also G. Salim, "Rashid ad-Din Fazlellah's Contribution to the Advancement of Education in His Time. With Particular Reference to His Interest in Medical Training," *Journal of Regional Cultural Interest*, VI, 137–42.

19. The story of Rashid's execution is told with many significant variants by almost all contemporary chroniclers and their early successors. Yet it is not even clear whether

he died at the age of seventy or nearly eighty, and hence also whether he was born *ca.* 1240 or 1250. Even contemporaries were spinning many legends around his intriguing personality. For example, the story about the enormous gift of 1,500,000 dinars in cash which Ghazan offered him is presented in a typical anecdotal form. On one occasion, we are told, in discussing with Ghazan his *History* (which was partially inspired by the monarch), the author allegedly mentioned Alexander the Great and Aristotle as his chief adviser, to whom the Macedonian world conqueror donated 1,000,000 dinars. Rashid is said to have drawn a parallel with Ghazan whom he considered greater than Alexander and the il-khan's relationship with himself who, he intimated, was likewise greater than Aristotle. Evidently to show his superiority over the widely celebrated ancient conqueror Ghazan increased the donation from 1,000,000 to 1,500,000 dinars. All this undoubtedly was part of an Oriental fantasy, based upon the reality that, even before coming to power, Rashid had amassed a great fortune, from which, as we recall, he could for a time maintain the expenses of the Empire when the Treasury had run out of cash. See *supra*, nn. 16 and 18; and *infra*, n. 52.

20. On Ghiyath's rise to power and assassination, see especially the sources cited by A. Ben-Jacob in *Yehudei Babel*, pp. 73 and 78; and I. P. Petrushevsky's comments in his "The Socio-Economic Conditions," *CHI*, V, 495 f. See also idem, *Zemledelie i agrar nie otnosheniya v Irane XIII–XIV vv* (Agriculture and Agrarian Developments in Iran in the XIII–XIV Centuries).

21. See E. S. Kennedy, "The Exact Sciences in Iran under the Saljuks and Mongols," *CHI*, V, 659–79, esp. p. 679; A. Ben-Jacob, *Yehudei Babel*, pp. 80 ff.; B. Spuler, *Die Mongolen in Iran*, pp. 127 ff. On the antecedents of Persia's national state see W. Hinz, *Irans Aufstieg zum Nationalstaat im fünfzehnten Jahrhundert.*

22. See E. Kohlberg, "The Development of the Imami Shi'i Doctrine of the *jihad,*" *ZDMG*, CXXVI, 61–86, esp. p. 65. Ismai'l's career and how he founded the Safavid state have often been studied. The older Strasbourg dissertation by E. D. Rose, "Early Years of Shāh Ismā'il, Founder of the Ṣafawi Dynasty," *JRAS*, 1896, pp. 249–340; and G. Sarwar, *History of the Shah Ismail Ṣafawi* with a Foreword by Hadi Ḥasan will supply the basic information. Among the new materials one might mention a Freiburg dissertation by E. Glassen (née Wendt), *Die Frühen Safawiden, nach Qāzi Ahmad Qumī.* It is not surprising that even the Shi'ites of the Ottoman Empire, especially Anatolia, felt the strong impact of the new religious state. See idem, "Shah Isma'il, ein Mahdi der anatolischen Turkmenen?" *ZDMG*, CXXI, 61–69; and H. Sohrweide, "Der Sieg der Safawiden in Persien und seine Rückwirkung auf die Schiiten Anatoliens im 16. Jahrhundert," *Der Islam*, XLI, 95–223 (also Diss. Hamburg, 1964). On the other hand, H. J. Kissling pointed out the international significance of Isma'il's important victories opening up new communications to India. See his "Šah Isma'il Ier. La Nouvelle Route des Indes et les Ottomans," *Turcica*, VI, 89–102, offering a general "geopolitical" survey of conditions in the early sixteenth century. On the background see also M. M. Mazzaoui, *The Origin of the Safawids: Shi'ism, Ṣufism, and the Gulat.*

23. To the literature listed in our earlier notes add the analysis of the developments under the first Safavids in C. Brockelmann's *History of the Islamic Peoples*, with a Review of Events 1939–1947 by M. Perlmann, trans. by J. Carmichael and M. Perlmann, pp. 317 ff.; A. Bausani's *The Persians from the Earliest Days to the Twentieth Century*, trans. from the Italian by J. B. Donne, pp. 135–53; and *infra*, n. 24.

Throughout the sixteenth and early seventeenth centuries, Persia was almost constantly involved in a war against the Ottoman Empire. This struggle is well exemplified by the destinies of Baghdad. Conquered in 1508 by Isma'il I, the city was incorporated into the Ottoman Empire by Suleiman the Magnificent in 1534. By 1623, after the aforementioned stormy period in Ottoman history, it was retaken by 'Abbas I, to be again annexed by Sultan Murad IV in 1638. Thenceforth it remained a part of the Ottoman Empire until after World War I. See E. Niewohner-Eberhard, "Machtpolitik. Aspekte des Osmanisch-Safawidischen Kampfes um Bagdad im 16/17 Jahrhundert," *Turcica*, VI, 103–27; and on the intellectual level her *Osmanische Polemik gegen die Safawiden im 16. Jahrhundert nach arabischen Handschriften.* On the equally prolonged struggle with the Uzbeks see, for instance, M. B. Dickson, *Shah Ṭahmasb and the Uzbeks (The Duel for Khurasan with 'Ubayd Khan, 930–946/1524–1540).* The production and consumption of wine is discussed *infra*, n. 58.

All along Christian Europe, especially the Papacy and Venice, were politically involved in the outcome of these conflicts, especially in view of the growing Turkish menace. But their participation expressed itself more in words than in deeds. See, for instance, G. Scarcia, "Venezia e la Persia tra Usun Ḥasan e Ṭahmasp (1454–1572)," *Veltro*, CXLI/2, pp. 61–76; C. Pérez-Bustamente, "Españoles, Persas y Turcos en los comienzos del siglo XVII," *Boletín* of the Academía de Historia, CLXVI, 77–89, esp. pp. 80 f.; and, more generally, B. von Palombini's well-documented study, *Bündiswerben abendländischer Mächte um Persien 1453–1600.* Of considerable interest also is the somewhat older study by K. Bayani, *Les Relations de l'Iran avec l'Europe Occidentale à l'époque Safavide (Portugal, Espagne, Angleterre, Hollande et France; avec documents inédits).*

24. On the dismal conditions in Persia before the accession of 'Abbas I, see H. R. Roemer's "Problèmes de l'histoire safavide avant la stabilisation de la dynastie sous Šāh 'Abbās," *Actes* of the Ve Congrès International d'Arabisants et de l'Islamisants, 1970, pp. 399–409; idem, *Der Niedergang Irans nach dem Tode Isma'ils des Grausamen, 1557–1581.* This period of disarray was followed by "The Consolidation of the Safawid Power in Persia" as described by R. M. Savory in *Der Islam*, XLI, 71–94; and in his additional "Notes on the Safawid State," *IS*, I, 96–103. Of the vast literature on 'Abbas I, we need but mention the somewhat older but relatively the best biography by L. L. Bellan, *Chah Abbas I, sa vie, son histoire;* and such additional data as were translated into German by H. Müller in his Mainz dissertation, *Shah Abbas der Grosse in der Chronik des Qāzī Aḥmad.* 'Abbas' favorable attitude toward England, as expressed in the passage quoted in the text from S. Purchas, *His Pilgrimages*, III, 219, is analyzed, among others, by R. W. Ferrier in "An English View of Persian Trade in 1618. Reports from the Merchants Edward Pettras and Thomas Barker," *JESHO*, XIX, 182–214; in his "The European Diplomacy of Shah 'Abbas I and the First Persian Embassy to England," *Iran*, XI, 75–92; and A. C. Wood, *A History of the Levant Company*, 2d impression, pp. 115 ff. See also *infra*, n. 60.

25. See Pope Clement VIII's suggestion for an alliance in his letter to the shah of 1592, reproduced in the *Chronicle of the Carmelites in Persia and the Papal Mission in the Seventeenth and Eighteenth Centuries*, I, 68 f. (English), II, 1273 f. (Latin); A. C. Wood, *A History of the Levant Company*, pp. 48 f., 115 ff.; J. J. Chardin, *Voyages*, ed. by L. Langlès. As we shall see, this French merchant-traveler has also offered some pertinent observations on the Jews of Persia. On Sir Anthony Sherley, whom Franz Babinger considered a "Hochstappler" (confidence man) and his brother Robert, see F. Babinger, *Sherleiana I. Sir Anthony Sherleys persische Botschaftsreise (1599–1601); II, Sir Anthony Sherleys marokkanische Sendung (1605–06).* Reprinted from *MSOS*, XXXV/II;

idem, "Sir Anthony Sherley, ein politischer Hochstapler um 1600," *Forschungen und Fortschritte,* IX/2, pp. 155–57; and the literature cited *infra,* n. 60.

26. K. M. Röhrborn, *Provinzen und Zentralgewalt Persiens im 16. und 17. Jahrhundert* showing the great administrative diversity existing among the provincial systems. This diversity continued despite the modicum of the shahs' successful efforts to run the country's affairs in a centralized fashion. They were aided by such works as the anonymous handbook for administration published by V. Minorsky in his much-quoted ed. and trans. of *Tadhkirat al-Mulūk: a Manual of Safavid Administration.* An example of what the neighboring rich Turkish archives may offer in elucidating the contemporary conditions in Iran is presented in B. Lewis's "Registers on Iran and Adharbayjan in the Ottoman *Defter-i-Khaqani,*" *Mélanges d'Orientalisme offerts à Henri Massé,* pp. 259–63 (includes statements on fiscal rules and documents of *waqfs* and fiefs). See also P. Schwarz, *Iran im Mittelalter nach den arabischen Geographen* (with references to Jews, pp. 720, 859). Because of the absolutist traditions of the Mongolian and pre-Mongolian rulers, it was not at all surprising that R. M. Savory found clear evidence for efforts by the Safavid rulers to conduct a totalitarian governmental system. See his "Some Reflections on Totalitarian Tendencies in the Ṣafavid State," *Der Islam,* LIII, 226–41, with references to Minorksy's ed. of *Tadhkirat.* But Savory himself, in another context, had pointed out that Persian absolutism was theoretically justified by the identification of every shah as being a Shadow of God whose orders had to be obeyed, like divine commandments, even if they appeared unjust. Yet his rule still left a considerable measure of personal freedom to the subjects. See his essays, cited *supra,* n. 24. See also A. K. S. Lambton, "Quis custodiet custodes. Some Reflections on the Persian Theory of Government," *Studia Islamica,* VI, 125–46, esp. p. 129. Of some interest also is the analysis by W. Hinz, "Die Persische Geheimkanzlei im Mittelalter," *Westöstliche Abhandlungen. Festschrift Rudolf Tschudi, überreicht,* pp. 342–54. Regrettably, little is to be found in these works having direct bearing on the position of the Jews and other minorities.

27. See J. P. Perry, "Forced Migrations in Iran during the Seventeenth and Eighteenth Centuries," *IS,* VIII, 199–215, mentioning a total of 141 such forced relocations which affected "at least 100,000 families"; those from Julfa beginning as early as 1602, pp. 203, 206 ff.

28. See K. Bayani, *Les Relations de l'Iran avec l'Europe Occidentale;* H. R. Roemer, "Die Safawiden. Ein orientalischer Bundesgenosse des Abendlandes im Türkenkampf," *Der Islam,* XL, 35–65; and B. Palombini's aforementioned *Bündniswerben.* See also, more generally, R. K. Ramazani, *The Foreign Policy of Iran: a Developing Nation in World Affairs, 1500–1941.*
Of the very large number of travelogues pertaining to Safavid Persia, we need mention here only the following additional works: T. Herbert, *Some Years Travels to Divers Parts of Africa and Asia the Great,* ed. by W. Foster, London, 1677 (esp. pp. 54, 60, 214); Adam Olearius, *Ausführliche Beschreibung der kundbaren Reyse nach Muscow und Persien,* Schleswig, 1663, also in French and English translations; Raphaël du Mans, originally Jacques Dutertre, *État de la Perse en 1660,* ed. with Notes and an Appendix by C. Shefer; Jean Baptiste Tavernier, *Les Six Voyages;* English trans., *Six Voyages through Turkey into Asia;* Pedro Teixeira, *The Travels;* M. D. Thévenot, *Suite du voyage;* and others. See also A. Gabriel, *Vergessene Persienreisende;* and the analyses by L. Lockhart, "Persia as Seen by the West," *The Legacy of Persia,* ed. by A. J. Arberry, pp. 318–58, esp. pp. 351 f.; S. Schuster-Walser, *Das Ṣafawidische Persien im Spiegel europäischer*

Reiseberichte (1502–1722). Untersuchungen zur Wirtschafts- und Handelspolitik. Very valuable, particularly through its rich documentation, also is *A Chronicle of the Carmelites in Persia.* Although unlike most other Muslim countries Safavid Persia often treated Jews differently than it did other non-Muslim minorities, much can be learned from the story of the Carmelite Order also with reference to the Jewish status. Many insights can also be obtained through the graphic presentations of Persian life preserved in European collections and analyzed in G. Houmayoun's *Iran in europäischen Bildzeugnissen vom Ausgang des Mittelalters bis ins 18. Jahrhundert* (diss. Cologne).

29. To the extensive historiographic literature concerning early modern Persia listed in the well-known works by Carl Brockelmann, Franz Rosenthal, and others, we might mention here the following recent publications: Ḥasan-i Rūmlū, *A Chronicle of the Early Safawīs: Being the Ahsanu't-tawarikh,* ed. and trans. into English by C. N. Seddon (with numerous omissions and condensations, but with a chronology of events in the years 900–984/1494–1575–76); E. Glassen (née Wendt), *Die Frühen Safawiden, nach Qāzi Ahmad Qumi* (Diss. Freiburg); H. Müller, ed. and trans., *Die Chronik Ḥulāsat-Tawārīh i Qumi: der Abschnitt über Schah Abbas I.* See also J. R. Walsh, "The Historiography of Ottoman-Safawid Relations in the Sixteenth and Seventeenth Centuries" in B. Lewis and P. M. Holt, eds., *Historians of the Middle East,* pp. 197–211, esp. p. 200; W. Hinz, "Beiträge zur Geschichte der Safawiden," *MSOS,* 1933, pp. 99–100; idem, "Eine Neuentdeckte Quelle zur Geschichte Irans im 16. Jahrhunderts," *ZDMG,* LXXIX, 315–28 (an historical work by Qadhi Aḥmad).

We must not be oblivious, however, of the shortcomings of the Persian historiography of the period. As stressed by a modern historian, Fereydoun Adamiyat, from the fourteenth to the nineteenth century history had declined along with other branches of learning; "the events were merely chronicled without analyzing either their causes or their effects." See his "Problems in Iranian Historiography," trans. from the Persian by T. M. Ricks, *IS,* IV, 132–56, esp. pp. 135 f. On Adiabene, see *supra,* Vol. I, p. 168.

The major Jewish sources on the crucial developments under 'Abbas I and 'Abbas II are recited in poetic form (which as usual lacks precision in many details) by Babai b. Luṭf in his *Kitab-i-Anusi* (The Book of Forced Conversion: The Story of the Events in which the Persian Jews were Forced to Become Muslims), published by W. Bacher in a summarized French prose translation in his *Les Juifs de Perse au XVIIe et au XVIIIe siècles d'après les chroniques poétiques de Babaï b. Loutf et de Babaï b. Farhad,* reprinted from *REJ,* LI, 121–36, 265–79; LII, 77–97, 234–71; LIII, 85–110. See also the excerpts from the original text with a different French trans., published earlier by M. Seligsohn in his "Quartre poésies judéo-persanes sur les persécutions des Juifs d'Ispahan," *ibid.,* XLIV, 87–103, 244–59 (corresponding to Bacher's summary in *Les Juifs,* xxii–xxv, pp. 34–38); and by Bacher himself in his "Un Épisode de l'histoire des Juifs de Perse," *ibid.,* XLVII, 262–82; "Élegie d'un poète judéo-persan contemporain de la persécutions de Schah Abbas II," *ibid.,* XLVIII, 94–105. Other excerpts have more recently been reproduced by E. Spicehandler in "The Persecution of the Jews of Isfahan under Shah Abbas II (1642–66)," *HUCA,* XLVI, 331–56, esp. pp. 346 ff. (without translation); and by V. B. Moreen in *An Introductory Study of the* Kitab-i Anusi *by Babai ibn Lutf* (Harvard diss., typescript), pp. 255 ff., Apps. A and F (transcripts and English trans.) and C, D, E, and G (English trans. only) with notes thereon. Professor Moreen has graciously let me consult her manuscript. But it came at a time when the present chapter had long been completed and I could refer here to only a few of her data and findings. It is to be hoped, however, that both her study and Professor Spicehandler's complete critical edition of Babai b. Luṭf's text, announced in his *HUCA* article in 1975, will before long appear in print. See also the additional data in V. B. Moreen's most recent essays, "The Persecution of Iranian Jews during the Reign of Shah 'Abbas II (1642–1666)," *HUCA*, LII, 275–309; "The Downfall of Muḥammad ['Alī] Beg, Grand Vizier of Shah 'Abbas II (Reigned 1642–1666)," *JQR*, LXII, 81–99.

Much of the information included in these tracts, containing a mixture of legends and facts, rumors and personal observations, is largely confirmed by a contemporary Armenian chronicler, Arakel (more correctly, Arakhial) of Tabriz (d. 1686), who described the events which led to the expulsion of the Armenians from Isfahan, followed by the second persecution of Jews by 'Abbas II up to March 10, 1660, about a year before it was terminated. His work, originally published in Armenian in Amsterdam in 1669, was translated into French by M. I. Brosset under the title, *Livre d'Histoire*, and published in the *Collection des Historiens Arméniens* (St. Petersburg), I, 269–618, esp. Chaps. xxxiii (pp. 482–89 on the Armenians), and xxxiv (pp. 489–96 on the Jews). This valuable material escaped Bacher's attention, but was used by later scholars in its Russian translation from the Amrmenian by X. Kutchuk-Ionnesov entitled "An Armenian Chronicle of the Jews in Persia in the Seventeenth Century and on the Messiah Shabbetai Zevi" (Russian), *Evreiskaya Starina*, X, 60–86, esp. pp. 62–76, and in another French translation prepared by Abraham Galanté from a Turkish rendition by one of his friends which he published under the title, "Un Chapitre inédit de l'histoire juive," in the Istanbul Jewish periodical, *Haménora*, May–June, 1935 (also available in a reprint).

30. See V. B. Moreen, "The Status of Religious Minorities in Safavid Iran between 1617 and 1661," *Journal of Near Eastern Studies*, XL, 119–34 (Princeton Conference Paper); V. Gregorian, "Minorities of Isfahan: the Minority Community of Isfahan, 1587–1722," *IS*, VII, 652–80; and, more generally, T. Nagel, *Studien zum Minderheitenproblem in Iran*, II: *Rechtsleitung und Kalifat. Versuch über eine Grundfrage der islamischen Geschichte* (Bonner Orientalische Studien, n.s. XXVII/2). Though mainly concerned with developments under early Islam, this work sheds light also about the conditions in the following centuries. On the emergence of various sectarian subdivisions within the Shi'a, including the Persian Twelver brand, see D. Donaldson, *The Shi'ite Religion: a History of Islam in Persia and Irak*.

31. See K. Kévonian, "Marchands arméniens au XVIIe siècle. À propos d'un livre arménien publié à Amsterdam en 1699," *CMRS*, XVI, 199–244 (referring to the Armenian work, *The Treasury of Measures . . . Weights, and Coins of the Entire World* by Lukas Vanandec'i [of Vanand]), esp. pp. 210, 232 nn. 109–115; P. G. Forand, "Accounts of Western Travelers concerning the Role of Armenians and Georgians in the 16th Century Iran," *Muslim World*, XL, 264–76; and, on the general developments in Georgia, see W. E. D. Allen, *A History of the Georgian People from the Beginning down to the Russian Conquest in the 19th Century*. The specific changes in the Jewish status are described by Babai b. Luṭf in his *Kitab-i Anusi*, V, xii, in the summary trans. by W. Bacher in *Les Juifs de Perse au XVIIe et au XVIIIe siècle*, pp. 21 ff., 34; M. Seligsohn, "Quatre poésies judéo-persanes," *REJ*, XLIV, 87–103, 244–59; V. B. Moreen, *An Introductory Study of the Kitab-i Anusi*, pp. 151 ff., 194 ff. (MS). See also Pietro della Valle, *Viaggi . . . Lettere della Persia*, ed. by F. Gaeta and L. Lockhart (Il Nuovo Ramusio, VI); or in its French trans., *Voyages*, Paris, 1664 ed., III, 86 f.; and C. Gray, ed. and trans., *A Narrative of Italian Travels in Persia in the Fifteenth and Sixteenth Centuries*. Della Valle, whose *Viaggi* immediately won wide recognition, was frequently reprinted and before long was highly praised by no less an authority than Edward

Gibbon ("no traveller knew and described Persia as well as Pietro della Valle") may be considered an impartial witness. In general, his description betrays rather some dislike for Jews combined with an element of envy about their staunchness of belief and readiness to suffer martyrdom for it. See also P. O. Bretenholz, *Pietro della Valle (1586–1652). Studien zur Geschichte der Orientkenntnis und des Orientbildes im Abendland;* and W. Blunt, *Pietro's Pilgrimage: a Journey to India and Back at the Beginning of the Seventeenth Century.* It is noteworthy that, though admiringly describing the city of Farahabad, which often served as 'Abbas' winter residence, De la Valle makes no reference to the Jewish legend. See T. W. Juynboll's "Farahabad" in *EI,* 2d ed., p. 783.

32. See K. M. Röhrborn, *Provinzen und Zentralgewalt Persiens im 16. und 17. Jahrhundert,* pp. 93 f., 118 ff.; R. M. Savory's "Notes," cited *supra,* n. 24; and, on the impact of the national state on the Jewish minority in the Middle Ages and early modern times, see my "Nationalism and Intolerance," *Menorah Journal,* XVI, 405–415; XVII, 148–58; and *supra,* Vol. XI, Chap. L, esp. pp. 198 f., 383 n. 10. Röhrborn also contrasts this attitude toward Shi'ite "heretics" with the greater leniency of such shahs as 'Abbas II toward the popular majority of Christians and other non-Shi'ites in Georgia. In this province the central government had to be satisfied with a governor of the Shi'ite Twelver denomination. Frequently even some of the governors' relatives were not converted to the state religion. At times the governors favored Christian subjects and were suspected of secretly professing Christianity. See Röhrborn, pp. 93 f. See also W. Hinz's aforementioned (n. 21) *Irans Aufstieg zum Nationalstaat im fünfzehnten Jahrhundert;* and J. Aubin's "Le Chiisme et le nationalité persane," *Revue du monde musulman,* IV, 457–90.

33. See S. H. Longrigg, *Four Centuries of Modern Iraq,* pp. 51 ff., 57; Sieur de la Boullaye le Gowz, *Les Voyages et observations,* p. 325; Muḥammad al-Jazari, *Ta'rikh al-Iraq* (History of Iraq), IV, 180. The effects of the changes from the Turkish to Persian domination and vice versa on the Iraqi population, including the Jews, were momentous. The deep hatred between the Turkish Sunnis and the Safavid Shi'ites had been of long standing; it helps explain the extremely sanguinary battles during 'Abbas I's regime. As early as 1540, six years after Suleiman's conquest of Baghdad, the Iraqi Sunni jurist, Ḥusain b. 'Abdallah ash-Shirwani, wrote an anti-Persian tract, dedicated to the sultan. In it he vigorously argued that the Persians were to all intents and purposes "infidels" to the faith of Islam, against whom the Ottoman Empire was to fight an enduring "holy war." See E. Eberhard, *Osmanische Polemik gegen die Safawiden nach arabischen Handschriften,* pp. 54 ff., 170 ff. As often before, Jews thus found themselves in the unenviable position of having to take sides. In this case, their sympathies, overt or clandestine, doubtless were predominantly on the Ottoman side. This situation has frequently been described in the literature; for example, in E. Niewohner-Eberhard's "Machtpolitik," *Turcica,* VI, 103–127. It appears that even when Baghdad was under Persian domination, Iraqi Jewry was able to maintain its close contacts with its Turkish coreligionists, particularly with residents of Aleppo, through both commercial and intellectual exchanges. See A. Ben-Jacob, *Yehudei Babel,* pp. 84 ff.; R. Yom Ṭob Ṣahalon, *Teshubot le-qehilat 'Aana* (Responsa to the Community of 'Anah), ed. with an Intro. including a historical sketch of that West-Iranian Jewish community, allegedly identical with the well-known Nehardea of ancient times, by M. Benayahu (reprinted from *Qobeṣ 'al Yad,* V), esp. Nos. 1, 4, 6–7, 10–11. On Nehardea, see A. Neubauer, *Géographie de Talmud,* pp. 350 ff.

34. See Arakel's *Livre d'Histoire,* xxxiv, trans. by M. I. Brosset, p. 492; or A. Galanté's *Marranes Iraniens,* p. 11; Babai b. Luṭf, *Kitab,* quoted here in V. B. Moreen's

trans. in *An Introductory Study*, pp. 30 f.; L. Arnold, "Le Credo de Shi'isme duodeci-man," *Travaux et jours*, XVII, 35–54; *A Chronicle of the Carmelites in Persia*, I, 350; *supra*, Vol. XVII, pp. 233 ff., 404 f. nn. 5–7. On Shah Ṣafi's generally stagnating regime, which sharply contrasted with his father's four decades of dynamic rule, see G. Ret-telbach's *Hulasat as-Siyar. Der Iran unter Schah Safi (1629–1642) nach der Chronik des Muḥammad Ma'sum b. Hulaǧagi Isfahani* (Beiträge zur Kenntnis Südosteuropas und des Nahen Orients, XXIX). Like the previously available sources, this work mentions no formal abrogation of 'Abbas I's anti-Jewish decrees. Fortunately, the two persecutions did not last long enough for us to judge whether the children of such "New Muslims" were fully brought up in the Jewish faith or had remained partially or totally assimi-lated to the Persian environment for the rest of their lives. It stands to reason that the strong cohesiveness of the Persian Jewish family, which was still observed by visi-tors in the nineteenth and twentieth centuries, prevented in most cases such decisive breaks between parents and children. On the Muslim doctrine of Taqiyya (Conceal-ment), see F. Mejer's "Anlass und Anwendungsbereich der Taqiyya," *Der Islam*, LXVII, 246–80; and *supra*, Vol. XVII.

35. Arakel in M. I. Brosset's trans., pp. 489–92, 494 f.; in A. Galanté's rendition, pp. 10 ff., 15 f.; Jean Chardin, *Voyages en Perse*, ed. by Langlès, VI, 134 f., 315 f.; and, more generally, P. Luft, *Iran unter Abbas II (1642–1666)*. On the city of Kashan, which was not only the birthplace and residence of Babai b. Luṭf, but also played a promi-nent role in 'Abbas I and II's anti-Jewish persecutions, see V. F. Costello's *Kashan: a City and Region of Iran*, ed. by J. C. Dewdney. There is some conflict between the list of Jewish communities affected by the persecution as given by Arakel and those men-tioned more fully by Babai b. Luṭf. See Bacher, *Les Juifs de Perse*, pp. 38 ff., 43–47, 62, 64, 66 f. Regrettably, no detailed information has come from other sources in order for us fully to judge whose assertions are correct. Moreover, it must be borne in mind that Arakel finished his recital on March 10, 1660, while Babai completed his poetic narrative considerably later and may have had fuller information.

36. See Arakel, *Livre d'Histoire*, in M. I. Brosset's trans. pp. 494 f.; in A. Galanté's trans. pp. 13 f.; J. Chardin, *Voyages en Perse*, VI, 135; J. de Thévenot, *Voyages . . . en Europe, Asie et Afrique*, Vol. IV, Chap. XIV. It is small wonder that the sudden cessa-tion of the anti-Jewish persecution by 'Abbas II was soon attributed, through some-one's fertile imagination, to another miraculous intervention by the ghost of Patriarch Jacob's legendary granddaughter, Seraḥ bat Asher; see *infra*, n. 44. On somewhat similar, though unrelated, developments in Bukhara, see R. Löwenthal, "The Judeo-Muslim Marranos in Bukhara," *Central-Asian Collectanea*, I. It may be noted in this connection that, in contrast to the Jews, most forced converts among the Armenians during the persecution of 1620–21 "embraced Islam with sincerity," at least according to Eskandar Beg Monshi's assertion in his contemporary *History of Shah Abbas the Great*, English trans. by R. M. Savory, II, 1181 f.

37. The developments in Kashan in the 1720s are described in considerable detail by Babai b. Farhad in his continuation of Babai b. Luṭf's chronicle which W. Bacher published in the same summary in French prose under a new title, *Livre des événements de Kachan relativement à la seconde persécution religieuse*, as an Appendix to Babai b. Luṭf's work in *REJ*, LIII, 85–108; reprinted in his *Les Juifs de Perse*, pp. 90–113. However, no critical edition of the Judeo-Persian original is as yet available. On the Shabbetian impact see Chardin, *Voyages*, VI, 135; A. Freimann, *Inyenei Shabbetai Zevi* (Matters Pertaining to S. Z.), p. 143 n. 51; M. Benayahu, "Sabbatian Liturgical Com-

positions and Other Documents from a Persian MS" (Hebrew), *Sefunot*, III–IV, 7–38; and G. Scholem's comprehensive work, *Sabbatai Sevi: The Mystical Messiah, 1626–1676*, pp. 637 ff., 752 f.

This connection with the Shabbetian movement made a tremendous impression in the Christian world (see, for example, D. C. Waugh's recent analysis of the "News of the False Messiah: Reports on Shabbetai Zevi in Ukraine and Muscovy," *JSS*, XLI, 301–322) which in 1683 induced Robert Burton (pseud. for Nathaniel Crouch) to fantasize about a further persecution of Persian Jews in 1663–66. He wrote about "the fatal and final Extirpation and Destruction of the *Jews* out of the Empire of Persia begun in 1663 and continuing till 1666." This otherwise unsubstantiated account, published in Burton's *Two Journeys to Jerusalem*, London, 1683, misled Jacques Basnage in his noteworthy *Histoire des Juifs, depuis Jesus-Christ jusqu'à present. Pour servir de continuation a l'Histoire de Joseph*, new ed. rev., IX, 754 ff., 758 ff., to include the story of that persecution as a matter of fact. Another fabricated report, included in the *Historia de tribus hujus seculi famosis impostoribus*, London, 1669, similarly misguided the German author, Johann Jakob Schudt, to devote to this alleged persecution several pages in his widely quoted *Jüdische Merckwürdigkeiten*, I, 26–32. See W. Bacher's *Les Juifs de Perse*, pp. 110 f.; and E. Spicehandler's "The Persecution," *HUCA*, XLVI, 334 f. Similarly, the connection with the Shabbetian movement, if any, of Babai b. Luṭf's poem in Judeo-Persian exalting the prophet Elijah, a figure playing a great role in many medieval Jewish messianic speculations, cannot be substantiated until the date of that poem's composition is fully ascertained. See J. P. Asmussen, "Babai b. Lutf's jüdisch-persisches Elija-Lied," *Festschrift Wilhelm Eiler. Ein Denkmal der internationalen Forschung*, pp. 131–35, reproducing the Hebrew text in facsimile and in a Latin translation, but without a German translation.

38. Gaspar Corrêa, *Lendas da India* (Legends from India), II, 419 f.; and, more generally, J. Aubin, "Les Princes d'Ormuz du XIIIe au XVe siècle," *JA*, CCXLI, 77–137 (with two extensive genealogical tables); and idem, "Le Royaume d'Ormuz au début du XVIe siècle," *Mare Luso-Indicum*, II, 75–179. See also the more popular presentation by A. T. Wilson, *The Persian Gulf, an Historical Sketch from the Earliest Times to the Beginning of the 20th Century;* and *infra*, n. 40. Aubin's drastic conclusion, however, that Ormuz was born in 1300 and died in 1622 ("Royaume," p. 78) is somewhat overstated.

39. Saadiah Gaon, *K. al-Amanat w'al-I'tiqadat* (Beliefs and Opinions), Intro., vi, ed. by S. Landauer, p. 21; in the Hebrew translation by Yehudah ibn Tibbon, ed. by D. Slucki, p. 48; and in the English translation by S. Rosenblatt, p. 26; cited *supra*, Vol. III, pp. 114, 284 n. 49; Hai Gaon's responsum, cited by J. Mann from a British Museum MS in "The Responsa of the Babylonian Geonim as a Source of Jewish History," *JQR*, VII, 457–90; VIII–XI, esp. VII, 471 f. n. 15; Zechariah b. Saadiah adh-Dhahri (or az-Zahiri), *Sefer ha-Musar* (Book of Moral Conduct), ed. by Y. Ratzaby, esp. pp. 28, 90, 145. On the riches amassed by Isaac (Ishaq) in India, see Buzurg ibn Shariyar's narrative in his *Kitab 'Ajā'ib al-Hind*, ed. by P. A. van der Lith, with a French trans. by L. M. David, and in the English trans. by P. Quennel entitled *The Book of the Marvels of India*.

The story of the Jews of Ormuz under Portuguese domination was described *supra*, Vol. XV, pp. 357 ff., 543 ff. and need not be repeated here. However, a few additional details have come to light through the publication of additional volumes of J. Wicki, *Documenta Indica*. See also W. J. Fischel, "New Sources for the History of the Jewish Diaspora in Asia in the Sixteenth Century," *JQR*, XL, 379–99; and, more broadly, idem, "The Region of the Persian Gulf and the Jewish Settlements in Islamic Times," *Alexander Marx Jub. Vol.*, English sec., pp. 203–230; his well-documented survey of the Jewish settlements in the Persian Gulf in *Ha-Yehudim be-Hodu* (The Jews in India: Their Contribution to the Economic and Political Life), pp. 50–65; and his frequently quoted *Jews in the Economic and Political Life of Mediaeval Islam*, new ed. with an additional intro., "The Court Jew in the Islamic World."

40. See García de Silva y Figueroa, *Comentarios de la embajada* [ed. by M. Serrano y Sanz], II, 530; or in the condensed French trans. by A. de Wicqfort, *L'Ambassade*, p. 42; Ludovicus Frois' report to his Lisbon colleagues, dated Goa, December 1, 1560, as reproduced in J. Wicki's ed. of the *Documenta Indica*, IV (*MHSI*, LXXVIII), 721 ff. No. 94, esp. pp. 738 f.; *supra*, Vol. XV, pp. 364 ff., 545 ff. nn. 113 ff., esp. n. 117; the English dispatch of early 1625 reproduced in the London Public Record Office's *Calendar of State Papers*, Colonial Series, IV: East India, China and Japan, 1622–1624, ed. by W. N. Sainsbury, pp. 60 ff. No. 143 end, 286 ff. No. 462. See also *ibid.*, pp. 441 ff. No. 677; and *Calendar . . . , VI: 1625–29*, pp. 2 ff. No. 2; "Bandar-Abbas," *EI*, 2d ed., *s.v.* The exaggeration inherent in the English agents' sweeping statements about Ormuz' destruction is somewhat controverted by another dispatch reproduced in *Calendar . . . 1625–1629*, pp. 60 ff. No. 121. Written on April 27, 1625 by a ship captain who briefly visited the town, it no longer stressed the wholesale devastation wrought three years earlier. Similarly tempered is the description by W. Foster in *The English Factories in India*, p. 85. See also other sources cited by Aubin in "Le Royaume," pp. 82 ff. On the grand vizier's order to convert the Jews of Shiraz, Lar, and Bandar, see the report by Babai b. Luṭf summarized in W. Bacher's *Les Juifs de Perse*, pp. xxxvi–xxxvii, 46 ff.; and *supra*, nn. 29 ff.

41. The Turkish mufti's irate exclamation is cited by P. Sykes in his *History of Persia*, pp. 178 f. with the sequel: "The Persian reply was still more insulting, but is too coarse to print." See also, more generally, A. Bausani, *The Persians*, p. 148.

42. See J. A. Boyle, "Dynastic and Political History of the Il-Khans," *CHI*, V, 353; Babai b. Luṭf, *Kitab-i Anusi*, xii in W. Bacher's rendition, *Les Juifs de Perse*, pp. 25 f.; G. Scholem, *Bibliographia kabbalistica; . . . Mit einem Anhang Bibliographie des Zohar und seiner Kommentare*; idem, *Einige kabbalistische Handschriften im Britischen Museum*, prepublished reprint from the *Soncino Blätter*, IV. It may be noted that, since from time to time there were among the Shi'ite mullahs scholars interested in the Hebrew Bible (they sometimes even consulted Jewish compeers), the ecclesiastical officials did not willingly collaborate in these anti-Jewish measures. At least one of them, Sheikh Baha ad-Din of Isfahan, strongly advised the shah against the forcible conversion of Jews. See Bacher, pp. 26 f.; and, more generally, E. N. Adler's older description of his 1896–97 journeys to Teheran, Bukhara, and Samarkand and a detailed review of the Hebrew manuscripts acquired on those occasions in his "Ginze Paras u-Madai (The Treasures of Persia and Media; The Persian Jews: Their Books and Their Ritual)," *JQR*, X, 584–625 (also reprint); W. J. Fischel, "The Bible in Persian Translation: a Contribution to the History of Bible Translation in Persia and India," *Harvard Theological Review*, XLV, 3–45; and idem, "The History of the Persian Jews during the Safavid Dynasty" (Hebrew), *Zion*, II, 282.

The last quarter century has witnessed a considerable revival of scholarly interest in the intellectual heritage of Persian Jewry. In addition to some data supplied in our earlier notes (1, 5, 37) suffice it to mention here several major publications by such specialists as Jes Peter Asmussen, B. Blieske, Bodil Hjerbild Carlsen, Gilbert Lazard,

Ernest Mainz, Amnon Netzer, and Herbert H. Paper. See especially Asmussens's "Judeo-Persica, I–IV," *Acta Orientalia*, XXVIII, 245–63; XXIX, 40–60, 247–51; XXX, 15–24; his *Jewish Persian Texts, Introduction, Selection and Glossary;* and his *Studies in Judeo-Persian Literature;* Blieske's *Sahin-e Sirazis Ardašir Buch;* Brinner's English trans. of Nissim b. Jacob ibn Shahin's *An Elegant Composition Concerning Relief after Adversity;* Carlsen's *Jonas in Judeo-Persian (Acta Iranica,* 3d ser. Textes et Mémoires, V [*Acta Iranica,* 12]); Lazard's succinct "Remarques sur le style des anciennes traductions persanes de Coran et de la Bible," *BEO,* XXX, 45–49; idem, "La Dialectologie du Judéopersan," *Studies in Bibliography and Folklore,* VIII, nos. 2–4, pp. 77–98; and other studies included in that special Spring issue, ed. by E. Spicehandler; Mainz's "Les Lamentations en Judéo-Persan," *Studia Iranica,* II, 193–202; idem, "L'Ecclesiaste en judéopersan," *ibid.,* III, 209–218; idem, "Vocabulaire judéo-persan," *Studia Iranica,* VI, 75–95; Netzer's "Danial-Name: an Exposition of Judeo-Persian," in *Islam and Its Cultural Divergence. In Honor of Gustave von Grunebaum,* ed. by G. L. Tikku, pp. 145–64 (based on a British Museum MS); and his comp. of *An Anthology of the Persian Poetry of the Jews;* Paper's "Judeo-Persian Bible Translations: Some Sample Texts," *Studies in Bibliography and Booklore,* VIII, 99–114; and his *A Judeo-Persian Pentateuch: the Text of the Oldest Judeo-Persian Pentateuch Translation, British Museum MS Or. 5446.*

Of interest also is M. Nehmad's *Ha-Glimah ha-hadashah shel Mullah Abraham* (The New Garment of M. A.: Five Folktales from Jewish Persian Tradition), ed. with additional notes by O. Schnitzler. The field of Persian-Jewish epigraphy has likewise been enriched by G. Gnoli's *Le Iscrizioni giudeo-persiche del Gur (Afghanistan);* and E. L. Rapp's *Die Jüdisch-persisch-hebräischen Inschriften aus Afghanistan,* Münchner Studien zur Sprachwissenschaft, 3d ser. Q.

43. See E. Eberhard, *Osmanische Polemik gegen die Safawiden,* pp. 101 ff., 112; H. Massé, "Aspects du pèlerinage à la Mecque dans la poèsie persane," *Mélanges Franz Cumont (Annuaire* of the Institut de Philosophie . . . Orientale, XX), 859–65; Joshua 24:32; P. Ponafidine, *Life in the Moslem East,* trans. from the Russian by (his widow) E. C. Ponafidine, esp. pp. 47 ff. To be sure, these residua of the ancient *weli* worship had occasionally *been attacked by medieval Jewish rationalists, including the tenth-century Karaite, Sahl b. Masliah. But the masses generally paid no heed to these strictures. See *supra,* Vols. III, pp. 137 f., 297 nn. 19–20; V, pp. 37, 308 n. 43; VII, pp. 76, 251 n. 17. It may be noted that in the course of generations some of the centers of Jewish pilgrimages suffered serious damage from natural and man-made causes. Impoverished Persian Jewry, unable to defray the mounting costs of repair, from time to time appealed to its coreligionists in other countries for subventions. The West-Asian and European responses and the letters of recommendation for the Persian messengers, written by some Jewish leaders from Baghdad and Aleppo to Amsterdam, were, as a rule, quite helpful. One such letter of 1859, signed by three rabbis and fifteen lay leaders of the Jewish community of Aleppo, soliciting generous gifts for the repair of the tombs, includes the following pathetic comparison: "He who sees the Gentile graves, located near the Jewish tombs, in their glory cannot but shed tears about the ruins of the aforementioned places of rest of our righteous great of the past." See the Hebrew text, reproduced from a contemporary booklet, published in Ancona, 1859, by D. S. Sassoon in his "The History of the Jews in Basra," *JQR,* XVII, esp. pp. 456 ff., 462 f.

44. See B. Spuler, *Die Mongolen in Persien,* p. 249, pointing out that the appropriation of Ezekiel's tomb by the Muslims took place with Rashid ad-Din's tacit approval. On the intriguing legends concerning Serah bat Asher, see E. E. Herzfeld, *Archaeolog-*

ical History of Iran, pp. 106 f. (rather peremptorily rejecting the presence of Jews in Isfahan and Hamadan in the pre-Achaemenid period); J. Horowitz, *Die Josephslegende,* pp. 125–32; and, more fully, L. Ginzberg, *The Legends of the Jews,* V, 39, 115 f., 181 f., 330; VI, 356 n. 293, 359 n. 321, 376 n. 438, and other passages listed in VII (Index), p. 424, *s.v.* Seraḥ. To the extensive bibliography here presented add, Y. Ben-Zvi, "A Hebrew Inscription in Persia Near the Cave of Seraḥ bat Asher" (Hebrew), in his *Meḥqarim u-meqorot* (Studies and Sources), pp. 289–91, referring to the legend concerning Seraḥ's miraculous intervention with 'Abbas I. See also W. J. Fischel, "Isfahan," *Joshua Starr Mem. Vol.,* pp. 117 ff.; and on the extent to which even the nineteenth-century rabbis of the area appreciated the care of the graves of saints, see D. S. Sassoon's reproduction of letters, the first of which has the incipit, *"Ve-haya ma'aseh ha-ṣedaqah shalom* (And the work of righteousness shall be peace; Isa. 32:17)," in his "The History of the Jews of Basra," *JQR,* XVII, 407 66, esp. pp. 459 ff. It refers to a messenger from the Jewish communal leaders in Baghdad to those of Aleppo engaged in raising funds for the proper maintenance of the tombs of Ezekiel, Ezra, and High Priest Joshua. This effort later involved also the rabbis of Jerusalem and even the Jewish leadership of Amsterdam and The Hague in the years 1855–59.

45. Barzaeus' letter to the Jesuit headquarters, dated Ormuz, December 1, 1549, is reproduced by J. Wicki in *Documenta Indica,* I, 606. On the events in Lar and the *fatwa* secured by Abu'l Ḥasan Lari, see Babai's *Kitab* in Bacher's summary, quoted *infra,* n. 46.

46. Jean Chardin, *Voyages,* VI, 317. 'Abbas I's order concerning the "badge of shame" and the role played therein by the Jewish convert, Abu'l Ḥasan Lari, are described in W. Bacher's "Un Épisode de l'histoire des Juifs de Perse," *REJ,* XLVII, 262–82; and idem, *Les Juifs de Perse,* pp. 55 ff. These badges were observed by European visitors, even those coming from countries where such badges were also worn. See especially J. Chardin, *Voyages,* VI, 317; and Jean de Thévenot, *Voyages en Europe, Asie et Afrique.* On the absence of both the badge and a Jewish quarter in Ormuz, see the report submitted by Gaspar Barzaeus to the Jesuit headquarters dated Ormuz, December 1, 1549 and reproduced by J. Wicki, in his ed. of *Documenta Indica,* I, 606.

47. See Sir John Malcolm, *The History of Persia from the Most Early Period to the Present Time,* esp. II, 49 f., and 479 f.; A. Bausani, *The Persians,* p. 150. On the dubious nature of Benjamin of Tudela's and Abraham ibn Ezra's figures relating to Persia, see *infra,* n. 50.

48. See 'Ala ad-Din Juwaini, *Ta'rikh-i Jahan-gusha,* ed. with an Intro., Notes and Indices from several old manuscripts by Mirza Muḥammad ibn 'Abdal-Wahhab-i Qazwini, I, 17 f.; in the English translation by A. J. Boyle, *The History of the World Conqueror,* I, 25; Rashid ad-Din, *Jami' aṭ-Ṭawarikh,* ed. by A. A. Alizade, pp. 447 f.; both quoted in Boyle's "Dynastic and Political History," *CHI,* V, 484, 491. On the 40,000 Shi'ite and Baghdadian victims, respectively, see P. Sykes, *History of Persia,* 3d ed., p. 162. The numerous internal difficulties facing the regime of Selim I, which forced him to adopt cruel measures against political and religious dissidents, are analyzed by I. Beldiceanu-Steinherr in "Le Règne de Selim Ier; Tournant dans la vie politique et religieuse de l'Empire Ottoman," *Turcica,* VI, 34–48; and A. Ben-Jacob, *Yehudei Babel,* p. 87.
Some of the cities affected by the mass slaughter revealed considerable recuperative power, however. Even Tabriz, which had suffered from the constant fluctuations in

the recurrent Turko-Persian wars, could ultimately reach a population of 550,000 inhabiting 15,000 houses and maintaining 15,000 shops, 250 mosques, and 300 cara-vansaries. See G. N. Curzon, *Persia and the Persian Question*, II, 250. The possible lesser losses of the peasant population did not prevent, however, so thorough a devastation of the countryside, too, that many villages completely disappeared after the Mongo-lian invasion. See the noteworthy comparison between the numbers recorded early in the thirteenth century by Yaqut and those mentioned about 1340 by Ḥamd Allah Mustaufi Qazwini. For example, the 660 villages in the Hamadan region were re-duced to only 212 in the following century. See the interesting table in J. A. Boyle in *CHI*, V, 497.

49. See R. A. McDaniel, "Economic Change and Economic Resiliency in Nineteenth Century Persia," *IS*, IV, 36–49, esp. pp. 40 f.; G. N. Curzon, *Persia*, I, 262, 518; R. W. Bulliet, *The Patricians of Nishapur*; idem, "Medieval Nishapur: a Topography and De-mographic Reconstruction," *Studia Iranica*, V, 67–89; Ḥamd Allah Mustaufi Qazwini, *Nuzhat al-qulub* (a geographical work), in part trans. by G. Le Strange in his *Description of the Province of Qais*, I, 34; also cited by Boyle in *CHI*, V, 484 f.; C. Issawi, ed., *The Economic History of Iran, 1800–1914*. Needless to say, the estimate of 40,000,000 for Persia's total population in the 1670s, mentioned by the otherwise very restrained Jean Chardin, is much too high.

While we do not have any accurate figures, and even the few attempts to come to grips with the size of the surviving population after 1270 are purely conjectural, one must be grateful to John Masson Smith's daring attempt to ascertain some approxi-mations of the population which survived the Hulagu conquests. By using a new method of deriving population figures from the recorded or postulated number of Mongolian soldiers, Smith came to the conclusion that, in an area covering approxi-mately half of the Persian territories, an original population of 2,500,000 was reduced by the Mongolian invasion by 90 percent, that is to a mere 250,000 persons. See his "Mongol Manpower and Persian Population," *JESHO*, XVIII, 271–99. To be sure, Smith's argumentation has some flaws, on which we need not expatiate here, but one may agree with him that, by the latter part of the thirteenth century, the population, reinforced by Turkish and Mongolian settlers, had staged a marvelous recovery.

50. See Benjamin of Tudela's *Itinerary*, ed. by M. N. Adler, esp. pp. 48, 51, 53 ff. (Hebrew), 51, 56 ff. (English). The contrast in the general accuracy of Benjamin's figures in areas he had first visited and the obvious exaggerations during his journey further into Central Asia, has long been recognized. See, for instance, Adler's Notes to his edition; and, more generally, *supra*, Vols. III, pp. 283 f. n. 48; VI, pp. 222 ff., 435 f. nn. 88–90. Some of the *Itinerary*'s exaggerations, moreover, may be attributed to its later copyists. For example, the 80,000 Jews of Ghazni appear in some versions (for instance, in the manuscript underlying the text of the *Itinerary*, previously ed. by A. Asher) as 8,000, which may well have been a plausible approximation.

51. See *A Chronicle of the Carmelites in Persia*, I, 364 f., II, 1040 f.; Muḥammad Ṭahir Waḥid, *'Abbas nama* (A History of 'Abbas II), ed. by I. Dehgan, in the passage exten-sively reproduced by V. B. Moreen in both Arabic and English trans. in her *An Intro-ductory Study* (MS), pp. 77 ff.; Jean Chardin, *Voyages*, VIII, 255 f.; Pedro Teixeira, *Travels*, ed. by W. F. Sinclair and D. Ferguson, p. 252; and *supra*, n. 39. Remarkably, Chardin's general accuracy did not extend to his aforementioned estimate of a total of 40,000,000 population in all of Persia. This contention can only be explained by his being overwhelmed by the magnitude and diversity of the country's area. Al-

though he spent eighteen months in 1667–68 and again four years in 1672–77 in Persia, he seems to have traveled only short distances from the capital. Moreover, as a professional jeweler he came to Persia principally on business and we are grateful to him for spending a disproportionate amount of time on minutely describing all quarters in Isfahan and on furnishing us a great many other illuminating details. See esp. his *Voyages*, Amsterdam, 1745 ed., III, 426 ff.; and, on his role within the array of "European Visitors to the Safavid Court," R. Stevens's pertinent essay in *IS*, VII (*Proceedings* of the Harvard Colloquium 21–24 January 1974), 421–57, esp. pp. 425 f.

With respect to the apparently small number of Sephardic Jews and repentant New Christians who emigrated to the Persian area or further East, one may note the opposition of the Jesuits to the immigration of "white Jews" into the Portuguese colonies including Ormuz. Even before the establishment of the Inquisition in Goa in 1560, this rejection was supported by the Jesuit leaders in Europe. No lesser a personality than Jacobus Laynez, Loyola's successor as the prior general of the entire Jesuit Order, though himself a New Christian, approved of that policy. At the end of 1562, in the midst of his arduous labors at the Council of Trent at which he played a prominent role, Laynez informed the Jesuit leader Melchior Eames Barreto in Cochin that he had asked friends in Portugal to secure from the king an order prohibiting the immigration of *judíos blancos* from Turkey and Persia to Portugal's Indian possessions. See his letter, dated Trent, December 10, 1562, as reproduced by J. Wicki in his *Documenta Indica*, Vol. V (*MHSI* LXXXIII), pp. 652 ff. No. 93. See also *ibid.* (*MHSI*, XCIV), 646 ff., 709 ff.; and *supra*, Vols. XIV, pp. 14 f., 306 f. n. 13; XV, 364 ff., 547 nn. 116–17.

52. Rashid ad-Din's twenty children are known to us by their names mentioned in his *Mukatabat-i Rashidi* (Rashid's Correspondence), ed. by M. Shafi', pp. 220 ff. No. 36; *Sbornik letopisei* (A Collection of Letters), ed. by L. A. Khetegurov *et al.* Rashid ad-Din's aforementioned enormous personal wealth was also shown by the large legacy he left behind for a *waqf*. This foundation included the beautiful suburb near Tabriz called Rub'-i Rashidi. It accommodated some 30,000 houses, 24 caravansaries, 1,500 shops, numerous mills, workshops for weaving and papermaking, a mint, and several bath houses, gardens, and so forth. To increase the local industry Rashid brought in craftsmen from various towns, as when he once requested his son to send him 50 woolweavers from Antioch and Cilicia, and 20 from Cyprus. At the same time he successfully promoted learning by settling in the suburb 400 theologians and jurists and attracting to it 1,000 students. He also brought in some 50 of the most qualified doctors from Syria, Egypt, India, and China who worked in a hospital established by him. See these data collected from Rashid's correspondence by I. P. Petrushevsky in his "Rashid ad-Din's Feudal Household" (Russian), *Veprosi istorii*, 1951, no. 4, pp. 87–104; and his "Socio-Economic Condition of Iran under the Il-Khans" in *CHI*, V, 509 f., 513 f., 521 f. On the provisions for the *waqf*, see B. Fragner, "Zu einem Autograph des Mongolenwezirs Rasid ad-Din Fazlallah, der Stiftungsurkunde für das Tabrizer Gelehrtenviertel Rab'i Rasidi," *Festgabe deutscher Iranisten zum 2500 Jahrfeier Irans*, ed. by W. Eilers, pp. 35–46, esp. pp. 39 ff., 45.

53. See G. Le Strange, *The Lands of the Eastern Caliphate, Mesopotamia, Persia, and Central Asia from the Moslem Conquest to the Time of Timur*, pp. 284 f., citing Hamd Allah Mustaufi Qazwini's *Nuzhat al-qulub;* W. J. Fischel, "The Region of the Persian Gulf and the Jewish Settlements in Islamic Times," *Alexander Marx Jub. Vol.*, English section, pp. 203–230. On Hamd Allah who was a fairly trustworthy reporter of contemporary affairs, see E. G. Browne, *A History of Persian Literature under Tartar Dominion*

(*A.D. 1265–1502*), pp. 87 ff. The extraordinary fertility of some Persian nomadic tribes was noted especially by the anthropologist F. Barth in his *Nomads of South Persia: the Basseri Tribe of the Khausch Confederacy* (also in the *Bulletin* of the University of Oslo Universiteits Ethnografiske Museum, VI). Because of the nearly total absence of written records and the varying trustworthiness of many oral traditions, the general history of the various Persian nomadic tribes, and particularly also their developments during the medieval and early modern periods are but superficially known. See D. Ehmann's valiant efforts in his *Bahtiyaren—Persische Bergnomaden im Wandel der Zeiten*. According to Ehmann, as late as the 1960s 10 percent of Persia's population still lived the life of nomads (p. 3). See also, more generally, V. Minorsky's suggestive essay, "Geographical Factors in Persian Art," *BSOAS*, IX, 621–52, factors which basically applied also to other fields of endeavor.

54. See A. Ashraf, "Historical Obstacles to the Development of a Bourgeoisie in Iran," *IS*, II, 54–79, esp. p. 61; G. Le Strange, *The Lands of the Eastern Caliphate*, p. 203; L. Golomber, "Urban Patterns in Pre-Safavid Isfahan," *IS*, VII, 18–44, with R. Holod's comments thereon, *ibid.*, pp. 45–48, esp. pp. 20 f. and 24; and the two complementary essays by W. J. Fischel, "Yahudiyah: on the Beginning of the Jewish Settlement in Persia" (Hebrew), *Tarbiz*, VI, 523–36; and "Isfahān: the Story of a Jewish Community in Persia," *The Joshua Starr Mem. Vol.*, pp. 111–28, esp. p. 118. Incidentally, Isfahan was not the only one to be called the "Jewish city" in the area. According to Le Strange (p. 424), the flourishing town of Maimana on the Balkh road was originally likewise named Yahudiyah or Yahudan, or even Yahudan Kubra (the great Jewry), as it is designated by the geographer Yaqut. Its foundation was also attributed to the exiles from Jerusalem in the days of Nebukadrezzar. When it became a predominantly Muslim city, its inhabitants renamed it Maimana (the Auspicious City) as a good augury for the future.

As for Isfahan, Colomber's observations have been largely anticipated in Sir William Ouseley's valuable travelogue entitled *Travels in Various Countries of the East, More Particularly Persia*, esp. III, 24. Ouseley also refers to popular local exaggerations concerning the size of Isfahan's population; some residents equated their city with "half the world." Even the generally cautious Chardin reported an estimate of Isfahan's population as amounting to 1,100,000, although his own feeling lowered it to 600,000. Referring to early-nineteenth-century realities Ouseley more cautiously added: "I strongly doubt whether at this time [1811] 200,000 would be found resident in the city." See also the various other essays presented to the aforementioned Harvard Colloquium which were included in the bulky volume VII of *IS* specially devoted to Isfahan.

55. References to the number of Jews in the individual cities are quite rare. To be sure, for example, Don García de Silva y Figueroa (in his *Comentarios de la embajada* or in its French rendition by A. de Wicqfort, *L'Ambassade de . . . en Perse*, esp. pp. 41 f.) mentions that in 1617 he found in Ormuz 2,500–3,000 Jewish families. This seems an overstatement, since before the Ottoman attack on the city in 1551 the total population apparently embraced only about 12,000 families and it probably did not substantially increase after its recovery from that assault. De Silva y Figueroa could be more accurate when he spoke of neighboring Muscat as comprising only 15–20 Jewish families in its territory. This small number is easily explainable because of Muscat's extremely hot and dry climate. Apparently Ormuz' lack of fresh water and its population's limited consumption of rain water discouraged Jews and others much less than Muscat's drought. Other writers generally limit themselves to such inexact

statements as that there were "more Jews than Christians" in the province of Jibal, or that more Jews lived in Lar than in Shiraz without indicating their number. All such observations are of course of little help to a demographer. See the data collected by W. J. Fischel in his "The Region of the Persian Gulf," *Alexander Marx Jub. Vol.*, English section, pp. 214 ff.; and his other essays.

The difficulty is further compounded by the fact that these scattered references relate to different periods, and are not fully comparable. Nevertheless, a careful collection of all such data found in historical and geographic works by Persians and Arabs and in travelogues by Western visitors might supply somewhat more detailed and dependable data on the Persian-Jewish population under the Il-Khans and Safavids. In any case, even if its maximum after 1670 should have amounted to 50,000 in a total population of some 5,000,000, its dispersal over 30 communities of frequently diverse lifestyles and traditions would explain the relatively minor role played in Persian society by Jews, especially professing Jews, after Sa'd ad-Daula. See also L. Lockhart, *Famous Cities in Persia:* With a Foreword by Lord Cadman of Silverdale.

56. See H. M. Durand, *Nadir Shah;* J. Chardin, *Voyages*, VI, 133 f. On the abysmal situation of source material for Persia's economic history and the paucity of detailed investigations in this field, see the observations by B. Lewis, "Sources for the Economic History of the Middle East" in M. A. Cook, ed., *Studies in the Economic History of the Middle East*, pp. 78–92, esp. pp. 78 n. 1, 80 f., and 84; N. R. Keddie, "The Economic History of Iran, 1800–1914 and Its Political Impact: an Overview," *IS*, V, 58–78; idem, "An Assessment of American, British, and French Works since 1940 in Modern Iranian History," *ibid.*, VI, 152–65; and especially on the Il-Khan period, I. P. Petrushevsky, "The Socio-Economic Condition of Iran," *CHI*, V, 483–537. While Petrushevsky's main strength lies in the field of medieval Persian agriculture (see *infra*, n. 58) his analyses of other phases of the Il-Khan economy often are equally perceptive. Of considerable value also are studies dealing with the somewhat later periods, such as Keddie's studies in *IS*, V–VI; T. M. Ricks's, "Towards a Social and Economic History of Eighteenth Century Iran," *ibid.*, VI, 110–26; and particularly the collection of essays edited by C. Issawi in *The Economic History of Iran, 1800–1914.* That none of these authors have hardly anything significant to say about medieval and early modern Jewry's contributions to the economy of Persia is merely another illustration of the underlying reasons: the lack of documentary evidence.

57. See Muḥammad Abu ar-Rayham b. Aḥmad al-Biruni, *India*, ed. and trans. by E. Sachau, 2d ed., I, 206; F. Braudel, *La Méditerranée*, II, 484; and C. Issawi's succinct observations in his Introduction to his *Economic History of Iran.* Nor can we overlook the impact of Persia's wars, both in the West and East, and of its frequent domestic uprisings, with very few genuinely peaceful intervals, which characterized its history ever since the dissolution of the Great Caliphate.

58. Much information about the agricultural situation in Persia has been assembled particularly by A. K. S. Lambton, *Landlord and Peasant in Persia: a Study of Land Tenure and Land Revenue Administration* and I. P. Petrushevsky (or Petrushevskii), *Zemledelie i agarnyie otnosheniya v Irane XIII–XIV vekov* (Agriculture and Agrarian Developments in Iran in the Thirteenth–Fourteenth Centuries). Of considerable interest also are E. Ehlers, *Traditionelle und moderne Formen der Landwirtschaft in Iran* (pointing out that fundamental changes in Persian agriculture and its comparatively high ratio of pastoral lands converted into grain-producing fields did not come until the twentieth century, esp. in the 1930s and 1960s, p. 20); the twin essays by F. Nomani, "Notes on

the Economic Obligations of Peasants in Iran, 300–1600," *IS*, X, 62–83; and "Notes on the Origins and Development of the Extra-Economic Obligations of Peasants in Iran," *ibid.*, IX, 121–41; and C. Cahen's more general observations in his "Notes pour une histoire de l'agriculture dans les pays musulmans médiévaux," *JESHO*, XIV, 63–68 (with a succinct survey of the Muslim agronomic literature outside Spain).

We must also constantly bear in mind that the agricultural organization was under the control of semi-feudal lords, although the term feudalism, so readily bandied about in some of the scholarly literature on the subject, evokes too many European parallels which do not apply to Persia. Nor must we forget the large areas occupied by nomadic tribes, whose extensive exploitation of the land greatly lowered the average intensity of agricultural cultivation. See L. M. Helfgott, "Tribalism as a Socioeconomic Formation in Iranian History," *IS*, X, 36–61; J. Aubin, "Réseau pastoral et réseau caravanier. Les grand'routes du Khurassan à l'époque mongole," *Le Monde iranien et l'Islam* (Publication of the École Pratique des Hautes Études, VIe section), 1971, pp. 105–30. Nor must we overlook the role of the *waqfs* in the agricultural field. Because of the frequent confiscations of landed property, under the theory that all land belonged to the shah, the *waqfs* upheld a certain continuity of production by maintaining the management and actual cultivation of the property under the direction of the same families for several generations. On the other hand, they also reduced incentives for innovation and thus perpetuated backwardness of agricultural technology.

The minor role played by Jews in the entire agricultural system is well illustrated by the little knowledge we possess even on their role in the production of wine, on which see, for instance, I. P. Petrushevsky's "Wine Cultivation and Manufacture in Iran in the Thirteenth and Fourteenth Centuries" (Russian), *Vizantiyskii Vremennik*, XI. Certainly, there was no dearth of customers. According to Arakel (or his interpolator), "one encountered intoxicated persons on the streets everywhere." See his *Livre d'Histoire*, xxxviii, in M. I. Brosset's trans., p. 482. This spread of drunkenness in Persia made the Shi'ite country a ready target for Ottoman controversialists. See E. Eberhard, *Osmanische Polemik gegen die Safawiden im 16. Jahrhundert nach arabischen Handschriften*, pp. 75 f. Not that there were few Muslim transgressors of that old Islamic prohibition in the Ottoman Empire or other Muslim lands. See *supra*, Chap. LXXVIII. But seemingly the proportion of such "sinners" in Persia was well above the Islamic average. It is very likely, therefore, that quite a few Jews made a living from producing and selling wine and arrack also to Muslims. Even in the twentieth century, anthropologists like Erich Brauer noted that in the western parts of Afghanistan (formerly under Persian sovereignty), famed for the quality of their wines, the producers were mainly Jews, because the modern (1924) Afghan Criminal Law Code still forbade Muslims to make or sell wine. Of course, Jews were free to drink wine, not only for their ritual purposes, but, unlike their Kurdish coreligionists, the Afghan and Persian Jews rarely became heavy drinkers. See E. Brauer's "The Jews in Afghanistan: an Anthropological Report," *JSS*, IV, 121–38, esp. p. 126; idem, *Yehudei Qurdistan* (The Jews of Kurdistan: an Ethnological Study). See also, *supra*, n. 23.

59. H. L. Rabino di Borgomale, *Coins, Medals, and Seals of the Shahs of Iran (1500–1941)*, esp. pp. 10 ff. and 14 f.; Jean Chardin, *Voyages*, IV, 182 f. The diffusion of the currency is well illustrated by Rabino's Table 3, which, based upon the author's observation of coins available in various collections, lists some one hundred Persian localities which operated mints, though not all at the same time. Most of them were active under the leading shahs, Isma'il I, Ṭahmasp I, 'Abbas I, and again, under

Nadir. Astonishingly, the confusion in the currency did not lead to a repetition of the aforementioned Il-Khan experiment at producing paper currency along Chinese patterns. However, currency depreciation through the reduction of the silver content in the leading coins occurred from time to time. For example, Persia's sudden diminution of the silver content by 50 percent in 1585 speedily imitated that by the Ottoman Turks a year earlier, creating a monetary crisis in both countries. See F. Braudel, *La Méditerranée*, II, 477; Ö. L. Barkan, "The Price Revolution of the Sixteenth Century: a Turning Point in the Economic History of the Near East," *IJMES*, VI, 3–28, esp. pp. 9 f.; R. W. Olson, "The Sixteenth Century 'Price Revolution' and the Effect on the Ottoman–Safavid Relations," *Acta Orientalia*, XXXVII, 45–55, esp. pp. 54 f. On the "quasi-mercantilistic" policies of the Safavid shahs, see also A. Banani's "Reflections on the Social and Economic Structure of Safawid Persia at Its Zenith," *IS*, XI, 83–116.

60. See Anthony Jenkinson's *Journal* reproduced in *Early Voyages and Travels to Russia and Persia*, ed. by E. D. Morgan and C. H. Coote, works issued by The Hakluyt Society, LXXII–LXXIII, esp. I, 141 ff.; D. W. Davies, *Elizabethan Errant: The Strange Fortunes of Sir Thomas Sherley and His Three Sons, As well in the Dutch Wars as in Muscovy, Morocco, Persia, Spain, and the Indies*, pp. 74 ff., 114 ff., 166 ff., 225 ff. Despite the commiseration with the Sherley brothers prevailing in the large pertinent literature on them, a recent author has argued that the various mishaps to Robert's career were largely of his own making. See R. Steven, "Robert Sherley: the Unanswered Question," *Iran*, XVII, 115–25.

The story of the Anglo-Dutch rivalries in the seventeenth-century trade with Persia has been amply documented in the sources accumulated by the respective Companies. See esp. the vast documentation reproduced by F. C. Danvers and W. M. Foster, eds., *Letters Received by the East India Company from Its Servants in the East*, regrettably covering only the period from 1600 to 1619; H. Dunlop, *Bronnen tot de Geschiedenis der Oostindische Compagnie in Perzie, I: 1611–1638*. See also the comprehensive analyses offered by W. Foster in his *England's Quest of Eastern Trade;* R. Mukherjee, *The Rise and Fall of the East India Company: a Sociological Appraisal*, esp. pp. 101 ff. on the "English-Dutch Rivalry." Trade was high on the agenda of political missions such as those described by U. Vermeulen, "L' Ambassade néerlandaise de Jan Smit en Perse (1628–1630)," *Persica*, VII, 155–63; idem, "La Mission de Jan L [uykassem] van Hasselt comme agent de Shah de Perse à Provinces Unies (1629–1631)," *ibid.*, VIII, 133–43. See also A. C. Wood, *A History of the Levant Company*. The extreme paucity of references to Persian Jews in all these works is a clear testimony of the negligible role played by them as agents or interpreters for the foreign businessmen—a sharp contrast to the contemporary situation in the Ottoman Empire. Some such negative evidence may at times be more enlightening than a few sporadic references to minor Jewish participation in significant developments. See *supra*, Vol. XV, pp. 42 f., 397 f. n. 51; and H. I. Bloom, *The Economic Activities of the Jews of Amsterdam*, pp. 85 ff.

61. See N. R. Keddie, "The Economic History of Iran, 1800–1914, and Its Political Impact: an Overview," *IS*, V, 58–78, esp. p. 68; C. Cahen, "Considérations sur l'utilisation des ouvrages de droit musulman par l'historien," *Atti* of the Terzo Congresso di Studi Arabi e Islamici held in Ravello, September 1–8, Naples, 1967, pp. 239–47, esp. p. 244; *supra*, Chap. LXIV, n. 111; P. Sykes, *A History of Persia*, p. 183.

62. See J. B. Tavernier, *Voyages en Perse*, pp. 239, 259; Cornelius de Bruyn, *Travels into Muscovy, Persia, and Diverse Parts of the East*, II, 46; Babai b. Luṭf, *Kitab* in

W. Bacher's *Les Juifs de Perse;* and sparse other data assembled by W. J. Fischel, particularly in "The Region of the Persian Gulf," *Alexander Marx Jub. Vol.,* English section, pp. 222 f. To be sure, for the most part the production of silk was a branch of agriculture and was largely pursued by male and female workers in rural districts. But some cities like Shiraz, Lar and Herat were likewise distinguished by their production of that precious fiber. However, its output began declining in the sixteenth century. See M. Reut, "La Production de la soie à Hérat," *Studia Iranica,* VIII, 107–116 (from an unpublished Paris dissertation); J. L. Bacque-Grammont, "Notes sur la saisie des soies d'Iran en 1518," *Turcica,* VIII, 237–53; *supra,* n. 58; and *infra,* n. 64.

63. W. M. Fluor, "The Guilds in Iran: an Overview from the Earliest Beginnings till 1972," *ZDMG,* CXXV, 99–116. While we do not have comprehensive and detailed studies of the medieval and early modern Persian guilds similar to those published on the corresponding corporations in the Ottoman Empire, especially Egypt, much can be learned from the earlier guilds and their antecedents in Islam's classical age, as well as from their subsequent evolution in the eighteenth and nineteenth centuries. See C. Cahen, "Y-a-t'il des corporations professionelles dans le monde musulman classique?" in *The Islamic City,* ed. by A. H. Hourani and S. M. Stern, pp. 51–63, reprinted in his *Les Peuples Musulmans,* pp. 307–321; T. Fahd, "Les Corps de métiers au IV–Xe siècle à Bagdad d'après le Chapitre XII d'al-Qadiri fi-t-Ta'bir de Dinawari," *JESHO,* VIII, 186–212; and the study by the pioneer of investigations in this field, L. Massignon in "Les Corps de métiers et la cité islamique" [1920], reprinted in his *Opera minora,* I, 396–421. Of special interest also is M. Makri's ed. and trans. of "Un Traité persan relatif à la Corporation prolétaire de porteurs d'eau musulman," *Revue du monde musulman,* XLV, 131–56. Although composed in Lahore, India, perhaps as early as in the fourteenth century, this valuable record doubtless reflects also similar conditions in Persia. The occupation of water carriers, considered a lowly occupation in the West, was held in higher esteem in Muslim lands, especially those suffering from water shortages. There is little doubt that, at least in larger eastern communities, there also were some Jews who made a living furnishing water to the inhabitants of the Jewish street. But they were hardly numerous enough to form a Jewish guild of their own.

On the modern Persian guilds see the data assembled by N. A. Kuznetsova, *Materialy k kharakteristike remeslenogo v iranskom gorode XVIII-nachala XIX veku* (Materials for the Character of the Handicraft in the Iranian City of the Eighteenth and Early Nineteenth Centuries; with numerous flashbacks to the seventeenth century); or in the English excerpts therefrom in C. Issawi's ed. of *The Economic History of Iran, 1800–1914.* See also the important general reviews by B. Lewis, "The Islamic Guilds," *Economic History Review,* VIII, 20–37; and G. Baer, "Guilds in Middle Eastern History," in M. A. Cook, ed., *Studies in the Economic History of the Middle East,* pp. 11–30.

64. See J. Aubin, *Le Royaume d'Ormuz,* p. 162; Johann Andreas Eisenmenger, *Entdecktes Judenthum, oder Gründlicher und wahrhafter Bericht, welchergestalt die verstockte Juden die Hochheilige Dreyeinigkeit erschrecklicher Weise lästern und vorunehren etc. samt den Grosen Irrthümer der Jüdischen Religion und Theologie,* II, 1001. To be sure, this antisemitic classic contains many erroneous and even consciously libelous statements. The mention of an otherwise unknown vizier, Eliezer, reinforces the likelihood of the spuriousness of this report. Misleading anecdotes of this kind and numerous other inflammatory statements were, indeed, the reason why the imperial government held back the release of these volumes—after the effort of the Jewish communities to bribe the author with a gift of 4,000 guilders to withhold publication had failed—which

resulted in a long trial and delay in its distribution for about a dozen years. See G. Wolf, "Der Prozess Eisenmenger," *MGWJ*, XVIII, 378–84, 425–32, 465–73; and L. Löwenstein, "Der Prozess Eisenmenger," *Magazin für die Wissenschaft des Judentums*, XVIII, 209–240. Yet, it appears that the "Eliezer" story had a kernel of truth. It may have induced the nascent Hamburg Sephardic community to persuade Duke Frederick of Holstein to send his mission to Persia, so extensively described by one of its participants, the Gottorf court librarian, Adam Olearius, in his *Ausführliche Beschreibung der kundbaren Reise nach Moskow und Persien*. See also H. Kellenbenz, *Sephardim an der unteren Elbe*, p. 153. Eisenmenger also claims that the duke had sent, through the head of his mission, Otto Brigmann, a letter to the Persian Jewish leader David Jan asking him "to be helpful to his envoy should something be needed so that the king of Persia fulfill the envoy's request." Since we hear nothing about a Jewish leader David in Isfahan, one wonders whether Eisenmenger did not confuse him with David Passi of Istanbul who, in the late sixteenth century, had indeed played a significant role at the Porte. See *supra*, Chap. LXXVII.

Neither the quantity nor the price of Eliezer's alleged shipment is given by Eisenmenger. But insofar as the story reflects reality, 70 camel loads probably averaged 244 kilograms per camel according to some general estimate by Charles Issawi who, however, also asserts that, in modern Arabia, camels carried loads of up to 500 kilograms each. See also, more generally, R. Lefebvre de Noëttes, *La Force motive animale à travers les âges*. At any rate the median figure, suggested by Issawi, suffices to give us an inkling of the size of the alleged shipment by the Persian Jewish trader. As to the price, the nearest figure I could thus far ascertain was close to the usual range of 20–25 dinars but occasionally going up to 31 dinars per kilogram in pre-Mongolian Iraq. See E. Ashtor, *Histoire des prix et des salaires dans l'Orient médiéval*, pp. 142 ff. See also A. C. Wood, *A History of the Levant Company*, pp. 49 f.

65. See G. F. Hourani, *Arab Seafaring in the Indian Ocean in Ancient and Early Medieval Times; Mare Luso-Indicum. Études et documents sur l'histoire de l'Océan Indien et des pays riverains à l'époque de la domination portuguese, passim;* and A. Houtun-Schindler, "Notes on the Karun River," *Proceedings* of the Royal Geographic Society, XII. On the general Turko-Persian relations before and after the peace treaty of 1590, which ended a twelve-year war, disastrous for Persia, see B. Kütükoglu, "Les Relations entre l'Empire Ottoman et l'Iran dans la seconde moitié du XVIe siècle," *Turcica*, VI, 128–45.

66. See A. Bakhtiar, "The Royal Bazaar of Isfahan," *IS*, VII, 320–47 (although written by an architect from a primarily architectural point of view, this essay gives a picture of the orderliness and intensity of the trade conducted in this establishment); Thomas Herbert, *Some Years Travels into Divers Parts of Africa and Asia The Great. Describing More Particularly the Empire of Persia and Industan*, London, 1677 ed. (earlier, 1634 ed. has a more elaborate title), p. 218 (praises the wares sold by Isfahan Jews); John Fryer, *A New Account of East India and Persia (1672–1681)*, ed. by W. Crooke, II, 247; Arakel, *Livre d'Histoire*, xxxiv, ed. by M. I. Brosset in the *Collection des Historiens Arméniens*, I; B. Spuler, *Die Mongolen in Iran*, p. 434; and the succinct, more general comments by M. Murtada al-Musawi on "Persian Trade under the Safavids (1514–1722)," *Sumer*, XXV, 99–102; and A. K. S. Lambton in her "Persian Trade under the Early Qajars" in D. S. Richard, ed., *Islam and the Trade of Asia*, pp. 215–44. On the development of the Armenian community and its competitive skills which made it a dominant factor in Isfahan's and Persia's trade in general, see the observations by V. Gregorian, "Minorities of Isfahan: the Armenian Community of Isfahan 1587–1722," *IS*, VII, 652–80; R. W. Ferrier, "The Armenians and The East India Company

in Persia in the Seventeenth and Eighteenth Centuries," *Economic History Review,* 2d ser. XXVI, 38–62, esp. pp. 40 f., 44; K. Kévonian's aforementioned (n. 31) well-documented essay in *CMRS,* XVI, 199–244, together with Lukas of Vanand's Armenian work to which it referred. As was mentioned here in another context, Chancellor Jan Zamoyski's effort to attract the Jews to his city of Zamość ended in failure, in part because of the Armenian competition. See M. Zakrzewska-Dubrazowa, *Ormianie zamojscy i ich rola* (The Armenians of Zamość and Their Role in Commercial Exchanges between Poland and the Orient), with the review thereof by Y. Dashkevich in the *Revue des études arméniennes,* III, 478–88; and *supra,* Vol. XVI, esp. pp. 51 f., 240 f., 338 f. n. 55, 430 n. 31.

67. Jean Chardin, *Voyages,* VI, 27, 132; W. Blunt, *Pietro's Pilgramage,* p. 135; L. D. Loeb, "The Jewish Musician and Music of Fars," *Asian Music,* IV, 3–14; Theodor Salmon, *Historie und Geographie des gegenwärtigen Staats in Persien,* p. 262. The Jewish role in Persia's entertainment world has also been observed by late-nineteenth-century European visitors. See, for example, E. G. Browne's *A Year amongst the Persians: Impressions as to the Life and Thought of the People of Persia,* pp. 241 ff., and 320 ff. See also W. J. Fischel, "The Region of the Persian Gulf," *Alexander Marx Jub. Vol.,* English sec., p. 222.

68. I. P. Petrushevsky, "The Socio-Economic Condition of Iran," in *CHI,* V, pp. 529 ff.; B. Spuler, *Die Mongolen in Iran,* pp. 306 ff.; A. K. S. Lambton, *Landlord and Peasant in Persia,* pp. 32 ff., 126 ff. Despite the large amount of information about the exploitation of the people by the governmental officials, including the arbitrary system of taxation, the evidence concerning the Jewish taxpayers and possibly also tax farmers is very scant. Among the popular proverbs we find in Persia's Kurdistan the refrain, also heard in other Muslim countries, that "a Jew does not pay his tax until he is beaten." Another proverb, circulating among the Persian Jews, is somewhat more disguised: "A dog does not eat the flesh of a dog," alluding to the unequal treatment of Jews by the gentile officials who were said to have always sided with their own coreligionists against the Jewish minority. See Y. Sahar, "Multilingual Proverbs in the Neo-Aramaic Speech of the Jews of Zakho, Iraqi Kurdistan," *IJMES,* IV, 215–35, esp. pp. 224 No. 61, and 225 No. 71; and *supra,* Chap. LXXVIII, nn. 97 ff.

Not surprisingly, a truly detailed study of a functioning Persian fiscal system could be presented only for a district, the Turkish records of which, stemming from the period of the Ottoman domination, have been preserved. See R. Mantran, "Règlements fiscaux ottomans la province de Bassora (2ᵉ moitié du XVIᵉ siècle)," *JESHO,* X, 224–77, offering the Turkish text with a facsimile and French translation of a document dating from 1574 (pp. 247 ff., 252 ff.). Among other rare documents relating to the medieval Persian tax system, we may refer to a remarkable account book covering the administration of several provinces described by W. Hinz in "Das Rechnungswesen orientalischer Reichsfinanzämter im Mittelalter," *Der Islam,* XXIX, 1–27, 113–41 which, however, by its total silence on Jews may merely imply that in Persia they played no special role as taxpayers or tax farmers. See also idem, "Zwei Steuerbefreiungs-Urkunden," *Documenta islamica inedita,* pp. 211–20, referring to fourteen similar documents found by V. Minorsky and published in his "*Soyurghal* [Grant] of Qasi'm b. Jahangir Aq-qoyunlu," *BSOAS,* IX, 927–60. None of them refers to Jews, which offers another contrast to conditions in the Ottoman Empire or Muslim Spain.

69. See *supra,* Chap. LXXVIII, n. 36; Vol. XII, pp. 10 ff., 246 ff. nn. 6 ff.; and, on the Jewish population in Poland, Vol. XVI, pp. 206 ff., 413 ff. nn. 48 ff.

CHAPTER LXXX: ON ISLAM'S PERIPHERY

1. See, for the time being, R. Lowenthal, "The Jews of Bukhara," *REJ*, CXX, 345–51, or in French, "Les Juifs de Boukhara," *CMRS*, II, 104–108; idem, "The Judeo-Tats in the Caucasus," *Historia Judaica*, XIV, 61–82, with an extensive bibliography; idem, "The Extinction of the Krimchaks in World War II," *American Slavic and East-European Review*, X, 130–36; J. Brutzkus, "History of the Jewish Mountaineers in Daghestan (Caucasia)" (Yiddish), *YIVO Historishe Shriftn*, II, 26–42, with an English summary, pp. vi f.; the earlier valuable anthropological studies by S. Weissenberg, "Die Kaukasischen Juden in anthropologischer Beziehung," *Archiv für Anthropologie*, XXXVI, 237–45; "Die Zentralasiatischen Juden in anthropologischer Beziehung," *Mitteilungen* of the Anthropologische Gesellschaft in Wien, XIII, 257–69; and, more generally, C. A. Burney and D. M. Lang, *The Peoples of the Hill: Ancient Ararat and Caucasus;* and on the basis of recent observations, A. L. Eliav (pseud. Ben-Ami), "The Jews of the Asian Borderlands" in his *Between Hammer and Sickle*, pp. 147–73.

2. I. Ben Zvi, *Nidḥei Yisrael*, new ed. rev.; or in the English trans. entitled *The Exiles and the Redeemed*, trans. by I. H. Abbady.

3. I Kings 10:1–13 (with no indication of the queen's name); E. A. W. Budge, *The Queen of Sheba and Her Only Son Menelyk: a Complete Translation of the* Kebra Nagast [Glory of Kings], with an Intro. (the original was ed. by C. Bezold, in *Abhandlungen of the Bavarian Academy*, 1905; although the editor's insistence that the sources of this important work be fully examined has not yet been fulfilled; p. xxxviii). For comparison with Jewish and Muslim legends, see L. Ginzberg, *Legends of the Jews*, esp. IV, 143 ff.; VI, 288 ff.; and W. M. Watt, *The Queen of Sheba in Islamic Tradition: Solomon and Sheba*, ed. by J. B. Pritchard. The linguistic aspects have been analyzed, among others, by T. Nöldeke in his *Neue Beiträge zur Semitischen Sprachwissenschaft*, pp. 31–46 (listing numerous Semitic loanwords in Ethiopian dialects); more recently supplemented by H. J. Polotsky in his "Aramaic, Syriac, and Ge‘ez," *Journal of Semitic Studies*, IX, 1–10 (from Papers read at the Second International Conference of Ethiopian Studies held at the University of Manchester, July 1963). Polotsky reached the conclusion that, "in the light of the linguistic evidence it seems hardly possible that the Aramaic words should have been introduced [into the Ge‘ez Bible translation] by Syriac-speaking missionaries or Bible translators; some of the words are characteristically non-Syriac, while none of them are characteristically and exclusively Syriac." See also E. Ullendorff, "Hebraic-Jewish Elements in Abyssinian (Monophysite) Christianity," *Journal of Semitic Studies*, I, 216–56; idem, *Ethiopia and the Bible*, Schweich Lectures of the British Academy, 1967, with the dissenting views expressed by L. Ricci in his review of that work in *Rassegna di Studi Etiopici*, XXIV, 273–83; and, more generally, Ullendorff, *The Ethiopians: an Introduction to Country and People*, pp. 98, 194 (citing the constitution of 1955, Arts. 2 and 4); M. Rodinson's informed but overskeptical questioning in his "Sur la question des 'influences juives' en Ethiopie," *Journal of Semitic Studies*, IX, 11–19 (from Papers read at the aforementioned Second International Conference of Ethiopian Studies). On the ancient period, see the older, but still valuable, comprehensive review by A. Kammerer, *Essai sur l'histoire antique d'Abyssinie. Le*

Royaume d'Aksum et ses voisins d'Arabie et de Méroc; and the references to the Egyptian-Jewish settlements, *infra,* nn. 6 middle and 13.

4. See H. Norden, *Africa's Last Empire: Through Abyssinia to Lake Tana and the Country of the Falasha,* p. 187; and *supra,* Vols. I, p. 321; II, pp. 211 f., 407; III, pp. 64, 66 ff., 116, 198, 251 f. n. 79, etc.; VII, p. 18. It may be noted that the Abyssinian invasion into Dhu Nuwas' kingdom was part of the great imperial confrontation between the Byzantine and Sassanian Empires. See E. Glaser's interpretation of *Die Abessinier in Arabien und Afrika. Auf Grund neuentdeckter Inschriften,* p. 175. This nexus was cut short by the Islamic conquest of Persia, Syria, and Egypt which made Abyssinia rather inaccessible to the Christian world and, particularly in Western Europe, turned it into a semi-mythical country of Prester John. Yet, the interrelations between Ethiopia and southern Arabia continued unabated.

5. E. Ullendorff, *The Ethiopians,* pp. 32, 41 f., and the sources cited there; G. W. B. Huntingford, *The Galla of Ethiopia: The Kingdoms of Kafa and Janjero* (Ethnographic Survey of North-Eastern Africa, II). See, more generally, A. Z. Aešcoly, *Recueil des textes Falasha. Introduction, textes éthiopiens.* Édition critique et traduction, 2d ed.; idem, *Sefer ha-Falashim* (The Book of Falashas: The Ethiopian Jews, Their Culture and Traditions); W. Leslau, *Falasha Anthology: Black Jews of Ethiopia,* trans. from Ethiopic Sources, with an Intro.; and some detailed older investigations by C. Conti Rossini, "Appunti di storia e letteratura Falascia," *RSO,* VIII, 563–610; and idem, "Nuovi appunti sui giudei d'Abissinie," *Rendiconti* of the R. Accademia Nazionale dei Lincei, 5th ser. XXXI, 221–40. These records represent only fragmentary survivals of what probably was a much larger literature, mostly written or assembled in the Middle Ages or early modern times, which has not yet been recovered and may not be recovered in the foreseeable future. Of considerable help, therefore, are the chronicles and other historical writings written by the non-Jewish Ethiopians. See E. Cerulli, *La Letteratura etiopica. L'Oriente cristiano nell'unità delle sue tradizioni,* 3d ed. enlarged.

6. See A. E. Mourant's 1962 study, cited by D. Soen in "The Falashas—Black Jews of Ethiopia," *Bulletin* of the International Committee on Urgent Anthropological and Ethnological Research, X, 67–74; A. Z. Aešcoly, "Ethiopic Jews in Hebrew Literature" (Hebrew), *Zion,* I, 316–36, 411–35; idem, "The Falashas: a Bibliography" (Hebrew), *Kirjath Sepher,* XII, 254–65, 370–83, 498–505; XIII, 250–65, 383–93, 506–512. Eldad ha-Dani's stories have been assembled from various Hebrew texts by A. Epstein in his critical edition of *Eldad ha-Dani.* See *supra,* Vols. III, pp. 116 f., 208, 286, 329; VI, pp. 122, 220 f., 241, 433 f. nn. 85–86; VIII, pp. 179, 228, and the literature listed there, including some of the older studies about the medieval Christian descriptions of the country of Prester John. See also the comments on Eldad's stories in P. Borchardt's "Die Falaschenjuden in Abessinien im Mittelalter," *Anthropos Ephemeris internationale,* XVIII/9, pp. 236–58; and C. Conti Rossini, "Leggende geografiche giudaiche nel IX secolo, I: Sefer Eldad," *Bolletino* of the R. Società Geografica Italiana, LXXII, 160–90; and *infra,* n. 12. See also *infra,* n. 21.

A passage, evidently referring to the Falashas, in Benjamin of Tudela's *Itinerary,* is marred by a geographically confusing array of names, often clearly misspelled, either by himself or by later copyists. It refers to an area in which "there are high mountains, where there are Jews who are not subject to Gentile domination. They possess towns and castles on the top of the mountains, from which they descend to the flat land called Lubia [or, Nubia] which is under Christian rule. The Jews fight with its inhabitants, capture much booty and return to their mountains, where no one can fight against them." These and further remarks of the famed traveler (*Itinerary*, ed. by M. N. Adler, pp. 61 f.) have intrigued many scholars. See esp. C. Conti Rossini's "Piccoli studi etiopici. Itinerario di Beniamino da Tudela e l'Etiopia," *Zeitschrift für Assyriologie*, XXVII, 358–78, esp. pp. 358 ff.; A. Z. Aescoly's observations in *Zion*, I. 326 ff.; and R. L. Hess's more recent critique of "The Itinerary of Benjamin of Tudela: a Twelfth-Century Jewish Description of Northern Africa," *Journal of African History*, VI, 15–24, concluding that, though Benjamin "did not visit the eastern Sudan, nevertheless his informants provided good information about this area in the twelfth century, a period for which there is otherwise little knowledge available" (p. 15). But many of their and other scholars' interpretations still are highly debatable.

Regrettably, some of these discussions have reflected the heritage of the period of the ultracritical schools of interpretation (including biblical criticism) which were ready to dismiss almost entirely any historical testimony based on oral traditions. Modern scholars have grown up in civilizations placing their major reliance on "documentary evidence" and observed the procedures of their own courts of justice, which completely disregarded "hearsay" testimony in favor of that derived from deeds and other written records. Some of them were even ready to accept the saying of the early modern glossators, *Quod non est in actis non est in mundo,* despite its limited validity even in the field of jurisprudence. A dramatically opposing view was held by the ancient rabbis even in the domain of Oral Law. They were so deeply convinced of the superior reliability of the *controlled* oral traditions over the written word that they coined the phrase that "Oral Law should not be committed to writing lest it lead to deep dissensions." Living under the Hellenistic civilization, with its proliferation of writings of all kinds, they thus voiced the fear that, if sacred traditions were written down, they would become subject to scribal errors by copyists and to more conscious interpolations or omissions because of some religious or sociopolitical bias, or even to outright falsifications. In contrast, oral traditions, especially if handed down by trained "memorizers" under the control of a central academy, would far more faithfully preserve even the original verbiage of the acknowledged authoritative leaders. Their confidence ultimately bore fruit, when under the great stress of external conditions they saw themselves forced to prepare, over a period of three generations of select competent redactors, a carefully edited text of the Babylonian Talmud.

Even with regard to the Bible more recent scholars have been prone to abandon the extreme criticism dominant early in this century and to acknowledge the "great tenacity of oral traditions in all ancient civilizations and their frequently surprising historical accuracy." Most of us are certainly no longer inclined to deny the very existence of such historical personalities as the patriarch Abraham, Moses, or Jesus, as was fashionable in certain circles early in this century. See *supra*, Vols. I, pp. 304 f. n. 10; II, pp. 353 ff.; and *passim.* To the literature listed there add, especially, J. Vansina's *De la tradition orale;* and with reference to the area here under discussion A. Finnegan, *Oral Tradition in Africa.* See also U. Bankämper, "The Correlation of Oral Traditions and Historical Records in Southern Ethiopia: a Case Study of the Hadiya/Sidamo Post," *Journal of Ethiopian Studies*, XI, no. 2, pp. 29–49, reaching the conclusion that "the unquestionably important value of oral tradition is especially based on the fact that they can particularly fill out the skeleton of fixed data, the 'history of events' [such as warlike deeds, negotiations, and dynastic policy] with the flesh of relevant information from the wide context of culture history" (p. 49).

With respect to the origin of the Falashas, such an overskeptical attitude toward oral traditions and legends is reflected not only in some of the writings of Carlo Conti

Rossini, a leader in Ethiopian studies in the first decades of this century, but also to some extent in the otherwise highly meritorious survey in R. L. Hess's fairly recent essay, "Toward a History of the Falasha" in D. F. McCall *et al.*, eds., *Eastern African History* (Boston University Papers on Africa, III), pp. 107–132. Such oral transmission over many centuries concerning laws, mores, or historical events, when recorded in however embellished and distorted a fashion in later hagiographic and other literature, must indeed be carefully weighed and the historic kernels identified. At times such identification can be made only with the aid of plausible hypotheses. Particularly useful are those hypothetical assumptions which, starting from different angles, happen to converge so as to present a sensible, rounded reconstruction of past developments. Unfortunately, with the present state of Ethiopian archaeology, which still is in the early stages of evolution, we may not expect fuller confirmation, denial, or modification of such hypotheses through early inscriptions, structural remnants, or artifacts, as happened time and again in the fields of biblical or Graeco-Roman research. But to shun the required strenuous efforts and to hide behind a wall of allegedly impenetrable darkness can turn into sheer escapism.

The following facts stand out: there were some connections between ancient Israel and Ethiopia from time immemorial. It is not a mere accident that we find in the Hebrew Bible some fifty references to Kush or Kushi (Ethiopia or Ethiopian). Among them is the mention that Moses himself had a Kushite wife (Num. 12:1) which aggrieved his siblings Miriam and Aaron, and was to cause much anxiety among such modern exponents of racism as some South African theologians supporting the policy of *apartheid*. Characteristically, the prophet Isaiah, speaking of the Assyrian conquest of Egypt, states: "So shall the king of Assyria lead away the captives of Egypt and the exiles of Ethiopia" (20:4). When the Book of Esther describes the vastness of the Persian Empire under Ahasuerus (Xerxes), it declares that the Empire extended "from India even unto Ethiopia, over a hundred and seven and twenty provinces." We are further told that, in his attempt to destroy the Jewish people, Haman argued before the king that "there is a certain people scattered abroad and dispersed among the peoples in *all* the provinces of thy kingdom" whose laws differed from those of all other subjects. He also secured from the king the order, which was sent "to the governors that were over *every* province," demanding the extermination of Jews (Esther 1:1, 3:8, 12–14). Such a great dispersion is generally confirmed by the data assembled by Antonin Causse showing that the Jewish diaspora extended over many lands even before the first destruction of the Temple of Jerusalem. See his *Les Dispersée d'Israel; les origines de la Diaspora et son rôle dans la formation du judaïsme;* and *supra,* Vol. I, p. 338 n. 44. The presence of Jews, in fact of an entire Jewish colony of soldiers and farmers in the Elephantine, Upper Egypt, established for the purpose of protecting the country against Ethiopian invasions possibly as early as in the days of Psammetichus I (663–609) and almost certainly antedating 586 B.C.E., makes it very likely that some Jews found their way also across the border into Ethiopia itself. See *supra,* Vol. I, pp. 110 f., 346 ff. nn. 12–13. In this connection one may recall the statement in Herodotus, ii. 30 (ed. and trans. by A. D. Godley for the Loeb Classical Library) concerning the Egyptian garrison of Libyan soldiers who, under Psammetichus I, had escaped to Ethiopia; and iii. 19 ff. referring to Cambyses sending spies to Elephantine to fetch persons "who understand the Ethiopian language." See W. Witakowski, "The Origin of the Jewish Colony at Elephantine," *Orientalia Suecana,* XXVIII–XXIX, 34–41, esp. p. 35; E. C. B. McLaurin, "Date of the Foundation of the Jewish Colony at Elephantine," *Journal of Near Eastern Studies,* XXVII, 89–96; and, more broadly, B. Porten, *Archives from Elephantine, the Life of an Ancient Jewish Military Colony.*

This likelihood of an early Jewish settlement in Ethiopia increases during the period of the Second Commonwealth. We recall the flight of Jeremiah's adherents soon after the Fall of Jerusalem to already well-established Jewish communities in Egypt. The Jewish population doubtless increased further after Alexander the Great founded Alexandria to which we are told he "invited" Jews of Palestine to settle. Soon thereafter, as we shall see, Ptolemy I, son of Lagos, equipped 30,000 Palestinian Jews as soldiers, and stationed them among the garrisons all over Egypt. (The important developments under Alexander and his Ptolemaic successors are mentioned *infra*, n. 13.) It stands to reason that the Jewish warriors participating in Egypt's defense against Ethiopia often took Ethiopian prisoners but also lost some prisoners to the enemy. As to the Elephantine soldiers, at least, we know that they were dedicated Jews, although at times their religion differed from the patterns then prevailing in Jerusalem. Remarkably, in that colony was found a copy of the famous circular, issued by the Persian King of Kings Darius II in 419 B.C.E., enjoining the Jews strictly to observe the Passover holiday, specifying certain ritualistic requirements fully consonant with the biblical commandments. Nor must we forget that during the last two pre-Christian centuries and beyond, many Jews were in a missionary mood, spreading the Jewish religion among the pagans. The latter may well have included a great many Phoenicians and Carthaginians, the most enterprising mercantile Semitic nation of antiquity, whose disappearance from the historic scene was plausibly attributed to the successful Jewish religious propaganda resulting in their ultimate amalgamation with the Jewish people.

Nor must we underestimate the great commotion created by the anti-Roman Jewish uprisings in Egypt and neighboring lands. That under Trajan (115–17 C.E.), especially, ended only after the Jews had successfully fought against the local population and had been defeated only by the strong Roman military intervention. During the early period of Jewish supremacy, some Egyptians may actually have joined the victors by adopting Judaism. During the Roman campaign—we have the noteworthy testimony of a local papyrus, dated some 85 years after the event, recording the annual celebration of the area's liberation from the Jewish military occupation, a sort of anti-Jewish Purim festival—there must have occurred, as usual during hostilities, a mass flight of some Jews (embracing converts to Judaism) to neighboring countries, very likely including Ethiopia. Some of these refugees, particularly merchants of the type of Ananias who, shortly before, had succeeded in converting the royal house of Adiabene to the Jewish faith, doubtless engaged in proselytizing among the local Ethiopians as well.

At the same time other Jews may also have penetrated the Ethiopian provinces from the Red Sea area. Since the days of Ophir that channel of communication with the Indian Ocean must have loomed large in many Jewish minds. Some Jews participated not only in such Roman expeditions as those of Aldus Gallus but also in peaceful journeys through the Red Sea. See the older, but still informative studies by J. D. Lieblein, *Handel und Schiffahrt auf dem Roten Meere in alten Zeiten;* and A. Kammeier, *Essai sur l'histoire antique d'Abyssinie;* and the literature cited *supra*, nn. 3–4; Vols. I, pp. 173 ff., 273 ff. nn. 10–13; II, pp. 79 f., 94 ff., 362 f. n. 33, 370 nn. 7–11; and *infra*, nn. 30–31, 64. This movement undoubtedly continued in the better known contacts between South Arabian Jews and Africa before and after the reign of the Jewish king Dhu Nuwas in the following Islamic centuries. During all these obscure centuries of Ethiopian history many Jews must have found their way into Ethiopia just as Ethiopian returnees from other lands may well have brought with them religious practices and doctrines they had learned from Jews abroad. Ethiopia may indeed have been included in the famous geographer Strabo's (died after 21 C.E.) much-quoted sweeping statement about the Jews: "This people has already made its way into every city, and it is not easy to find any place in the habitable world which has not received this nation and in which it has not made its power felt," quoted in Josephus' *Antiquities,*

XIV, 7, 2.115, edited and trans. by R. Marcus for the Loeb Classical Library, VII, 509.

Such a presence of Jews may also help explain the adoption of Christianity by the monarchy and masses of population in fourth-century Ethiopia. It has long been observed that early Christianity made its greatest conquests in areas with existing Jewish communities. Even Paul, the great "Apostle to the Gentiles," is recorded only as addressing Jewish, rather than Gentile gatherings. As observed somewhat irreverently by a Protestant theologian Ernst von Dobschütz, "Paul tries over and over again to come to terms with the synagogue, until sooner or later each one throws him and all his adherents out, whereupon he opens a competitive establishment on his own premises." So widely accepted was this notion that the mere fact that Paul planned to visit Spain was taken—in the absence of direct evidence—as an indication that there were Jewish communities in that country as early as the first century C.E. This indication was later confirmed by archaeological findings. To students of early Christianity it appears, therefore, with a high degree of probability, that such a *preparatio evangelica* had also taken place in Ethiopia before the fourth century and that, hence, the early Ethiopian Christians took over many traditions of local Jews with all their divergences from the normative Judaism previously established in its Palestino-Babylonian centers. For example, the Ethiopic Enoch, together with the more recently analyzed Ethiopic Book of Jubilees, noteworthy products of the Apochryphal and Pseudepigraphic literature, may have been influenced by already established Jewish foci dating back to the pre-Maccabean period. See W. Baars and R. Zuurmond's announcement of 1964 concerning "The Project for a New Edition of the Ethiopic Book of Jubilees," *American Journal of Semitic Studies*, IX, 67–74 (from the Papers read at the Second International Conference of Ethiopian Studies held at the University of Manchester, July 1963). The authors hoped to publish such an edition "in about six years time," (p. 74).

In short, this reconstruction of the early Falasha history, or perhaps prehistory, is based on brief allusions and hints in external sources, linguistic borrowings, and particularly a long oral tradition, though not by direct documentary evidence, but also with no persuasive contrary documentation. It is likely better to explain a great many features of the ancient Hebraic impact on Ethiopic Christianity, influences manifest in the Falasha heritage until the present day. At the same time contemporary scholarship ought to concentrate on clearing up as many obscure phases in the Falasha evolution as possible. The call to such "urgent" investigations, sounded in 1968 by Dan Soen, in his succinct article on "The Falashas" in the *Bulletin* of the International Committee on Urgent Anthropological and Ethnological Research, X, 67–74, still awaits more resolute collective action.

7. See A. Z. Aescoly's essays in *Zion*, I; and *Kirjath Sepher*, XII–XIII. On the derivation of the name Simen from Teiman and the final struggle for Jewish independence under King Suseyos (1607–1632), see F. M. Esteves Pereira's ed. and trans. of that king's chronicle, cited *infra*, n. 14, esp. text Chap. xxxiv, and trans., II, 216 ff. and 331. The Ethiopic studies and sources made available to Europeans from the fifteenth century on are briefly sketched, under the heading "Exploration and Study," in E. Ullendorff's *The Ethiopians*, pp. 1–22 with the literature listed there. This aspect is treated also by many other writers but a more up-to-date comprehensive bibliography would now be very timely.

8. See E. Cerulli, "Eugenio IV e gli Etiopi al Concilio di Firenze," *Rendiconti* of the R. Accademia dei Lincei, 7th ser., IX, 347–68; Francisco Alvares (Alvarez), *Verdadera*

informação das terras do Preste João das Indias, ed. with an Intro. and Notes by A. R. Machado; idem, *Narrative of the Portuguese Embassy to Abyssinia during the Years 1520–27,* trans. and ed. with notes by Stanley of Alderley (Works issued by the Hakluyt Society, LXIV), esp. pp. 78 f., 353. In his presentation Alvarez to a large extent relied upon what he had heard from local informants as well as from earlier Portuguese visitors to Ethiopia. His volume became an important handbook for most subsequent researchers in Ethiopian history. See also C. F. Beckingham, "Notes on an Unpublished MS of Francisco Alvarez," *Annales d'Ethiopie,* IV, 139–54, esp. p. 147; and *supra,* Vol. XIII, pp. 110, 114 f., 364 ff. nn. 53 and 58. In this connection one may also mention the wholly legendary Hebrew letters allegedly sent to Pope Eugenius and a Roman emperor Frederick published (among others) by A. Neubauer in his "Matters Relating to the Ten Tribes and the Sons of Moses" (Hebrew), *Qobeṣ 'al yad* of the Mekize Nirdamim Society, IV, 7–24. Disregarding the enormous exaggeration concerning the power and wealth of the Jewish King Daniel in Ethiopia (for instance, that he had under his reign 300 kings and 3,000 lords), this alleged correspondence attests Italian Jewish reactions to the spreading rumors about an independent Jewish kingdom in Ethiopia. See the comments on Neubauer's text by D. Kaufmann in his "Rumour about the Ten Tribes in Pope Martin V's Time," *JQR,* [o.s.] IV, 503–508; and by A. Z. Aescoly in his "Ethiopian Jews in Hebrew Literature" (Hebrew), *Zion,* III, 328 f.

All earlier writings, however, were overshadowed by the researchers of a distinguished seventeenth-century scholar and diplomat, Job Ludolf. See his *Historia ethiopica,* almost immediately after publication translated into English by J. P. under the title *History of Abessinia;* supplemented by Ludolf's *Commentarius ad Historiam Ethiopicam.* These volumes have been extensively used by Ludolf's successors and even today offer much valuable information. On the papal attitudes to the Ethiopian visitors in Rome, whom they often had to support financially from the Roman Treasury, and for whom they ultimately built a special church called Santo Stefano dei Monti, which often served also as a focus of Ethiopian studies, see, for instance, R. Lefevre, "Documenti pontifici sui rapporti con l'Etiopia nei secoli XV e XVI," *Rassegna di studi etiopici,* V, esp. Nos. xv, xvii, xlviii–ix, lxxxi; idem, "Documenti e notizie su Taifa Scyon e la sua attività romana nel secolo XVI," *ibid.,* XXIV, 74–153, esp. pp. 105 f. This distinguished Ethiopian monk, who lived for several years in Jerusalem and later in Rome, where he died in 1550, served also as informant concerning the Ethiopic Book of Enoch for Guillaume Postel's important work *De originibus seu de hebraicae linguae et gentis antiquitate,* Basel, 1553; and *supra,* Vol. XII, pp. 177 f., 403 f. n. 20. See also, A. Bartnicki and J. Mantel-Niećko's more general analysis, cited *infra,* n. 21. On Postel's mission and its yield of Ethiopic manuscripts now in part at the Vatican Library, see G. Levi della Vida, *Ricerche sulla formazione del più antico fondo dei manoscritti orientali della Biblioteca Vaticana* (Studi e Testi, XCII), pp. 307 ff.; and the literature listed there, esp. pp. 307 n. 1 and 325 n. 1.

9. Elijah of Ferrara, *Letter,* first published by E. Ashkenazi in his *Dibre ḥakhamim* (Sayings of the Sages), republished and frequently commented on in the following years. It is quoted here from a Hebrew excerpt, reproduced from a Paris MS by A. E. Aescoly in *Zion,* I, 231; and from the English trans. in E. N. Adler's *Jewish Travellers,* pp. 151 ff. Similarly Obadiah Yaré di Bertinoro's *Epistles,* which have been frequently cited here from their best reproduction (with the aid of an unpublished critical edition prepared by E. S. Artom) in A. Yaari's *Iggerot Ereṣ Yisrael,* pp. 133, 141, and the notes thereon, pp. 542 f.; likewise quoted here from Adler's English trans., pp. 209 ff., esp. pp. 238 f. On the presence of numerous Ethiopians in Jerusalem and

even in Ormuz, see E. Cerulli, *Etiopi in Palestina, Storia della comunità etiopica di Gerusalemme;* J. Wicki, ed., *Documenta Indica,* I (*MHSI,* LXX), 698 ff., esp. p. 706. Characteristically, the latter reference is included in Gaspar Francisco Barzaeus' aforementioned conversionist discourse in the Ormuz synagogue. See *supra,* Vol. XV, pp. 357 ff., 542 f. nn. 109–110.

10. See R. David Ibn abi Zimra, *Resp.,* Vol. VI, Nos. 5 and 9; also reproduced by A. Z. Aešcoly in *Zion,* I, 334; given here in a variant from I. M. Goldman's English trans. in his *The Life and Times of Rabbi David Ibn Abi Zimra,* pp. 57 ff. Not all rabbis agreed with R. David's argument that the Falashas' strict adherence to the literal meaning of the Pentateuchal laws could be historically explained without their necessarily being followers of Karaism. Remarkably, however, none of them suggested that the Falashas should be equated with Samaritans, with whom they shared, for example, the practice of not circumcising a newly born boy on a Sabbath, but rather postponing the operation for a day. See A. d'Abbadie's observations with A. Z. Aešcoly's comments thereon in the latter's "Notices sur les Falachas ou Juifs d'Abyssinie d'après le 'Journal de Voyage' d'Antoine d'Abbadie," *Cahiers d'Études Africaine,* II, no. 5, pp. 84–147, esp. pp. 98 f. Of course, both the Falashas and the Samaritans followed the literal interpretation of the Pentateuch only. Yet, the rabbis, whose general sympathy for the Falashas appears clearly in their writings, did not wish to place them on a par with the Samaritans, whose Jewishness many of them, like R. Ibn abi Zimra, denied altogether. See Goldman, p. 57; and *infra,* n. 13.

11. J. Halévy, "Excursion chez les Falachas en Abyssinie," *Bulletin* of the Société de Géographie, XVII, 270–94, also in English in *Travels in Abyssinia,* trans. by J. Picciotto; and such important monographs as his ed. of *Prières de Falachas ou des Juifs d'Abyssinie* (from the thirteenth-century prayerbook prepared by one Abba Sikion or Sikoin); supplemented by his collection of "Nouvelles prières des Falacha," *Revue sémitique,* XIX, 96–104, 215–19, 344–48 (texts), 348–64 (French translation); and "La Guerre de Sarza Dangel contre les Falachas: Texte éthiopien traduit en français et en hebreu," *ibid.,* XIV, 392–427; XV, 119–63, 263–87. Coming from the pen of a distinguished semitist, these publications made a considerable impression on the Jewish and non-Jewish public. On Halévy's influence as an innovative scholar and as a teacher at the École des Hautes Études of Paris, see Isidore Lévy's and M. Schorr's necrologies in *RH,* CXXVI, 215–18; and *Deutsche Literaturzeitung,* 1917, pp. 595–602, 628–37; and D. Sidersky, *Quelques portraits des mes maîtres des études sémitiques: Ernest Renan - Marquis de Vogue - Clermont Ganneau - Philippe Berger - Joseph Halévy,* pp. 59–63.

In connection with Halévy's publication of the Falasha prayers, one ought to mention also some recent studies of Falasha liturgical music, such as K. K. Shelemay's " 'Historical Ethnomusicology' Reconstructing Falasha Liturgical History," *Ethnomusicology,* XXIV, 233–58. Incidentally, I wish to take this occasion to thank Professor Shelemay for turning my attention to a couple of recent publications on the Falashas which might otherwise have eluded me. For the entire area of Falasha liturgy, including the synagogue chant, my analysis, similar to that presented in Vol. VII, Chap. XXXI for the period before 1200 C.E., must be postponed to a later volume. On the general "Awakening of West-European Jewry to the Assistance of the Falashas," see the pertinent Hebrew article under this title by M. Eliav in *Tarbiz,* XXXV, 61–76.

12. See *Eldad ha-Dani,* ed. by A. Epstein; with D. H. Müller's additional readings in his *Die Recensionen und Versionen des Eldad ha-Dani nach den alten Drucken . . . und den Handschriften* (*Denkschriften* of the Vienna Academy, XLI); and other sources listed

supra, n. 6. On Eldad ha-Dani's possible origin from Ethiopia, see the debates already aired by Epstein in his Introduction and further comments by A. Z. Aescoly in his essay in *Zion*, I, 324 ff. Some scholars, especially S. Krauss, tried to deny altogether the relevance of Eldad's report for Ethiopia and to seek the regions described by him around Nishapur. See Krauss's "New Light on Geographical Data in Eldad Hadani and Benjamin of Tudela" (Hebrew), *Tarbiz*, VIII, 208–232, with "Corrigenda" thereto, *ibid.*, p. 368.

13. Gen. 49:10. The idea of connecting some settlement of the Jews in Ethiopia with the conquest of Alexander the Great was advanced by a pioneer in modern Falasha research, Louis Marcus, in his "Notice sur l'époque de l'établissement des Juifs dans l'Abyssinie," *JA*, III, 409–431; IV, 51–73 (part of a larger work on colonies). It was summarily dismissed, however, by later specialists. Yet, this proposal is not without merit. We must remember, as mentioned before (n. 6), that no sooner did Alexander establish the great new emporium of Alexandria than he invited the Jews from Palestine to settle there. This move was subsequently expanded (according to the *Letter of Aristeas*, 12–14 in R. H. Charles's English trans. in *The Apocrypha and Pseudepigrapha of the Old Testament*, II, 96) by the forcible deportation of no less than "a hundred thousand" Palestinian Jews to Egypt by his successor Ptolemy I. "Of these he armed thirty thousand picked men and settled them in garrisons in the country districts." From there Jews spread all over Egypt, and on his mission to Emperor Caligula, Philo emphasized that there were flourishing Jewish communities in Egypt "down to the boundaries of Ethiopia." *In Flaccum*, vi.43. All along some Egyptian Jews may well have penetrated Ethiopia, possibly finding some Jews who had emigrated there from Upper Egypt during the Achaemenid domination of that country. This is indeed clearly indicated in the continuation of the *Letter of Aristeas* stating: "And even before this time [of Ptolemy I] large numbers of Jews had come into Egypt with the Persian, and in an earlier period still others had been sent to Egypt to help Psammetichus in his campaign against the king of Ethiopia." See *supra*, n. 6; and Vol. I, pp. 110 f., 168 ff., 172, 185, 346 f. nn. 12–13, 370 ff. nn. 6 ff., 377 n. 22. This Falasha nexus with Egypt may also explain the absence of the Ḥanukkah celebration in Ethiopia often cited as evidence for the Falasha pre-Maccabean origin. See also *infra*, n. 43.

Of special interest may also be the fact that Alexander and his successors also transplanted some Samaritans from Palestine into the Egyptian metropolis and other parts of the country. These Jewish sectarians, who were a remnant of the preexilic Israelites, may well have boasted of their ancestry in the new environment. If later some Samaritans settled in Ethiopia—which is wholly within the realm of possibility—they may have contributed their share to the legends about the origin of the Falashas from exiles from the First and Second Jewish Commonwealths. See *supra*, n. 6; Vol. II, pp. 34 f., 339 n. 32, 341 n. 42.

14. The chronicles which dealt with the wars of the Falashas and their ultimate defeat and subjugation have been reviewed by "Rechtsanwalt" [I.?] Metz in his "Über die Quellen zur Geschichte der Falaschas," *MGWJ*, XXVIII, 70–78, 130–39, 189–92, 279–85, 359–68; a sequel to his historical survey, "Zur Geschichte der Falascha (Abyssinischen Juden)," *ibid.*, XXVII, 385–99, 433–52. These sources were subsequently often reedited in more critical editions. See, for instance, J. Halévy, "La Guerre de Sarza Dengel contre les Falachas," *Revue sémitique*, XIV, 392–427; XV, 119–63, 263–87. The various articles on individual Solomonid monarchs by Halévy's pupil, J. Perruchon, in his "Notes pour l'histoire d'Ethiopie," *ibid.*, I, 274–86; IV, 87–90, 177–85, 273–78; V, 75–80, 173–89; his ed. of *Les Chroniques de Zar'a Ya'acob et de Ba'eda Mar-*

yam, rois de l'Ethopie de 1434 à 1478 (from which the passage in the text is quoted, pp. 96 f.); his "Histoire d'Eskender, d'Amda Seyon II et de Na'od, rois d'Ethiopie. Texte éthiopien inédit comprenant en outre un fragment de la chronique de Ba'eda Maryam, leur prédécesseurs, et traduction," *JA*, 9th ser., III, 319–66; C. Conti Rossini, ed., *Historia regis Sarsa Dengel, Malak Sagad* (*Corpus Scriptorum Christianorum Orientalium*, II/3), esp. p. 110, on the negus' calling the Falashas together peacefully and then exterminating them. See also T. Tamrat's succinct summary of the efforts at "the evangelization of the Falashas" in his *Church and State in Ethiopia, 1270–1527*, pp. 196–206, 231–42.

The subjection of the Falashas, left unfinished by Sarṣa Dengel, was completed by Susneyos (Susenyos or Sacinius) whose reign left behind extensive documentation. See F. M. Estaves Pereira's ed. and Portuguese trans. of the *Chronica de Susenyos, rei de Ethiopia* (includes a volume of the Ge'ez original from a Bodleian MS and a volume of trans. and extensive notes containing one on the variant spelling of the monarch Susneyos' name; II, 265). See the graphic description of "La Guerra coi Falascia dell'Amba Seccana," in an Italian translation from *La Cronaca del Re Malac Sagad* in E. Cerulli's *La Letteratura etiopica*, 3d ed., pp. 153–56; and H. C. Maydon's modern study of *Simen, Its Heights and Abysses: a Record of Travel and Sport in Abyssinia with Some Account of the Sacred City of Aksum and the Ruins of Gondar*, esp. p. 7. Although he undertook his journey of 1922–23 mainly as a sportsman in quest of a rare bird called Walia Ibis, Maydon was an interested observer. He described Simen as "that lofty and remote barrier of mountains culminating in a series of towering precipices." However, on his visit to Simen (of which he presents a rough and admittedly rather inaccurate map) he found no Falashas there, in contrast to Gondar, where he saw separate Muslim and Jewish quarters (pp. 85, 89, 114, and 185).

15. C. Singer, "The Falashas," *JQR*, [o.s.] XVII, 142–47. Haimanot's letter concludes with a somewhat longer explanation of the strict Falasha observance of the laws of purity as stated in the Mosaic legislation. The writer added that, since the people lived among Christians who did not observe the Levitical laws, they did not touch the cooking utensils of any Gentile household and refused to eat any food prepared by non-Jews. "Whenever they trespass against any of these laws they wash and shave themselves and live in separation for several days, eating uncooked beans." Their failure to observe the commandment of the phylacteries was perhaps derived from their general abhorrence of amulets which their neighbors carried in profusion and which included texts or inscriptions doubtless considered idolatrous by the Falashas. As to the veneration of saints, we have indications that some groups added at least three other persons, one woman and two men, to the biblical record. See the fuller analyses of the Falasha religious observances and secular mores in A. E. Aescoly's *Sefer ha-Falashim*, pp. 22–84; and W. Leslau, *Coutumes et croyances des Falachas* (*Juifs d'Abyssinie*), *Travaux et mémoires* of the Institut d'Ethnologie of the University of Paris, LXI.

It may also be noted that many Christians, including some Abyssinian divines, reciprocated in voicing respect for the Jewish religion. On one occasion, for example, when in 1560 Emperor Menas (Ada Saged, 1558–63), instigated by Portuguese missionaries, wished to attack the Falashas' fortress of Simen, he was allegedly restrained by an Abyssinian hermit's warning that the time for the conversion of their Jewish compatriots had not yet come. See the citation from a contemporary chronicle, in Metz's "Zur Geschichte der Falaschas," *MGWJ*, XXVII, 439.

16. See A. Z. Aescoly, *Sefer ha-Falashim*, pp. 28 ff., 52 ff., 62 ff.; W. Leslau, *Coutumes et croyances des Falachas*, pp. 57 ff., 64 ff., 70 ff. A relatively modern innovation

seems to have been introduced in the fifteenth century, namely the establishment of Jewish monasteries. At that time we hear of a Jewish monastic leader, Abba Sabra and his disciple Ṣega Amlak, said to have been the son of Emperor Zar'a Ya'qob (1434–68). See A. Z. Aescoly, *Recueil des textes falachas,* p. 201; J. A. Quirin, *The Beta Israel (Falasha) in Ethiopian History: Caste Formation and Cultural Change,* Dissertation at the University of Minnesota, 1977 (typescript), cited by Steven B. Kaplan in his comprehensive study of *The Monastic Holy Man and the Christianization of Ethiopia (1270–1468).* Dissertation at the Hebrew University, 1982 (typescript shown me by the author), esp. pp. 112 ff. See also E. Cerulli's earlier survey, "Il Monachismo in Etiopia," *Orientalia Christiana Analecta,* CLIII, 259–78. At any rate, no Falasha monks are mentioned in the sources before that date. On the various theories concerning the presence of monks among the Falashas, who were quite different from the various kinds of hermits and Nazirites, discussed already in the Bible (Num. 6:1 ff.) and at considerable length in a special tract, Nazir, in the Talmud, see the explanations offered by P. Luzzatto, J. M. Flad, J. Halévy, and C. Conti Rossini, mentioned by Leslau, *Coutumes,* p. 61 n. 1.

17. See Enoch 25:6, in R. H. Charles' *The Apocrypha and Pseudepigrapha,* I, 205; W. Leslau, *Coutumes,* pp. 57 ff., 75 ff.; A. Freimann, *'Inyenei Shabbetai Zevi* (Matters Pertaining to Shabbetai Zevi), p. 64; H. Zotenberg, "Un Document sur les Falachas," *JA,* 6th ser. IX, 265–68. It may be noted that the Ethiopian Christians also had their false messiahs. One of them appeared in 1603–1604, calling himself Za Chrestos and pretending to be "Christ God." He quickly attracted a large following. Although he was executed on royal order, many of his adherents believed in his forthcoming resurrection. They contended that "Christ was twice born in the flesh; the first time from the offspring of Shem from the Holy Virgin Mary and the second time from the issue of Canaan, from a lady called Amata Uanghel. This happened in order that Israel not be the only one thus honored and solely enjoy that glory among the peoples." Fourteen years after Za Chrestos' death the government was forced violently to suppress that heresy. See E. Cerulli, *La Letteratura etiopica,* pp. 158 ff.

Among the Falashas the messianic ideal was kept alive also after their subjection to the Christian regime. Curiously, the name of the messiah given by them, although of Levitic origin, was Theodoros, which Filossene (Philoxène) Luzzatto explained as being the Greek equivalent of the Hebrew Nathaniel, Netanyahu, Jonathan, or Mattathias. See his *Mémoire sur les Juifs d'Abyssinie ou Falachas* (reprinted *from Archives Israélites,* XII–XV), pp. 37 ff. From the legends current among them, Antoine d'Abbadie had been told by a learned Falasha that Theodoros, the great king, will have one eye on his face and the other on his skull. By a simple turn of his head his gaze would slay thousands of people on each side, and he would rule over the whole earth. Only afterward would the Messiah come. See A. Z. Aescoly, "Notice sur les Falacha ou Juifs d'Abyssinie d'après le 'Journal de Voyage' d'Antoine d'Abbadie," *Cahiers d'Études Africaines,* II, no. 5, pp. 84–147, esp. pp. 104 f. Aescoly deduces therefrom that "Theodoros" represented the idea of the expected first messiah of the House of Joseph. Only after him would the ultimate Messiah of the House of David usher in the messianic age. However, these hypotheses cannot be fully verified because of the lack of direct documentation, since the Falashas appear not to have strongly emphasized the messianic element in their faith, the expectation for the Redeemer not even being included in any of their prayers. This low-keyed messianic hope may perhaps also explain the Falashas' failure to stage the mass emigration to Israel after 1948, similar to that of their Yemenite neighbors. Of course, the Ethiopian regime was not as hostile to its Jewish citizens as were the Yemenite and other South Arabian states toward the Jews living in their midst.

18. See Patriarch Alphonso Mendez' *Expeditionis ethiopicae libri I–II,* Chaps. XII: "Patriarchae disputatio cum Hebraeo europaeo de Messiae divinitate"; XIII: "Altera Patriarchae disputatio cum eodem Iudaeo de integritate sanctissimae Dei genetricis Mariae," in C. Beccari's ed., *Rerum Aethiopicarum Scriptores Occidentales inediti a saeculo XVI ad XIX* (this vast collection offers a multitude of details, esp. in Vols. II, III, VI and VIII; see the Index, Vol. XV, pp. 124 *s.v.* Falascia; 185 *s.v.* Judaei), VIII, 231– 55; with the comments thereon by A. Z. Aescoly in *Sefer ha-Falashim,* pp. 158 f. n. 2; and his summation of observations found in D'Abbadie's *Journal* in *Cahiers d'Études Africaines,* II, no. 5, pp. 104 f.; J. M. Flad, *Kurze Schilderung der bisher fast unbekannten abessinischen Juden,* esp. p. 16; W. Leslau, "A Falasha Religious Dispute," *PAAJR,* XVI, 71–95, offering the Falasha text (from a MS found by him in Ethiopia) with an English trans. and commentary. Here a Falasha monk and a European missionary debated primarily the doctrine of Trinity and the practice of sacrifices among the Falashas. In his comments and Appendices Leslau also offers interesting data on the other aspects of the Falasha religion, including the sacrifices (p. 73 n. 10), and on the work of nineteenth-century Christian missionaries, such as Flad, in the Falasha communities. See also, more generally, Leslau's brief survey of "The Religious Life of the Falashas" (Yiddish), *YIVO Bleter,* XXXIV, 209–220.

Although on principle justified in his critical approach, Leslau has at times gone a bit too far in discounting the information available in existing accounts. He declared: "Most of the reports . . . about the Falashas have been incomplete and characterized by a Christian or Jewish missionary tendency which appreciably diminishes their usefulness and objectivity." See his *Falasha Anthology,* p. x. Certainly, on the Jewish side even propagandists like Jacob Faitlovich were more interested in helping these newly discovered coreligionists financially and educationally than in altering any of their religious doctrines or practices. The French missions, too, pursued, as the Alliance Israélite did in other countries, mainly programs of Westernizing and modernizing the culture of the Falashas and in improving their economic well-being by teaching them new crafts and professions. On the relationship of the Ethiopian Christian masses to Jews and Judaism—a much-discussed subject in the existing literature—see, for instance, E. Ullendorff, *The Ethiopians,* pp. 97 ff.

It may be mentioned in this connection that, despite its bent toward special pleading in favor of a particular saint or saints and its frequent reference to miracles and divine interventions for the edification of pious Christian readers, the vast hagiographic literature, forming a substantial part of Ethiopia's literary heritage, supplies at times significant data and insights also on the political and socioeconomic developments in the country. See Steven B. Kaplan's recent analysis of "Hagiographies and the History of Medieval Ethiopia," *History in Africa,* VIII, 107–123. Certainly, an effort to come to grips with this aspect of the hagiographic materials also for the history of the Falashas may well shed some new light on many hitherto unexplored elements in their history.

19. H. Vivian, *Abyssinia: Through the Land to the Court of the Lion of Judah,* p. 329; D. H. Müller, *Die Recensionen und Versionen des Eldad-ha-Dani,* p. 13; Azariah de' Rossi, *Sefer Me'or 'Eynaim* (Enlightening the Eyes: Historical Essays), ed. by I. E. Benjacob, I, 189; ed. by D. Cassel, p. 193. Azariah evidently had in mind Lodovico Guicciardini's *Descrittione . . . di tutti i Paesi Bassi;* and Abraham Ortelius' *Theatrum orbis terrarum,*

which he apparently quoted from the second edition, published in 1572, that is, but two years before the appearance of his own work. See my "Azariah de' Rossi's Historical Method" (in the English trans. from the French in *REJ*, LXXXVI, 151–75; LXXXVII, 43–78) in my *History and Jewish Historians: Essays and Addresses*, ed. by A. Hertzberg and L. A. Feldman, pp. 205–37, 422–42, esp. pp. 229 f., 437 n. 138.

The contrasting estimates by James Bruce and Henry A. Stern appeared in Stern's *Wanderings among the Falashas in Abyssinia, Together with a Description of the Country and Its Various Inhabitants*, 2d ed., with an Intro. by R. L. Hess, esp. p. 194; J. Bruce, *Travels to Discover the Source of the Nile*, Vol. I, toward end. On Bruce's major discoveries, see the biographical sketches by E. Ullendorff, "James Bruce of Kinnaird," *Scottish Historical Review*, II, 128–43; and J. M. Reid, *Traveller Extraordinary: The Life of James Bruce of Kinnaird*. To be sure, Bruce's main objective, the discovery of the sources of the Nile, had (unbeknown to him) already been accomplished in 1588 by Giovanni Gabriel, son of an Italian father and an Abyssinian mother, and again in 1618 by the Spaniard Pero Paez. Yet the Scotsman's own explorations in detail, as well as the numerous manuscripts and artifacts he had brought back with him which have since served as a source of important information (at the British Museum, the Bodleian Library, and so forth), have proved to be as important as his description of the Nile's sources. See also the brief discussion in C. Rathjen's *Die Juden in Abessinien*, pp. 65 ff.; and, more generally, C. Conti Rossini, "Studi su popolazione dell'Etiopia," *RSO*, VI; and M. Wolde-Aragay, "Population Movements as a Possible Factor in the Muslim-Christian Conflict in Medieval Ethiopia," *Symposion Leo Frobenius*. Of interest also is R. Pankhurst's analysis of "Some Factors Influencing the Health of Traditional Ethiopia," *Journal of Ethiopian Studies*, IV, 31–70. After showing the "depressing" elements of climate, epidemics, and so forth, the author concludes that nonetheless "Ethiopian society had at an early time evolved many useful practices for the prevention and cure of disease" (p. 70). Presumably, the Falashas shared many of these behavioral patterns.

20. See A. Z. Aešcoly, *Sefer ha-Falashim*, pp. 19 f.; W. Leslau, *Coutumes et croyances des Falachas*, pp. 94 ff.; and J. Faitlovich, "Les Falachas d'après les explorateurs. Notes apologétiques," *Rivista israelitica*, IV, 92–101. Faitlovich points to the strong marital ties characterizing the Falashas. Celibacy was practically unknown among them; even hermits were expected to be married. He also emphasizes the generally prevalent feminine morality which, as we know from other sources, often aroused the admiration of hostile observers. Some of the chroniclers referred, for example, to the case of a Jewish woman captive who was conducted by an official through a mountainous area. At a propitious moment the woman jumped into an abyss, carrying her captor to death with her. See *ibid.*, pp. 97 and 100 f.

21. See A. Bartnicki and J. Mantel-Niecko, "The Role and Significance of the Religious Conflicts and People's Movements in the Political Life of Ethiopia in the Seventeenth and Eighteenth Centuries," *Rassegna di Studi Etiopici*, XXIV, 5–39, esp. p. 20; and the numerous references in R. Pankhurst's *Economic History of Ethiopia, 1800–1935*, listed in the Index, *s.v.* famines, pests, venereal diseases, and wars. For instance, the devastating impact of the spread of malaria, even in recent years when that disease had elsewhere come under effective medical control, is well illustrated by E. Schafer's "Epidemiological Investigation of a Malaria Epidemic in Begemdir and Semien Provinces in Ethiopia," *Journal of Health* of the Public Health College of the Haile Selassie I University in Gondar, VI, 11 ff. See also the brief comment by A. E. Mourant *et al.* in their *The Genetics of the Jews*, p. 39 referring to the Rh frequencies among

the Falashas, which "suggest that they, like the other Ethiopian population, are at least 50 percent of Negroid ancestry" and asking for a closer examination of the seriological factors among them; *supra*, n. 6.

22. See N. Nahoum, "Mission chez les Falachas d'Abyssinie," *Bulletin* of the Alliance Israélite Universelle, XXXIII, 100–137; C. Rathjen, *Die Juden in Abessinien*, pp. 64 f. On the extraordinary expansion of the Portuguese Empire, despite its small population in the mother country, see *supra*, Vols. XI, pp. 243 ff., 406 nn. 66 ff.; XII, pp. 23 ff., 257 nn. 21–22; XV, Chap. LXVI. The Falashas were indeed fortunate not to come under Portuguese control or even to feel the effects of a conversion of the native majority to Catholicism. Otherwise, they might have received some of the harsh treatment extended to their coreligionists in Portugal's Asian and African colonies after the establishment of the Inquisition in Goa in 1560. See *supra*, Vol. XV, pp. 356 ff., 364 ff., 543 ff. nn. 108 ff.

23. See H. A. Stern, *Wanderings among the Falashas in Abyssinia*, pp. 193 f.; J. Bruce, *Travels to Discover the Source of the Nile*, IV, 121; V, 13; A. Z. Aescoly, "Les Noms magiques dans les apocryphes chrétiens des Ethiopiens," *JA*, CCXX, 87–128; D. Lifschitz, *Textes éthiopiens magico-religieux* (*Travaux et Memoires* of the Institut d'Ethnologie in Paris, XXXVIII); A. D'Abbadie, "Rapport sur les Falachas," *Archives Israélites*, 1846; idem, *Douze ans dans la Haute Ethiopie*, p. 165; C. Conti Rossini, "Manoscritti ed opere abissine in Europa," *Rendiconti* of the R. Accademia dei Lincei, ser. 5, Vol. VIII, 606–637; E. Ullendorff, *The Ethiopians*, pp. 45 f. In this connection one may note Lifschitz's observation that "one finds a very large number of amulets written in Abyssinia. Almost all Abyssinians, men and women, wear on their neck, or in their belt, a box made of leather and more rarely of silver, containing a booklet or parchment roll of magical content" (p. 8). However, in the long list of magical names enumerated by her and Aescoly, one finds practically none of Hebrew origin, except for some names of angels derived from the Bible. We recall that, perhaps in opposition to this custom, the Falashas did not even observe the liturgical commandment of phylacteries, as did the Jews of other lands. Nor do we hear of Falasha artisans engaged in supplying amulets. See also the older, but still valuable study by W. H. Worrell, "Studien zum abessinischen Zauberwesen," *Zeitschrift für Assyriologie*, XXIII, 149–83; XXIV, 59–96; XXIX, 85–141.

According to E. Rüppell, in 1832–33 the Falashas almost monopolized the production of earthenware and the building of houses. See his *Reise in Abessinien*, II, 1810. (The reliability of this author as an explorer is emphasized in R. Merten's biography, *Eduard Rüppell, Leben und Werk eines Forschungsreisenden*.) In his *Wanderings among the Falashas*, Henry Aaron Stern actually came across two villages entirely inhabited by Jewish potters. This did not necessarily enhance the Falashas' social standing, however, and in his *Africa's Last Empire*, pp. 154, 191, 194 f., H. Norden quotes a popular saying by the Christian Abyssinians: "Pottery means Falasha, and Falasha means disgrace." D'Abbadie also noted that, in contrast to other Abyssinians, the Falashas held their blacksmiths in high repute. He saw therein another proof that they were of a different racial origin from the other local tribes, and not merely native converts to Judaism. See his *Journal*, cited by A. Z. Aescoly in the *Cahiers d'Études Africaines*, II, no. 5, p. 99. In this connection Aescoly also refers to the renown in which Jewish forgers of arms were held in Arabia in the days of Mohammed. See also, more generally, R. Pankhurst, *Economic History of Ethiopia, 1800–1935*, esp. pp. 40 f., 68 nn. 54 ff. Incidentally, the author points out that the publication of this volume in Addis

Ababa, being the largest English book issued in the Ethiopian capital, was an historic event in Ethiopian printing.

24. See E. Haberland, "Zum Problem der Jäger und besonderen Kasten in Nordost- und Ostafrika," *Paideuma. Mitteilungen zur Kulturkunde,* VIII, 136–55, esp. p. 136; C. Conti Rossini, *Principi di diritto consuetudinario dell'Eritrea,* pp. 111 ff., cited by R. Pankhurst, *Economic History,* pp. 135 f.; and, more generally, *ibid.,* Chaps. on "Land Tenure" (pp. 135–83), and on "Agriculture" (pp. 184–230); and V. Krempel, *Die Soziale und Wirtschaftliche Stellung der Falascha in der christlich-amharischen Gesellschaft von Nordwest-Äthiopien* (Dissertation of the Free University of Berlin; 1972), esp. pp. 78 ff., 98 ff., 112, 117 ff., 131 ff., 139, 150 f., 165 ff., offering a good analysis of contemporary conditions, with only occasional historical flashbacks. There is little information in the sources about the extent and forms of the earlier Falasha land tenure. But it appears that, like other peasants, they controlled the land in each area by virtue of inheritance from generation to generation, although in the period after 1630, their tribute to the Crown may have included specific payments from crops they harvested. Before that time, as a more or less independent tribe, they may have considered themselves the owners of the land they cultivated, at least insofar as they had not been deprived of it in the fifteenth-century turmoil. However, this is one of the most obscure aspects of medieval Falasha life.

25. See the two complementary studies by C. T. Beke, and by A. C. Cooke, both entitled "Routes in Abyssinia" in the *Journal of the Royal Geographical Society,* XII, 12–15, 215–58; XIV, 1–76; and in book form, respectively; the succinct description of Ethiopia's "climatic wonders" in E. H. Schrenzel's *Abessinien, Land ohne Hunger, Land ohne Zeit,* pp. 104 ff.; T. Tamrat's observations in his *Church and State in Ethiopia,* pp. 80 ff. (it may be assumed that the facilities of communication were no better in the preceding centuries); and A. H. Wyle's observation and the British consular report of 1900, cited by R. Pankhurst in his *Economic History of Ethiopia,* pp. 346, 408. According to H. A. Stern, the Falashas were forbidden by the Ethiopian government to engage in commerce. See his *Wanderings among the Falashas,* pp. 193 f. This assertion is not confirmed by any other source, however. Carl Rathjens doubts even whether the Falashas themselves believed in a Mosaic prohibition of trade, and refers to the observations of another traveler, C. Rohlfs, who had personally encountered a few Falasha traders. See Rathjens, *Die Juden in Abessinien,* p. 68; and Rohlfs, *Meine Mission nach Abessinien.* Of course, the situation may have changed since 1650. In any case, the long predominance of Muslim traders in Ethiopian commerce also in medieval times is evidenced by the numerous Arabic loanwords which had penetrated the various Ethiopian dialects; they are especially frequent among the technical terms in commercial exchanges. See the important pertinent studies by W. Leslau, listed by Pankhurst, p. 451 n. 15; to which may be added Leslau's more recent study, *Hebrew Cognates in Amharic.* Not surprisingly, there also were some Ethiopian words which were borrowed by neighboring Arabs. See the examples, cited by T. Nöldeke in his *Neue Beiträge zur semitischen Sprachwissenschaft,* pp. 46 ff.; and W. Leslau's *Ethiopic and South Arabic Contributions to the Hebrew Lexicon.*

26. See especially S. Strelcyn's studies, "Les Traités médicaux éthiopiens," *Cahiers d'Études africaines,* II, no. 5, pp. 148–59 (four years later updated by him in "Les Écrits médicaux éthiopiens," *Journal of Ethiopian Studies,* III, no. 1, pp. 82–103); "Ethiopian Medical Treatises as a Source for the Study of Early Amharic," *Proceedings* of the First International Congress of Africanists, held in Accra in 1962, ed. by L. Bown and M.

Crowders, pp. 105–112, and particularly his comprehensive and detailed study *Médecine et plantes d'Ethiopie. Les Traités médicaux ethiopiens (Prace Orientalistyczne* of the Polish Academy, XIV), with comments thereon by L. Ricci in his review of that volume in *Rassegna di Studi Etiopici*, XXIV, 264–73. Not surprisingly, both author and reviewer are stressing the philological, rather than the medical or sociohistorical, aspects of that literature. See also R. H. P. Pankhurst, "An Historical Examination of Traditional Ethiopian Medicine and Surgery; the Introduction of Modern Medicine in Ethiopia," *Ethiopia Observer*, IX, 114–60; "The Beginnings of Modern Medicine in Ethiopia," in the same volume; and D. Harel, "Medical Works among the Falashas in Ethiopia," *Israel Journal of Medicine and Science*, III, 483–90. This still is clearly one of the numerous gray areas in Ethiopian history awaiting further elucidation by specialists.

27. Antoine d'Abbadie's *Journal* cited by A. Z. Aeŝcoly in the *Cahiers d'Etudes Africaines*, II, no. 5, pp. 100 ff.; W. Leslau, *Coutumes et Croyances*, pp. 58 ff., also referring to the debate between A. Z. Aeŝcoly and Jacques Faitlovich concerning the alleged claim of Falasha priests to be descendants of the tribe of Levi. Faitlovich's denial of this claim is accepted by Leslau (p. 58 n. 4).

28. See W. Plowden, *Travels in Abyssinia*, pp. 137 f.; M. Parkyns, *Life in Abyssinia*, I, 101; V. L. Grottanelli, "Ricerche antropogeografiche sulla regione del Lago Tana," in *Missione di studio al Lago Tana*, published by the Italian Academy in Rome, 1938, all cited in R. Pankhurst's *Economic History of Ethiopia*, pp. 504 f., 515. Pankhurst's chapter on "Taxation and Government Revenue" in that volume, pp. 504–544, offers the best review of that subject for the nineteenth and twentieth centuries. In the earlier periods, it may be assumed, there was even greater arbitrariness, moderated by more paternalism in various degrees in different parts of the country and different periods. For the Falashas the crucial break occurred, of course, about 1630, when they lost their national independence and began paying the Crown tributes fluctuating in size.

29. See I Kings 10:22, 22:49; J. H. Lord, *The Jews in India and the Far East* (Being a Reprint of Articles contributed to "Church and Synagogue" with Appendices), pp. 49 ff.; J. Hornell, "Naval Activity in the Days of Solomon and Rameses III," *Antiquity*, XXI, 66–73, esp. p. 72; the older and more recent theories about the origin of the Bene-Israel, reviewed by H. S. Kehimkar in *The History of the Bene Israel of India*, pp. 4 ff.; S. Samuel, *A Treatise on the Origin and Early History of the Beni-Israel of Maharashtar State*, pp. 5 ff.; and *supra*, Vols. I, p. 221 n. 3; VII, pp. 18 and 226 f. To be sure, the location of the biblical Ophir is still controversial. The authors of *The Cambridge Shorter History of India* adroitly circumvented the issue by writing: "It was ultimately, if not directly, from south India that the ships of Tarshish brought to Solomon ivory, apes, and peacocks." See that *History*, by J. Allan *et al.*, and ed. by H. H. Dodwell with additional Chapters on *The Last Phase (1919–1947)* by R. R. Sethi, esp. p. 140. See *supra*, Vol. I, pp. 184, 321; Vol. III, pp. 116, 286 n. 52.

30. See A. Hamilton, *A New Account of the East Indies, Observations and Remarks*, reproduced in John Pinkerton's *Voyages and Travels in All Parts of the World Digested on a New Plan*, VIII, 238–572, esp. pp. 379 ff.; *supra*, Vols. I, p. 64; III, pp. 114 f., 173, 284 f. n. 50. We may also remember the curious identification of the Jews by Greek observers as being descendants of Indians. See *supra*, Vol. I, p. 184. "India as described by Medieaval European Travelers, I: Jewish Dwelling Places," is analyzed by L. Sternbach in a pertinent essay under this title in *Barutiya Vidya*, VII, 10–28; and,

more fully, by W. J. Fischel in his *Ha-Yehudim be-Hodu,* with extensive bibliographical references. Fischel subsequently added a careful review of "The Exploration of the Jewish Antiquities of Cochin on the Malabar Coast," *JAOS,* LXXXVII, 230–46. This essay includes a reexamination of the intriguing inscriptions on the copper plates recording the early Jewish privileges, their decipherment, and Western translations, a task first accomplished by the distinguished French student of Zoroastrianism, Abraham Hyacynth Anquetil-Duperron, who at the beginning of 1758 spent almost a month in Cochin. On this occasion he enjoyed the full cooperation of the Jewish community whose chief (*mudeliar*), Joseph Hallague, went out of his way to lend him the precious plates for minute study at home. See his French trans. of the Zoroastrian Scripture, *Zenda-Avesta,* I, pp. cxlvii–cxcii, 151–52. This work, published in 1777, was used to good advantage by several successors, including those mentioned *supra,* Vol. III, and G. S. Oppert, a retired professor of Sanskrit of the Presidential College in Madras and one of the Jewish scholarly pioneers in the study of Indian Jewry. See his "Über die jüdischen Kolonien in Indien," in *Semitic Studies in Memory of Alexander Kohut,* pp. 396–409. Incidentally, Anquetil-Duperron, with the assistance of an unnamed Jew from Calicut, succeeded in deciphering also the somewhat similar copper plates in the possession of the St. Thomas Christians in Malabar, but he was unable to view the plates obtained by the Muslim minority. See M. Rae, *The Syrian Church in India.* On Anquetil's high competence in this field see R. Schwab, *Vie d'Anquetil-Duperron suivie de l'usage civile et religieuse de Parses,* with a Preface by Sylvain Lévi and two essays by J. Jamshedji Modi.

31. Benjamin of Tudela, *Itinerary,* ed. by M. N. Adler, pp. 58 ff. (Hebrew), 63 ff. (English); and the relatively few documents published more than twenty years ago, cited *supra,* Vol. III, pp. 284 f. nn. 49–50. See also *infra,* n. 47; and especially S. D. Goitein's preliminary study "From the Mediterranean to India: Documents on the Trade to India, South Arabia, and East Africa from the Eleventh and Twelfth Centuries," *Speculum,* XXIX, 181–97; and his more recent "From Aden to India: Specimens of the Correspondence of India Traders of the Twelfth Century," *JESHO,* XXIII, 43–66 includes the Arabic text of two pertinent letters from the Genizah (pp. 46 ff.) and an English trans. and commentaries (pp. 51 ff.) and mentions transcripts of some 400 other documents of this type in his possession. On Solomon ibn Ya'ish's successful business career in India, see *supra,* Chap. LXXVII, n. 25.

32. See the distinguished collection and English trans. of H. M. Elliot, *The History of India as Told by Its Own Historians,* posthumously ed. by J. Dawson, VIII, 576 ff., 585 (Nawar Muhabbat Khan's *Akbar I*); F. Bernier, *Travels in the Mogul Empire A.D. 1656–1668,* trans. on the Basis of I. Brock's version and annotated by A. Constable; 2d ed., rev. by V. A. Smith, pp. 428 f. (see the passage more fully quoted *infra,* n. 50); Mohbul Hasan, *Kashmir under the Sultans. Abdul Halim Memorial Volume,* esp. pp. 58 ff., 71 ff., 162 ff. The date of Sikandar's reign is given here at variance from that mentioned by M. Hasan, which had long been accepted from E. von Zambaur's comprehensive chronologies of the Muslim dynasties in his *Manuel de généalogie et de chronologie pour l'historire de l'Islam.* Although I have generally followed the dates given in that manual, I believe that in this case those established by T. W. Haig in "The Chronology and Genealogy of the Muhammadan Kings of Kashmir," *JRAS,* 1918, pp. 451–68; and accepted by *The Cambridge History of India,* III, 277 ff., 698 ff.; and by C. E. Bosworth in *The Islamic Dynasties,* pp. 196 ff. are more correct. See also R. C. Majumdar, *The Delhi Sultanate,* with a Foreword by K. M. Munshi, pp. 415 ff., mentioning also without further elaboration or documentation Ibn Baṭṭuṭa's report that on his

way to Quilon he had passed through a Jewish settlement in Kunjakari living under a Jewish chief, but paying tax to the Hindu ruler of Quilon!

Of the very large literature on the manifold aspects of medieval Indian life and culture written by both Indian and Western scholars, we need but cite here: S. Lane-Poole, *Medieval India under Mohammadan Rule*, describing Maḥmud of Ghazni's and other early Arab conquests of India as "episodes" in its histories, "a triumph without results" (pp. 26 ff.); I. Prasad, *History of Medieval India from 647 A.D. to the Mughal Conquest*, with a Foreword by L. F. Bushbrock-Williams or in the French trans. *L'Inde du VIIe au XVIe siècle*, trans. from the 2d ed. by H. de Saucy; and K. S. Lai, *Studies in Medieval Indian History*.

33. Emperor Babur's statements quoted by E. D. Ross in *The Cambridge History of India*, IV, ed. by R. Burn, pp. 1–20, esp. p. 14. See also Babur's *Memoirs . . . , Written by Himself in the Chagatai Túrki*, and trans. by J. Leyden and W. Eskiney, annotated and revised by L. King; and the biographical sketch in *The Great Moghuls* by B. Gascoigne. The general history of the Mughal Empire has been treated in many works. See especially R. F. Tripathi, *Rise and Fall of the Mughal Empire;* and A. L. Scrivastava, *The Moghul Empire, 1526–1803 A.D.*, 4th ed. rev. Many older works are listed in S. R. Sharma, *A Bibliography of Mughal India (1525–1707 A.D.)*. With a Foreword by J. Sarkan. A fuller and more up-to-date bibliography is greatly needed.

34. V. A. Smith, *Akbar the Great Moghul, 1542–1605,* 2d ed., p. 256; L. Binyon, *Akbar*. In this well-written biographical sketch, Binyon emphasizes, among the emperor's achievements, that "the principles and the practices worked out by Akbar and his ministers were largely adopted under the English system of government" (p. 3).

35. See P. du Jarrie, *Akbar and the Jesuits: an Account of the Jesuit Missions to the Coast of Malabar*, ed. and trans., with an Intro. and Notes by C. H. Paine; and the survey by J. Correia-Afonso in his *Jesuit Letters and Indian History 1542–1773*, 2d ed., with a Foreword by Valerian Cardinal Gracias. See also, more generally, R. Krishnamurti's observations on *Akbar: the Religious Aspect;* and *infra*, nn. 36 and 41. Despite his general tolerance of religious diversity and the vagueness of his own beliefs, Akbar severely handled an opponent in this area. He enjoyed therein the support of many Islamic religious leaders. According to Badaoni, on September 23, 1579, these leaders declared that "any opposition on the part of his [the emperor's] subjects to such an order passed by His Majesty shall involve damnation in the world to come and loss of property and religious privileges in this" (II, 279 ff. cited by Krishnamurti in his *Akbar*, pp. 30 f.). Regrettably, no records of these disputations have been kept and whatever summaries are included in the biographical and historical literature do not present any adequate picture. However, their level doubtless resembled that of some later disputations which were summarized in *The Dabistan*. See *infra*, n. 38. For one example, the record of a debate, later held with the participation of a Jew, describes first the controversy between a Sunnite and a Shi'ite Muslim. Among other arguments here presented was the contention of the Shi'ite that the Sunnites did not understand the nature of a prophet's purity, since they really believed that King David had caused Uriah to be killed in order to get his wife. A Jew who happened to be present at that discussion confirmed the Sunnite's assertion by pointing out that this story is actually recorded in the Pentateuch (he really meant in the Bible). "Upon which the Shiâh rejoined: 'The Pentateuch is altered.' The Jew retorted: 'We may as well, and with a better right, say that your book is altered, while there is no reason to be urged that the Pentateuch is corrupted.' The Shiâh had no answer to give, and the author of this

book saw in the treatises of several of the modern learned, that they have appropriated this answer to themselves." See *The Dabistan*, translated from the Original Persian by D. Shea and A. Troyer. With an Intro. by A. V. W. Jackson. Reprinted in Lahore, 1973, pp. 353 f.

36. See Abu'l Fazl i 'Allami, *The Akbarnama*, trans. from the Persian by M. Beveridge, II, 316 f.; J. C. Powell-Price, *A History of India*, pp. 284 ff. (includes a judicious assessment of Akbar's personality); and other sources listed by W. J. Fischel in his "Jews and Judaism at the Court of the Moghul Emperors in Medieval India," *PAAJR*, XVIII, 137–77, esp. pp. 141 ff. To support his ambitious claim that a new era had begun under his regime, the emperor used a millennarian argument—similar to that widespread in the Christian world, before 1000 C.E.—that Mohammed's mission was to be terminated at the year 1000 of the Muslim calendar. Hence, 1000 A.H. which coincided with 1592 C.E. could well be used as a justification for a new calendar. In fact Akbar ordered Maulana Ahmad and, upon his death, Badaoni to write a *Tarikh-i-Alfi* (Annals of the Millennium) which Badaoni also managed to publish in 1592. One wonders whether Akbar and some other Muslim millennarians took their cue from the anti-Jewish calculation by the Almohades and others that Mohammed's concession to the "People of the Book" was to last only 500 years, at which time the Jewish Messiah was to appear and Christ reappear; otherwise those concessions were to be withdrawn. Needless to say, the emperor's calendar reform did not last beyond his lifetime which ended in 1605. See H. G. Keene, *A Sketch of the History of Hindustan from the First Muslim Conquest to the Fall of the Mughol Empire*, pp. 119 f., 136.

37. See W. J. Fischel, "The Bible in Persian Translation," *Harvard Theological Review*, XLV, 3–45; Rodolfo Acquaviva's report of July 18, 1586; Alessandro Valignano's *Summarium Indicum alterum*, both reproduced by J. Wicki in his ed. of *Documenta Indica*, XII (= *MHSI*, CV, 1972), 48 f.; XIII (–*MHSI*, CXIII, 1975), 134–319, esp. p. 146. On Valignano's high ranking in both the Jesuit Order and its historiography, see *supra*, Vol. XV, pp. 548 f. n. 118.

38. See *Dabistan*, pp. 299 ff.; and B. J. Hasrat's *Dārā Shikuh: Life and Works*, pp. 100 ff. It appears that Sarmad, despite his own claim of having been a rabbi, forgot most of what he may have learned in his youth from Jewish sources and accepted many of the age-old Muslim controversialists' attributions to Jewish lore. In the information, for instance, which he gave to the author of *Dabistan* he correctly stated that "the Yahuds agree in denying the appearance of *Aisia* (Jesus) *as a prophet;* They say that he was a deceiver; and they reject what the *Aisuyan* (Christians) adduce from the Old Testament about the appearance of Aisya." He also confirmed the authenticity of the biblical story of David's connivance in the death of Uriah. But at the same time he conceded the alleged biblical predictions of the appearance of Mohammed, stating that it was "written in their [the Jews'] sacred book that, when the children of Isráil shall perform iniquitous acts, Mohammed will appear." He merely added the reservation that this particular biblical passage could have the simple meaning of a prophet exhorting the Israelites to convert themselves to his religion. See *supra*, Vols. V, pp. 86 ff., 329 ff. nn. 5 ff.; XVII, pp. 179 ff., 379 ff. nn. 66 ff., and other passages.

39. See Muhammad Dara Shikuh, *Majma' ul-Bakrain or The Mingling of the Two Oceans*, ed. and trans. into English by Mahfun al-Haq (Bibliotheca Indica, Arabic and Persian Series), pp. 26–29; L. Massignon and A. M. Kassim, "Un Essai de Bloc Islamo-Hindou au XVII siècle; L'Humanisme Mystique du Prince Dârâ," *Revue du Monde Musulman*,

LXIII, 1–14; B. J. Hasrat, *Dārā Shikuh, passim.* See also A. Sajida, "The Historians of Awangzib: a Comparative Study of Three Primary Sources," in Donald P. Little, ed. of *Essays on Islamic Civilization. Presented to Niyazi Berkes,* pp. 57–73.

It may be noted that Akbar's immediate successor, Nur as-Din Jihangir (1605–1627) was much more ambivalent than his father concerning his Muslim beliefs and practices. In his letter of October 30, 1616 to the Lord Bishop of Canterbury, the English ambassador, Sir Thomas Roe, reported that "the present King, beeing the issue of this New fancy, and neuer circumcised, bread up without any religion at all, continewes so to this hower, and is an Atheist. Sometyme he will make profession of a Moore: but alway obserue the hollidayes, and doe all Ceremonyes with the Gentilles too." While atheism was a clear overstatement, since even Akbar prayed daily to a deity, Roe was right in saying that Jihangir was more a practicing than a believing Muslim. As a result, his regime continued the policy of religious toleration introduced by his father. In another context (in an entry in his private *Journal* under the date of February 11, 1617), Roe described at some length the experience he had with Jihangir who was, at that moment, completely inebriated. "The good king fell to dispute of the lawes of Moses, Jesus and Mahomett; and in drinck was so kinde that hee turned to mee, and said: Am I a king? You shal be wellcome: Christians, Moores, Iewes, hee meddled not with their faith: They Came all in loue [love] and hee would protect them from wrong: they liued vnder his safety and none should oppresse them; and this often repeated; but in extreame drunkennes hee fell to weeping and to diuers Passions, and soe kept vs till midnight." *The Embassy of Sir Thomas Roe to the Court of the Great Mogul, 1615–1619, as Narrated in his Journal and Correspondence.* Ed. by W. Foster, *Publications* of the Hakluyt Society, I, 313 f., 382. See also F. Guerrero, *Jahangzir and the Jesuits,* ed. by C. N. Payne. Yet the growing Muslim reaction made the humanism of Dara Shikuh obsolete and his brother Awrangzib, being a devout Muslim, used the Islamic reaction to eliminate rivals like Dara and to establish the Muslim predominance during his half-century-long reign.

40. The story of Goa, the Portuguese Inquisition, and its antecedents has been reviewed *supra,* Vol. XV, pp. 364 ff., 547 ff. Of course, being in the focus of attention of Portuguese and other European, as well as Indian, historical scholarship, considerable additional literature has appeared in the last several years. However, it did not shed much new light on the position of the Jews in that Portuguese colony in the sixteenth and seventeenth centuries. To be sure, Kenneth S. Latourette's assertion that "by the close of the sixteenth century practically all in the vicinity of Goa were professing Christians," based on an old and somewhat uncritical study by M. Müllbauer, *Geschichte der katholischen Missionen in Ostindien von der Zeit Vasco da Gamas bis zur Mitte des achtzehnten Jahrhunderts,* pp. 81 ff. is questionable. But the ruling circles remained Christian for centuries, professing Jews not being tolerated at all, while Marranos were in constant peril of detection and ultimately execution. It is not surprising, therefore, that this area completely disappeared from the arena of Jewish history. Unlike the other European-dominated provinces in India, the Goa regime was not succeeded either by Dutch or by British rule and this remnant of the Portuguese colonial empire in Asia was only eliminated by a direct belligerent action of the independent Indian state in 1961. See K. N. Latourette, *A History of Expansion of Christianity,* IV, 249 ff., 256; and particularly A. Baião, *A Inquisição de Goa, 1509–1630.*

41. See R. Mac Phee, "An Investigation into the Muslim Character of the Mughal State," *Journal of Indian History,* LIV, 93–106, contending that "the term Muslim cannot be applied to the Mughal dynasty in any but the most superficial sense of the

word" (p. 93). His argument depends on how one uses the nomenclature of "Muslim state." The Mughal Empire definitely was under a Muslim regime if considered from the point of view of the powers that were, even if the majority of the population did not profess Islam and the traditional caste structure of Indian society continued unabated under the Mughal emperors. However, such differences between rulers and ruled existed in many other states with the basic coloring conferred upon them by their dominant group, which was in complete control over the legislative, administrative, and military powers.

42. Questions concerning the origin and early developments of the group which called itself by the biblical name Bene-Israel (Children of Israel), rather than Jews, has occupied the minds of scholars for several generations. The most comprehensive analysis has been offered by one of its own members, Haeem Samuel Kehimkar. Born in 1830 in Alibag, some 25 miles southeast of Bombay, Kehimkar spent his lifetime in trying to educate his coreligionists and to ameliorate their communal life. He not only founded a school, later called the Sir Elly Kadoori School, and the Bene-Israel Benevolent Society, which greatly contributed to the awakening of the consciousness of their heritage among the scattered Bene-Israel communities, but in 1897 he also wrote the basic book, *The History of the Bene Israel of India,* which, however, did not appear in print until 1937. While some of his theories, like those of his predecessors, have been rejected by other scholars, he has helped collect many ascertainable data and contributed much to an emerging consensus at least on a few general assumptions. Some of the later studies have been reviewed by another member of the community, Shellim Samuel, in *A Treatise on the Origin and Early History of the Beni-Israel of Maharashtra State.* A lawyer, economist, and civic leader, Samuel helped clarify some specific points under discussion for many years. Among the latest publications, dealing mainly with the contemporary situation, but also shedding some additional light on the history of the group, one may mention the on-the-spot researches conducted by S. Strizower of Melbourne, Australia, summarized in "The Bene Israel and the Jewish People," in the *Salo Wittmayer Baron Jubilee Volume,* II, 850–86; and by J. G. Roland of New York, in "The Jews of India: Communal Survival or the End of a Sojourn?" *JSS,* XLII, 75–90, referring also to more recent publications in the field.

43. See II Macc. 1–8; III Macc. 7:19; with the comments thereon by E. Bickermann in "Ein Jüdischer Festbrief von Jahre 124 v. Chr. (II Macc. I, 1–9)," *Zeitschrift für die neutestamentliche Wissenschaft,* XXXII, 233–54. The internal conflicts generated after the Maccabean revolt between the kings and the Pharisaic group have ingeniously been analyzed by V. (A.) Aptowitzer in his *Parteipolitik der Hasmonäerzeit im rabbinischen und pseudepigraphischen Schrifttum.* While some of Aptowitzer's reconstructions have been criticized by other scholars, his main thesis of the deep breach between the politically minded later Hasmoneans and the mainly religiously oriented Pharisaic leaders appears incontrovertible.

It is not surprising, therefore, that the Ḥanukkah festival played a diminishing role even in ancient Palestine, being elevated again into a national holiday in Babylonian circles in defiance of the Zoroastrian majority. These changing attitudes of the population toward the Festival of Lights found expression even in the varying shapes of the lamps employed by the population. See L. Ginzberg, *Ginze Schechter and Genizah Studies in Memory of Solomon Schechter,* I, 476; G. E. Wright, "Lamps, Politics and the Jewish Religion," *Biblical Archaeologist,* II, 22–24; and, more generally, O. S. Rankin, *The Origins of the Festival of Hanukkah, the Jewish New-Age Festival,* with L. Finkelstein's comments thereon in the review of this work in his "Hanukkah and Its Origin," *JQR,*

XXII, 169–73. See also *supra*, Vol. I, pp. 220 f., 395 n. 13, 398 ff. (also in the 1st ed., Vol. III, p. 3 n. 2). It is small wonder, then, that neither the Falashas nor the Bene-Israel, whose general religious outlook and practice depended more on the Palestino-Egyptian than the Babylonian Jewish traditions, paid little heed to a festival which was not prescribed in the Bible and whose actual observance was subject to some controversy among their purported ancestors.

44. See S. Weil's succinct intro., "The Bene Israel of India," in the recently published booklet, *The Jews from the Konkan: the Bene Israel Communities in India,* an exhibition of photographs, principally supplied by C. Berkson and displayed by the Beth Hatefutsoth. The debates of the Israeli rabbinate from 1938 on, the decision adopted by the Chief Rabbinate in Jerusalem in 1951, and particularly the comprehensive survey of, and quotations from, earlier responsa stemming from many lands as reproduced in the Chief Rabbinate's Hebrew publication entitled *"Benei-Yisrael" Pisqei halakhah u-mequorot* (B.-Y. Halakhic Decisions and Sources for the Clarfication of the Law and the Problem of Their Origin), ed. by R. Yitzhak Nissim, Chairman, Vol. I, esp. pp. 7 ff.; the list of festivals and fast days observed by the Bene-Israel compiled by H. S. Kehimkar in *The History of the Bene Israel,* pp. 16 ff. The omission of the Feast of Weeks, here explained by the absence of synagogues, is less convincing than the fact mentioned in the Bible that it was the Festival of First Fruits (Num. 28:26) brought to the Temple in Jerusalem which in the Indian environment had no corresponding celebration fifty days after the beginning of Passover. It may also be noted that by quoting the passage in the Babylonian Talmud (Rosh Ha-Shanah 19b) which explained that "so long as the Second Temple stood it was not permissible to observe the four fasts of national mourning, because they were days of joy, but since the Temple fell, it is allowed, because they are days of mourning," Kehimkar found support for his thesis that the type of observance of these sorrowful occasions by the Bene-Israel dated from the tannaitic times, rather than from earlier periods. This argument is, of course, quite weak, since the days of mourning have been observed by the Jewish communities of all other countries, because of the historic continuity of their life as Jews.

45. See G. Philips, extensively quoted in K. P. Padmanabha Menon's *A History of Kerala, Written, in the Form of Notes on [Jacob Canter] Visscher's Letters from Malabar,* and ed. by T. K. Krishna Menon, I, 163 f. On the great and persistent tribal and caste divisions in the area, see also L. K. A. K. Iyer's *Cochin Tribes and Castes,* 2d ed. In this connection one ought to mention P. Hardy's pertinent observation about the general superiority of medieval Indian Muslim historiography over that of contemporary Europe. This superiority lay principally in the fact, already noted by H. H. Dodwell, that the Muslim chronicles "were written for the most part not by monks but by men of affairs, often by contemporaries who had seen and taken part in the events they recounted." See P. Hardy's "Some Studies in Pre-Mughal Muslim Historiography," in C. H. Philips, ed. *Historians of India, Pakistan and Ceylon,* pp. 115–27. However, we also remember the limitations of that historical literature, discussed in this and earlier chapters.

46. See M. Rae, *The Syrian Church in India;* S. G. Pothan, *The Syrian Christians in Kerala,* also reproducing (in the Appendix, pp. 102 ff.) the copper plates of Cochin Jewry in English; A. Valignano, *Historia del principio y progreso de la Compañía de Jesús en las Indias Orientales (1542–1564),* ed. by J. Wicki, p. 343. In view of the ability of so many Eastern Christians to find their way from Syria and Tunisia to India in the

early Middle Ages there is a great probability that a similar migration took place among the Jews of western Asia. In fact, as Pothan pointed out, in many observances, especially in marriage customs, the St. Thomas Christians followed ancient Jewish, rather than Western Christian patterns (pp. 67 ff.). Not surprisingly, the fourteenth-century Franciscan visitors in the area, Andreas of Perugia and Odoricus de Pordenone, confirmed not only the Jewish presence in Malabar but also the fact that neither Jews nor Muslims were willing to be converted to Christianity. According to Odoricus, both Cranganore (which he called Çinflin) and Pandarani (Falandria) were inhabited by some Jews and Christians who always were at war with one another. This may be an exaggeration, but the government's neutrality in such conflicts within a general freedom of conscience, also attested by Andreas of Perugia, doubtless reflected existing realities in the religious sphere. See Andreas de Perugia, "Epistola," and Odoricus de Pordenone, "Relatio," both critically ed. by A. van den Wyngaert in his *Sinica Franciscana*, Vol. I: *Itinera et relationes fratrum minorum saeculi XIII et XIV*, pp. 369–77, esp. p. 376; and pp. 381–495, esp. pp. 439 f. (also in the English translation by H. Yule, ed., *Cathay and the Way Thither, Being a Collection of Medieval Notices on China. New edition, revised throughout in the Light of Recent Discoveries* by H. Cordier. (*Works* of the Hakluyt Society, XXXIII, XXXVII–VIII, XLI).

47. Maimonides' "Letter to the Jews of Lunel," quoted in the English translation by E. N. Ezekiel from Bombay in his letter to the London *Jewish Chronicle* of September 28, 1906 and reproduced in J. H. Lord's *The Jews in India and the Far East*, App. iii, p. 12. On that famous correspondence between the sage of Fusṭaṭ and the Jewish scholars of Lunel, see *supra*, Vol. VI, pp. 106, 380 n. 122.

48. The responsa by R. David Ibn abi Zimra and R. Jacob Castro, reproduced by A. Marx in his "Contribution à l'histoire des Juifs de Cochin," *REJ*, LXXXIX, 293–304, reprinted in English (without the texts) in Marx's *Essays in Jewish History and Booklore*, pp. 174–77; further interpreted, with reference to Ibn abi Zimra's general attitude toward various deviant groups of Jews, by I. M. Goldman in *The Life and Times of Rabbi David Ibn Abi Zimra*, pp. 59 f.; and the collection of some other responsa written by rabbis over the ages in the aforementioned compilation, *"Benei Yisrael." Pisqei halakhah*. This array of somewhat divergent opinions clearly reflects the inner conflict of the respondents between adhering to the rigidity of the law which would treat the "Black" Jews in Cochin as descendants of slaves not duly discharged by a writ of liberation, and thereby make their entry into the Jewish community extremely difficult, and the attempt to regard this distant group as part of the Jewish people. This sentimental dilemma is already illustrated by Ibn abi Zimra's argument that, because of the absence of the five legal requirements of the halakhah or even of one of them, the Cochin Jews should be treated "not as slaves but rather as candidates for conversion who, together with their wives and children, are ready to enter into the community of the Lord." In his opinion even the more rigid interpreters would be prepared to "rely on the emergency nature of the Cochin situation to permit this segment to be integrated into the community of Israel so as to remove from them the mutual hatred and dissension." See Marx, p. 300.

49. See Zechariah b. Saadiah adh-Dhahri (or az-Zahiri), *Sefer ha-Musar* (Book of Moral Conduct) ed. by Y. Ratzaby, esp. pp. 28, 90, 145; Mosseh Pereyra de Paiva, *Notisias dos Judeos de Cochin*, Amsterdam 1687, republished by M. Amzalak. Among the nineteenth-century visitors we need but mention R. David D'Beth Hillel, *The Trav-*

els of Rabbi David D'Beth Hillel: from Jerusalem through Arabia, Koordistan, part of Persia and India to Madras, pp. 116–29; Benjamin II, *Eight Years in Asia and Africa,* Hannover, 1859, pp. 143–47; R. Jacob Saphir, *Eben Sapir* (Travelogue), II, 42–50. The Sassoon manuscript referred to in the text contains a small Hebrew treatise by G. A. Rahavi, "Dibrei yemei ha-Yehudim be-Cochin" (A History of the Jews in Cochin), as described in the Sassoon catalogue, *Ohel David* (David's Tent), I, 370 No. 268. This essay has been used to good advantage by G. Bar-Giyora in his "Sources for the History of the Conflicts between the White and Black Jews in Cochin" (Hebrew), *Sefunot,* I, 242–75. See also the same author's "A Contribution to the History of the Synagogues in Cochin" (Hebrew) *ibid,* II, 214–45; and his earlier observations in his *Massa' be-Hodu* (Travel through India).

It may be noted that, unlike their counterparts in Ethiopia and China, the Cochin Jews seem to have had in their midst persons able to write letters for them in an acceptable Hebrew style. Apart from those mentioned in our other notes, see the two epistles published by G. A. Kohut in his "Correspondence between the Jews of Malabar and New York a Century Ago," in *Semitic Studies in Memory of Alexander Kohut,* ed. by him, pp. 420–34. These letters and two others written in 1795 by the New York spokesmen Solomon b. Joseph Simson and Alexander Hirsch, however, contribute but few new data or insights on the position of Indian Jewry at the end of the eighteenth century.

50. Some of these travelogues and reports have been, and will be, mentioned in the notes to the present chapter. Unfortunately, perhaps because they were overwhelmed by the subcontinent's immensity of territory, population density, and great variations in class, religion, and culture, most visitors to India were far less specific with details regarding Jewish life than were their counterparts—and sometimes even they themselves—in their observations of the developments within the Jewish communities in the Ottoman Empire or Persia. They also often depended on certain assumptions concerning the appearance of the Indian Jew rather than on fully ascertainable facts. Typical of such generalizations is the following discourse of one of the best of them, François Bernier (1620–88). After securing a degree of doctor of medicine in Montpellier and associating with the famed philosopher Pierre Gassendi, Bernier gave vent to his wanderlust and spent ten years in the Middle East and particularly in India (1656–66). Discussing the population of Kashmir, Bernier was pleased to answer the inquiry of another distinguished traveler, Jean de Thévenot, concerning the presence of Jews in that mountainous region. He believed that the Jewish descendants of the early Israelitic exiles may well have disappeared from that area but he added:

—

There are, however, many signs of *Judaism* to be found in this country. On entering the kingdom after crossing the *Pire-penjale* mountains, the inhabitants in the frontier villages struck me as resembling *Jews.* Their countenance and manner, and that indescribable peculiarity which enables a traveller to distinguish the inhabitants of different nations, all seemed to belong to that ancient people. You are not to ascribe what I say to mere fancy, the *Jewish* appearance of these villagers having been remarked by our *Jesuit Father,* and by several other *Europeans,* long before I visited *Kachemire.*

A second sign is the prevalence of the name *Mousa,* which means *Moses,* among the inhabitants of this city, notwithstanding they are all *Mahometans.*

A third is the common tradition that *Solomon* visited this country, and that it was he who opened a passage for the waters by cutting the mountain of *Baramoulé.*

A Fourth, the belief that *Moses* died in the city of *Kachemire,* and that his tomb is within a league of it.

And a fifth may be found in the generally received opinion that the small and extremely ancient edifice seen on one of the high hills was built by *Solomon;* and it is therefore called the *Throne of Solomon* to this day.

Bernier seems generally to have relied on his visual conceptions. He went, for example, to very great lengths and much expense to smuggle himself into one of the Kashmir buildings where he could see some of the beautiful women for which the country was famous. See his *Travels in the Mogul Empire* A.D. *1656–1668,* translated on the Basis of Irving Brock's Version and Annotated by Archibald Constable, 2d ed. rev. by V. A. Smith, pp. 405, 430.

51. See R. David Ibn abi Zimra's *Resp.* in A. Marx's "Contribution" in *REJ,* LXXXIX, 299 f.; Mosseh Pereyra de Paiva, *Notisias,* ed. by M. A. Amzalak; Jacob Saphir, *Eben Sapir.*

52. On the Paradesi synagogue, see G. Bar Giyora in *Sefunot,* II, 214 ff. It undoubtedly was that synagogue (called "Paradesi" or of Foreigners, by the local population because the White Jews who built it were relative newcomers in the city) which was visited and briefly described in 1556 by Didacus or Diogo do Soveral, a Jesuit missionary who had entered the Order in 1543, shortly after its foundation. See his letter of January 2, 1556 to the Order's headquarters, reproduced by J. Wicki in his ed. of *Documenta Indica,* III (*MHSI,* LXXIV), 431 ff. No. 75 item 7, also mentioning the presence in the city of seven pagodas and a number of mosques. The contrasting cleavage between Sephardim and Ashkenazim in the West was demonstrated on many occasions. See, for instance, H. J. Zimmels, *Ashkenazim and Sephardim: Their Relations, Differences and Problems,* esp. pp. 49 ff., 164 ff. European Jewish arrivals in India begin sporadically appearing in the literature relating to the Portuguese and other Western expansion into India. Apart from the well-known story of Gaspar da Gama (see *supra,* Vol. XV, pp. 356 ff., 543 nn. 108 ff.); and the additional data supplied by W. J. Fischel in his *Ha-Yehudim be-Hodu,* pp. 15 ff.; we also have a reference to a Jewish woman from Seville, who had come to Cranganore (via Cairo and Mecca), and was seen there by the famed navigator Pedro Alvares Cabral in his journey of 1501. See his *The Voyage to Brazil and India from Contemporary Documents and Narratives,* trans. and ed. by W. B. Greenlee, p. 86. For Spanish-speaking Jews encountered by John Huyghen van Linschoten in the 1580s, see *infra,* n. 55.

53. See Mosseh Pereyra de Paiva, *Notisias dos Judeos de Cochim;* the various statistical data collected by D. G. Mandelbaum in "The Jewish Way of Life in Cochin," *JSS,* I, 423–60, esp. pp. 433, 453 f.; J. H. Lord in *The Jews in India and the Far East,* esp. pp. 1 ff., Apps. I–II; and *infra,* n. 57. Regrettably, fairly reliable statistical data stem only from the period of British domination in the nineteenth and twentieth centuries. While the progressive decline of the Jewish population in all of India is clearly demonstrated by the available evidence, specific data for various periods and regions until the seventeenth century are largely in the realm of conjecture. The low figure of less than 5,000 for the total Jewish population in all of India in the 1970s which, even

without Pakistan and Bangladesh, has been the recognized second most populous country in the world, is given by J. G. Roland in "The Jews of India," *JSS*, XLII, 79 f. Although the generally unfriendly attitude of the Indian government to Israel, and indirectly also to Judaism, may have played some role in increasing the emigration of many Baghdadi Jews and Bene-Israel, there also were fundamental forces at work to make the decline of the Jewish population more explainable. However, the recent developments shed but little light on the medieval and early modern evolution under the different conditions analyzed in the present volume.

54. See E. J. W. Macfarlane, "Preliminary Note . . . on Blood Groups," *Current Science*, IV, 653–54, cited by Mandelbaum in *JSS*, I, 446; Indira Gandhi, "Great Heritage," in the *Commemoration Volume: Cochin Synagogue Quatercentenary Celebration, December 15, 16, 17, 18 and 19, 1968* (with an Intro. by S. S. Koder), Cochin [1969], pp. 5–8. Among the biological factors which, at least in the earlier generations, impeded the growth of the Jewish, as well as of the general, population, was the spread of certain diseases peculiar to these areas. Jews, like their neighbors, were often afflicted by elephantiasis, which resulted in the swelling of each leg up to the circumference of a person's waistline. Called in Malayalam *perikkal* (a great leg), it was frequently designated as the "Cochin leg" in the Anglo-Indian dialect. See C. R. Boxer, ed., *South China in the Sixteenth Century. Being the Narrative of Galeote Pereira, Fr. Gaspar de Cruz, O.P., Fr. Martin de Rada O. E. S. A. (1550–1575)*, p. 87 n. 2. At times almost one-sixth of the Cochin Jewish population was found to suffer from that disease. Similarly, a disproportionate number of Jewish individuals, male and female, were suffering from a variety of mental disorders. While the proportion of mental diseases among other Jews is often likewise higher than the average in other ethnic groups, the explanation, usually given, that it is caused by the Jewish concentration in metropolises and the great tensions existing in the modern complex civilizations, cannot apply to the tiny settlements of Jews in Malabar. However, the prevailing endogamy and the general refusal of even the small Jewish castes to intermarry with coreligionists of other Jewish groups may have led to excessive inbreeding over generations. Small as the population was, the linguistic disparities between the Marathi and the Malayalam speaking groups must have contributed to the strong separatism between them. See J. H. Lord's brief observations in *The Jews in India*, pp. 14 f. App. V.

55. See *The Voyage of John Huyghen van Linschoten to the East Indies. From the Old English translation of 1598. The First Book, Containing His Description of the East in Two Volumes*, ed. by A. C. Burnell and P. A. Tiele, respectively, esp. I, 286; Ruy Gonsalves da Caminha's report of January 30, 1548 in G. Schurhammer's *Die Zeitgenössischen Quellen zur Geschichte Portugiesisch Asiens und seiner Nachbarländer (Ostafrika, Abessinien, Arabien, Persien, Vorder- und Hinterindien, Malaischen Archipel, Philipinen, China und Japan zur Zeit des hl. Franz Xavier, 1538–1552*. Unveränderter Neudruck der ersten Auflage, mit vollständigem Index und Supplement bis 1962. (Bibliotheca Instituti Historici S. I., XX), pp. 240 f. No. 3665; Adriaan Mones' 1781 memorandum, quoted here in the English trans. from A. Galletti *et al.*, *The Dutch in Malabar*, pp. 197 f., 222 f. See also Mandelbaum in *JSS*, I, 436. Van Linschoten's observations, quoted in the text, must be treated with caution. His reports generally tended to be overoptimistic, and they were criticized on this score by a later Dutch traveler, Gerrit de Veer, in his *True Description of Three Voyages by the North-East towards Cathay and China Undertaken by the Dutch in the Years 1594, 1595 and 1596*, published in Amsterdam in 1598 and trans. into English by William Phillip. This book was ed. with an Intro. and Notes by C. T. Beke; see p. 40. Greater credence may be given to Adriaan Mones

whose generally sympathetic attitude toward Indian Jews was quite typical of the Dutch regime which, at that time, was nearing its end. Not unjustly was this Dutch period (1663–1795) called the "golden age" of Indian Jewry. Among its benefits one may mention the publication in Amsterdam, 1757, of the prayer book entitled *Seder Tefilloth, Gelegenheitsgebeden volgens den ritus der Joden in Ceylonen en Cochin.* See M. M. Kleerkooper and W. P. van Stockum, *De Boekhandel te Amsterdam voornamentlijk in de 17ᵉ eeuw.* On the growingly important role played by the Amsterdam Jews in the Dutch East India Company, see H. I. Bloom, *The Economic Activities of the Jews of Amsterdam in the Seventeenth and Eighteenth Centuries,* pp. 85 ff.; and the data discussed by me *supra,* Vol. XV, pp. 41 ff., 397 nn. 50 ff.

The following British regime, though not hostile to the Jews, left their inner developments with less guidance and, while utilizing the local Jewish manpower in public service and army to good advantage, it helped little in the development of Jewish culture. Much of the impetus came from abroad, particularly from Jewish circles in London, but these occasional outbursts of cultural activities, exemplified in the publication of a presentable Jewish press in English or local languages, as well as in the sporadic appearance of Hebraic prayer books with or without Marathi translations, did not suffice to develop a genuine native Hebrew culture, thus reinforcing the overwhelming factors of assimilation. But all these relatively recent developments have little bearing on the much less well-documented Indian-Jewish cultural history of the period before 1650.

56. See François Pyrard de Laval, *The Voyage to the East Indies, the Maldives . . . ,* pp. 283 ff.; J. Lancaster, *The Voyages . . . to Brazil and the East Indies 1591–1603,* new ed. with intro. and notes by W. Foster, pp. 75 ff., 97 n. 1, 124. See also B. L. Abrahams, "A Jew in the Service of the East India Company in 1601," *JQR,* [o.s.] IX, 173–75; and other data, cited by W. J. Fischel in his *Ha-Yehudim be-Hodu,* pp. 125 ff.

57. See W. J. Fischel, "Abraham Navarro—Jewish Interpreter and Diplomat in the Service of the English East India Company (1682–1692)," *PAAJR,* XXV, 39–68; XXVI, 25–39; idem, "Cochin in Jewish History," *ibid.,* XXX, 37–59; idem, *Ha-Yehudim be-Hodu,* pp. 97 ff., 127 ff.; idem, "The Immigration of 'Arabian' Jews to India in the Eighteenth Century," *PAAJR,* XXXIII, 1–20; C. Roth, *The Sassoon Dynasty;* S. Jackson, *The Sassoons;* and *supra,* n. 53. On various general aspects of economic life, particularly the domestic and international trade which attracted some Jews to India, especially to the Mughal Empire, Malabar, and later Bombay, see W. H. Moreland, *India at the Death of Akbar: an Economic Study,* emphasizing the prosperity of the country about 1600 c.e. during the last years of the emperor's reign. While the seventeenth century was, in general, a period of retrogression, there was a certain revival in the eighteenth century. See R. Mantran, "L 'Europe ottomane et le commerce asiatique aux 16ᵉ et 17ᵉ siècles" in D. S. Richards, ed., *Islam and the Trade of Asia: a Colloquium,* pp. 169–79, citing an unnamed consular report of 1669 which asserted that only few Turks traveled to Persia and India for purposes of trade and that the northern route was entirely dominated by the Armenians (pp. 173 f.). Cf. S. Gopel's monograph on *Commerce and Crafts in Gujarat (16ᵗʰ and 17ᵗʰ Centuries).* This English trans. of a Russian 1965 dissertation at the USSR Academy of Science, not surprisingly reaches the conclusion that merchant capitalism "had brought nothing but misery to the craftsman." See also, more generally, B. G. Gokhala, "The Merchant Community of XVIIᵗʰ Century India," *Journal of Indian History,* LIV, 117–41. Much can further be learned from the later developments, as analyzed by A. Das Gupta in his "Trade and Politics in 18ᵗʰ

Century India," in Richards, pp. 181–214; and his more specific *Malabar in Asia's Trade, 1740–1800*.

58. See Gregory I's decree of 591 cited *supra*, Vol. II, pp. 282, 423 n. 56. See also *supra*, Vol. III, pp. 114 f., 284 f. n. 50; and K. P. Padmanabha Menon, *History of Kerala*, pp. 308 f. The new British law of 1878 was an example of the adverse conse-quences which arose from an excessive readiness of the conquerors to preserve the existing caste system in India. The Jews, though not officially a caste, had to be treated on a par with the divisions among the majority and, hence, were practically eliminated from the officers corps to their own disadvantage as well as that of the British rulers. On the variety of other substantial services rendered by the Jews to the British au-thorities in India, often while endangering their lives, see, for instance, the eleven letters of recommendation written by British officials at various dates, reproduced in Hebrew trans. by W. J. Fischel in his *Ha-Yehudim be-Hodu*, pp. 199 ff.; and, more generally, H. S. Kehimkar's chapter on "The Bene-Israel as Gallant and Faithful Sol-diers," in *The History of the Bene Israel*, pp. 187–225.

59. See W. J. Fischel, "The Exploration of the Jewish Antiquities," *JAOS*, LXXXVII, 237; C. V. Subrahmanya Alyar, "The Jews of Cochin," *Malabar Quarterly Review*, I, 130, cited by Mandelbaum in *JSS*, I, 433; and Menasseh ben Israel, *Humble Addresses to the Lord Protector . . .* , reproduced in L. Wolf's *Menasseh ben Israel's Mission to Oliver Cromwell*, pp. 73 ff., esp. p. 85; G. Bar-Giyora, "The Synagogues in Cochin" (Hebrew), *Sefunot*, II, 214–45. Since the Jewish population of Cochin apparently never exceeded 2,500 persons, the presence of seven synagogues in rather close proximity can only be explained by the caste system which made, for example, the "white" segment of little more than 200 persons almost alone in attendance at the largest (Paradesi) syn-agogue. The black Jews were either not admitted at all or confined to the anterooms. Conversely, the older "Angadi" synagogue, with its interesting inscriptions, including a mural slab dating from 1344 C.E., was in the exclusive possession of the black com-munity. With the progressive decline in the total numbers to less than 1,000 persons, some of these houses of worship were, to all intents and purposes, abandoned and allowed to decay. See J. H. Lord, *The Jews in India*, p. 84.

60. The great variations in the responsa of the various rabbis prompted by their different backgrounds and personal temperaments are illustrated in the aforemen-tioned (n. 44) collection of decisions, published by the Israeli Chief Rabbinate and ed. by Y. Nissim under the title, *Benei Yisrael, Pisqei halakhah*.

61. On the other hand, it must be noted, some voices were heard from leaders of the Jewish community of Cochin, such as S. S. Koder, asking for the return of some of their emigré coreligionists to their native land. These leaders felt that such return-ing emigrants, having for a time lived in Israel among Jews and received a better training in Jewish lore and traditions, would help keep alive the sparks of Judaism and prevent the total extinction of the Indian Jewish communities. The precipitous decline of the total number of Jewish inhabitants to less than 5,000, scattered over many cities, including the metropolitan areas of Calcutta and Bombay, clearly showed signs of serious disintegration of Jewish communal life throughout the subcontinent.

62. See K. S. Latourette, *A History of the Expansion of Christianity*, Vol. III: *Three Centuries of Advance A.D. 1500–A.D. 1800*, esp. pp. 336 ff., 348. See also *infra*, nn. 65 and 74.

63. See L. Boulnois, *The Silk Road,* English trans. from the French by D. Chamberlain (the French original appeared in 1963); the arguments presented by Yitzhak Ben-Zvi on the basis of ancient library and archaeological sources in his "The Stone Tablets of the Old Synagogue in Kai-Feng-Fu" (Hebrew) *Sefunot,* V (*Isaiah Sonne Mem. Vol.,* 27–66, with an English summary, pp. 5–6; and D. D. Leslie's brief comments thereon in his "Notes on the Inscriptions of Kai-Feng-Fu" (Hebrew), *ibid.,* pp. 67–73; G. Lambert, "Le Livre d'Isaïe parle-t'il des Chinois?" *Nouvelle Revue théologique,* LXXV, 965–72, interpreting the passage in Isaiah 49:12, with the aid of the Dead Sea Isaiah Scroll, as referring to *Sevaniyim,* that is the inhabitants of Aswan, Egypt, rather than to *Sinim,* or Chinese; the Jesuit reports summarized by G. Brotier in his "Mémoire sur les Juifs établis en Chine," first published in the *Lettres édifiantes et curieuses,* 1st ed., Vol. XXXI (1774), pp. 296–372, 388–90, here cited in the abridged English translation by W. C. White in his *Chinese Jews. A Compilation of Matters Relating to the Jews of K'aifeng Fu,* I: Historical, II: Inscriptional, III: Genealogical, I, 49–68, esp. p. 66. On the Christians in China see A. C. Moule, *Christians in China Before the Year 1550;* and K. S. Latourette, *A History of Christian Missions in China.* The story of the more numerous Muslims in China was, as late as 1910, called by M. Broomhall "a neglected problem." See his *Islam in China: a Neglected Problem,* with a Preface by J. Mott *et al.;* A. J. A. Vissière, *Études sino-mahométanes;* complemented by H. M. G. Ollone *et al., Recherches sur les musulmans chinois;* and especially the comprehensive work by Tazaka Kōdō, *Chugaku ni okeru kaikyō no denrai to somo kotsu* (Islam in China: Its Introduction and Development; Japanese). On the inscriptions in Chinese mosques, see the study by P. Bertholet, cited *infra,* n. 68.

64. G. Ferrand, trans., *Voyage du marchand arabe Sulayman en Inde et en Chine, rédigé en 851, suivi de remarques par Abû Zaid Ḥasan (vers 916),* trans. from the Arabic with an Introduction, Glossary, and Index; the critique thereof by P. Pelliot in his review of that report in *T'oung Pao,* XXI, 399–413; T. Lewicki, "Les Premiers commerçants arabes en Chine," *Rocznik orientalistyczny,* XI, 173–86 (citing sources attesting the presence of Arabs [and indirectly perhaps also of Jews from Arab lands] in China in the eighth century); E. N. Adler, "A Jewish Merchant in China at the Beginning of the Tenth Century," *Abhandlungen* in honor of H. P. Chajes, pp. 1–5, offering a translation of the aforementioned tale by Buzurg ibn Shahriyar concerning the Jew Isaac of Oman who allegedly returned from China (in this version, rather than India) with his ship laden with treasures worth millions of dinars. Isaac was subsequently killed in Sumatra. See *supra,* Chap. LXXIX, n. 39; L. I. Rabinowitz, "Eldad Ha-Dani and China," *JQR,* XXXVI, 23–38 (pointing out, against various critics, that the name Eldad was not infrequent among the Chinese Jews as is attested by Bishop White's list of names, claiming that Eldad himself had been ransomed by "a Jewish merchant of the tribe of Issachar" in Sin [China]); and other sources discussed *supra,* Vols. III, pp. 115 f., 285 f. n. 51; VI, pp. 220 f., 433 f. nn. 84–85 (on Eldad), 222 ff., 435 f. nn. 88–89. On Ibn Khurdadhbah and his Radanites see L. I. Rabinowitz's stimulating discussion, *Jewish Merchant Adventurers: a Study of the Radanites;* and the various weighty arguments on diverse possibilities quoted *supra,* Vol. IV, pp. 180 f., 328 n. 39.

65. See P. Y. Saeki, *The Nestorian Documents and Relics in China,* esp. pp. 238 ff. Apart from overemphasizing the fact that "all authorities agree in saying that there were Jews in China as early as the T'ang Dynasty," the author enumerates eleven Chinese designations of the ethnoreligious group "Jews." Eight of these are variants of *Yuhud* or *Djuhud,* but characteristically, one designation, *Ching-Chen,* means in

Chinese pure or true, certainly a flattering description. Two others are related to the term "sinews," evidently an allusion to the Jewish practice of deveining the hind part of slaughtered animals. See the next note. See also R. Israeli's recent survey, *Muslims in China: a Study in Cultural Confrontation.*

As usual the debate on origins is endless. This is true of many entire nations as well as of a variety of subgroups. The pros and cons of Chinese Jewry's origin from India and Yemen, or Persia, have been discussed in almost all major works on this subject. Some references to this aspect have already been indicated in our earlier treatment of Persia and India in this volume. Other literature can easily be found in the comprehensive works on the Chinese Jews by W. C. White, and more recently by D. D. Leslie, a leading student in this field, in his *The Survival of the Chinese Jews: the Jewish Community of Kaifeng.* T'oung Pao, Archives concernant l'histoire, les langues, la géographie, l'ethnographie et les arts de l'Asie Orientale, X; and the literature cited by him. See also the more recent study by M. Pollak, *Mandarins, Jews, and Missionaries: the Jewish Experience in the Chinese Empire.* Earlier works have been listed in the bibliographies raisonées by R. Loewenthal in his "The Jews in China: an Annotated Bibliography," *Chinese Social and Political Science Review,* XXIV, 113–234; and in his "The Early Jews of China: a Supplementary Bibliography," *Folklore Studies* (Peking), VI, 353–98.

66. Gen. 32:25 ff.; the laws of deveining the hindparts of slaughtered animals in Joseph Karo's *Shulḥan 'Arukh,* Y. D. Terefot, 65, 5–14; J. J. Berman, *Shechitah; a Study in the Cultural and Social Life of the Jewish People,* pp. 209 ff. The confusion in the Kaifeng Jewish tradition concerning the Jewish arrival from Palestine under the Han or under the Sung dynasty is understandable when we consider how faulty the general knowledge of Jewish chronology was among the Chinese Jews. In the remarkable inscription of 1489 found in the Kaifeng synagogue, the entire earlier chronology of the Jewish people, beginning with the biblical heroes Abraham, Moses, and Ezra, is very defective. Abraham's life is placed at a date corresponding to 977 B.C.E., while Moses is said to have flourished in 510 B.C.E. True, even modern scholars have failed to reach a consensus on the dating of these founders of the Jewish religion. Yet, few doubt that Abraham, if he existed at all, which is very likely, must have lived between the eighteenth and sixteenth centuries, Moses not later than in the thirteenth century B.C.E. See *supra,* Vol. I, pp. 301 ff. nn. 4 and 14. Evidently, the Jews were influenced by their Chinese neighbors who had many different traditions about the origin of man, as well as about the Great Deluge. In contrast to the biblical story of Noah's ark, which described the destruction of all humanity except those spared by taking refuge on that ark, some ancient Chinese historians claimed that large areas of both China and India had escaped the flood. We shall presently see (n. 69) that such divergences also affected the relations between the Jewish and Chinese lunar calendars.

67. See W. C. White, *Chinese Jews,* II, 11 f., asserting that as early as 1279 "on each of its four sites it [the synagogue] was thirty-five chang," that is 350 feet, and *ibid.,* p. 24 n. 18, stating that in his (White's) time the synagogue site still measured 350 by 250 feet. Most of these measurements as well as sketches of the synagogue's exterior and interior go back to Jean Domenge, whose letters, provided with his own sketches, have greatly enriched our knowledge of the synagogue's *realia.* Regrettably, only a few of these letters extant in the Archives of the Society of Jesus, Paris province, have thus far been published in their original Latin or in some translations. See the list in D. D. Leslie's 1972 publication, *The Survival of the Chinese Jews,* pp. 180 f. (No subse-

quent editions or translations have come to my attention.) Domenge's successors, for the most part, derived their information from Abbé Gabriel Brotier's summary in his "Mémoire sur les Juifs établis en Chine," *Lettres édifiantes et curieuses*, 1st ed., XXXI, 296–372, 388–90. To the measurements of the synagogue mentioned above one might add Domenge's observation that the synagogue chamber itself was 60 by 40 feet, whereas with the other buildings it occupied a space of 150 by 300–400 feet. See Leslie, pp. 79 n. 1, and 180 f.

68. See Nicolò Langobardi's observation quoted by Jérôme Tobar in his *Inscriptions juives de K'ai-fong-fou.* (This still is the basic collection and interpretation of these inscriptions, although since its publication in 1912 it has been supplemented by later studies, including D. S. D. Sassoon's "Inscriptions in the Synagogue of Kai-fung-foo," *JQR,* XI, 127–44 on the basis of two Sassoon MSS.) Of comparative interest also is P. Bertholet's study of "Inscriptions arabes et persanes des mosquées chinoises de Kai-fong-fou et de Si-ngan-fou," ed. by C. Huart in *T'oung-Pao,* 2d ser. IV, 3 (one inscription dated in 1455 grandiloquently mentions a Muslim "sheikh ul-Islam" in Singanfu).

It may be noted that Langobardi's bias not only against Jews but also against the Nestorians is clearly revealed in that letter, which expresses the hope that "the Christians of the Cross," together with the Jews, will find their way into full-fledged Catholicism. It should be noted, however, that not only the vanishing Nestorian sect but also some Confucian Chinese sometimes expressed their sympathy for Judaism. It was quite possible, therefore, that the synagogue inscription of 1512, which sounded like an outright apologia for Judaism, was actually written by some such Chinese sympathizer. See W. C. White's English translation of that inscription in his *Chinese Jews,* II, 42 ff. White's suggestion that Tso T'ang, an important government official, who composed that inscription, "may possibly have been a Jew" (*ibid.,* p. 47 n. 1) is not supported by any evidence. See Leslie, *The Survival,* p. 29.

69. See A. Väth, *Johann Adam Schall von Bell, S. J., Missionär in China, Kaiserlicher Astronom und Ratgeber am Hofe von Peking 1592–1606.* To be sure, there were enough similarities between the Chinese lunar calendar and that used by medieval Jews for some Jewish savants (there were some in the country, as we shall see *infra,* n. 78) to use their people's millennial experience to help solve some riddles in the Chinese computations. However, despite the general conformity in medieval Jewish life there still were some possibilities for differences of opinion which in practice could degenerate into serious deviations. We need but recall the famous Saadiah-Ben Meir Controversy early in the tenth century, on which, and on the general developments in the history of the Jewish calendar, see *supra,* Vols. V, pp. 30, 196 f., 304 ff. n. 34; VIII, 184 ff., 368 ff. ("Solilunar Harmonization"). There also were sufficient discrepancies between the Chinese and Jewish lunar months to make mutual accommodation difficult. See, for instance, the list of festivals in the letter by Chao Nien-tsu published by J. Finn, in his *The Orphan Colony of the Jews in China.* See also his earlier remarkable work on *The Jews in China, Their Synagogue, Their Scriptures, Their History* (reproduced by H. Kublin in his compilation, *Jews in Old China: Some Western Views: Selections from Journals East and West. With a Preface and Introductions,* pp. 1–91); and D. D. Leslie's *Survival,* pp. 86 ff., 99.

70. See Max Weber, *The Religion of China: Confucianism and Taoism,* English trans. and ed. by H. H. Gerth, p. 115, cited by L. I. Kramer, Jr., "The K'aifeng Jews: a Disappearing Community," *JSS,* XVIII, 125–44, esp. p. 139; reproduced in H. Kublin's *Studies,* pp. 1–22, esp. p. 17; the N'gai Ai T'ien and Ai Hsien-sheng *lien,* repub-

lished in Chinese with an English trans. by W. C. White, *Chinese Jews*, II, 143 No. xxxiii (the first sentence was composed by the grandfather, the second by the grandson); "Lettre de Père Jean-Paul Gozani, Mission de la Cie de Jésus, au Père Joseph Suarez de la même Cie, traduite de Portuguese," *Lettres édifiantes et curieuses*, XVIII, 31–48, and translated into English by W. C. White, I, 39–46, esp. p. 43. See also M. Pollack, *Manderins, Jews, and Missionaries*, p. 289.

Some scholars pointed out that, unlike the Nestorians, Jews did not transliterate the name of the biblical Tetragrammaton, but rather adopted the Chinese designations T'ien, Tao, or T'i, all meaning Lord or Supreme Ruler. Sometimes they used the circumlocution of Heaven. This was, however, not an accommodation to the Chinese practice. Jews of all countries have, ever since ancient times, shunned the pronunciation of the name of God and replaced it even in reading Scripture by the word Adonai or in ancient Greek *Kyrios*. Hence the Chinese equivalent must have greatly appealed to them. See P. D'Elia, "Contributo alla storia del monoteismo del'antica Cina," *RSO*, XXVII, 128–49, esp. pp. 129 f.; and J. Bettray, *Die Akkommodationsmethode des P. Matteo Ricci*, pp. 278 f.; and on the use of *Kyrios* and its equivalents, see *supra*, Vol. II, pp. 17 f., 335 n. 20 and the literature listed there. The Talmud and rabbinic literature also frequently used such circumlocutions as "fear of Heaven" for the "fear of God." Possibly, the Nestorians had inherited this usage from the Jews, along with some other Jewish practices which allowed such leaders of the Roman Empire or Church as Theodosius the Great, Justinian, and Gregory the Great to equate Nestorians with the "Jewish perfidy." See *supra*, Vol. III, pp. 8, 229 n. 1, and 243 n. 35.

71. J. P. Gozani in W. C. White's English trans., *Chinese Jews*, I, 43. The Catholic "Rites Controversy" continued intermittently for a century (1643–1742) and on occasion involved both the Chinese emperor and the pope as well as even outsiders, like the philosopher Gottfried Wilhelm von Leibniz. Nevertheless it left considerable doubt on the extent to which the Christian leaders in China were to be permitted to make ritual concessions to the Chinese majority. This controversy has been analyzed, among others, by A. Thomas in his *Histoire de la Mission de Pékin depuis les origines jusqu'à l'arrivée des Lazaristes*, esp. pp. 163 ff., 181 ff., 202 ff.; F. R. Merkel, *G. W. Leibnitz und die China Mission*, pp. 98 ff.; K. S. Latourette, *A History of Christian Missions in China*, pp. 48 ff.; and more briefly in his *A History of the Expansion of Christianity*, III, 349 ff. There were no similar repercussions in Jewish life, even after the Western Jewish leaders had learned about the presence of the Kaifeng community and its purported deviations from normative Judaism. If anything, Jews generally rejoiced about the survival of some coreligionists in the Far East and through visitors took a rather sympathetic position concerning the Kaifeng "aberrations" from the highway of Jewish law. We do not even learn of any discussions concerning the admissibility of Kaifeng Jews to the Western communities on a par with the reservations voiced by some Western rabbis with respect to certain Indian coreligionists. The Western attitude toward their Chinese coreligionists was more in line with the tolerant treatment of Eldad ha-Dani's reported differences from the existing practices in Kairuwan, recommended by R. Ṣemaḥ Gaon. See *supra*, Vol. VI, pp. 220 f., 434 n. 86.

Obviously, the Kaifeng Jews were unfamiliar with the reasons why ancient Judaism had rejected ancestor worship, which was so widespread particularly in Egypt. We recall that, probably for this reason, the ancient sages declared the corpse of a deceased person to be supremely impure ("a grandfather of impurity"). See *supra*, Vol. I, p. 148. However, the rabbis did not object to the memorialization of immediate ancestors for whom *kaddish* was to be recited during the first eleven months and on subsequent anniversaries, as well as through certain memorial prayers (*hazkarat ne-*

shamot) on specified holidays. Nor did they resent, but often rather fostered, pilgrimages to the graves of their forefathers or distinguished leaders of past ages. Such pilgrimages were particularly frequent, as we recall, in the Persian-speaking areas, from which many Kaifeng Jews had originally come. Characteristically, however, the Jewish people did not observe special memorial days for most of its ancient and medieval heroes, similar to the Washington and Lincoln birthdays. In fact, they actually allowed the dates of the demise of most of these great personalities to sink into oblivion.

72. See T. A. Layton's letter of January 15, 1849 to J. Finn, published by the latter in his *The Orphan Colony of Jews in China*, pp. 21–27; E. I. Ezra, "Chinese Jews," *The East Asia Magazine*, I, 278–96; A. Sopher, *Chinese Jews;* D. A. Brown, "Brown Meets the Chinese Jews," *American Hebrew*, 1933; the first two reprinted in H. Kublin's *Jews in Old China*. Compiled with an Intro., pp. 213–95; and the third (partially) in W. C. White's *Chinese Jews*, I, 150–64. It may be assumed that physical assimilation progressed in the course of generations so that the well-informed student of Chinese Jewish history, Rudolf Loewenthal, could assert "that for the past fifty or a hundred years there existed no pure Jews" in Kaifeng. This despite the persistence of clan names which some of those twentieth-century survivors still bore—as was noted by the Japanese officials, Teichò Mikami and Shizu Sogabe—during the Japanese occupation of Kaifeng in 1940. See R. Loewenthal, "The Nomenclature of Jews in China," *Collectancea Commissionis Synodalis*, XVII, 254–370, reprinted in H. Kublin, comp., *Studies of the Chinese Jews: Selections from Journals East and West*, pp. 55–84, esp. p. 66; Teichò Mikami, "Report on the Actual Conditions of the Kaifeng Jewish Community" (Japanese), *Shina Bukyò Shigaku*, V, no. 1 (Tokyo, June 25, 1941), pp. 76–77; Shizu Sogabe, "The Kaifeng Jews" (Japanese), *Gaigo Jiho* (Revue Diplomatique), XCVII, no. 4 (Tokyo, February 15, 1941), pp. 65–67. See also M. Pollack, *Mandarins*, pp. 242 ff., 401 f. n. 8.

No one seems to have seriously questioned the permissibility of the Kaifeng Jews marrying more than one wife. We have the documentation for such multiple marriages in the case of Chang Mei "the Handsome" whose six wives are mentioned in the *Book of the Dead*, as reproduced by W. C. White in his *Chinese Jews*, III, 24 f. Nos. 525, 541–45, 556. But this number was doubtless exceptional; it may have resulted from the extraordinary loss of lives during the catastrophic flood of 1642. Some of Chang's marriages may have resulted from his wish thus to save orphaned girls from non-Jewish families by converting them to Judaism before their wedlock. See *ibid.*, III, 115 ff. Five of Chang's wives were indeed originally Muslim or Chinese women; they are identified as being "daughters of Adam." Evidently the Kaifeng Jews thus wished to indicate their birth outside the Jewish fold. That they chose the descent from Adam, rather than the phrase frequently used in rabbinic sources, "children of Noah" (if they were at all familiar with that rabbinic term) may have originated from their reluctance to consider what the rabbis called the six or seven commandments of the children of Noah. In any case, polygamy was not unknown to the oriental Jews, particularly in Muslim countries, since they were not descendants of Jews who had accepted the "ban of Rabbenu Gershom, Light of the Exile." We recall that among the Spanish and Turkish Sephardim polygamy was not a very rare occurrence.

73. Antoine Gaubil, *Correspondance de Pekin, 1722–1759*, ed. by R. Simon, cited by D. D. Leslie, *Survival*, p. 38; Nicolò Langobardi's letter to Claudio Acquaviva, Superior General of the Jesuit Order, dated November 22, 1610, in *Opere storiche del P. Matteo Ricci S. I.*, ed. by P. Tacchi-Venturi, II, 328 ff., 344; T. Mikami and S. Sogabe, cited in n. 72. Yet, as late as 1957, on his visit to Kaifeng, the Czech scholar Timoteus

Pakora reported that he found in the city 100 families with 200 dependents, that is probably children, who "class themselves as Jews." See his "Jews in China" (Czech), *Nový Orient*, XII/6, 93–94, quoted by D. D. Leslie in his *Survival*, p. 74. Remarkably, the largest emigration of Jews from Europe to China in the 1930s and 1940s, which led to the establishment of a significant Jewish community in Shanghai, did not result in the influx of Jews into Kaifeng. On the other hand, a few Kaifeng Jews, too, found their way into Shanghai. Even more astonishing is that the Jewish world migrations after the establishment of the State of Israel did not seem to bring any significant number of Kaifeng Jews to the new state, although Yitzhak Ben Zvi, its second president, had long evinced an interest in such exotic survivals of Jews in various parts of the world. See his aforementioned (n. 63) essay in *Sefunot*, V; and his *Niḏḥei Yisrael*, or in English trans. by D. E. Abbady, *The Exiled and the Redeemed*. See also M. Pollack, *Mandarins*, pp. 247, 350.

74. The story of N'gai Ai Tien's visit to Matteo Ricci has frequently been retold, most recently in a dramatic fashion by M. Pollack in his *Mandarins*, pp. 3 ff. All accounts are based upon Ricci's own reports in both his diary (*Commentarii*) and in his letter to Claudio Acquaviva of July 26, 1605. They have been reproduced in his *Opere storiche*, ed. by P. Tacchi-Venturi, I, 466 ff., II, 289 ff.; translated into English by R. Loewenthal in *The Early Jews in China*, pp. 396 ff., and cited in H. Kublin's *Studies*, pp. 209 ff. These reports have been subjected to a careful examination by Paul Pelliot, who reached the conclusion that the *Commentarii*, written a considerable time after the event, were far less accurate than the letter sent to Rome about a month after N'gai Ai Tien's visit on June 24–30, 1605. See Pelliot's "Le Juif Ngai, informateur du P. Matthieu Ricci," *T'oung Pao*, 2d ser. XX, 32–39, reproduced in English translation by A. E. H. Petrie in White's *Chinese Jews*, III, 16–19; and in the fuller French original in Kublin's *Studies*, pp. 91–100. This searching inquiry has since been corrected in some details by Berthold Laufer, D. D. Leslie, and others. Ricci's reports were followed by those of his student Langobardi and other Jesuits, especially Gozani, Domenge, Gaubil, Brotier, reviewed by D. D. Leslie in his *Survival*, esp. pp. 177 ff. On these disciples see also L. Pfister, *Notices biographiques et bibliographiques sur les Jésuites de l'ancienne Mission . . . en Chine 1552–1773;* and more recently supplemented and updated by J. Dehergne's *Répertoire des Jésuites de Chine de 1550 à 1800*. Needless to say, behind the scholarly curiosity evinced by the Jesuits always lurked the hope that the Jews, and other Chinese, would be converted to Christianity. This hope was still vigorously defended in 1937 by H. Bernard in his extensive biography, *Le Père Matthieu Ricci et la Société chinoise de son temps (1552–1610)*, esp. II, 284.

75. See L. Wallach, "The Origin of the Testimonia Biblica in Early Christian Literature," *Review of Religion*, VIII, 130–36; and other sources cited *supra*, Vols. II, pp. 386 n. 23; V, pp. 344 f. n. 49, 351 n. 68, and so forth. Although as was mentioned here on several previous occasions, Muslim polemists had also taken over the accusation of Jewish forgeries of the Bible, which in that late period the Papacy and other official organs of the Church, to whom these China messages had been addressed, did not seriously expect to prove with the aid of Chinese Jewish sources. That is perhaps also why the Vatican Library is in possession of fewer Chinese Hebrew writings than are other institutions of this magnitude in England and, to a lesser extent, in France.

76. See A. H. Godbey's rather speculative, but stimulating, accumulation of data concerning the various legends about *The Lost Tribes;* Menasseh ben Israel's *Humble*

Addresses, ed. by L. Wolf, p. 85; and *supra,* n. 59; J. Finn, *The Jews in China, Their Synagogue, Their Scriptures, Their History, etc.;* reproduced in H. Kublin's *Jews in Old China,* pp. 78 f.

77. See A. Neubauer, "Jews in China," *JQR,* [o.s.] VIII, 123–39, reprinted in H. Kublin, *Studies,* pp. 139–57; A. S. Oko, *A History of the Hebrew Union College Library and Museum,* pp. 5 f. (reprinted from his article in the *American Jewish Year Book,* XLV, 67–96: "Jewish Book Collections in the United States," esp. pp. 78 ff.). The earlier acquisition (after 1850) of the original Kai-feng Pentateuch and copies by several Western libraries and individuals, including the New York Public Library and the well-known Philadelphia collector, Judge Mayer Sulzberger, is mentioned by M. N. Adler in his "Chinese Jews," *JQR,* [o.s.] XIII, 18–41, esp. pp. 32 ff. This essay also offers interesting data on the various efforts of English Jewry, including the Adler family, to offer assistance to the distant "orphan colony" in Kaifeng and to learn more about its history and way of life. More intensive was the investigation of the Hebrew material included in the *Book of the Dead,* initiated by B. Laufer's aforementioned "A Chinese-Hebrew Manuscript, a New Source for the History of the Chinese Jews," *American Journal of Semitic Languages,* XLVI, 189–97, also reprinted in H. Kublin's *Studies,* pp. 159–69. The high quality of this essay induced Bishop White not only to reprint it but also, jointly with R. J. Williams, to examine the Hebrew names of that codex with additional notes by Williams. See White's *Chinese Jews,* III, 28 ff., 75 ff., 83 ff. The manuscript used by Laufer was carefully reexamined by D. D. Leslie in "The Chinese-Hebrew Memorial Book of the Jewish Community of K'aifeng," *Abr-Nahrain,* IV, 19–45; V, 1–28; VI, 1–52.

Indeed, it has been Leslie who in this area, too, has contributed the most incisive and extensive data and observations. Beginning with his Hebrew "Notes on the Inscriptions from Kai-Feng Fou," *Sefunot,* V, 67–73, complementing Isaac Ben Zvi's aforementioned essay (n. 63) on "The Stone Tablets," *ibid.,* pp. 27–66 with an English summary, pp. 5 f., Leslie has examined "The Judeo-Persian Colophons to the Pentateuch of the K'aifeng Jews," *Abr-Nahrain,* VIII, 1–35, and published other pertinent articles. Most comprehensively, he reproduced in the appendix to *The Survival of the Chinese Jews* a number of facsimile reproductions of the Hebrew texts and, in his important chapter "On Hebrew Manuscripts," *ibid.,* pp. 141–59, he furnished a general review of the existing manuscripts and books, including an indication of their present location. In this connection he also warned that not all manuscripts attributed to Kaifeng really stemmed from there. He stated, for example, that C. Roth's "An Illuminated Hebrew Scroll of Esther from China," *Oriental Art,* I, 176–81 (revised version in White, *Chinese Jews,* 1968 ed., to which Roth wrote the Introduction), is possibly based on a scroll which did not come from Kaifeng. See *The Survival,* p. 149. There is no question, however, about the authentic Kaifeng origin of the *Haggadah of the Chinese Jews,* ed. by B. D. Drenger, to which Roth likewise contributed an Introduction.

78. See M. N. Adler's "Chinese Jews," *JQR,* [o.s.] XIII, 38 f.; Anatole Gaubil's Letter dated November 8, 1749 in his *Correspondance,* pp. 267, 598 ff.; D. D. Leslie, *The Survival,* pp. 50, 182; White, *Chinese Jews,* III, 201 ff. App. D, esp. Nos. 671, 672, 684, 687–704, 707, 708, 710 and 713. White's statement concerning the fifteen provinces (a map of which, dated *ca.* 1550, is reproduced in C. R. Boxer's *South China,* facing p. xix), is accepted without demurrer by L. Carrington Goodrich, an authoritative historian of China, in his review of White's work in *JSS,* VI, 70–72, esp. p. 71, reprinted in H. Kublin's *Studies,* pp. 201–203, esp. p. 202; W. A. P. Martin's remark on

the Jewish moneylenders in *The Chinese: Their Education, Philosophy and Letters,* pp. 292 ff., 295, is but one of several in which he could not suppress his personal anti-Jewish sentiments.

Our information about the occupational changes within the small Jewish community of Kaifeng over the years is necessarily very hazy. Thus far even with the data collected from the local gazetteers we know, for the most part, only individuals who reached a certain status in society as "rabbis," physicians, military commanders, higher public officials, and the like. The 6 archway inscriptions, 18 *piens* (horizontal) and 17 *liens* (vertical), tablets reproduced and commented on by White in *Chinese Jews,* III, 110–52, mentioned exclusively ranking individuals. Even in these cases, the donors' occupation is not always indicated. Only here and there do we get more extensive biographical data from the available sources. But only one Jewish leader, Chao Ying-Ch'eng, a high official in the Chinese administration and a communal leader of importance in the 1660s, received a biographical description of some length in the local gazetteer. His biography has also been the subject of a fairly detailed essay by D. D. Leslie entitled "The K'aifeng Jew Chao Ying-Ch'eng and His Family," *T'oung Pao,* LIII, 147–79, reprinted in H. Kublin's *Studies,* pp. 101–137. See also the aforementioned briefer sketch of "Le Juif N'gai," by P. Pelliot, in the same journal, 2d ser. XX, 32–39, also reprinted in Kublin's *Studies,* pp. 91–100.